FOREWORD

This manual (Volume 2) contains repair pr̲o̲c̲e̲d̲ures for the chassis and body, and electrical service procedures, for the 1993 COROLLA.

Applicable models: AE101, 102 series

For maintenance and engine repair procedures, refer to VOLUME 1 (Pub. No. RM294U1).

The manual is divided into 12 sections with a thumb index for each section at the edge of the pages.

Please note that the publications below have also been prepared as relevant service manuals to the components and systems in this vehicle.

Manual Name	Pub. No.
● 1993 Corolla Electrical Wiring Diagram	EWD153U
● 1992 A131L, A132L Automatic Transaxle Repair Manual	RM269U
● 1993 A245E Automatic Transaxle Repair Manual	RM311U
● 1993 Corolla New Car Features	NCF087U

All information in this manual is based on the latest product information at the time of publication. However, specifications and procedures are subject to change without notice.

TOYOTA MOTOR CORPORATION

© **1992 TOYOTA MOTOR CORPORATION**
All rights reserved. This book may not be reproduced or copied, in whole or in part, without the written permission of Toyota Motor Corporation.

NOTE: The screen toned sections below are in VOLUME 1
(Pub.No.RM294U1).

CLUTCH

CL

DESCRIPTION

The diaphragm spring turnover type clutch providing lighter release performance.

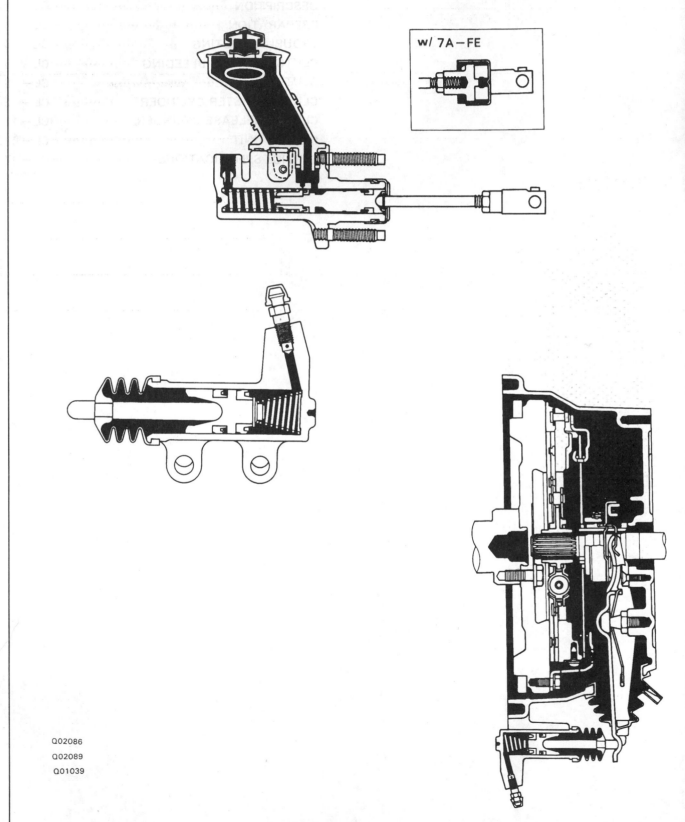

w/ 7A—FE

Q02086
Q02089
Q01039

PREPARATION
SST(SPECIAL SERVICE TOOLS)

CL003-08

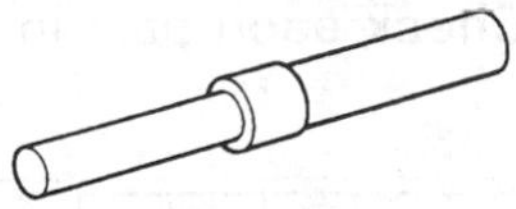	09301–00210	Clutch Guide Tool	
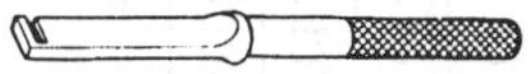	09333–00013	Clutch Diaphragm Spring Aligner	
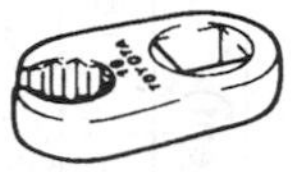	09023–00100	Union Nut Wrench 10 mm	Clutch line tube

EQUIPMENT

CL004-01

Calipers	
Dial indicator	
Torque wrench	

TROUBLESHOOTING

You will find the cause of trouble more easily by properly using the table shown below. In this table, the numbers indicate the priority of the probable cause of trouble. Check each part in the order shown. If necessary, repair or replace the part.

Trouble \ See Page	CL-6	CL-5	CL-8	CL-11	–	CL-13	MX-38	CL-13	CL-13	CL-13	CL-13	CL-13	CL-13	CL-13	CL-13	CL-16	CL-13	CL-15	CL-13	–
Parts Name	Clutch pedal (Freeplay out of adjustment)	Clutch line (Air in line)	Master cylinder cup (Damaged)	Release cylinder cup (Damaged)	Engine mounting (Loosen)	Release bearing (Worn, dirty or damaged)	Input shaft bearing (Worn or damaged)	Clutch disc (Out of true)	Clutch disc (Runout is excessive)	Clutch disc (Lining broken)	Clutch disc (Dirty or burred)	Clutch disc (Oily)	Clutch disc (Worn out)	Clutch disc torsion rubber (Damaged)	Clutch disc (Harden)	Clutch disc (Lack of spline grease)	Diaphragm spring (Damaged)	Diaphragm spring (Out of tip alignment)	Pressure plate (Distortion)	Flywheel (Distortion)
Clutch grabs/chatters					1				2			2	2	2	2			2		
Clutch pedal spongy		1	2	2																
Clutch noisy						1	2							3						
Clutch slips	1											2	2					3	4	5
Clutch does not disengage	1	2	3	4		5		6	6	6	6	6				6	7	7	8	

V00004

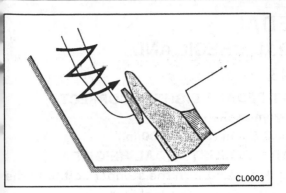

CL0003

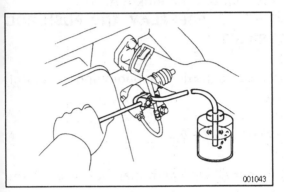

001043

CLUTCH SYSTEM BLEEDING

CL006-04

HINT: If any work is done on the clutch system or if air is suspected in the clutch lines, bleed the system of air.

NOTICE: Do not let brake fluid remain on a painted surface. Wash it off immediately.

1. **FILL CLUTCH RESERVOIR WITH BRAKE FLUID**
   Check the reservoir frequently. Add fluid if necessary.

2. **CONNECT VINYL TUBE TO BLEEDER PLUG**
   Insert the other end of the tube in a half—full container of brake fluid.

3. **BLEED CLUTCH LINE**
   (a) Slowly pump the clutch pedal several times.
   (b) While pressing on the pedal, loosen the bleeder plug until the fluid starts to run out. Then close the bleeder plug.
   (c) Repeat this procedure until there are no more air bubbles in the fluid.

CL

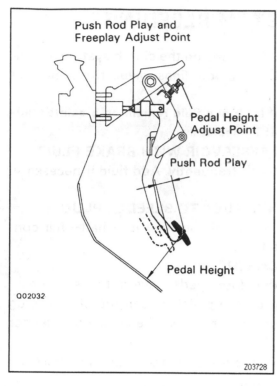

Push Rod Play and
Freeplay Adjust Point

Pedal Height
Adjust Point

Push Rod Play

Pedal Height

Q02032

Z03728

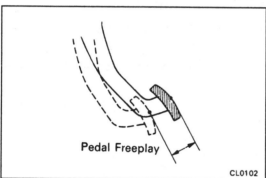

Pedal Freeplay

CL0102

CLUTCH PEDAL
CLUTCH PEDAL CHECK AND ADJUSTMENT
CL02T–01

1. **CHECK THAT PEDAL HEIGHT IS CORRECT**
    Pedal height from asphalt sheet:
    142.5 — 152.5 mm (5.61 — 6.00 in.)

2. **IF NECESSARY, ADJUST PEDAL HEIGHT**
    Loosen the lock nut and turn the stopper bolt until the height is correct. Tighten the lock nut.

3. **CHECK THAT PEDAL FREEPLAY AND PUSH ROD PLAY ARE CORRECT**
    (Pedal freeplay)
    Push in on the pedal until the beginning of clutch resistance is felt.
    Pedal freeplay:
    5.0 — 15.0 mm (0.197 — 0.591 in.)
    (Push rod play)
    Push in on the pedal with a finger softly until the resistance begins to increase a little.
    Push rod play at pedal top:
    1.0 — 5.0 mm (0.039 — 0.197 in.)

4. **IF NECESSARY, ADJUST PEDAL FREEPLAY AND PUSH ROD PLAY**
    (a) Loosen the lock nut and turn the push rod until the freeplay and push rod play are correct.
    (b) Tighten the lock nut.
    (c) After adjusting the pedal freeplay, check the pedal height.
    (d) Connect the air duct and install the lower finish panel.

5. **INSPECT CLUTCH RELEASE POINT**
    (a) Pull the parking brake lever and install wheel stopper.
    (b) Start the engine and idle the engine.
    (c) Without depressing the clutch pedal, slowly shift the shift lever into reverse position until the gears contact.

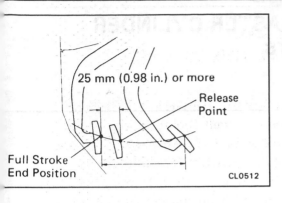

25 mm (0.98 in.) or more

Release Point

Full Stroke End Position

CL0512

(d) Gradually depress the clutch pedal and measure the stroke distance from the point the gear noise stops (release point) up to the full stroke end position.

Standard distance:

25 mm (0.98 in.) or more

(From pedal stroke end position to release point)

If the distance not as specified, perform the following operation.

- Inspect pedal height.
- Inspect push rod play and pedal freeplay.
- Bleed the clutch line.
- Inspect the clutch cover and disc.

CL

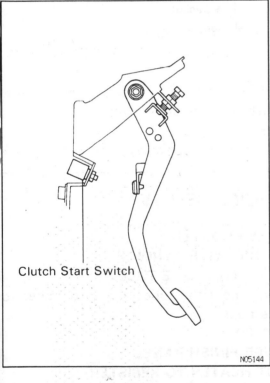

Clutch Start Switch

N05144

6. CHECK CLUTCH START SYSTEM

(a) Check that the engine does not start when the clutch pedal is released.

(b) Check that the engine starts when the clutch pedal is fully depressed.

If necessary, adjust or replace the clutch start switch.

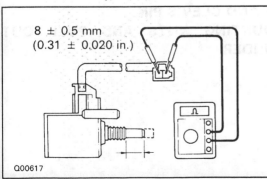

8 ± 0.5 mm
(0.31 ± 0.020 in.)

Q00617

7. INSPECT CONTINUTIY OF CLUTCH START SWITCH

(a) Check that there is continuity between teminnals when the switch is ON (pushed).

(b) Check that there is no continuity between terminals when the switch is OFF (free).

If continuty is not as specified, replace the switch.

CL

CLUTCH MASTER CYLINDER
COMPONENTS

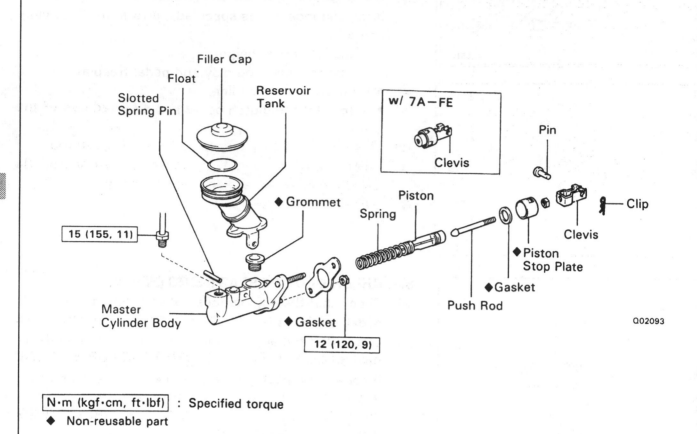

Filler Cap
Float
Reservoir Tank
Slotted Spring Pin
w/ 7A—FE
Clevis
Pin
Grommet
Piston
Spring
Clip
Clevis
15 (155, 11)
Piston Stop Plate
Gasket
Push Rod
Master Cylinder Body
Gasket
12 (120, 9)
Q02093

N·m (kgf·cm, ft·lbf) : Specified torque
◆ Non-reusable part

Z03731

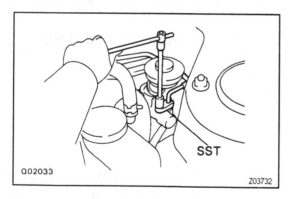

SST
Q02033
Z03732

MASTER CYLINDER REMOVAL

1. **REMOVE BRAKE BOOSTER**
2. **DRAW OUT FLUID WITH SYRINGE**
3. **DISCONNECT CLUTCH LINE TUBE**
   Using SST, disconnect the tube. Use a container to catch the brake fluid.
   SST 09023—00100
4. **REMOVE LOWER FINISH PANEL**
5. **REMOVE DUCT HEATER TO RESISTER**
6. **REMOVE CLIP AND CLEVIS PIN**
7. **REMOVE MOUNTING NUTS AND PULL OUT MASTER CYLINDER**

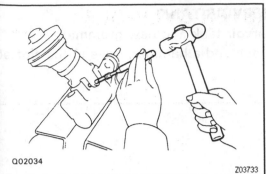

CL00A-07

MASTER CYLINDER DISASSEMBLY

1. **REMOVE RESERVOIR TANK**
(a) Using a pin punch and a hammer, drive out the slotted spring pin.
(b) Remove the reservoir tank and grommet.

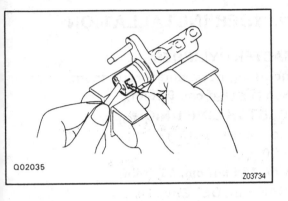

2. **REMOVE PUSH ROD**
(a) Using a minimum driver, loosen the staked part of the plate.
(b) Remove the stop plate, gasket and the push rod.
HINT: Tape the minimum driver tip before use. Be careful not to damage the cylinder body.

3. **REMOVE PISTON**

CL00B-01

MASTER CYLINDER INSPECTION

HINT: Clean the disassembled parts with compressed air.

1. **INSPECT MASTER CYLINDER BORE FOR SCORING OR CORROSION**
If a problem is found, clean or replace the cylinder.

2. **INSPECT PISTON AND CUPS FOR WEAR, SCORING, CRACKS OR SWELLING**
If either one requires replacement, use the parts from the cylinder kit.

3. **INSPECT PUSH ROD FOR WEAR OR DAMAGE**
If necessary, replace the push rod.

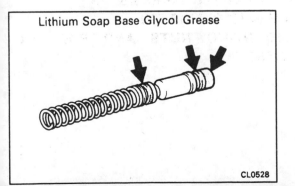

Lithium Soap Base Glycol Grease

CL00C-05

MASTER CYLINDER ASSEMBLY

1. **COAT PARTS WITH LITHIUM SOAP BASE GLYCOL GREASE, AS SHOWN**

2. **INSERT PISTON INTO CYLINDER**

3. **INSTALL PUSH ROD ASSEMBLY WITH NEW STOP PLATE AND NEW GASKET**

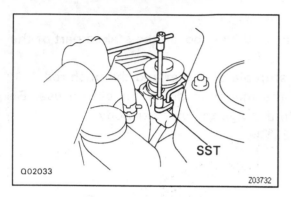

Protrusion
1.5 – 3.5 mm
(0.059 – 0.138 in.)

Q02038   Z03735

4. INSTALL RESERVOIR TANK

(a) Install the reservoir tank and new grommet.

(b) Using a pin punch and a hammer, drive in the slotted spring pin.

MASTER CYLINDER INSTALLATION

1. INSTALL MASTER CYLINDER
Install the mounting nuts, and torque them.
Torque: 13 N·m (130 kgf·cm, 9 ft·lbf)

2. CONNECT CLUTCH LINE UNION
Using SST, connect the union.
SST 09023–00100
Torque: 15 N·m (155 kgf·cm, 11 ft·lbf)

3. INSTALL BRAKE BOOSTER

4. CONNECT PUSH ROD AND INSTALL PIN
Install the clip in the push rod pin.

5. ADJUST CLUTCH PEDAL

6. INSTALL DUCT HEATER TO RESISTER

7. INSTALL LOWER FINISH PANEL

8. BLEED CLUTCH SYSTEM

SST

Q02033   Z03732

CLUTCH RELEASE CYLINDER
COMPONENTS

CL00E—0A

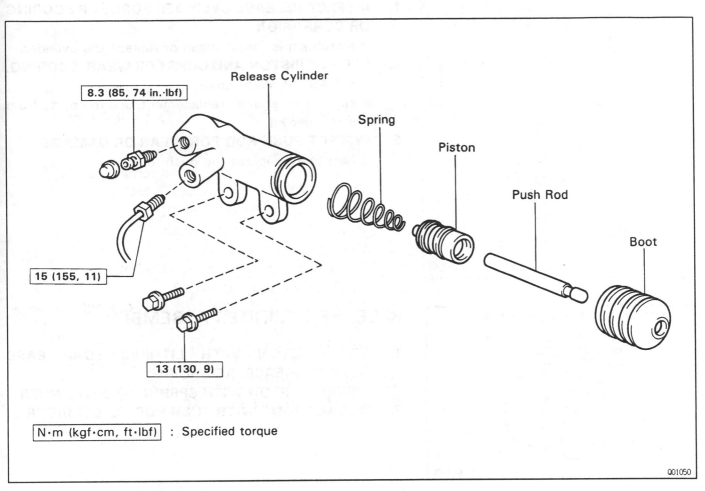

8.3 (85, 74 in.·lbf)

Release Cylinder

Spring

Piston

Push Rod

Boot

15 (155, 11)

13 (130, 9)

N·m (kgf·cm, ft·lbf) : Specified torque

Q01050

CL00F—05

RELEASE CYLINDER REMOVAL

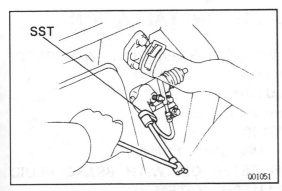

SST

001051

1. **DISCONNECT CLUTCH LINE TUBE**
   Using SST, disconnect the tube. Use a container to catch the brake fluid.
   SST 09023—00100
2. **REMOVE TWO BOLTS AND PULL OUT RELEASE CYLINDER**

CL00G—03

RELEASE CYLINDER DISASSEMBLY

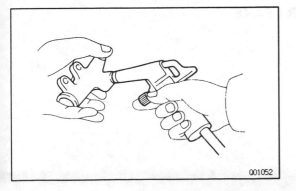

001052

1. **PULL OUT BOOT WITH PUSH ROD**
2. **REMOVE PISTON**
   Using compressed air, remove the piston with the spring from the cylinder.

RELEASE CYLINDER INSPECTION

CL00U-01

HINT: Clean the disassembled parts with compressed air.

1. **INSPECT RELEASE CYLINDER BORE FOR SCORING OR CORROSION**
   If a problem is found, clean or replace the cylinder.
2. **INSPECT PISTON AND CUPS FOR WEAR, SCORING, CRACKS OR SWELLING**
   If either one requires replacement, use the parts from the cylinder kit.
3. **INSPECT PUSH ROD FOR WEAR OR DAMAGE**
   If necessary, replace the push rod.

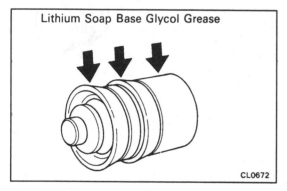

Lithium Soap Base Glycol Grease

CL0672

RELEASE CYLINDER ASSEMBLY

CL00H-01

1. **COAT PISTON WITH LITHIUM SOAP BASE GLYCOL GREASE, AS SHOWN**
2. **INSTALL PISTON WITH SPRING INTO CYLINDER**
3. **INSTALL BOOT WITH PUSH ROD TO CYLINDER**

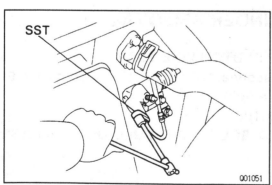

SST

001051

RELEASE CYLINDER INSTALLATION

CL00J-06

1. **INSTALL RELEASE CYLINDER WITH TWO BOLTS**
   Torque: 13 N·m (130 kgf·cm, 9 ft·lbf)
2. **CONNECT CLUTCH LINE TUBE**
   Using SST, connect the tube.
   SST 09023—00100
   Torque: 15 N·m (155 kgf·cm, 11 ft·lbf)
3. **FILL CLUTCH RESERVOIR WITH BRAKE FLUID AND BLEED CLUTCH SYSTEM**
4. **CHECK FOR LEAKS**

CLUTCH UNIT
COMPONENTS

CL00K-08

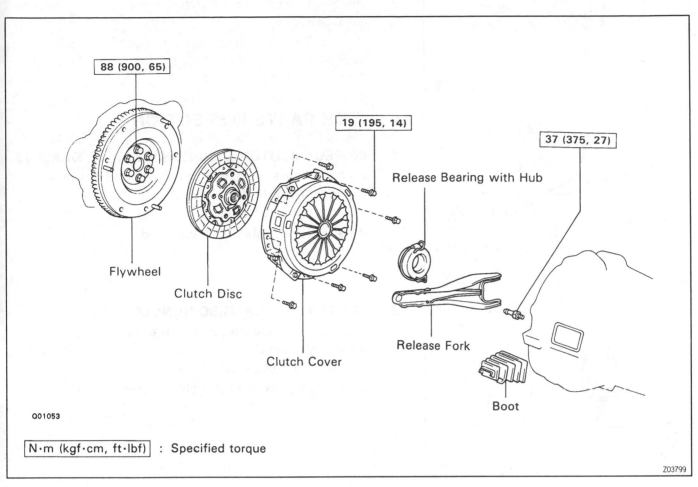

88 (900, 65)

19 (195, 14)

37 (375, 27)

Release Bearing with Hub

Flywheel

Clutch Disc

Clutch Cover

Release Fork

Boot

Q01053

N·m (kgf·cm, ft·lbf) : Specified torque

Z03799

CL00L-09

CLUTCH UNIT REMOVAL

1. **REMOVE TRANSAXLE FROM ENGINE**
   (See page MX−9)

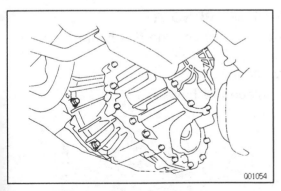

Q01054

2. **REMOVE CLUTCH COVER AND DISC**
   (a) Place matchmarks on the flywheel and clutch cover.
   (b) Loosen each set bolt one turn at a time until spring tension is released.
   (c) Remove the set bolts, and pull off the clutch cover with the clutch disc.
   NOTICE: Do not drop the clutch disc.

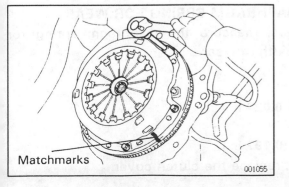

Matchmarks

Q01055

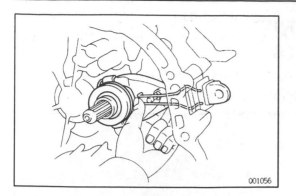

001056

3. REMOVE RELEASE BEARING AND FORK FROM TRANSAXLE

Remove the release bearing together with the fork and then separate them.

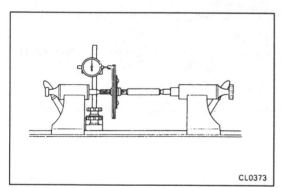

001057

CLUTCH PARTS INSPECTION

CL00M–03

1. INSPECT CLUTCH DISC FOR WEAR OR DAMAGE

Using calipers, measure the rivet head depth.
Minimum rivet depth:
    0.3 mm (0.012 in.)
If necessary, replace the clutch disc.

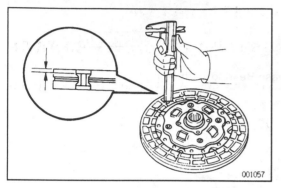

CL0373

2. INSPECT CLUTCH DISC RUNOUT

Using a dial indicator, check the disc runout.
Maximum runout:
    0.8 mm (0.031 in.)
If necessary, replace the clutch disc.

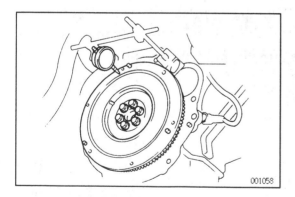

001058

3. INSPECT FLYWHEEL RUNOUT

Using a dial indicator, check the flywheel runout.
Maximum runout:
    0.1 mm (0.004 in.)
If necessary, replace the flywheel.

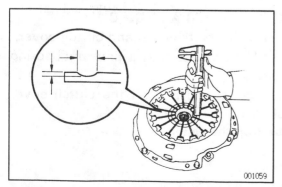

001059

4. INSPECT DIAPHRAGM SPRING FOR WEAR

Using calipers, measure the diaphragm spring for depth and width of wear.
Maximum:
Depth
    0.6 mm (0.024 in.)
Width
    5.0 mm (0.197 in.)
If necessary, replace the clutch cover.

CL

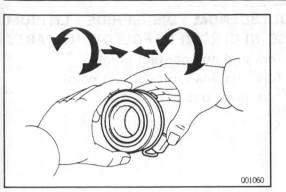

001060

5. INSPECT RELEASE BEARING

Turn the bearing by hand while applying force in the axial direction.

HINT: The bearing is permanently lubricated and requires no cleaning or lubrication.

If necessary, replace the release bearing.

CL00N—05

CLUTCH UNIT INSTALLATION

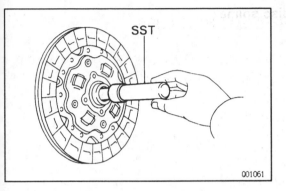

001061

1. INSTALL CLUTCH DISC AND CLUTCH COVER ON FLYWHEEL

(a) Insert the SST in the clutch disc, and then set them and the clutch cover in position.
    SST 09301—00210

CL

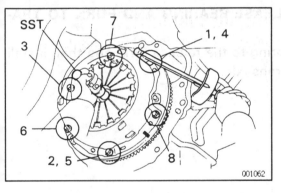

001062

(b) Align the matchmarks on the clutch cover and flywheel.

(c) Torque the bolts on the clutch cover in the order shown.
    Torque: 19 N·m (195 kgf·cm, 14 ft·lbf)
    HINT: Temporarily tighten the No.1 and No.2 bolts.

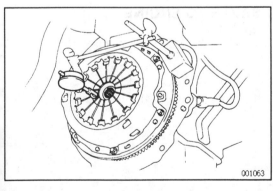

001063

2. CHECK DIAPHRAGM SPRING TIP ALIGNMENT

Using a dial indicator with roller instrument, check the diaphragm spring tip alignment.
Maximum non—alignment:
      0.5 mm (0.020 in.)

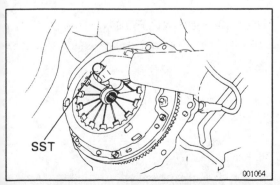

001064

If alignment is not as specified, using SST, adjust the diaphragm spring tip alignment.
SST 09333—00013

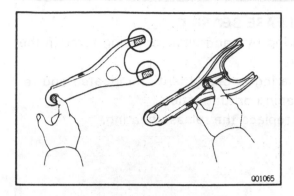

3. **APPLY MOLYBDENUM DISULPHIDE LITHIUM BASE GREASE (NLGI NO.2) TO FOLLOWING PARTS**
   - Release fork and hub contact point
   - Release fork and push rod contact point
   - Release fork pivot point

   - Clutch disc spline

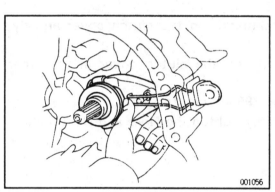

4. **INSTALL RELEASE BEARING AND FORK TO TRANSAXLE**
   Install the bearing to the release fork, and then install them to the transaxle.

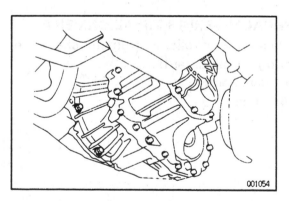

5. **INSTALL TRANSAXLE TO ENGINE**
   (See page MX—9)

SERVICE SPECIFICATIONS
SERVICE DATA

CL02U-01

Pedal height from asphalt sheet	142.5−152.5 mm (5.61−6.00 in.)
Push rod play at pedal top	1.0−5.0 mm (0.039−0.197 in.)
Pedal freeplay	5.0−15.0 mm (0.197−0.591 in.)
Clutch release point from pedal full stroke end position	25 mm (0.98 in.) or more
Disc rivet head depth (Minimum)	0.3 mm (0.012 in.)
Disc runout (Maximum)	0.8 mm (0.031 in.)
Diaphragm spring tip non−alignment (Maximum)	0.5 mm (0.020 in.)
Diaphragm spring finger wear (Maximum depth)	0.6 mm (0.024 in.)
Diaphragm spring finger wear (Maximum width)	5.0 mm (0.197 in.)
Flywheel runout (Maximum)	0.1 mm (0.004 in.)

TORQUE SPECIFICATIONS

CL00Q-0A

CL

Part tightened	N·m	kgf·cm	ft·lbf
Clutch line union	15	155	11
Master cylinder installation nut	12	120	9
Bleeder plug	8.3	85	74 in.·lbf
Clutch cover x Flywheel	19	195	14
Release cylinder installation bolt	13	130	9
Flywheel set bolt	88	900	65

CL

MANUAL TRANSAXLE

DESCRIPTION
PRECAUTIONS

When working with FIPG materials, you must be observe the following.

- Using a razor blade and gasket scraper, remove all the old sealant (FIPG) material from the gasket surfaces.
- Thoroughly clean all components to remove all the loose material.
- Clean both sealing surfaces with a non–residue solvent.
- Apply the seal packing in approx. 1 mm (0.04 in.) bead along the sealing surface.
- Part must be assembled within 10 minutes of application. Otherwise, the sealant (FIPG) material must be removed and reapplied.

DESCRIPTION

- Transaxle type C50 and C52 are constant mesh synchronizer for forward gears, and a sliding mesh reverse gear.
- The input shaft is composed of the 1st and 2nd speed gears and the reverse drive gear, and the output shaft is composed of the drive gear (for use with ring gear).

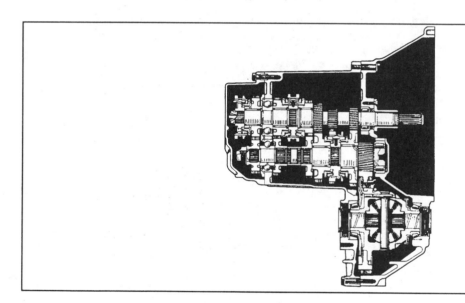

Type of Transaxle		C50	C52
Type of Engine		4A–FE	7A–FE
Gear Ratio	1st	3.545	3.166
	2nd	1.904	←
	3rd	1.310	←
	4th	0.969	←
	5th	0.815	←
	Reverse	3.250	←
Differental Gear Ratio		3.722	←
Oil Capacity		2.6 liters (2.7 US qts, 2.3 Imp. qts)	←
Oil Viscosity		SAE 75W–90	←
Oil Grade		API GL–3, GL–4 or GL–5	←

OPERATION

- **The illustrations below show the engagements of transaxle gears.**

MX00E—05

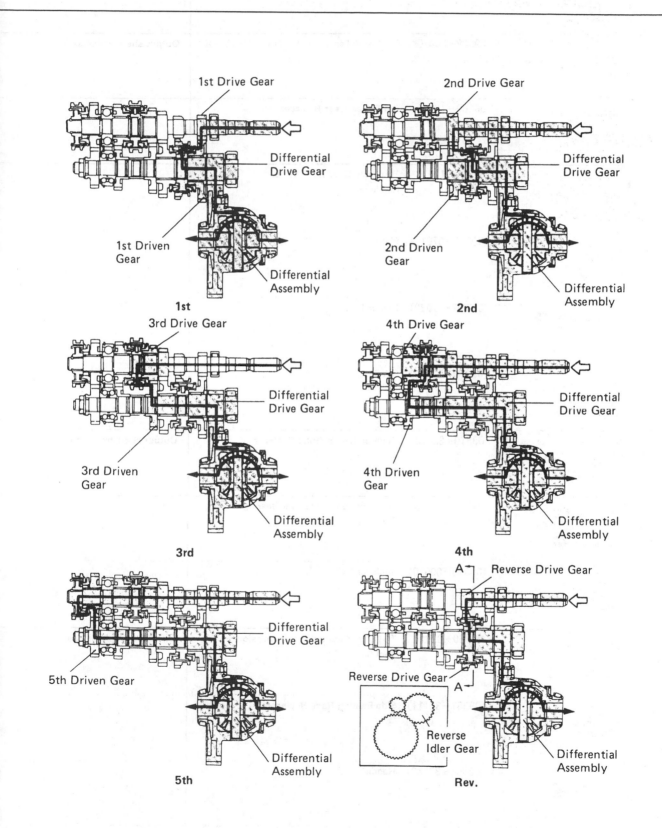

MX

000688

PREPARATION
SST(SPECIAL SERVICE TOOLS)

MX06E−01

	09213−36020	Timing Gear Remover	Fifth driven gear
	09308−00010	Oil Seal Puller	Output shaft front bearing
	09309−12020	5th Driven Gear Replacer	
	09310−17010	Transaxle Gear Remover & Replacer	
	(09310−07010)	Plate	
	(09310−07020)	Center Bolt	
	(09310−07030)	Set Bolt	
	09310−35010	Countershaft Bearing Replacer	Output shaft front bearing
	09316−60010	Transmission & Transfer Bearing Replacer	
	(09316−00020)	Replacer "A"	
	09350−32014	TOYOTA Automatic Transmission Tool Set	Differential side oil seal
	(09351−32111)	Side Bearing Race Replacer	
	(09351−32130)	Handle	

(09351—32150)	Oil Seal Replacer	
09502—10012	Differential Preload Puller	
09550—10012	Replacer Set "B"	Differential side bearing
(09252—10010)	No. 1 Replacer Handle	
(09556—10010)	Differential Drive Pinion Front Bearing Remover	
(09560—10010)	Knuckle Outer Bearing Replacer	
09564—32011	Differential Preload Adaptor	
09608—12010	Front Hub & Drive Pinion Bearing Replacer Set	Input shaft front bearing Input shaft front oil seal
(09608—00020)	Remover & Replacer Handle	
(09608—00030)	Replacer	
(09608—00080)	Replacer	
09608—20012	Front Hub & Drive Pinion Bearing Tool Set	Input shaft rear bearing Differential side bearing outer race
(09608—03020)	Handle	
(09608—03060)	Replacer	

MX

	(09608−03070)	Replacer	
	(09608−03090)	Replacer	
	09612−65014	Steering Worm Bearing Puller	Input shaft front bearing Differential side bearing outer race
	09636−20010	Upper Ball Joint Dust Cover Replacer	No.3 hub sleeve assembly
	09950−00020	Bearing Remover	

MX06F−01

RECOMMENDED TOOLS

	09025−00010	Small Torque Wrench	Differential preload
	09031−00030	Pin Punch	
	09905−00012	Snap Ring No. 1 Expander	

MX06G−01

EQUIPMENT

Dial indicator with magneticbase	
Feeler gauge	
Micrometer	
Torque wrench	

MX06H−01

LUBRICANT

Item	Capacity	Classification
Manual transaxle oil (w/Differential oil)	2.6 liters (2.7 US qts, 2.3 Imp. qts)	GL−3, GL−4 or GL−5 SAE 75W−90

MX06J—01

SSM(SPECIAL SERVICE MATERIALS)

08826—00090	Seal Packing 1281, Three bond 1281 or equivalent	Transmission case x Transaxle case Transmission case x Case cover
08833—00080	Adhesive 1344, THREE BOND 1344, LOCTITE 242 or equivalent	Transmission case cover bolt Straight screw plug Control shaft cover bolt

TROUBLESHOOTING

MX00D-02

You will find the troubles easier using the table well shown below. In this table, each number shows the priority of causes in troubles. Check each part in order. If necessary, replace these parts.

See Page	—	MX-2	—	MX-23	MX-23	MX-23	MX-73	MX-23	MX-23	MX-23	MX-23	MX-40,47	MX-40,47			
Parts Name / Trouble	Oil (Level low)	Oil (Wrong)	Oil (Level too high)	Gasket (Damaged)	Oil seal (Worn or damaged)	O-Ring (Worn or damaged)	Control cable (Faulty)	Locking ball spring (Damaged)	Shift fork (Worn)	Gear (Worn or damaged)	Bearing (Worn or damaged)	Synchronizer ring (Worn or damaged)	Shifting key spring (Damaged)			
Noise	1	2								3	3					
Oil leakage			1	2	2	3										
Hard to shift or will not shift							1					2	3			
Jumps out of gear								1	2	3	3					

V00019

ASSEMBLY REMOVAL AND INSTALLATION

Removal and installation the parts as shown below.

MX06K–01

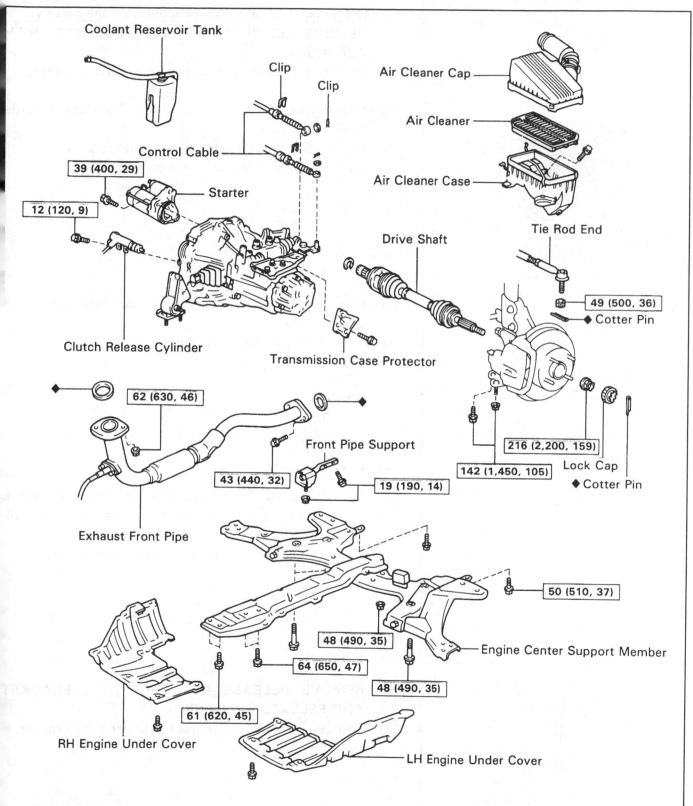

N·m (kgf·cm, ft·lbf) : Specified torque

◆ Non-reusable part

002217

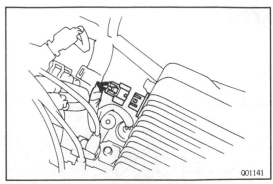

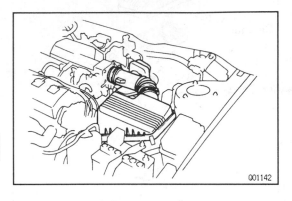

MX

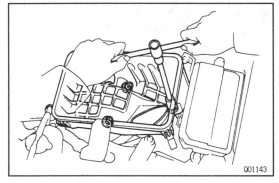

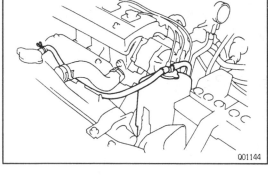

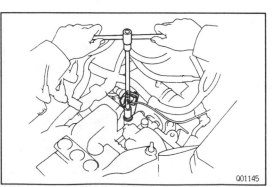

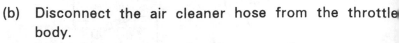

TRANSAXLE REMOVAL

1. **DISCONNECT NEGATIVE BATTERY CABLE**
   CAUTION: Work must be started after approx. 90 seconds or longer from the "LOCK" position and the negative (−) terminal cable is disconnected from the battery.

2. **REMOVE AIR CLEANER CASE ASSEMBLY WITH AIR HOSE**

(a) Disconnect the intake air temp sensor connector.

(b) Disconnect the air cleaner hose from the throttle body.

(c) Disconnect the four air cleaner cap clips.

(d) Remove the air cleaner cap and element.

(e) Disconnect the two wire harness clamps from air cleaner case.

(f) Remove the three bolts and air cleaner case.

3. **REMOVE COOLANT RESERVOIR TANK WITH HOSE**

(a) Disconnect the coolant reservoir hose from the radiator.

(b) Remove the coolant reservoir tank with hose.

4. **REMOVE RELEASE CYLINDER TUBE BRACKET AND RELEASE CYLINDER**

(a) Remove the bolt and release cylinder tube bracket.

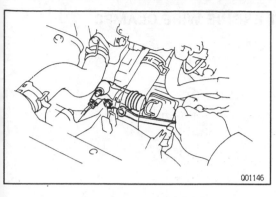

(b) Remove the two bolts and clutch release cylinder.

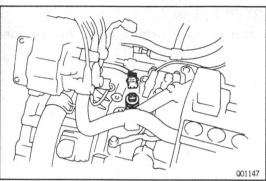

5. DISCONNECT BACK − UP LIGHT SWITCH CON-NECTOR

MX

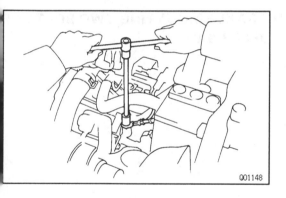

6. REMOVE EARTH CABLE

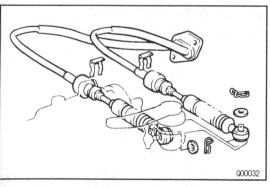

7. DISCONNECT CONTROL CABLES
(a) Remove the clips and washers.
(b) Remove the retainer from the cables.
(c) Disconnect the control cables from the control lever housing support bracket.

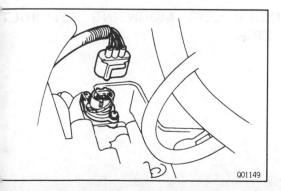

8. DISCONNECT VEHICLE SPEED SENSOR CONNEC-TOR

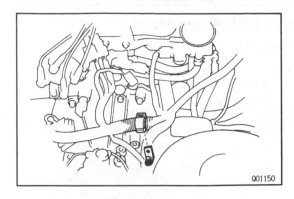

9. DISCONNECT ENGINE WIRE CLAMPS

10. REMOVE STARTER SET BOLT
Remove the starter set bolt from the transaxle upper side.

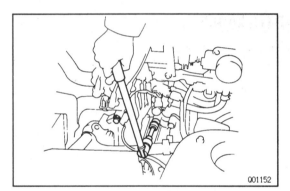

11. REMOVE TRANSAXLE MOUNTING TWO BOLTS OF TRANSAXLE UPPER SIDE

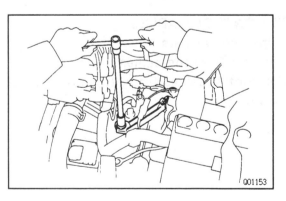

12. REMOVE ENGINE LEFT MOUNTING STAY
Remove the two bolts and engine left mounting stay.

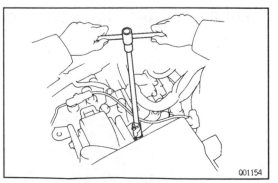

13. REMOVE ENGINE LEFT MOUNTING SET BOLT FROM REAR SIDE

MX

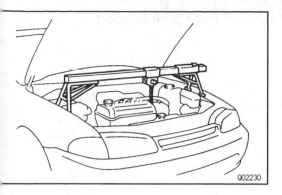

14. **INSTALL ENGINE SUPPORT FIXTURE**
15. **REMOVE FRONT WHEELS**
16. **RAISE VEHICLE**
    NOTICE: Be sure the vehicle is securely supported.
17. **REMOVE UNDER COVERS**
18. **DRAIN TRANSAXLE OIL**

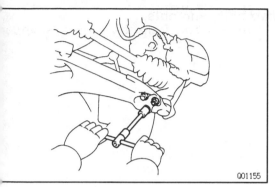

19. **DISCONNECT LOWER BALL JOINT FROM LOWER ARM**
(a) Remove the bolt and two nuts.
(b) Disconnect the lower ball joint from the lower arm.

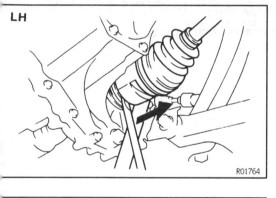

20. **REMOVE DRIVE SHAFT**
    (See SA Section)

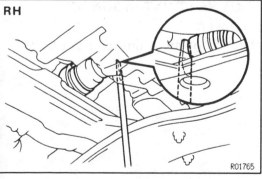

21. **REMOVE EXHAUST FRONT PIPE**
(a) Remove the two bolts.

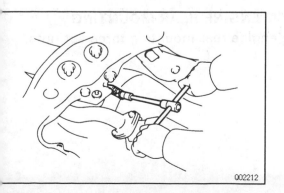

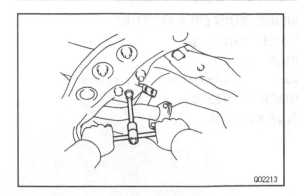

(b)   Remove the nut and front pipe support.

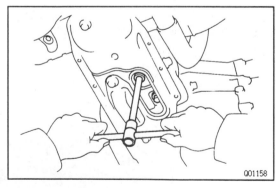

(c)   Remove the two bolts and nuts.

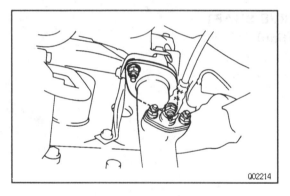

(d)   Remove the three nuts.
(e)   Remove the exhaust front pipe.

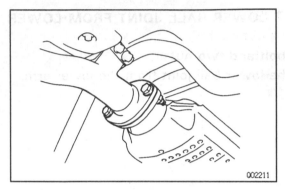

22. DISCONNECT ENGINE FRONT MOUNTING
(a)   Remove the hole cover.
(b)   Remove the engine front mounting two set bolts.

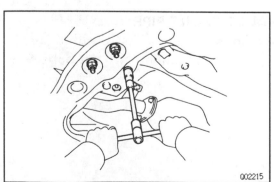

23. DISCONNECT ENGINE REAR MOUNTING
Remove the engine rear mounting three set nuts.

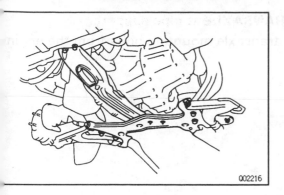

24. REMOVE ENGINE CENTER SUPPORT MEMBER
Remove the eight set bolts and the engine center support member.

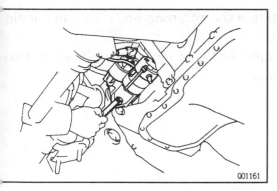

25. REMOVE STARER
(a) Disconnect the connector and wire from the starter.
(b) Remove the starter set bolt from the lower side.
(c) Remove the starter.

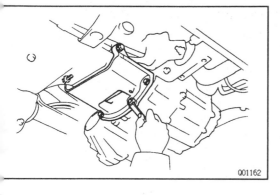

26. (4A−FE Engine)
REMOVE STIFFENER PLATE
(a) Remove the five set bolts.
(b) Remove the stiffener plate.

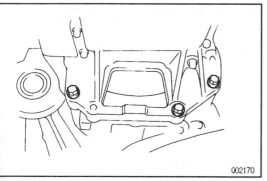

27. (7A−FE Engine)
REMOVE TRANSAXLE MOUNTING BOLTS FROM ENGINE REAR END PLATE SIDE

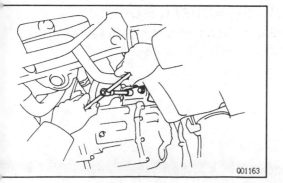

28. DISCONNECT ENGINE LEFT MOUNTING
(a) Raise the transaxle and engine slightly with a jack.
(b) Remove the engine left mounting two set bolts from front side.

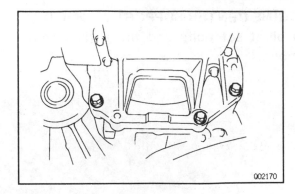

002170

29. REMOVE TRANSAXLE

(a) Remove the transaxle mounting bolts from the engine front side.

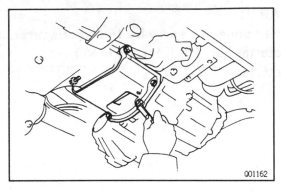

001162

(b) Remove the transaxle mounting bolts from the engine rear side.

(c) Lower the engine left side and remove the transaxle from the engine.

TRANSAXLE INSTALLATION

MX06M–01

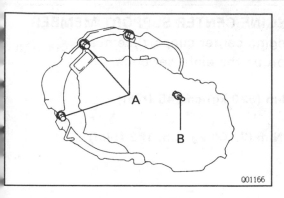

001166

1. INSTALL TRANSAXLE

(a) Align the input shaft spline with the clutch disc and install the transaxle to the engine.

(b) Torque the bolts.

Bolt A

Torque: 64 N·m (650 kgf·cm, 47 ft·lbf)

Bolt B

Torque: 46 N·m (470 kgf·cm, 34 ft·lbf)

2. CONNECT ENGINE LEFT MOUNTING

(a) Raise the transaxle and engine slightly with a jack. Connect the engine left mounting.

(b) Install and torque the engine left mounting two set bolts.

Torque: 56 N·m (570 kgf·cm, 41 ft·lbf)

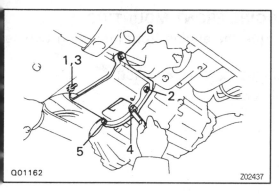

001163

MX

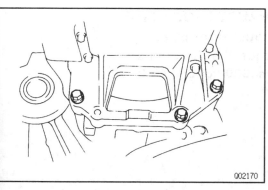

Q01162   Z02437

3. (4A–FE Engine)
INSTALL STIFFENER PLATE

(a) Temporarily tighten the No.1 bolt.

(b) Torque the five bolts on the stiffener plate in the order shown.

Torque: 23 N·m (230 kgf·cm, 17 ft·lbf)

4. (7A–FE Engine)
INSTALL AND TORQUE TRANSAXLE MOUNTING BOLTS TO ENGINE REAR END PLATE SIDE

Torque: 23 N·m (230 kgf·cm, 17 ft·lbf)

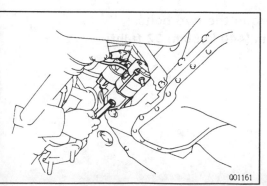

002170

5. INSTALL STARTER

(a) Install the starter.

(b) Install and torque the starter set bolt to the lower side.

Torque: 39 N·m (400 kgf·cm, 29 ft·lbf)

(c) Connect the connector and wire to the starter.

001161

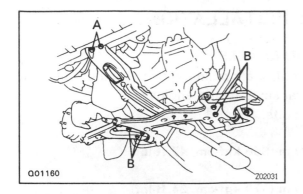

Q01160   Z02031

6. INSTALL ENGINE CENTER SUPPORT MEMBER

Install the engine center support member.
Install and torque the eight set bolts.
Bolt A
Torque: 61 N·m (620 kgf·cm, 45 ft·lbf)
Bolt B
Torque: 206 N·m (2,100 kgf·cm, 152 ft·lbf)

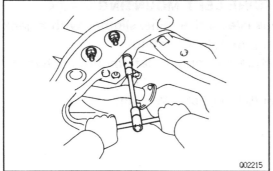

Q02215

7. CONNECT ENGINE REAR MOUNTING

Install and torque the engine rear mounting three set nuts.
Torque: 48 N·m (490 kgf·cm, 35 ft·lbf)

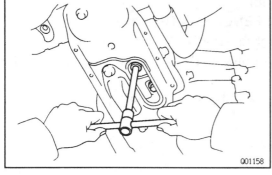

Q01158

8. CONNECT ENGINE FRONT MOUNTING

(a) Install and torque the engine front mounting two set bolts.
Torque: 64 N·m (650 kgf·cm, 47 ft·lbf)
(b) Install the hole cover.

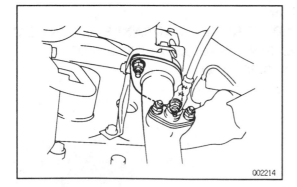

Q02214

9. INSTALL EXHAUST FRONT PIPE

(a) Install the exhaust front pipe.
(b) Install and torque the three nuts.
Torque: 62 N·m (630 kgf·cm, 46 ft·lbf)

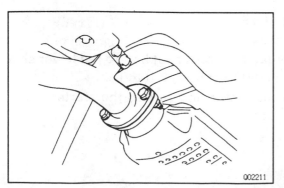

Q02211

(c) Install and torque the two bolts.
Torque: 43 N·m (440 kgf·cm, 32 ft·lbf)

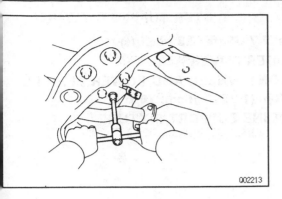

(d) Install the front pipe support and torque the nut.
Torque: 19 N·m (195 kgf·cm, 14 ft·lbf)

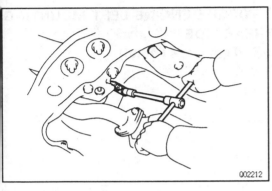

(e) Install and torque the two bolts.
Torque: 19 N·m (195 kgf·cm, 14 ft·lbf)

MX

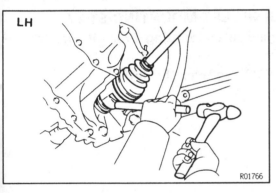

LH

10. INSTALL DRIVE SHAFT
(See SA Section)

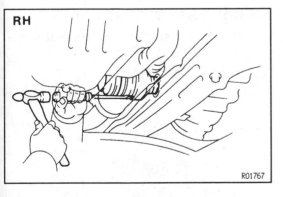

RH

11. CONNECT LOWER BALL JOINT TO LOWER ARM
(a) Connect the lower ball joint to the lower arm.
(b) Install and torque the bolt and two nuts.
Torque: 142 N·m (1,450 kgf·cm, 105 ft·lbf)
12. FILL TRANSAXLE WITH GEAR OIL
   Oil grade:
        API GL3, GL-4 or GL-5
   Viscosity:
        SAE 75W-90

Capacity:
   2.6 liters (2.7 USqts, 2.3 Imp.qts)

13. INSTALL UNDER COVERS

14. INSTALL FRONT WHEEL AND LOWER VEHICLE
Torque: 103 N·m (1,050 kgf·cm, 76 ft·lbf)

15. REMOVE ENGINE SUPPORT FIXTURE

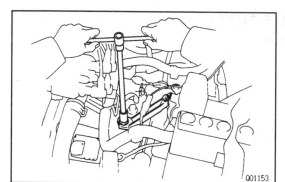

16. INSTALL AND TORQUE ENGINE LEFT MOUNTING SET BOLT TO REAR SIDE
Torque: 56 N·m (570 kgf·cm, 41 ft·lbf)

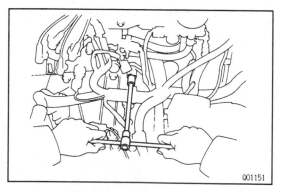

17. INSTALL ENGINE LEFT MOUNTING STAY
Install the engine left mounting bracket and torque the two bolts.
Torque: 21 N·m (210 kgf·cm, 15ft·lbf)

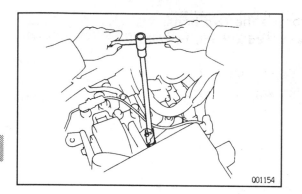

18. INSTALL AND TORQUE STARTER SET BOLT
Install and torque the starter set bolt to the transaxle upper side.
Torque: 39 N·m (400 kgf·cm, 29 ft·lbf)

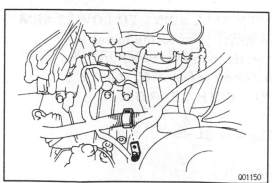

19. CONNECT ENGINE WIRE CLAMP

20. CONNECT VEHICLE SPEED SENSOR CONNECTOR

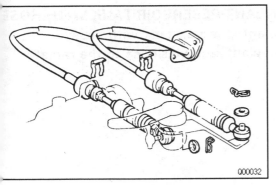

21. CONNECT CONTROL CABLES

(a) Connect the control cables to the control lever housing.

(b) Install the clips to cables.

(c) Install the clips and washers.

MX

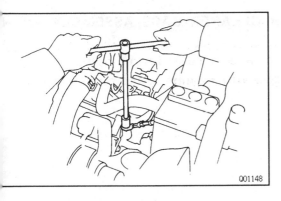

22. INSTALL EARTH CABLE

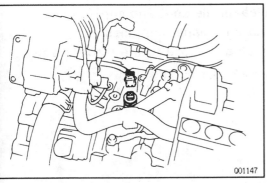

23. CONNECT BACK — UP LIGHT SWITCH CONNECTOR

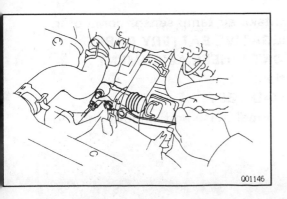

24. INSTALL RELEASE CYLINDER AND RELEASE CYLINDER TUBE BRACKET

(a) Place the release cylinder and torque the two bolts.
Torque: 12 N·m (120 kgf·cm, 9 ft·lbf)

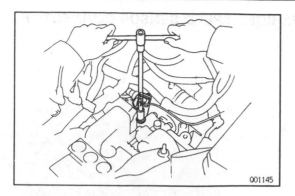

MX

(b)   Install the release cylinder tube bracket and bolt.

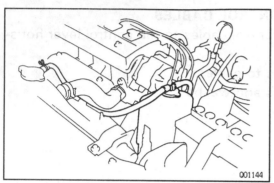

25. INSTALL COOLANT RESERVOIR TANK WITH HOSE
(a)   Install the coolant reservoir tank with hose.
(b)   Connect the coolant reservoir hose to the radiator.

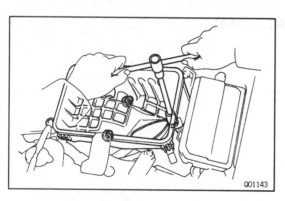

26. INSTALL AIR CLEANER CASE ASSEMBLY WITH AIR HOSE
(a)   Install the air cleaner case and three bolts.
(b)   Connect the two wire clamps to the air cleaner case.

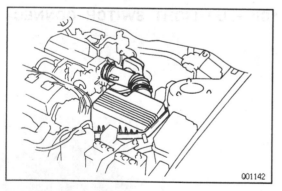

(c)   Install the air cleaner element and cap.
(d)   Connect the four air cleaner cap clips.
(e)   Connect the air cleaner hose to the throttle body.

(f)   Connect the intake air temp sensor connector.
27. CONNECT NEGATIVE BATTERY CABLE
28. INSPECT FRONT WHEEL ALIGNMENT
(See SA Section)
29. PERFORM ROAD TEST
Check for abnormal noise and smooth shifting.

COMPONENT PARTS REMOVAL
COMPONENTS

MX06W—01

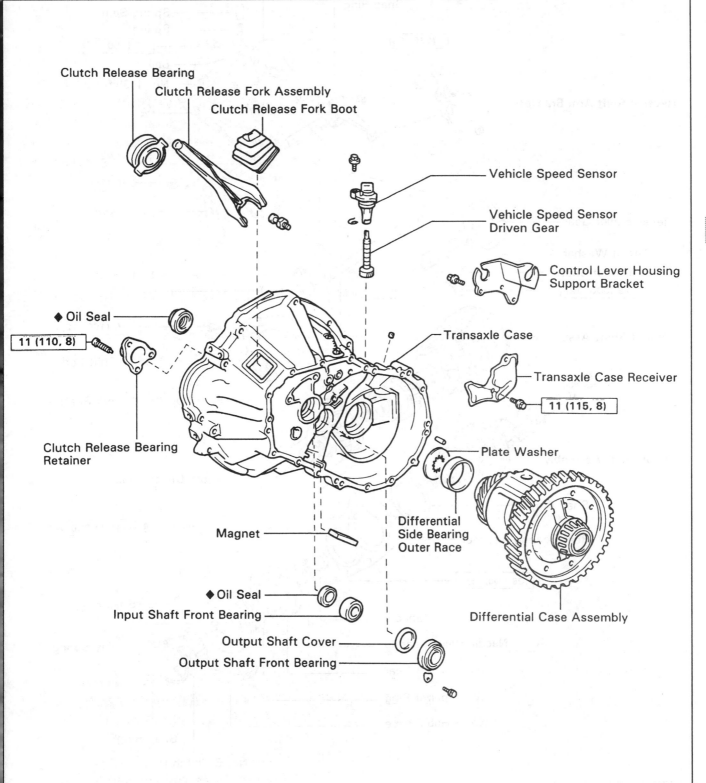

Clutch Release Bearing
Clutch Release Fork Assembly
Clutch Release Fork Boot

Vehicle Speed Sensor

Vehicle Speed Sensor Driven Gear

Control Lever Housing Support Bracket

MX

◆ Oil Seal

11 (110, 8)

Transaxle Case

Transaxle Case Receiver

11 (115, 8)

Clutch Release Bearing Retainer

Plate Washer

Magnet

Differential Side Bearing Outer Race

◆ Oil Seal
Input Shaft Front Bearing

Differential Case Assembly

Output Shaft Cover
Output Shaft Front Bearing

N·m (kgf·cm, ft·lbf) : Specified torque
◆ Non-reusable part

001575

MX

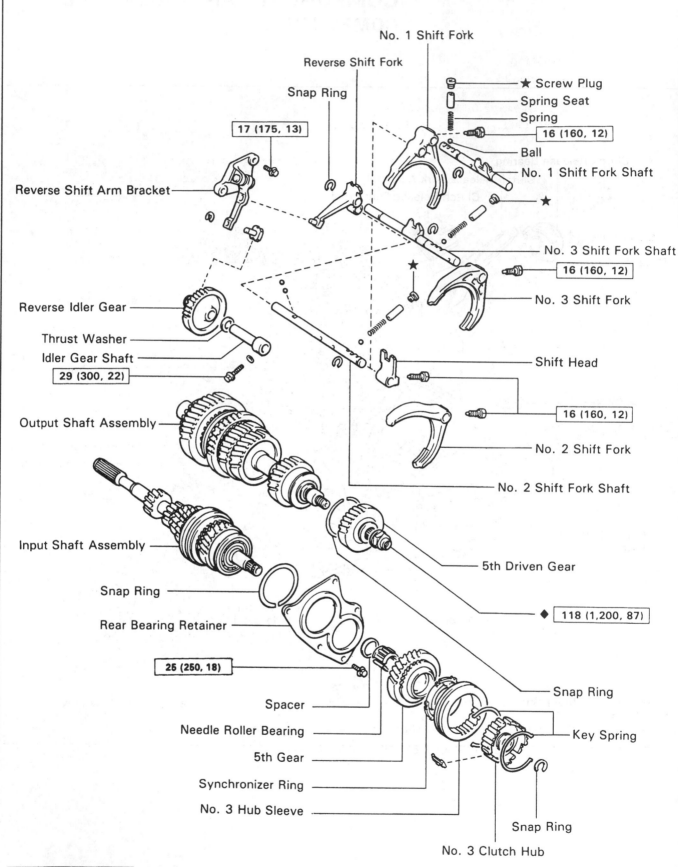

No. 1 Shift Fork

Reverse Shift Fork

Snap Ring

★ Screw Plug

Spring Seat

Spring

16 (160, 12)

Ball

No. 1 Shift Fork Shaft

★

17 (175, 13)

Reverse Shift Arm Bracket

No. 3 Shift Fork Shaft

16 (160, 12)

No. 3 Shift Fork

Reverse Idler Gear

★

Thrust Washer

Idler Gear Shaft

Shift Head

29 (300, 22)

16 (160, 12)

Output Shaft Assembly

No. 2 Shift Fork

Input Shaft Assembly

No. 2 Shift Fork Shaft

5th Driven Gear

Snap Ring

Rear Bearing Retainer

◆ **118 (1,200, 87)**

25 (250, 18)

Snap Ring

Spacer

Needle Roller Bearing

Key Spring

5th Gear

Synchronizer Ring

No. 3 Hub Sleeve

Snap Ring

No. 3 Clutch Hub

N·m (kgf·cm, ft·lbf) : Specified torque

◆ Non-reusable part

★ Precoated part

000985

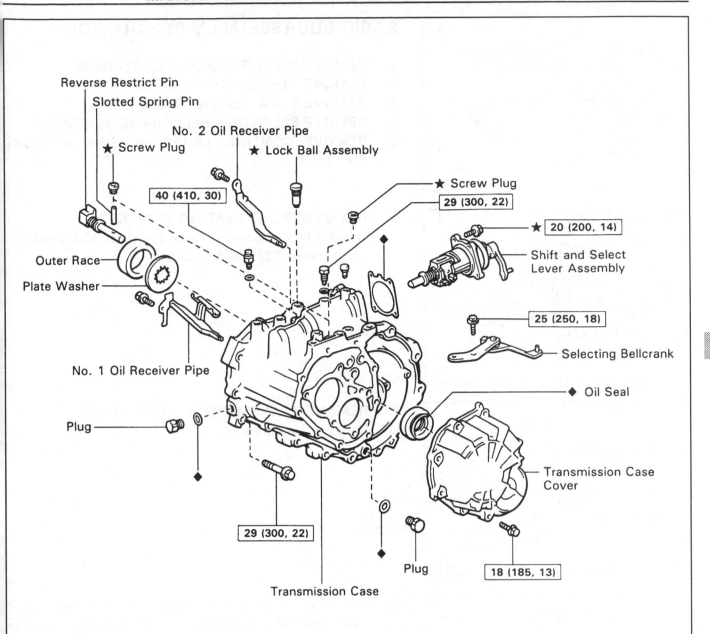

Reverse Restrict Pin
Slotted Spring Pin
No. 2 Oil Receiver Pipe
★ Screw Plug
★ Lock Ball Assembly
★ Screw Plug
40 (410, 30)
29 (300, 22)
★ 20 (200, 14)
Shift and Select Lever Assembly
Outer Race
Plate Washer
25 (250, 18)
Selecting Bellcrank
No. 1 Oil Receiver Pipe
◆ Oil Seal
Plug
Transmission Case Cover
29 (300, 22)
Plug
18 (185, 13)
Transmission Case

MX

N·m (kgf·cm, ft·lbf) : Specified torque

◆ Non-reusable part

★ Precoated part

000986

MX

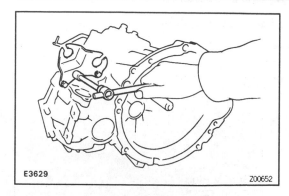

E3629   Z00652

BASIC SUBASSEMBLY SEPARATION

MX06N-01

1. **REMOVE RELEASE FORK AND BEARING**
2. **REMOVE VEHICLE SPEED SENSOR**
3. **REMOVE BACK-UP LIGHT SWITCH**
4. **REMOVE SELECTING BELLCRANK ASSEMBLY**
5. **REMOVE CONTROL LEVER HOUSING SUPPORT BRACKET**

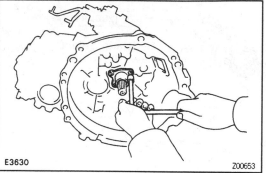

E3630   Z00653

6. **REMOVE FRONT BEARING RETAINER**
   Using a torx wrench, remove the three torx screws.
   Torx wrench T30 09042-00010

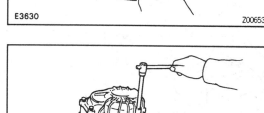

E3631   Z00654

7. **REMOVE TRANSMISSION CASE COVER**
   (a) Remove the nine bolts.

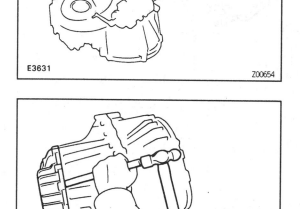

E3632   Z01196

(b) Carefully tap off the projection of the transmission case cover with a brass bar and hammer to remove the transmission case cover from the transmission case, and remove the transmission case cover.

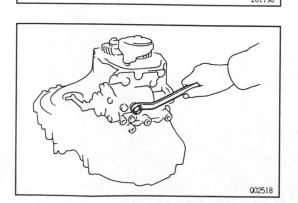

002518

8. **REMOVE SHIFT AND SELECT LEVER SHAFT ASSEMBLY**
   (a) Remove the lock bolt.

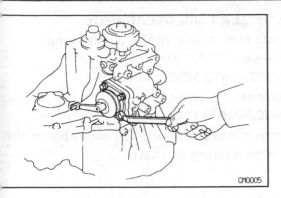

(b) Remove the four bolts and pull out the shift and select lever shaft assembly.

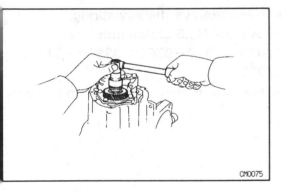

9. REMOVE LOCK NUT
(a) Engage the gear double meshing.
(b) Using a hammer and chisel, loosen the staked part of the nut.

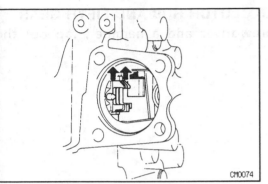

(c) Remove the lock nut.
(d) Disengage the gear double meshing.

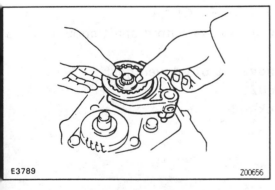

10. REMOVE NO. 3 HUB SLEEVE AND NO. 3 SHIFT FORK
(a) Remove the bolt from No.3 shift fork.
(b) Remove the No.3 hub sleeve and shift fork.

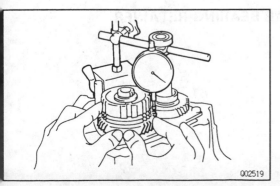

11. INSPECT FIFTH GEAR THRUST CLEARANCE
Using a dial indicator, measure the thrust clearance.
Standard clearance:
   0.10−0.57 mm (0.0039−0.0224 in.)
Maximum clearance:
   0.65 mm (0.056 in.)

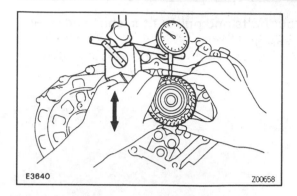

12. INSPECT FIFTH GEAR OIL CLEARANCE

Using a dial indicator, measure the oil clearance.

Standard clearance:

　0.015−0.058 mm (0.0006−0.0023 in.)

Maximum clearance:

　0.070 mm (0.0028 in.)

If the clearance exceeds the maximum, replace the gear, needle roller bearing or shaft.

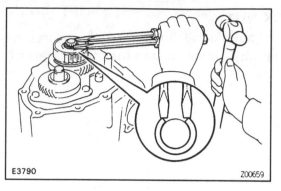

13. REMOVE NO.3 CLUTCH HUB AND FIFTH GEAR

(a) Using two screwdriver and a hammer, tap out the snap ring.

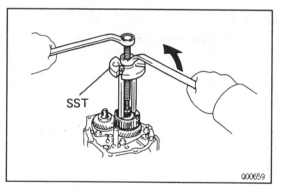

(b) Using a screwdriver, remove the key spring.
(c) Using SST, remove the No.3 clutch hub.
　　SST 09310−17010 (09310−07010, 09310−07020,
　　　09310−07030)
(d) Remove the synchronizer ring, 5th gear and needle roller bearing.

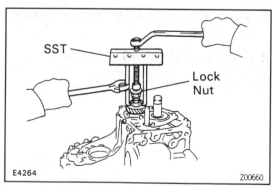

14. REMOVE FIFTH DRIVEN GEAR

(a) Install the lock nut to the output shaft shown in the illustration.
(b) Using SST, remove the 5th driven gear.
　　SST 09213−36020
(c) Remove the lock nut.

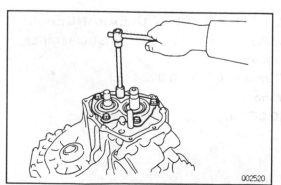

15. REMOVE REAR BEARING RETAINER

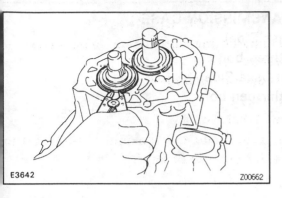

16. REMOVE BEARING SNAP RINGS
Using a snap ring expander, remove the two snap ring.
HINT: If it is difficult to remove the snap rings, pull up the shafts.

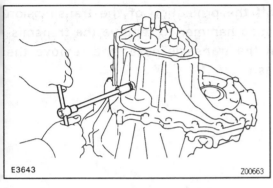

17. REMOVE REVERSE IDLER GEAR SHAFT LOCK BOLT

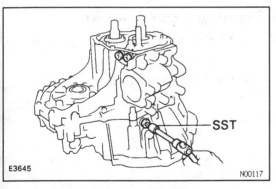

18. REMOVE SNAP RING FROM NO. 2 SHIFT FORK SHAFT
Using two screwdrivers and a hammer, tap out the snap ring.

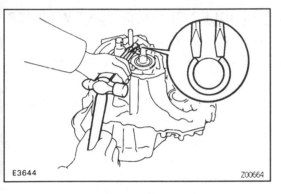

19. REMOVE PLUGS, SEATS, SPRINGS, BALLS AND LOCK BALL ASSEMBLY
(a) Using a hexagon wrench, remove the three plugs.
(b) Using a magnetic finger, remove the three spring seats, springs and balls.

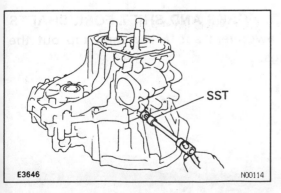

20. REMOVE LOCK BALL ASSEMBLY
Using a hexagon wrench, remove the lock ball assembly.

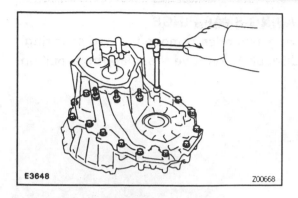

21. REMOVE TRANSMISSION CASE
(a) (Transaxle Case Side)
Remove the three bolts.
(b) (Transmission Case Side)
Remove the thirteen bolts.

(c) Carefully tap off the projection of the transmission case with a plastic hammer to remove the transmission case from the transaxle case, and remove the transmission case.

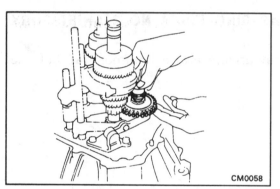

22. REMOVE REVERSE IDLER GEAR, THRUST WASHER AND SHAFT

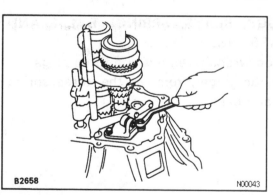

23. REMOVE REVERSE SHIFT ARM BRACKET
Remove the two bolts and bracket.

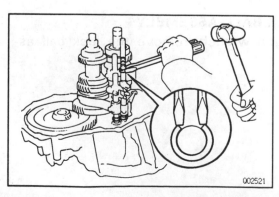

24. REMOVE SHIFT FORKS AND SHIFT FORK SHAFTS
(a) Using two screwdrivers and a hammer, tap out the three snap rings.

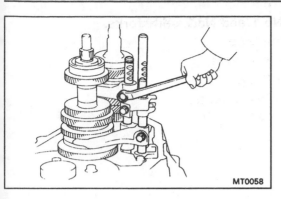

(b) Remove the three set bolts.

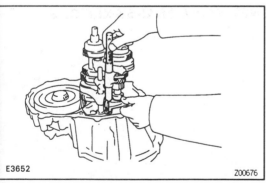

(c) Pull up No.3 shift fork shaft, remove the No.2 fork shaft and the shift head.

MX

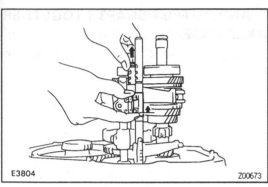

(d) Using a magnetic finger, remove the two balls from the reverse shift fork.

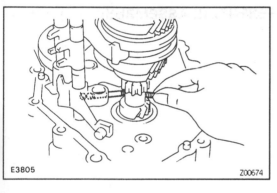

(e) Remove the No.3 shift fork shaft and reverse shift fork.

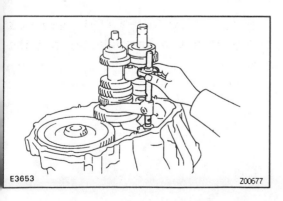

(f) Pull out the No.1 fork shaft.

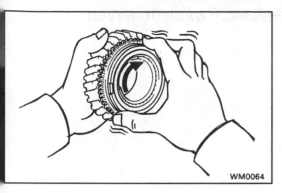

WM0064

COMPONENT PARTS INSPECTION

MX06P—01

1. **INSPECTION SYNCHRONIZER RING OF FIFTH GEAR**
(a) Check for wear or damage.
(b) Check the braking effect of the synchronizer ring.
   Turn the synchronizer ring in one direction while pushing it to the gear cone and check that the ring is locked.
   If the braking effect is insufficient, apply a small amount of fine lapping compaund between the synchoronizer ring and gear cone. Lightly rub the synchronizer ring and gear cone together.
   NOTICE:
   - **Wash off completely the fine lapping compound after rubbing.**
   - **Check again the braking effect of the synchronizer ring.**

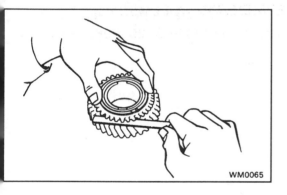

WM0065

(c) Measure the clearance between the synchronizer ring back and gear spline end.
   Minimum clearance:
   0.6 mm (0.024 in.)
   HINT:
   - When replacing either a synchronizer ring or gear, apply a small amount of fine lapping compaund between the synchronizer ring and gear cone. Lightly rub the synchronizer ring and gear cone together.
   - When replacing both the synchronizer ring and gear, there is no need to apply any compound or to rub them together.
   NOTICE: Wash off completely the fine lapping compound after rubbing.

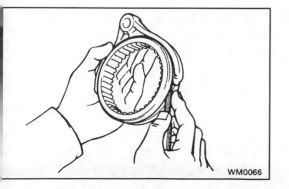

WM0066

2. **INSPECT CLEARANCE OF SHIFT FORK AND HUB SLEEVE**
Using a feeler gauge, measure the clearance between the hub sleeve and shift fork.
Maximum clearance:
1.0 mm (0.039 in.)
If the clearance exceeds the maximum, replace the shift fork or hub sleeve.

3. REMOVE TRANSAXLE CASE RECEIVER

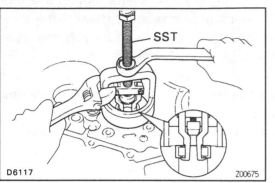

4. IF NECESSARY, REPLACE INPUT SHAFT FRONT BEARING
(a) Using SST, pull out the bearing.
SST 09612—65014

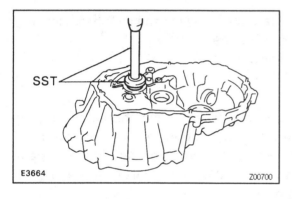

(b) Using SST and a press, install a new bearing.
SST 09608—12010 (09608—03020, 09608—00030)

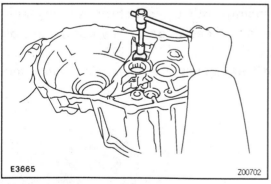

5. IF NECESSARY, REPLACE OUTPUT SHAFT FRONT BEARING
(a) Remove the bolt and bearing lock plate.

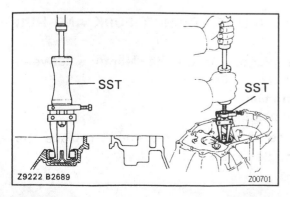

(b) Using SST, pull out the bearing.
SST 09308—00010
(c) Remove the output shaft front cover.

MX

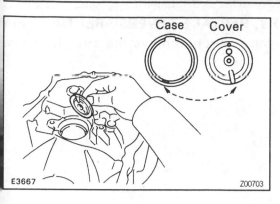

(d) Install the output shaft front cover.
HINT: Install the output shaft front cover projection into the case side hollow.

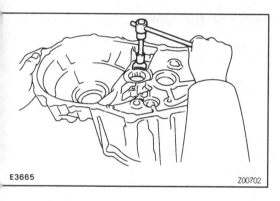

(e) Using SST and a press, install a new bearing.
SST 09310—35010

MX

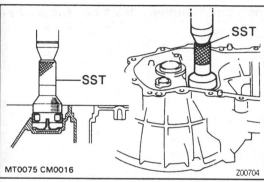

(f) Install the bearing lock plate and torque the bolt.
Torque: 11 N·m (115 kgf·cm, 8 ft·lbf)

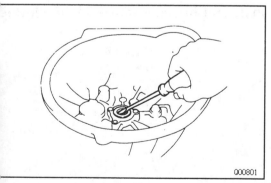

6. IF NECESSARY, REPLACE INPUT SHAFT FRONT OIL SEAL

(a) Using a screwdriver, pry out the oil seal.

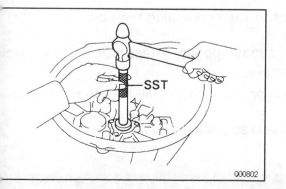

(b) Using SST, drive in a new oil seal.
SST 09608—12010 (09608—00020, 09608—00080)
(c) Coat the lip of the oil seal with MP grease.

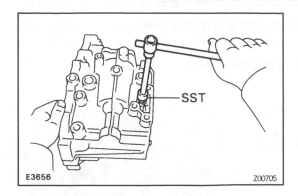

7.   **IF NECESSARY, REPLACE REVERSE RESTRICT PIN**

(a)   Using a hexagon wrench, remove the straight screw plug.

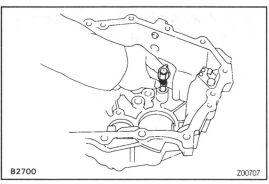

(b)   Using a pin punch and hammer, drive out the slotted spring pin.

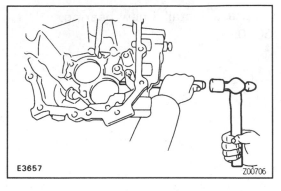

(c)   Replace the reverse restrict pin.

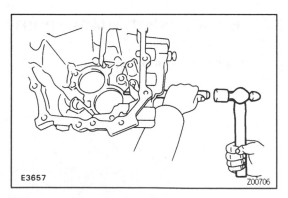

(d)   Using a pin punch and hammer, drive in the slotted spring pin.

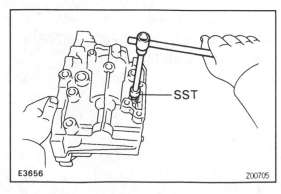

(e)   Apply sealant to the screw plug threads.
     Sealant:
        Part No. 08833−00080, THREE BOND 1344, LOC-
        TITE 242 or equivalent

(f)   Using a hexagon wrench, install the straight screw plug.
     Torque: 13 N·m (130 kgf·cm, 9 ft·lbf)

8. INSTALL AND TORQUE TRANSAXLE CASE RE-CEIVER
Torque: **11N·m (115 kgf·cm, 8 ft·lbf)**

INPUT SHAFT
COMPONENTS

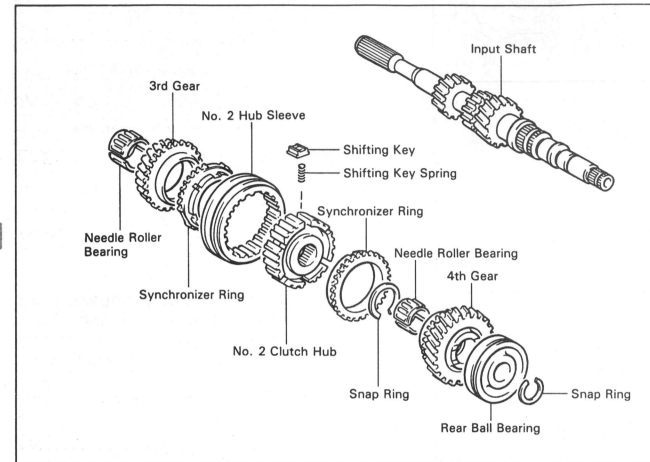

MX04B—02

- Input Shaft
- 3rd Gear
- No. 2 Hub Sleeve
- Shifting Key
- Shifting Key Spring
- Synchronizer Ring
- Needle Roller Bearing
- Needle Roller Bearing
- 4th Gear
- Synchronizer Ring
- No. 2 Clutch Hub
- Snap Ring
- Snap Ring
- Rear Ball Bearing

000803

MX06Q—01

INPUT SHAFT DISASSEMBLY

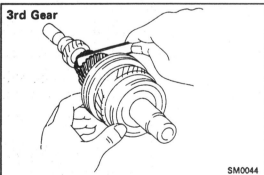

3rd Gear

SM0044

4th Gear

SM0043

1. **INSPECT THIRD AND FOURTH GEAR THRUST CLEARANCE**

   Using a feeler gauge, measure the thrust clearance.

   Standard clearance:

   3rd gear

   > 0.10—0.35 mm (0.0039—0.0138 in.)

   4th gear

   > 0.10—0.55 mm (0.0039—0.0217 in.)

   Maximum clearance:

   3rd gear

   > 0.40 mm (0.0157 in.)

   4th gear

   > 0.60 mm (0.0236 in.)

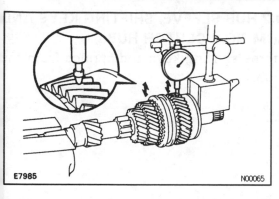

2. **INSPECT THIRD AND FOURTH GEAR OIL CLEARANCE**

Using a dial indicator, measure the oil clearance between the gear and shaft.

Standard clearance:

    0.015 — 0.058 mm (0.0006 — 0.0023 in.)

Maximum clearance:

    0.070 mm (0.0028 in.)

If the clearance exceeds the minimum, replace the gear, needle roller bearing and shaft.

3. **REMOVE SNAP RING**

Using two screwdrivers and a hammer, tap out the snap ring.

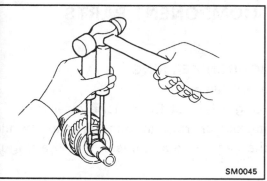

4. **REMOVE REAR BALL BEARING, FOURTH GEAR, NEEDLE ROLLER BEARING, SPACER AND SYNCHRONIZER RING FROM INPUT SHAFT**

(a) Using SST and a press, remove the rear ball bearing.
     SST 09950 — 00020

(b) Remove the 4th gear, meesle roller bearing, spacer and synchronizer ring.

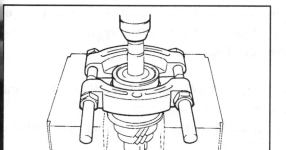

5. **REMOVE SNAP RING**

Using two screwdrivers and a hammer, tap out the snap ring.

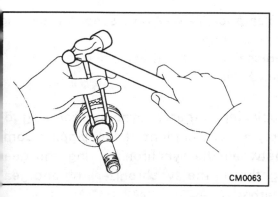

6. **REMOVE NO.2 HUB SLEEVE ASSEMBLY, THIRD GEAR, SYNCHRONIZER RING AND NEEDLE ROLLER BEARING**

Using SST and a press, remove the No.2 hub sleeve, 3 rd gear, synchronizer ring and needle roller bearing.
SST 09950 — 00020

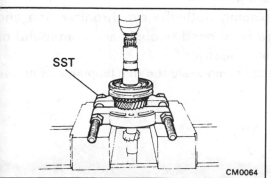

7. REMOVE NO.2 HUB SLEEVE, SHIFTING KEYS AND SPRINGS FROM NO.2 CLUTCH HUB

Remove the three shifting keys and springs from the No.2 clutch hub.

MX06R—01

INPUT SHAFT COMPONENT PARTS INSPECTION

1. INSPECT SYNCHRONIZER RING

(a) Check for wear or damage.

(b) Check the braking effect of the synchronizer ring.

Turn the synchronizer ring in one direction while pushing it to the gear cone and check that the ring is locked.

If braking effect is insufficient, apply a small amount of fine lapping compaund between the synchronizer ring and gear cone.Lightly rub the synchronizer ring and gear cone together.

NOTICE:

- **Wash off completely the fine lapping compound after rubbing.**
- **Check again the braking effect of the synchronizer ring.**

(c) Measure the clearance between the synchronizer ring back and gear spline end.

Minimum clearance:

0.6 mm (0.024 in.)

HINT:

- When replacing either a synchronizer ring o gear, apply a small amount of fine lapping compound between the synchronizer ring and gea cone. Lightly rub the synchronizer ring and gea cone together.
- When replacing both the synchronizer ring and gear, there is no need to apply any compound o to rub them together.

NOTICE: Wash off completely the fine lapping compound after rubbing.

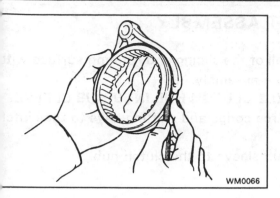

2. **INSPECT CLEARANCE OF SHIFT FORK AND HUB SLEEVE**

Using a feeler gauge, measure the clearance between the hub sleeve and shift fork.

Maximum clearance:

1.0 mm (0.039 in.)

HINT:

- When replacing either a synchronizer ring or gear, applya small amount of fine lapping compaund between the synchronizer ring and gear cone. Lightly rub the synchronizer ring and gear cone together.
- When replacing both the synchronizer ring and gear, there is no need to apply any compound or to rub them together.

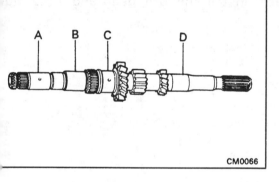

3. **INSPECT INPUT SHAFT**

(a) Check the input shaft for wear or damage.

(b) Using a micrometer, measure the outer diameter of the input shaft journal surface.

Minimum outer diameter:

Part A

24.870 mm (0.9791 in.)

Part B

28.970 mm (1.1405 in.)

Part C

30.970 mm (1.2193 in.)

Part D

24.970 mm (0.9831 in.)

If the outer diameter exceeds the minimum, replace the inutput shaft.

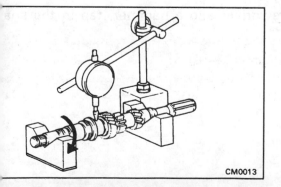

(c) Using a dial indicator, check the shaft runout.

Maximum runout:

0.05 mm (0.0020 in.)

If the runout exceeds the maximum, replace the input shaft.

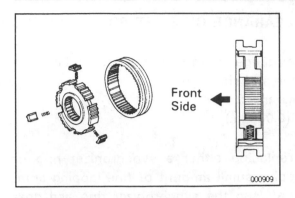

MX

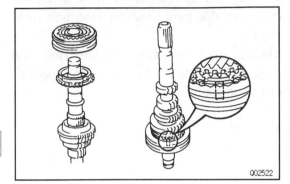

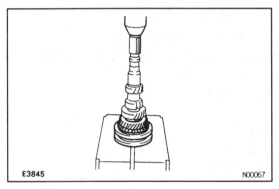

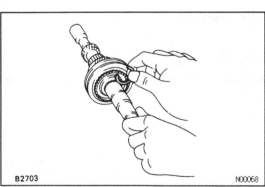

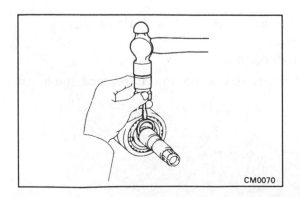

MX06S—01

INPUT SHAFT ASSEMBLY

HINT: Coat all of the sliding and rotating surface with gear oil before assembly.

1. INSTALL NO.2 CLUTCH HUB INTO HUB SLEEVE

(a) Install the three sprigs and shifting keys to the clutch hub.

(b) Install the hub sleeve to the clutch hub.

2. INSTALL THIRD GEAR, NEEDLE ROLLER BEARING SYNCHRONIZER RING AND NO. 2 HUB SLEEVE ASSEMBLY TO INTPUT SHAFT

(a) Apply gear oil to the needle roller bearing.

(b) Place the synchronizer ring on the gear and align the ring slots with the shifting keys.

(c) Using a press, install the 3rd gear and No.2 hub sleeve.

3. INSTALL SNAP RING

(a) Select a snap ring that will allow minimum axial play

Mark	Thickness mm (in.)	Mark	Thickness mm (in.)
0	2.30 (0.0906)	3	2.48 (0.0976)
1	2.36 (0.0929)	4	2.54 (0.1000)
2	2.42 (0.0953)	5	2.60 (0.1024)

(b) Using a screwdriver and a hammer, tap in the snap ring.

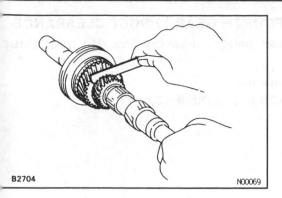

B2704 N00069

4. INSPECT THIRD GEAR THRUST CLEARANCE

Using a feeler gauge, measure the 3rd gear thrust clearance.

Standard clearance:

0.10−0.35 mm (0.0039−0.0138 in.)

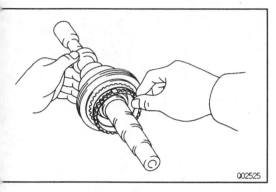

002525

5. INSTALL SYNCHRONIZER RING, NEEDLE ROLLER BEARING, SPACER, FOURTH GEAR AND REAR BALL BEARING

(a) Apply gear oil to the needle roller bearing.
(b) Place the synchronizer ring on the gear and align the ring slots with the shifting keys.

MX

SST

SM0049

(c) Using SST and a press, install the rear ball bearing.
SST 09608−20012(09608−03070)

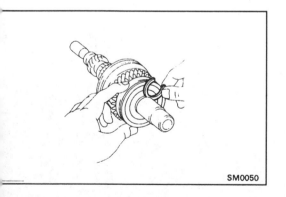

SM0050

6. INSTALL SNAP RING

(a) Select a snap ring that will allow minimum axial play.

Mark	Thickness mm (in.)	Mark	Thickness mm (in.)
A	2.29 (0.0902)	D	2.47 (0.0972)
B	2.35 (0.0925)	E	2.53 (0.0996)
C	2.41 (0.0949)	F	2.59 (0.1020)

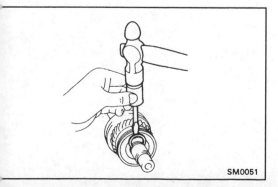

SM0051

(b) Using a screwdriver and a hammer, tap in the snap ring.

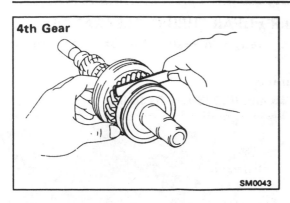

4th Gear

SM0043

7. **MEASURE FOURTH GEAR THRUST CLEARANCE**
Using a feeler gauge, measure the 4th gear thrust clearance.
Standard clearance:
0.10 – 0.55 mm (0.0039 – 0.0217 in.)

OUTPUT SHAFT
COMPONENTS

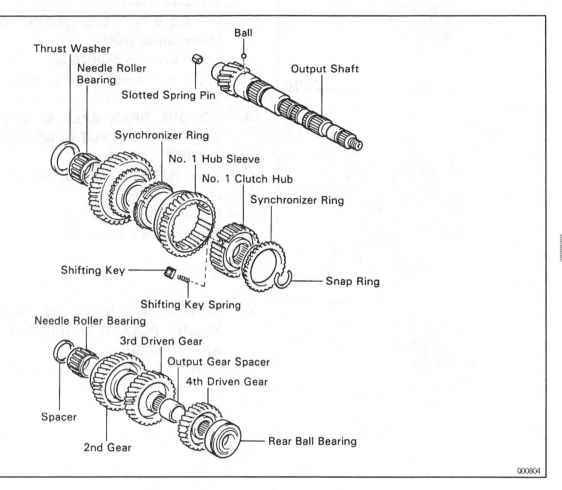

MX043-02

MX

MX044-02

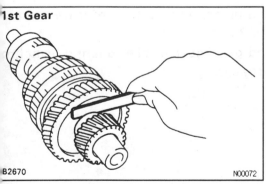

OUTPUT SHAFT DISASSEMBLY

1. **INSPECT FIRST AND SECOND GEAR THRUST CLEARANCE**
    Using a feeler gauge, measure the thrust clearance.
    Standard clearance:
    1st gear
    0.10 — 0.40 mm (0.0039 — 0.0157 in.)
    2nd gear
    0.10 — 0.45 mm (0.0039 — 0.0177 in.)
    Maximum clearance:
    1st gear
    0.45 mm (0.0177 in.)
    2nd gear
    0.50 mm (0.0197 in.)

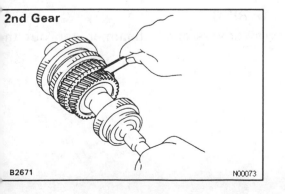

MX

SM0137

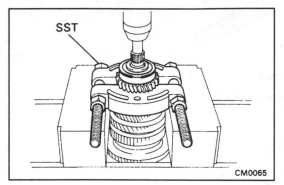

SST

CM0065

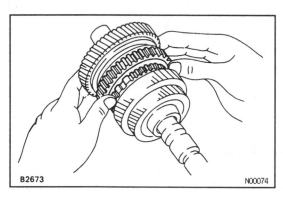

B2673   N00074

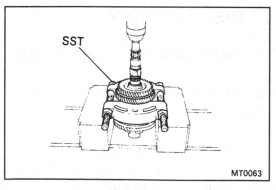

SST

MT0063

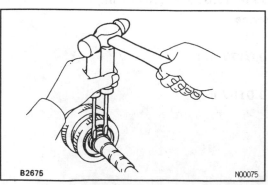

B2675   N00075

2. INSPECT FIRST AND SECOND GEAR OIL CLEARANCE

Using a dial indicator, measure the oil clearance between the gear and shaft.

Standard clearance:

0.015—0.058 mm (0.0006—0.0023 in.)

Maximum clearance:

0.070 mm (0.0028 in.)

If the clearance exceeds the minimum, replace the gear, needle roller bearing and shaft.

3. REMOVE REAR BALL BEARING, FORTH DRIVEN GEAR AND OUTPUT GEAR SPACER FROM OUTPUT SHAFT

(a) Using SST and a press, remove the rear ball bearing and 4th driven gear.

SST 09950—00020

(b) Remove the output spacer.

4. REMOVE THIRD DRIVEN GEAR, SECOND GEAR, NEEDLE ROLLER BEARING, SYNCHRONIZER RING AND SPACER

(a) Shift No.1 hub sleeve into the 1st gear.

(b) Using SST and a press, remove the 3rd driven gear.

SST 09950—00020

(c) Remove the 2nd gear, needle roller bearing, synchronizer ring and spacer.

5. REMOVE SNAP RING

Using two screwdrivers and a hammer, tap out the snap ring.

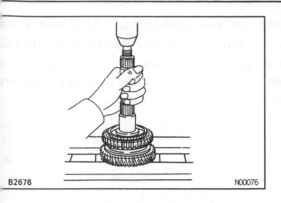

B2676   N00076

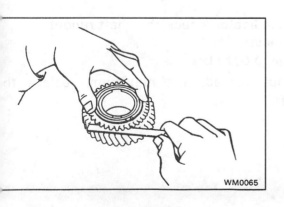

000818

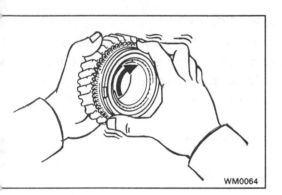

WM0064

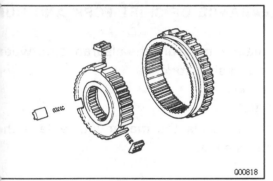

WM0065

6. **REMOVE NO. 1 HUB SLEEVE ASSEMBLY, FIRST GEAR, SYNCHRONIZER RING, NEEDLE ROLLER BEARING, THRUST WASHER AND BALL**
(a) Using a press, remove the No.1 hub sleeve, 1st gear and synchronizer ring.
(b) Remove the needle roller bearing, thrust washer and ball.

7. **REMOVE NO.1 HUB SLEEVE, SHIFTING KEYS AND SPRINGS FROM NO.1 CLUTCH HUB**
Remove the three shifting keys and springs from the No.1 clutch hub.

MX

OUTPUT SHAFT COMPONENT PARTS INSPECTION

MX045-02

1. **INSPECT SYNCHRONIZER RING**
(a) Check for wear or damage.
(b) Check the braking effect of the synchronizer ring.
   Turn the synchronizer ring in one direction while pushing it to the gear cone and check that the ring is locked.
   If the braking effect is insufficient, apply a small amount of fine lapping compound between the synchronizer ring and gear cone. Lightly rub the synchronizer ring and gear cone together.
   NOTICE:
   - **Wash off completely the fine lapping compound after rubbing.**
   - **Check again the braking effect of the synchronizer ring.**
(c) Measure the clearance between the synchronizer ring back and gear spline end.

Minimum clearance:
   0.6 mm (0.024 in.)
HINT:
   - When replacing either a synchronizer ring or gear, apply a small amount of fine lapping compound between the cynchronizer ring and gear cone. Lightly rub the synchronizer ring and gear cone together.

MX

- When replace the synchronizer ring and gear there is no need to apply any compound or to rub them torether.

NOTICE: Wash off completely the fine lapping compound after rubbing.

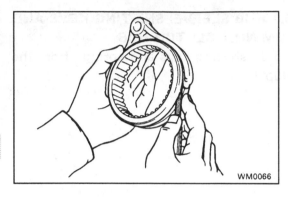

2. INSPECT CLEARANCE OF SHIFT FORK AND HUB SLEEVE

Using a feeler gauge, measure the clearance between the hub sleeve and shift fork.

Maximum clearance:

1.0 mm (0.039 in.)

If the clearance exceeds the maximum, replace the shift fork or hub sleeve.

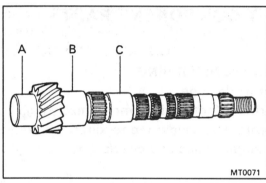

3. INSPECT OUTPUT SHAFT

(a) Check the output shaft for wear or damage.

(b) Using a micrometer, measure the outer diameter of the output shaft journal surface.

Minimum outer diameter:

Part A

32.970 mm (1.2980 in.)

Part B

37.970 mm (1.4949 in.)

Part C

31.970 mm (1.2587 in.)

If the outer diameter exceeds the minimum, replace the output shaft.

(c) Using a dial indicator, check the shaft runout.

Maximum runout:

0.05 mm (0.0020 in.)

If the runout exceeds the maximum, replace the output shaft.

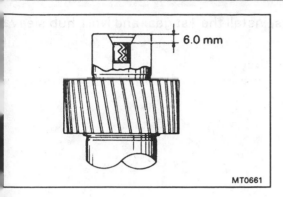

6.0 mm

MT0661

OUTPUT SHAFT ASSEMBLY

MX046-02

HINT: Coat all of the sliding and rotating surface with gear oil before assembly.

1. **IF OUTPUT SHAFT WAS REPLACED, DRIVE IN SLOTTED SPRING PIN**

If the output shaft was replaced, drive the slotted spring pin in the output shaft to a depth of 6.0 mm (0.236 in.).

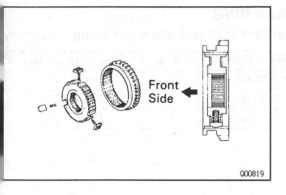

Front Side

000819

2. **INSTALL NO.1 CLUTCH HUB INTO HUB SLEEVE**
(a) Install the three sprigs and shifting keys to the clutch hub.
(b) Install the hub sleeve to the clutch hub.

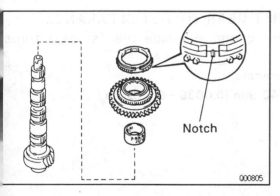

E3685

N00077

3. **INSTALL BALL, THRUST WASHER, FIRST GEAR, NEEDLE ROLLER BEARING, SYNCHRONIZER RING AND NO.1 HUB SLEEVE ASSEMBLY TO OUTPUT SHAFT**
(a) Install the ball to the shaft.
(b) Fit the thrust washer groove securely over the locking ball when installing the thrust on the shaft.
(c) Apply gear oil to the needle roller bearing.

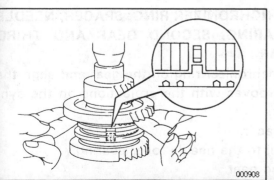

Notch

000805

(d) Install the needle roller bearing, 1st gear and synchronizer ring.

MX

(e) Place the synchronizer ring on the gear and align the clutch hub grooves with the projections on the synchronizer ring.

000908

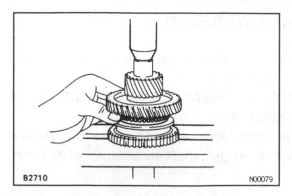

B2710   N00079

(f)   Using a press, install the 1st gear and No.1 hub sleeve

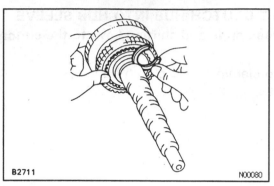

B2711   N00080

4.   INSTALL SNAP RING

(a)   Select a snap ring that will allow minimum axial play

Mark	Thickness mm (in.)	Mark	Thickness mm (in.)
A	2.50 (0.0984)	D	2.68 (0.1055)
B	2.56 (0.1008)	E	2.74 (0.1079)
C	2.62 (0.1031)	F	2.80 (0.1102)

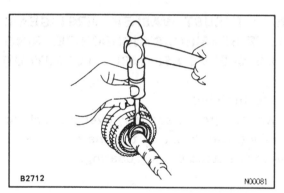

B2712   N00081

(b)   Using a screwdriver and hammer, tap in the snap ring

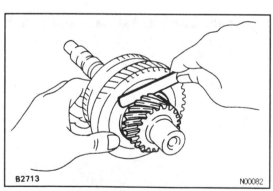

B2713   N00082

5.   INSPECT FIRST GEAR THRUST CLEARANCE

Using a feeler gauge, measure the 1st gear thrus
clearance.

Standard clearance:
   0.10 – 0.40 mm (0.0039 – 0.0157 in.)

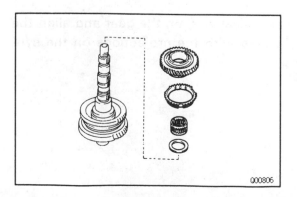

000806

**6.   INSTALL SYNCHRONIZER RING, SPACER, NEEDLE
   ROLLER BEARING, SECOND GEAR AND THIRD
   DRIVEN GEAR**

(a)   Place the synchronizer ring on the gear and align the
   clutch hub grooves with the projections on the syn
   chronizer ring.

(b)   Install the spacer.

(c)   Apply gear oil to the needle roller bearing.

(d)   Install the 2nd gear.

MX

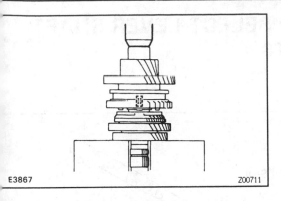

(e) Using a press, install the 3rd driven gear.

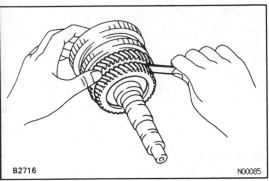

7. INSPECT SECOND GEAR THRUST CLEARANCE
Using a feeler gauge, measure the 2nd gear thrust clearance.
Standard clearance:
  0.10 – 0.45 mm (0.0039 – 0.0177 in.)

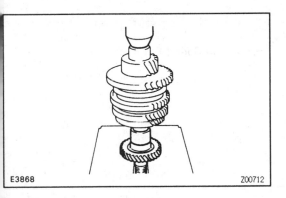

8. INSTALL OUTPUT GEAR SPACER AND FOURTH DRIVEN GEAR
(a) Install the output gear spacer.
(b) Using a press, install the 4th driven gear.

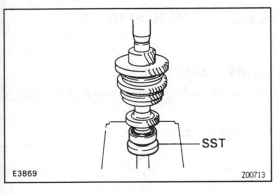

9. INSTALL REAR BALL BEARING
Using SST and a press, install the rear ball bearing.
SST 09316 – 60010 (09316 – 00020)

MX

SHIFT AND SELECT LEVER SHAFT
COMPONENTS

MX00A–02

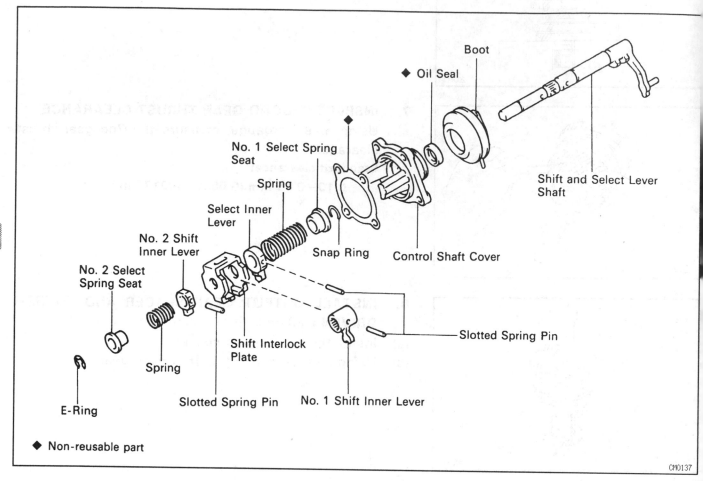

◆ Oil Seal

Boot

No. 1 Select Spring Seat

Spring

Select Inner Lever

No. 2 Shift Inner Lever

No. 2 Select Spring Seat

Spring

E-Ring

Slotted Spring Pin

Shift Interlock Plate

No. 1 Shift Inner Lever

Snap Ring

Control Shaft Cover

Shift and Select Lever Shaft

Slotted Spring Pin

◆ Non-reusable part

CM0137

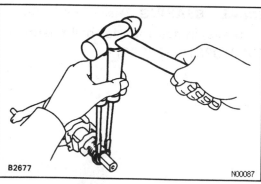

B2677　　N00087

SHIFT AND SELECT LEVER SHAFT DISASSEMBLY

MX00B–02

1.　REMOVE NO.2 SHIFT INNER LEVER
(a)　Using two screwdrivers and hammer, tap out the snap ring.
(b)　Remove the compression spring and seat.

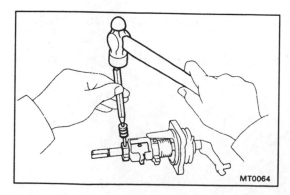

MT0064

(c)　Using a pin punch and hammer, drive out the slotted spring pin from the No.2 shift inner lever.
(d)　Remove the No.2 shift inner lever.

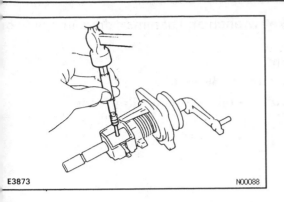

E3873   N00088

2. REMOVE SHIFT INTERLOCK PLATE AND NO. 1 SHAFT INNER LEVER

(a) Using a pin punch and hammer, drive out the slotte dspring pin from the No.1 shaft inner lever.

(b) Remove the shift interlock plate and No.1 shift inner lever.

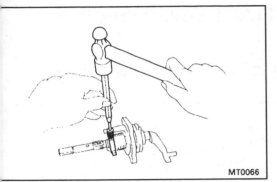

MT0066

3. REMOVE SELECT INNER LEVER

(a) Using a pin punch and hammer, drive out the slotted spring pin from the select inner lever.

(b) Remove the select inner lever, No. 1 compression spring and No.1 select spring seat.

MX

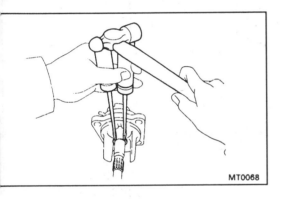

MT0068

4. REMOVE SNAP RING

Using two screwdrivers and hammer, tap out the snap ring.

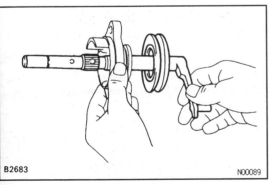

B2683   N00089

5. REMOVE CONTROL SHAFT COVER AND DUST BOOT

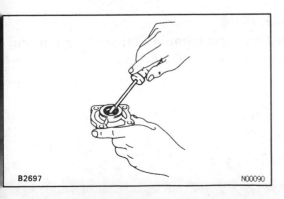

B2697   N00090

6. IF NECESSARY, REPLACE CONTROL SHAFT COVER OIL SEAL

(a) Using a screwdriver, remove the oil seal.

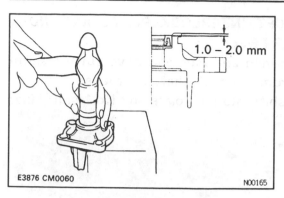

1.0 – 2.0 mm

E3876 CM0060   N00165

(b) Using a socket wrench and hammer, drive in a new oil seal.
Drive in depth:
    1.0 – 2.0 mm (0.039 – 0.079 in.)

(c) Coat the lip of the oil seal with MP grease.

SHIFT AND SELECT LEVER SHAFT ASSEMBLY

MX00C – 02

1. APPLY MP GREASE TO PARTS, AS SHOWN

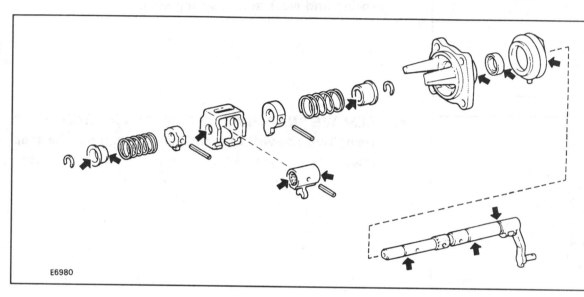

E6980   N00091

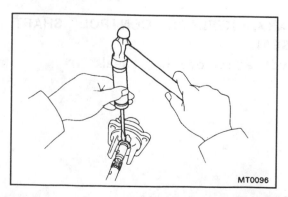

B2741   N00092

2. INSTALL SHIFT AND SELECT LEVER SHAFT

Install the boot and shaft to the control shaft cover.
HINT: Make sure to install the boot in correct direction.
Position the air bleed of the boot downward.

3. INSTALL SNAP RING

Using a screwdriver and hammer, tap in the snap ring.

MT0096

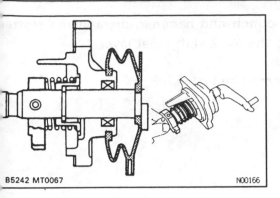

B5242 MT0067   N00166

4. INSTALL SELECT INNER LEVER

(a) Install the No.1 select spring seat, No.1 select spring and select inner lever.

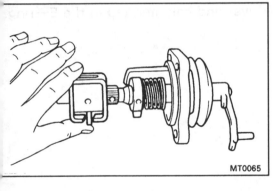

0 ± 0.5 mm

B2680 E3878   N00167

(b) Using a pin punch and hammer, drive in the slotted spring pin to the select inner lever.
Drive in depth:
    0±0.5 mm (0±0.020 in.)

MX

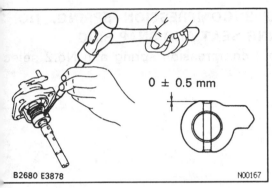

MT0065

5. INSTALL SHIFT INTERLOCK PLATE AND NO. 1 SHIFT INNER LEVER

(a) Install the shift interlock plate No.1 shift inner lever.

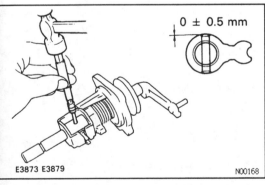

0 ± 0.5 mm

E3873 E3879   N00168

(b) Using a pin punch and hammer, drive in the slotted spring pin to the No.1 shift inner lever.
Drive in depth:
    0±0.5 mm (0±0.020 in.)

(c) Check that the shift interlock plate turns smoothly.

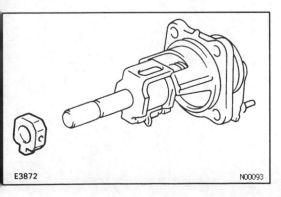

E3872   N00093

6. INSTALL NO.2 SHIFT INNER LEVER

(a) Install the No.2 shift inner lever.

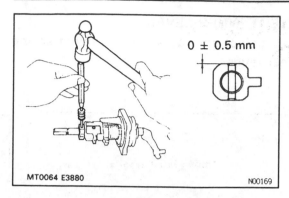

0 ± 0.5 mm

MT0064 E3880　　　N00169

(b) Using a pin punch and hammer, drive in the slotte
spring pin to the No.2 shift inner lever.
Drive in depth:
　　0±0.5 mm (0±0.020 in.)

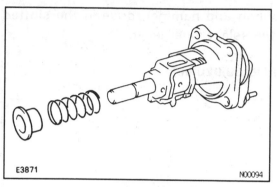

E3871　　　N00094

7. INSTALL NO. 2 COMPRESSION SPRING, NO.
SELECT SPRING SEAT AND SNAP RING
(a) Install the No.2 compression spring and No.2 selec
spring seat.

MX

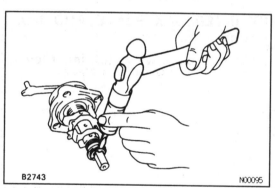

B2743　　　N00095

(b) Using a screwdriver and hammer, tap in the E−ring.

DIFFERENTIAL CASE
COMPONENTS

MX047-02

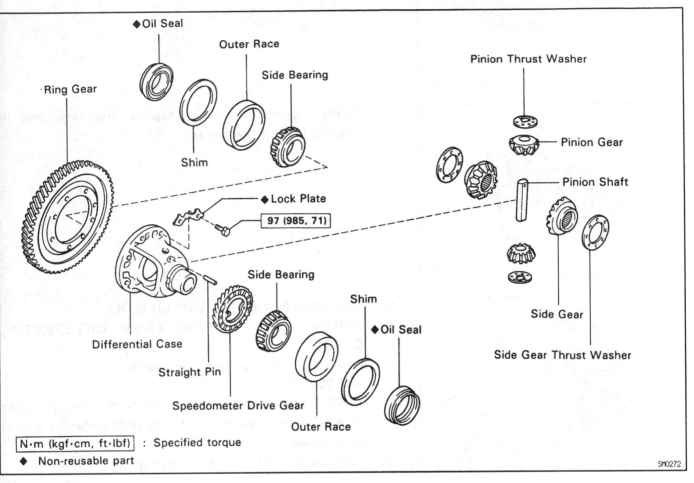

◆Oil Seal

Outer Race

Side Bearing

Ring Gear

Shim

◆ Lock Plate

97 (985, 71)

Pinion Thrust Washer

Pinion Gear

Pinion Shaft

Side Bearing

Shim

◆Oil Seal

Differential Case

Side Gear

Side Gear Thrust Washer

Straight Pin

Speedometer Drive Gear

Outer Race

| N·m (kgf·cm, ft·lbf) | : Specified torque |

◆   Non-reusable part

SM0272

MX048-02

DIFFERENTIAL CASE DISASSEMBLY

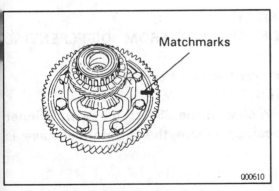

Matchmarks

Q00610

1.   REMOVE RING GEAR
(a)   Place the matchmarks on the ring gear and case.

(b)   Loosen the staked part of the lock plate.

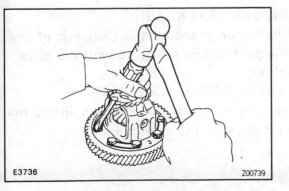

E3736

Z00739

MX

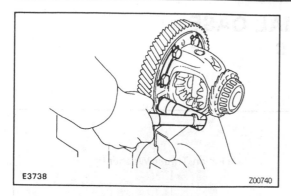

E3738   Z00740

(c) Remove the eight bolts and four lock plates.

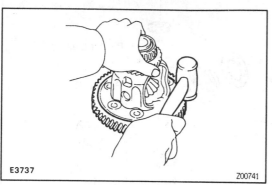

E3737   Z00741

(d) Using a copper hammer, tap on the ring gear to remove it from the case.

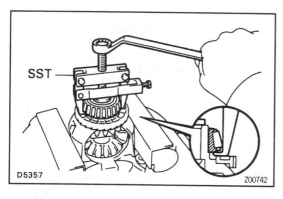

SST

D5357   Z00742

**2. (SPEED SENSOR DRIVE GEAR SIDE)
REMOVE SIDE BEARING FROM DIFFERENTIAL CASE**

(a) Using SST, remove the side bearing.
SST 09502−10012
HINT: Apply the claw of the SST to the bearing inner race at the position where the speedometer drive gear is indented.

(b) Remove the speedometer drive gear.

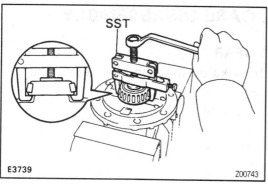

SST

E3739   Z00743

**3. (RING GEAR SIDE)
REMOVE SIDE BEARING FROM DIFFERENTIAL CASE**

Using SST, remove the side bearing.
SST 09502−10012
HINT: Apply the claw of the SST to the bearing inner race at the position where the differential case is indented.

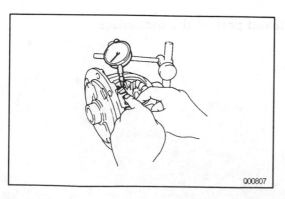

000807

4. INSPECT SIDE GEAR BACKLASH

Using a dial indicator, measure the backlash of one side gear while holding one pinion toward the case.

Standard backlash:

0.05−0.20 mm (0.0020−0.0079 in.)

If the backlash does not meet specification, install the correct thrust washer to the side gears.

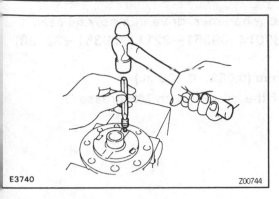

5. DISASSEMBLY DIFFERENTIAL CASE
(a) Using a pin punch and hammer, drive out the pinion shaft lock pin.

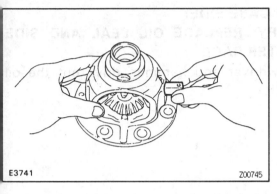

(b) Remove the pinion shaft from the case.
(c) Remove the two pinions and two side gears with the four thrust washers from each gear.

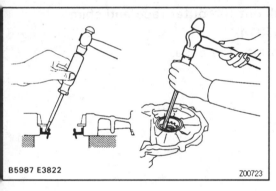

6. (TRANSMISSION CASE SIDE)
IF NECESSARY, REPLACE OIL SEAL AND SIDE BEARING OUTER RACE
(a) Using a screwdriver and hammer, drive out the oil seal.

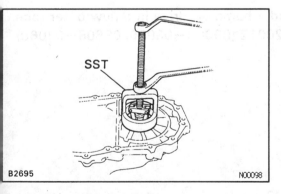

(b) Using SST, pull out the outer race and shim.
SST 09612—65014
(c) Place the shim into the case.

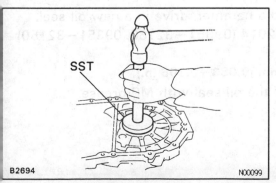

(d) Using SST and a hammer, drive in a new outer race.
SST 09608—20012 (09608—03020, 09608—03090)

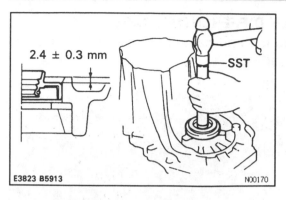

(e) Using SST and a hammer, drive in a new oil seal.
SST 09350−32014 (09351−32111, 09351−32130)
Drive in depth:
   2.1−2.7 mm (0.083−0.106 in.)

(f) Coat the lip of the oil seal with MP grease.

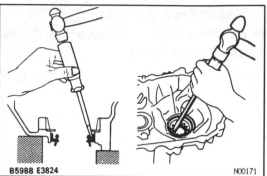

7. (TRANSAXLE CASE SIDE)
IF NECESSARY, REPLACE OIL SEAL AND SIDE BEARING OUTER RACE

(a) Using a screwdriver and hammer, drive out the oil seal.

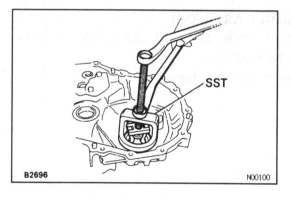

(b) Using SST, pull out the outer race and shim.
SST 09612−65014

(c) Place the shim into the case.

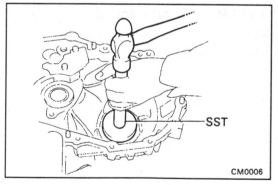

(d) Using SST and a hammer, drive in a new outer race.
SST 09608−20012 (09608−03020, 09608−03060)

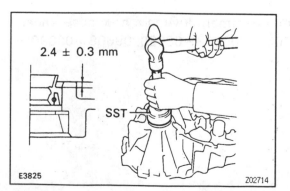

(e) Using SST and a hammer, drive in a new oil seal.
SST 09350−32014 (09351−32130, 09351−32150)
Drive in depth:
   2.1−2.7 mm (0.083−0.106 in.)

(f) Coat the lip of the oil seal with MP grease.

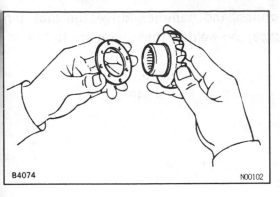

B4074　　　　　　　　　　　　　N00102

MX049-02

DIFFERENTIAL CASE ASSEMBLY

1. ASSEMBLY DIFFERENTIAL CASE

(a) Install the correct thrust washers and side gear.
Referring to the table below, select thrust washers which will ensure that the backlash is within specification.

Standard backlash:
　　0.05–0.20 mm (0.0020–0.0079 in.)

Thickness mm (in.)	Thickness mm (in.)
0.95 (0.0374)	1.10 (0.0433)
1.00 (0.0394)	1.15 (0.0453)
1.05 (0.0413)	1.20 (0.0472)

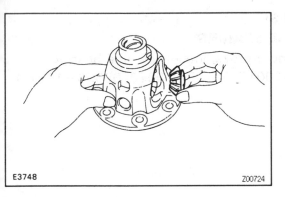

E3748　　　　　　　　　　　　　Z00724

(b) Install the thrust washers and side gears in the differential case.

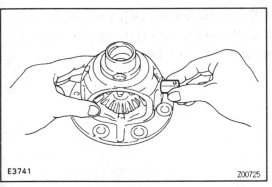

E3741　　　　　　　　　　　　　Z00725

(c) Install the pinion shaft.

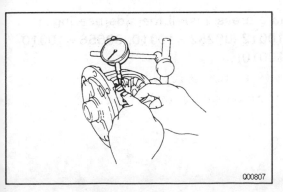

Q00807

(d) Using a dial indicator, check the side gear backlash. Measure the side gear backlash while holding one pinion gear toward the case.

Standard backlash:
　　0.05–0.20 mm (0.0020–0.0079 in.)

If the backlash is not within specification, install a thrust washer of different thickness.

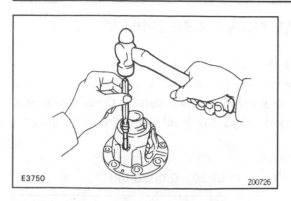

(e) Using a pin punch and hammer, drive the lock pin through the case and hold in the pinion shaft.

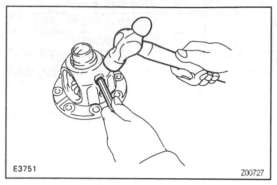

(f) Stake the differential case.

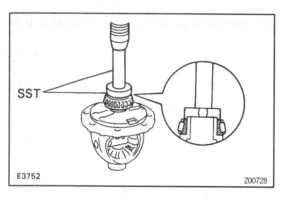

2. **(RING GEAR SIDE)**
    INSTALL SIDE BEARING
    Using SST and a press, install the side bearing.
    SST 09550−10012 (09252−10010, 09556−10010)

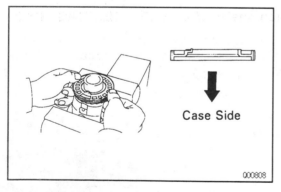

Case Side

3. **(SPEED SENSOR DRIVE GEAR SIDE)**
    INSTALL SIDE BEARING
(a) Install the speedometer drive gear.

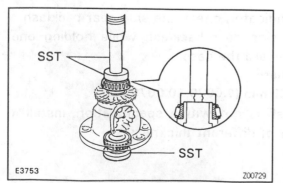

(b) Using SST and a press, install the side bearing.
    SST 09550−10012 (09252−10010, 09556−10010, 09560−10010)

MX

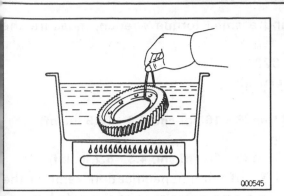

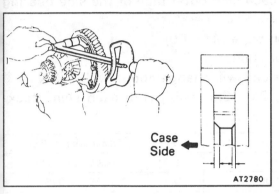

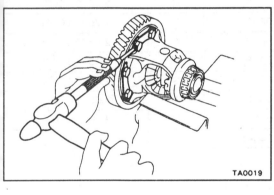

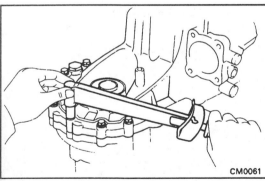

4. INSTALL RING GEAR ON DIFFERENTIAL CASE
(a) Clean the contact surface of the differential case.
(b) Heat the ring gear in boiling water.
(c) After the moisture on the ring gear has completely evaporated, quickly install the ring gear to the differential case.

HINT: Align the matchmarks on the differential case and contact the ring gear.
(d) Temporary install the four lock plates and eight bolts.
NOTICE: The ring gear set bolts should not be tightened until the ring gear has cooled sufficiently.
(e) After the ring gear has cooled sufficiently, torque the ring gear set bolts.
Torque: 97 N·m (985 kgf·cm, 71 ft·lbf)

Case
Side

MX

(f) Using a hammer and drift punch, stake the locking plate.
HINT: Stake one claw flush with the flat surface of the nut. For the claw contacting the protruding portion of thenut, stake only the half on the tightening side.

5. MEASURE DIFFERENTIAL SIDE BEARING PRE-LOAD
(a) Install the differential to the transaxle case.
(b) Install the transmission case.
(c) Install and torque the case bolts.
Torque: 29 N·m (300 kgf·cm, 22 ft·lbf)

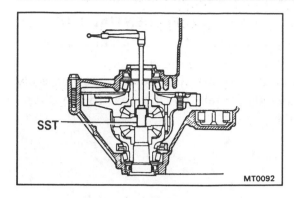

SST

MT0092

(d) Using SST and a small torque wrench, measure the preload.
SST 09564—32011
Preload (at starting):
New bearing
　　0.8—1.6 N·m (8—16 kgf·cm, 6.9—13.9 in.·lbf)
Reused bearing
　　0.5—1.0 N·m (5—10 kgf·cm, 4.3—8.7 in.·lbf)
If the preload is not within specification, remove the transmission case side outer race of the side bearing with SST.
(See step 7 on page MX—60)
Select another shim.
HINT: The preload will change about 0.3—0.4 N·m (3—4 kgf·cm, 2.6—3.5 in.·lbf) with each shim thickness.

Mark	Thickness mm (in.)	Mark	Thickness mm (in.)
A	2.10 (0.0827)	L	2.60 (0.1024)
B	2.15 (0.0846)	M	2.65 (0.1043)
C	2.20 (0.0866)	N	2.70 (0.1063)
D	2.25 (0.0886)	P	2.75 (0.1083)
E	2.30 (0.0906)	Q	2.80 (0.1102)
F	2.35 (0.0925)	R	2.85 (0.1122)
G	2.40 (0.0945)	S	2.90 (0.1142)
H	2.45 (0.0965)	T	2.95 (0.1161)
J	2.50 (0.0984)	U	3.00 (0.1181)
K	2.55 (0.1004)		

MX

COMPONENT PARTS INSTALLATION
BASIC SUBASSEMBLY REASSEMBLY

MX06T−01

HINT: Coat all of the sliding and rotating surface with gear oil before assembly.

1. **MEASURE DIFFERENTIAL SIDE BEARING PRE-LOAD**

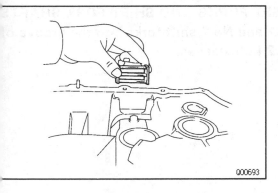

2. **INSTALL MAGNET TO TRANSAXLE CASE**

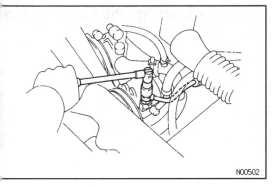

3. **INSTALL DIFFERENTIAL CASE ASSEMBLY**

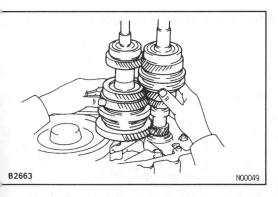

4. **INSTALL INPUT AND OUTPUT SHAFTS**
   Install the input and output shafts together.

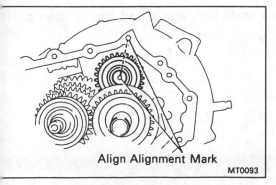

Align Alignment Mark

5. **INSTALL REVERSE IDLER GEAR, THRUST WASHER AND SHAFT**
   Install the reverse idler gear, thrust washer and shaft as shown.

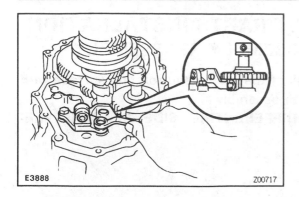

6. **INSTALL REVERSE SHIFT ARM BRACKET**
(a) Install the reverse shift arm bracket as shown.
(b) Install and torque the two bolts.
    Torque: 17N·m (175 kgf·cm, 13 ft·lbf)

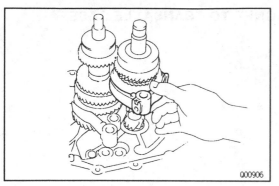

7. **INSTALL SHIFT FORKS AND SHIFT FORK SHAFTS**
(a) Place the No.1 and No.2 shift forks into the groove of No.1 and No.2 hub sleeves.

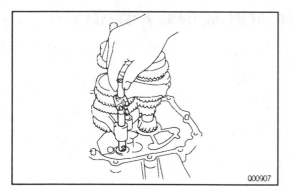

(b) Install the No.1 shift fork shaft into the No.1 shift fork hole.

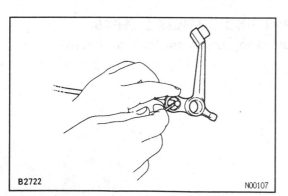

(c) Install the two balls into the reverse shift fork hole.

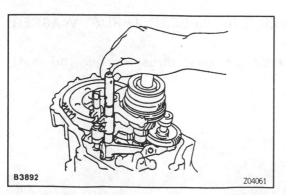

(d) Install the No.3 shift fork shaft and the reverse shift fork.

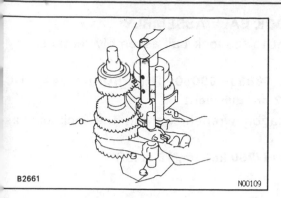

(e) Install the No.2 shift fork shaft and the shift head.

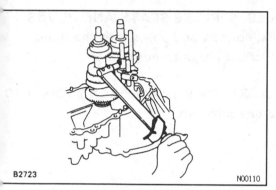

(f) Install and torque the three bolts.
Torque: 16 N·m (160 kgf·cm, 12 ft·lbf)

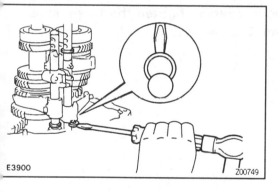

(g) Using a screwdriver and hammer, tap in the three snap rings.

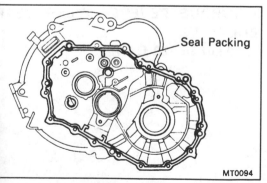

Seal Packing

8. INSTALL TRANSAXLE CASE

(a) Remove the any packing material and be careful not to drop oil on the contacting surface of the transmission case and transaxle case.

(b) Apply seal packing to the transaxle case as shown in the figure.
Seal packing:
   Part No. 08826 – 00090, THREE BOND 1281 or equivalent

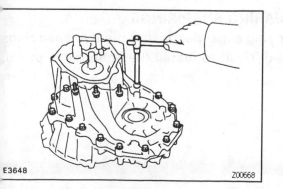

(c) Install and torque the sixteen bolts.
Torque: 29 N·m (300 kgf·cm, 22 ft·lbf)

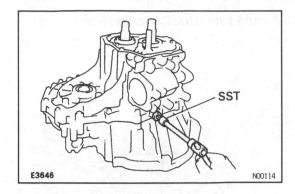

9. INSTALL LOCK BALL ASSEMBLY

(a) Apply sealant to the lock ball assembly threads.
Sealant:

Part No. 08833−00080, THEE BOND 1344, LOC
TITE 242 or equivalent

(b) Using a hexagon wrench, tighten the lock ball as
sembly.
Torque: 25 N·m (250 kgf·cm, 18 ft·lbf)

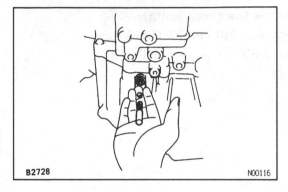

10. INSTALL BALLS, SPRINGS, SEATS AND PLUGS

(a) Install the balls, springs and seats into the holes.

(b) Apply sealant to the plugs threads.
Sealant:

Part No. 08833−00080, THREE BOND 1344, LAC
TATE 242 or equivalent

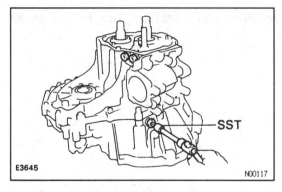

(c) Using a hexagon wrench, tighten the three plugs.
Torque: 25 N·m (250 kgf·cm, 18 ft·lbf)

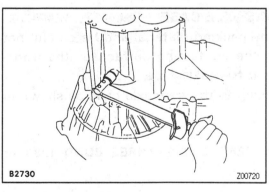

**11. INSTALL AND TORQUE REVERSE IDLER GEAR
SHAFT LOCK BOLT**
Torque: 29 N·m (300 kgf·cm, 22 ft·lbf)

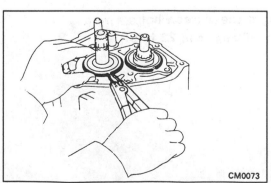

12. INSTALL BEARING SNAP RINGS
Using a snap ring expander, install the two snap rings
HINT: If it is difficult to install the snap rings, pull up
the shafts.

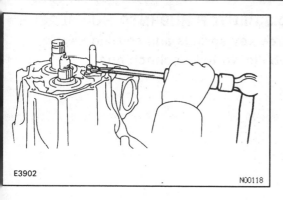

13. INSTALL SNAP RING TO NO.2 FORK SHAFT
Using a screwdriver and hammer, tap in the snap ring.

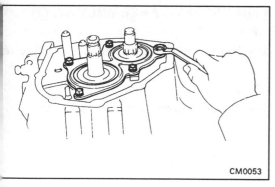

14. INSTALL REAR BEARING RETAINER
Install and torque the five bolts.
Torque: 27 N·m (280 kgf·cm, 20 ft·lbf)

MX

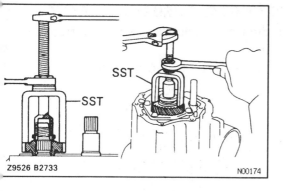

15. INSTALL FIFTH DRIVEN GEAR
Using SST, install the 5th driven gear.
SST 09309—12020

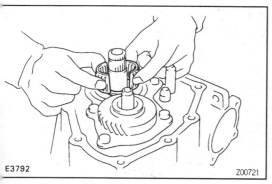

16. INSTALL SPACER, NEEDLE ROLLER BEARING, FIFTH GEAR AND SYNCHRONIZER RING
(a) Install the spacer.
(b) Apply gear oil to the needle roller bearing.
(c) Install the needle roller bearing.

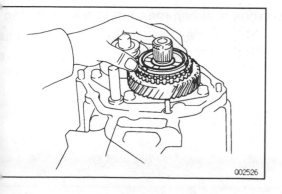

(d) Install the 5th gear and synchronizer ring.

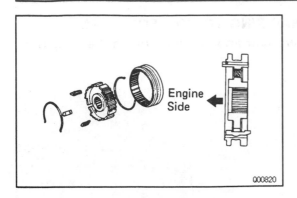

17. INSTALL NO.3 CLUTCH HUB INTO HUB SLEEVE
(a) Install the three key springs and shifting keys.
(b) Install the hub sleeve to the clutch hub.

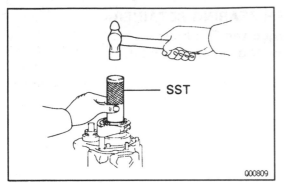

18. INSTALL NO.3 HUB SLEEVE ASSEMBLY WITH NO.3 SHIFT FORK
Using SST and a hammer, drive in No.3 hub sleeve with shift fork.
SST 09636−20010
NOTICE: Align the synchronizer ring slots with the shifting keys.

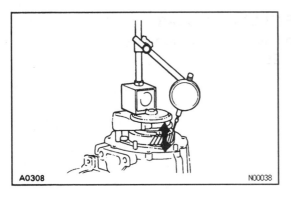

19. MEASURE FIFTH GEAR THRUST CLEARANCE
Using a dial indicator, measure the thrust clearance.
Standard clearance:
    0.10−0.57 mm (0.0039−0.0224 in.)

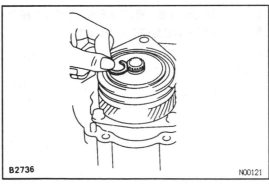

20. INSTALL SNAP RING
(a) Select a snap ring that will minimum axial play.

Mark	Thickness mm (in.)	Mark	Thicknessmm (in.)
A	2.25 (0.0886)	E	2.49 (0.0980)
B	2.31 (0.0909)	F	2.55 (0.1004)
C	2.37 (0.0933)	G	2.61 (0.1028)
D	2.43 (0.0957)		

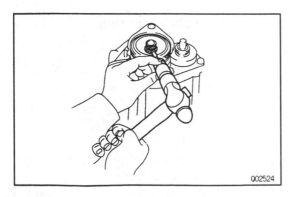

(b) Using a screwdriver and hammer, tap in the snap ring

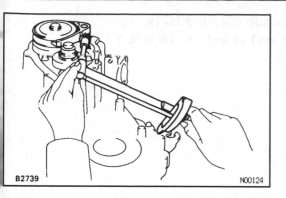

21. INSTALL AND TORQUE SET BOLT
Torque: 16 N·m (160 kgf·cm, 12 ft·lbf)

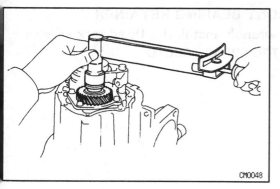

22. INSTALL LOCK NUT
(a) Install the gear double meshing.
(b) Install and torque the nut.
Torque: 118 N·m (1,200 kgf·cm, 87 ft·lbf)
(c) Disengage the gear double meshing.
(d) Stake the lock nut.

MX

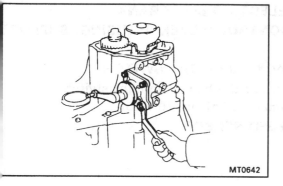

23. INSTALL SHIFT AND SELECT LEVER SHAFT AS-SEMBLY
(a) Place a new gasket in position on the control shaft cover.
(b) Apply sealant to the bolt threads.
Sealant:
    Part No.08833−00080, THREE BOND 1344, LOC-TITE 242 or equivalent
(c) Install the shift and select lever shaft and torque the bolts.
Torque: 20 N·m (200 kgf·cm, 14 ft·lbf)

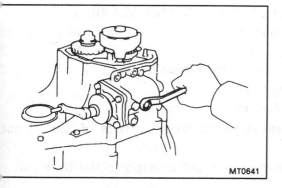

24. INSTALL AND TORQUE LOCK BOLT
Torque: 29 N·m (300 kgf·cm, 22 ft·lbf)

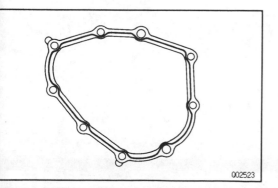

25. INSTALL TRANSMISSION CASE COVER
(a) Apply seal packing to the transmission case cover shown in the illustration.
Seal packing:
    Part No. 08826 − 00090, THREE BOND 1281 or equivalent

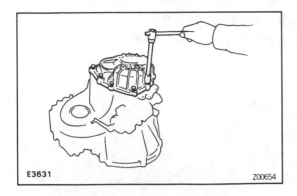

(b) Install and torque the nine bolts.
Torque: 18 N·m (185 kgf·cm, 13 ft·lbf)

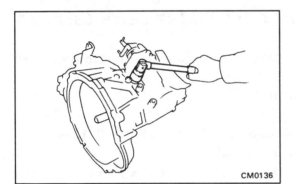

26. INSTALL FRONT BEARING RETAINER
Using a torx wrench, install the three torx screws.
Torx wrench T30 09042–00010

MX

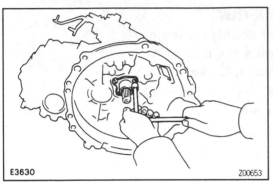

27. INSTALL SELECTING BELLCRANK
28. INSTALL CONTROL LEVER HOUSING SUPPORT BRACKET
29. INSTALL BACK–UP LIGHT SWITCH
Install and torque the back–up light switch.
Torque: 40 N·m (410 kgfcm;, 30 ft·lbf)
30. INSTALL SPEED SENSOR

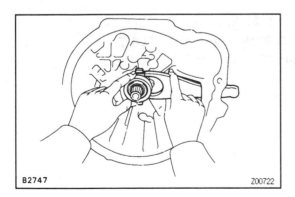

31. INSTALL RELEASE FORK AND BEARING
(a) Apply molybdenum disulphide lithium base grease to the following parts.
- **Release bearing hub inside groove**
- **Input shaft spline**
- **Release fork contact surface**

(b) Apply MP grease to the front surface of the release bearing.
(c) Install the release fork and bearing to the transaxle.

SHIFT LEVER AND CONTROL CABLE
COMPONENTS
MX04B–03

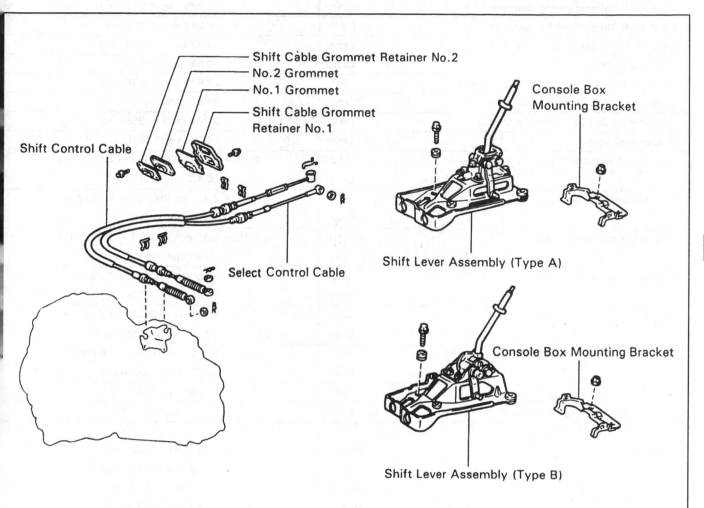

- Shift Cable Grommet Retainer No.2
- No.2 Grommet
- No.1 Grommet
- Shift Cable Grommet Retainer No.1
- Shift Control Cable
- Select Control Cable
- Console Box Mounting Bracket
- Shift Lever Assembly (Type A)
- Console Box Mounting Bracket
- Shift Lever Assembly (Type B)

MX

HINT: There are two shapes of shift lever assembly. However, both function the same way.

001563

SERVICE SPECIFICATIONS
SERVICE DATA

MX06U-01

Input shaft roller bearing journal diameter	Limit	24.970 mm (0.9831 in.)
Input shaft 3rd gear journal diameter	Limit	30.970 mm (1.2193 in.)
Input shaft 4th gear journal diameter	Limit	28.970 mm (1.1405 in.)
Input shaft 5th gear journal diameter	Limit	24.870 mm (0.9791 in.)
Input shaft runout	Limit	0.05 mm (0.0020 in.)
Output shaft roller bearing journal diameter	Limit	32.970 mm (1.2980 in.)
Output shaft 1st gear journal diameter	Limit	37.970 mm (1.4949 in.)
Output shaft 2nd gear journal diameter	Limit	31.970 mm (1.2587 in.)
Output shaft runout	Limit	0.05 mm (0.0020 in.)
Gear thrust clearance 1st	STD	0.10 — 0.40 mm (0.0039 — 0.0157 in.)
	Limit	0.45 mm (0.0177 in.)
Gear thrust clearance 2nd	STD	0.10 — 0.45 mm (0.0039 — 0.0177 in.)
	Limit	0.50 mm (0.0197 in.)
Gear thrust clearance 3rd	STD	0.10 — 0.35 mm (0.0039 — 0.0138 in.)
	Limit	0.40 mm (0.0157 in.)
Gear thrust clearance 4th	STD	0.10 — 0.55 mm (0.0039 — 0.0217 in.)
	Limit	0.60 mm (0.0236 in.)
Gear thrust clearance 5th	STD	0.10 — 0.57 mm (0.0039 — 0.0244 in.)
	Limit	0.65 mm (0.0256 in.)
Gear oil clearance 1st, 2nd, 3rd, 4th and 5th	STD	0.015 — 0.058 mm (0.0006 — 0.0023 in.)
	Limit	0.070 mm (0.0028 in.)
Shift fork to hub sleeve clearance	Limit	1.0 mm (0.039 in.)
Synchronizer ring to gear clearance	Limit	0.6 mm (0.024 in.)
Input shaft snap ring thickness		
No.2 clutch hub	Mark 0	2.30 mm (0.0906 in.)
	Mark 1	2.36 mm (0.0929 in.)
	Mark 2	2.42 mm (0.0953 in.)
	Mark 3	2.48 mm (0.0976 in.)
	Mark 4	2.54 mm (0.1000 in.)
	Mark 5	2.60 mm (0.1024 in.)
Rear bearing	Mark A	2.29 mm (0.0902 in.)
	Mark B	2.35 mm (0.0925 in.)
	Mark C	2.40 mm (0.0949 in.)
	Mark D	2.47 mm (0.0972 in.)
	Mark E	2.53 mm (0.0996 in.)
	Mark F	2.59 mm (0.1020 in.)

Output shaft snap ring thickness		
No.1 clutch hub	Mark A	2.50 mm (0.0984 in.)
	Mark B	2.56 mm (0.1008 in.)
	Mark C	2.62 mm (0.1031 in.)
	Mark D	2.68 mm (0.1055 in.)
	Mark E⟩	2.74 mm (0.1079 in.)
	Mark F	2.80 mm (0.1102 in.)
No.3 clutch hub	Mark A	2.25 mm (0.0886 in.)
	Mark B	2.31 mm (0.0909 in.)
	Mark C	2.37 mm (0.0933 in.)
	Mark D	2.43 mm (0.0957 in.)
	Mark E	2.49 mm (0.0980 in.)
	Mark F	2.55 mm (0.1004 in.)
	Mark G	2.61 mm (0.1028 in.)

Differential side bearing preload (at starting)			
New bearing	0.8 — 1.6 N·m	8 — 16 kgf·cm	6.9 — 13.9 in.·lbf
Reused bearing	0.5 — 1.0 N·m	5 — 10 kgf·cm	4.3 — 8.7 in.·lbf

MX

Differential pinion to side gear backlash	0.05 — 0.20 mm (0.0020 — 0.0079 in.)

Differential side gear thrust washer thickness	
None Mark	0.95 mm (0.0374 in.)
None Mark	1.00 mm (0.0394 in.)
None Mark	1.05 mm (0.0413 in.)
None Mark	1.10 mm (0.0433 in.)
None Mark	1.15 mm (0.0453 in.)
None Mark	1.20 mm (0.0472 in.)

Differential side bearing adjusting shim thickness	
Mark A	2.10 mm (0.0827 in.)
Mark B	2.15 mm (0.0846 in.)
Mark C	2.20 mm (0.0866 in.)
Mark D	2.25 mm (0.0886 in.)
Mark E	2.30 mm (0.0906 in.)
Mark F	2.35 mm (0.0925 in.)
Mark G	2.40 mm (0.0945 in.)
Mark H	2.45 mm (0.0965 in.)
Mark J	2.50 mm (0.0984 in.)
Mark K	2.55 mm (0.1004 in.)
Mark L	2.60 mm (0.1024 in.)
Mark M	2.65 mm (0.1043 in.)
Mark N	2.70 mm (0.1063 in.)
Mark P	2.75 mm (0.1083 in.)
Mark Q	2.80 mm (0.1102 in.)
Mark R	2.85 mm (0.1122 in.)
Mark S	2.90 mm (0.1142 in.)
Mark T	2.95 mm (0.1161 in.)
Mark U	3.00 mm (0.1181 in.)

TORQUE SPECIFICATIONS

MX06V—0

Part tightened		N·m	kgf·cm	ft·lbf
Transaxle x Engine	12 mm bolt	64	650	47
	10 mm bolt	46	470	34
Stiffener plate set bolt		23	230	17
Engine center support member x Body	10 mm bolt	61	620	45
	14 mm bolt	206	2,100	152
Stabilizer bar bushing bracket set bolt		50	510	37
Engine rear mounting x Engine center support member		48	490	35
Engine front mounting x Engine center support member		64	650	47
Engine left mounting x Engine left munting bracket		21	210	15
Exhaust front pipe x Exhaust manifold		62	630	46
Exhaust front pipe x Exhaust center pipe		43	440	32
Front pipe support	Nut	19	195	14
	Bolt	19	195	14
Lower ball joint x Lower arm		142	1,450	105
Transaxle x Starter		39	400	29
Transaxle x Clutch release cylinder		12	120	9
Transmission case x Transaxle case		29	300	22
Transmission case x Case cover		18	185	13
Rear bearing retainer		27	280	20
Output shaft bearing lock plate		11	115	8
5th driven gear lock nut		118	1,200	87
Differential case x Ring gear		97	985	71
Reverse idler shaft lock blot		29	300	22
Reverse shift arm bracket set bolt		17	175	13
Oil receiver pipe set bolt		17	175	13
Shift fork set bolt		16	160	12
Reverse restrict pin screw plug		13	130	9
Shift and select lever shaft lock bolt		29	300	22
Filler plug		39	400	29
Drain plug		39	400	29
Back—up light switch		40	410	30
Straight screw plug (shift fork shaft)		25	250	18
Lock ball assembly		39	400	29
Control shaft cover set bolt		20	200	14

MX

A131L AUTOMATIC TRANSAXLE

AX

DESCRIPTION
GENERAL DESCRIPTION

The A131L automatic transaxle described in this AX section is a lock−up three−speed automatic transaxle developed exclusively for use with a transversely−mounted engine.

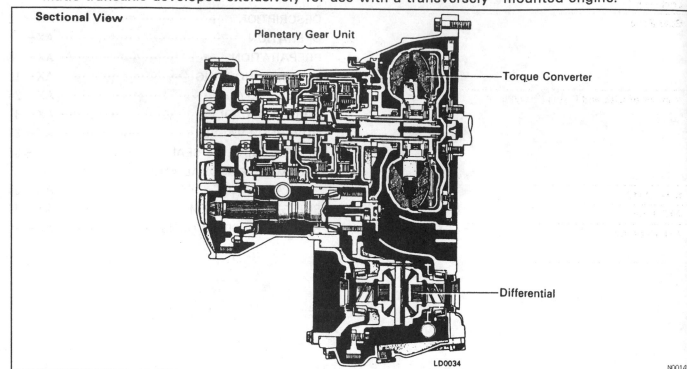

Sectional View

Planetary Gear Unit

Torque Converter

Differential

LD0034

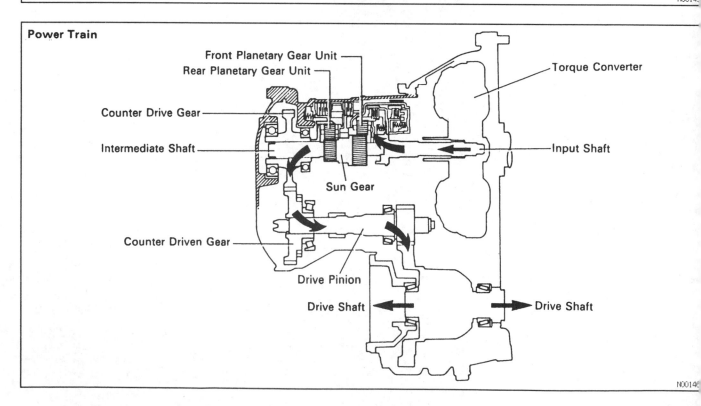

Power Train

Front Planetary Gear Unit

Rear Planetary Gear Unit

Counter Drive Gear

Intermediate Shaft

Sun Gear

Counter Driven Gear

Drive Pinion

Drive Shaft

Torque Converter

Input Shaft

Drive Shaft

N00146

ENERAL SPECIFICATIONS

Type of Transaxle		A131L
Type of Engine		4A—FE
Stall Torque Ratio		2.3 : 1
Lock—up Mechanism		Equipped
Gear Ratio	1st Gear	2.810
	2nd Gear	1.549
	3rd Gear	1.000
	Reverse Gear	2.296
Number of Disc and Plates (Disk/Plate)		
	Forward Clutch (C_1)	3/3
	Direct Clutch (C_2)	2/3
	2nd Brake (B_2)	3/3
	First and Reverse Brake (B_3)	6/5
Band Width	2nd Coast Brake (B_1)	25 mm (0.98 in.)
ATF Type		ATF DEXRON® II
ATF Capacity	Transmission	5.5 Litter (5.8 US qts, 4.8 Imp.qts)
	Differential	1.4 Litter (1.1 US qts, 0.9 Imp.qts)

AX

OPERATION

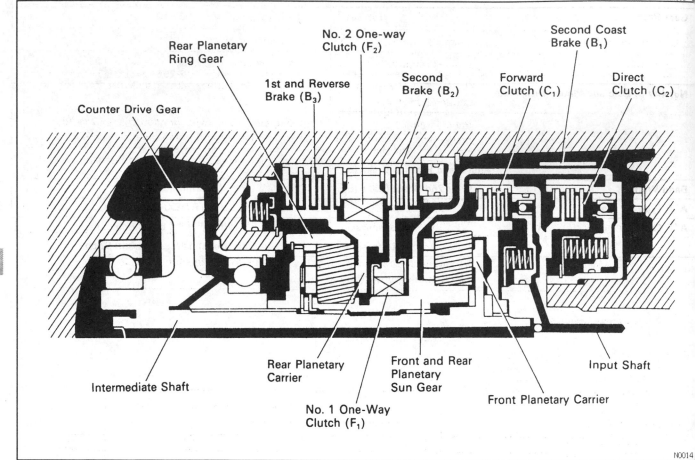

Shift lever position	Gear position	C₁	C₂	B₁	B₂	B₃	F₁	F₂
P	Parking							
R	Reverse		○			○		
N	Neutral							
D	1st	○						○
D	2nd	○			○		○	
D	3rd	○	○		○			
2	1st	○						○
2	2nd	○		○	○		○	
L	1st	○				○		○
L	*2nd	○		○	○		○	

○--- Operating

* Down-shift in L range, 2nd gear only — no up-shift.

1. FUNCTION OF COMPONENTS

	Component	Function
C_1	Forward Clutch	Connects input shaft and front planetary ring gear.
C_2	Direct Clutch	Connects input shaft and front & rear planetary sun gear.
B_1	2nd Coast Brake	Prevents front & rear planetary sun gear from turning either clockwise or counterclockwise.
B_2	2nd Brake	Prevents outer race of F_1 from turning either clockwise or counterclockwise thus preventing the front & rear planetary sun gear from turning counterclockwise.
B_3	1st & Reverse Brake	Prevents rear planetary carrier from turning either clockwise or counterclockwise.
F_1	No. 1 One-Way Clutch	When B_2 is operating, this clutch prevents the front & rear planetary sun gear from turning counterclockwise.
F_2	No. 2 One-Way Clutch	Prevents rear planetary carrier from turning counterclockwise.
	Planetary Gears	These gears change the route through which driving force is transmitted in accordance with the operation of each clutch and brake in order to increase or reduce the input and output speed.

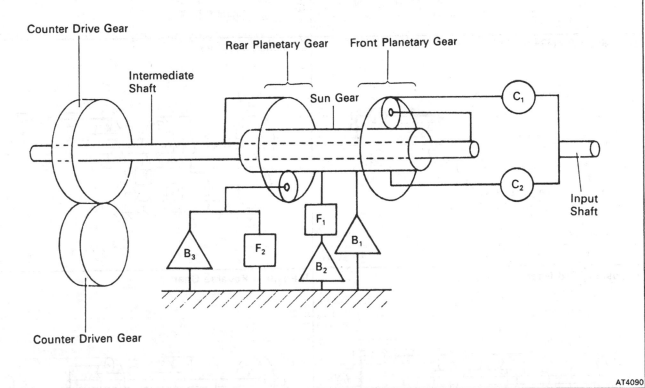

AT4090

V00185

AX

Power from the engine transmitted to the input shaft via the torque converter is then transmitted to the planetary gears by the operation of the clutch.

By operation of the brake and one—way clutch, either the planetary carrir or the planetary su gear are immobilized, altering the speed of revolution of the planetary gear unit.

Shift change is carried out by altering the combination of clutch and brake operation.

Each clutch and brake operates by hydraulic pressure; gear position is decided according to th throttle opening angle and vehicle speed, and shift change automatically occurs.

The conditions of operation for each gear position are shown on the following illustrations:

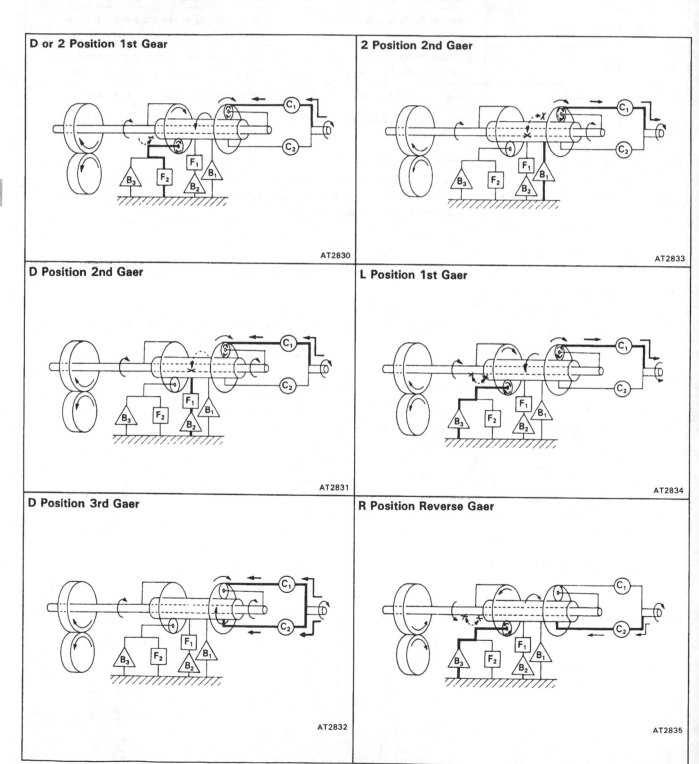

D or 2 Position 1st Gear

AT2830

2 Position 2nd Gaer

AT2833

D Position 2nd Gaer

AT2831

L Position 1st Gaer

AT2834

D Position 3rd Gaer

AT2832

R Position Reverse Gaer

AT2835

HYDRAULIC CONTROL SYSTEM

The hydraulic control system is composed of the oil pump, the valve body, the accumulators, the clutches and brakes, and the governor valve as well as fluid passage which connect all of these components.

Based on the hydraulic pressure created by the oil pump, the hydraulic control system governs the hydraulic pressure acting on the torque converter, clutches and brakes in accordance with the increases as vehicle speed increases.

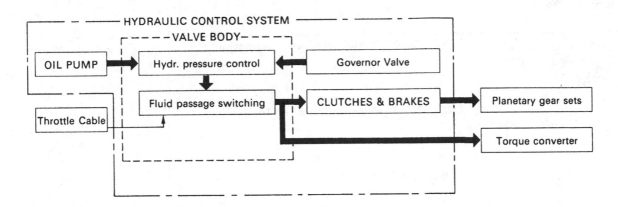

V00179

AX

PREPARATION
SST(SPECIAL SERVICE TOOLS)

AX04T-03

	09043−38100	Hexagon 10 mm Wrench	Oil pan drain plug
	09201−60011	Valve Guide Bushing Remover & Replacer	Speedometer driven gear oil seal
	09308−00010	Oil Seal Puller	Side gear shaft oil seal
	09350−32014	TOYOTA Automatic Transmission Tool Set	
	(09351−32010)	One−way Clutch Test Tool	
	(09351−32020)	Stator Stopper	
	(09351−32130)	Handle	
	(09351−32150)	Oil Seal Replacer	
	09992−00094	Automatic Transmission Oil Pressure Gauge Set	Line pressure

AX04U−02

EQUIPMENT

Straight edge	Check torque converter installation.
Dial indicator or dial indicator with magnetic base	Measure inside diameter or piston stroke.
Torque wrench	
Voltmeter	
Ammeter(A)	
Ohmmeter	

AX06D−02

LUBRICANT

Item	Capacity	Classification
Automatic transaxle fluid Dry fill Drain and refill	5.5 liters (5.8 US qts, 4.8 Imp.qts) 2.5 liters (2.6 US qts, 2.2 Imp.qts)	ATF DEXRON® II
Differential oil	1.4 liters (1.1 US qts, 0.9 Imp.qts)	ATF DEXRON® II

AX04W−02

SSM(SPECIAL SERVICE MATERIALS)

08833−00070 Adhesive 1324, THREE BOND 1324 or equivalent	Torque converter mounting bolt

AX

TROUBLESHOOTING
GENERAL INFORMATION

AX068-03

1. Troubles occurring with the automatic transaxle can be caused by either the engine or the transaxle itself. These two areas should be distinctly before proceeding with troubleshooting.

2. Troubleshooting should begin with the simplest operation, working up in order of difficulty but first determine whether the trouble lies within the engine or transaxle.

3. Proceed with the inspection as follows:

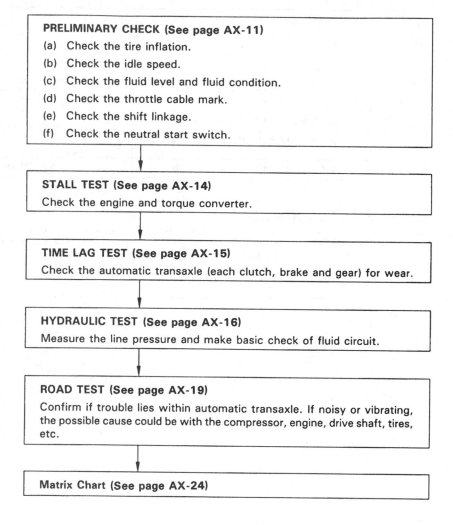

PRELIMINARY CHECK (See page AX-11)

(a) Check the tire inflation.

(b) Check the idle speed.

(c) Check the fluid level and fluid condition.

(d) Check the throttle cable mark.

(e) Check the shift linkage.

(f) Check the neutral start switch.

STALL TEST (See page AX-14)

Check the engine and torque converter.

TIME LAG TEST (See page AX-15)

Check the automatic transaxle (each clutch, brake and gear) for wear.

HYDRAULIC TEST (See page AX-16)

Measure the line pressure and make basic check of fluid circuit.

ROAD TEST (See page AX-19)

Confirm if trouble lies within automatic transaxle. If noisy or vibrating, the possible cause could be with the compressor, engine, drive shaft, tires, etc.

Matrix Chart (See page AX-24)

V00638

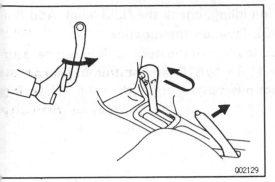

002129

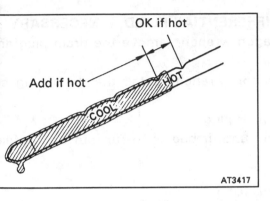

AT3417

AX056-06

PRELIMINARY CHECK

1. **CHECK FLUID LEVEL**

   HINT: The vehicle must have been driven so that the engine and transaxle are at normal operating temperature.

   (fluid temperature: 70—80°C or 158—176°F)

   (a) Park the vehicle on a level surface, set the parking brake.

   (b) With the engine idling, shift the selector into each gear from P position to L position and return to P position.

   (c) Pull out the transaxle dipstick and wipe it clean.

   (d) Push it back fully into the tube.

   (e) Pull it out and check that the fluid level is in the HOT range.

   If the level is at the low side of the hot range, add fluid.

   Fluid type:
   　　ATF DEXRON® II
   NOTICE: Do not overfill.

AX

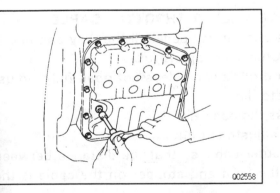

002558

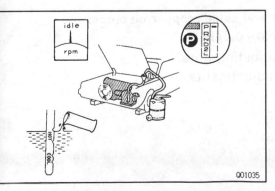

001035

2. **CHECK FLUID CONDITION**

   If the fluid smells burnt or is black, replace it.

3. **REPLACE ATF**

   NOTICE: Do not overfill.

   (a) Using a hexagen wrench, remove the drain plug and drain the fluid.

   (b) Using a hexagon wrench, install the drain plug securely.

   (c) Add new fluid through the filler tube.
   Fluid:
   　　ATF DEXRON® II
   Capacity:
   　　5.5 liters (5.7 US qts, 4.8 Imp.qts)
   Drain and refill:
   　　2.5 liter (2.6 US qts, 2.2 Imp.qts)

   (d) Start the engine and shift the selector into all positions from P through L and then shift into P.

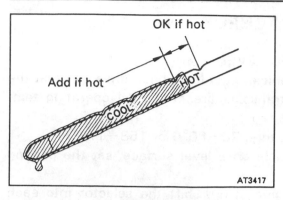

AT3417

(e) With the engine idling, check the fluid level. Add flui
up to the COOL level on the dipstick.

(f) Check the fluid level with the normal fluid temperatur
(70–80°C or 158–176°F) and add as necessary.
NOTICE: Do not overfill.

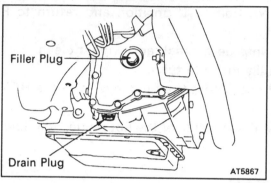

AT5867

4. REPLACE DIFFERENTIAL FLUID IF NECESSARY

(a) Using a hexagon wrench, remove the drain plug an
drain the fluid.

(b) Using a hexagon wrench, install the drain plug se
curely.

(c) Remove the filler plug.

(d) Add new fluid until it begins to run out of the fille
hole.
Fluid type:
ATF DEXRON® II

5. CHECK DIFFERENTIAL FLUID LEVEL
Remove the filler plug and check differential fluid
level.

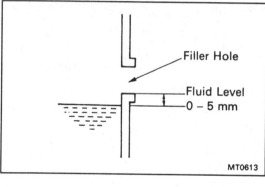

MT0613

6. INSPECT AND ADJUST THROTTLE CABLE

(a) Depress the accelerator pedal all the way and check
that the throttle valve opens fully.
HINT: If the throttle valve does not open fully, adjust
the accelerator link.

(b) Fully depress the accelerator.

(c) Loosen the adjustment nuts.

(d) Adjust the outer cable so that the distance between
the end of the boot and stopper on the cable is the
standard.
Standard boot and cable stopper distance:
0–1 mm (0–0.04in.)

(e) Tighten the adjusting nuts.

(f) Recheck the adjustments.

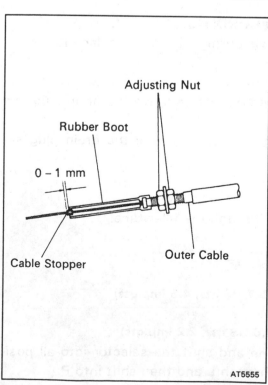

AT5555

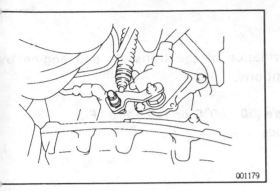

001179

7. **INSPECT AND ADJUST SHIFT CONTROL CABLE**
When shifting the shift lever from the N position to other positions, check that the lever can be shifted smoothly and accurately to each position and that the position indicator correctly indicates the position.

(a) Remove the No.2 engine under cover.
(b) Loosen the nut on the manual shift lever.
(c) Push the manual lever fully toward the right side of the vehicle.
(d) Return the lever two notches to the NEUTRAL position.
(e) Set the shift lever in N position.
(f) While holding the lever lightly toward the R position side, tighten the swivel nut.

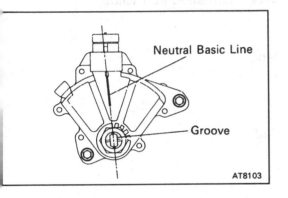

Neutral Basic Line

Groove

AT8103

8. **ADJUST PARK/NEUTRAL POSITION SWITCH**
If the engine will start with the shift selector in any position other than N or P position, adjustment is required.

(a) loosen the park/neutral position switch bolts and set the shift selector to the N position.
(b) Align the groove and neutral basic line.
(c) Hold is position and tighten the bolts.
Torque: 5.4 N·m (55 kgf·cm, 48 in.·lbf)

9. **INSPECT IDLE SPEED (N RANGE)**
Idle speed:
650−750 RPM

STALL TEST

AX057-06

The object of this test is to check the overall performance of the transaxle and engine by measuring the maximum engine speeds in D and R positions.

NOTICE:

- **Perform the test at normal operating fluid temperature (50–80°C or 122–176 °F).**
- **Do not continuously run this test longer than 5 seconds.**

MEASURE STALL SPEED

(a) Chock the front and rear wheels.

(b) Mount an engine tachometer.

(c) Fully apply the parking brake.

(d) Keep your left foot pressed firmly on the brake pedal.

(e) Start the engine.

(f) Shift into the D position. Step all the way down on the accelerator pedal with your right foot. Quickly read the highest engine rpm at this time.

   Stall speed:

   2,400±150 rpm

(g) Perform the same test in the R position.

   EVALUATION

(a) If the engine speed is the same for both positions but lower than specified value:
- Engine output may be insufficient
- Stator one–way clutch is not operating properly

(b) If the stall speed at the D position is higher than specified:
- Line pressure too low
- Forward clutch slipping
- One–way clutch No.2 not operating properly

(c) If the stall speed at the R position is higher than specified:
- Line pressure too low
- Direct clutch slipping
- First and reverse brake slipping

(d) If the stall speed in the R and D positions is higher than specified:
- Line pressure too low
- Improper fluid level

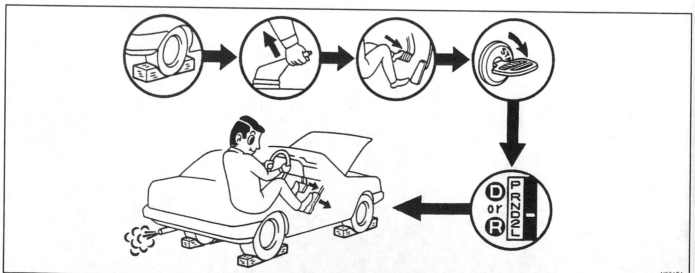

N00151

AX058-04

TIME LAG TEST

When the shift lever is shifted while the engine is idling, there will be a certain time elapse or lag before the shock can be felt. This is used for checking the condition of the forward clutch, direct clutch and first and reverse brake.

NOTICE:

- **Perform the test at normal operating fluid temperature (50–80°C or 122–176°F).**
- **Be sure to allow a one minute interval tests.**
- **Make three measurements and take the average value.**

MEASURE TIME LAG

(a) Fully apply the parking brake.

(b) Start the engine and check the idle speed. (Cooling fan and A/C OFF)

Idling speed:

N position 650–750 RPM

(c) Shift the shift lever from N to D position. Using a stop watch, measure the time it takes from shifting the lever until the shock is felt.

Time lag:

Less than 1.2 seconds

(d) In same manner, measure the time lag for N→R.

Time lag:

Less than 1.5 seconds

EVALUATION

If N→D time lag is longer than specified.

- Line pressure too low
- Forward clutch worn
- Line pressure too low
- Direct clutch worn
- First and reverse brake worn

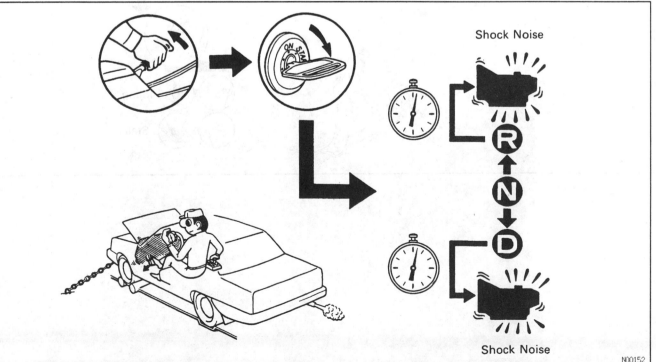

Shock Noise

Shock Noise

N00152

HYDRAULIC TEST

AX098—01

1. MEASURE LINE PRESSURE

(a) Warm up the transaxle fluid.

(b) Remove the transaxle case test plug and mount the oil pressure gauge (SST).
SST 09922—00094
NOTICE:
- **Perform the test at normal operating fluid temperature (50 — 80°C or 122 — 176°F).**
- **Check that the throttle cable is adjusted within specifications.**
- **Check that the tire pressures are adjusted according to specifications.**

(c) Fully apply the parking brake and chock the four wheels.

(d) Start the engine and check the idle speed.

(e) Shift into the D position, step down strongly on the brake pedal with your left foot and while manipulating the accelerator pedal with the right foot, measure the line pressure at the engine speeds specified in the table.

(f) In the same manner, perform the test in the R position.

D position	Idling	373—422 kPa (3.8—4.3 kgf/cm², 54—61 psi)
	Stall	902—1,049 kPa (9.2—10.7 kgf/cm², 131—152 psi)
R position	Idling	549—706 kPa (5.6—7.2 kgf/cm², 80—102 psi)
	Stall	1,412—1,647 kPa (14.4—16.8 kgf/cm², 205—239 psi)

(g) If the measured pressures are not up to specified values, recheck the throttle cable adjustment (See page AX—12) and retest.

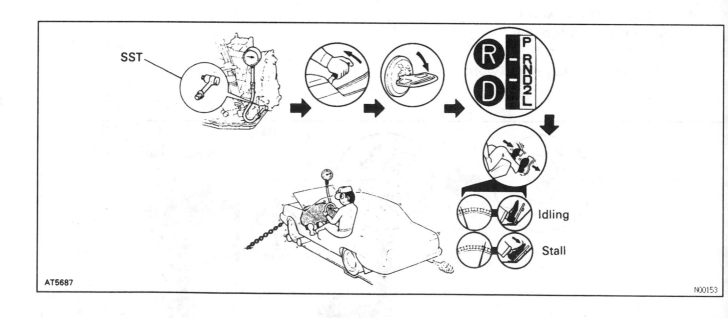

AT5687　　　　　　　　　　　　　　　　　　　　　　　　　　　　　　　　N00153

EVALUATION

(a) If the measured values at all position are higher than specified:
- Throttle cable out of adjustment
- Throttle valve defective
- Regulator valve defective

(b) If the measured values at all position are lower than specified:
- Throttle cable out of adjustment
- Throttle valve defective
- Regulator valve defective
- Oil pump defective

(c) If pressure is low in the D position only:
- D position circuit fluid leakage
- Forward clutch defective

(d) If pressure is low in the R position only:
- R position circuit fluid leakage
- First and reverse brake defective
- Direct clutch defective

2. MEASURE GOVERNOR PRESSURE

(a) Warm up the transaxle fluid.

(b) Remove the transaxle case test plug and mount the oil pressure gauge (SST).
SST 09992−00094

NOTICE:

- **Perform the test at normal operating fluid temperature (50−80°C or 122−176°F).**
- **Check that the throttle cable is adjusted within specifications.**
- **Check that the tire pressures are adjusted according to specifications.**

(c) Check the parking brake to see that it is not applied.

(d) Start the engine.

(e) Shift into the D position and measure the governor pressures at the speeds specified in the table.

EVALUATION

If governor pressure is defective:

- Line pressure defective
- Fluid leakage in governor pressure circuit
- Governor valve operation defective

Differential gear ratio: 3.526

Vehicle speed (Reference)	Governor pressure
30 km/h (19 mph)	39−118 kPa (0.4−1.2 kgf/cm², 6−17 psi)
60 km/h (37 mph)	157−235 kPa (1.6−2.4 kgf/cm², 23−34 psi)
90 km/h (56 mph)	284−363 kPa (2.9−3.7 kgf/cm², 41−53 psi)

Differential gear ratio: 3.722

Vehicle speed (Reference)	Governor pressure
30 km/h (19 mph)	88−167 kPa (0.9−1.7 kgf/cm², 13−24 psi)
60 km/h (37 mph)	177−255 kPa (1.8−2.6 kgf/cm², 26−37 psi)
90 km/h (56 mph)	314−392 kPa (3.2−4.0 kgf/cm², 46−57 psi)

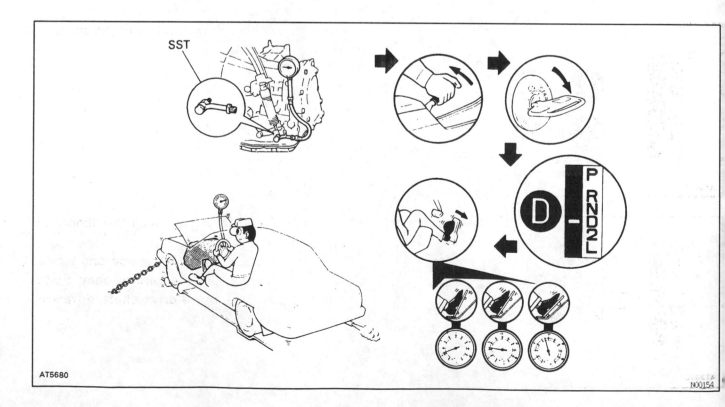

AT5680

N00154

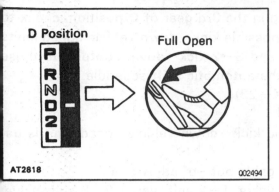

AT2818 Q02494

AX06A—07

ROAD TEST

NOTICE: Perform this test at normal fluid temperature (50—80°C or 122—176°F).

1. **D POSITION TEST**

Shift into D position and while driving with the accelerator pedal held constant at the throttle valve full open, check on the following points:

(a) Check to see that the 1—2 and 2—3 up—shifts take place and also that the shift points conform to those shown in the automatic shift schedule.
(See page AX—23)

EVALUATION

If there is no 1—2 up—shift:

- Governor valve is defective
- 1—2 shift valve stuck

If there is no 2—3 up—shift:

- 2—3 shift valve stuck

If the shift point is defective:

- Throttle cable out—of adjustment
- Throttle valve, 1—2 shift valve, 2—3 shift valve, etc. defective

AX

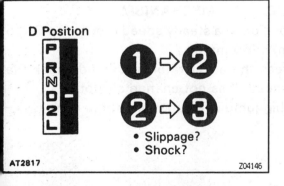

AT2817 Z04146

(b) In the same manner, check the shock and the slip at 1—2 and 2—3 up—shifts.

EVALUATION

If the shock is severe:

- Line pressure is too high
- Accumulator is defective
- Check ball is defective

(c) Run in the 3rd gear of D position, check the abnormal noise and vibration.

HINT: Check for cause of abnormal noise and vibration must be made with extreme care as they could also be due to unbalance in the drive shaft, differential, tires, torque converter etc.

AT2816 Z04147

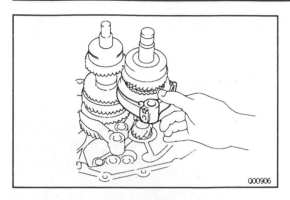

(g)   Remove the No.1 and No.2 shift forks.

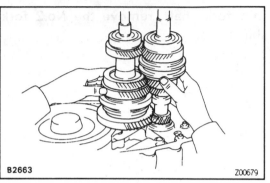

25. REMOVE INPUT AND OUTPUT SHAFTS TOGETHER FROM TRANSAXLE CASE

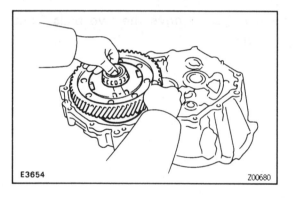

26. REMOVE DIFFERENTIAL ASSEMBLY

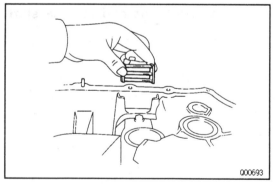

27. REMOVE MAGNET FROM TRANSAXLE CASE

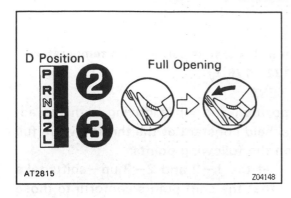

(d) While running in the 3rd gear of D position, check to see that the possible kick—down vehicle speed limits for the 3—1 and 3—2 kick—down conform to those indicated in the automatic shift schedule.
(See page AX—23)

EVALUATION

If the possible kick—down vehicle speed limit is defective:

- Throttle cable out—of adjustment
- Throttle valve, 1—2 shift valve, 2—3 shift valve, etc. defective

(e) Check the abnormal shock and slip at kick—down.

AX

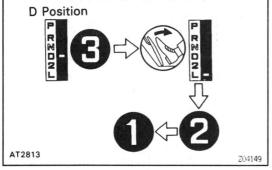

(f) While running about 60 km/h (37 mph) in the 3rd gear of D position, release your foot from the accelerator pedal and shift into L position. Then check to see if the 2—1 down—shift point conform to those indicated in the automatic shift schedule.
(See page AX—23)

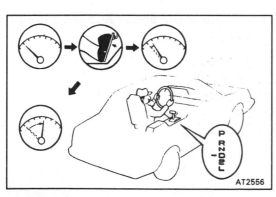

2. INSPECT LOCK—UP MECHANISM

(a) Drive in D position at a steady speed (Lock—up ON) of about 80 km/h (50 mph).

(b) Lightly depress the accelerator pedal and check that the engine speed does not change abruptly.
If there is a big jump in engine rpm, there is no lock—up.

3. 2 POSITION TEST

(a) While running in 2 positon, 2nd gear, release the accelerator pedal and check the engine braking effect

EVALUATION

If there is no engine braking effect:

- Second coast brake is defective

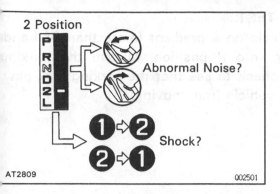

(b) Check the abnormal noise during acceleration and-deceleration.

(c) Check the shock at up—shift and down—shift.

4. L POSITION TEST

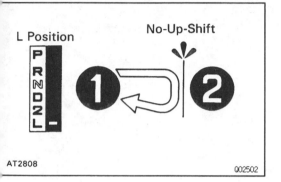

(a) While running in L position, check to see that there is no up—shift to 2nd gear.

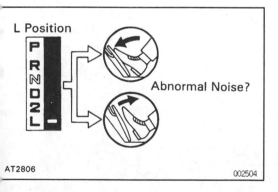

(b) While running in L position, release the accelerator pedal and check the engine braking effect.
EVALUATION
If there is no engine brake effect:
• First and reverse brake is defective

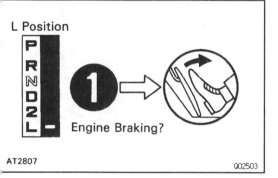

(c) Check the abnormal noise during acceleration and deceleration.

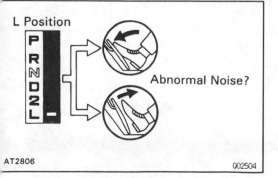

5. R POSITION TEST

Shift into R position and, while running at full throttle, check the slipping.

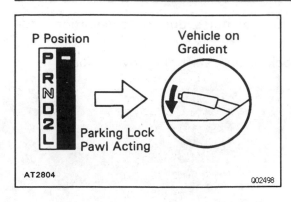

P Position

Vehicle on Gradient

Parking Lock Pawl Acting

AT2804

Q02498

6. P POSITION TEST

Stop the vehicle on a gradient (more than 9%) and after shifting into P position, release the parking brake. Then check to see that the parking lock pawl prevents the vehicle from moving.

AX

AX099-01

AUTOMATIC SHIFT SCHEDULE

Differential Gear Ratio: 3.526

Position	Gear Position	Vehicle Speed
D Position	1→2	53−71 (33−44)
	2→3	103−118 (64−73)
	3→2	97−115 (60−71)
	2→1	38−49 (24−30)
	Lock−up ON	71−82 (44−51)
	Lock−up OFF	67−78 (42−48)
L Position	2→1	41−53 (25−33)

Differential Gear Ratio: 3.722

Position	Gear Position	Vehicle Speed
D Position	1→2	50−67 (31−42)
	2→3	97−116 (60−72)
	3→2	92−112 (57−70)
	2→1	36−47 (22−29)
	Lock−up ON	68−78 (42−48)
	Lock−up OFF	63−74 (39−46)
L Position	2→1	39−50 (24−31)

AX04Y−03

TROUBLESHOOTING MATRIX CHART

You will find the troubles easier using the table well shown below. In this table, each number shows the priority of causes in troubles. Check each part in order. If necessary, replace these parts.

NOTICE: Refer to A131l, A132L Automatic Transaxle Repair Manual (Pub.No. RM058E) when ★ mark appers in the column for page numbers.

Suspect Area / Symptom	Torque converter	Parking lock pawl	Manual valve	Governer valve	1-2 Shift valve	2-3 Shift valve	Forward clutch (C1)	Direct clutch (C2)	No. 2 one-way clutch (F2)	Front planetary gear	Rear planetary gear	1st and reverse brake (B3)	Second brake (B2)	2nd coast brake (B1)	No. 1 one-way clutch (F1)	C1 accumulator	Low coast modulator valve	B2 accumulator	2nd coast modulator valve	Throttle modulator valve	Throttle valve	Primary regulator valve
See page	AX-40	★	★	AX-33	★	★	★	★	★	★	★	★	★	★	★	★	★	★	★	★	★	★
Does not move in any forward range				1			2	6	3			4	5		5							
Does not move in reverse range					3	4		5		2	2	6			1							
Does not move in any forward range or reverse range	4	1	2							3	3											
No-up shift 1st → 2nd					1								2		3							
No-up shift 2nd → 3rd						1		2														
No-down shift 3rd → 2nd								2													1	
No-down shift 2nd → 1st					2																1	
Shift point too high or too low				1	2	2																
Harsh engagement "N" → "R"								1				2										
Harsh engagement "N" → "D"							1									2						
Harsh engagement "N" → "L"							2					4			3	1						
Harsh engagement 1st → 2nd ("D" range)													2					1				
Harsh engagement 1st → 2nd ("2" range)													3					2	1			
Harsh engagement 1st → 2nd → 3rd																				1		
Harsh engagement 2nd → 3rd								1														
Harsh engagement 3rd → 2nd																				1		2

V01143

Symptom		Torque converter	Forward clutch (C_1)	Direct clutch (C_2)	No. 2 one-way clutch (F_2)	1st and reverse brake (B_3)	Second brake (B_2)	No. 1 one-way clutch (F_1)	Pressure relief valve	Oil strainer	Second coast brake (B_1)	1-2 Shift valve	2-3 Shift valve	Lock-up relay valve	Lock-up signal valve
See page		AX-40	★	★	★	★	★	★	★	AX-26	★	★	★	★	★
Slip	Forward & Reverse	1							2	3					
	"R" range			1		2									
	1st		1		2										
	2nd						1	2							
	3rd			1	2										
No engine	1st ("L" range)					1									
	2nd ("2" range)										1				
No kick-down												1	2		
Poor acceleration		1													
No lock-up		3												1	2

V01142

AX

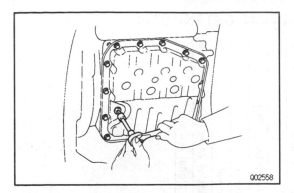

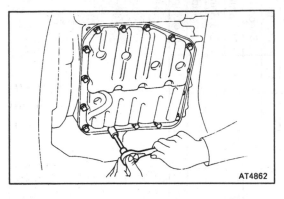

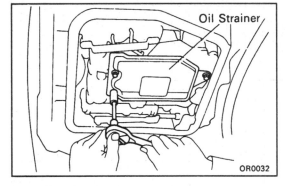

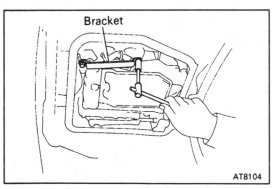

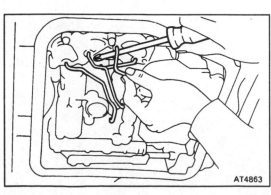

VALVE BODY
VALVE BODY REMOVAL

1. **CLEAN TRANSAXLE EXTERIOR**
   To help prevent contamination, clean the exterior of the transaxle.

2. **DRAIN TRANSAXLE FLUID**
   Using a heagon wrench, remove the drain plug and drain the fluid into suitable container.

3. **REMOVE OIL PAN AND GASKET**
   NOTICE: Some fluid will remain in the oil pan. Remove all pan bolts, and carefully remove the oil pan assembly. Discard the gasket.

4. **REMOVE OIL STRAINER**
   Remove the three bolts, and the oil strainer.
   NOTICE: Be careful as some oil will come out with the strainer.

5. **REMOVE OIL TUBES**
   (a) Remove the two bolts and apply tube bracket.

   (b) Pry up the both tube ends with a large screwdrive and remove the four tubes.

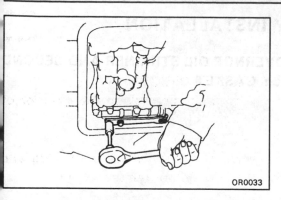

OR0033

6. REMOVE MANUAL DETENT SPRING

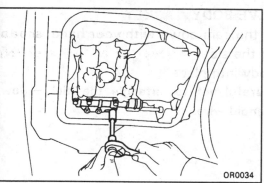

OR0034

7. REMOVE MANUAL VALVE AND VALVE BODY

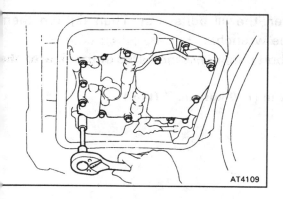

AT4109

8. REMOVE VALVE BODY
(a) Remove the fourteen bolts.

AX

(b) Disconnect the throttle cable.
(c) Remove the valve body.

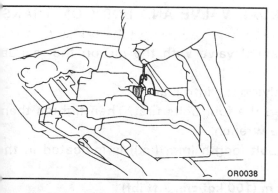

OR0038

9. REMOVE SECOND BRAKE APPLY GASKET AND GOVERNOR OIL STRAINER

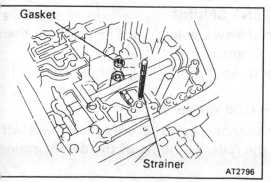

Gasket

Strainer

AT2796

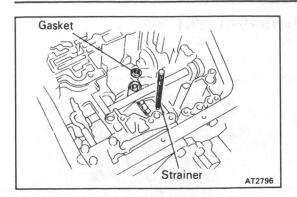

Gasket
Strainer
AT2796

AX003–05

VALVE BODY INSTALLATION

1. **INSTALL GOVERNOR OIL STRAINER AND SECOND BRAKE APPLY GASKET**

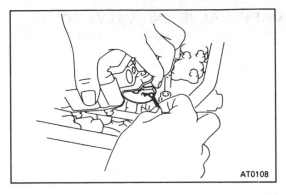

AT0108

2. **INSTALL VALVE BODY**
   (a) While holding the cam down with your hand, slip the cable end into the slot.
   (b) Bring valve body into place.
   NOTICE: Be careful not to entangle the kick — down switch and solenoid wire.

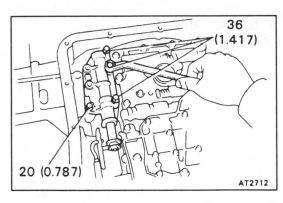

25 (0.984) 36 (1.417)
20 (0.787)
36 (1.417)
25 (0.984)
25 (0.984)
50 (1.969)
25 (0,984)
25 (0.984) 50 (1.969) AT0361

   (c) Finger tighten the all bolts first. Then tighten them with a torque wrench.
   HINT: Each bolt (mm(in.)) is indicated in the figure.

   Torque: 10 N·m (100 kgf·cm, 7 ft·lbf)

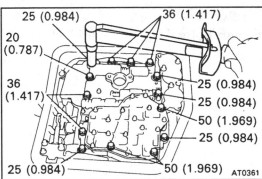

36 (1.417)
20 (0.787)
AT2712

3. **PLACE MANUAL VALVE AND BODY ON TRANSMISSION**
   (a) Align the manual valve with the pin on the manual valve lever.
   (b) Install the valve body into place.
   (c) Finger tighten the four bolts first. Then tighten them with a torque wrench.
   HINT: Each bolt length (mm (in.)) is indicated in the figure.
   Torque: 10 N·m (100 kgf·cm, 7 ft·lbf)

4. **INSTALL DETENT SPRING**
   (a) Finger tighten the two bolts first. Then tighten them with a torque wrench.
   HINT: Each bolt length (mm (in.)) is indicated in the figure.
   Torque: 10 N·m (100 kgf·cm, 7 ft·lbf)

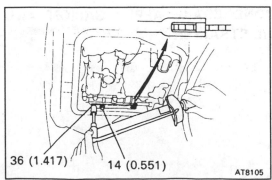

36 (1.417) 14 (0.551)
AT8105

   (b) Check that the manual valve lever is in contact with the center of the roller at the tip of the detent spring

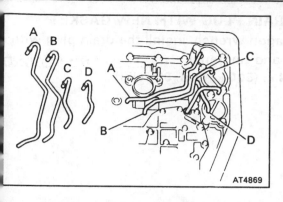

5. INSTALL OIL TUBES

(a) Tap the tubes with a plastic hammer to install them into the positions indicated in the figure.

NOTICE: Be careful not to bend or damage the tubes.

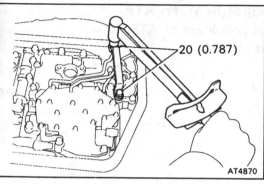

(b) Install the apply tube bracket.

HINT: Each bolt length (mm (in.)) is indicated in the figure.

20 (0.787)

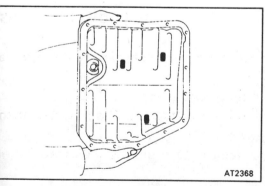

6. INSTALL OIL STRAINER

HINT: Each bolt length (mm (in.)) is indicated in the figure.

45 (1.772)　　45 (1.772)　　50 (1.969)

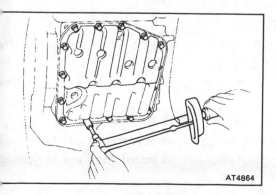

7. INSTALL MAGNETS IN PAN

8. INSTALL OIL PAN WITH GASKET

NOTICE: Make sure that the magnet does not interfere with the oil tubes.

Torque: 4.9 N·m (50 kgf·cm, 43 in.·lbf)

AX

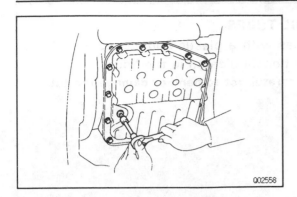

9. INSTALL DRAIN PLUG WITH NEW GASKET
Using a hexagon wrench, install the drain plug with a
new gasket and tighten it.
Torque: 49 N·m (500 kgf·cm, 36 ft·lbf)

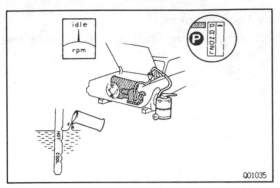

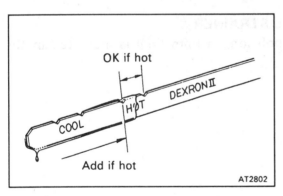

10. FILL TRANSMISSION WITH ATF
Add only about two liters of ATF.
NOTICE: Do not overfill.
Fluid type:
ATF DEXRON® II

11. CHECK FLUID LEVEL
(See page AX−11)

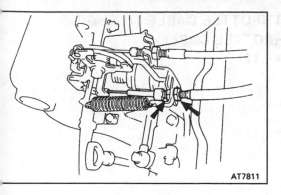

THROTTLE CABLE
THROTTLE CABLE REMOVAL

1. **DISCONNECT THROTTLE CABLE FROM ENGINE**
   Disconnect the cable from the throttle linkage.

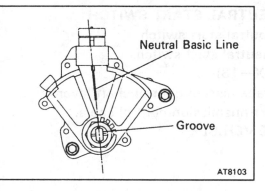

Neutral Basic Line

Groove

2. **REMOVE NEUTRAL START SWITCH**
   (a) Disconnect the transmission control cable from the transmission control shaft lever.
   (b) Remove the transmission control shaft lever.
   (c) Remove the neutral start switch.
3. **REMOVE VALVE BODY**
   (See page AX—26)

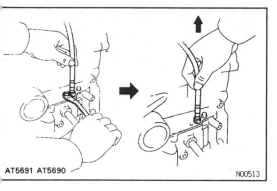

4. **REMOVE THROTTLE CABLE**
   (a) Remove the retaining bolt and plate.
   (b) Pull out the cable from the transmission case.

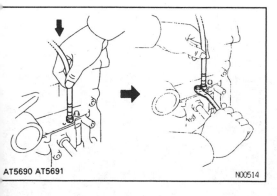

THROTTLE CABLE INSTALLATION

1. **INSTALL CABLE INTO TRANSMISSION CASE**
   (a) Be sure to push it in all the way.
   (b) Install the retaining plate and bolt.
2. **INSTALL VALVE BODY**
   (See page AX—28)

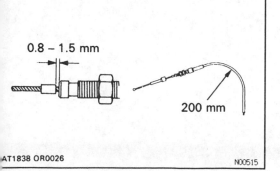

0.8 – 1.5 mm

200 mm

3. **IF THROTTLE CABLE IS NEW, STAKE STOPPER ON INNER CABLE**
   HINT: New cables do not have a cable stopper staked.
   (a) Bend the cable so there is a radius of about 200 mm (7.87 in.).
   (b) Pull the inner cable lightly until a slight resistance is felt, and hold it.
   (c) Stake the stopper, 0.8—1.5 mm (0.031—0.059 in.) from the end of outer cable.

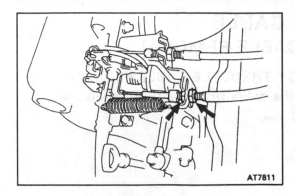

AT7811

4. **CONNECT THROTTLE CABLE TO ENGINE**
5. **ADJUST THROTTLE CABLE**
   (See page AX—12)

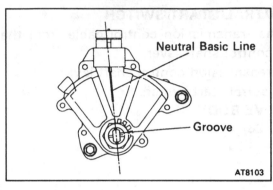

Neutral Basic Line

Groove

AT8103

6. **INSTALL NEUTRAL START SWITCH**
(a) Install the neutral start switch.
(b) Adjust the neutral start switch.
   (See page AX—13)
(c) Install the transmission control shaft lever.
(d) Connect the transmission control cable.
7. **TEST DRIVE VEHICLE**

AX

GOVERNOR VALVE
GOVERNOR VALVE REMOVAL

AX006—03

1. **REMOVE TRANSAXLE DUST COVER**
2. **DISCONNECT LH DRIVE SHAFT**
   (See SA Section)

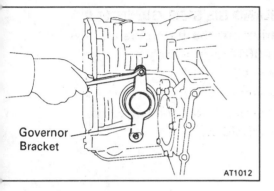

3. **REMOVE GOVERNOR BRACKET**

Governor
Bracket

AT1012

AX

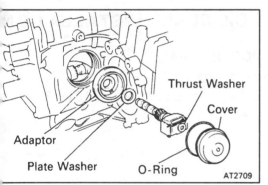

Thrust Washer

Cover

Adaptor

Plate Washer   O-Ring

AT2709

4. **REMOVE GOVERNOR COVER WITH O—RING**
5. **REMOVE GOVERNOR BODY WITH THRUST WASHER**
6. **REMOVE PLATE WASHER**
7. **REMOVE GOVERNOR BODY ADAPTOR**

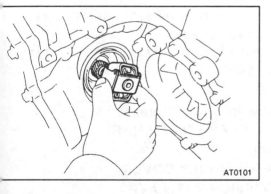

AT0101

AX007—03

GOVERNOR VALVE INSTALLATION

1. **INSTALL GOVERNOR BODY ADAPTOR**
2. **INSTALL PLATE WASHER**
3. **INSTALL GOVERNOR BODY WITH THRUST WASHER**
4. **INSTALL GOVERNOR COVER WITH O—RING**

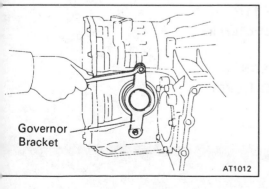

Governor
Bracket

AT1012

5. **INSTALL GOVERNOR BRACKET**
6. **CONNECT LH DRIVE SHAFT**
   (See SA Section)
7. **INSTALL TRANSAXLE DUST COVER**
8. **ADD FLUID TO DIFFERENTIAL IF NECESSARY**
   (See page AX—12)
   Fluid type:
   ATF DEXRON® II

DIFFERENTIAL OIL SEAL
DIFFERENTIAL OIL SEALS REMOVAL

1. **DRAIN TRANSAXLE FLUID**
   Remove the drain plug and drain the fluid into suitable container.
2. **REMOVE ENGINE UNDER COVER**
3. **REMOVE LH AND RH DRIVE SHAFTS**
   (See SA Section)

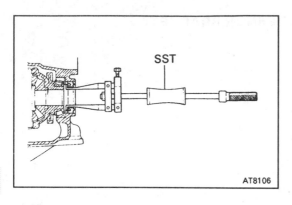

AT8106

4. **REMOVE LH AND RH SIDE OIL SEALS**
   Using SST, drive out the both side oil seals.
   SST 09308—00010

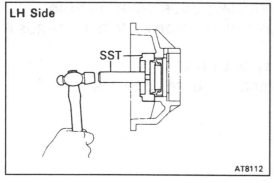

LH Side

SST

AT8112

DIFFERENTIAL OIL SEALS INSTALLATION

1. **INSTALL LH SIDE OIL SEAL**
   (a) Using SST, drive in a new oil seal.
   SST 09350—32014 (09351—32150, 09351—32130)
   Oil seal drive in depth:
   0 mm (0 in.)
   (b) Coat the oil seal lip with MP grease.

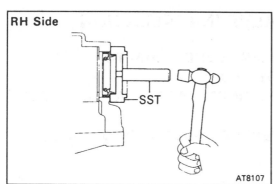

RH Side

SST

AT8107

2. **INSTALL RH SIDE OIL SEAL**
   (a) Using SST, drive in a new oil seal until its surface is flush with the case surface
   SST 09350—32014 (09351—32150, 09351—32130)
   Oil seal drive in depth:
   0±0.5 mm
   (b) Coat the oil seal lip with MP grease.
3. **INSTALL LH AND RH DRIVE SHAFT**
   (See SA Section)
4. **INSTALL ENGINE UNDER COVER**
5. **FILL TRANSMISSION WITH ATF**
   (See page AX—11)
   NOTICE: Do not overfill.
   Fluid type:
   ATF DEXRON® II
6. **CHECK FLUID LEVEL**

ASSEMBLY REMOVAL AND INSTALLATION

Remove and install the parts as shown below.

AX06E—03

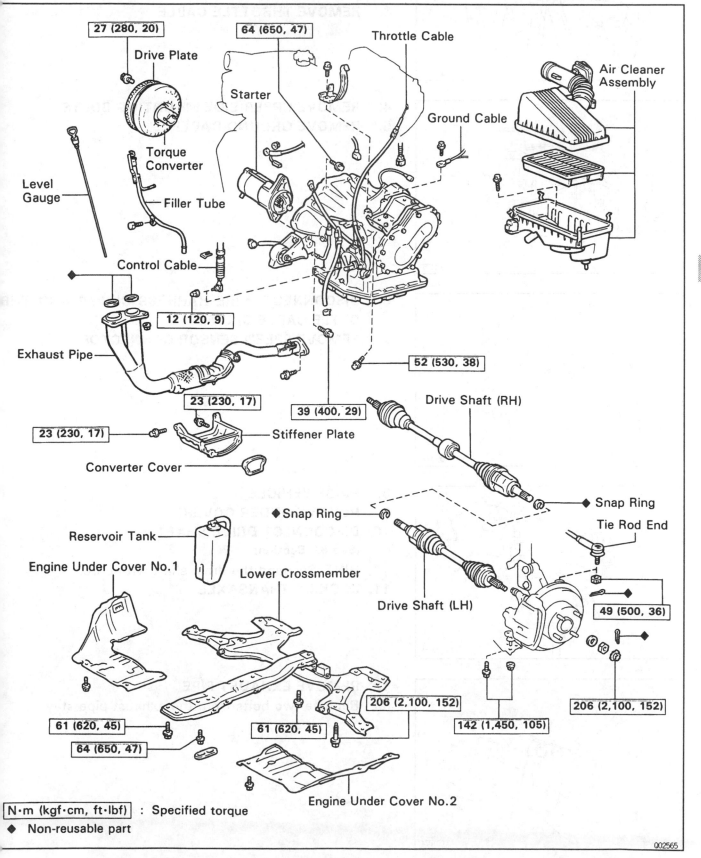

27 (280, 20)
Drive Plate

64 (650, 47)

Throttle Cable

Air Cleaner
Assembly

Starter

Ground Cable

Torque
Converter

Filler Tube

Level
Gauge

Control Cable

12 (120, 9)

Exhaust Pipe

52 (530, 38)

Drive Shaft (RH)

23 (230, 17)

23 (230, 17)

Stiffener Plate

39 (400, 29)

Converter Cover

Snap Ring

Snap Ring
Tie Rod End

Reservoir Tank

Engine Under Cover No.1

Lower Crossmember

Drive Shaft (LH)

49 (500, 36)

206 (2,100, 152)

61 (620, 45)

61 (620, 45)

142 (1,450, 105)

206 (2,100, 152)

64 (650, 47)

Engine Under Cover No.2

N·m (kgf·cm, ft·lbf) : Specified torque

◆ Non-reusable part

002565

AX

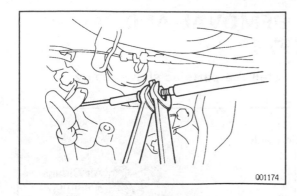

TRANSAXLE REMOVAL

1. **DISCONNECT NEGATIVE (−) TERMINAL FROM BATTERY**
2. **REMOVE LEVEL GAUGE**
3. **REMOVE THROTTLE CABLE**

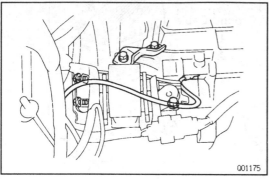

4. **REMOVE UPPER SIDE MOUNTING BOLTS**
5. **REMOVE GROUND CABLE**

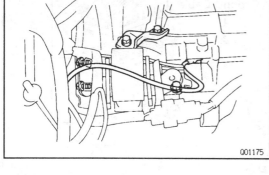

6. **DISCONNECT WIRE HARNESS CLUMP AND THROTTLE CABLE CLUMP**
7. **REMOVE SPEED SENSOR CONNECTOR**

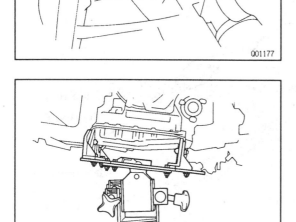

8. **RAISE VEHICLE**
9. **REMOVE UNDER COVER**
10. **DISCONNECT DRIVE SHAFT**
    (See SA Section)
    HINT: Suspend the drive shaft with cord.
11. **JACK UP TRANSAXLE**

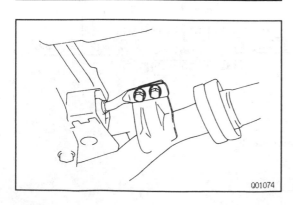

12. **REMOVE EXHAUST PIPE**
(a) Remove two bolts from the exhaust pipe stay.

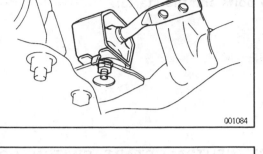

(b) Remove the nut and the exhaust pipe stay from the suspension member.

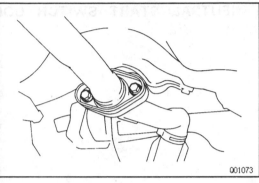

(c) Remove two bolts from the exhaust pipe.

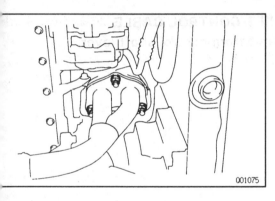

(d) Remove three nuts and the exhaust pipe.

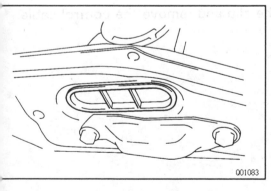

13. INSTALL ENGINE SUPPORT FIXTURE
14. REMOVE SUSPENSION MEMBER
(a) Remove the hole cover.

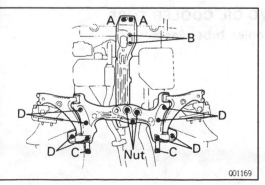

(b) Remove fourteen bolts and three nuts.
(c) Remove the suspension member.

AX

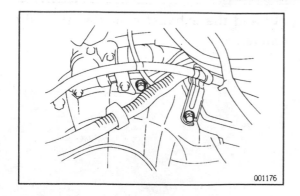

15. REMOVE STARTER
(a) Remove the nut and disconnect the connector.
(b) Remove two bolts and the starter.

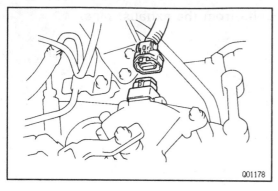

16. DISCONNECT NEUTRAL START SWITCH CONNECTOR

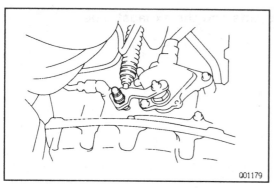

17. REMOVE SHIFT CONTROL CABLE
(a) Remove the nut from control shaft lever.

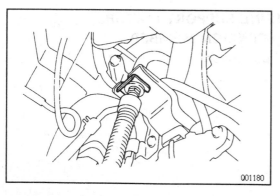

(b) Disconnect the clip and remove the control cable.

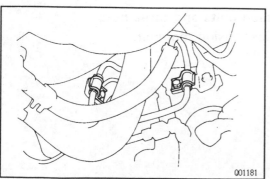

18. REMOVE TWO OIL COOLER TUBE
(a) Remove oil cooler tube clamp.

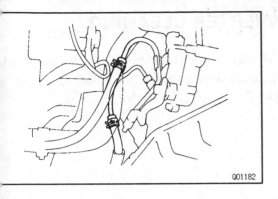

(b) Pull out the two oil cooler tubes.

19. REMOVE FILLER TUBE

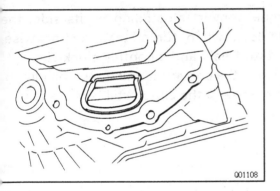

20. REMOVE TRANSAXLE

(a) Remove the converter cover.

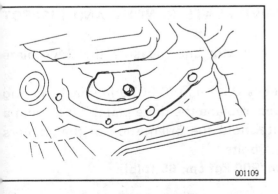

(b) While turning the crankshaft to gain across and remove the six bolts.

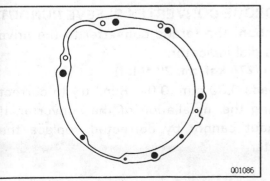

(c) Remove seven bolts and the transaxle.

TORQUE CONVERTER CLEANING

If the transmission is contaminated, the torque converter and transmission cooler should be thoroughly flushed with ATF.

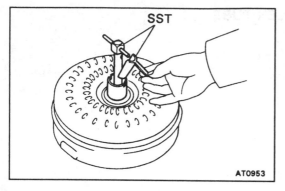

AT0953

TORQUE CONVERTER AND DRIVE PLATE INSPECTION

1. **INSPECT ONE–WAY CLUTCH**
(a) Install SST in the inner race of the one–way clutch.
SST 09350–32014 (09351–32010)
(b) Install SST so that it fits in the notch of the converter hob and outer race of the one–way clutch.
SST 09350–32014 (09351–32020)

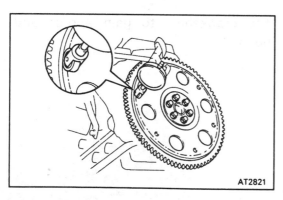

AT8110

(c) With the torque converter standing on its side, the clutch should lock when turned counterclockwise, and should rotate freely and smoothly clockwise.
If necessary, clean the converter and retest the clutch.
Replace the converter if the clutch still fails the test.

AT2821

2. **MEASURE DRIVE PLATE RUNOUT AND INSPECT RING GEAR**
Set up a dial indicator and measure the drive plate runout.
If runout exceeds 0.20 mm (0.0079 in.) or if the ring gear is damaged, replace the drive plate. If installing a new drive plate, note the orientation of the spacers and tighten the bolts.
Torque: 88 N·m (900 kgf·cm, 65 ft·lbf)

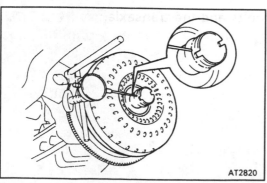

AT2820

3. **MEASURE TORQUE CONVERTER SLEEVE RUNOUT**
(a) Temporarily mount the torque converter to the drive plate. Set up a dial indicator.
Torque: 27 N·m (275 kgf·cm, 20 ft·lbf)
If runout exceeds 0.30 mm (0.0118 in.) try to correct it by reorienting the installation of the converter. If excessive runout cannot by corrected, replace the torque converter.

HINT: Mark the position of the converter to ensure correct installation.

(b) Remove the torque converter from the drive plate.

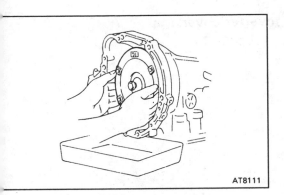

AX06F-02

TRANSAXLE INSTALLATION

1. INSTALL TORQUE CONVERTER IN TRANSAXLE

If the torque converter has been drained and washed, refill with new ATF.

Fluid type:
   ATF DEXRON® II

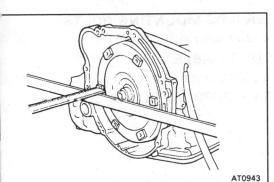

AT8111

2. CHECK TORQUE CONVERTER INSTALLATION

Using calipers and a straight edge, measure from the installed surface to the front surface of the transmission housing.

Correct distance:
   More than 23.0 mm (0.906 in.)

AT0943

3. JACK UP TRANSAXLE

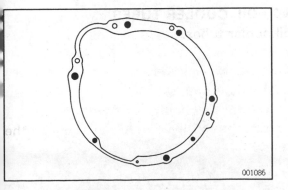

001072

4. ALIGN TRANSAXLE AT INSTALLATION POSITION

(a) Align the two knock pins on the block with the converter housing.

(b) Temporarily install one bolt.

5. INSTALL TRANSAXLE HOUSING MOUNTING BOLTS

Install the transaxle housing mounting bolts.

Torque: 64 N·m (650 kgf·cm, 47 ft·lbf)

001086

AX

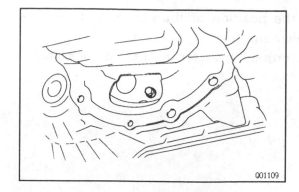

001109

6. INSTALL TORQUE CONVERTER MOUNTING BOLTS

(a) First, install the gray bolt.Then install five black bolts while turning the crankshaft to gain across.

(b) Tighten the bolts evenly.
Torque: 18 N·m (185 kgf·cm, 13 ft·lbf)

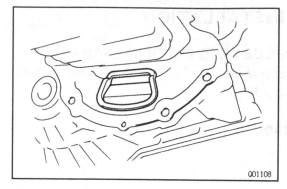

001108

(c) Install the converter cover.

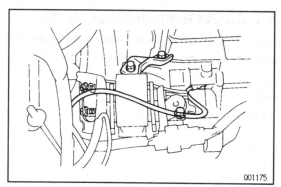

001175

7. INSTALL UPPER SIDE MOUNTING BOLTS
Torque: 23 N·m (230 kgf·cm, 17 ft·lbf)

8. INSTALL GROUND CABLE
Torque: 13 N·m (185 kgf·cm, 18 ft·lbf)

9. REMOVE ENGINE SUPPORT FIXTURE

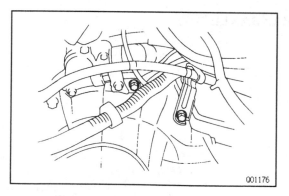

001176

10. INSTALL STARTER

(a) Install the starter with two bolts.
Torque: 39 N·m (400 kgf·cm, 29 ft·lbf)

(b) Install the nut and connect the connector.

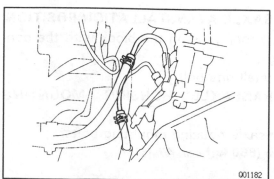

001182

11. INSTALL TWO OIL COOLER TUBES

(a) Install two oil cooler tubes.

(b) Install two oil cooler tube clamps.

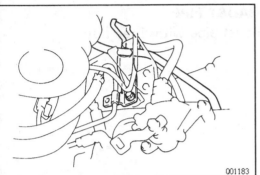

12. INSTALL FILLER TUBE

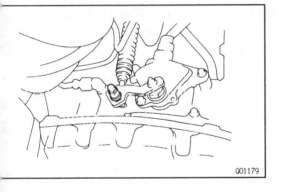

13. INSTALL SHIFT CONTROL CABLE
(a) Temporarily install the nut to the control shaft lever.

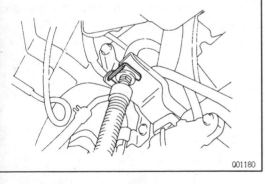

(b) Install the clip to the shift control cable.

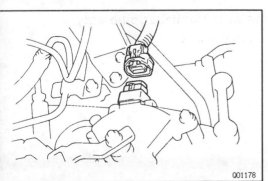

14. INSTALL NEUTRAL START SWITCH CONNECTOR

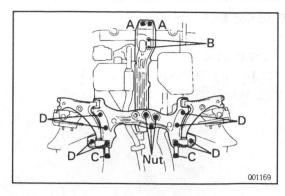

15. INSTALL SUSPENSION MEMBER

(a) Temporarily install the fifteen bolts and three nuts.

(b) Torque the bolts and nuts.

Torque:

   A bolt: 61 N·m (620 kgf·cm, 45 ft·lbf)

   B bolt: 64 N·m (650 kgf·cm, 47 ft·lbf)

   C bolt: 206 N·m (2,100 kgf·cm, 152 ft·lbf)

   D bolt: 206 N·m (2,100 kgf·cm, 152 ft·lbf)

   Nut: 57 N·m (580 kgf·cm, 42 ft·lbf)

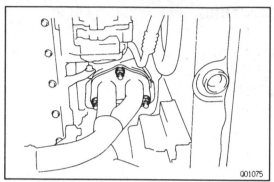

16. INSTALL EXHAUST PIPE

(a) Install the exhaust pipe with three nuts.

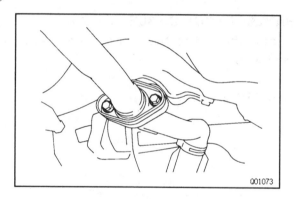

(b) Install two bolts.

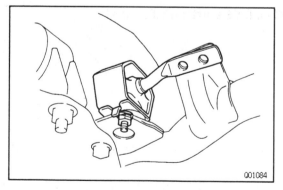

(c) Install the exhaust pipe stay to the suspensio member with the nut.

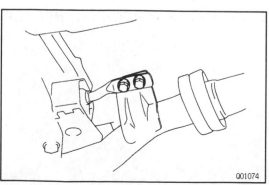

(d) Install two bolts to the exhaust pipe stay.

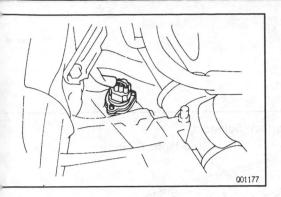

17. INSTALL DRIVE SHAFT
(See SA Section)

18. INSTALL UNDER COVER

19. CONNECT SPEED SENSOR CONNECTOR

20. INSTALL LEVEL GAUGE

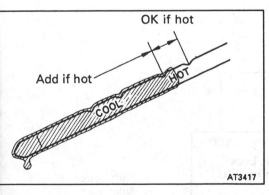

21. INSTALL AND ADJUST THROTTLE CABLE
(See page AX–12)

22. ADJUST SHIFT CABLE
(See page AX–13)

23. ADJUST NEUTRAL START SWITCH
(See page AX–13)

AX

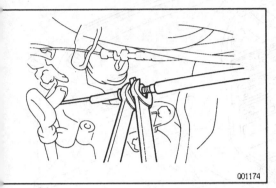

24. FILL TRANSAXLE
Fluid type:
ATF DEXRON® II
Capacity:
5.5 liters (5.7 US qts, 4.8 lmp.qts)

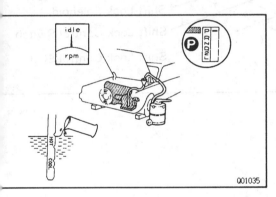

25. CHECK FLUID LEVEL
(See page AX–11)

SHIFT LOCK SYSTEM
COMPONENT

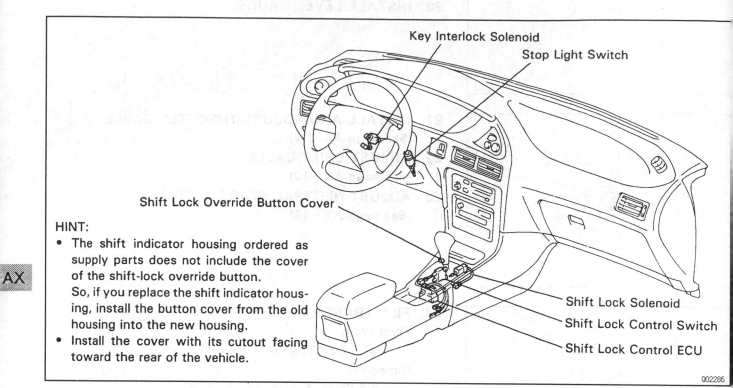

HINT:
- The shift indicator housing ordered as supply parts does not include the cover of the shift-lock override button.
  So, if you replace the shift indicator housing, install the button cover from the old housing into the new housing.
- Install the cover with its cutout facing toward the rear of the vehicle.

WIRING DIAGRAM

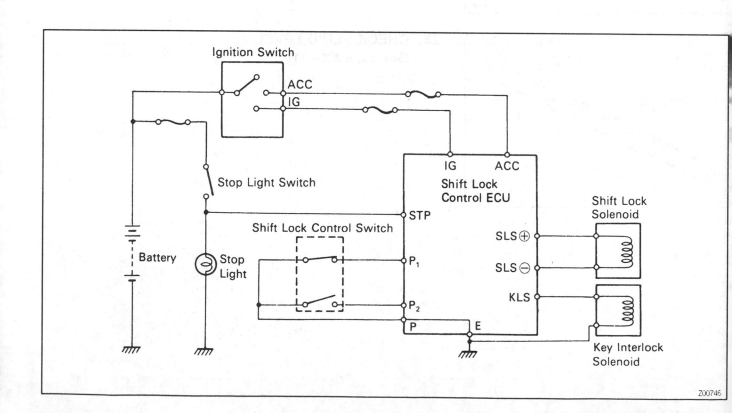

SHIFT LOCK SOLENOID INSPECTION

AX051-02

INSPECT SHIFT LOCK SOLENOID

(a) Disconnect the solenoid connector.

(b) Using an ohmmeter, measure the resistance between terminals.

Standard resistance:

30 − 35 Ω

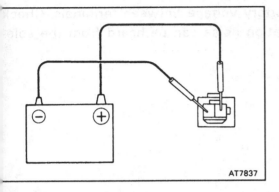

AT7835

(c) Apply the battery voltage between terminals. Check that an operation noise can be heard from the solenoid.

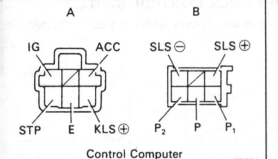

AT7837

SHIFT CONTROL ECU INSPECTION

AX052-01

INSPECT SHIFT LOCK CONTROL ECU

Using a voltmeter, measure the voltage at each terminals.

HINT: Do not disconnect the ECU connector.

A

IG   ACC

STP   E   KLS⊕

B

SLS⊖   SLS⊕

P_2 P P_1

Control Computer

AT7834

Connector	Terminal	Measuring condition		Voltage (V)
A	ACC – E	Ignition switch ACC position		10 – 14
	IG – E	Ignition switch ON position		10 – 14
	STP – E	Depress brake pedal		10 – 14
	KLS – E	① Ignition switch ACC position and P range		0
		② Ignition switch ACC position and except P range		8 – 14
		③ (Approx-after one second)		6 – 9
B	SLS ⊕ – SLS ⊖	① Ignition switch ON position and P range		0
		② Depress brake pedal		8.5 – 13.5
		③ (Approx-after 20 seconds)		5.5 – 9.5
		④ Except P range		0
	P_1 – P	① Ignition switch ON, P range and depress brake pedal		0
		② Except P range		9 – 13.5
	P_2 – P_1	③ Ignition switch ACC position and P range		9 – 13.5
		④ Except P range		0

V00183

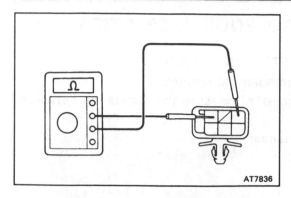

AT7836

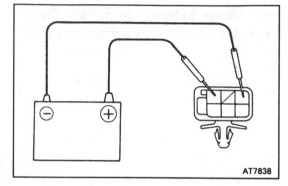

AT7838

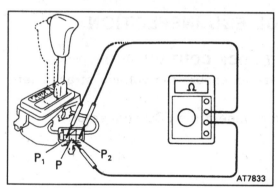

P₁ P P₂

AT7833

KEY INTER LOCK SOLENOID INSPECTION

AX053-02

1. INSPECT KEY INTER LOCK SOLENOID
(a) Disconnect the solenoid connector.
(b) Using an ohmmeter, measure the resistance between terminals.

Standard resistance:

12.5 – 16.5 Ω

(c) Apply the battery voltage between terminals. Check that an operation noise can be heard from the solenoid.

2. INSPECT SHIFT LOCK CONTROL SWITCH
Check whether there is continuity between each terminals.

○—○: Continuity

Terminal Shift Position	P	P₁	P₂
P range (Release button is pushed)	○—	—○	
P Range (Release button is pushed)	○—	—○	
	○—	—	—○
R,N,D,2,L range	○—	—	—○

V00567

SERVICE SPECIFICATIONS
SERVICE DATA

AX09A-03

Governor Pressure	(Vehicle speed reference)			
Differential Gear Ratio: 3.526				
30km/h (19 mph)		39−118 kPa	0.4−1.2 kgf/cm²	6−17 psi
60km/h (37 mph)		157−235 kPa	1.6−2.4 kgf/cm²	23−34 psi
90 km/h (56 mph)		284−363 kPa	2.9−3.7 kgf/cm²	41−53 psi
Differential Gear Ratio: 3.722				
30km/h (19 mph)		88−167 kPa	0.9−1.7 kgf/cm²	13−34 psi
60km/h (37 mph)		177−255 kPa	1.8−2.6 kgf/cm²	26−37 psi
90 km/h (56 mph)		314−39kPa	3.2−4.0 kgf/cm²	46−57 psi
Line Pressure (Wheel locked)	Engine Idling			
	D range	373−422 kPa	3.8−4.3 kgf/cm²	54−61 psi
	R range	549−706 kPa	5.6−7.2 kgf/cm²	80−102 psi
	AT stall			
	D range	902−1,049 kPa	9.2−10.7 kgf/cm²	131−152 psi
	Rrange	1,412−1,647 kPa	14.4−16.8 kgf/cm²	205−239 psi
Engine stall revolution		2,400±150 rpm		
Time lag	N range→D range	Less than 1.2 seconds		
	N range→R range	Less than 1.5 seconds		
Engine idle speed (Cooling fan and A/C OFF) N range		650−750 RPM		
Throtttle cable adjustment		Between boot end face and inner cable stopper		
(Throttle valve fully opened)		0−1 mm	0−0.04 in.	
Torque converter runout	Limit	0.30 mm	0.0118 in.	
Drive plate runout	Limit	0.20 mm	0.0079 in.	

AUTOMATIC SHIFT SCHEDULE

Differential Gear Ratio: 3.526

Range	Gear Position	Vehicle Speed km/h (mph)
D Range	1→2	53—71 (33—44)
	2→3	103—118 (64—73)
	3→2	97—115 (60—71)
	2→1	38—49 (24—30)
	Lock—up ON	71—82 (44—51)
	Lock—up OFF	67—78 (42—48)
L Range	2→1	41—53 (25—33)

Differential Gear Ratio: 3.722

Range	Gear Position	Vehicle Speed km/h (mph)
D Range	1→2	50—67 (31—42)
	2→3	97—116 (60—72)
	3→2	92—112 (57—70)
	2→1	36—47 (22—29)
	Lock—up ON	68—78 (42—48)
	Lock—up OFF	63—74 (39—46)
L Range	2→1	39—50 (24—31)

AX058-06

TORQUE SPECIFICATIONS

Part tightened	N·m	kgf·cm	ft·lbf
Engine mounting	52	530	38
Transaxle housing x Engine	64	650	47
Drive plate x Crankshaft	88	900	65
Torque converter x Drive plate	27	275	20
Valve body	10	100	7
Oil pan	4.9	50	43 in.·lbf
Oil pan drain plug	49	500	36
Ball joint x Lower arm	142	1,450	105
Lower crossmember x Body	206	2,100	152
Center member x Transaxle mounting bracket	61	620	45
Center member x Body	61	620	45
Starter	39	400	29
Stiffener plate	23	230	17
Tie rod end	49	500	36
Drive shaft	206	2,100	152

A245E AUTOMATIC TRANSAXLE

AX

DESCRIPTION
GENERAL DESCRIPTION

AX016-03

The A245E new automatic transaxle is a greatly improved version of the A240 series automatic transaxle.

It has the following features;

- Space is no longer required for the governor valve,so the transaxle case has been redesigned specifically for electronic control. The No.2 speed sensor has also been eliminated to reduce the weight.
- The oil pan ground clearance has been increased by relocating the 2nd coast brake piston from the side of the transaxle case to the top, and relocating the valve body upward.
- The shift response has been improved by changing the shape of the fluid passages, improving operation of the brake and clutch pistons, and adding C_1 accumulator back pressure.
- Fuel consumption has been reduced and power output increased by more precise shift control and monitoring of the throttle openig angle.

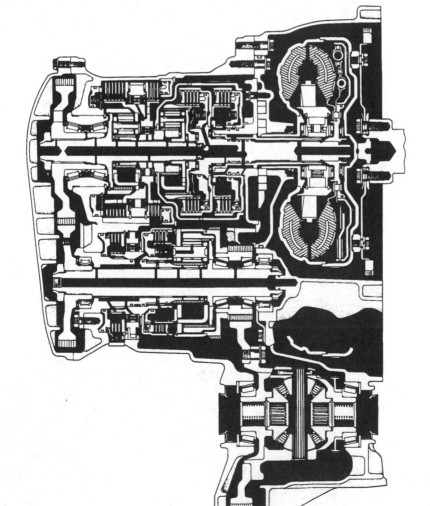

V01569

SPECIFICATIONS

Type of Transaxle		A245E
Type of Engine		7A—FE
Torque Converter Stall Torque Ratio		2.3:1
Lock—up Mechanism		Equipped
Gear Ratio	1st Gear	3.643
	2nd Gear	2.008
	3rd Gear	1.296
	O/D Gear	0.892
	Reverse Gear	2.977
Number of Discs and Plates(Disc/Plate)		
	Forward Clutch (C_1)	4/4
	Direct Clutch (C_2)	3/3
	UD Clutch (C_3)	3/3
	2nd Brake (B_2)	3/3
	First & Reverse Brake (B_3)	6/6
	U/D Brake (B_4)	3/3
Band Width	2nd Coast Brake (B_1)	25 mm (0.98 in.)
ATF Type		ATF DEXRON® II
ATF Capacity	Total	7.6 litter (8.0 US qts, 6.7 Imp. qts)
	Drain & Refill	3.3 litter (3.5 US qts, 2.9 Imp. qts)

AX

OPERATION
FUNCTION OF COMPONENTS

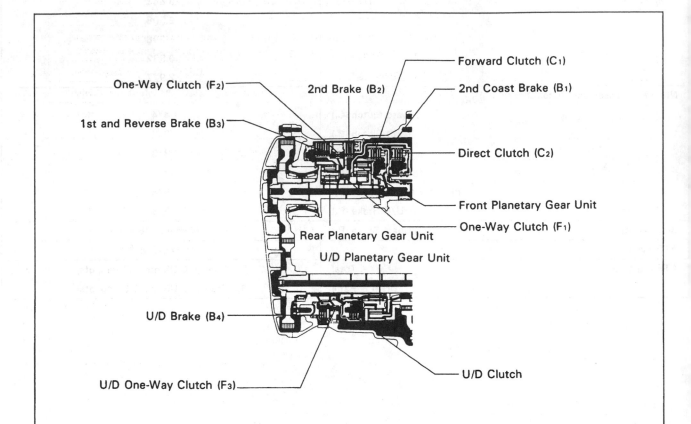

Range (i.e.,) Shift Lever Position	Gear	No. 1 Solenoid Valve	No. 2 Solenoid Valve	C₁	C₂	C₃	B₁	B₂	B₃	B₄	F₁	F₂	F₃
P	Park	ON	OFF							●			
R	Reverse	ON	OFF		●				●	●			
N	Neutral	ON	OFF							●			
D	1st	ON	OFF	●						●		●	●
	2nd	ON	ON	●				●		●	●		●
	3rd	OFF	ON	●	●			●		●			●
	O/D	OFF	OFF	●	●	●		●					
2	1st	ON	OFF	●						●		●	●
	2nd	ON	ON	●			●	●		●	●		●
	3rd*	OFF	ON	●	●			●		●			●
L	1st	ON	OFF	●					●	●		●	●
	2nd*	ON	ON	●			●	●		●	●		●

● : Operating

* : Down-Shift only in the 3rd gear for the 2 range and 2nd gear for the L-range - no up-shift

Component		Function
C_1	Forward Clutch	Connects input shaft and front planetary ring gear.
C_2	Direct Clutch	Connects input shaft and front & rear planetary sun gear.
C_3	U/D Clutch	Connects underdrive sun gear and underdrive planetary carrier.
B_1	2nd Coast Brake	Prevents front & rear planetary sun gear from turning either clockwise or counterclockwise.
B_2	2nd Brake	Prevents outer race of F_1 from turning either clockwise or counterclockwise thus preventing the front & rear planetary sun gear from turning counterclockwise.
B_3	1st & Reverse Brake	Prevents rear planetary carrier from turning either clockwise or counterclockwise.
B_4	U/D Brake	Prevents underdrive sun gear from turning either clockwise or counterclockwise.
F_1	No.1 One-Way Clutch	When B_2 is operating, this clutch prevents the front & rear planetary sun gear from turning counterclockwise.
F_2	No.2 One-Way Clutch	Prevents rear planetary carrier from turning counterclockwise.
F_3	U/D One-Way Clutch	Prevents underdrive planetary sun gear from turning clockwise.
Planetary Gears		These gears change the route through which driving force is transmitted in accordance with the operation of each clutch and brake in order to increase or reduce the input and output speed.

AX

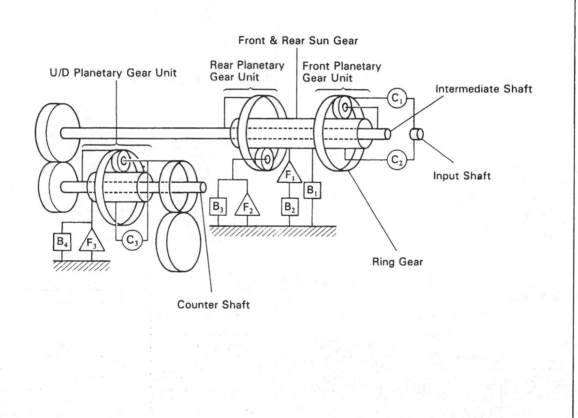

V00643

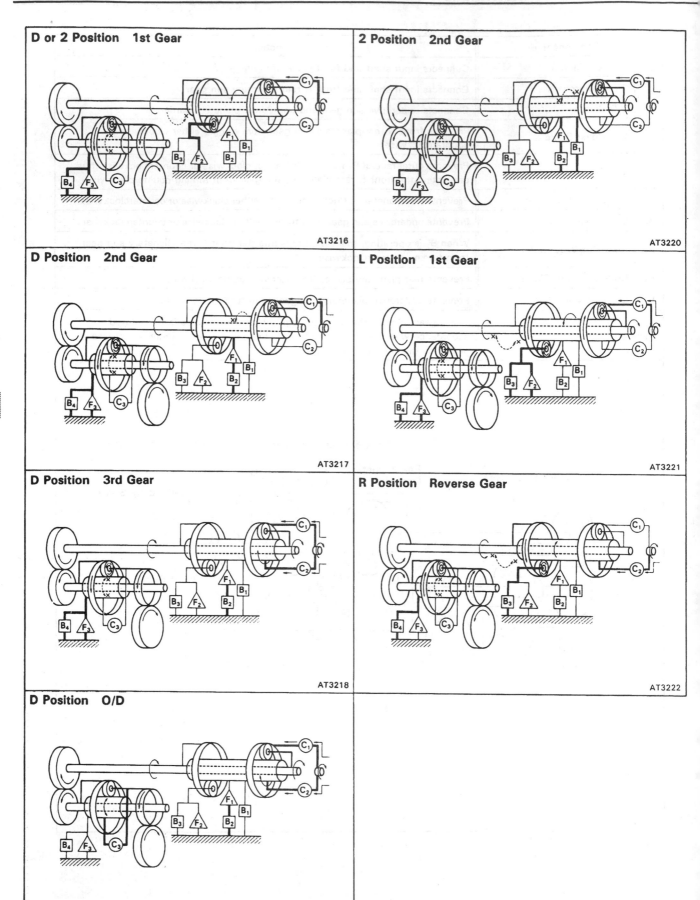

D or 2 Position   1st Gear

AT3216

2 Position   2nd Gear

AT3220

D Position   2nd Gear

AT3217

L Position   1st Gear

AT3221

D Position   3rd Gear

AT3218

R Position   Reverse Gear

AT3222

D Position   O/D

AT3219

V01577

HYDRAULIC CONTROL SYSTEM

The hydraulic control system is composed of the oil pump, the valve body, the solenoid valves, the accumulators, the clutches and brakes as well as the fluid passages which connect all of these components.

Based on the hydraulic pressure created by the oil pump, the hydraulic control system governs the hydraulic pressure acting on the torque converter, clutches and brakes in accordance with the vehicle driving conditions.

There are three solenoid valves on the valve body.

The No.1 and No.2 solenoid vales are turned on and off by signals from the ECM to operate the shift valves and change the gear shift position.

The SL solenoid valve is operated by signals from the ECM to engage or disengage the lock—up clutch of the torque converter.

HYDRAULIC CONTROL SYSTEM

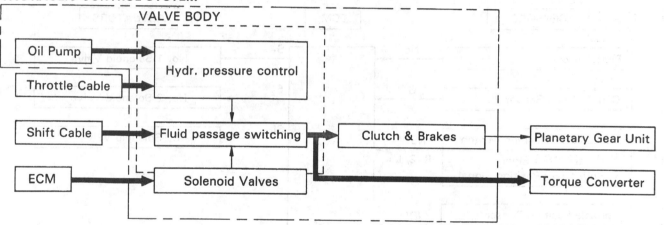

LINE PRESSURE

Line pressure is the most basic and important pressure used in the automatic transaxle, because it is used to operate all of the clutches and brakes in the tranxaxle.

If primary regulator valve does not operate correctly, line pressure will be either toohigh or too low. Line pressure that is too high will lead to shifting shock and consequent engine power loss due to the greater effort required of the oil pump; line pressute that is too low will cause slippage of clutches and brakes, which will, in extreme cases, prevent the vehicle fron moving.The refore, if either of these problems are noted, the line pressure should be measured to see if it is within standard.

THROTTLE PRESSURE

Throttle pressute is always kept in accordance with the opening angle of the engine throttle valve.

This throttle pressure acts on the primary refulator valve and, accordingly, line pressure is regulated in responde to the throttle valve opening.

In the fully hydraulic controlled automatic transaxle, throttle pressure is used for regulating line pressure and as signal pressure for up—shift and down—shift fo the transaxle. In the ECT, however throttle pressure is used onlu for regulating line pressure. Consequently, improper adjudtment of transaxle throttle cable may result in a line pressure that is too high or roo low. This, in turn, will lead to shfting shock or clutch and brakeslippage.

AX0CB−01

ELECTRONIC CONTROL SYSTEM

The electronic control system, which is controls the shift points and the operation of the lock—up clutch, is composed of the following three parts:

1. **Sensor**

   These sensors sense the vehicle speed, throttle opening and other conditions and send thid data to the ECM in the from of electrical signals.

2. **ECM**

   The ECM determines the shift and lock—up timing based upon the signals from sensors, and controls the solenoid valves of the hydraulic control unit accordingly.

3. **Actuators**

   These are three solenoid valves that control hydraulic pressure acting on the hydraulic valves to control shifting and lock—up timing.

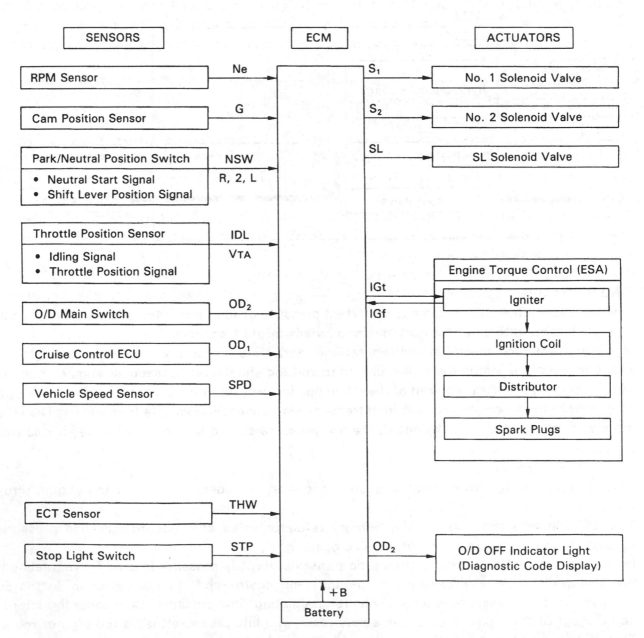

V01576

Function of ECM

- ### Control of Shift Timing

The ECM has programmed into its memory the optimum shift pattern for each shift lever position (D, 2, L position).

Based on the appropriate shift pattern, the ECM turns No.1 and No.2 solenoid valves ON or OFF in accordance with the vehicle speed signal from the vehicle speed sensor and the throttle opening signal from the throttle position sensor. In this manner, the ECM operates each shift valve, opening or closing the fluid passaged to the clutches and brakes to permit up—shift or down—shift of the transaxle.

HINT: The electronic control system prevides shft timing and lock—up control only while the vehicle is traveling forward, In REVERSE, PARK, and NEUTRAL, the transaxle is mechanically, not electronically controlled.

- ### Control of Overdrive

Driving in overdrive is possible if the O/D main switch is ON and the shft lever is in the D position. However, when the vehicle is being driven using the cruise control system (CCS), if the actual vehicle speed drops to about 10 km/h (6 mph) below the set speed while the vehicle is running in overdrive, the CCS ECU sends a signal to the ECM to release the oberdrive and prevent the transaxle from shifting back into overdrive until the actual vehicle speed reaches the speed set in the CCS momory.

On this model, if the coolant temperature falls below 55°C (131°F), the ECM prevents the transaxle from up shi fting into orerdrive.

AX

- ### Control of Lock—up System

The ECM has programmed in its memory a lock—up clutch operation pattern. Based on this lock—up pattern, the ECM turns lock—up solenoid valve ON or OFF in accordance with the vehicle speed signals recived from the vehcle speed sensor and the throttle opening signals from the throttle position sensor.

Depending on ehther lock—up solenoid valvs is ON or OFF, the lock—up relay valve performs changeover of the fluid passages for the converter pressure acting on the torque converter to engage or disengage the lock—up clutch.

(Mandatory Cancellation of Lock—up System)

If any of the followng conditions exist, the ECM turns OFF lock—up solenoid valve to disengage the lock—up clutch.

(1) The brake light switch comes on (during braking).

(2) The coolant temperature falls below 55°C (131°F).

The purpose of (1) is to prevent the engine from stalling if the front wheel lock up. The purpose of (2) is improve general driveability, and to speed up engine warm—up.

Also, wehile the lock—up system is in operation, the ECM will temporarily turn it OFF during up—shift or down—shift in order to decrease shfting shock.

ARRANGEMENT OF COMPONENTS

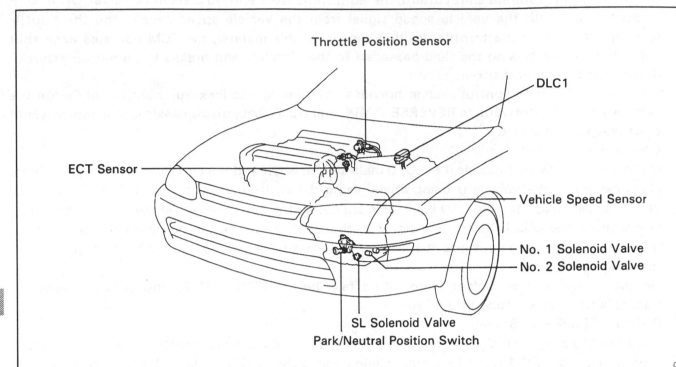

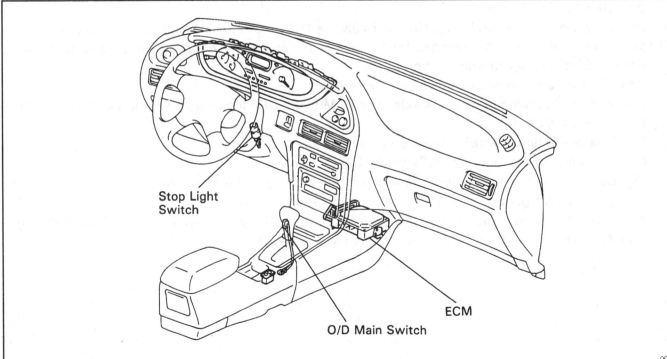

SYSTEM DIAGRAM

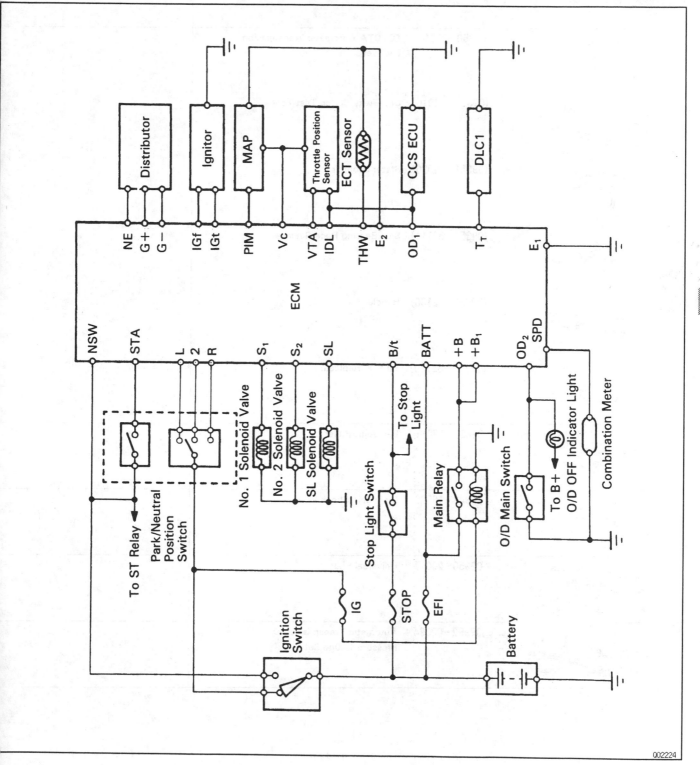

AX

002224

PREPARATION
SST (SPECIAL SERVICE TOOLS)

AX01C-02

	09308-00010	Oil Seal Puller
	09350-32014	TOYOTA Automatic Transmission Tool Set
	(09351-32010)	One-way Clutch Test Tool
	(09351-32020)	Stator Stopper
	(09351-32111)	Side Bearing Race Replacer
	(09351-32130)	Handle
	(09351-32150)	Oil Seal Replacer
	09628-62011	Ball Joint Puller
	09843-18020	Diagnosis Check Wire
	09950-20017	Universal Puller
	09992-00094	Automatic Transmission Oil Pressure Gauge Set

RECOMMENDED TOOLS

	09031–00030 Pin Punch	Pin diameter 3mm(0.12in.)
	09082–00015 TOYOTA Electrical Tester	

AX01E–02

EQUIPMENT

Straight edge	Check torque converter installation.
Vernier calipers	Check torque converter installation.
Dial indicator or dial indicator with magnetic base	Measure drive plate runout.
Torque wrench	

AX01Q–03

AX

LUBRICANT

Item	Capacity	Classification
Automatic transaxle fluid (w/o differential oil)		ATF DEXRON® II
Dry fill	7.6 liters (8.0 US qts, 6.7 Imp. qts)	
Drain and refill	3.3 liters (3.5 US qts, 2.9 Imp. qts)	

AX01F–02

SSM (Special Service Materials)

	08833–00070 Adhesive 1324, THREE BOND 1324 or equivalent	Torque converter mounting bolt

ON—VEHICLE REPAIR
VALVE BODY REMOVAL

1. CLEAN TRANSAXLE EXTERIOR

To help prevent contamination, clean the exterior of the transaxle.

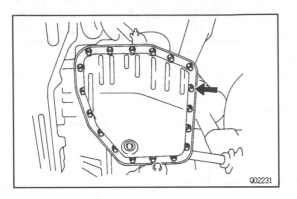

2. DRAIN TRANSAXLE FLUID

Remove the drain plug, gasket and drain the fluid into a suitable container.

3. REMOVE OIL PAN AND GASKET

NOTICE: Some fluid will remain in the oil pan. Remove all pan bolts, and carefully remove the oil pan assembly. Discard the gasket.

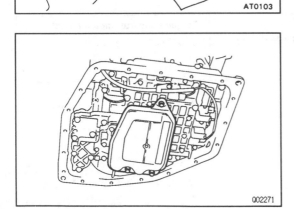

4. EXAMINE PARTICLES IN PAN

Remove the magnets and use them to collect any steel chips. Look carefully at the chips and particles in the pan and the magnet to anticipate what type of wear you will find in the transaxle.

- Steel (magnetic): bearing, gear and plate wear

- Brass (non—magnetic): bushing wear

5. REMOVE OIL STRAINER

NOTICE: Be careful as some fluid will come out with the oil strainer.

Remove the three bolts, the oil strainer and gasket.

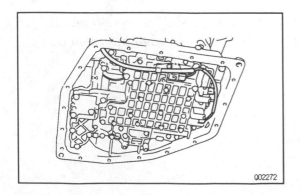

6. DISCONNECT SOLENOID CONNECTORS

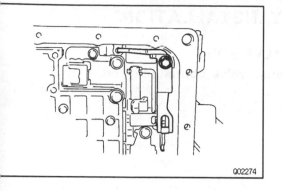

002274

7. REMOVE MANUAL DETENT SPRING

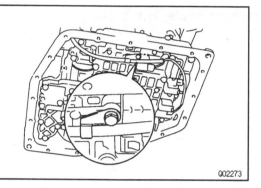

002273

8. REMOVE VALVE BODY
(a) Remove the wire retainer.

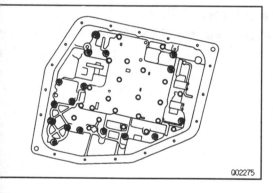

002275

(b) Remove the seventeen bolts.

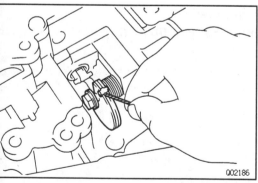

002186

(c) Disconnect the throttle cable from the cam.

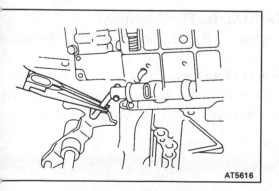

AT5616

(d) While disconnecting the manual valve connecting rod from the manual valve lever, remove the valve body.

AX09D—03

VALVE BODY INSTALLATION

1. INSTALL VALVE BODY

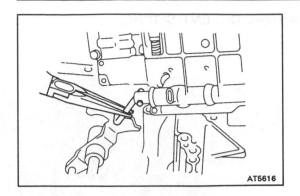

(a) Connect manual valve connecting rod.

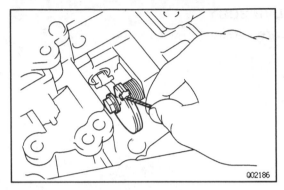

(b) Connect the throttle cable to the cam.

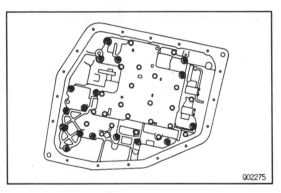

(c) Install seventeen bolts.
   Torque: 10 N·m (100 kgf·cm, 7 ft·lbf)

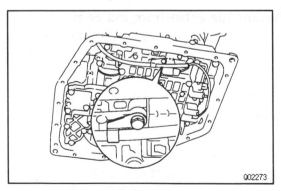

(d) Install the wire retainer.
   Torque: 6.4 N·m (65 kgf·cm, 56 in.·lbf)

2. INSTALL MANUAL DETENT SPRING

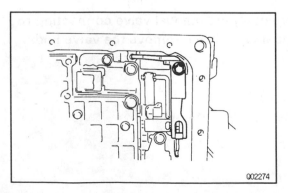

(a) Install and tighten 16 mm length bolt with torqu⌐
   wrench.
   Torque: 10 N·m (100 kgf·cm, 7 ft·lbf)

(b) Check that the manual valve lever is in contact wit⌐
   the center of the roller at the tip of the detent spring

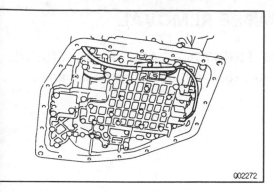

3. CONNECT SOLENOID CONNECTORS

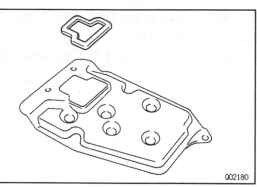

4. INSTALL OIL STRAINER

(a) Install a new gasket to the oil strainer.

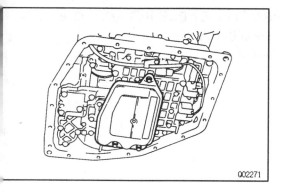

(b) Install the oil strainer and torque the three bolts.

AX

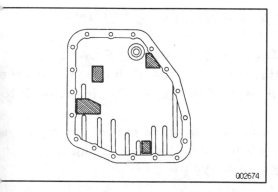

5. INSTALL FOUR MAGNETS IN OIL PAN
    NOTICE: Make sure that the magnets do not interfere with the oil tubes.

6. INSTALL OIL PAN

(a) Install a new gasket to the oil pan and install the oil pan.

(b) Tighten the eighteen bolts.
    Torque: 5.3 N·m (55 kgf·cm, 48 in.·lbf)

7. INSTALL OIL PAN DRAIN PLUG
    Torque: 17 N·m (175 kgf·cm, 13 ft·lbf)

8. FILL TRANSAXLE WITH ATF
    (See page AX—54)
    NOTICE: Donot over fill.
    Fluid type:
        ATF DEXRON® II

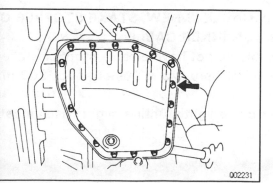

9. CHECK FLUID LEVEL (See page AX—54)

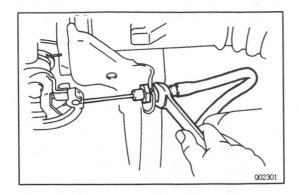

AX01G—02

THROTTLE CABLE REMOVAL

1. **DISCONNECT THROTTLE CABLE FROM ENGINE**
   Disconnect the cable from the throttle linkage.

2. **REMOVE PARK/NEUTRAL POSITION SWITCH**
   (a) Remove the manual shaft lever.
   (b) Pry out the lock wahser and remove the manual valve shaft nut.
   (c) Remove the two bolts and pull out the park/neutral position switch.

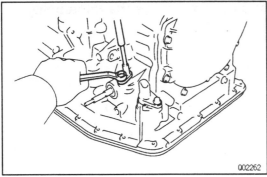

3. **REMOVE THROTTLE CABLE RETAINING BOLT**
4. **REMOVE VALVE BODY**
   (See age AX—14)

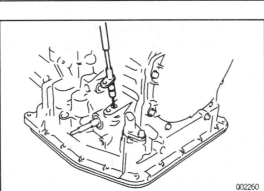

AX0A2—0

THROTTLE CABLE INSTALLATION

1. **INSTALL CABLE INTO TRANSAXLE CASE**
   Install the throttle cable to the hole on the case being careful not to damage the O—ring. Check for full seating.
   NOTICE: In subsequent work, do not roll the case over the cable to avoid breaking the cable fitting.

2. **INSTALL VALVE BODY**
   (See page AX—16)

3. **IF THROTTLE CABLE IS NEW, STAKE STOPPER O PAINT MARK ON INNER CABLE**
   HINT: New cable do not have a cable stopper staked
   (a) Bend the cable so there is a radius of about 200 mr (7.87 in.).
   (b) Pull the inner cable lightly until a slight resistance i felt, and hold it.

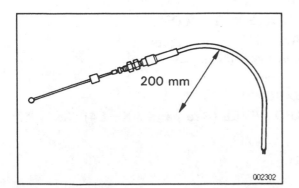

200 mm

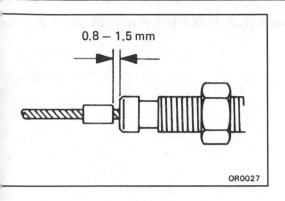

0.8 – 1.5 mm

OR0027

(c) Stake the stopper, 0.8–1.5 mm (0.031–0.059 in.) from the end of outer cable.

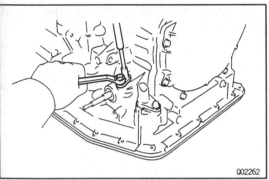

Q02262

4. INSTALL THROTTLE CABLE RETAINING BOLT

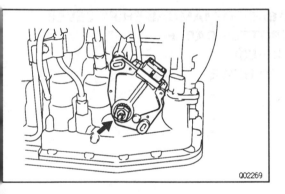

Q02269

5. INSTALL PARK/NEUTRAL POSITION SWITCH

(a) Install the park/neutral position switch to the manual valve shaft.
(b) Install the packing, nut stopper and nut.
(c) Tighten the nut.
   Torque: 12 N·m (125 kgf·cm, 108 in.·lbf)

AX

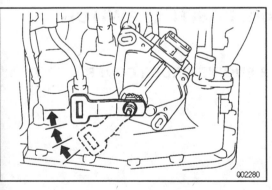

Q02280

(d) Temporarily install the manual shaft lever.
(e) Turn the lever clockwise until it stops, then turn it counterclockwise three notches.
(f) Remove the manual shift lever.

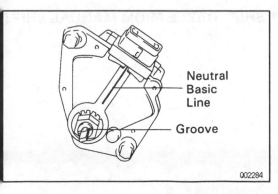

Neutral
Basic
Line

Groove

Q02284

(g) Align the groove and neutral basic line as shown.
(h) Install and tighten the two bolts.
   Torque: 5.4 N·m (55kgf·cm, 48 in.·lbf)

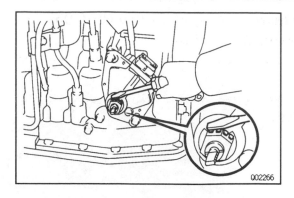

(i)　Using a screwdriver, stake the nut with the nut stopper.

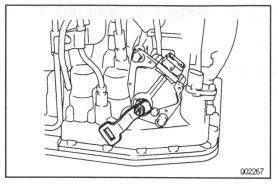

(j)　Install the manual shift lever with the washer, and tighten the nut.

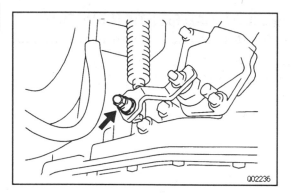

6.　**INSTALL CABLE TO MAMUAL SHIFT LEVER**
7.　**ADJUST THROTTLE CABLE**
　　(See page AX−55)
8.　**TEST DRIVE VEHICLE**

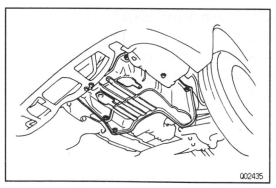

AX09E−01

PARK/NEUTRAL POSITION SWITCH REMOVAL

1.　**REMOVE NO.2 ENGINE UNDER COVER**

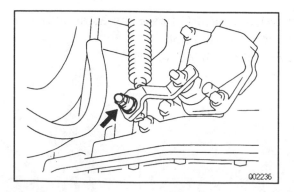

2.　**DISCONNECT SHIFT CABLE FROM MANUAL SHIFT LEVER**

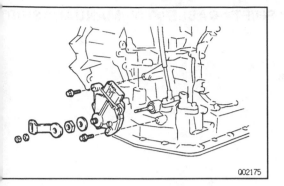

002175

3. REMOVE PARK/NEUTRAL POSITION SWITCH
(a) Remove the manual shift lever.
(b) Pry off the lock plate and remove the manual valve shaft nut.
(c) Remove the two bolts and pull out the park/neutral position switch.

002261

AX09F—01

PARK/NEUTRAL POSITION SWITCH INSTALLATION

1. INSTALL PARK/NEUTRAL POSITION SWITCH
(a) Install the park/neutral position switch to the manual valve shaft.
(b) Install a new lock plate and tighten the nut.
(c) Stake the nut with lock plate.

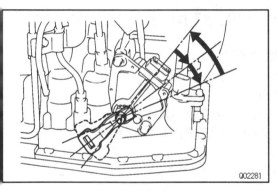

002281

(d) Temporarily install the manual shift lever.
(e) Turn the lever counterclockwise until it stops, then turn it clockwise two notches.
(f) Remove the manual shift lever.

AX

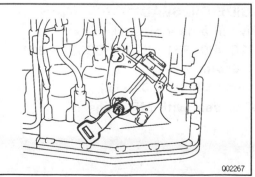

Neutral
Basic
Line

Groove

002284

(g) Adjust the park/neutral position switch.
(See page AX—19)
HINT: Align the groove and neutral basic line.
(h) Install and tighten the two bolts.
Torque: 5.4 N·m (55 kgf·cm, 48 in.·lbf)

2. INSTALL MANUAL SHIFT LEVER

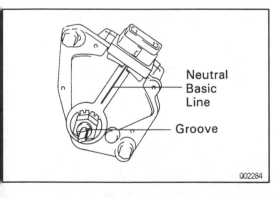

002267

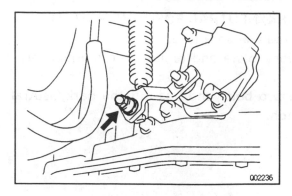

3. **CONNECT SHIFT CABLE TO MANUAL SHIFT LEVER**

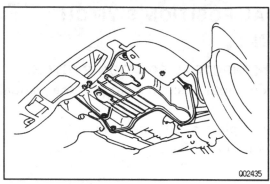

4. **INSTALL NO.2 ENGINE UNDER COVER**

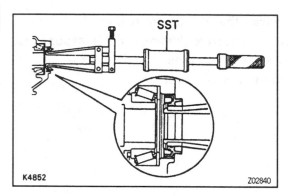

DIFFERENTIAL OIL SEAL REPLACEMENT

1. **DRAIN TRANSAXLE FLUID**
   Remove the drain plug and drain the fluid into a suitable container.
2. **REMOVE ENGINE UNDER COVER**
3. **REMOVE LH AND RH DRIVE SHAFTS**
   (See SA Section)
4. **REMOVE BOTH OIL SEALS**
   Using SST, pull out the oil seals.
   SST 09308−00010

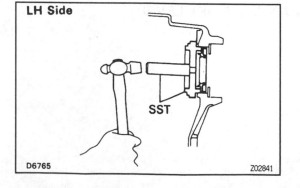

5. **INSTALL LH SIDE OIL SEAL**
   (a) Using SST, drive in a new oil seal.
       SST 09350−32014(09351−32111,09351−32130)
       Oil seal drive in depth:
           5.3± 0.5 mm (0.209± 0.020 in.)
   (b) Coat the lip of oil seal with MP grease.

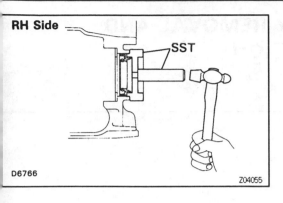

RH Side

SST

D6766

Z04055

6. INSTALL RH SIDE OIL SEAL

(a) Using SST, drive in a new oil seal until SST makes contact with the case surfacfe.
SST 09350−32014(09351−32150,09351−32130)
Oil seal drive in depth:
3.1± 0.5 mm (0.122± 0.020 in.)

(b) Coat the lip of oil seal with MP grease.

7. INSTALL BOTH DRIVE SHAFTS
(See SA Section)

8. FILL TRANSAXLE WITH ATF
(See page AX−54)
NOTICE: Do not over fill.
Fluid type:
ATF DEXRON ® II

9. CHECK TRANSAXLE FLUID LEVEL

10. INSTALL ENGINE UNDER COBER

AX

ASSEMBLY REMOVAL AND INSTALLATION

CONPONENTS

AX01J—0

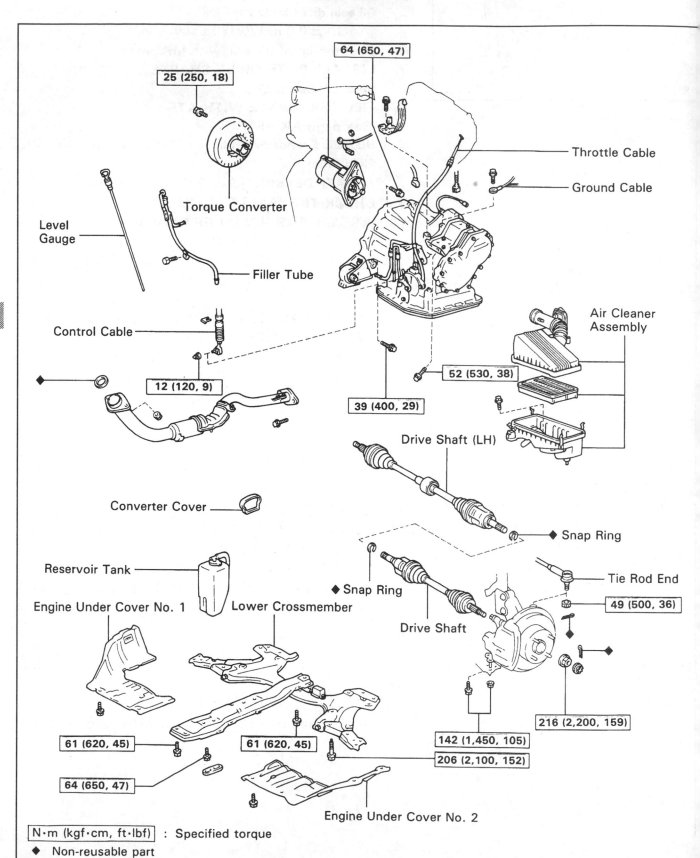

64 (650, 47)

25 (250, 18)

Throttle Cable

Ground Cable

Torque Converter

Level Gauge

Filler Tube

Control Cable

12 (120, 9)

52 (530, 38)

Air Cleaner Assembly

39 (400, 29)

Drive Shaft (LH)

Converter Cover

Snap Ring

Reservoir Tank

Snap Ring

Tie Rod End

Engine Under Cover No. 1   Lower Crossmember

Drive Shaft

49 (500, 36)

61 (620, 45)

61 (620, 45)

216 (2,200, 159)

64 (650, 47)

142 (1,450, 105)

206 (2,100, 152)

Engine Under Cover No. 2

N·m (kgf·cm, ft·lbf) : Specified torque

◆ Non-reusable part

002167

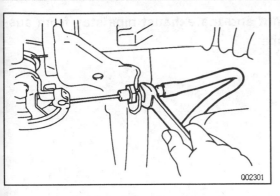

AX09G-03

TRANSAXLE REMOVAL

1. **SDISCONNECT NEGATIVE (−) TERMINAL FROM BATTERY**
2. **REMOVE LEVEL GAUGE**
3. **REMOVE RESERVOIR TANK**
4. **DISCONNECT THROTTLE CABLE**

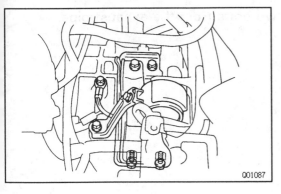

5. **REMOVE AIR CLEANER**
6. **REMOVE ENGINE LEFT MOUNTING UPPER SIDE BOLTS**
7. **REMOVE ENGINE LEFT MOUNTING STAY**
8. **REMOVE GROUND CABLE**
9. **DISCONNECT WIRE HARNESS CLAMP AND THROTTLE CABLE CLAMP**
10. **REMOVE STARTER UPPER SIDE MOUNTING BOLT**

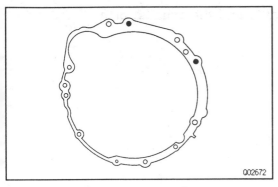

11. **REMOVE TRANSAXLE MOUNTING TWO BOLTS OF TRANSAXLE SIDE**

12. **RAISE VEHICLE**
13. **REMOVE UNDER COVER**
14. **REMOVE DRIVE SHAFT**
    (See SA Section)
    HINT: Suspend the drive shaft with cord.
15. **JACK UP TRANSAXLE**

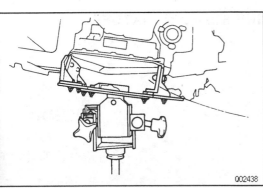

16. **REMOVE EXHAUST PIPE**
(a) Remove the two bolts from the exhaust pipe stay.

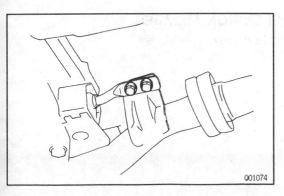

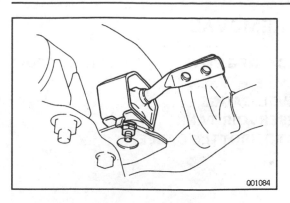

(b) Remove the nut and the exhaust pipe stay from suspension member.

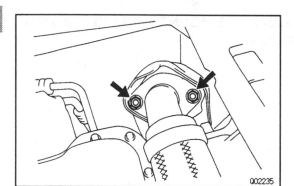

(c) Remove the two bolts from the exhaust pipe.

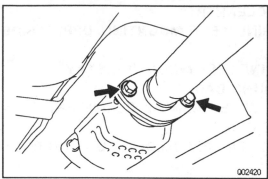

(d) Remove two nuts and the exhaust pipe.

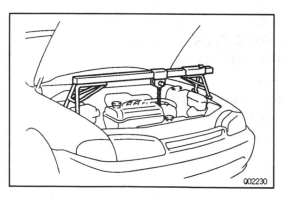

17. INSTALL ENGINE SUPPORT FIXTURE

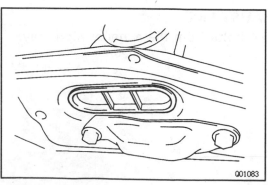

18. REMOVE SUSPENSION MEMBER

(a) Remove the hole cover.

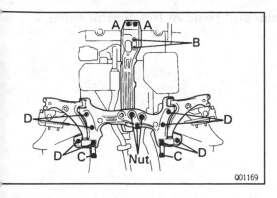

(b) Remove fourteen bolts ans three nuts.

(c) Remove the suspension member.

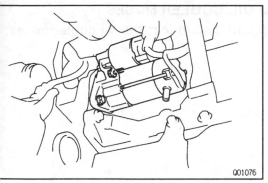

19. REMOVE STARTER

(a) Remove the nut and disconnect the connector.

(b) Remove the bolt and starter.

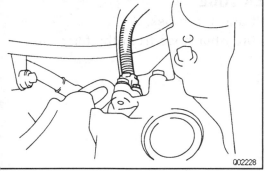

20. DISCONNECT VEHICLE SPEED SENSOR CONNECTOR

21. DISCONNECT SOLENOID CONNECTOR AND PARK/NEUTRAL POSITION SWITCH CONNECTOR

(a) Disconnect the solenoid connector and park/neutral position switch connector.

(b) Remove wire harness clamps.

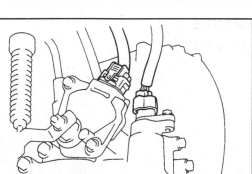

22. REMOVE SHIFT CONTROL CABLE

(a) Remove the nut from control shaft lever.

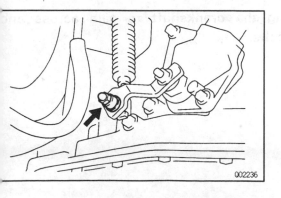

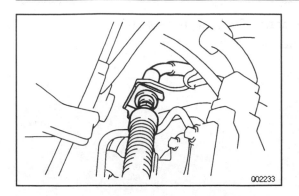

(b)   Remove the clip and remove the control cable.

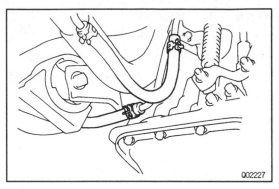

23. REMOVE TWO OIL COOLER HOSES
Loosen the clip and disconnect the oil cooler hoses.

24. REMOVE FILLER TUBE
(a)   Remove the bolt and the tubes.
(b)   Disconnect the breather hose from the filler tube.

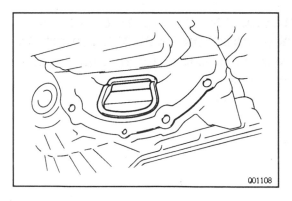

25. REMOVE TRANSAXLE
(a)   Remove converter cover.

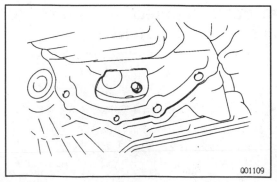

(b)   While turning the crankshaft to gain across and
remove six bolts.

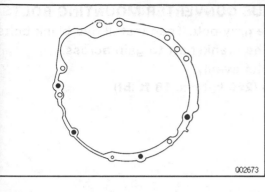

(c) Remove four bolts and the transaxle.

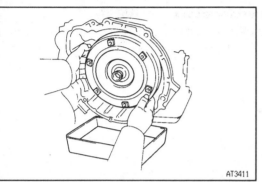

AX09H-02

TRANSAXLE INSTALLATION

1. INSTALL TORQUE CONVERTER IN TRANSAXLE

If the torque converter has been drained and washed,
refill with new ATF.

Fluid type:
ATF DEXRON® II

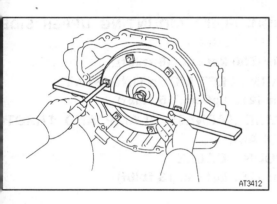

2. CHECK TORQUE CONVERTER INSTALLATION

Using calipers and a straight edge, measure from the
installed surface to the front surface of the transsxle
housing.

Correct distance:
More than 22.8 mm (0.898 in.)

AX

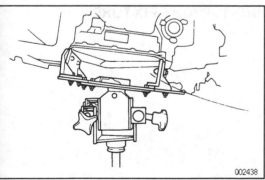

3. JACK UP TRANSAXLE

4. ALIGN TRANSAXLE AT INSTALLATION POSITION

(a) Align the two knock pins on the block with the converter housing.

(b) temporarily install one bolt.

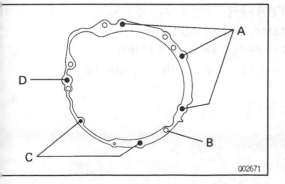

**5. INSTALL TRANSAXLE MOUNTING BOLTS OF
TRANSAXLE SIDE**

Install the transaxle housing mounting bolts.

Torque:
A Bolt : 64 N·m (650 kgf·cm, 47 ft·lbf)
B Bolt : 25 N·m (250 kgf·cm, 18 ft·lbf)
C Bolt : 23 N·m (230 kgf·cm, 17 ft·lbf)
D Bolt : 46 N·m (470 kgf·cm, 34 ft·lbf)

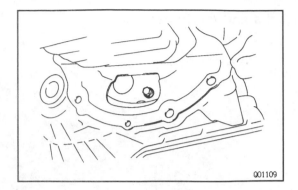

6. INSTALL TRQUE CONVERTER MOUNTING BOLTS
(a) First, install the gray bolt. Then install five black bolts while turning the crankshaft to gain across.
(b) Tighten the bolts evenly.
   Torque: 25 N·m (250 kgf·cm, 18 ft·lbf)

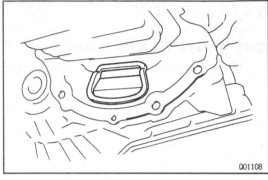

(c) Install the converter cover.

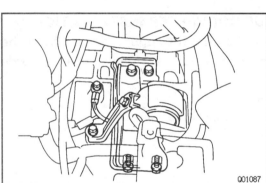

7. INSTALL ENGINE LEFT MOUNTING UPPER SIDE BOLTS
   Torque: 52 N·m (530 kgf·cm, 38 ft·lbf)
8. INSTALL ENGINE LEFT MOUNTING STAY
   Torque: 21 N·m (210 kgf·cm, 15 ft·lbf)
9. CONNECT WIRE HARNESS CLAMP AND THROT-TLE CABLE CLAMP
10. INSTALL GROUND CABLE
   Torque: 18 N·m (185 kgf·cm, 13 ft·lbf)

11. REMOVE ENGINE SUPPORT FIXTURE

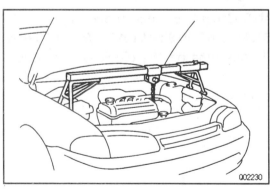

12. INSTALL STARTER
(a) Install the starter with two bolts.
   Torque: 39 N·m (400 kgf·cm, 29 ft·lbf)
(b) Install the nut and connect the connector.

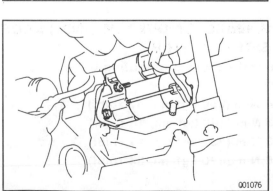

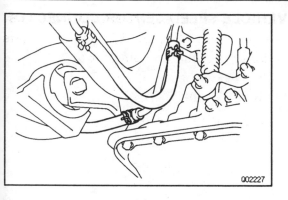

13. INSTALL TWO OIL COOLER HOSES

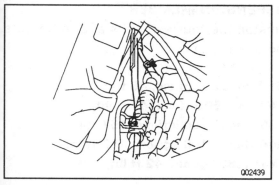

14. INSTALL FILLER TUBE

(a) Install the filler tube with the bolt.

(b) Connect the breather hose to the filler tube.

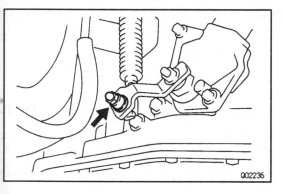

15. INSTALL SHIFT CONTROL CABLE

(a) Temporarily install the nut to the control shaft lever.

AX

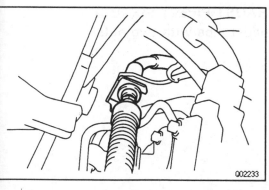

(b) Install the clip to the shift control cable.

16. CONNECT SOLENOID CONNECTOR AND PARK / NEUTRAL POSITION SWITCH

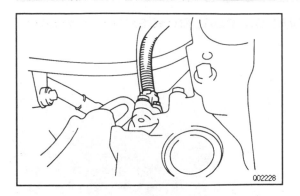

17. CONNECT VEHICLE SPEED SENSOR CONNECTOR

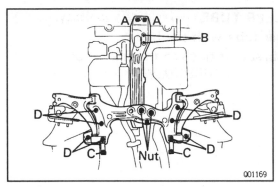

18. INSTALL SUSPENSION MEMBER

(a) Temporarily install the fourteen bolts and three nuts.

(b) Torque the bolts and nuts.

Torque:

A bolt: 61 N·m (620 kgf·cm, 45 ft·lbf)

B bolt: 64 N·m (650 kgf·cm, 47 ft·lbf)

C bolt: 206 N·m (2,100 kgf·cm, 152 ft·lbf)

D bolt: 206 N·m (2,100 kgf·cm, 152 ft·lbf)

Nut: 57 N·m (580 kgf·cm, 42 ft·lbf)

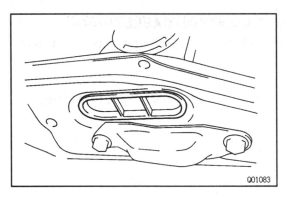

(c) Install hole cover.

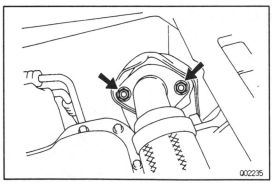

19. INSTALL EXHAUST PIPE

(a) Install the exhaust pipe with two nuts.

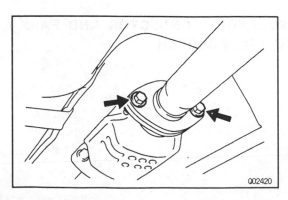

(b) Install the two bolts.

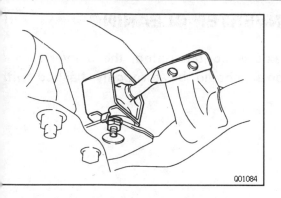

(c) Install the exhaust pipe stay to the suspension member with the nut.

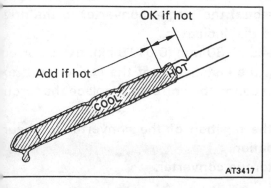

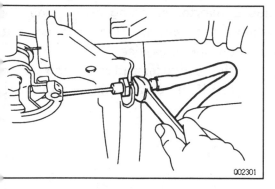

(d) Install the two bolts to the exhaust pipe stay.

20. INSTALL DRIVE SHAFTS
   (See SA Section)

21. INSTALL ENGINE UNDER COVER

22. INSTALL AIR CLEANER

23. INSTALL LEVEL GAUGE

24. INSTALL RESERVOIR TANK

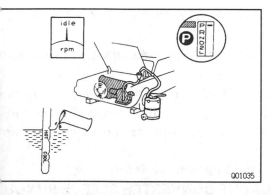

AX

25. INSTALL AND ADJUST THROTTLE CABLE
   (See page AX−55)

26. ADJUST SHIFT CABLE
   (See page AX−21)

27. ADJUST PARK/NEUTRAL POSITION SWITCH
   (See page AX−19)

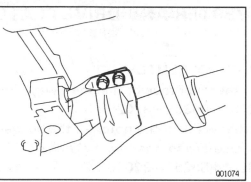

28. FILL TRANSAXLE
   Fluid type:
      ATF DEXRON® II
   Capacity:
      7.6 liters (8.0 US qts, 6.7 Imp.qts)

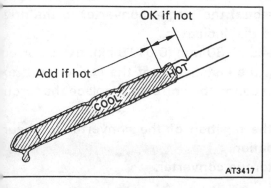

29. CHECK FLUID LEVEL
   (See page AX−54)

TORQUE CONVERTER CLEANING

AX09J−01

If the transaxle is contaminated, the converter and
transaxle cooler should be throughly flashed with
ATF.

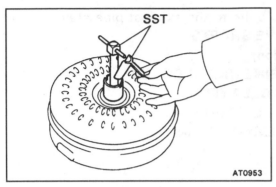

TORQUE CONVERTER AND DRIVE PLATE INSPECTION

AX09K−01

1. **INSPECT ONE−WAY CLUTCH**
(a) Install SST into the inner race of the one−way clutch
 SST 09350−32014(09351−32020)
(b) Install SST so that is fits in the notch of the converte
 hub and outer race of the one−way clutch.
 SST 09350−32014(09351−32020)

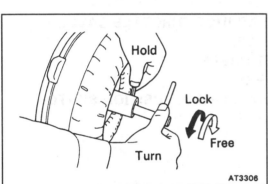

(c) With the torque converter standing on its side, th
 clutch locks when turned counterclockwise, and rot
 ates freely and smoothly clockwise.
 If necessary, clean the converter and retest the clutch
 Replace the converter if the clutch still fails the test

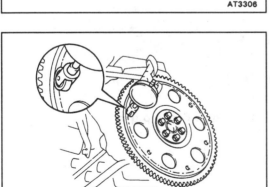

2. **MEASURE DRIVE PLATE RUNOUT AND INSPEC
 RING GEAR**
 Set up a dial indicator and measure the drive plat
 runout.
 If runout exceeds 0.20 mm (0.0079 in.) or if the rin
 gear is damaged replace the drive plate. if installing
 new drive plate, note the orientation of spacers an
 tighten the bolts.
 Torque: 64 N·m (650 kgf·cm, 47 ft·lbf)

3. **MEASURE TORQUE CONVERTER SLEEVE RUNOU**
(a) Temporarily mount the torque converter to the driv
 plate. Set up a dial indicator.
 If runout exceeds 0.30 mm (0.0118 in.), try to correc
 by reorienting the installation of the converter. If e>
 cessive runout cannot be corrected replace the torqu
 converter.
 HINT: Mark the position of the converter to ensur
 correct installation.

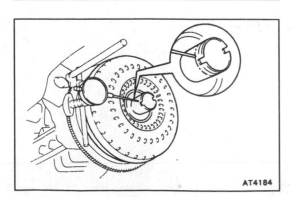

(b) Remove the torque converter.

SHIFT LOCK SYSTEM
COMPONENT PARTS LOCATION

AX01L–02

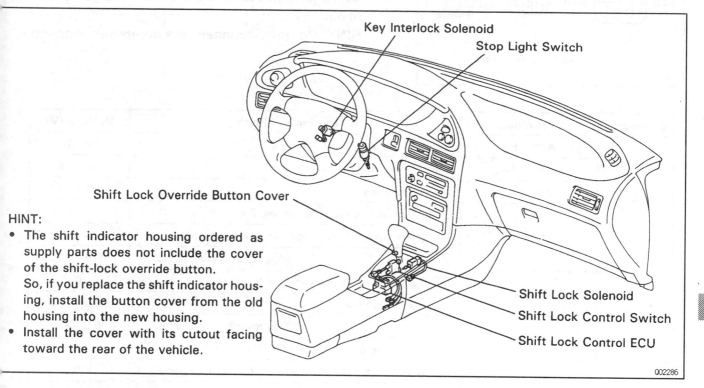

HINT:
- The shift indicator housing ordered as supply parts does not include the cover of the shift-lock override button.
 So, if you replace the shift indicator housing, install the button cover from the old housing into the new housing.
- Install the cover with its cutout facing toward the rear of the vehicle.

Q02286

WIRING DIAGRAM

AX01M–02

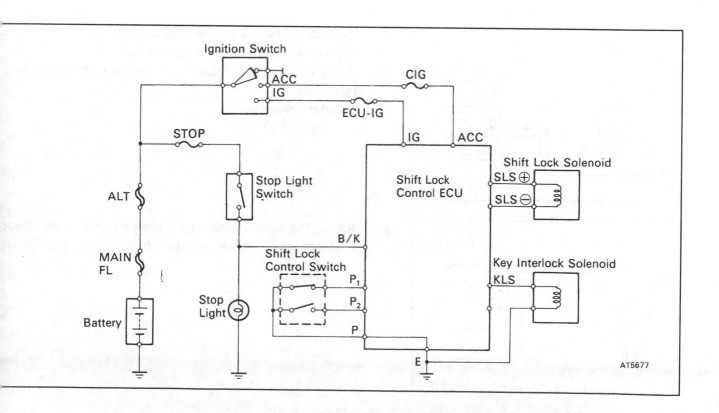

AT5677

AX

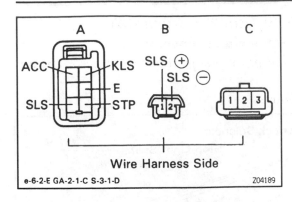

A   B   C

ACC — KLS

SLS ⊕

SLS ⊖

E

SLS — STP

Wire Harness Side

e-6-2-E GA-2-1-C S-3-1-D   Z04189

ELECTRIC CONTROL COMPONENTS INSPECTION

1. INSPECT SHIFT LOCK CONTROL ECM

Using a voltmeter, measure the voltage at each terminal.

HINT: Do not disconnect the computer connector.

Connector	Terminal	Measuring condition	Voltage (V)
A	ACC – E	Ignition switch ACC position	10 – 14
	IG – E	Ignition switch ON position	10 – 14
	B/K – E	Depress brake pedal	10 – 14
	KLS – E	① Ignition switch ACC position and P range	0
		② Ignition switch ACC position and except P range	10 – 14
		③ (Approx-after one second)	6 – 9
B	SLS + – SLS-	① Ignition switch ON position and P range	0
		② Depress brake pedal	8.5 – 13.5
		③ (Approx-after 20 seconds)	5.5 – 9.5
		④ Except P range	0
C	P_1 – P	① Ignition switch ON, P range and depress brake pedal	0
		② Shift except P range under conditions above	9 – 13.5
	P_2 – P	① Ignition switch ACC position and P range	9 – 13.5
		② Shift except P range under condition above	0

V0036

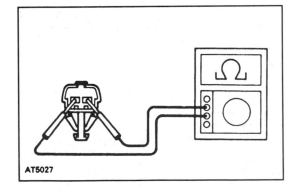

AT5027

2. INSPECT SHAFT LOCK SOLENOID

(a) Disconnect the solenoid connector.

(b) Using an ohmmeter, measure the resistance between terminals.

Standard resistance:

     21 – 27 Ω

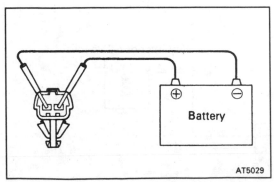

Battery

AT5029

(c) Apply the battery voltage between terminals. Check that operation noise can be heard from the solenoid.

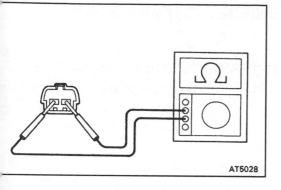

3. INSPECT KEY INTERLOCK SOLENOID

(a) Disconnect the solenoid connector.

(b) Using an ohmmeter, measure the resistance between terminals.
    Standard resistance:
        12.5—16.5 Ω

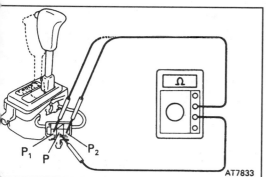

(c) Apply the battery voltage between terminals. Check that an operation noise can be heard from the solenoid.

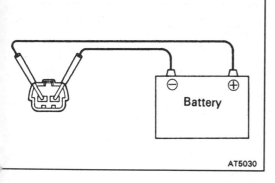

4. INSPECT SHIFT LOCK CONTROL SWITCH

Inspect that there is continuity between each terminal.

Shift Position	Terminal P	P_1	P_2
P range (Release button is not pushed)	O———	———O	
P Range (Release button is pushed)	O———	———O	
	O——————|———————O		O
R, N, D, 2, L range	O——————|———————O		O

V00370

AX

— MEMO —

AX

TROUBLESHOOTING

AX

HOW TO PROCEED WITH TROUBLESHOOTING

AX09M—01

For troubleshooting using a volt/ohm meter, see page AX—40 ～ 42.
For troubleshooting using both volt/ohm meter and ECT checker, see page AX—43 ～ 44.

HOW TO PROCEED WITH TROUBLESHOOTING USING VOLT/OHM METER

AX09N—01

1. **CUSTOMER PROBLEM ANALYSIS**
   Using the customer problem analysis check sheet for reference, ask the customer in as much detail as possible about the problem.

2. **CHECK AND CLEAR THE DIAGNOSTIC TROUBLE CODES (PRECHECK)**
   Before confirming the problem symptom, first check the diagnostic trouble code if there are any trouble codes stored in memory. When there are trouble codes, make a note of them, then clear them and proceed to "3. Problem Symptom Confirmation".

3. **PROBLEM SYMPTOM CONFIRMATION**
   Confirm the problem symptoms.

4. **SYMPTOM SIMULATION**
   If the problem does not reappear, be sure to simulate the problem by mainly checking the circuits indicated by the diagnostic trouble code in step 2., using "Problem Simulation method".

5. **DIAGNOSTIC TROUBLE CODE CHECK**
   Check the diagnostic trouble codes. Check if there is abnormality in the sensors or the wire harness.
   If a trouble code is output, proceed to "6. Diagnostic Trouble Code Chart".
   If the normal code is output, proceed to "7. Matrix Chart of Problem Symptoms".
   Be sure to proceed to "6. Diagnostic Code Chart" after the steps 2. and 3. are completed.
   If troubleshooting is attempted only by following the trouble code stored in the memory is output, errors could be made in the diagnosis.

6. **DIAGNOSTIC TROUBLE CODE CHART**
   If a trouble code is confirmed in the diagnostic trouble code check, proceed to the inspection procedure indicated by the matrix chart for each diagnostic trouble code.

7. **PRELIMINARY CHECK**
   Carry out a preliminary check of the transaxle oil level, throttle cable adjustment, etc.

8. **SHIFT POSITION SIGNAL CHECK**
   Carry out the shift position signal check when the transsxle gears do not up—shift, down—shift or lock—up. This is to check the output condition from the ECM to each solenoid. If the results are NG, then it is likely that the trouble is in the electrical system (particularly in the sors or the ECM).
   Proceed to Part 1 (Electrical System) under "11.Matrix Chart of ProblemSymptoms". If all the circuits specified in Part 1 are OK, check the ECM and replace it.

9. **MECHANICAL SYSTEM TEST**
   (Stall Test, Time Lag Test, Line Pressure Test)
   If the malfunction is found in the stall test, time lag test or line pressure test, check the part indicated in the respective tests.

10. **MANUAL SHIFTING TEST**
    If the results of the manual driving test are NG, it is likely that the trouble is in the mechanical system or hydraulic system. Proceed to Part 2 (Mechanical System) under the Matrix Chart of Problem Symptoms.

11. MATRIX CHART OF PROBLEM SYMPTOMS

If the normal code is confirmed in the diagnostic trouble code check, perform inspection according to the inspection order in the matrix chart of problem symptoms. Perform diagnosis of each circuit or part in the order shown in the Matrix Chart. The Matrix Chart contains 3 chapters, Electronically Controlled Circuits in Chapter 1, On—vehicle Inspection in Chapter 2 and Off—vehicle Inspection in Chapter 3. If all the circuits indicated in Chapter 1 are normal, proceed to Chapter 2. If all the parts indicated in Chapter 2 are normal, proceed to Chapter 3. If all the circuits and parts in Chapter 1 — Chapter 3 are normal and the trouble still occurs, check and replace the ECM.

12. CIRCUIT INSPECTION

Perform diagnosis of each circuit in accordance with the inspection order confirmed in 6. and 11. judge whether the cause of the problem is in the sensor, actuators, wire harness and connectors, or the ECM. In some cases, the Flow Chart instructs that a throttle signal check or brake signalcheck be performed. These are diagnosis functions used to check if signals are being input correctly to the ECM.

13. PART INSPECTION

Check the individual parts of the mechanical system and hydraulic system in the order of the numbers indicated in the Matrix Chart.

14. REPAIRS

After the cause of the problem is located, perform repairs by following the inspection and replacement procedures in this manual or '93 A245E Automatic Transaxle Repair Manual (Pub. No. RM311U).

AX

15. CONFIRMATION TEST

After completing repairs, confirm not only that the malfunction is eliminated, but also conduct a test drive, etc., to make sure the automatic transaxle is operateing correctly.

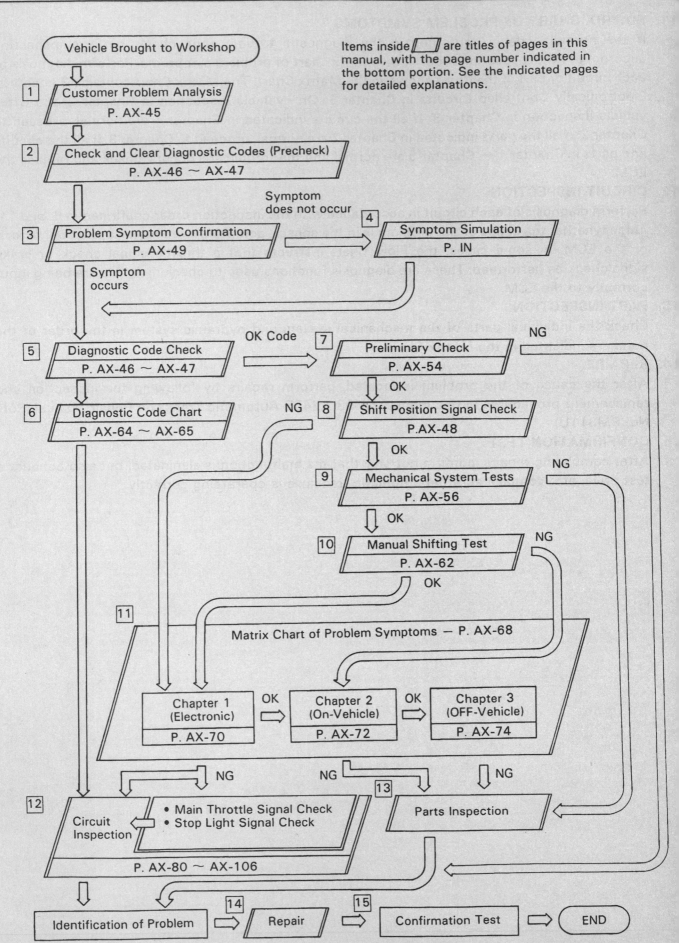

Items inside ▱ are titles of pages in this manual, with the page number indicated in the bottom portion. See the indicated pages for detailed explanations.

Vehicle Brought to Workshop

1 | **Customer Problem Analysis** — P. AX-45

2 | **Check and Clear Diagnostic Codes (Precheck)** — P. AX-46 ~ AX-47

3 | **Problem Symptom Confirmation** — P. AX-49

Symptom does not occur →

4 | **Symptom Simulation** — P. IN

Symptom occurs ↓

5 | **Diagnostic Code Check** — P. AX-46 ~ AX-47

OK Code →

7 | **Preliminary Check** — P. AX-54 — NG

OK ↓

6 | **Diagnostic Code Chart** — P. AX-64 ~ AX-65 — NG

8 | **Shift Position Signal Check** — P. AX-48

OK ↓

9 | **Mechanical System Tests** — P. AX-56 — NG

OK ↓

10 | **Manual Shifting Test** — P. AX-62 — NG

OK →

11 | **Matrix Chart of Problem Symptoms** — P. AX-68

Chapter 1 (Electronic) — P. AX-70 | OK → | **Chapter 2 (On-Vehicle)** — P. AX-72 | OK → | **Chapter 3 (OFF-Vehicle)** — P. AX-74

NG | NG | NG

12 | **Circuit Inspection**
• Main Throttle Signal Check
• Stop Light Signal Check
P. AX-80 ~ AX-106

13 | **Parts Inspection**

Identification of Problem | 14 → **Repair** | 15 → **Confirmation Test** → **END**

V014

HOW TO PROCEED WITH TROUBLESHOOTING USING VOLT/OHM METER AND ECT CHECKER

AX09P—01

For the explanation of steps 1. ～ 7. and 9. ～15., see the explanation of steps with the same title on page AX—40.

8. CIRCUIT INSPECTION BY CHECKER

Connect ECT checker to the vehicle and check all the circuits which can be inspected using the checker.

If the malfunctioning circuit can be defected using the checker, proceed to 11. Matrix chart of Problem Symptoms — Part 2 (on Vehicle) or 12. Circuit Inspection by Volt/ ohm meter and perform troubleshooting.

For instructions on how to connect the checker to the vehicle and how to use the checker, please refer to the Instruction Manual for ECT checker.

AX

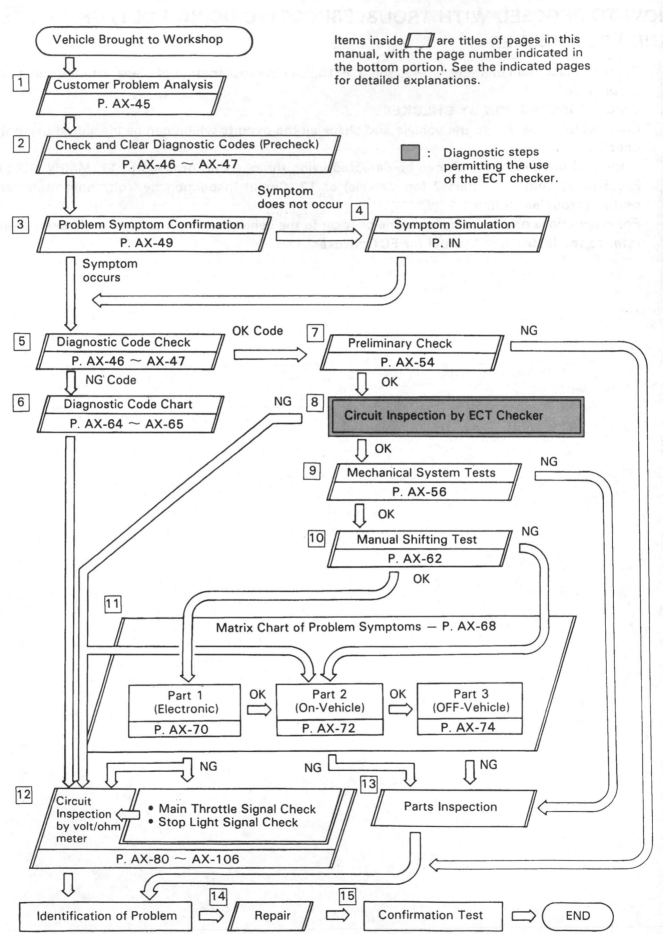

Vehicle Brought to Workshop

Items inside ▱ are titles of pages in this manual, with the page number indicated in the bottom portion. See the indicated pages for detailed explanations.

1. Customer Problem Analysis — P. AX-45

2. Check and Clear Diagnostic Codes (Precheck) — P. AX-46 ~ AX-47

▨ : Diagnostic steps permitting the use of the ECT checker.

3. Problem Symptom Confirmation — P. AX-49

Symptom does not occur

4. Symptom Simulation — P. IN

Symptom occurs

5. Diagnostic Code Check — P. AX-46 ~ AX-47

OK Code

7. Preliminary Check — P. AX-54

NG

NG Code

OK

6. Diagnostic Code Chart — P. AX-64 ~ AX-65

NG

8. Circuit Inspection by ECT Checker

OK

9. Mechanical System Tests — P. AX-56

NG

OK

10. Manual Shifting Test — P. AX-62

NG

OK

11. Matrix Chart of Problem Symptoms — P. AX-68

Part 1 (Electronic) — P. AX-70

OK

Part 2 (On-Vehicle) — P. AX-72

OK

Part 3 (OFF-Vehicle) — P. AX-74

NG

NG

NG

12. Circuit Inspection by volt/ohm meter
• Main Throttle Signal Check
• Stop Light Signal Check
P. AX-80 ~ AX-106

13. Parts Inspection

Identification of Problem

14. Repair

15. Confirmation Test

END

AX

CUSTOMER PROBLEM ANALYSIS

AX09Q-01

	ECT Check Sheet	Inspector's Name :

		Registration No.	
Customer's Name		Registration Year	/ /
		Frame No.	
Date Vehicle Brought In	/ /	Odometer Reading	km Mile

Condition of Problem Occurrence	Date of Problem Occurrence	/ /
	How Often does Problem Occur?	□ Continuous □ Intermittent (times a day)

Symptoms	□ Vehicle does not move. (□ Any range □ Particular range)
	□ No up-shift (□ 1st → 2nd □ 2nd → 3rd □ 3rd → O/D)
	□ No down-shift (□ O/D → 3rd □ 3rd → 2nd □ 2nd → 1st)
	□ Lockup malfunction
	□ Shift point too high or too low.
	□ Harsh engagement (□ N → D □ Lockup □ Any drive range)
	□ Slip or shudder
	□ No Kickdown
	□ Others ( )

Check Item	CHECK engine warning light	□ Normal □ Remains ON

Diagnostic Code Check (O/D OFF Indicator Light)	1st Time	□ Normal Code □ Malfunction Code (Code)
	2nd Time	□ Normal Code □ Malfunction Code (Code)

AX

V01427

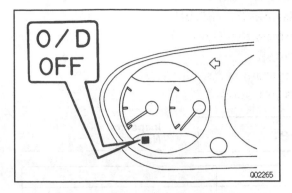

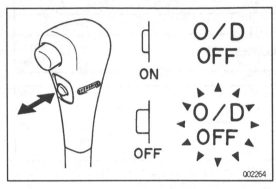

DIAGNOSIS SYSTEM

The automatic transaxle has built—in self—diagnosti functions. If the malfunction occurs in the system, th ECM stores the trouble code in memory and the O/ OFF (Overdrive OFF) indicator light blinks to infor the driver. The diagnostic trouble code stored i memory can be read out by the following procedure.

O/D OFF INDICATOR LIGHT INSPECTION

1. Turn the ignition switch to ON.
2. Check if the O/D OFF indicator light lights up whe the O/D main switch is pushed out to OFF and goe off when the O/D main switch is pushed in to ON.

   HINT:
   • If the O/D OFF indicator light does not light up stay on all the time, carry out the check for "O/ OFF Indicator Light Circuit" on page AX—98.
   • If the O/D OFF indicator light blinks, a trouble coc is stored in the ECM memory.

DIAGNOSTIC TROUBLE CODE CHECK

1. Turn the ignition switch ON, but do not start th engine.
2. Push in the O/D main switch to ON.
   HINT: Warning and diagnostic trouble codes can b read only when the O/D main switch is ON. If it OFF, the O/D OFF indicator light up will light conti uously and will not blink.

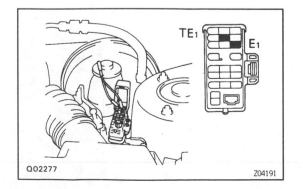

3. Using SST, connect terminals TE1 and E1 of th DLC1.
   SST 09843—18020

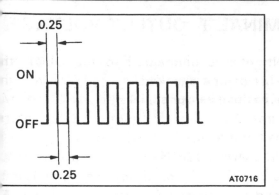

AT0716

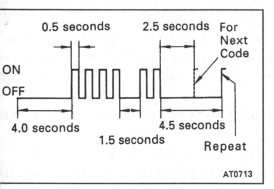

AT0713

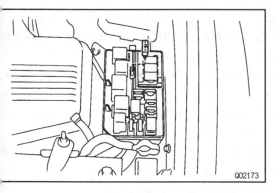

002173

4. **Read the diagnostic trouble code indicated by the number of times the O/D OFF indicator light blinks (See next page).**
HINT: If the system is operating normally, the light will blink 2 times per second.

The trouble code is indicated as shown in the illustration at left (Diagnostic trouble code "42" is shown as an example).
HINT: When 2 or more trouble codes are stored in memory, the lower-numbered code is displayed first. If no diagnostic trouble code is output, or if a diagnostic trouble code is output even though no diagnostic trouble code output operation is performed, check the TE1 terminal circuit on page AX–104.

AX09T–01

CANCELLING DIAGNOSTIC TROUBLE CODE

After repair of the trouble area, the diagnostic trouble code retained in the ECM memory must be cancelled out by removing the EFI fuse for 10 seconds or more, with the ignition switch off.
Check that the normal code is output after connecting the fuse.

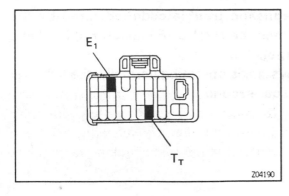

Z04190

CHECK TERMINAL T$_T$ OUTPUT VOLTAGE

When a voltmeter is connected to the DLC1, the following items can be checked.
1. **Throttle position sensor signal**
2. **Brake signal**
3. **Shift position signal**

1. **VOLTMETER CONNECTION**
Connect the positive (+) probe of the voltmeter to terminal T$_T$ and the negative (−) probe to terminal E$_1$ of the DLC1.
HINT: If a voltmeter with small internal resistance is used, the correct voltage will not be indicated, so use a voltmeter with an internal resistance of at least 10 Ω.

2. **TURN IGNITION SWITCH TO ON (DO NOT START THE ENGINE)**

3. **CHECK THROTTLE POSITION SENSOR SIGNAL**
Check if the voltage changes from approximately 0 to approximately 8 V when the accelerator pedal gradually depressed from the fully closed position.

4. **CHECK BRAKE SIGNAL (LOCK−UP CUT SIGNAL)**

(a) Open the throttle valve fully to apply approximately V to terminal T$_T$.

(b) In this condition, check terminal T$_T$ voltage when the brake pedal is depressed and released.
T$_T$ terminal voltage:
　　0 V (When brake pedal is depressed)
　　8 V (When brake pedal is released)

5. **START THE ENGINE**

6. **CHECK SHIFT POSITION SIGNAL**
(VEHICLE SPEED ABOVE 60 KM/H OR 37 MPH)
Check up−shifting together with terminal T$_T$ voltage

HINT: Check for light shocks from up−shifting and for changes in the tachometer.

Gear Position	Terminal T$_T$ output voltage
1st Gera	Below 0.4 V
2nd Gear	1.7~2.4 V
2nd Lock−up	2.7~3.4 V
3rd Gear	3.7~4.4 V
3rd Lock−up	4.7~5.7 V
O/D	5.7~6.7 V
O/D Lock−up	6.7~7.7 V

If Terminal T$_T$ Output voltage check cannot be performed, perform the check of T$_T$ terminal circuit on page AX−106.

PROBLEM SYMPTOM CONFIRMATION

AX09U−01

Taking into consideration the results of the customer problem analysis, try to reproduce the symptoms of the trouble. If the problem is that the transaxle does not up−shift, does not down−shift, or the shift point is too high or too low, conduct the following road test the automatic shift schedule and simulate the problem symptoms.

ROAD TEST

AX09V−02

NOTICE: Perform the test at normal ATF operating temperature (50 − 80 °C or 122 − 176 °F).

1. **D POSITION TEST**

   Shift into the D position and keep the accelerator pedal constant at the full throttle valve opening position, and check the following points:

   (a) Check up−shift operation

   Check that 1−2, 2−3 and 3−O/D up−shift takes place, at the shift point shown in the automatic shift schedule (See page AX−53)

   HINT:

   (1) O/D Gear Up−shift Prohibition Control
      - Coolant temp. is 55°C (131°F) or less
      - If there is a 10 km/h (6 mph) difference between the set cruise control speed and vehicle speed.
      - O/D main switch is pushed ON
        (During the O/D OFF indicator light lights up.)

   (2) O/D Gear Lock−up Prohibition Control
      - Brake pedal is depressed.
      - Coolant temp. is 55 °C (131 °F) or less.

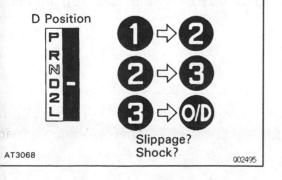

(b) Check for shift shock and slip.

   Check for shock and slip at the 1−2, 2−3 and 3−O/D up−shifts.

AX

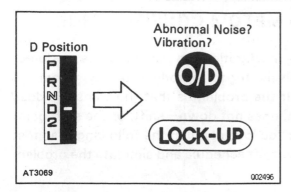

(c) Check for abnormal noise and vibration.
Run at the D position lock−up or O/D gear and chec
for abnormal noise and vibration.
HINT: The check for the cause of abnormal noise an
vibration must be perform very thoroughly as it coul
also be due to loss of balance in the, differentia
torque converter, etc.

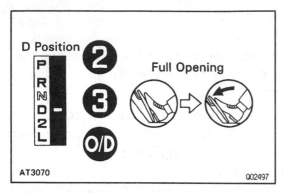

(d) Check kick−down operation
While running in the D position, 2nd, 3rd and O/
gears, check to see that the possible kick−dow
vehicle speed limits for 2 → 1, 3 → 2 and O/D →
kick−downs conform to those indicated on the au
tomatic shift schedule. (See page AX−53)

(e) Check abnormal shock and slip at kick−down.

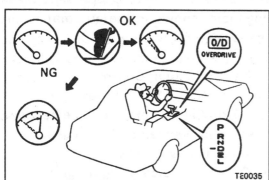

(f) Check the lock−up mechanism.
  (1) Drive in D position, O/D gear, at a steady spee
(lock−up ON) of about 70 km/h (43 mph).

  (2) Lightly depress the accelerator pedal and chec
that the RPM does not change abruptly.
If there is a big jump in RPM, there is no lock−up.

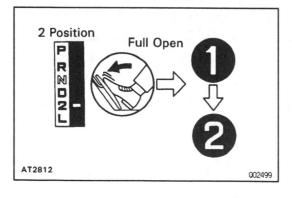

2. 2 POSITION TEST
Shift into the 2 position and, while driving with th
accelerator pedal held constantly at the full throttl
valve opening position and check on the followin
points:

(a) Check up−shift operation
Check to see that the 1 → 2 up−shift takes place an
that the shift point conforms to the automatic shif
schedule. (See page AX−53)
HINT:
There is no O/D up−shift and lock−up in the
position.

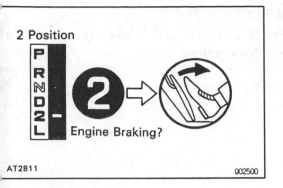

AT2811   002500

(b) Check engine braking
While running in the 2 position and 2nd gear, release the accelerator pedal and check the engine braking effect.

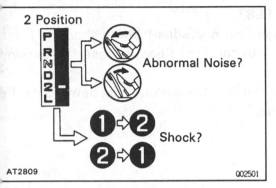

AT2809   002501

(c) Check for abnormal noise at acceleration and deceleration, and for shock at up—shift and down—shift.

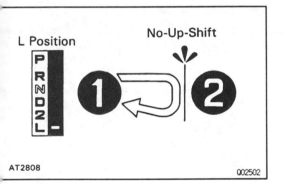

AT2808   002502

3. L POSITION TEST
Shift into the L position and while driving with the accelerator pedal held constantly at the full throttle valve opening position, and check the following points:

(a) Check no up—shift
While running in the L position, check that there is no up—shift to 2nd gear.

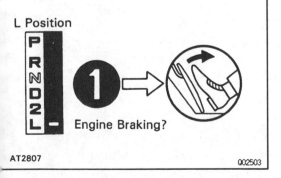

AT2807   002503

(b) Check engine braking
While running in the L position, release the accelerator pedal and check the engine braking effect.

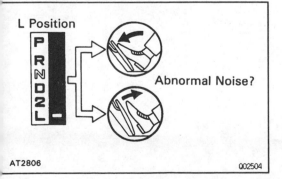

AT2806   002504

(c) Check for abnormal noise during acceleration and deceleration.

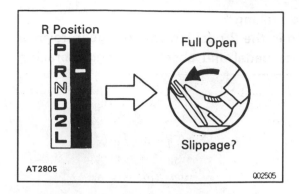

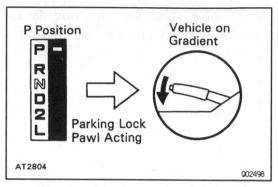

4. R POSITION TEST

Shift into the R position and while starting at ful throttle, check for slipping.

5. P POSITION TEST

Stop the vehicle on a gradient (more than 5 °) and after shifting into the P position, release the parking brake.

Then check to see that the parking lock pawl holds the vehicle in place.

AX

AUTOMATIC SHIFT SCHEDULE

AX09W-01

SHIFT POINT

Shift position	Shifting point			Vehicle speed km/h (mph)
D position	Throttle valve fully opened		1→2	56−62 (35−39)
			2→3	104−111 (65−69)
			3→O/D	139−151 (86−94)
			O/D→3	133−145 (83−90)
			3→2	98−106 (61−66)
			2→1	43−49 (27−30)
	Throttle valve fully closed		3→O/D	35−41 (22−25)
			O/D→3	17−22 (11−14)
2 position	Throttle valve fully opened		3→2	102−109 (63−68)
			2→1	43−49 (27−30)
L position	Throttle valve fully opened		2→1	47−53 (29−33)

LOCK−UP POINT

D position km/h (mph) Throttle valve opening 5%	Lock−up ON	Lock−up OFF
3rd Gear	65−72 (40−45)	58−64 (36−40)
O/D Gear	65−72 (40−45)	58−64 (36−40)

AX

HINT:

(1) There is no lock−up in the 2 and L positions.

(2) In the following cases, the lock−up will be released regardless of the lock−up pattern.

- **When the throttle valve is completely closed.**
- **When the brake light switch is ON.**

(3) Shift−up to O/D will not occur when the engine coolant temp. is below 55 °C (131 °F).

(4) When the vehicle speed drops to 10 km/h (6 mph) or more below the cruise control set vehicle speed, shift down from O/D to 3rd occurs.

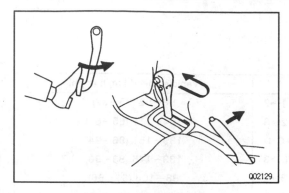

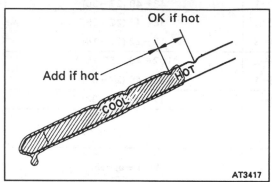

AX

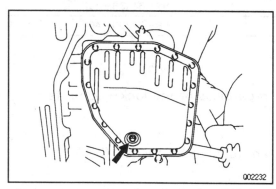

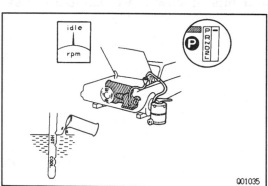

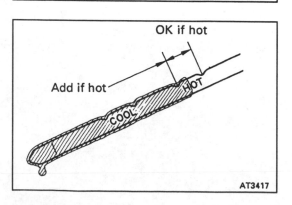

PRELIMINARY CHECK

AX09X−02

1. **CHECK FLUID LEVEL**
   HINT:
   - Drive the vehicle so that the engine and transaxle are at normal operating temperature.
     (Fluid temperature: 70 − 80 °C or 158 − 176 °F)
   - Only use the COOL position on the dipstick as a rough reference when the fluid is replaced or the engine does not run.

   (a) Park the vehicle on a level surface and set the parking brake.
   (b) With the engine idling and the brake pedal depressed, shift the shift lever into all positions from P to L position and return to P position.
   (c) Pull out the oil livel gauge and wipe it clean.
   (d) Push it back fully into the tube.
   (e) Pull it out and check that the fluid level is in the HOT position.
   If the level is at the low side, add fluid.
   Fluid type:
   DEXRON ® II or Equivalent
   NOTICE: Do not overfill.

2. **CHECK FLUID CONDITION**
   If the fluid smells burnt or is black, replace it.

3. **REPLACE TRANSAXLE FLUID**
   (a) Remove the drain plug and drain the fluid.
   (b) Reinstall the drain plug securely.
   (c) With the engine OFF, add new fluid through the oil filler tube.
   Fluid type:DEXRON ® II or Equivalent
   Capacity:
   Total: 7.6 liters (8.0 US qts, 6.7 Imp. qts)
   Drain and refill:3.3 liters (3.5 US qts, 2.9 Imp. qts)

   (d) Start the engine and shift the shift lever into all positions from P to L position and then shift into P position.
   (e) With the engine idling, check the fluid level. Add fluid up to the COOL level on the dipstick.
   (f) Check the fluid level at the normal operating temperature (70 − 80 °C or 158 − 176 °F) and add as necessary.
   NOTICE: Do not overfill.

4. **CHECK FLUID LEAKS**
   Check for leaks in the transaxle.
   If there are leaks, it is necessary to repair or replace O−rings, seal packings, oil seals, plugs or other parts.

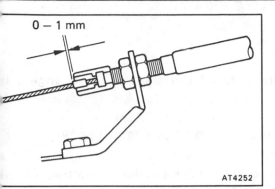

0 – 1 mm

AT4252

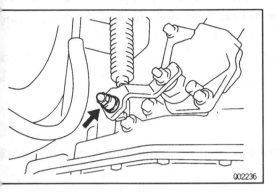

002236

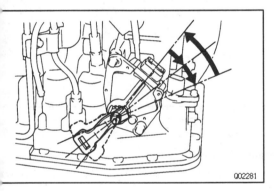

002281

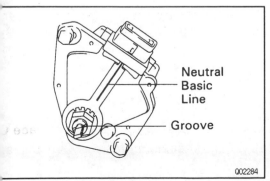

Neutral
Basic
Line

Groove

002284

5. INSPECT AND ADJUST THROTTLE CABLE

(a) Check that the throttle valve is fully closed.

(b) Check that the inner cable is not slack.

(c) Measure the distance between the outer cable end and stopper on the cable.
Standard distance:
    0 – 1 mm (0 – 0.04 in.)
If the distance is not standard, adjust the cable by the adjusting nuts.

6. INSPECT AND ADJUST SHIFT LEVER POSITION

When shifting the shift lever from the N position to other positions, check that the lever can be shifted smoothly and accurately to each position and that the position indicator correctly indicates the position.

If the indicator is not aligned with the correct posotion, carry out the following adjustment procedures:

(a) Loosen the nut on the control shaft lever.

(b) Push the control shaft lever fully downward.

(c) Return the control shaft lever two notches to N position.

(d) Set the shift lever to N position.

(e) While holding the shift lever lightly toward the R position side, tighten the shift lever nut.

(f) Start the engine and make sure that thevehicle moves forward when shifting the lever from the N to D position and reverses when shifting it to the R position.

7. INSPECT AND ADJUST PARK/NEUTRAL POSITION SWITCH

Check that the engine can be started with the shift lever only in the N or P position, but not in other positions.

If not as started above, carry out the following adjustment procedure:

(a) Loosen the park/neutral position switch bolt and set the shift lever to the N position.

(b) Align the groove and neutral basic line.

(c) Hold in position and tighten the bolt.
Torque: 12 N·m (125 kgf·cm, 9 ft·lbf)
For continuity inspection of the park/neutral position switch, see page AX–94.

8. INSPECT IDLE SPEED
Idle speed:
    650 – 750 RPM
(In N position and air conditioner OFF)

AX

MECHANICAL SYSTEM TESTS

AX09Y–

STALL TEST

The object of this test is to check the overall performance of the transaxle and engine b measuring the stall speeds in the D and R positions.

NOTICE:

- **Perform the test at normal operating fluid temperature (50 — 80 °C or 122 — 176 °F).**
- **Do not continuously run this test longer than 5 seconds.**
- **To ensure safety, conduct this test in a wide, clear, level area which provides good traction.**
- **The stall test should always be carried out in pairs. One technician should observe the condition of wheels or wheel stoppers outside the vehicle while the other is performing the test.**

MEASURE STALL SPEED

(a) Chock the four wheels.

(b) Connect a tachometer to the engine.

(c) Fully apply the parking brake.

(d) Keep your left foot pressed firmly on the brake pedal.

(e) Start the engine.

(f) Shift into the D position. Press all the way down on the accelerator pedal with your right foo Quickly read the stall speed at this time.

Stall speed:

2,450 ± 150 RPM

(g) Perform the same test in R position.

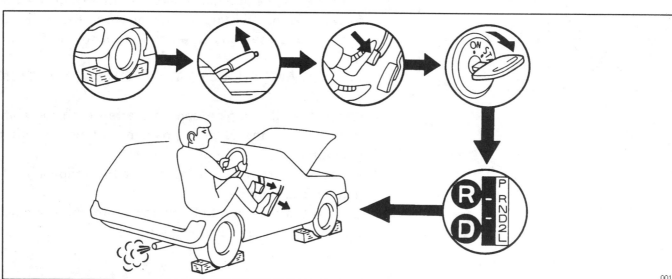

00103

EVALUATION

Problem	Possible cause
(a) Stall speed low in D and R positions.	• Engine output may be insufficient. • Stator one—way clutch is operating properly HINT: If more than 600 RPM below the specified value, the 〈rtn〉 torque converter could be faulty.
(b) Stall speed high in D position.	• Line pressure too low • Forward clutch slopping • No.2 one—way clutch not opetating properly • U/D one—way clutch not operating properly
(c) Stall speed high in R position.	• Line pressure too low • Direct clutch slipping • First and reverse brake slipping • U/D brake slipping
(d) Stall speed high in D and R position.	• Line pressure too low • Improper fluid level • U/D one—way clutch not operating properly

TIME LAG TEST

When the shift lever is shifted while the engine is idling, there will be a certain time lapse or lag before the shock can be felt. This is used for checking the condition of the U/D direct clutch forwardclutch, direct clut, and first and reverse brake.

NOTICE:

- Perform the test at normal operating fluid temperature (50 − 80 °C or 122 − 176 °F).
- Be sure to allow a one minute interval between tests.
- Make three measurements and take the average value.

MEASURE TIME LAG

(a) Fully apply the parking brake

(b) Start the engine and check idle speed.

Idle speed:

650 RPM (In N position and air conditioner OFF)

(c) Shift the shift lever from N to D position. Using a stop watch, measure the time it takes from shifting the lever until the shock is felt.

In same manner, measure the time lag for N → R.

Time lag:

N → D Less than 1.2 seconds

N → R Less than 1.5 seconds

AX

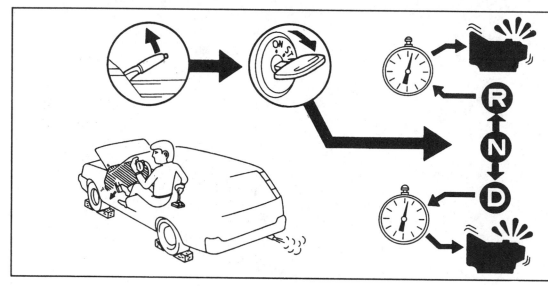

001036

EVALUATION

If N → D or N → R time lag are longer than specified:

Problem	Possible cause
N→D time lag is longer	• Line pressure too low • Forward clutch worn • U/D one−way clutch not operating properly
N→R time lag is longer	• Line pressure too low • Direct clutch worn • First and reverse brake worn • U/D brake worn

AX

MEASURE LINE PRESSURE

NOTICE:
- Perform the test at normal operating fluid temperature (50 – 80 °C or 122 – 176 °F).
- The line pressure test should always be carried out in pairs. One technician should observe the conditions of wheels or wheel stoppers outside the vehicle while the other is performing the test.
- Be careful to prevent the oil pressure gauge hose from interfering with the exhaust pipe.

(a) Warm up the transaxle fluid.

(b) Remove the test plug on the transaxle case left side an d connect the oil pressure gauge (SST).

SST 09992 – 00094 (Oil pressure gauge)

HINT: Connecting the oil pressure gauge will be made easier by moving LH side heat insulator aside.

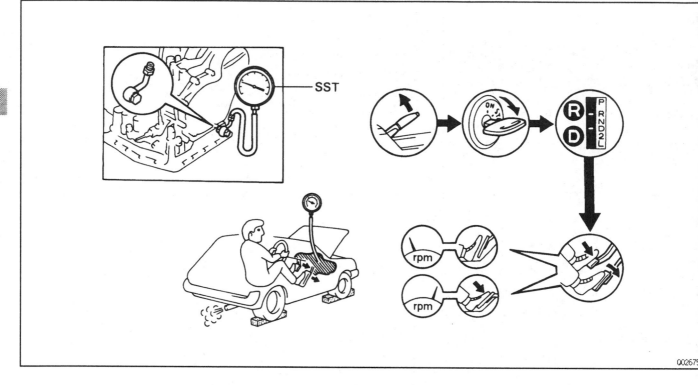

(c) Fully apply the parking brake and chock the four wheels.

(d) Start the engine and check idling RPM.

(e) Keep your left foot pressed firmly on the brake pedal and shift into D position.

(f) Measure the line pressure when the engine is idling.

(g) Press the accelerator pedal all the way down. Quickly read the highest line pressure when engine speed reaches stall speed.

(h) In the same manner, perform the test in R position.

SPECIFIED LINE PRESSURE

Line pressure kPa (kgf/cm², psi)	D position	R position
Idling	373—441 (3.8—4.5, 54—64)	598—716 (6.1—7.3, 87—104)
Stall	980—1,138 (10.0—11.6, 142—165)	1,393—1,716 (14.2—17.5, 201—249)

If the measured pressures are not up to specified values, recheck the throttle cable adjustment and perform a retest.

EVALUATION

Problem	Possible cause
If the measured values at all positions are higher.	• Throttle cable out of adjustment • Throttle valve defective • Regulator valve defective
If the measured values at all positions are lower.	• Throttle cable out of adjustment • Throttle valve defective • Regulator valve defective • Oil pump defective • U/D direct clutch defective
If pressrue is low in the D position only.	• D position circuit fluid leakage • Forard clutch defective
If pressure is low in the R position only.	• R position circuit fluid keakage • Direct clutch defedtive • First and reverse brake defective

AX

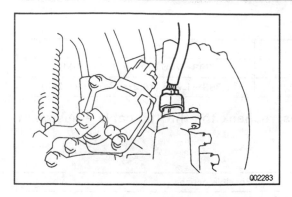

002283

AX09Z-01

MANUAL SHIFTING TEST

HINT: With this test, it can be determined whether the trouble is within the electrical circuit or is a mechanical problem in the transaxle.

1. **DISCONNECT SOLENOID WIRE**
2. **INSPECT MANUAL DRIVING OPERATION**

   Check that the shift and gear positions correspond with the table below.

   HINT: If the L, 2 and D position gear positions are difficult to distinguish, perform the following road test.

   - While driving, shift through the L, 2 and D positions. Check that the gear change corresponds to the shift position.

   If any abnormality is found in the above test, the problem is in the transaxle itself.

3. **CONNECT SOLENOID WIRE**
4. **CANCEL OUT DIAGNOSTIC TROUBLE CODE**

   (See page AX—47)

— **MEMO** —

DIAGNOSTIC TROUBLE CODE CHART

AX0CC–01

If a trouble code is displayed during the diagnostic trouble code check, check the circuit listed for that code in the table below and proceed to the page given.

Code No.	Blinking Pattern	Circuit	Diag. Code Detection Condition
42		Speed sensor	If the SPD signal is not input for two second or longer after condition A or B (described below occurs, DTC 42 is recorded and the O/D OFF indicator light lights up simultaneously. **CONDITION A** • 30 seconds or more elapses after the PNP switch goes OFF. • The throttle opening ratio and engine rpm are higher than the certain valve. **CONDITION B** • 1 second or more elapses after the PNP switch goes OFF. • AN SP signal of 14 km/h (8.7 mph) or more is input. • The stop light switch is OFF (brake pedal is released).
62		No. 1 solenoid valve	(a) Solenoid resistance of 8 Ω or less is detected (*) 8 times or more when No. 1 solenoid is energized. (b) Solenoid resistance of 100 kΩ or more is detected (*) 8 times or more when No. 1 solenoid is not energized. (*) If the above failuers are detected less than 8 times, the ECM memorizes the malfunction code but the O/D OFF indicator light does not blink.
63		No. 2 solenoid valve	(a) Solenoid resistance of 8 Ω or less is detected (*) 8 times or more when No. 2 solenoid is energized. (b) Solenoid resistance of 100 kΩ or more is detected (*) 8 times or more when No. 2 solenoid is not energized. (*) If the above failuers are detected less than 8 times, the ECM memorizes the malfunction code but the O/D OFF indicator light does not blink.
64		SL solenoid valve	(a) Solenoid resistance is 8 Ω or lower (short circuit) when solenoid energized. (b) Solenoid resistance is 100 kΩ or higher (open circuit) when solenoid is not energized. (*) ECM memorizes diag. code 64 if above (a) or (b) condition is detected once or more, but ECM does not start O/D OFF indicator light blinking.

V01430

AX

Trouble Area	O/D OFF Light *1 Blinks	Memory *2	See Page
• Harness or connector between speed sensor and ECM • Speed sensor • Combination meter • ECM	○	○	AX-80
• Harness or connector between No. 1 solenoid and ECM • No. 1 solenoid • ECM	○	○	AX-84
• Harness or connector between No. 2 solenoid and ECM • No. 2 solenoid • ECM	○	○	AX-84
• Harness or connector between SL solenoid valve and ECM • SL solenoid valve • ECM	×	○	AX-88

V01431

HINT:

- If the malfunction returns to normal while a malfunction warning is being output, the O/D OFF indicator light stops blinking and goes off.
  However, the trouble code is retained in memory until it is cleared from memory.

- If the diagnosis system output a trouble code even though the O/D OFF indicator was not blinking, there is intermittent trouble. Check all the connections in the circuits corresponding to that code.

- Codes 42, 62, 63 and 64 are limited to short or open circuits in the electrical system comprised of the solenoids, wire harnesses, and connectors. The ECM is unable to detect mechanical trouble (sticking, for example) in the solenoid valves.

STANDARD VALUE OF ECM TERMINAL

AX0CD–01

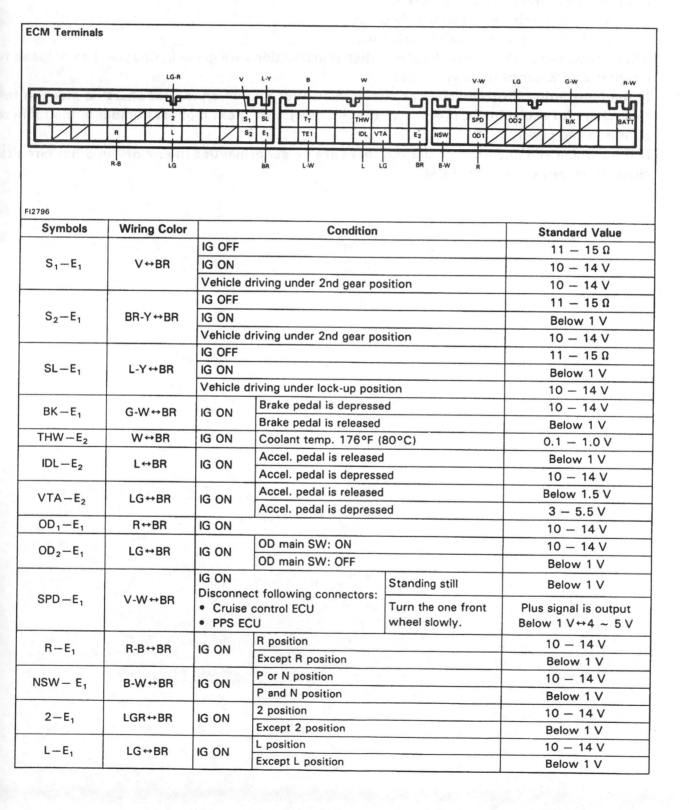

ECM Terminals

FI2796

Symbols	Wiring Color	Condition		Standard Value
S_1-E_1	V↔BR	IG OFF		11 — 15 Ω
		IG ON		10 — 14 V
		Vehicle driving under 2nd gear position		10 — 14 V
S_2-E_1	BR-Y↔BR	IG OFF		11 — 15 Ω
		IG ON		Below 1 V
		Vehicle driving under 2nd gear position		10 — 14 V
$SL-E_1$	L-Y↔BR	IG OFF		11 — 15 Ω
		IG ON		Below 1 V
		Vehicle driving under lock-up position		10 — 14 V
$BK-E_1$	G-W↔BR	IG ON	Brake pedal is depressed	10 — 14 V
			Brake pedal is released	Below 1 V
$THW-E_2$	W↔BR	IG ON	Coolant temp. 176°F (80°C)	0.1 — 1.0 V
$IDL-E_2$	L↔BR	IG ON	Accel. pedal is released	Below 1 V
			Accel. pedal is depressed	10 — 14 V
$VTA-E_2$	LG↔BR	IG ON	Accel. pedal is released	Below 1.5 V
			Accel. pedal is depressed	3 — 5.5 V
OD_1-E_1	R↔BR	IG ON		10 — 14 V
OD_2-E_1	LG↔BR	IG ON	OD main SW: ON	10 — 14 V
			OD main SW: OFF	Below 1 V
$SPD-E_1$	V-W↔BR	IG ON Disconnect following connectors: • Cruise control ECU • PPS ECU	Standing still	Below 1 V
			Turn the one front wheel slowly.	Plus signal is output Below 1 V↔4 ~ 5 V
$R-E_1$	R-B↔BR	IG ON	R position	10 — 14 V
			Except R position	Below 1 V
$NSW-E_1$	B-W↔BR	IG ON	P or N position	10 — 14 V
			P and N position	Below 1 V
$2-E_1$	LGR↔BR	IG ON	2 position	10 — 14 V
			Except 2 position	Below 1 V
$L-E_1$	LG↔BR	IG ON	L position	10 — 14 V
			Except L position	Below 1 V

V01533

AX0CE–01

MATRIX CHART OF PROBLEM SYMPTOMS

If a normal code is displayed during the diagnostic trouble code check but the trouble still occurs, check the circuits for each symptom in the order given in the charts on the following pages and proceed to the page given for troubleshooting.

The Matrix Chart is divided into 3 chapters.

Chapter 1: Electronic Circuit Matrix Chart

Chapter 2: On–vehicle Repair Matrix Chart

Chapter 3: Off–vehicle Repair Matrix Chart

When troubleshooting, check Chapter 1 first. If instructions are given in Chapter 1 to proceed to Chapter 2 or 3, proceed as instructed.

1. **If the instruction "Proceed to next circuit inspection shown on matrix chart" is given in the flow chart for each circuit, proceed to the circuit with the next highest number in the table to continue the check.**

2. **If the trouble still occurs even though there are no abnormalities in any of the other circuits, then check or replace the ECM.**

– MEMO –

Chapter 1. Electronic Circuit

See Page		AX-80	AX-84	AX-88	AX-92	AX-94	AX-96	AX-98
Suspect Area Symptom		Speed sensor circuit	No. 1, No. 2 Solenoid circuit	SL Solenoid circuit	Throttle position sensor circuit	Park/Neutral Position Switch	Stop light switch circuit	O/D switch O/D OFF indicator light circuit
Vehicle does not move in any forward range and reverse range								
Vehicle does not move in particular range or ranges								
No up-shift	1st → 2nd	3	1		2	5		
	2nd → 3rd	3	1		2	5		
	3rd → O/D	3	2		4	5		1
No down-shift	O/D → 3rd	3	1		2			
	3rd → 2nd	3	1		2			
	2nd → 1st	3	1		2			
No lock-up		3		1	2	5	4	
No lock-up off		3		1	2		4	
Shift point too high or too low		3			1			
Up-shifts to 2nd while in L range Up-shifts to 3rd while in L range						1		
Up-shifts to O/D from 3rd while O/D switch is OFF								1
Up-shifts to O/D from 3rd while engine is cold						3		
Harsh engagement	N → D			1	2	3		
	Lock-up	3		1	2			
	Any driving range	3		1	2			
Slip or Shudder	Forward and reverse							
	Particular range							
No engine braking								
Poor acceleration		2	3	4	1			
No kick-down		2	3		1			
No pattern select								
Large shift shock or Engine stalls when starting off or stopping.				1			2	

O/D cancel signal circuit (AX-102)	ECT sensor circuit (TR-506)	ECM (IN-27)	ON-Vehicle repair matrix chart (AX-72)	OFF-Vehicle repair matrix chart (AX-74)
			1	2
			1	2
		7	4	6
		7	4	6
6	7	10	8	9
		5	4	—
		5	4	—
		6	4	5
	6	9	7	8
		7	5	6
		4	—	—
		2	—	—
		2	—	—
	1	4	2	3
		6	4	5
		6	4	5
		6	4	5
			1	2
			1	2
			1	2
		6	—	5
		5	4	—
		1	—	—
		4	—	3

AX

Chapter 2. On−Vehicle Repair
(★ : A245E AUTOMATIC TRANSAXLE Repair Manual Pub No. RM311U)

See Page → Trouble		Oil strainer (AX-14)	Pressure relief valve ★	1-2 shift valve ★	2-3 shift valve ★	3-4 shift valve ★	Manual valve ★	Throttle valve ★	Primary regulator valve ★	Lock-up relay valve ★	Low coast modulator valve ★	2nd coast modulator valve ★	Accumulator control valve ★	B₂ Accumulator ★	B₄ Accumulator ★	C₁ Accumulator ★
Does not move in any forward range																
Does not move in reverse range																
Does not move in any range							2	3	1							
No up-shift	1st→2nd			1												
	2nd→3rd				1											
	3rd→O/D					1										
No down-shift	O/D→3rd					1										
	3rd→2nd				1											
	2nd→1st			1												
Shift point too high or too low																
Up-shift 3rd→O/D with O/D switch OFF																
Harsh engagement	"N"→"R"															
	"N"→"D"															1
	"N"→"L"										2					1
	1st→2nd ("D" position)												1	2		
	1st→2nd ("2" position)											3	2	1		
	1st→2nd→3rd→O/D							1	2							
	2nd→3rd												2			
	3rd→O/D													1		
	O/D→3rd														1	
	3rd→2nd															
Slip	Forward & Reverse								1							
	"R" position															
	1st															
	2nd															
	3rd															
	O/D															
No engine braking	1st ("L" position)										1					
	2nd ("2" position)											1				
No kick-down				1	1	1										
Poor acceleration									1							
No lock-up										2						

V0143 4

C$_2$ Accumulator (★)	C$_3$ Accumulator (★)	No. 1 Solenoid (★)	No. 2 Solenoid (★)	Torque converter clutch (★)	ECM (IN-27)	OFF-Vehicle matrix chart (AX-74)
						1
						1
						4
		2	3			4
		2	3			4
		2	3			4
			2			3
		2				3
		2				3
					1	
					1	
1						2
						2
						3
						3
						4
1						3
	1					2
						2
1						2
						2
						1
						1
						1
						1
						1
						2
						2
		2	2			
						2
				1		3

Chapter 3. Off–Vehicle Repair
(★ : A245E AUTOMATIC TRANSAXLE Repair Manual Pub No. RM311U)

Trouble \ Parts Name	Torque converter	Oil pump	Second coast brake (B_1)	Second brake (B_2)	First and reverse brake (B_3)	U/D brake (B_4)	Forward clutch (C_1)	Direct clutch (C_2)	U/D clutch (C_3)	No. 1 one-way clutch (F_1)	No. 2 one-way clutch (F_2)	U/D one-way clutch (F_3)	Front planetary gear	Rear planetary gear	ON-Vehicle matrix chart
See Page	AX-34	★	★	★	★	★	★	★	★	★	★	★	★	★	AX-72
Does not move in any forward range							1								
Does not move in reverse range					2	3		1							
Does not move in any range	1	2										3	4	5	6
No up-shift 1st→2nd				1						2					3
No up-shift 2nd→3rd								1							2
No up-shift 3rd→O/D									1						2
No down-shift O/D→3rd						1						2			3
No down-shift 3rd→2nd								1							2
No down-shift 2nd→1st											1				2
Shift point too high or too low															1
Up-shift 3rd→O/D with O/D switch OFF															1
Harsh engagement "N"→"R"					2			1							3
Harsh engagement "N"→"D"							1								
Harsh engagement "N"→"L"					2		1								3
Harsh engagement 1st→2nd ("D" position)				1						2					3
Harsh engagement 1st→2nd ("2" position)			1	2						3					4
Harsh engagement 1st→2nd→3rd→O/D															1
Harsh engagement 2nd→3rd								1							2
Harsh engagement 3rd→O/D									1						2
Harsh engagement O/D→3rd						1									2
Harsh engagement 3rd→2nd								1							2
Slip Forward & Reverse	1	2													3
Slip "R" position					2			1							
Slip 1st							1				2	3			
Slip 2nd				2			1			3		4			
Slip 3rd							1	2				3			
Slip O/D							1	2	3						
No engine braking 1st ("L" position)					1										2
No engine braking 2nd ("2" position)			1												2
No kick-down															1
Poor acceleration	1						2								3
No lock-up	1														

AX0CF–01

LOCATION OF CONNECTORS

Location of Connectors in Engine Compartment

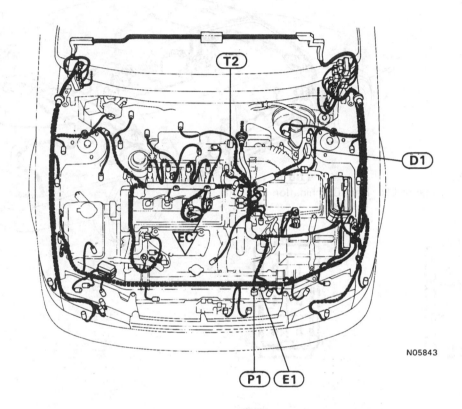

N05843

Data Link Connector

lei-23-1

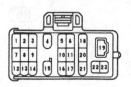

ECT Solenoid

le-3-1-G

Park/Neutral Position Switch

le-10-1-B

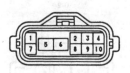

Throttle Position Sensor

IV-4-1-A

AX

V01527

Location of Connectors in Body

(Sedan)

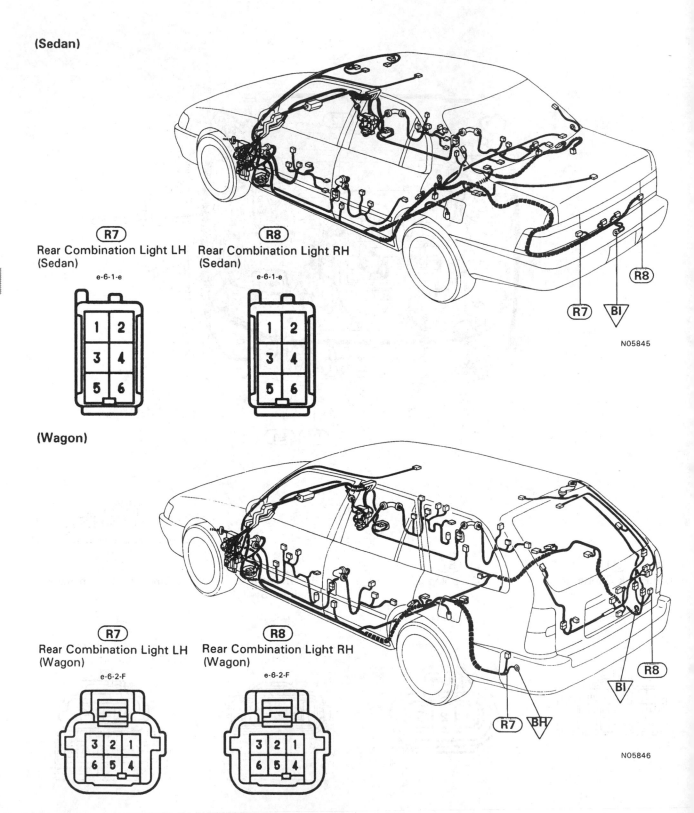

N05845

(R7)
Rear Combination Light LH
(Sedan)
e-6-1-e

(R8)
Rear Combination Light RH
(Sedan)
e-6-1-e

(Wagon)

(R7)
Rear Combination Light LH
(Wagon)
e-6-2-F

(R8)
Rear Combination Light RH
(Wagon)
e-6-2-F

N05846

AX

V01528

Location of Connectors in Instrument Panel

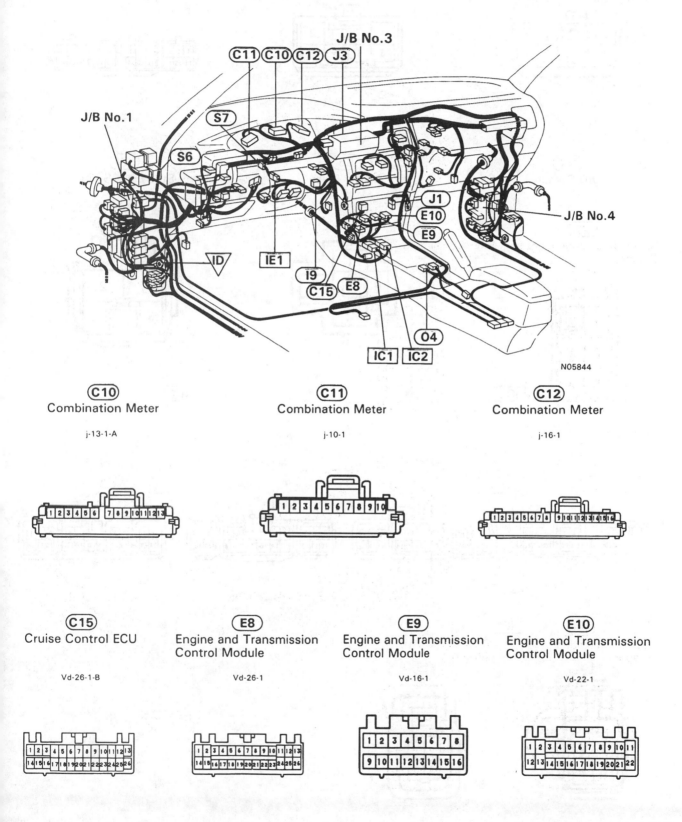

AX

N05844

(C10) Combination Meter	(C11) Combination Meter	(C12) Combination Meter
j-13-1-A	j-10-1	j-16-1

(C15) Cruise Control ECU	(E8) Engine and Transmission Control Module	(E9) Engine and Transmission Control Module	(E10) Engine and Transmission Control Module
Vd-26-1-B	Vd-26-1	Vd-16-1	Vd-22-1

V01529

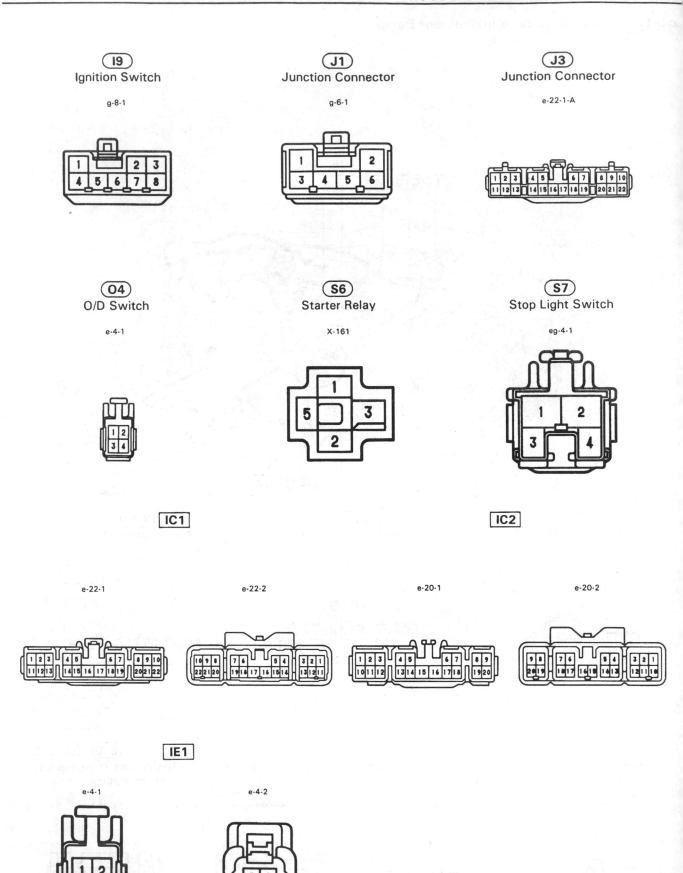

(I9) Ignition Switch
g-8-1

(J1) Junction Connector
g-6-1

(J3) Junction Connector
e-22-1-A

(O4) O/D Switch
e-4-1

(S6) Starter Relay
X-161

(S7) Stop Light Switch
eg-4-1

IC1

IC2

e-22-1   e-22-2   e-20-1   e-20-2

IE1

e-4-1   e-4-2

J/B No.1

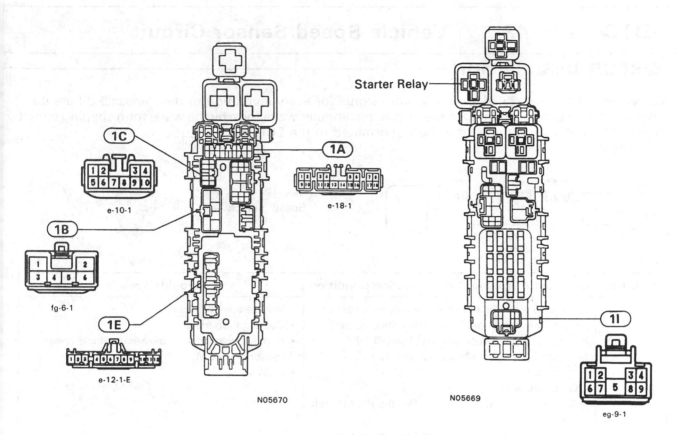

Starter Relay

1C — e-10-1

1A — e-18-1

1B — fg-6-1

1E — e-12-1-E

N05670

N05669

1I — eg-9-1

AX

J/B No.3

J/B No.4

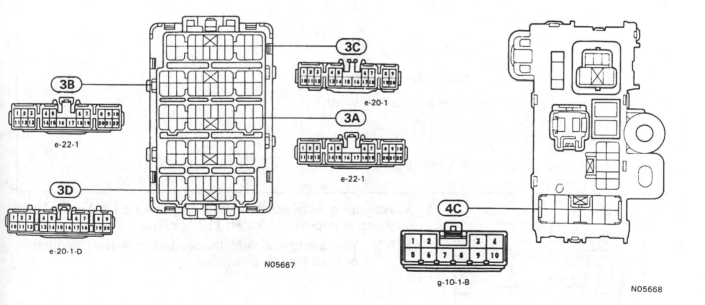

3C — e-20-1

3B — e-22-1

3A — e-22-1

3D — e-20-1-D

N05667

4C — g-10-1-B

N05668

CIRCUIT INSPECTION

DTC	42	Vehicle Speed Sensor Circuit

CIRCUIT DESCRIPTION

The vehicle speed sensor outputs a 4-pulse signal for every revolution of the transaxle differential. After this signal converted into a more precise rectangular wave form by the wave form shaping circuit inside the combination meter, it is then transmitted to the ECM.

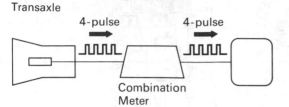

Transaxle

4-pulse   4-pulse

Combination
Meter

Q00765

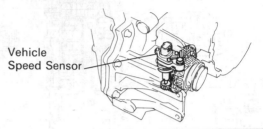

Vehicle
Speed Sensor

V01558

DTC No.	Diagnostic Trouble Code Detection Condition	Trouble Area
42	If the VSS signal is not input for two seconds or longer after condition A or B (described below) occurs, DTC 42 is recorded and the OD OFF indicator light lights up simultaneously. **CONDITION A** • 30 seconds or more elapses after the PNP switch goes OFF. • The throttle opening ratio and engine rpm are within the shadded area. RPM 4,000 3,000 2,000 25 50 100 (%) Throttle Opening Ratio **CONDITION B** • 1 second or more elapses after the PNP switch goes OFF. • A VSS signal of 14 km/h (8.7 mph) or more was input. • The stop light switch is OFF (brake pedal is released). V01547	• Vehicle speed sensor • Combination meter. • Harness or connector between vehicle speed sensor and ECM. • ECM

< Reference >

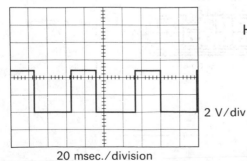

2 V/div

20 msec./division

V01496

● Waveform between terminals SPD and E1 when vehicle speed is approx. 20 km/h (12 MPH).

HINT: The greater the vehicle speed, the greater the number of VSS signals produced.

— CIRCUIT DESCRIPTION

Fail Safe Function
If the vehicle speed sensor fails, shift control takes place so that the throttle opening ratio and RPM are controlled according to the shift control map.

Shift Control Map (Reference)

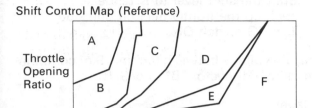

Throttle Opening Ratio

RPM

A Zone: Shift down 2 gears
B Zone: Shift down 1 gear
C Zone: No change
D Zone: Shift up 1 gear
E Zone: Shift up 2 gears
F Zone: Shift up 3 gears

V01546

— DIAGNOSTIC CHART

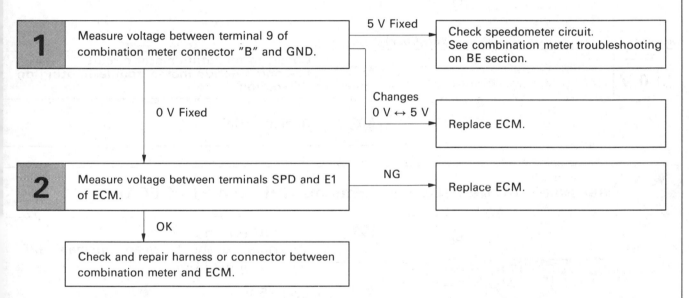

1 Measure voltage between terminal 9 of combination meter connector "B" and GND.

5 V Fixed → Check speedometer circuit. See combination meter troubleshooting on BE section.

Changes 0 V ↔ 5 V → Replace ECM.

0 V Fixed

2 Measure voltage between terminals SPD and E1 of ECM.

NG → Replace ECM.

OK

Check and repair harness or connector between combination meter and ECM.

AX

WIRING DIAGRAM

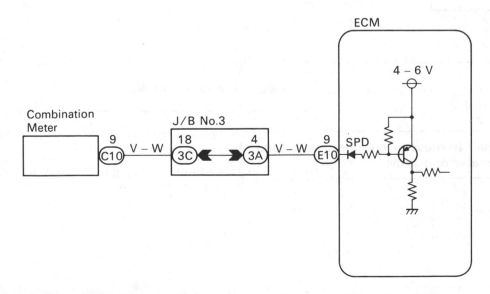

ECM

4 – 6 V

Combination Meter

9
C10   V – W

J/B No.3
18
3C   4   3A   V – W

9
E10   SPD

INSPECTION PROCEDURE

1 | Measure voltage between terminal 9 of combination meter connector "B" and GND.

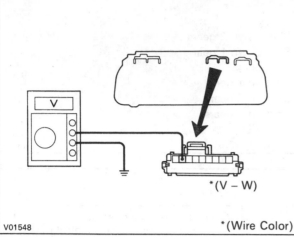

V01548   *(Wire Color)

*(V – W)

P
1. Shift the shift lever to N range.
2. Jack up the front wheel on one side.
3. Turn IG switch ON.

C Measure voltage between terminal 9 of combination meter connector "B" and GND.

Voltage:
        Constantly 0 V .... Go to next step
        Constantly 5 V .... Go to NG 1
        Changes 0 V ↔ 5 V ... Go to NG 2

0 V

NG 1 〉 Check combination meter circuit
See combination meter troubleshooting on BE section.

NG 2 〉 Replace ECM.

---

2 | Measure voltage between terminals SPD and E1 of ECM.

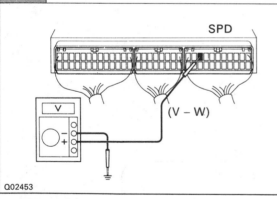

SPD

(V – W)

Q02453

P
1. Turn IG switch ON.
2. Measure voltage between terminals SPD and E1 of the ECM.

OK Voltage: 5 V

OK

NG 〉 Replace ECM.

Check and repair harness or connector between combination meter and ECM.

– MEMO –

DTC	62, 63	No.1 and No.2 Solenoid Valve Circuit

CIRCUIT DESCRIPTION

Shifting from 1st to O/D is performed in combination with ON and OFF of the No.1 and No.2 solenoid valves controlled by ECM. If an open or short circuit occurs in either of the solenoid valves, the ECM controls the remaining normal solenoid to allow the vehicle to be operated smoothly (Fail safe function).

Fail Safe Function
If either of the solenoid valve circuits develops a short or an open, the ECM turns the other solenoid ON and OFF to shift to the gear positions shown in the table below. The ECM also turns the lock-up solenoid valve OFF at the same time. If both solenoids malfunction, hydraulic control cannot be performed electronically and must be done manually.
Manual shifting as shown in the following table must be done. (In the case of a short circuit, the ECM stops sending current to the short circuited solenoid).

Position	NORMAL			NO.1 SOLENOID MALFUNCTIONING			NO.2 SOLENOID MALFUNCTIONING			BOTH SOLENOIDS MALFUNCTIONING
	Solenoid valve		Gear	Solenoid valve		Gear	Solenoid valve		Gear	Gear when shift selector is manually operated
	No.1	No.2		No.1	No.2		No.1	No.2		
D	ON	OFF	1st	x	ON	3rd	ON	x	1st	O/D
	ON	ON	2nd	x	ON	3rd	OFF	x	O/D	O/D
	OFF	ON	3rd	x	ON	3rd	OFF	x	O/D	O/D
	OFF	OFF	O/D	x	OFF	O/D	OFF	x	O/D	O/D
2	ON	OFF	1st	x	ON	3rd	ON	x	1st	3rd
	ON	ON	2nd	x	ON	3rd	OFF	x	3rd	3rd
	OFF	ON	3rd	x	ON	3rd	OFF	x	3rd	3rd
L	ON	OFF	1st	x	OFF	1st	ON	x	1st	1st
	ON	ON	2nd	x	ON	2nd	ON	x	1st	1st

x: Malfunctions

Check the No. 1 solenoid when diagnostic trouble code 62 is output and check the No. 2 solenoid when diagnostic trouble code 63 is output.

DTC No.	Diagnostic Trouble Code Detection Condition	Trouble Area
62, 63	(a) Solenoid resistance is 8 Ω or lower (short circuit when solenoid is energized. (b) Solenoid resistance is 100 kΩ or higher (open circuit) when solenoid is not energized. The ECM checks for an open or short circuit in the No.1 and No.2 solenoid circuit when it changes gear position The ECM records DTC 62 or 63 if condition (a) or (b) is detected once, but it does not blink the O/D OFF indicator light. After the ECM detects the condition (a) or (b) continuously 8 times or more, it causes the O/D OFF indicator light to blink until condition (a) or (b) disappears. After that, if the ECM detects condition (a) or (b) one, it starts blinking the O/D OFF indicator light again.	• Solenoid valve • Harness or connector between solenoid and ECM • ECM

— DIAGNOSTIC CHART

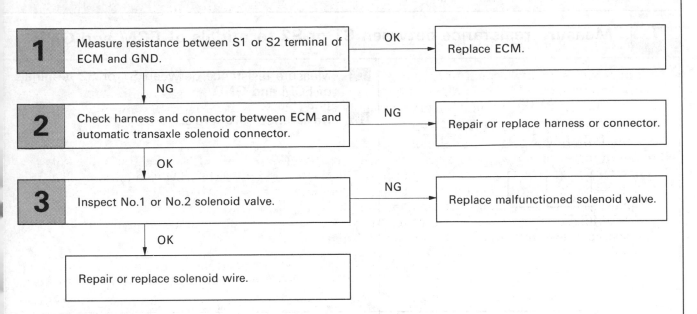

1 | Measure resistance between S1 or S2 terminal of ECM and GND. | OK → | Replace ECM.

↓ NG

2 | Check harness and connector between ECM and automatic transaxle solenoid connector. | NG → | Repair or replace harness or connector.

↓ OK

3 | Inspect No.1 or No.2 solenoid valve. | NG → | Replace malfunctioned solenoid valve.

↓ OK

Repair or replace solenoid wire.

WIRING DIAGRAM

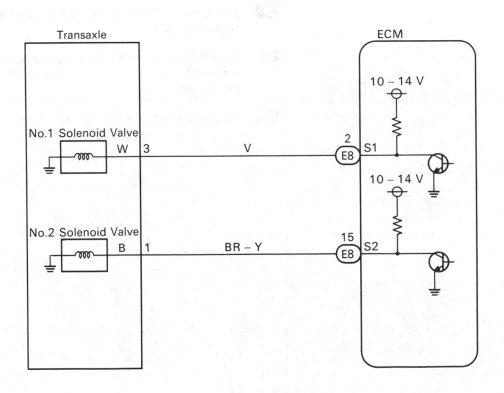

Transaxle

No.1 Solenoid Valve   W   3 —— V —— (E8) 2   S1   10 – 14 V

No.2 Solenoid Valve   B   1 —— BR – Y —— (E8) 15   S2   10 – 14 V

ECM

AX

INSPECTION PROCEDURE

1 | **Measure resistance between S1 or S2 terminals of ECM and GND.**

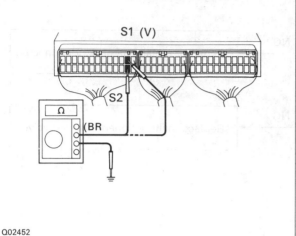

Q02452

C   Measure resistance between S1 or S2 terminals of ECM and GND.

OK   **Resistance: 10 – 16 Ω**

NG

OK ⟩ **Replace ECM.**

2 | **Check harness and connector between ECM and automatic transaxle solenoid connector.**

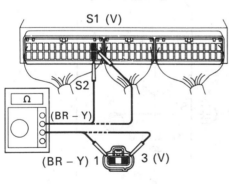

Q02447
Q02283

P   Disconnect the solenoid connector on the automatic transaxle.

C   Check harness and connector between S1 and S2 terminals of ECM and 3 terminals of solenoid connector.

OK   **There is no open and short circuit.**

OK

NG ⟩ **Repair or replace harness or connector.**

3   Check No.1 or No.2 solenoid valves.

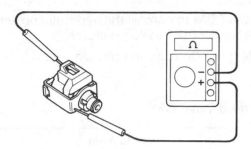

Electrical Check

P 1. Jack up the vehicle.
2. Remove oil pan.
3. Disconnect solenoid connector.
4. Remove No.1 or No.2 solenoid valve.

C Measure resistance between solenoid connector and body ground.

OK **Resistance: 10 – 16 Ω**

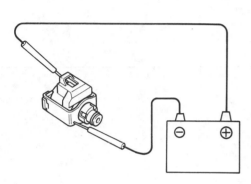

C Connect positive $\oplus$ lead to terminal of solenoid connector, negative $\ominus$ lead to solenoid body.

OK **The solenoid makes an operating noise.**

Mechanical Check

P 1. Remove the oil pan.
2. Remove the No.1 or No.2 solenoid valve.

C 1. Applying 490 kPa (5 kgf/cm^2, 71 psi) of compressed air, check that the solenoid valves do not leak the air.
2. When battery voltage is supplied to the solenoid valves, check that the solenoid valves open.

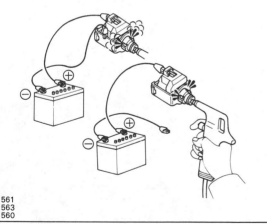

V01561
V01563
V01560

OK

NG ⟩ Replace solenoid valve.

Repair or replace solenoid wire.

DTC	64	SL Solenoid Valve Circuit

CIRCUIT DESCRIPTION

The SL solenoid valve is turned ON and OFF by signals from the ECM to control the hydraulic pressure acting on the lock-up relay valve, which then controls operation of the lock-up clutch.

If a malfunction occurs in this circuit and diagnostic trouble code 64 is stored in memory, the O/D OFF indicator light does not blink.

Fail Safe Function
If the ECM detects a malfunction, it turns the lock-up solenoid valve OFF.

DTC No.	Diagnostic Trouble Code Detection Condition	Trouble Area
64	(a) Solenoid resistance is 8 Ω or lower (short circuit) when solenoid energized. (b) Solenoid resistance is 100 kΩ or higher (open circuit) when solenoid is not energized. ECM memorizes diag. code 64 if about (a) or (b) condition is detected once or more, but ECM does not start O/D OFF indicator light blinking.	• SL solenoid valve. • Harness or connector between SL solenoid valve and ECM. • ECM

— DIAGNOSTIC CHART

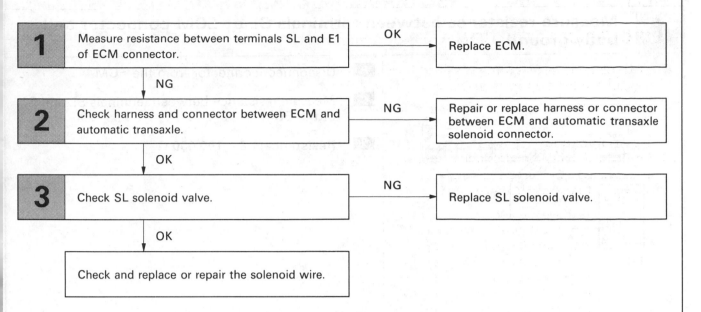

1	Measure resistance between terminals SL and E1 of ECM connector.	— OK →	Replace ECM.
2	Check harness and connector between ECM and automatic transaxle.	— NG →	Repair or replace harness or connector between ECM and automatic transaxle solenoid connector.
3	Check SL solenoid valve.	— NG →	Replace SL solenoid valve.

NG (after 1)
OK (after 2)
OK (after 3)

Check and replace or repair the solenoid wire.

WIRING DIAGRAM

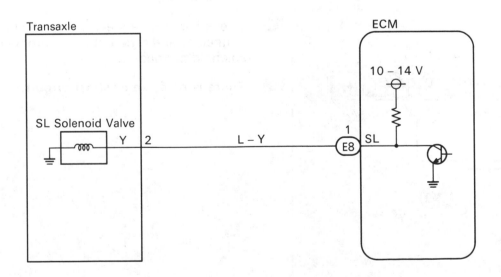

Transaxle

SL Solenoid Valve
Y   2   L – Y   E8   1   SL

ECM

10 – 14 V

INSPECTION PROCEDURE

1 **Measure resistance between terminals SL of ECM connector and body ground.**

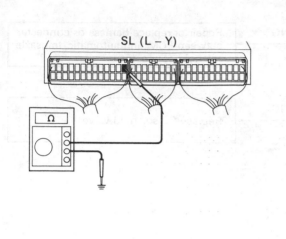

Q02451

P Disconnect connector from the ECM.

C Measure resistance between terminals SL and E1 of the ECM.

OK **Resistance: 8 – 100,000 Ω**

NG

OK ⟩ **Replace ECM.**

---

2 **Check harness and connector between ECM and automatic transaxle.**

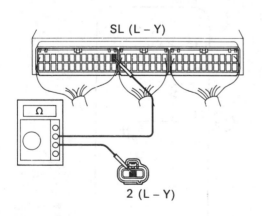

SL (L – Y)

2 (L – Y)

Q02446

P 1. Disconnect the connector from the PCM.
　　 2. Disconnect the solenoid connector from the transaxle.

C Check harness between terminal SL of the ECM connector and terminal 3 of automatic transaxle solenoid connector.

OK **There is no open or short circuit.**

OK

NG ⟩ **Repair or replace harness or connector between ECM connector and automatic transaxle solenoid connector.**

3 | **Check SL solenoid valve.**

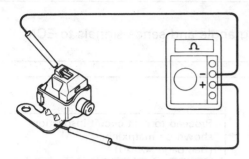

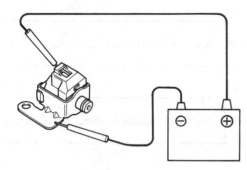

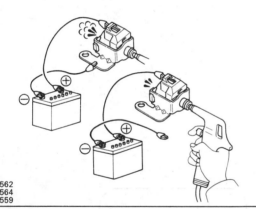

V01562
V01564
V01559

Electrical check

P 1. Jack-up the vehicle.
2. Remove oil pan.
3. Disconnect SL solenoid valve connector.
4. Remove SL solenoid valve.

C Measure resistance between SL solenoid connector terminal and its body ground.

OK **Resistance: 10 – 16 Ω**

C Check SL solenoid valve operation noise when apply battery voltage to the solenoid connector terminal and it's body.

OK **The SL solenoid valve makes operation noise.**

Mechanical Check

P Remove SL solenoid valve from valve body.

C 1. Applying 490 kPa (5 kgf/cm², 71 psi) of compressed air, check that the solenoid valves do not leak the air.
2. When battery voltage is supplied to the solenoid valves, check that the solenoid valves open.

AX

OK

NG ⟩ Replace SL solenoid valve.

Check and replace or repair the solenoid wire.

Throttle Position Sensor Circuit

CIRCUIT DESCRIPTION

The throttle position sensor detects the throttle valve opening angle and sends signals to ECM.

DIAGNOSTIC CHART

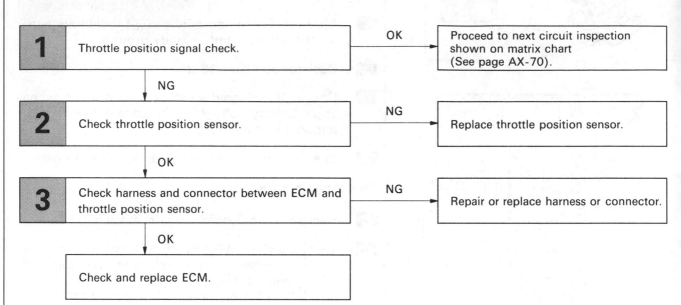

1 Throttle position signal check. — OK → Proceed to next circuit inspection shown on matrix chart (See page AX-70).

NG

2 Check throttle position sensor. — NG → Replace throttle position sensor.

OK

3 Check harness and connector between ECM and throttle position sensor. — NG → Repair or replace harness or connector.

OK

Check and replace ECM.

WIRING DIAGRAM

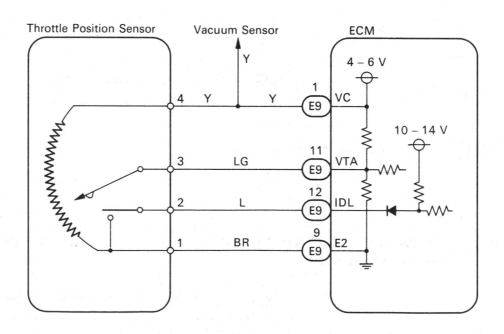

INSPECTION PROCEDURE

1 Throttle position signal check.

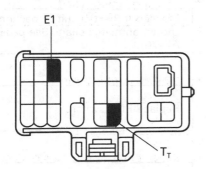

P Turn ignition switch ON (Do not start the engine).

C Check voltage at the terminal T_T of the DLC No.1 while gradually depressing the accelerator pedal from the fully closed position to the fully opened position.

OK Voltage changes from 0 V to 8 V by stages.

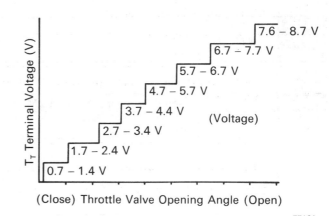

Hint Do not depress the brake pedal during this test. The voltage will stay at 0 V if depressed.

lej-23-1-A

AX

NG

OK ⟩ Proceed to next circuit inspection shown on matrix chart (See page AX-70).

2 Check throttle position sensor.

See engine troubleshooting section.

OK

NG ⟩ Replace throttle position sensor.

3 Check harness and connector between ECM and throttle position sensor (See IN Section).

OK

NG ⟩ Repair or replace harness or connector.

Check and replace ECM.

Park/Neutral Position Switch Circuit

CIRCUIT DESCRIPTION

The PNP switch detects the shift lever position and sends signals to ECM.
The ECM receives signals (R, NSW, 2 and L) from the PNP switch. When the signal is not sent to the ECM from the Neutral start switch, the ECM judges that the shift lever is in the D position.

DIAGNOSTIC CHART

1   Check voltage between terminal R, NSW, 2, L of ECM connector and body ground.   → OK →   Proceed to next circuit inspection shown on matrix chart (See page AX-70).

↓ NG

2   Check PNP switch   → NG →   Replace PNP switch.

↓ OK

3   Check harness and connector between ECM and PNP switch, PNP switch and battery (See IN Section).   → NG →   Repair or replace harness or connector.

↓ OK

Check and replace ECM.

WIRING DIAGRAM

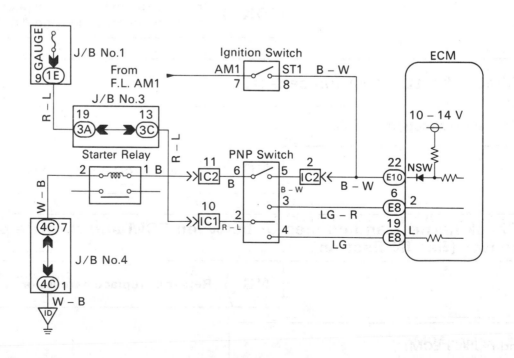

V01493

INSPECTION PROCEDURE

1   Check voltage between terminal R, NSW, 2, L of ECM connector and body ground.

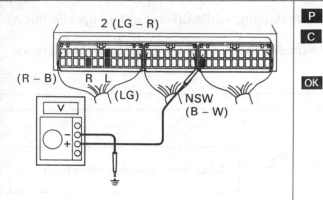

Q02450

P   Turn ignition switch ON.

C   Measure voltage between terminals R, NSW, 2, L of ECM connector and body ground when the shift lever is shifted to the following positions.

OK

Position	R-body ground	NSW-body ground	2-body ground	L-body ground
P, N	0 V	0 V	0 V	0 V
R	10 – 14 V*	10 – 14 V*	0 V	0 V
D	0 V	10 – 14 V	0 V	0 V
2	0 V	10 – 14 V	10 – 14 V	0 V
L	0 V	10 – 14 V	0 V	10 – 14 V

*: The voltage will drop slightly due to lighting up of the back up light.

NG

OK ⟩ Proceed to next circuit inspection shown on matrix chart (See page AX-70).

AX

2   Check PNP switch.

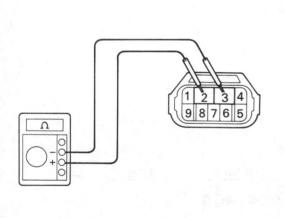

AT5528

P   Remove PNP switch (See page AX-21).

C   Check continuity between each terminal shown below when the shift lever is shifted to each position.

○—○ Continuity

Shift Position \ Terminal	3	2	9	1	4	6	5	7	8
P	○—○		○—○						
R			○——○						
N	○—○		○——		—○				
D			○———			—○			
2			○————				—○		
L			○—————						—○

OK

NG ⟩ Replace PNP switch.

3   Check harness and connector between ECM and PNP switch, PNP switch and battery.

OK

NG ⟩ Repair or replace harness and connector.

 Check and replace ECM.

Stop Light Switch Circuit

CIRCUIT DESCRIPTION

The purpose of this circuit is to prevent the engine from stalling, while driving in lockup condition, when brakes are suddenly applied.

When the brake pedal is operated, this switch sends a signal to ECM. Then the ECM cancels operation of the lockup clutch while braking is in progress.

DIAGNOSTIC CHART

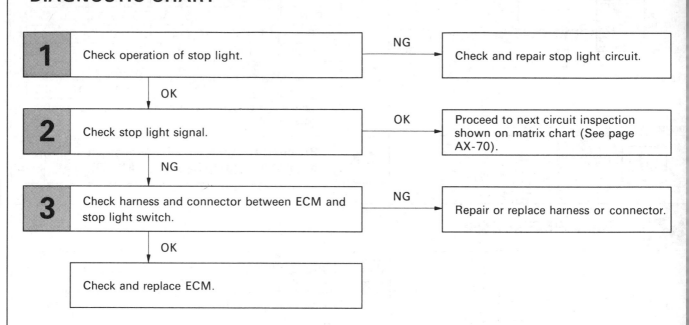

1 Check operation of stop light. — NG → Check and repair stop light circuit.

↓ OK

2 Check stop light signal. — OK → Proceed to next circuit inspection shown on matrix chart (See page AX-70).

↓ NG

3 Check harness and connector between ECM and stop light switch. — NG → Repair or replace harness or connector.

↓ OK

Check and replace ECM.

WIRING DIAGRAM

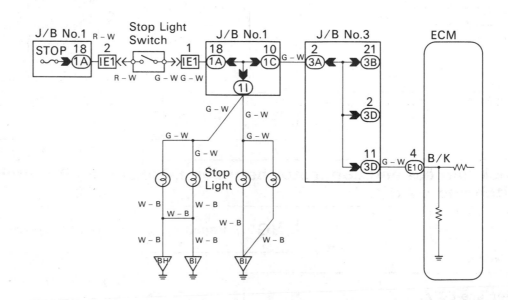

NSPECTION PROCEDURE

1 | Check operation of stop light.

C Check if the stop lights go on and off normally when the brake pedal is operated and released.

OK		**NG** 〉	Check and repair stop light circuit.

2 | Check stop light signal.

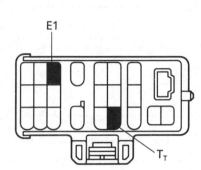

E1

T$_T$

IG ON

7.6 – 8.7 V

Brake Pedal

Accelerator Pedal

0 – 0.4 V

j-23-1-A
T1085

C
1. Connect voltmeter to the terminals T$_T$ and E1 of the DLC No.1.
2. Turn ignition switch ON (Do not start the engine).
3. Fully depress the accelerator pedal until the voltmeter indicates 6.7 – 8.7 V and hold it.
4. Depress and release the brake pedal and check the voltage.

OK

Brake pedal	Voltage
Depressed	0 – 0.4 V
Released	7.6 – 8.7 V

NG		**OK** 〉	Proceed to next circuit inspection shown on matrix chart (See page AX-70).

3 | Check harness and connector between ECM and stop light switch.

OK		**NG** 〉	Repair or replace harness or connector.

Check and replace ECM.

AX

O/D Main Switch & O/D OFF Indicator Light Circuit

CIRCUIT DESCRIPTION

The O/D main switch contacts go off when the switch is pushed in and come on when it is pushed out. In O/D main switch OFF position, the O/D OFF indicator lights up, and the ECM prohibits shifting to overdrive. The ECM also causes the O/D OFF indicator light to blink when a malfunction is detected. In this case, connecting the terminals in the DLC No.1 can display the DTC.

WIRING DIAGRAM

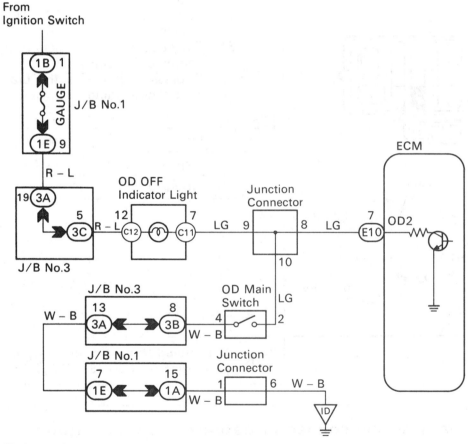

(*) O/D Main Switch
     Contacts go off with switch pushed in.
     Contacts go on with switch pushed out.

DIAGNOSTIC CHART

O/D OFF indicator light does not light up.

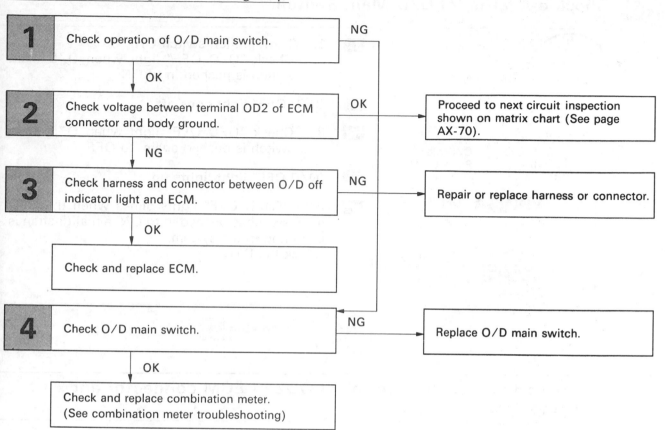

1 Check operation of O/D main switch.

— OK ↓

2 Check voltage between terminal OD2 of ECM connector and body ground.

— NG ↓

3 Check harness and connector between O/D off indicator light and ECM.

— OK ↓

Check and replace ECM.

4 Check O/D main switch.

— OK ↓

Check and replace combination meter.
(See combination meter troubleshooting)

— NG → Proceed to next circuit inspection shown on matrix chart (See page AX-70).

— NG → Repair or replace harness or connector.

— NG → Replace O/D main switch.

O/D OFF indicator light remains ON

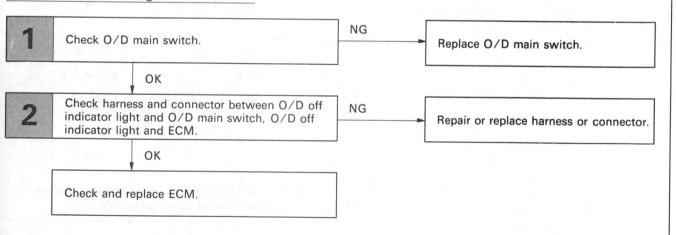

1 Check O/D main switch.

— NG → Replace O/D main switch.

— OK ↓

2 Check harness and connector between O/D off indicator light and O/D main switch, O/D off indicator light and ECM.

— NG → Repair or replace harness or connector.

— OK ↓

Check and replace ECM.

O/D OFF indicator light blinks

Perform diagnostic code check (See page AX-46).

AX

INSPECTION PROCEDURE

1   Check operation of O/D Main Switch.

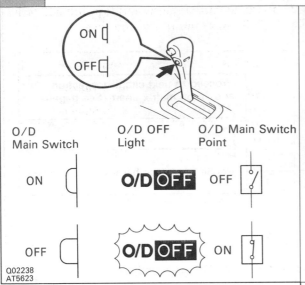

C   1. Turn ignition switch ON.
     2. Check "O/D OFF" light when O/D main switch is pushed in to ON.

OK   "O/D OFF" light goes off.

C   3. Check "O/D OFF" light when O/D main switch is pushed again, to OFF.

OK   "O/D OFF" light lights up.

Hint   If the "O/D OFF" lights blinks when the O/D main switch is pushed in to ON, a malfunction is occurring in the system.
Check the DTC.

OK   **NG** ⟩ Go to step **4** .

---

2   Check voltage between terminal OD2 of ECM connector and body ground.

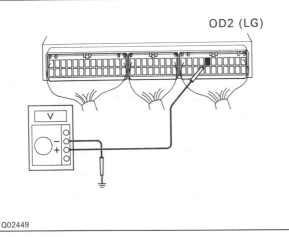

OD2 (LG)

P   Turn ignition switch ON.

C   Check voltage between terminal OD2 of ECM and body ground.

OK

O/D Main Switch	Voltage
OFF	Below 1 V
ON	10 ~ 14 V

Q02449

NG   **OK** ⟩ Proceed to next circuit inspection shown on matrix chart (See page AX-xx).

---

3   Check harness and connector between O/D off indicator light and ECM.

OK   **NG** ⟩ Repair or replace harness or connector.

Check and replace ECM.

4   Check O/D Main Switch.

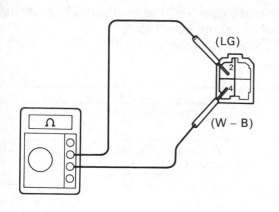

(LG)

(W – B)

AT5529

C 1. Disconnect O/D main switch connector.
    2. Measure resistance between terminals 2 and
        4 of O/D main switch connector.

OK

O/D Main Switch	Resistance
ON	∞ Ω (open)
OFF	0 Ω (continuity)

OK

NG ⟩ Replace O/D Main Switch.

**Check and replace combination meter.
(See combination meter troubleshooting
section.)**

AX

O/D Cancel Signal Circuit

CIRCUIT DESCRIPTION

While driving with cruise control activated, in order to minimize gear shifting and provide smooth cruising on an uphill overdrive may be prohibited temporarily in some conditions.
The Cruise Control ECU sends O/D cut signals to the ECM as necessary and the ECM cancels overdrive shifting until these signals are discontinued.

DIAGNOSTIC CHART

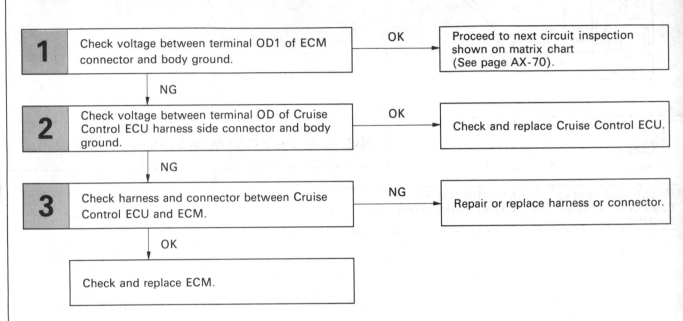

1	Check voltage between terminal OD1 of ECM connector and body ground.	OK →	Proceed to next circuit inspection shown on matrix chart (See page AX-70).

NG ↓

2	Check voltage between terminal OD of Cruise Control ECU harness side connector and body ground.	OK →	Check and replace Cruise Control ECU.

NG ↓

3	Check harness and connector between Cruise Control ECU and ECM.	NG →	Repair or replace harness or connector.

OK ↓

Check and replace ECM.

WIRING DIAGRAM

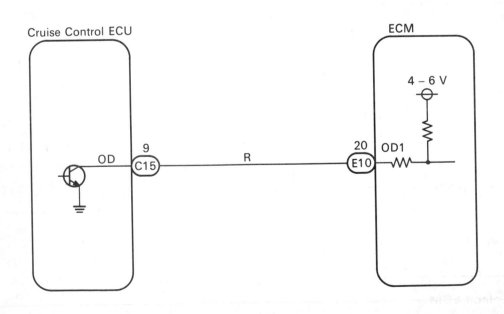

Cruise Control ECU

ECM

4 – 6 V

OD   9 (C15)   R   20 (E10)   OD1

INSPECTION PROCEDURE

1 | Check voltage between terminal OD1 of ECM connector and body ground.

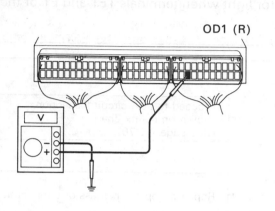

OD1 (R)

P	Turn ignition switch ON.
C	Measure voltage between terminal OD1 of ECM connector and body ground.
OK	Voltage: 4 – 6 V

N02448

| **NG** | | **OK** ⟩ Proceed to next circuit inspection shown on matrix chart (See page AX-70). |

AX

2 | Check voltage between terminal OD of Cruise Control ECU harness side connector and body ground.

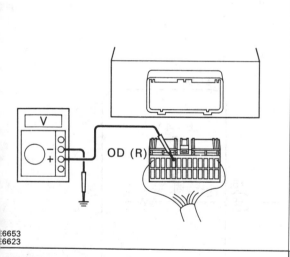

OD (R)

P	1. Disconnect Cruise Control ECU connector. 2. Turn ignition switch ON.
C	Measure voltage between terminal OD of Cruise Control ECU harness side connector and body ground.
OK	Voltage: 4 – 6 V

6653
6623

| **NG** | | **OK** ⟩ Check and replace Cruise Control ECU. |

3 | Check harness or connector between Cruise Control ECU and ECM.

| **OK** | | **NG** ⟩ Repair or replace harness or connector. |

Check and replace ECM.

TE1 Terminal Circuit

CIRCUIT DESCRIPTION

ECM displays diagnostic codes using the O/D OFF indicator light when terminals TE1 and E1 of the DLC1 are connected.

DIAGNOSTIC CHART

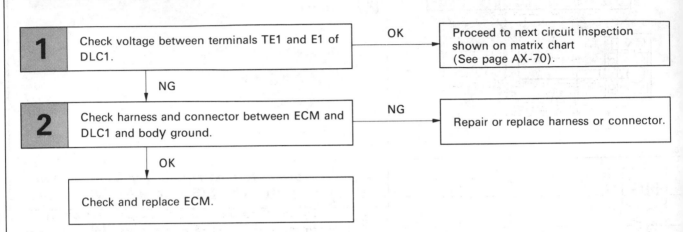

| **1** | Check voltage between terminals TE1 and E1 of DLC1. | OK → | Proceed to next circuit inspection shown on matrix chart (See page AX-70). |

↓ NG

| **2** | Check harness and connector between ECM and DLC1 and body ground. | NG → | Repair or replace harness or connector. |

↓ OK

| Check and replace ECM. |

WIRING DIAGRAM

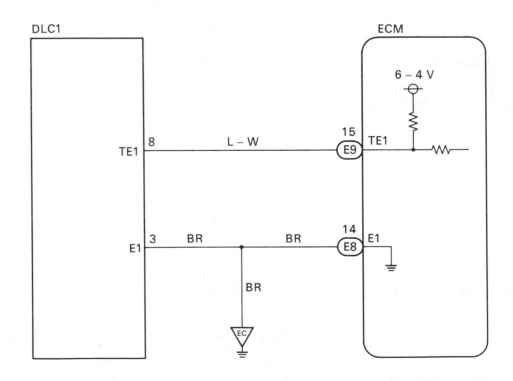

INSPECTION PROCEDURE

1   **Check voltage between terminals TE1 and E1 of DLC1.**

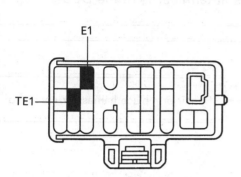

ej-23-1-A

	C Measure voltage between terminals TE1 and E1 of DLC1.
	OK Voltage: 4 – 6 V

NG

OK ⟩ Proceed to next circuit inspection shown on matrix chart (See page AX-70).

2   **Check harness and connector between ECM and DLC1, and body ground.**

OK

NG ⟩ Repair or replace harness or connector.

Check and replace ECM.

T_T Terminal Circuit

CIRCUIT DESCRIPTION

Checks of ECM input and output signals related to the throttle position sensor, brakes, shift position and other circuits can be performed by measuring the voltages at terminal T_T of the DLC1.

DIAGNOSTIC CHART

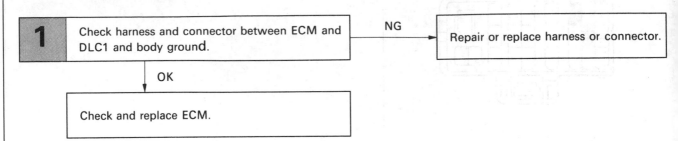

| **1** | Check harness and connector between ECM and DLC1 and body ground. | NG → | Repair or replace harness or connector. |

OK ↓

Check and replace ECM.

WIRING DIAGRAM

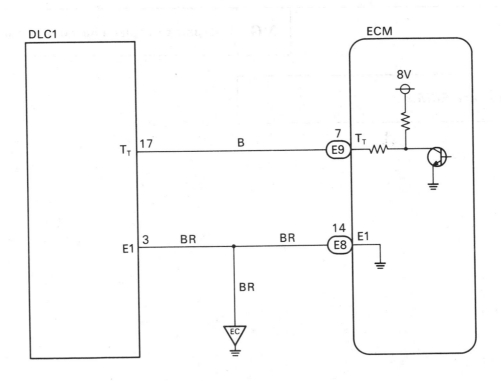

SERVICE SPECIFICATIONS
SERVICE DATA

AX0A5-01

Line pressure(whell locked)	Engine idling			
	D position	373—441	3.8—4.5	54—64
	R position	598—716	6.1—7.3	87—104
	AT stall			
	D position	980—1,138	10.0—11.6	142—165
	R position	1,393—1,716	14.2—17.5	201—249
Engine stall revolution		2,450±150 RPM		
Time lag	N position → D position	Less than 1.2 seconds		
	N position → R position	Less than 1.5 seconds		
Engine idle speed(Cooling fan and A/C OFF)				
	N position	650—750 RPM		
Throttle cable adjustment (Throttle valve fully opened)		Between boot and face and inner cable stopper		
		0—1 mm	0—0.04 in.	
Torque converter runout	Limit	0.30 mm	0.0118 in.	
Drive plate runout	Limit	0.20 mm	0.0079 in.	

SHIFT POINT

Shift position	Shifting point		Vehicle speed km/h (mph)
D position	Throttle valve fully opened	1→2	56—62 (35—39)
		2→3	104—111 (65—69)
		3→O/D	139—151 (86—94)
		O/D→3	133—145 (83—90)
		3→2	98—106 (61—66)
		2→1	43—49 (27—30)
	Throttle valve fully closed	3→O/D	35—41 (22—25)
		O/D→3	17—22 (11—14)
2 position	Throttle valve fully opened	3→2	102—109 (63—68)
		2→1	43—49 (27—30)
L position	Throttle valve fully opened	2→1	47—53 (29—33)

LOCK—UP POINT

D position km/h (mph) Throttle valve opening 5%	Lock—up ON	Lock—up OFF
3rd Gear	65—72 (40—45)	58—64 (36—40)
O/D Gear	65—72 (40—45)	58—64 (36—40)

TORQUE SPECIFICATIONS

Part tightened		N·m	kgf·cm	ft·lbf
Transaxle housing x Engine		64	650	47
Drive shaft x Crankshaft		64	650	47
Torque converter x Drive plate		25	250	18
Valve body x Transaxle case		10	100	7
Oil pan x Transaxle case		5.3	55	48in.·lbf
Oil pam drain plag		17	175	13
Park/neutral position switch x Transaxle case		5.4	55	48in.·lbf
Park/neutral position switch		12	125	108in.·lbf
Lower crossmember x Body		206	2,100	152
Center member x Transaxle mounting bracket		61	620	45
Center member x Body		61	620	45
Wire retainer		6.4	65	56in.·lbf
Manual defent spring		10	100	7
Transaxle housing x Engine	Bolt A	64	650	47
	Bolt B	25	250	18
	Bolt C	23	230	17
	Bolt D	46	470	34
Engine left mounting	Upper	52	530	38
	Lower	21	210	15
Ground cable		18	185	13
Starter		39	400	29
Suspension member	A Bolt	61	620	29
	B Bolt	64	650	45
	C Bolt	206	2,100	47
	D Bolt	206	2,100	152
	Nut	57	580	152
				42

SUSPENSION AND AXLE

SA

TROUBLESHOOTING

You will find the troubles easier using the table well shown below. In this table, each number shows the priority of causes in troubles. Check each part in order. If necessary, replace these parts.

Trouble \ Parts Name	Tires	Cold tire inflation pressure	Wheel alignment	Springs	Stabilizer bar	Shock absorber	Ball joint	Hub bearings	Steering linkage	Steering gear	Suspension parts	Overloaded	Wheel balance
See Page	—	SA-3	SA-3	SA-39,71	SA-55,84	SA-39,71	SA-52	SA-10,61	—	—	—	—	—
Wander/pulls	1		2					4	3	5	6		
Bottoming				2		3						1	
Sways/pitches	1				2	3							
Front wheel shimmy	1		4			3	5	6	7	8			2
Abnormal tire wear		1	2			4					3		

V0031

WHEEL ALIGNMENT

PRIMARY INSPECTION

1. **MAKE FOLLOWING CHECKS AND CORRECT ANY PROBLEMS**
(a) Check the tires for wear and for the proper inflation pressure.

Cold inflation pressure:

Tire size	Front	Rear
P175/65R14 81S	210 kPa (2.1 kgf/cm², 30 psi)	210 kPa (2.1 kgf/cm², 30 psi)
175/65R14 82S	210 kPa (2.1 kgf/cm², 30 psi)	210 kPa (2.1 kgf/cm², 30 psi)
P185/65R14 85S	210 kPa (2.1 kgf/cm², 30 psi)	210 kPa (2.1 kgf/;cm2;, 30 psi)
185/65R14 85S	210 kPa (2.1 kgf/cm², 30 psi)	210 kPa (2.1 kgf/;cm2;, 30 psi)

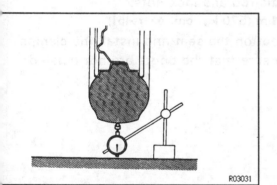

R03031

(b) Check the wheel bearings for looseness.
(c) Check the wheel runout.

Lateral runout:
1.0 mm (0.039 in.) or less

(d) Check the suspension for looseness.
(e) Check the steering linkage for looseness.
(f) Check that the shock absorbers work properly by using the standard bounce test.

2. **MEASURE VEHICLE HEIGHT**
Vehicle height:

Tire size	Front	Rear
P175/65R14 81S 175/65R14 82S	185 mm (7.28 in.)	245 mm (9.65 in.)
P185/65R14 85S 185/65R14 85S	190 mm (7.48 in.)	250 mm (9.84 in.)

Front

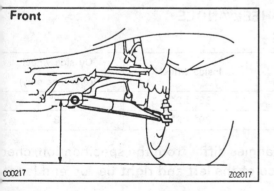

C00217   Z02017

Rear

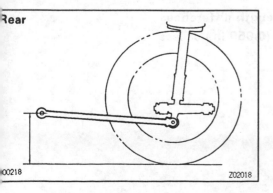

00218   Z02018

HINT:
● Measuring point
Front: Measure from the ground to the center of the front side lower arm mounting bolt.
Rear: Measure from the ground to the center of the strut rod mounting bolt.
● Before inspecting the wheel alignment, adjust the vehicle height to specification.
If the vehicle height is not standard, try to adjust it by pushing down on or lifting the body.

SA

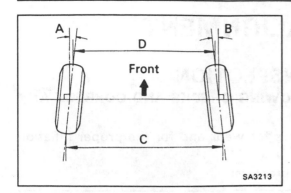

SA3213

FRONT WHEEL ALIGNMENT

SA05X–C

1. INSPECT TOE-IN

Toe-in (total):

A+B 0.1°±0.2°

(C-D 1±2 mm, 0.04±0.08 in.)

If the toe-in is not within the specification, adjust at the tie rod end.

2. ADJUST TOE-IN

C00219

(a) Remove the boot clamps.

(b) Loosen the tie rod end lock nuts.

(c) Turn the left and right tie rod ends an equal amount t adjust the toe-in.

HINT: Ensure that the lengths of the left and right ti rod end length are the same.

Tie rod end length difference:

1.0 mm (0.039 in.) or less

(d) Torque the tie rod end lock nuts.

Torque: 56 N·m (570 kgf·cm, 41 ft·lbf)

(e) Place the boot on the seat and install the clamps.

HINT: Make sure that the boots are not twisted.

3. INSPECT WHEEL ANGLE

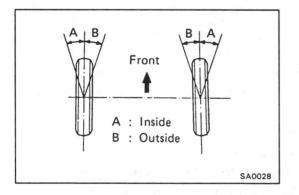

A : Inside
B : Outside

SA0028

Wheel angle:

Steering type	Inside wheel	Outside wheel (reference only)
Manual steering	39°±2°	33°
Power steering	39°±2°	33°

If the wheel angles differ from the specification, chec the difference of the left and right tie rod end lengt

Tie rod end length difference:

1.5 mm (0.059 in.) or less

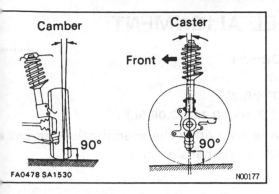

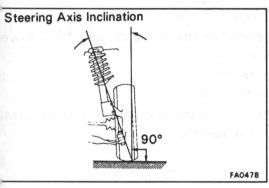

4. INSPECT CAMBER, CASTER AND STEERING AXIS INCLINATION

Camber:
  −10′±45′
Cross camber:
  30′or less
Caster:
  1°20′±45′
Cross caster:
  30′or less
Steering axis inclination:
  12°35′±45′

HINT: Camber, caster and steering axis inclination are not adjustable. If measurements are not within specification, inspect the suspension parts for damaged and/or worn out parts and replace them as necessary.

SA

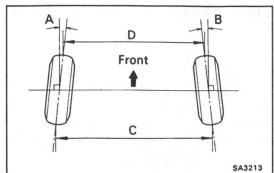

SA3213

REAR WHEEL ALIGNMENT

SA01S—03

1. **INSPECT TOE—IN**
   Toe—in (total):
       A+B 0.3° ±0.2°
       (C−D 3±2 mm, 0.12±0.08 in.)
   If the toe—in is not within the specification, adjust i
   at the No.2 lower suspension arm.

C00216

2. **ADJUST TOE—IN**
   (a) Measure the length of the left and right No.2 lowe
       suspension arm.
       Left—right difference:
           1 mm (0.04 in.) or less
       If the left—right difference is greater than the speci
       fication, adjust the length.

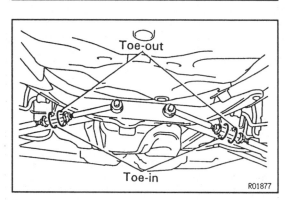

R01877

(b) Loosen the lock nuts.
(c) Turn the left and right adjusting tube an equal amoun
    to adjust toe—in.
- If the toe—in is out of specification toward th
  toe—out side, turn the adjusting tubes towar
  the "Toe—in" side shown in the illustration.
- If the toe—in is out of specification toward th
  toe—in side, turn the adjusting tubes toward th
  "Toe—out" side shown in the illustration.

HINT: One turn of the one side adjusting tube wi
adjust the toe—in about 1.2°(11 mm, 0.43 in.).
(d) Torque the lock nuts.
    Torque: 56 N·m (570 kgf·cm, 41 ft·lbf)
3. **INSPECT CAMBER**
    Camber:
        −55' ±45'
    Cross camber:
        30'or less

HINT: Camber is not adjustable. If measurement is no
within specification, inspect and replace the suspen
sion parts as necessary.

SA

FRONT AXLE

DESCRIPTION

The wheel bearings are double—row angular ball bearings having small rolling resistance and are free from maintenance.

The preload of the bearing can be determined only by tightening the drive shaft nut at a specified torque, improving serviceability.

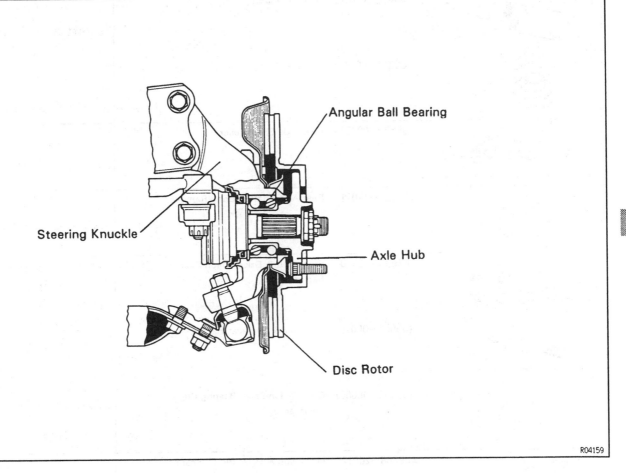

- Angular Ball Bearing
- Steering Knuckle
- Axle Hub
- Disc Rotor

R04159

SA

PREPARATION
SST(SPECIAL SERVICE TOOLS)

SA00K—02

09308—00010	Oil Seal Puller	
09316—60010	Transmission & Transfer Bearing Replacer	Dust deflector installation
(09316—00010)	Replacer Pipe	
(09316—00040)	Replacer "C"	
09520—00031	Rear Axle Shaft Puller	
09527—17011	Rear Axle Shaft Bearing Remover	
09608—12010	Front Hub & Drive Pinion Bearing Replacer Set	
(09608—00020)	Remover & Replacer Handle	
(09608—00060)	Drive Pinion Front Bearing Cup Replacer	
09608—20012	Front Hub & Drive Pinion Bearing Tool Set	
(09608—03020)	Handle	
(09608—03060)	Replacer	
(09608—03090)	Replacer	

SA

	09608—32010	Steering Knuckle Oil Seal Replacer	
	09620—30010	Steering Gear Box Replacer Set	Bearing inner race removal
	(09625—30010)	Steering Main Shaft Bearing Replacer	
	09628—10011	Ball Joint Puller	Hub bolt removal
	09628—62011	Ball Joint Puller	
	09950—00020	Bearing Remover	

SA00L—01

SA

RECOMMENDED TOOLS

	09042—00010	Torx Socket T30	Dust cover set bolt
	09905—00013	Snap Ring Pliers	Front axle hub bearing

SA00M—01

EQUIPMENT

Dial indicator	
Torque wrench	

FRONT AXLE HUB
COMPONENTS

SA003−(

275 (2,800, 203)

7.8 (80, 69 in.·lbf)
ABS Speed Sensor

Tie Rod End

Front Drive Shaft

49 (500, 36)
◆ Cotter Pin

88 (900, 65)

29 (300, 22)

◆ Cotter Pin

88 (900, 65)

Brake Cylinder

216 (2,200, 159)

Disc Rotor

Lock Nut Cap

142 (1,450, 105)

Snap Ring

Inner Race

◆ Bearing   Steering Knuckle

◆ Dust Deflector

◆ Oil Seal

8.3 (85, 74 in.·lbf)

Dust Cover

Inner Race

118 (1,200, 87)

◆ Oil Seal

◆ Cotter Pin

Lower Ball Joint

Axle Hub

Hub Bolt

N·m (kgf·cm, ft·lbf) : Specified torque

◆ Non-reusable part

R03850

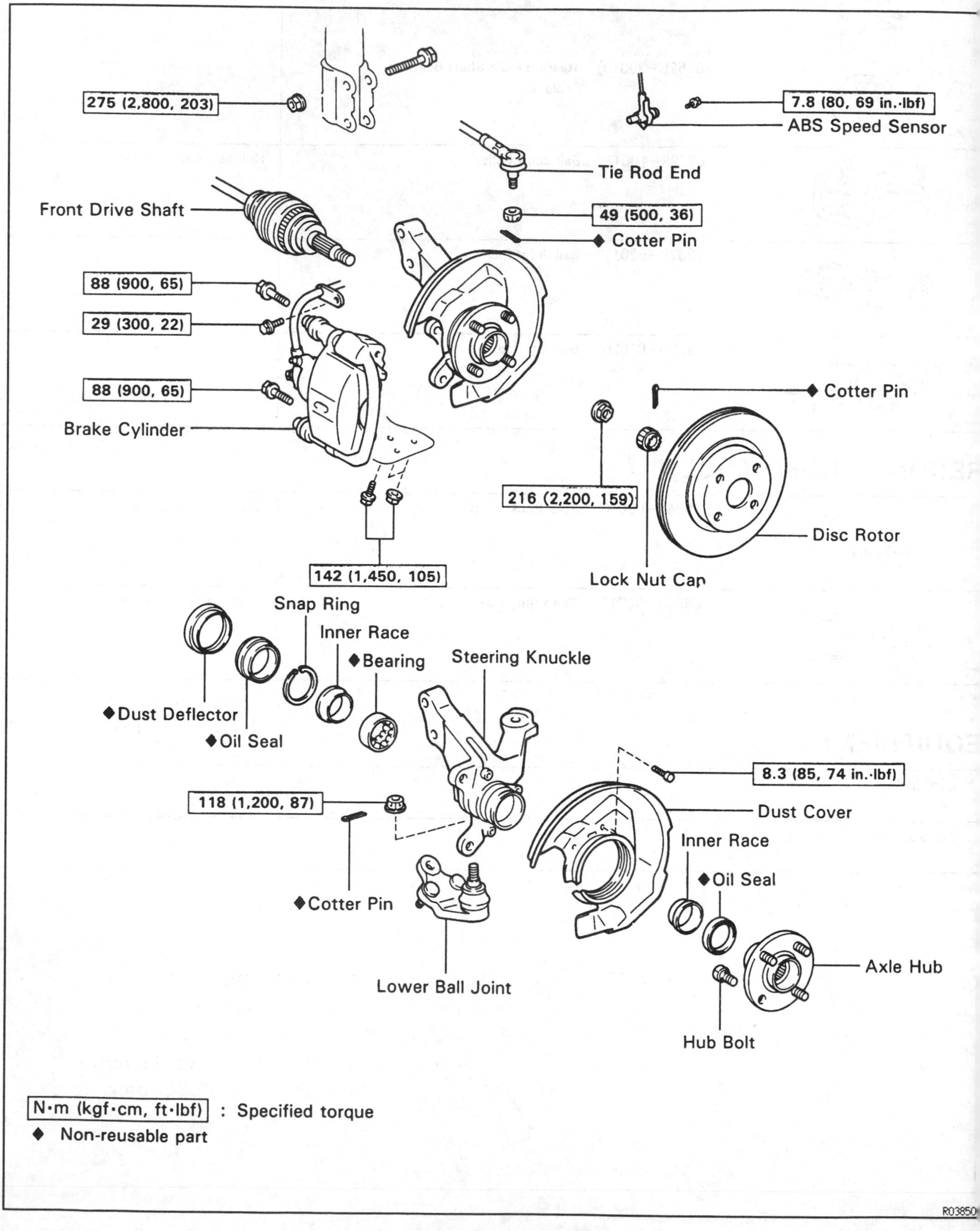

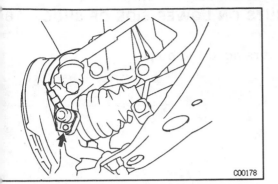

SA0H0-01

STEERING KNUCKLE WITH AXLE HUB REMOVAL

1. **JACK UP VEHICLE, REMOVE FRONT WHEEL**
2. **(w/ ABS)**
   REMOVE ABS SPEED SENSOR
   Remove the bolt and the speed sensor.

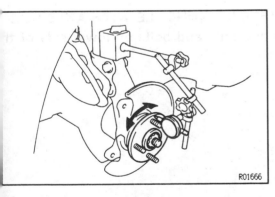

3. **CHECK BEARING BACKLASH AND AXLE HUB DEVIATION**
   (a) Remove the two brake cylinder set bolts.
   (b) Hang up the brake cylinder using wire, etc.
   (c) Remove the disc rotor.

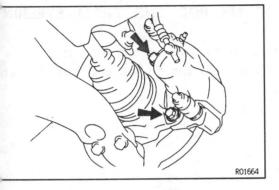

(d) Place the dial indicator near the center of the axle hub and check the backlash in the bearing shaft direction.
   Maximum:
   0.05 mm (0.0020 in.)
   If greater than the specified maximum, replace the bearing.

SA

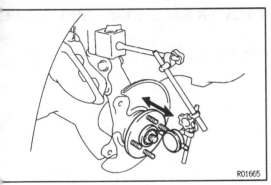

(e) Using a dial indicator, check the deviation at the surface of the axle hub outside the hub bolt.
   Maximum:
   0.07 mm (0.0028 in.)
   If greater than the specified maximum, replace the axle hub.

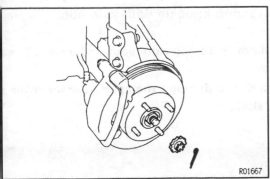

4. **REMOVE DRIVE SHAFT LOCK NUT**
   (a) Install the disc rotor and brake cylinder.
   (b) Remove the cotter pin and lock cap.
   (c) While applying the brakes, remove the nut.
   (d) Remove the brake cylinder and disc rotor.

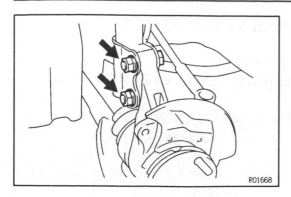

5. LOOSEN NUTS ON LOWER SIDE OF SHOCK ABSORBER

HINT: Do not remove the bolts.

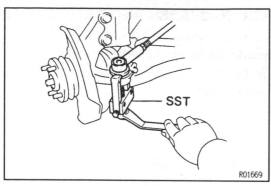

6. DISCONNECT TIE ROD END FROM STEERING KNUCKLE

(a) Remove the cotter pin and remove the nut.

(b) Using SST, disconnect the tie rod end from the steering knuckle.

SST 09628—62011

SA

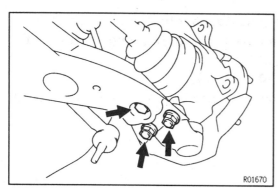

7. DISCONNECT LOWER BALL JOINT FROM LOWER ARM

Remove the bolt and the two nuts.

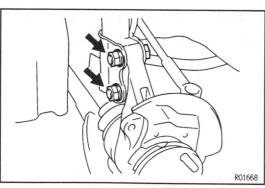

8. REMOVE STEERING KNUCKLE WITH AXLE HUB

(a) Remove the two nuts and bolts on lower side of the shock absorber.

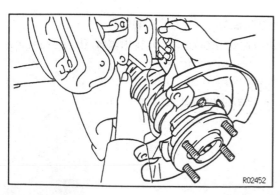

(b) Remove the steering knuckle with axle hub.

NOTICE:
- Be careful not to damage the boot and inner oil seal.
- (w/ ABS)

  Be careful not to damage the speed sensor rotor of the drive shaft.

FRONT AXLE HUB DISASSEMBLY

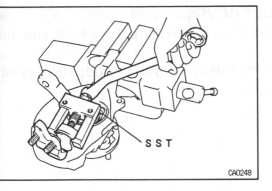

1. REMOVE DUST DEFLECTOR

Using a screwdriver, remove the dust deflector.

2. REMOVE LOWER BALL JOINT

(a) Remove the cotter pin and nut.

(b) Using SST, remove the lower ball joint.
SST 09628—62011

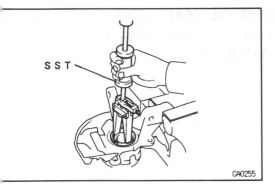

3. REMOVE INNER OIL SEAL

Using SST, remove the inner oil seal.
SST 09308—00010

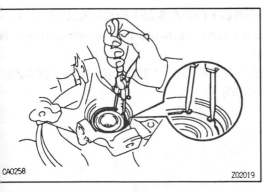

4. REMOVE SNAP RING

Using snap ring pliers, remove the snap ring.

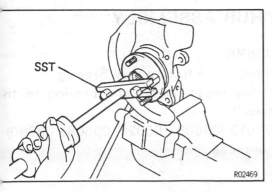

5. REMOVE AXLE HUB

(a) Using SST, remove the axle hub from the steering knuckle.
SST 09520—00031

(b) Remove the inner race (inside).

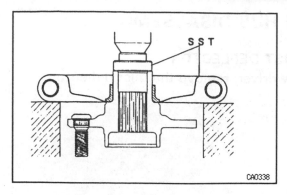

(c) Using SST and a press, remove the inner race (outside from the axle hub.
SST 09620−30010 (0925−30010),
09950−00020

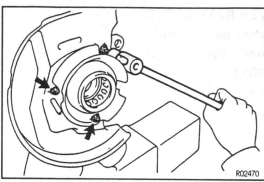

6. **REMOVE DUST COVER**
Using a torx wrench, remove the three bolts and dust cover.
Torx wrench: T30 (Part No.09042−00010 or locall manufactured tool)

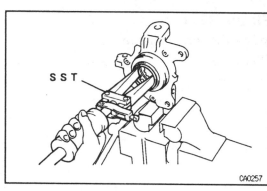

7. **REMOVE OUTER OIL SEAL**
Using SST, remove the outer oil seal.
SST 09308−00010

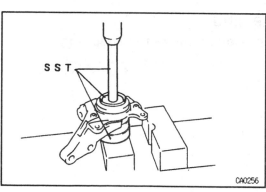

8. **REMOVE BEARING FROM STEERING KNUCKLE**
Using SST and a press, remove the bearing from the steering knuckle.
SST 09527−17011, 09608−12010 (09608−00020, 09608−00060)

SA

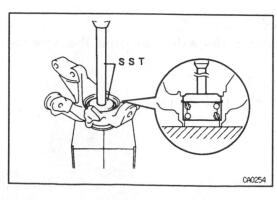

FRONT AXLE HUB ASSEMBLY

1. **INSTALL BEARING**
(a) Remove the inner races from a new bearing.
(b) Using SST and a press, install the bearing to th steering knuckle.
SST 09608−20012 (09608−03020, 09608−03090)
(c) Install the inner races.

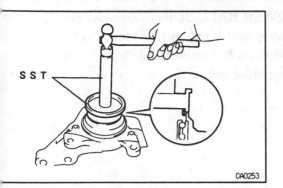

NOTICE: If the inner race and balls come loose from the bearing outer race, be sure to instal them on the same side as before.

2. **INSTALL OUTER OIL SEAL**
Using SST, install a new outer oil seal.
SST 09608–20012 (09608–03020),
    09608–32010

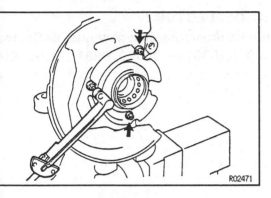

3. **INSTALL DUST COVER**
Using a torx wrench, install the dust cover with the three bolts.
Torx wrench: T30 (Part No.09042–00010 or locally manufactured tool)
Torque: 8.3 N·m (85 kgf·cm, 74 in.·lbf)

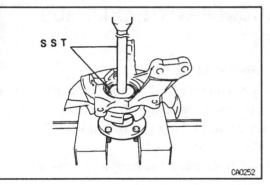

4. **INSTALL AXLE HUB**
Using SST and a press, install the axle hub.
SST 09608–20012 (09608–03020, 09608–03060)
NOTICE: Be careful not to damage the bearing.

SA

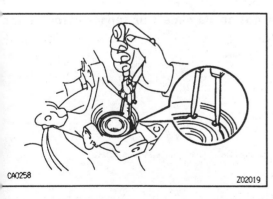

5. **INSTALL SNAP RING**
Using snap ring pliers, install the snap ring.
NOTICE: Be careful not to damage the bearing.

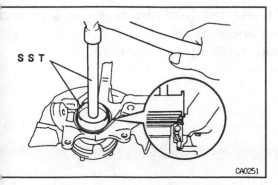

6. **INSTALL INNER OIL SEAL**
Using SST and a hammer, install a new inner oil seal.
SST 09608–20012 (09608–03020),
    09608–32010

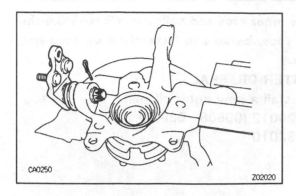

7. INSTALL LOWER BALL JOINT

(a) Install the lower ball joint and tighten the nut.
Torque: 118 N·m (1,200 kgf·cm, 87 ft·lbf)

(b) Install a new cotter pin.

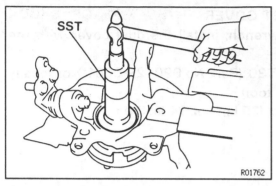

8. INSTALL DUST DEFLECTOR

Using SST and a hammer, install a new dust deflector.
SST 09316−60010 (09316−00010, 09316−00040)

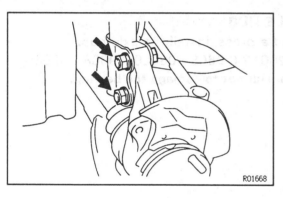

STEERING KNUCKLE WITH AXLE HUB INSTALLATION

1. INSTALL STEERING KNUCKLE

(a) Place the steering knuckle and temporarily install the two bolts and nut on lower side of shock absorber.
HINT: Coat the threads of nuts with engine oil.
NOTICE:

- **Be careful not to damage the boot and inner oil seal.**
- **(w/ ABS)**

Be careful not to damage the sensor rotor of the drive shaft.

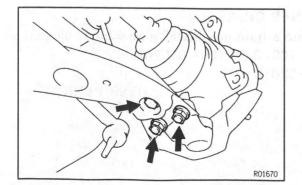

(b) Connect the lower ball joint the to lower arm and tighten the bolt and nuts.
Torque: 142 N·m (1,450 kgf·cm, 105 ft·lbf)

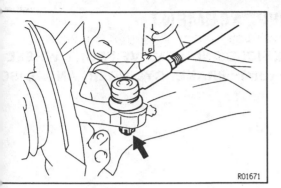

2. CONNECT TIE ROD END TO STEERING KNUCKLE
(a) Connect the tie rod end to the steering knuckle and tighten the nut.
Torque: 49 N·m (500 kgf·cm, 36 ft·lbf)
(b) Install a new cotter pin.

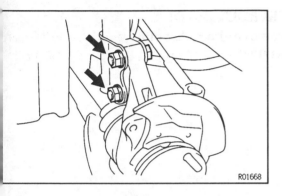

3. TORQUE BOLTS ON LOWER SIDE OF SHOCK ABSORBER
Torque: 275 N·m (2,800 kgf·cm, 203 ft·lbf)

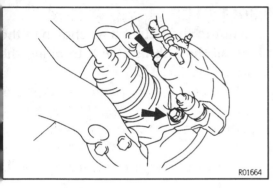

4. INSTALL FRONT BRAKE CYLINDER
(a) Install the disc rotor.
(b) Install the brake cylinder.
Torque: 88 N·m (900 kgf·cm, 65 ft·lbf)

SA

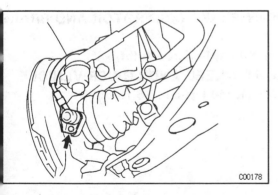

5. (w/ ABS)
INSTALL ABS SPEED SENSOR
Install the speed sensor with the bolt.
Torque: 7.8 N·m (80kgf·cm, 69 in.·lbf)

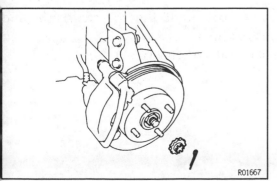

6. INSTALL DRIVE SHAFT LOCK NUT
(a) While applying the brakes, install the nut.
Torque: 216 N·m (2,200 kgf·cm, 159 ft·lbf)
(b) Install the lock cap and a new cotter pin.
7. INSTALL FRONT WHEEL AND LOWER VEHICLE
Torque: 103 N·m (1,050 kgf·cm, 76 ft·lbf)
8. INSPECT FRONT WHEEL ALIGNMENT
(See page SA−3)

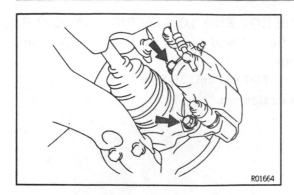

HUB BOLT REPLACEMENT

1. **JACK UP VEHICLE AND REMOVE FRONT WHEEL**
2. **REMOVE FRONT BRAKE CYLINDER AND DISC ROTOR**

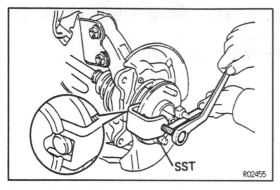

3. **REMOVE HUB BOLT**
   Using SST, remove the hub bolt.
   SST 09628—10011

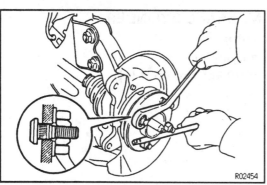

4. **INSTALL HUB BOLT**
   Install washer and nut to the hub bolt as shown in the illustration, and install the hub bolt with torquing the nut.

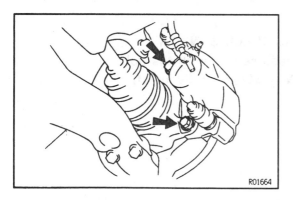

5. **INSTALL FRONT BRAKE DISC ROTOR AND BRAKE CYLINDER**
   Torque: 88 N·m (900 kgf·cm, 65 ft·lbf)
6. **INSTALL FRONT WHEEL AND LOWER VEHICLE**
   Torque: 103 N·m (1,050 kgf·cm, 76 ft·lbf)

FRONT DRIVE SHAFT

DESCRIPTION

The front drive shaft has a slideable tripod type CVJ (Constant Velocity Joint) on the differential side and Rzeppa type CVJ on the wheel side.

A dynamic damper has been mounted on the right—hand drive shaft to reduce vibration and noise.

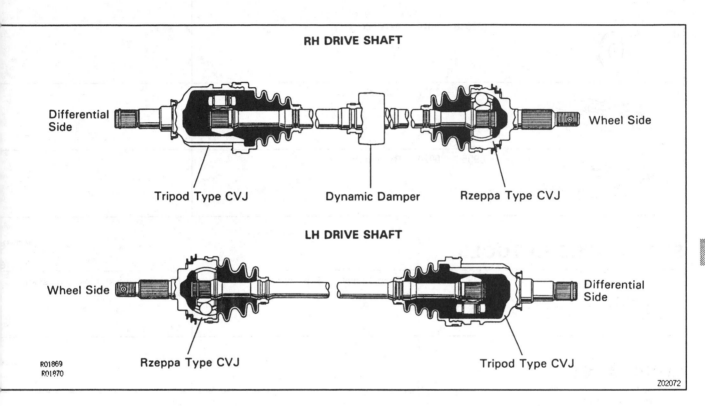

SA

PREPARATION
SST (SPECIAL SERVICE TOOLS)

	09608–16041	Front Hub Bearing Adjusting Tool
	(09608–02020)	Bolt & Nut
	(09608–02040)	Retainer
	09628–62011	Ball Joint Puller
	09950–00020	Bearing Remover

SA

RECOMMENDED TOOLS

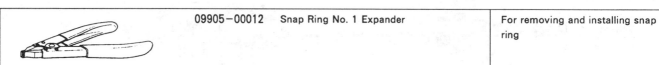

	09905–00012 Snap Ring No. 1 Expander	For removing and installing snap ring

EQUIPMENT

Torque wrench	

LUBRICANT

Item	Capacity	Classification
Outboard joint grease	120–130 g (4.2–4.6 oz.)	(TOYOTA type)
Inboard joint grease	180–190 g (6.3–6.7 oz.)	
Outboard joint grease	130–150 g (4.6–5.3 oz.)	(SAGINAW type)
Inboard joint grease	230–250 g (8.1–8.8 oz.)	

FRONT DRIVE SHAFT
COMPONENTS
(TOYOTA type)

SA007−05

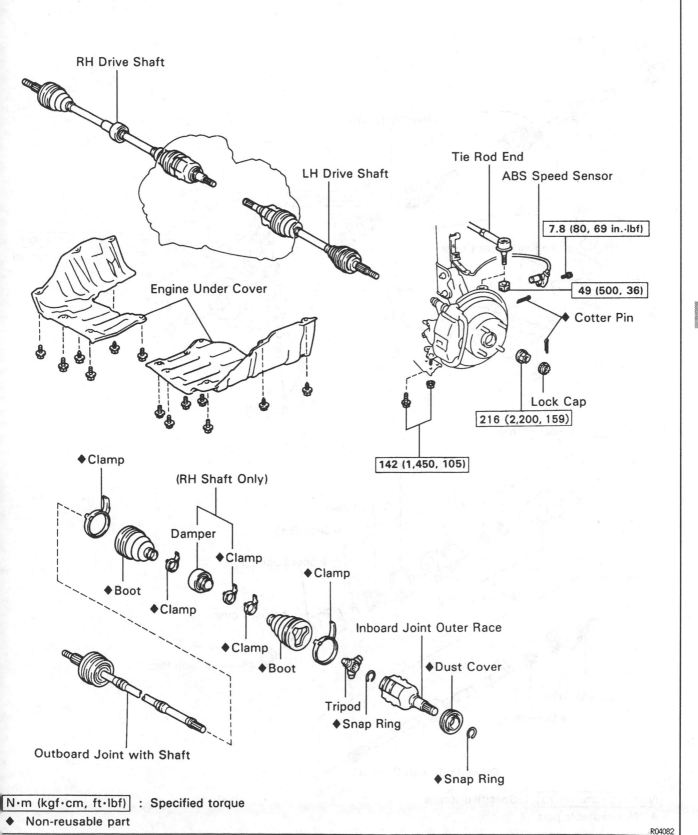

RH Drive Shaft

LH Drive Shaft

Tie Rod End

ABS Speed Sensor

7.8 (80, 69 in.·lbf)

Engine Under Cover

49 (500, 36)

Cotter Pin

Lock Cap

216 (2,200, 159)

142 (1,450, 105)

◆Clamp

(RH Shaft Only)

Damper

◆Clamp

◆Boot

◆Clamp

◆Clamp

◆Clamp

◆Boot

◆Clamp

Inboard Joint Outer Race

◆Dust Cover

Tripod

◆Snap Ring

Outboard Joint with Shaft

◆Snap Ring

N·m (kgf·cm, ft·lbf) : Specified torque

◆ Non-reusable part

R04082

SA

COMPONENTS
(SAGINAW type)

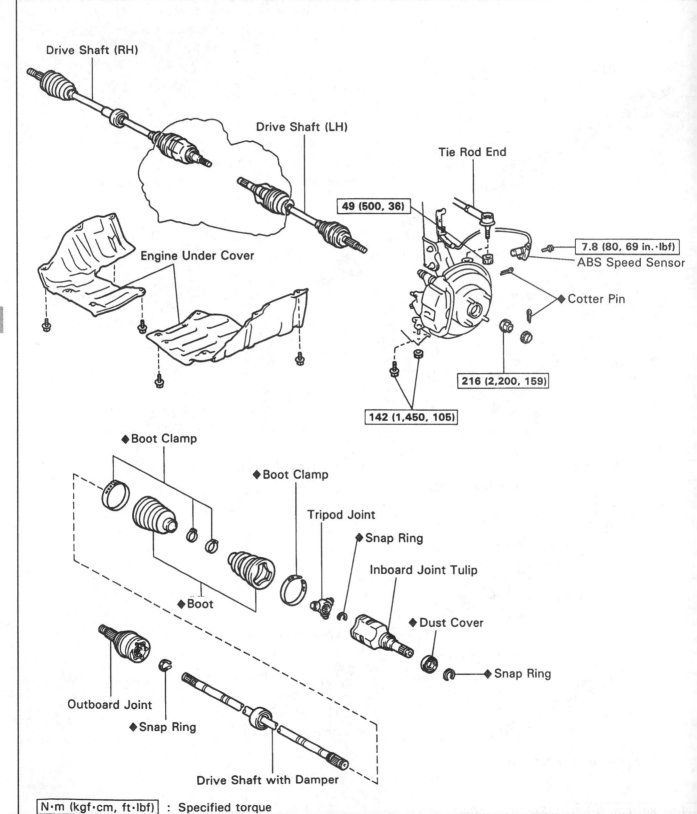

Drive Shaft (RH)

Drive Shaft (LH)

Tie Rod End

49 (500, 36)

7.8 (80, 69 in.·lbf)
ABS Speed Sensor

Engine Under Cover

Cotter Pin

216 (2,200, 159)

142 (1,450, 105)

◆Boot Clamp

◆Boot Clamp

Tripod Joint

◆Snap Ring

Inboard Joint Tulip

◆Dust Cover

◆Boot

◆Snap Ring

Outboard Joint

◆Snap Ring

Drive Shaft with Damper

N·m (kgf·cm, ft·lbf) : Specified torque

◆ Non-reusable part

R0416

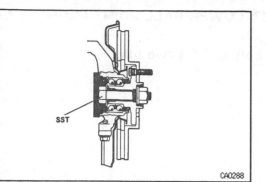

CA0288

SA0H2-01

FRONT DRIVE SHAFT REMOVAL

NOTICE:

- The hub bearing could be damage if it is subjected to the vehicle weight, such as when moving the vehicle with the drive shaft removed.

  Therefore, if it is absolutely necessary to place the vehicle weight on the hub bearing, first support it with SST.

SST 09608−16041 (09608−02020, 09608−02040)

- **(w/ ABS)**

  After disconnecting the drive shaft from the axle hub, work carefully so as not to damage the sensor rotor serrations on the drive shaft.

SA1735

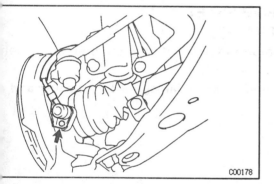

C00178

1. **JACK UP VEHICLE AND REMOVE FRONT WHEEL**
2. **REMOVE ENGINE UNDER COVERS**
3. **(M/T)**
   DRAIN TRANSAXLE OIL
   (A/T)
   DRAIN DIFFERENTIAL FLUID
4. **REMOVE ABS SPEED SENSOR**
   Remove the bolt and the speed sensor.

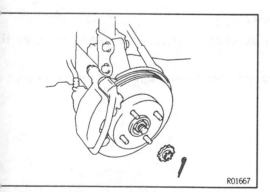

R01667

5. **REMOVE DRIVE SHAFT LOCK NUT**
(a) Remove the cotter pin and lock cap.
(b) While applying the brakes, remove the nut.

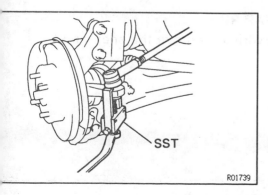

R01739

6. **DISCONNECT TIE ROD END FROM STEERING KNUCKLE**
(a) Remove the cotter pin and nut.
(b) Using SST, disconnect the tie rod end from the steering knuckle.
   SST 09628−62011

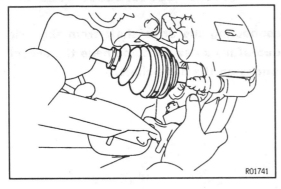

R01740

7. DISCONNECT LOWER BALL JOINT FROM LOWE ARM

Remove the bolt and the two nuts.

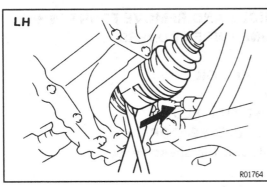

R01741

8. DISCONNECT DRIVE SHAFT FROM AXLE HUB

Using a plastic hammer, disconnect the drive sha from the axle hub.

NOTICE:

- Be careful not to damage the inner oil seal.
- (w/ ABS)
  Be careful not to damage the sensor rotor of th drive shaft.

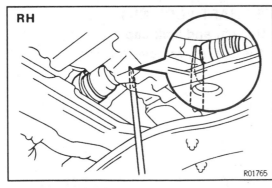

LH

R01764

9. REMOVE DRIVE SHAFT
[LH DRIVE SHAFT]

Using a hammer and hub nut wrench or an equivaler remove the drive shaft.

NOTICE: Be careful not to damage the dust cover and seal.

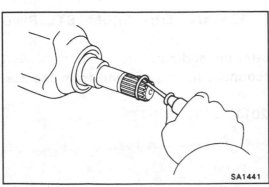

RH

R01765

[RH DRIVE SHAFT]

Using a hub nut wrench or an equivalent, remove th drive shaft.

NOTICE: Be careful not to damage the dust cover and seal.

10. REMOVE SNAP RING

Using a screwdriver, remove the snap ring.

SA1441

SA

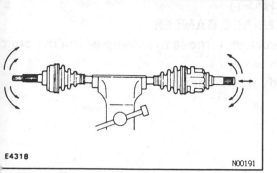

E4318   N00191

FRONT DRIVE SHAFT DISASSEMBLY (TOYOTA type)

SAOH3−02

1. CHECK DRIVE SHAFT

(a) Check to see that there is no play in the outboard joint.

(b) Check to see that the inboard joint slides smoothly in the thrust direction.

(c) Check to see that there is no obvious play in the radial direction of the inboard joint.

(d) Check the boot for damage.

2. REMOVE INBOARD JOINT BOOT CLAMPS

(a) Using a screwdriver, remove the two boot clamps.

(b) Slide the inboard joint boot toward the outboard joint.

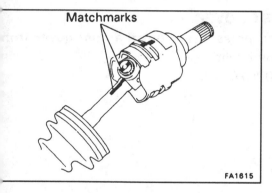

K1897   N00192

SA

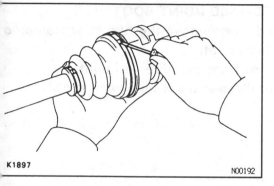

Matchmarks

FA1615

3. REMOVE INBOARD JOINT TULIP

(a) Place matchmarks on the inboard joint tulip, tripod and drive shaft.
NOTICE: Do not punch the marks.

(b) Remove the inboard joint tulip from the drive shaft.

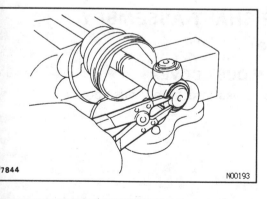

7844   N00193

4. REMOVE TRIPOD JOINT

(a) Using a snap ring expander, remove the snap ring.

(b) Place matchmarks on the shaft and tripod.
NOTICE: Do not punch the marks.

(c) Using a brass bar and hammer, remove the tripod joint from the drive shaft.
NOTICE: Do not tap the roller.

5. REMOVE INBOARD JOINT BOOT

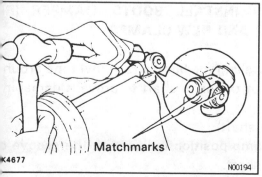

Matchmarks

K4677   N00194

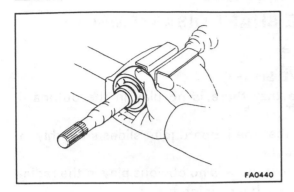

6. (RH DRIVE SHAFT)
REMOVE DYNAMIC DAMPER

(a) Using a screwdriver, remove the clamp of the dynamic damper.

(b) Remove the dynamic damper.

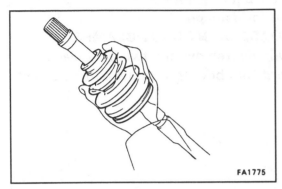

7. REMOVE OUTBOARD JOINT BOOT

(a) Using a screwdriver, remove the two boot clamps of the outboard joint boot.

(b) Remove the boot from the outboard joint.
NOTICE: Do not disassemble the outboard joint.

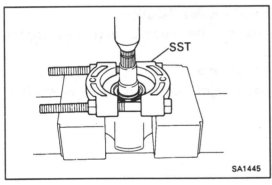

8. REMOVE DUST COVER
Using SST and press, press out the dust cover from the inboard joint tulip.
SST 09950–00020

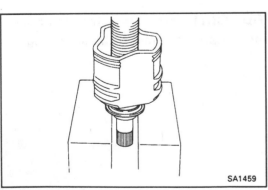

FRONT DRIVE SHAFT ASSEMBLY
(TOYOTA type)

1. INSTALL NEW DUST COVER
Using a press, press into a new dust cover.

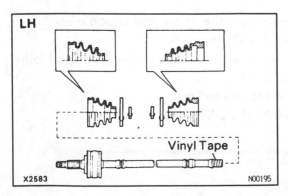

2. TEMPORARILY INSTALL BOOTS, DAMPER (RH DRIVE SHAFT) AND NEW CLAMPS
HINT:
- Before installing the boot, wrap vinyl tape around the spine of the drive shaft to prevent damaging the boot.
- (RH Drive shaft)
  Fix the clamp position in line with the groove of the drive shaft.

SA

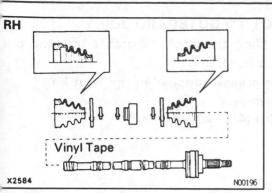

RH

Vinyl Tape

X2584   N00196

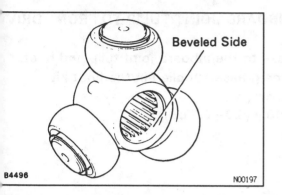

Beveled Side

B4496   N00197

3. INSTALL TRIPOD JOINT
(a) Place the beveled side of the tripod joint axial spine toward the outboard joint.

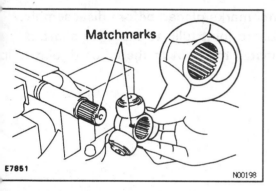

Matchmarks

E7851   N00198

(b) Align the matchmarks placed before removal.

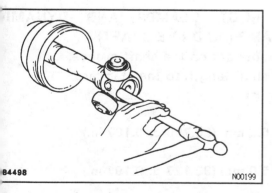

B4498   N00199

(c) Using a brass bar and hammer, tap in the tripod joint to the drive shaft.
NOTICE: Do not tap the roller.

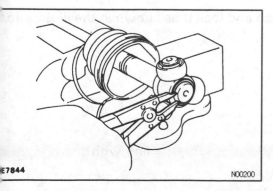

E7844   N00200

(d) Using a snap ring expander, install a new snap ring.

SA

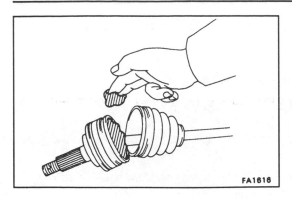

FA1616

4. INSTALL BOOT TO OUTBOARD JOINT

Before assembling the boot, fill grease into the out
board joint and boot.

HINT: Use the grease supplied in the boot kit.

Grease capacity:

120–130 g (4.2–4.6 oz.)

Grease color:

Black

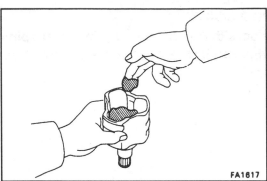

FA1617

**5. INSTALL INBOARD JOINT TULIP TO FRONT DRIVE
SHAFT**

(a) Pack in grease to the inboard joint tulip and boot.

HINT: Use the grease supplied in the boot kit.

Grease capacity:

180–190 g (6.3–6.7 oz.)

Grease color:

Yellow

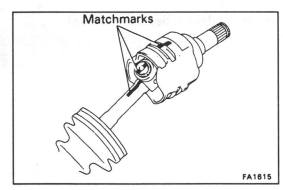

Matchmarks

FA1615

(b) Align the matchmarks placed before disassembly.

(c) Install the inboard joint tulip to the drive shaft.

(d) Temporarily install the boot to the inboard joint tulip

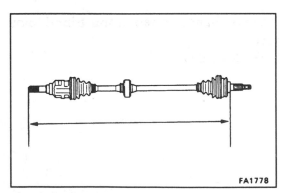

FA1778

**6. ASSEMBLY BOOT CLAMPS AND DYNAMIC
DAMPER CLAMP (RH DRIVE SHAFT)**

(a) Be sure the boots are on the shaft groove.

(b) Set the drive shaft length to the standard.

Standard length:

LH shaft

528.3 ± 5.0 mm (20.799 ± 0.197 in.)

RH shaft

842.7 ± 5.0 mm (33.177 ± 0.197 in.)

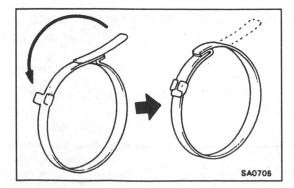

SA0705

(c) Bend the clamp and lock it as shown in the illustration

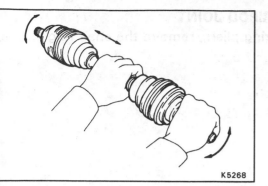

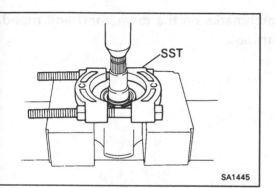

SAOHZ—01

FRONT DRIVE SHAFT DISASSEMBLY (SAGINAW type)

1. **CHECK DRIVE SHAFT**
   (a) Check to see that there is no play in the outboad joint.

   (b) Check to see that the inboard joint slides smoothy in the thrust direction.

   (c) Check to see that there is no obvious play in the radial direction of the inboard joint.

   (d) Check for damage to boots.

2. **REMOVE DUST COVER**

   Using SST and press, press out the dust cover from the inboard joint tulip.

   SST 09950—00020

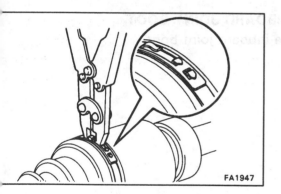

3. **REMOVE INBOARD JOINT BOOT CLAMPS**
   (a) Using a boot clamp tool, draw hooks together and remove the large clamp.

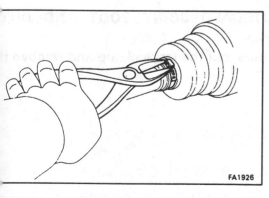

(b) Using side cutter, cut the small boot clamp and remove it.

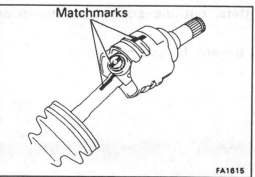

4. **REMOVE INBOARD JOINT TULIP**
   (a) Place the matchmarks on the inboard joint tulip, tripod and drive shaft.

   NOTICE: Do not punch the marks.

   (b) Remove the inboard joint tulip from the drive shaft.

SA

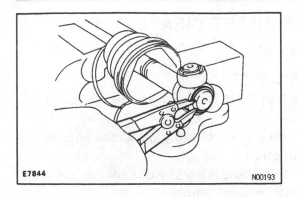

5. REMOVE TRIPOD JOINT
(a) Using snap ring pliers, remove the snap ring.

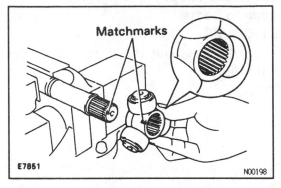

(b) Place the matchmarks on the drive shaft and tripod.
(c) Pull out the trupod.

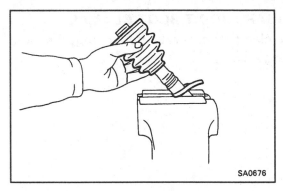

6. REMOVE INBOARD JOINT BOOT
Slide out the inboard joint boot.

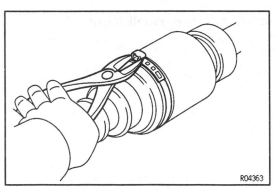

7. REMOVE OUTBOARD JOINT BOOT AND OUT BOARD JOINT
(a) Using side cutters, cut the large clamp and remove it

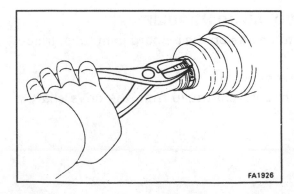

(b) Using side cutters, cut the small boot clamp an remove it.
(c) Move the boot toward damper temporary.

SA

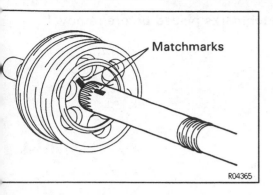

(d) Place the matchmarks on the outboard joint's inner-race and drive shaft.

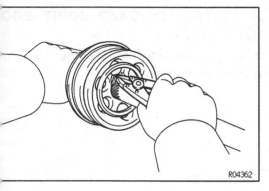

(e) Using snap ring pliers, expand the snap ring and push off the outboard joint.

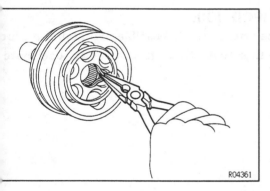

(f) Remove the snap ring.
(g) Slide out the outboard joint boot.
     NOTICE: Do not disassembly the outboard joint further.

SA

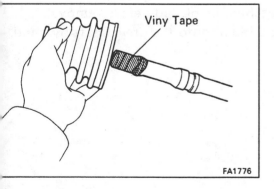

Viny Tape

FRONT DRIVE SHAFT ASSEMBLY (SAGINAW type)

SAOJO—01

1. TEMPORARILY INSTALL OUTBOARD JOINT BOOT AND NEW BOOT CLAMPS
     HINT: Before installing the boot, wrap vinyl tape around the spline of the drive shaft to prevent damaging the boot.

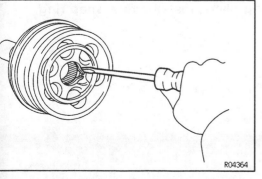

(a) Install a new snap ring to the outboard joint.

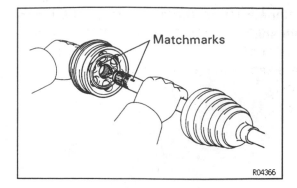

(b)   Align the matchmarks placed before removal.

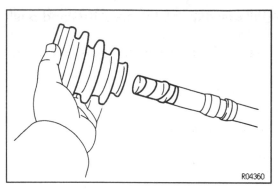

2.   **TEMPORARILY INSTALL INBOARD JOINT BOO**
     AND NEW BOOT CLAMPS
     Temporarily install the boot and two new boot clamp
     for the inboard joint to the drive shaft.

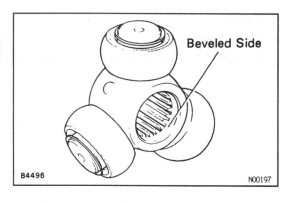

3.   **INSTALL TRIPOD JOINT**
     NOTICE: Please note that it is possible to install the tripo
     joint facing either way. To install correctly, use match
     marks.

SA

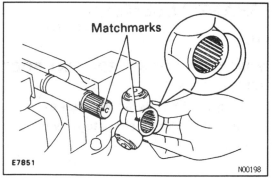

(a)   Align the matchmarks placed before removal.
(b)   Push the tripod joint onto the drive shaft by hand.

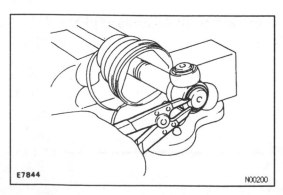

(c)   Using snap ring pliers, install a new snap ring.

FA1616

4. INSTALL BOOT TO OUTBOARD JOINT

Brfore assembling the boot, fill grease into the outboard joint and boot.

HINT: Use the grease supplied in the boot kit.

Greace capacity:
    130 — 150 g (4.6—5.3 oz.)
Greace color:
    Black

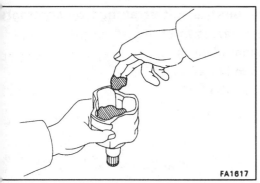

FA1617

5. INSTALL INBOARD JOINT TULIP TO FRONT DRIVE SHAFT

(a) Pack in the grease to the inboard joint tulip and boot.

HINT: Use the grease supplide in the boot kit.

Greace capacity:
    230 — 250 g (8.1—8.8 oz.)
Greace color:
    Yellow ocher

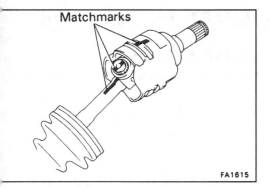

Matchmarks

FA1615

(b) Align the matchmarks placed before remove, and install the inboard joint tulip to the drive shaft.

(c) Install the boot to the inboard joint tulip.

SA

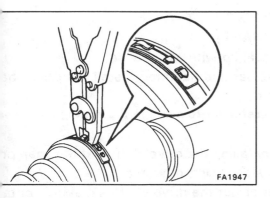

FA1947

6. ASSEMBLY BOOT CLAMPS

(a) Be sure the inboard boot(large side) is on the shaft groove.

(b) Using a boot clamp tool, place pincer jaws in closing hooks of large clamp.

(c) Secure clamp by drawing at closing hooks together.

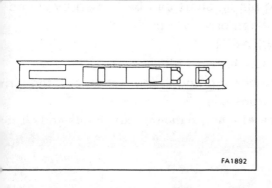

FA1892

(d) Check that the clamp at closed position is the same as in the illustration.

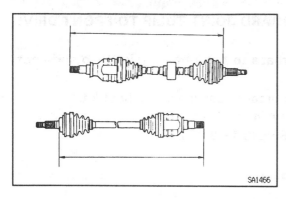

FA1929

(e) Be sure the inboard boot(small side) is on the sha
groove.

(f) Using a boot clamp tool, tighten the clamp.

(g) Be sure the outboard boot (large and small side) is c
the shaft groove.

(h) Using a boot clamp tool, tighten the clamp.

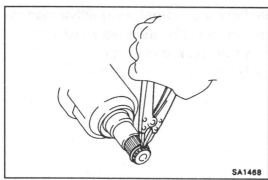

SA1466

(i) Insure that the boot is not stretched or contracte
when the drive shaft is at standard length.
Drive shaft standard length:
LH 540.2 mm (21.268 in.)
RH 857.4 mm (33.756 in.)

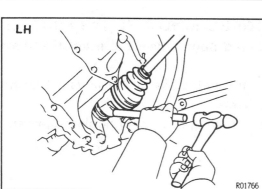

SA1468

FRONT DRIVE SHAFT INSTALLATION

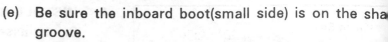

1. INSTALL NEW SNAP RING
Using a snap ring expander, install a new snap ring

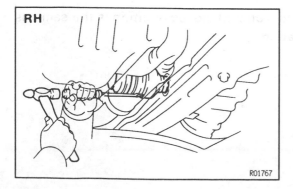

LH

R01766

RH

R01767

2. INSTALL DRIVE SHAFT
[LH DRIVE SHAFT]
(a) Coat the oil seal lip with MP grease.
(b) Using a brass bar and hammer, install the drive sha
to the transaxle.
NOTICE: Be careful not to damage the boots and oil se
HINT:
- Before installing the drive shaft, set the snap rir
opening side facing downward.
- Whether or not the drive shaft is making conta
with the pinion shaft can be known by sound
feeling when driving it in.
[RH DRIVE SHAFT]
(a) Coat the oil seal lip with MP grease.
(b) Using a screwdriver and hammer, install the driv
shaft to the transaxle.
NOTICE: Be careful not to damage the boots and oil se
HINT:

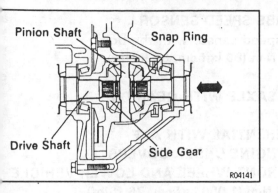

Pinion Shaft Snap Ring
Drive Shaft Side Gear

- Before installing the drive shaft, set the snap ring opening side facing downward.
- Whether or not the drive shaft is making contact with the pinion shaft can be known by sound or feeling when driving it in.

3. CHECK INSTALLATION OF FRONT DRIVE SHAFT

(a) Check that there is 2—3mm (0.08—0.12in.) of play in axial direction.

(b) Check that the drive shaft will not come out by trying to pull it completely out by hand.

4. CONNECT DRIVE SHAFT TO AXLE HUB
NOTICE:

- Be careful not to damage the boots and inner oil seal.

- (w/ ABS)
  Be careful not to damage the speed sensor rotor of the drive shaft.

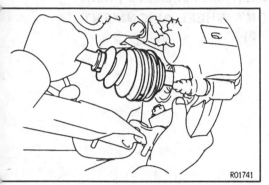

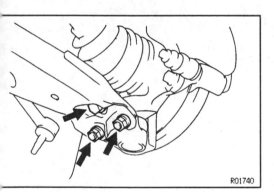

5. CONNECT LOWER BALL JOINT TO LOWER ARM

Connect the lower ball joint to the lower arm and tighten the bolt and two nuts.
Torque: 142 N·m (1,450 kgf·cm, 105 ft·lbf)

SA

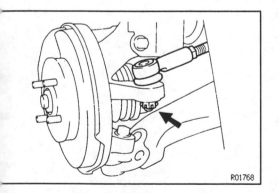

6. CONNECT TIE ROD END TO STEERING KNUCKLE

(a) Connect the tie rod end to steering knuckle and tighten the nut.
Torque: 49 N·m (500 kgf·cm, 36 ft·lbf)

(b) Install a new cotter pin.

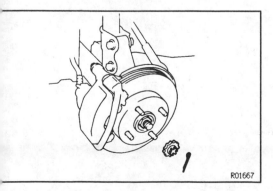

7. INSTALL DRIVE SHAFT LOCK NUT

(a) Tighten the lock nut.
Torque: 216 N·m (2,200 kgf·cm, 159 ft·lbf)

(b) Install the lock cap and a new cotter pin.

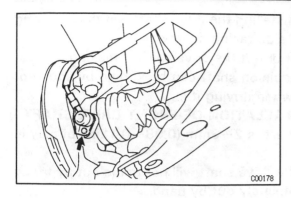

C00178

8. **INSTALL ABS SPEED SENSOR**
Install the speed sensor with the bolt.
Torque: 7.8 N·m (80 kgf·cm, 69 in.·lbf)

9. **(M/T)**
FILL TRANSAXLE WITH GEAR OIL
(A/T)
FILL DIFFERENTIAL WITH ATF

10. **INSTALL ENGINE UNDER COVERS**

11. **INSTALL FRONT WHEEL AND LOWER VEHICLE**
Torque: 103 N·m (1,050 kgf·cm, 76 ft·lbf)

12. **INSPECT FRONT WHEEL ALIGNMENT**
(See page SA—3)

FRONT SUSPENSION

DESCRIPTION

The front suspension is Mcpherson strut type suspension with L—shape lower arm which functions as a strut bar.

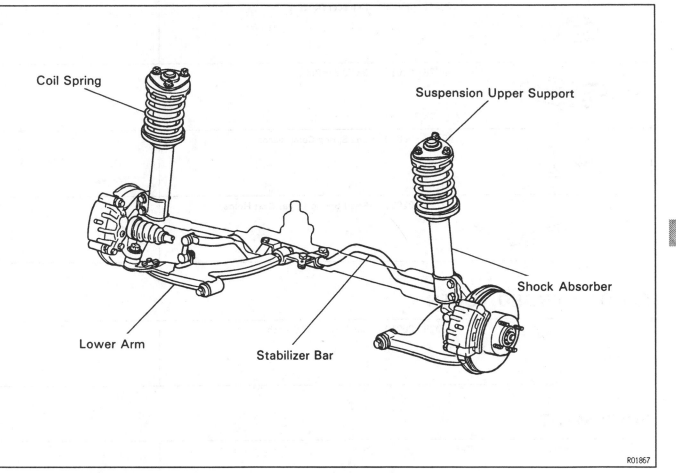

Coil Spring

Suspension Upper Support

Shock Absorber

Lower Arm

Stabilizer Bar

PREPARATION
SST (SPECIAL SERVICE TOOLS)

	09316−60010	Transmission & Transfer Bearing Replacer	Dust deflector installation
	(09316−00010)	Replacer Pipe	
	(09316−00040)	Replacer "C"	
	09628−62011	Ball Joint Puller	
	09727−30020	Coil Spring Compressor	
	09729−22031	Front Spring Upper Seat Holder	

RECOMMENDED TOOLS

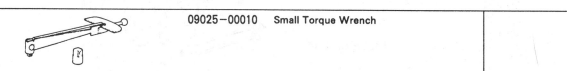	09025−00010	Small Torque Wrench	

EQUIPMENT

Torque wrench	

FRONT SHOCK ABSORBER
COMPONENTS

SA00A-03

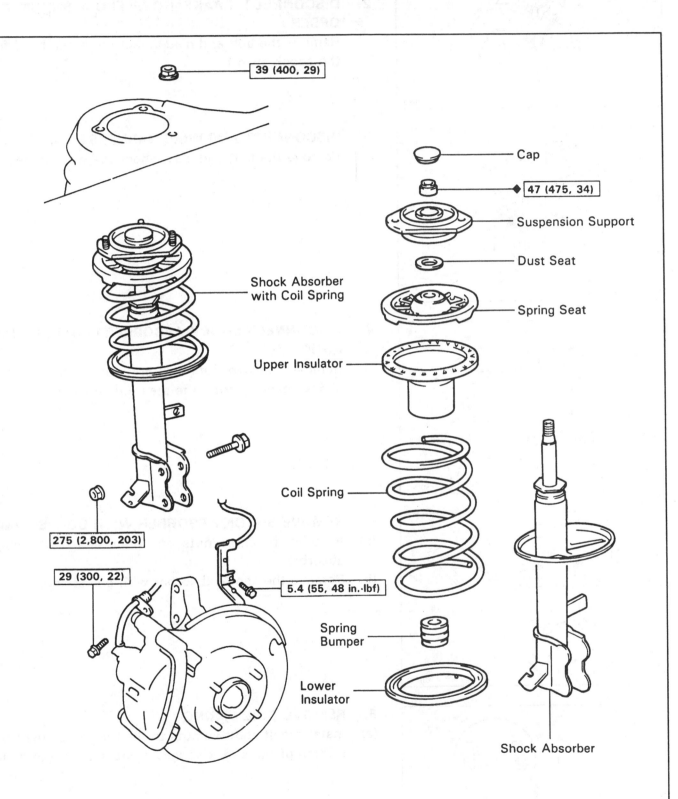

39 (400, 29)

Cap

◆ 47 (475, 34)

Suspension Support

Dust Seat

Shock Absorber
with Coil Spring

Spring Seat

Upper Insulator

Coil Spring

275 (2,800, 203)

29 (300, 22)

5.4 (55, 48 in.·lbf)

Spring
Bumper

Lower
Insulator

Shock Absorber

SA

N·m (kgf·cm, ft·lbf) : Specified torque

◆ Non-reusable part

R03852

FRONT SHOCK ABSORBER REMOVAL

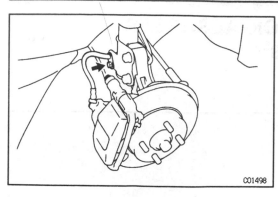

1. **JACK UP VEHICLE AND REMOVE FRONT WHEEL**
2. **DISCONNECT BRAKE HOSE FROM SHOCK ABSORBER**

   Remove the bolt and disconnect the brake hose from the shock absorber.

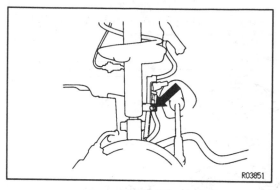

3. **DISCONNECT ABS WIRE HARNESS**

   Remove the bolt and disconnect the wire harness.

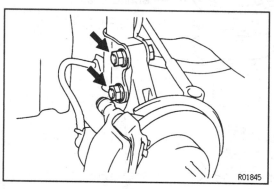

4. **DISCONNECT SHOCK ABSORBER FROM STEERING KNUCKLE**

   Remove the two nuts and bolts and disconnect the shock absorber from the steering knuckle.

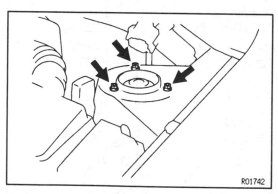

5. **REMOVE SHOCK ABSORBER WITH COIL SPRING**
   (a) Remove the three nuts on upper side of the shock absorber.
   (b) Remove the shock absorber with coil spring.

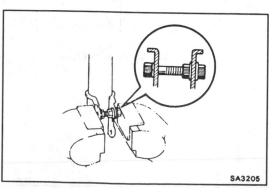

6. **REMOVE COIL SPRING**
   (a) Install a bolt and two nuts to the bracket at the lower portion of the shock absorber and secure it in a vice.

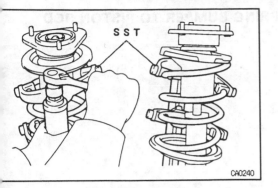

(b) Using SST, compress the coil spring.
SST 09727—30020

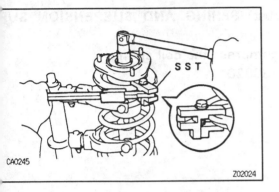

(c) Using SST to hold the spring seat, remove the nut.
SST 09729—22031
(d) Remove the following parts.
- Suspension support
- Dust seal
- Spring seat
- Upper insulator
- Coil spring
- Spring bumper
- Lower insulator

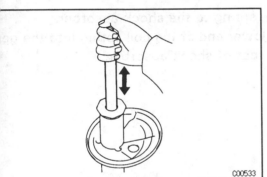

FRONT SHOCK ABSORBER INSPECTION

SA

INSPECT SHOCK ABSORBER

Compress and extend the shock absorber rod and check that there is no abnormal resistance or unusual operation sounds.

If there is any abnormality, replace the shock absorber with a new one.

NOTICE: When discarding the shock absorber, use the following procedure.

FRONT SHOCK ABSORBER DISPOSAL

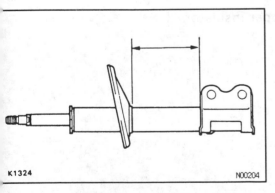

1. **FULLY EXTEND SHOCK ABSORBER ROD**
2. **DRILL HOLE TO REMOVE GAS FROM CYLINDER**
   Using a drill, make a hole in the cylinder as shown to remove the gas inside.
   CAUTION: The gas coming out is harmless, but be careful of chips which may fly up when drilling.

FRONT SHOCK ABSORBER INSTALLATION

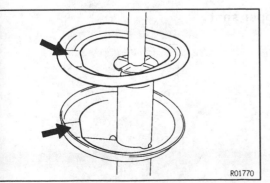

1. **INSTALL LOWER INSULATOR ONTO SHOCK ABSORBER**

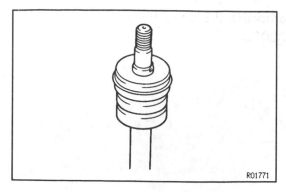

2. INSTALL SPRING BUMPER TO PISTON ROD

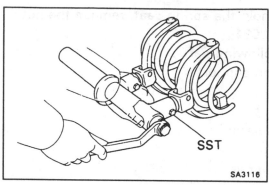

3. INSTALL COIL SPRING AND SUSPENSION SUP-PORT
(a) Using SST, compress the coil spring.
SST 09727−30020

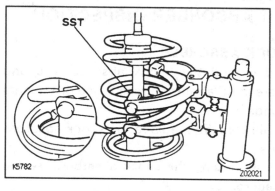

(b) Install the coil spring to the shock absorber.
HINT: Fit the lower end of the coil spring into the gap of the spring seat of shock absorber.

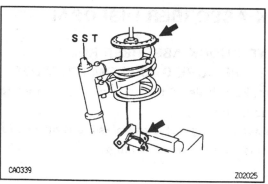

(c) Install the upper insulator.

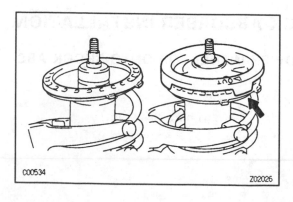

(d) Install the upper seat.

SA

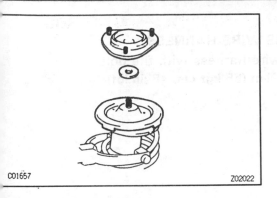

(e) Install the dust seal and suspension support.

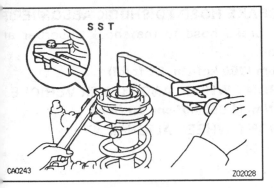

(f) Using SST to hold the spring seat, install a new nut.
SST 09729—22031
Torque: 47 N·m (475 kgf·cm, 34 ft·lbf)

(g) Remove the SST.

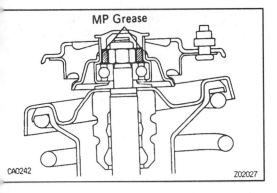

(h) Pack MP grease into the suspension support.

(i) Install the dust cover.

SA

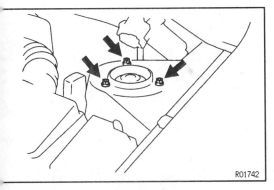

4. **INSTALL SHOCK ABSORBER WITH COIL SPRING**
Place the chock absorber and install the three nuts.
Torque: 39 N·m (400 kgf·cm, 29 ft·lbf)

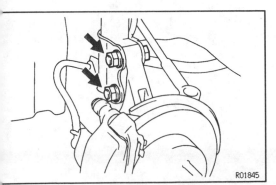

5. **CONNECT SHOCK ABSORBER TO STEERING KNU-CKLE**

(a) Coat the threads of the bolt with engine oil.

(b) Install the two bolts and nuts.

(c) Torque the bolts.
Torque: 275 N·m (2,800 kgf·cm, 203 ft·lbf)

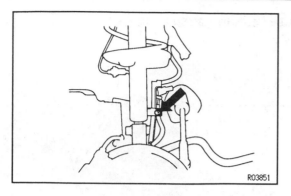

R03851

6. **(w/ ABS)**
CLAMP ABS WIRE HARNESS
Clamp the wire harness with the bolt.
Torque: 5.4 N·m (55 kgf·cm, 48 ;in.lbf)

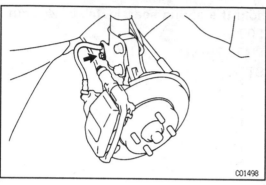

C01498

7. **CONNECT BRAKE HOSE TO SHOCK ABSORBER**
Connect the brake hose to the shock absorber ar
install the bolt.
Torque: 29 N·m (300 kgf·cm, 22 ft·lbf)

8. **INSTALL FRONT WHEEL AND LOWER VEHICLE**
Torque: 103 N·m (1,050 kgf·cm, 76 ft·lbf)

9. **INSPECT FRONT WHEEL ALIGNMENT**
(See page SA—3)

LOWER SUSPENSION ARM
COMPONENTS

SA00B-04

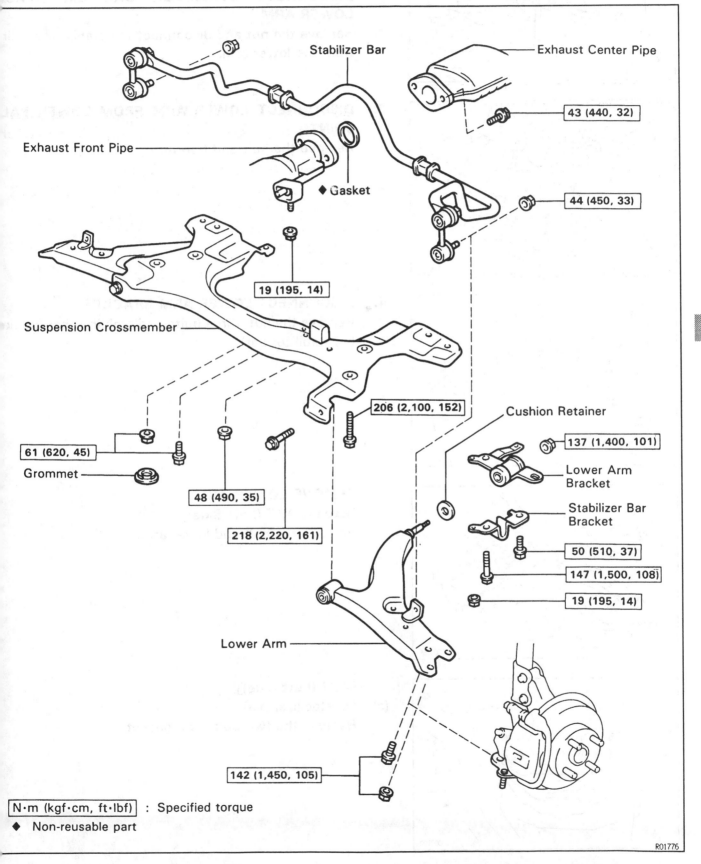

Stabilizer Bar

Exhaust Center Pipe

Exhaust Front Pipe

◆ Gasket

43 (440, 32)

44 (450, 33)

19 (195, 14)

Suspension Crossmember

206 (2,100, 152)

Cushion Retainer

137 (1,400, 101)

Lower Arm
Bracket

Stabilizer Bar
Bracket

50 (510, 37)

147 (1,500, 108)

19 (195, 14)

61 (620, 45)

Grommet

48 (490, 35)

218 (2,220, 161)

Lower Arm

142 (1,450, 105)

N·m (kgf·cm, ft·lbf) : Specified torque

◆ Non-reusable part

SA

R01776

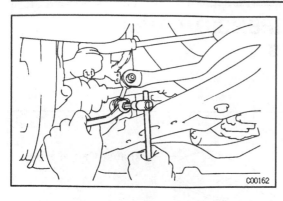

LOWER ARM REMOVAL

1. **JACK UP VEHICLE AND REMOVE FRONT WHEEL**
2. **(W/STABILIZER BAR)**
   DISCONNECT STABILIZER BAR LINK FROM LOWER ARM
   Remove the nut and disconnect the stabilizer bar link from the lower arm.

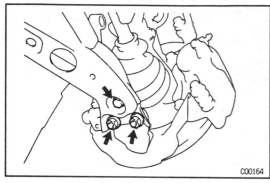

3. **DISCONNECT LOWER ARM FROM LOWER BALL JOINT**
   Remove the bolt and two nuts.

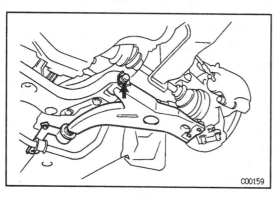

4. **DISCONNECT LOWER ARM BRACKET**
   Remove the nut, three bolts and stabilizer bar bracket (w/stabilizer bar).

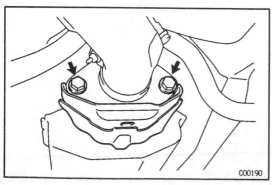

5. **REMOVE LOWER ARM**
   [Except A/T (Left Side)]
   Remove the bolt and lower arm.

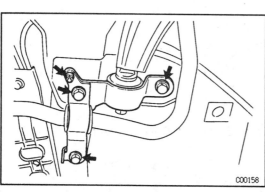

[A/T (Left Side)]
(a) (w/stabilizer bar)
   Remove the two bolts and gasket.

(b) Remove the nut.

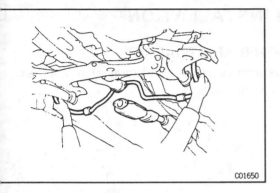

(c) (w/stabilizer bar)
     Remove the stabilizer bar.

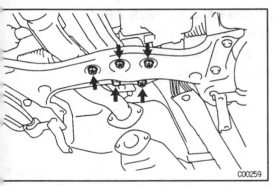

(d) Remove the grommet.
(e) Remove the four nuts and bolt.

SA

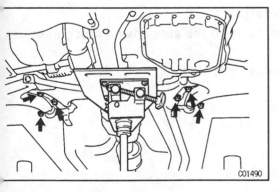

(f) Support the suspension cross member with a jack.
(g) Remove the six bolts and suspension cross member with the lower arms.

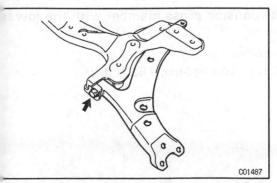

(h) Remove the bolt and lower arm.

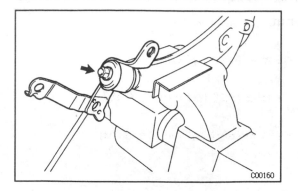

6. REMOVE LOWER ARM BRACKET

Remove the nut, lower arm bracket and cushion retainer.

LOWER ARM INSTALLATION

1. INSTALL LOWER ARM BRACKET

(a) Install the cushion retainer and lower arm bracket.

(b) Temporarily install the nut.

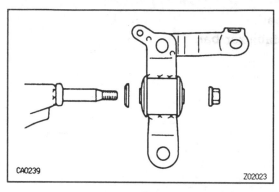

2. TEMPORARILY INSTALL LOWER ARM
[Except A/T (Left Side)]

(a) Install the lower arm to the body.

(b) Temporarily install the bolt.

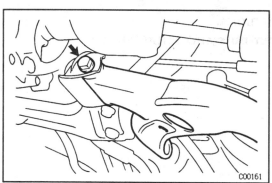

[A/T (Left Side)]

(a) Install the lower arm to the suspension cross member.

(b) Temporarily install the bolt.

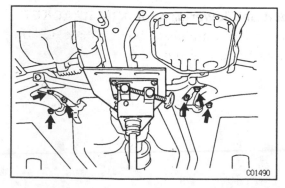

(c) Jack up the suspension cross member with the lower arms.

(d) Install the six bolts.
Torque: 206 N·m (2,100 kgf·cm, 152 ft·lbf)

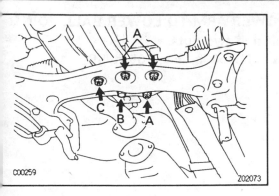

(e) Install the four nuts and bolt.
Nut A:
    Torque: 48 N·m (490 kgf·cm, 35 ft·lbf)
Bolt B:
    Torque: 61 N·m (620 kgf·cm, 45 ft·lbf)
Nut C:
    Torque: 61 N·m (620 kgf·cm, 45 ft·lbf)

(f) Install the grommet.

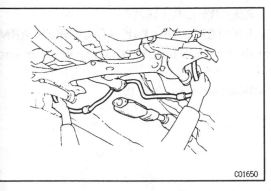

(g) (w/stabilizer bar)
Install the stabilizer bar.

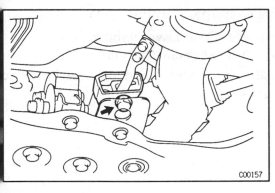

(h) Install the nut.
Toruqe: 19 N·m (195 kgf·cm, 14 ft·lbf)

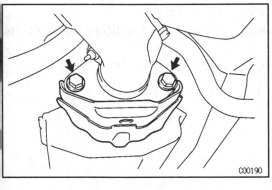

(i) (w/stabilizer bar)
Install a new gasket and the two bolts.
Torque: 43 N·m (440 kgf·cm, 32 ft·lbf)

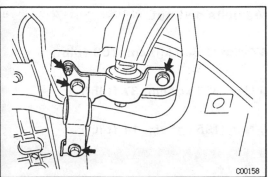

3. **TEMPORARILY INSTALL LOWER ARM BRACKET**
Temporarily install the stabilizer bar bracket (w/stabilizer bar), three bolts and nut.

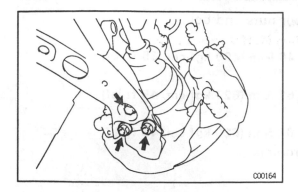

4. CONNECT LOWER ARM TO LOWER BALL JOINT

Install the bolt and two nuts.

Torque: 142 N·m (1,450 kgf·cm, 105 ft·lbf)

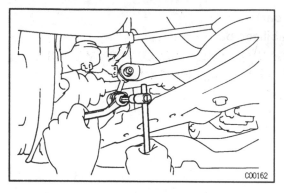

5. (W/STABILIZER BAR)
CONNECT STABILIZER BAR LINK TO LOWER ARM

Connect the stabilizer bar link to the lower arm and install the nut.

Torque: 44 N·m (450 kgf·cm, 33 ft·lbf)

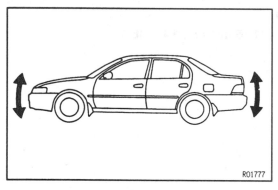

6. STABILIZE SUSPENSION

(a) Install the front wheel and lower vehicle.

Torque: 103 N·m (1,050 kgf·cm, 76 ft·lbf)

(b) Bounce the vehicle up and down several times to stabilize the suspension.

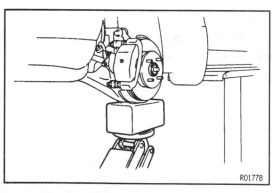

7. TORQUE BOLTS AND NUTS

(a) Jack up the vehicle and support the body with stands.

(b) Remove the front wheel.

(c) Support the lower arm with a jack.

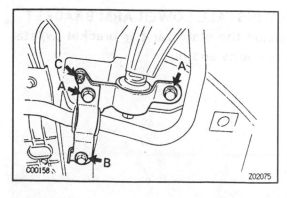

(d) Torque the three bolts and nut.

Bolt A:

   Torque: 147 N·m (1,500 kgf·cm, 108 ft·lbf)

Bolt B:

   Torque: 50 N·m (510 kgf·cm, 37 ft·lbf)

Nut C:

   Torque: 19 N·m (195 kgf·cm, 14 ft·lbf)

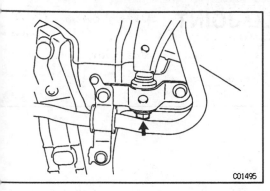

(e) Torque the nut.
Toruqe: 137 N·m (1,400 kgf·cm, 101 ft·lbf)

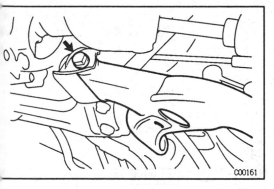

(f) Torque the bolt.
Torque: 218 N·m (2,220 kgf·cm, 161 ft·lbf)

8. INSTALL FRONT WHEEL AND LOWER VEHICLE
Torque: 103 N·m (1,050 kgf·cm, 76 ft·lbf)

9. INSPECT FRONT WHEEL ALIGNMENT
(See page SA−3)

SA

LOWER BALL JOINT
COMPONENTS

SA02Z—04

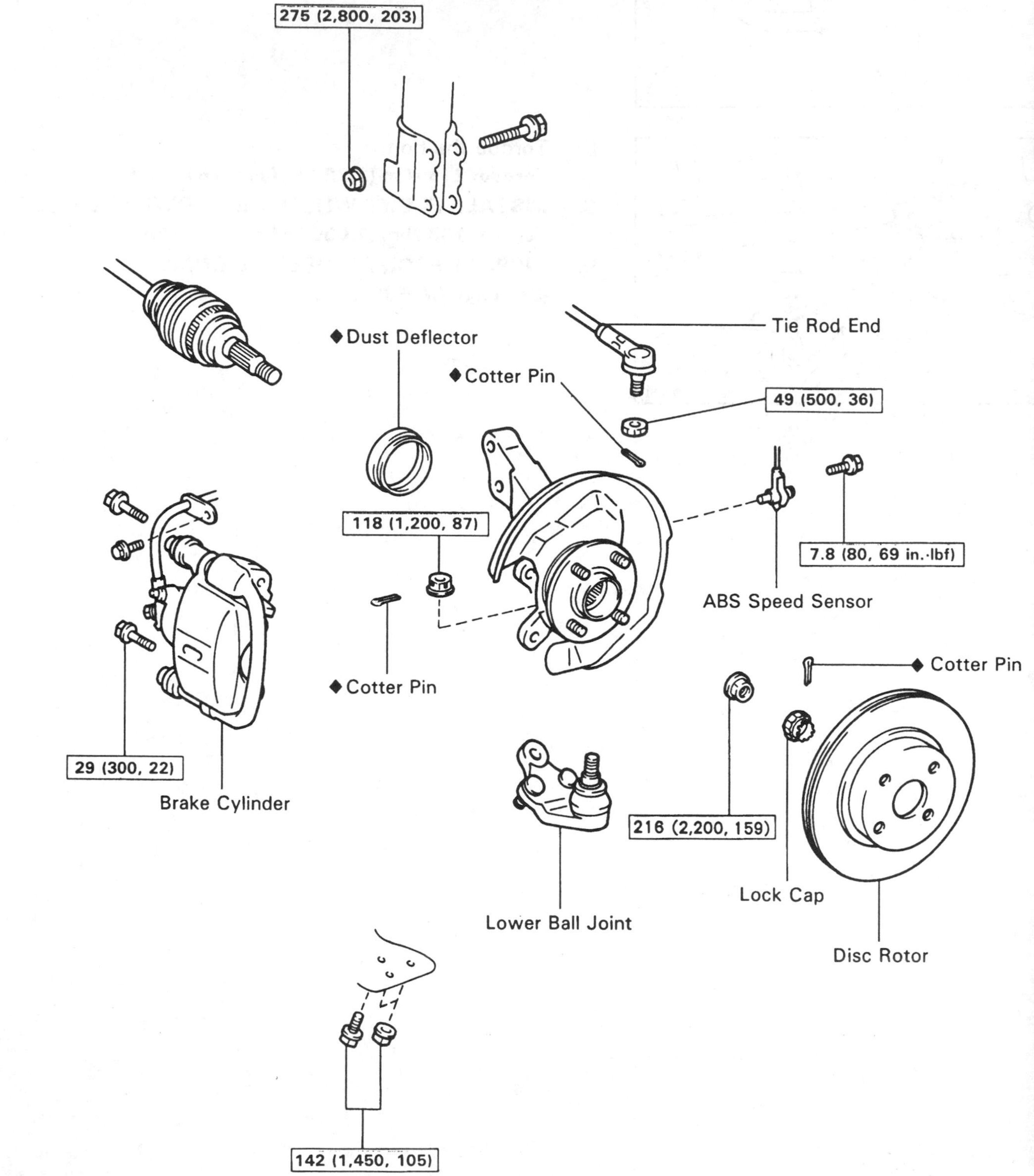

275 (2,800, 203)

◆ Dust Deflector

Tie Rod End

◆ Cotter Pin

49 (500, 36)

118 (1,200, 87)

7.8 (80, 69 in.·lbf)

ABS Speed Sensor

◆ Cotter Pin

29 (300, 22)

Brake Cylinder

◆ Cotter Pin

Lower Ball Joint

216 (2,200, 159)

Lock Cap

Disc Rotor

142 (1,450, 105)

N·m (kgf·cm, ft·lbf) : Specified torque

◆ Non-reusable part

R03853

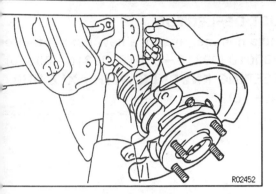

LOWER BALL JOINT REMOVAL

1. REMOVE STEERING KNUCKLE WITH AXLE HUB
(See page SA−11)

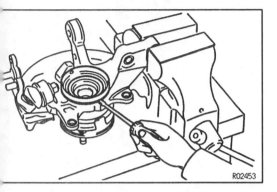

2. REMOVE LOWER BALL JOINT
(a) Using a screwdriver, remove the dust deflector.

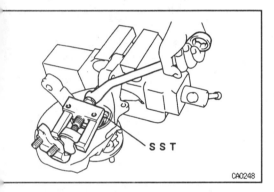

(b) Remove the cotter pin and nut.
(c) Using SST, remove the lower ball joint.
SST 09628−62011

LOWER BALL JOINT INSPECTION

INSPECT BALL JOINT FOR ROTATION CONDITION

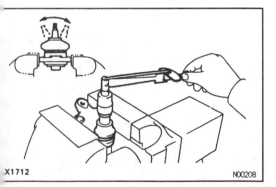

(a) As shown, flip the ball joint stud back and forth 5 times before installing the nut.
(b) Using a torque gauge, turn the nut continuously one turn per 2−4 seconds and take the torque reading on the 5th turn.
Turning torque:
1.0−2.9 N·m (10−30 kgf·cm, 8.7−26 in.·lbf)

LOWER BALL JOINT INSTALLATION

1. INSTALL LOWER BALL JOINT
(a) Install the lower ball joint and tighten the nut.
Torque: 118 N·m (1,200 kgf·cm, 87 ft·lbf)
(b) Install a new cotter pin.

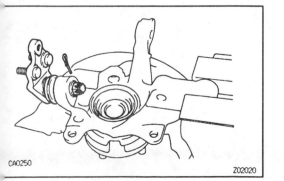

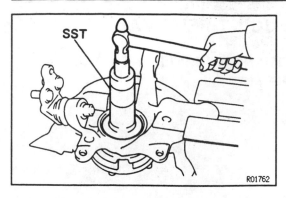

2. **INSTALL DUST DEFLECTOR**
Using SST and a hammer, install a new dust deflector.
SST 09316—60010 (09316—00010, 09316—00040)

3. **INSTALL STEERING KNUCKLE WITH AXLE HUB**
(See page SA—16)

SA

STABILIZER BAR
COMPONENTS

8A033—06

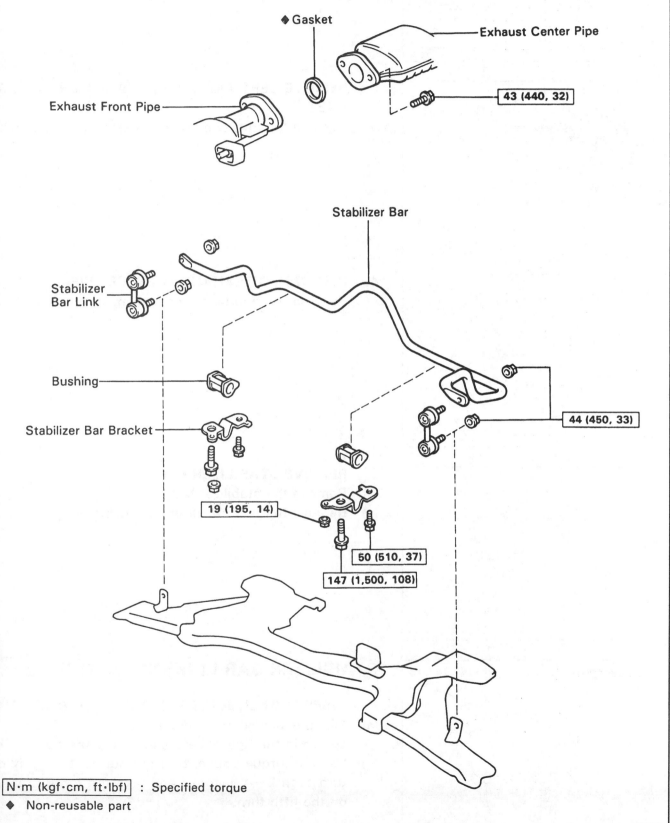

◆ Gasket

Exhaust Center Pipe

Exhaust Front Pipe

43 (440, 32)

Stabilizer Bar

Stabilizer
Bar Link

Bushing

Stabilizer Bar Bracket

44 (450, 33)

19 (195, 14)

50 (510, 37)

147 (1,500, 108)

N·m (kgf·cm, ft·lbf) : Specified torque
◆ Non-reusable part

R01807

SA

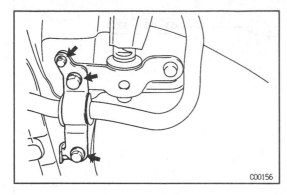

STABILIZER BAR REMOVAL

1. **JACK UP VEHICLE AND REMOVE LEFT AND RIGH** FRONT WHEELS
2. **REMOVE LEFT AND RIGHT STABILIZER BAR LINK**

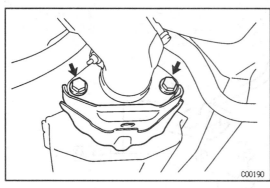

3. **REMOVE LEFT AND RIGHT STABILIZER BAR BRA CKET**
   Remove the nut, two bolts and stabilizer bar bracke

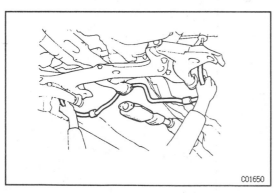

4. **DISCONNECT EXHAUST CENTER PIPE**
   Remove the two bolts and gasket.

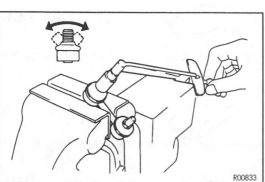

5. **REMOVE STABILIZER BAR**
   (a) Remove the stabilizer bar.
   (b) Remove the two stabilizer bar bushings.

STABILIZER BAR LINK INSPECTION

INSPECT BALL JOINT FOR ROTATION CONDITIO
(a) Flip the ball joint stud back and forth 5 times shown in the figure, before installing the nut.
(b) Using a torque gauge, turn the nut continuously or turn each 2—4 seconds and take the torque readir on the fifth turn.

Turning torque:

   0.05−1.0 N·m (0.5−10 kgf·cm, 0.4−8.7 in.·lbf)

If not within specification, replace the stabilizer bar link.

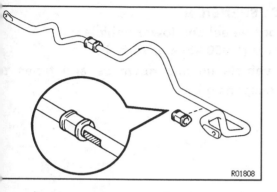

SA065−01

STABILIZER BAR INSTALLATION

1. INSTALL STABILIZER BAR BUSHINGS

Install the stabilizer bar bushings touching the line painted on the stabilizer bar.

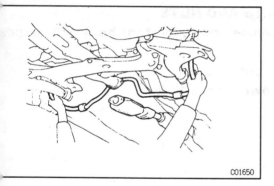

2. INSTALL STABILIZER BAR

SA

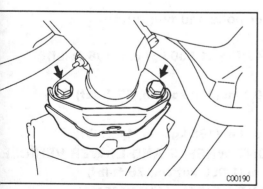

3. CONNECT EXHAUST CENTER PIPE

Install a new gasket and two bolts.
Torque: 43 N·m (440 kgf·cm, 32 ft·lbf)

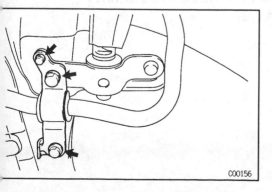

4. TEMPORARILY INSTALL STABILIZER BAR BRACKETS

Temporarily install the stabilizer bar bracket with the two bolts and nut.

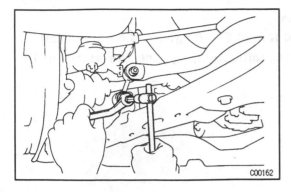

5. INSTALL STABILIZER BAR LINK
Torque: 44 N·m (450 kgf·cm, 33 ft·lbf)

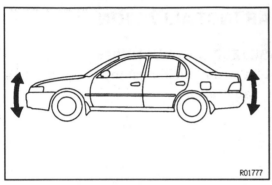

6. STABILIZE SUSPENSION
(a) Install the front wheel and lower vehicle.
Torque: 103 N·m (1,050 kgf·cm, 76 ft·lbf)
(b) Bounce the vehicle up and down several times t
stabilize the suspension.

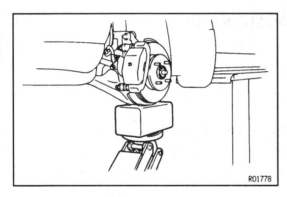

SA

7. TORQUE BOLTS AND NUTS
(a) Jack up the vehicle and support the body with stands
(b) Remove the front wheels.
(c) Support the lower arm with jack.

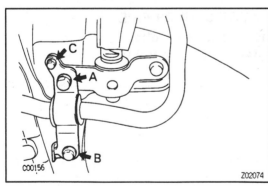

(d) Torque the four bolts and two nuts.
    Bolt A:
        Torque: 147 N·m (1,500 kgf·cm, 108 ft·lbf)
    Bolt B:
        Torque: 50 N·m (510 kgf·cm, 37 ft·lbf)
    Nut C:
        Torque: 19 N·m (195 kgf·cm, 14 ft·lbf)
8. INSTALL FRONT WHEELS AND LOWER VEHICLE
Torque: 103 N·m (1,050 kgf·cm, 76 ft·lbf)
9. INSPECT FRONT WHEEL ALIGNMENT
(See page SA−3)

REAR AXLE

DESCRIPTION

The rear axle uses double—row angular ball bearings combined with the oil seals for wheel bearings.

There is no need for bearing grease maintenance or preload adjustment.

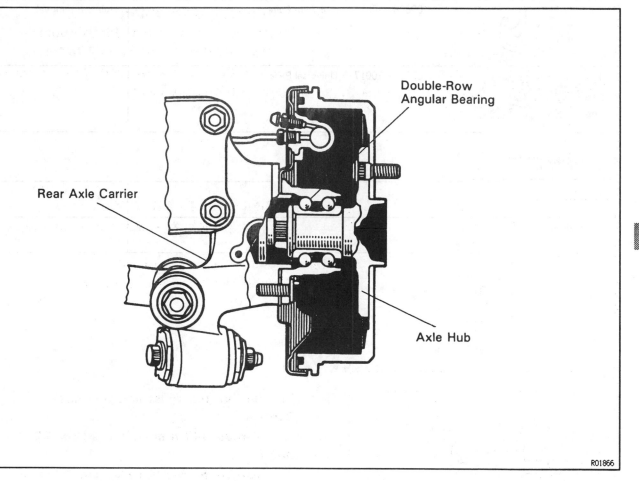

Double-Row Angular Bearing

Rear Axle Carrier

Axle Hub

R01866

PREPARATION
SST (SPECIAL SERVICE TOOLS)

SA038—03

	09608—30012	Front Hub & Drive Pinion Bearing Tool Set	
	(09608—04030)	Front Hub Inner Bearing Cone Replacer	Axle shaft installation
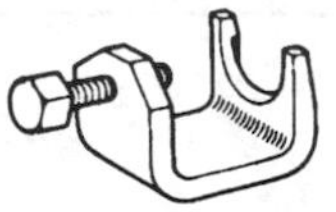	09628—10011	Ball Joint Puller	Hub bolt removal
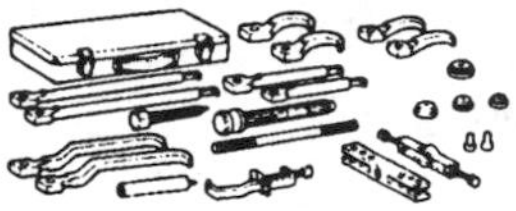	09950—20017	Universal Puller	

SA039—02

EQUIPMENT

Dial indicator	
Torque wrench	

SA

REAR AXLE HUB
COMPONENTS

SA03A−03

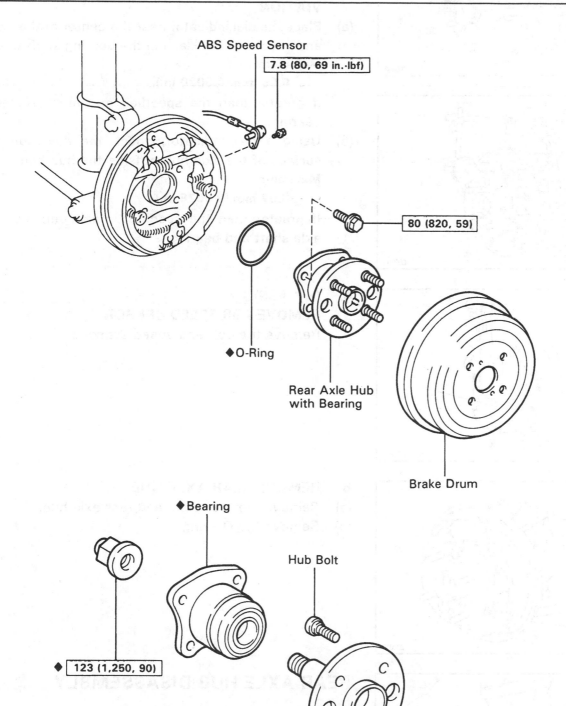

ABS Speed Sensor

7.8 (80, 69 in.·lbf)

◆O-Ring

80 (820, 59)

Rear Axle Hub
with Bearing

Brake Drum

◆Bearing

Hub Bolt

◆ 123 (1,250, 90)

Rear Axle Hub

SA

N·m (kgf·cm, ft·lbf) : Specified torque

◆ Non-reusable part

R03900

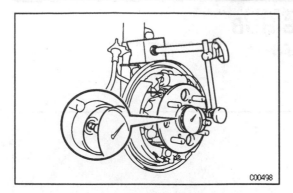

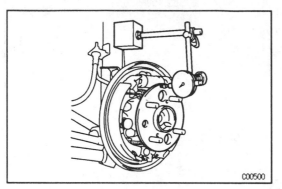

REAR AXLE HUB REMOVAL

1. **JACK UP VEHICLE AND REMOVE REAR WHEEL**
2. **REMOVE BRAKE DRUM**
3. **CHECK BEARING BACKLASH AND AXLE HUB DEVIATION**
(a) Place the dial indicator near the center of the axle hub and check the backlash in the bearing shaft direction.
   Maximum:
      0.05 mm (0.0020 in.)
   If greater than the specified maximum, replace the bearing.
(b) Using a dial indicator, check the deviation at the surface of the axle hub outside the hub bolt.
   Maximum:
      0.07 mm (0.0028 in.)
   If greater then the specified maximum, replace the axle shaft and bearing.

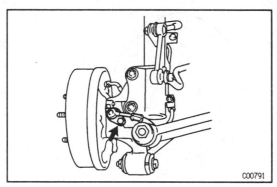

4. **(w/ ABS)**
   REMOVE ABS SPEED SENSOR
   Remove the bolt and speed sensor.

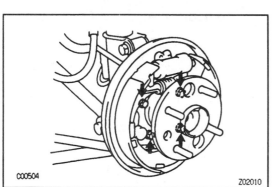

5. **REMOVE REAR AXLE HUB**
(a) Remove the four bolts and rear axle hub.
(b) Remove the O—ring.

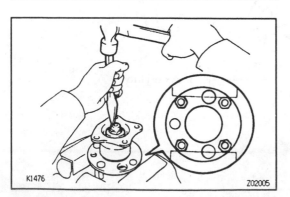

REAR AXLE HUB DISASSEMBLY

NOTICE: If equipped with ABS, do not disassemble the rear axle shaft and bearing.
1. **REMOVE LOCK NUT**
(a) Using a hammer and chisel, release the nut caulking.
(b) Remove the lock nut.

REAR AXLE CARRIER
COMPONENTS

SA03F-05

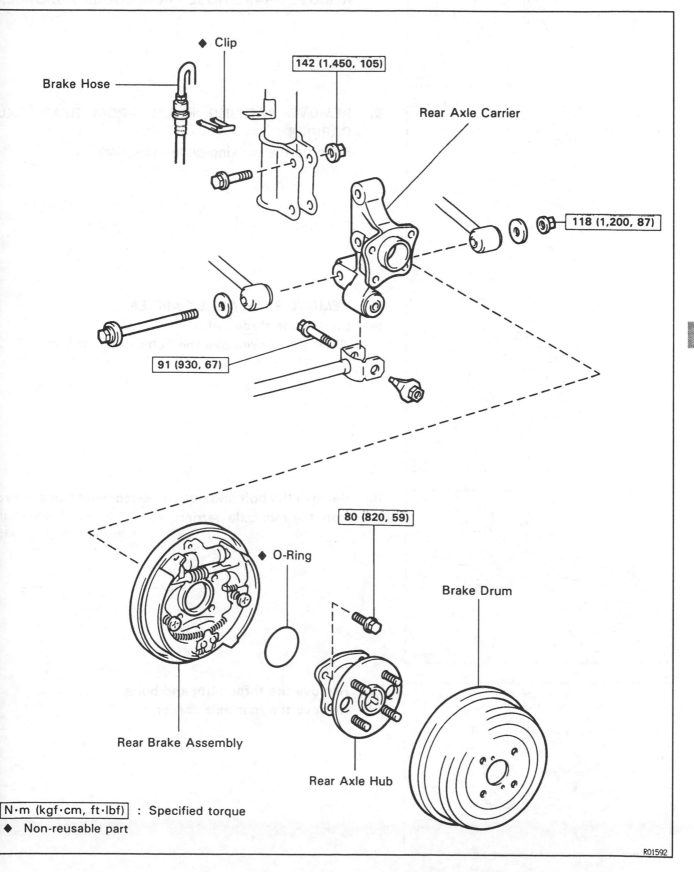

◆ Clip

Brake Hose

142 (1,450, 105)

Rear Axle Carrier

118 (1,200, 87)

91 (930, 67)

80 (820, 59)

◆ O-Ring

Brake Drum

Rear Brake Assembly

Rear Axle Hub

SA

N·m (kgf·cm, ft·lbf) : Specified torque

◆ Non-reusable part

R01592

SAQJ1–0

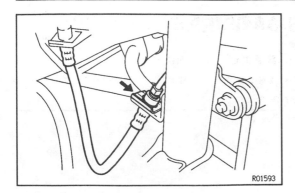

R01593

REAR AXLE CARRIER REMOVAL

1. **REMOVE REAR AXLE HUB**
   (See page SA–62)
2. **REMOVE BRAKE HOSE FROM SHOCK ABSORBER**

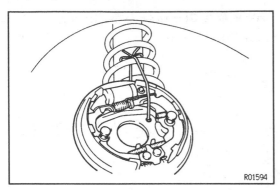

R01594

3. **REMOVE BACKING PLATE FROM REAR AXL CARRIER**
   Hang up the backing plate using wire, etc.

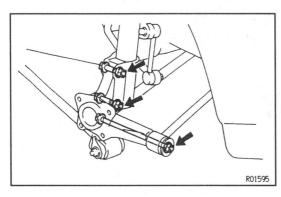

R01595

4. **REMOVE REAR AXLE CARRIER**
   (a) Loosen the three nuts.
   HINT: Do not remove the bolts.

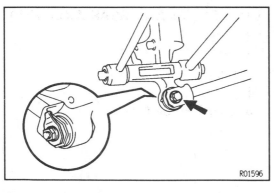

R01596

(b) Remove the bolt and nut and disconnect the strut ro from the rear axle carrier.

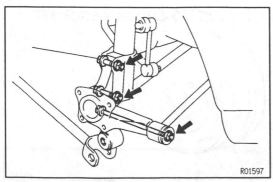

R01597

(c) Remove the three nuts and bolts.
(d) Remove the rear axle carrier.

SA

REAR AXLE CARRIER INSTALLATION

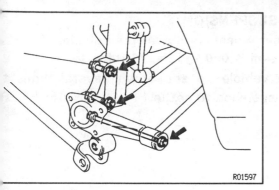

1. INSTALL REAR AXLE CARRIER
(a) Place the rear axle carrier and temporarily install the three bolts and nuts.

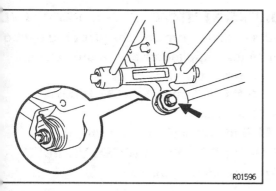

(b) Connect the strut rod to the rear axle carrier.
(c) Temporarily install the bolt and nut.

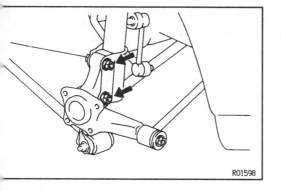

(d) Torque the two nuts.
Torque: 142 N·m (1,450 kgf·cm, 105 ft·lbf)

SA

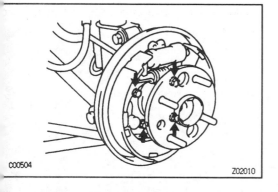

2. INSTALL BACKING PLATE AND REAR AXLE HUB
(a) Place the backing plate.
(b) Install a new O—ring.
(c) Install the rear axle hub.
(See page SA—63)
Torque: 80 N·m (820 kgf·cm, 59 ft·lbf)

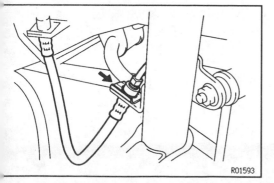

3. INSTALL BRAKE HOSE TO SHOCK ABSORBER

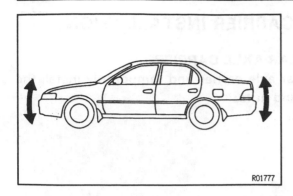

R01777

4.   STABILIZE SUSPENSION

(a)   Install the rear wheel and lower the vehicle.
Torque: 103 N·m (1,050 kgf·cm, 76 ft·lbf)

(b)   Bounce the vehicle up and down several times t
allow the suspension to settle.

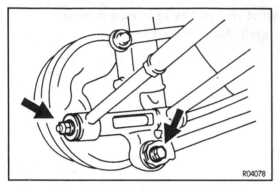

R04078

5.   TORQUE BOLT AND NUTS

Torque the nuts of lower arm and the strut rod set bo
with the vehicle load applied onto the suspension.
Axle carrier x Lower arm:
Torque: 118 N·m (1,200 kgf·cm, 87 ft·lbf)
Axle carrier x Strut rod:
Torque: 91 N·m (930 kgf·cm, 67 ft·lbf)

6.   INSTALL REAR WHEEL AND LOWER VEHICLE
Torque: 103 N·m (1,050 kgf·cm, 76 ft·lbf)

SA

REAR SUSPENSION

DESCRIPTION

The rear suspension is dual—link strut independent suspension composed of two lower arms in parallel at the side, and strut rods which extend forward.

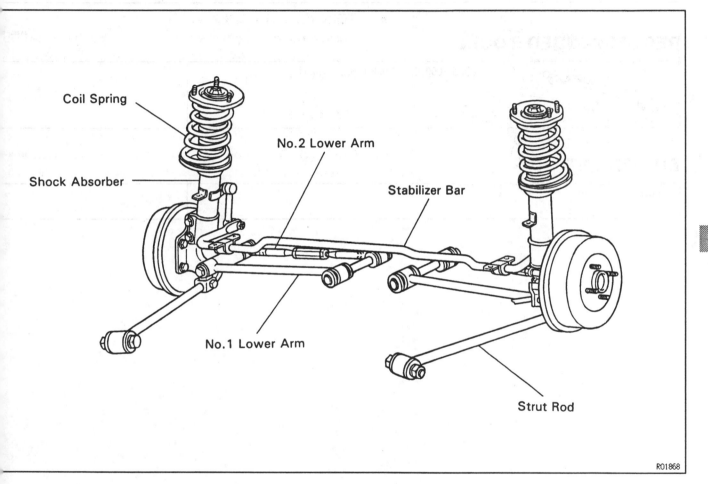

R01868

SA

PREPARATION
SST (SPECIAL SERVICE TOOLS)

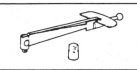	09727–30020	Coil Spring Compressor
	09729–22031	Front Spring Upper Seat Holder

RECOMMENDED TOOLS

	09025–00010	Small Torque Wrench

EQUIPMENT

Torque wrench	

REAR SHOCK ABSORBER
COMPONENTS

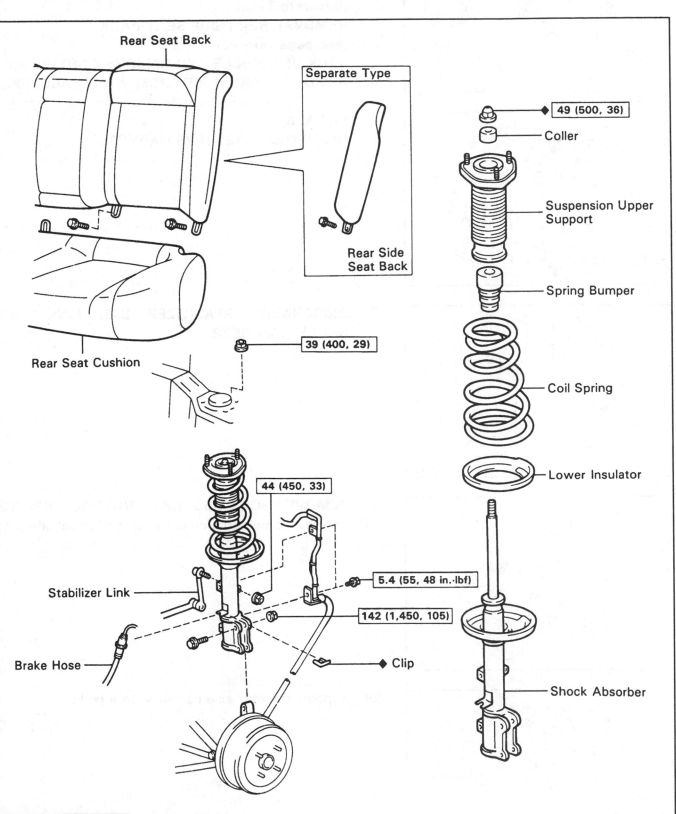

Rear Seat Back

Separate Type

Rear Side Seat Back

Rear Seat Cushion

39 (400, 29)

Stabilizer Link

44 (450, 33)

Brake Hose

5.4 (55, 48 in.·lbf)

142 (1,450, 105)

◆ Clip

◆ 49 (500, 36)

Coller

Suspension Upper Support

Spring Bumper

Coil Spring

Lower Insulator

Shock Absorber

SA

N·m (kgf·cm, ft·lbf) : Specified torque

◆ Non-reusable part

R03910

REAR SHOCK ABSORBER REMOVAL

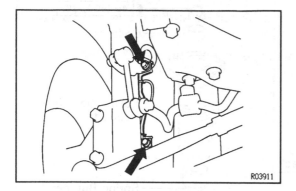

1. (Fixed Type)
   REMOVAL REAR SEAT
   (Separate Type)
   REMOVAL REAR SIDE SEAT BACK
   (See page BO—70)
2. JACK UP VEHICLE AND REMOVE REAR WHEEL
3. REMOVE BRAKE HOSE FROM SHOCK ABSORBER

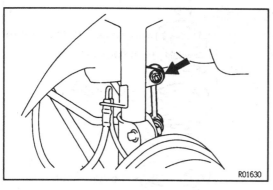

4. (w/ ABS)
   DISCONNECT ABS HIRE HARNESS

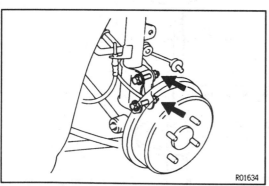

5. DISCONNECT STABILIZER BAR LINK FROM SHOCK ABSORBER

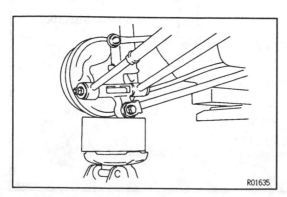

6. REMOVE SHOCK ABSORBER WITH COIL SPRING
   (a) Loosen the two nuts on lower side of shock absorber

(b) Support the rear axle carrier with a jack.

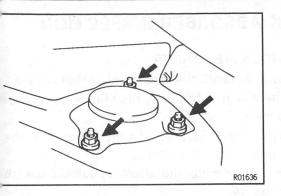

(c) Remove the three nuts of upper support.

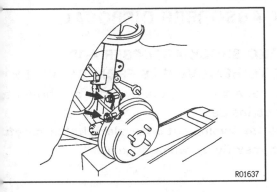

(d) Lower the rear axle carrier and remove the two nuts and bolts.
(e) Remove the shock absorber with coil spring.

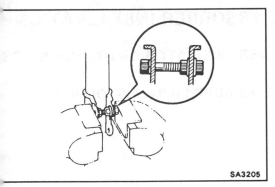

7. REMOVE COIL SPRING
(a) Install a bolt and two nuts to the bracket at the lower portion of the shock absorber and secure it in a vice.

SA

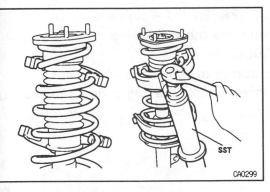

(b) Using SST, compress the coil spring.
SST 09727—30020

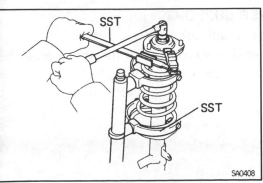

(c) Remove the nut.
(d) Remove the following parts.
- Collar
- Suspension upper support
- Coil spring
- Spring bumper
- Lower insulator

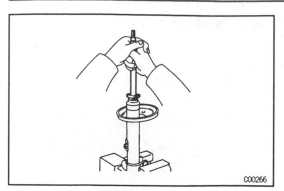

REAR SHOCK ABSORBER INSPECTION

INSPECT SHOCK ABSORBER

Compress and extend the shock absorber rod an
check that there is no abnormal resistance or unusua
operation sounds.

If there is any abnormality, replace the shock absorbe
with a new one.

NOTICE: When discarding the shock absorber, use th
following procedure.

REAR SHOCK ABSORBER DISPOSAL

1. **FULLY EXTEND SHOCK ABSORBER ROD**
2. **DRILL HOLE TO REMOVE GAS FROM CYLINDER**

Using a drill, make a hole in the cylinder as shown t
remove the gas inside.

CAUTION: The gas coming out is harmless, but be carefu
of chips which may fly up when drilling.

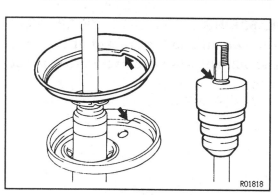

REAR SHOCK ABSORBER INSTALLATION

1. **INSTALL LOWER INSULATOR ONTO SHOCK ABS
   ORBER**
2. **INSTALL SPRING BUMPER TO PISTON ROD**

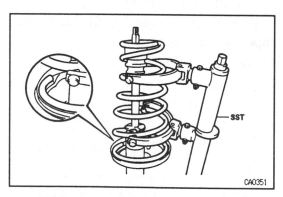

3. **INSTALL COIL SPRING**
   (a) Using SST, compress the coil spring
       SST 09727−30020
   (b) Install the coil spring to the shock absorber.
       HINT: Fit the lower end of the coil spring into the ga
       of the lower seat.

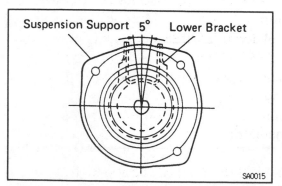

4. **INSTALL UPPER SUPPORT**
   (a) Install the upper insulator.
   (b) Align the suspension support with the shock absorbe
       lower bracket as shown.

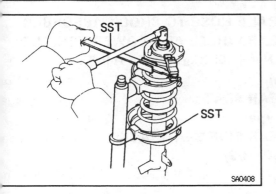

(c) Install the collar to the piston rod.
(d) Using SST to hold the upper support, install a new nut.
SST 09729−22031
Torque: 49 N·m (500 kgf·cm, 36 ft·lbf)
(e) Remove the SST.
HINT: After removing SST, again check the direction of the upper support.

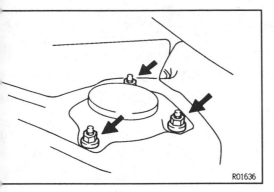

5. **INSTALL SHOCK ABSORBER WITH COIL SPRING**
Place the shock absorber and install the three nuts of upper support.
Torque: 39 N·m (400 kgf·cm, 29 ft·lbf)

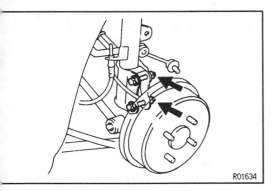

6. **CONNECT SHOCK ABSORBER TO REAR AXLE CARRIER**

SA

(a) Coat the threads of the bolts with engine oil.
(b) Install the two bolts and nuts.
Torque: 142 N·m (1,450 kgf·cm, 105 ft·lbf)

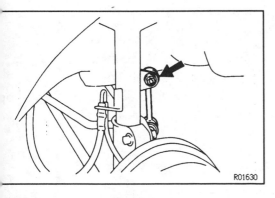

7. **CONNECT STABILIZER BAR LINK TO SHOCK ABSORBER**
Torque: 44 N·m (450 kgf·cm, 33 ft·lbf)

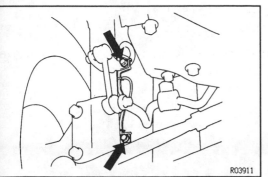

8. **(w/ ABS)**
CLAMP ABS WIRE HARNESS
Torque: 5.4 N·m (55 kgf·cm, 48 in.·lbf)

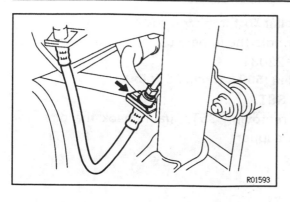

R01593

9. **INSTALL BRAKE HOSE TO SHOCK ABSORBER**
10. **INSTALL REAR WHEEL AND LOWER VEHICLE**
   Torque: 103 N·m (1,050 kgf·cm, 76 ft·lbf)
11. **(Fixed Type)**
   INSTALL REAR SEAT
   (Separate Type)
   INSTALL REAR SIDE SEAT BACK
   (See page BO—69)

LOWER SUSPENSION ARM AND STRUT ROD
COMPONENTS

SA038-02

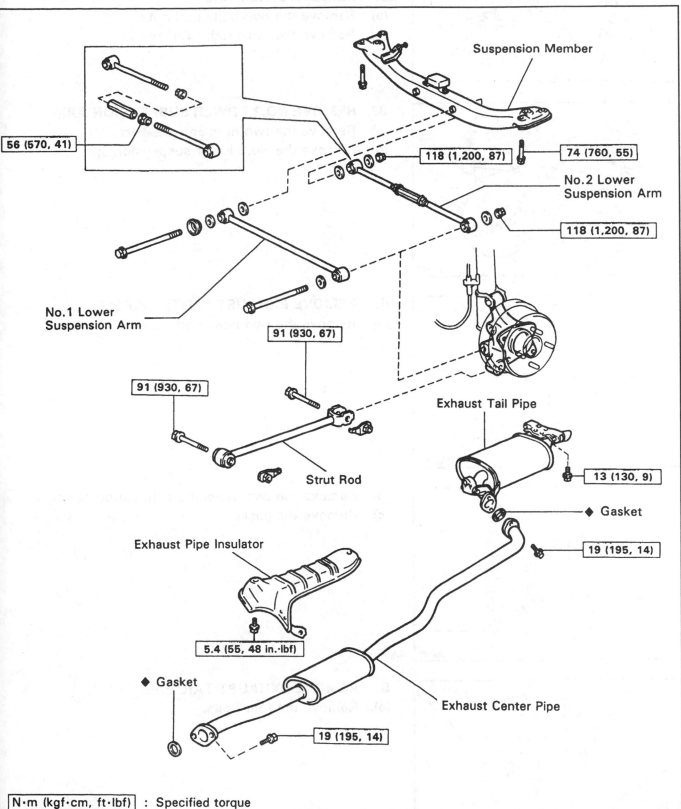

Suspension Member

56 (570, 41)

118 (1,200, 87)   74 (760, 55)

No.2 Lower
Suspension Arm

118 (1,200, 87)

No.1 Lower
Suspension Arm

91 (930, 67)

91 (930, 67)

Strut Rod

Exhaust Tail Pipe

13 (130, 9)

◆ Gasket

19 (195, 14)

Exhaust Pipe Insulator

5.4 (55, 48 in.·lbf)

◆ Gasket

Exhaust Center Pipe

19 (195, 14)

N·m (kgf·cm, ft·lbf) : Specified torque

◆ Non-reusable part

R01640

SA

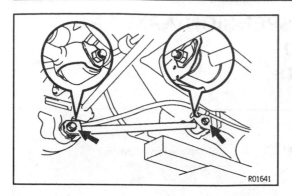

LOWER SUSPENSION ARM AND STRUT ROD REMOVAL

1.   JACK UP VEHICLE AND REMOVE REAR WHEEL

2.   REMOVE STRUT ROD

(a)   Remove the two bolts and nuts.

(b)   Remove the strut rod.

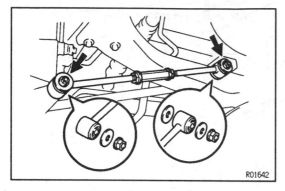

3.   REMOVE NO.2 LOWER SUSPENSION ARM

(a)   Remove the two nuts and washers.

(b)   Remove the No.2 lower suspension arm.

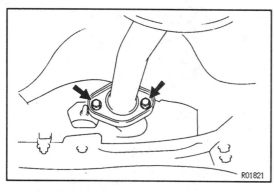

4.   REMOVE EXHAUST CENTER PIPE

(a)   Remove the two bolts and gasket.

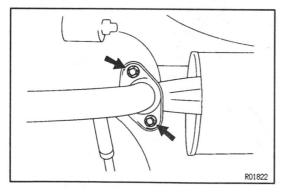

(b)   Remove the two bolts and exhaust center pipe.

(c)   Remove the gasket.

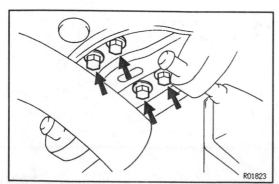

5.   REMOVE EXHAUST TAIL PIPE

(a)   Remove the four bolts.

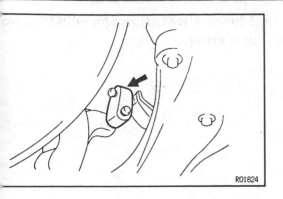

(b) Disconnect the exhaust tail pipe from the bracket.

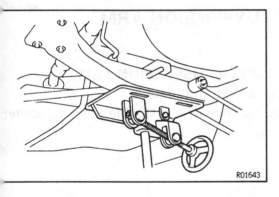

6. REMOVE EXHAUST PIPE INSULATOR
Remove the three bolts and exhaust pipe insulator.

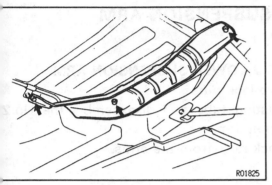

7. REMOVE NO.1 LOWER SUSPENSION ARM
(a) Support the suspension member with a jack.

SA

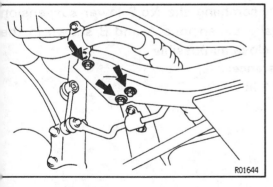

(b) Remove the six bolts.

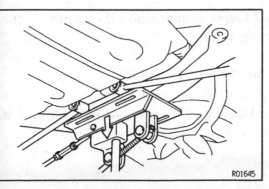

(c) Lower the suspension member.

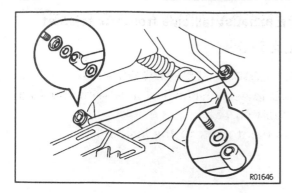

(d) Remove the No.1 lower suspension arm with the two bolts and the four washers.

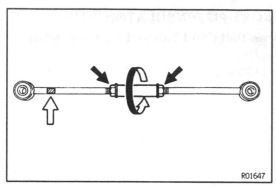

NO.2 LOWER SUSPENSION ARM DISASSEMBLY

DISASSEMBLE NO.2 LOWER SUSPENSION ARM
(a) Loosen the two lock nuts.
(b) Turn the adjusting tube and disassemble the No.2 lower suspension arm.
(c) Remove the lock nuts from the arms.

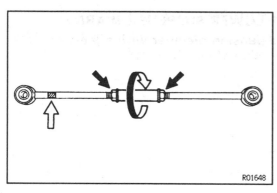

NO.2 LOWER SUSPENSION ARM ASSEMBLY

ASSEMBLE NO.2 LOWER SUSPENSION ARM
(a) Install the lock nuts to the arms.
(b) Turn the adjusting tube and assemble the No.2 lower suspension arm.

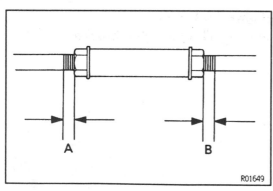

HINT: When assembling the No.2 lower suspension arm, try to make dimensions A and B shown in the illustration as close as possible.
Maximum difference:
   3 mm (0.12 in.)

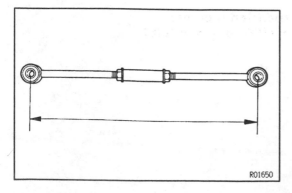

(c) Adjust the No.2 lower suspension arm length by turning the adjusting tube.
   Arm length:
      500±1.5 mm (19.69±0.059 in.)
(d) Temporarily tighten the two lock nuts.
   HINT: After adjusting the rear wheel alignment, torque the lock nuts.

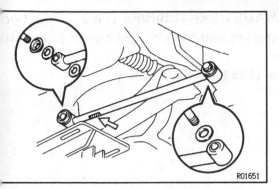

LOWER SUSPENSION ARM AND STRUT ROD INSTALLATION

1. INSTALL NO.1 LOWER SUSPENSION ARM

Install the No.1 lower suspension arm with the four washers and the two bolts.

HINT: Face the paint mark to the inside.

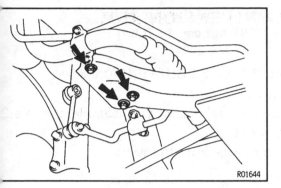

2. INSTALL SUSPENSION MEMBER TO BODY

(a) Jack up the suspension member.

(b) Install the six bolts.

Torque: 74 N·m (760 kgf·cm, 55 ft·lbf)

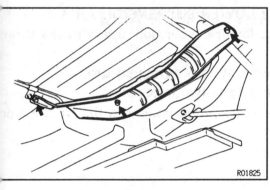

3. INSTALL EXHAUST PIPE INSULATOR

Install the exhaust pipe insulator with the three bolts.

Torque: 5.4 N·m (55 kgf·cm, 48 in·lbf)

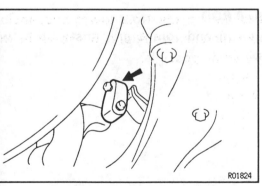

4. INSTALL EXHAUST TAIL PIPE

(a) Connect the exhaust tail pipe to the bracket.

(b) Install the four bolts.

Torque: 13 N·m (130 kgf·cm, 9 ft·lbf)

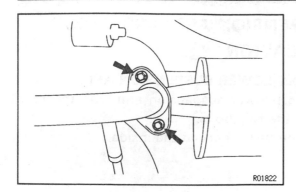

5. **INSTALL EXHAUST CENTER PIPE**
   (a) Install a new gasket and the exhaust center pipe with the two bolts.
   Torque: 19 N·m (195 kgf·cm, 14 ft·lbf)

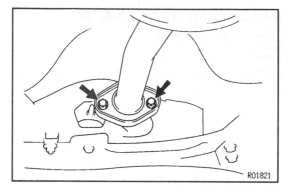

   (b) Install a new gasket and the two bolts.
   Torque: 19 N·m (195 kgf·cm, 14 ft·lbf)

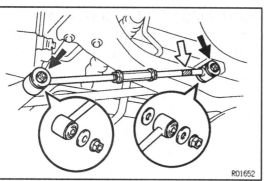

6. **INSTALL NO.2 LOWER SUSPENSION ARM**
   (a) Install the No.2 lower suspension arm with the three washers.
   HINT: Face the paint mark to the inside.
   (b) Temporarily install the two lock nut.

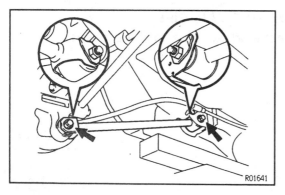

7. **INSTALL STRUT ROD**
   Place the strut rod and temporarily install the two bolts and nuts.

8. **STABILIZE SUSPENSION**
   (a) Install the rear wheel and lower the vehicle.
   Torque: 103 N·m (1,050 kgf·cm, 76 ft·lbf)
   (b) Bounce the vehicle up and down several times to stabilized suspension.

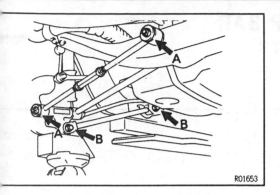

R01653

9. TORQUE BOLTS AND NUTS

(a) Jack up the vehicle and support the body with stands.

(b) Remove the rear wheel.

(c) Support the rear axle carrier with a jack.

(d) Torque the nuts of lower arm and the strut rod set bolts.

Nut A:
   Torque: 118 N·m (1,200 kgf·cm, 87 ft·lbf)

Bolt B:
   Torque: 91 N·m (930 kgf·cm, 67 ft·lbf)

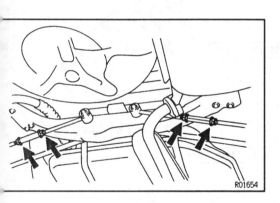

R01654

10. INSTALL REAR WHEEL AND LOWER VEHICLE
Torque: 103 N·m (1,050 kgf·cm, 76 ft·lbf)

11. INSPECT AND ADJUST REAR WHEEL ALIGNMENT
(See page SA−3)

12. TORQUE NO.2 LOWER SUSPENSION ARM LOCK NUTS
Torque: 56 N·m (570 kgf·cm, 41 ft·lbf)

STABILIZER BAR
COMPONENTS

SA03X—02

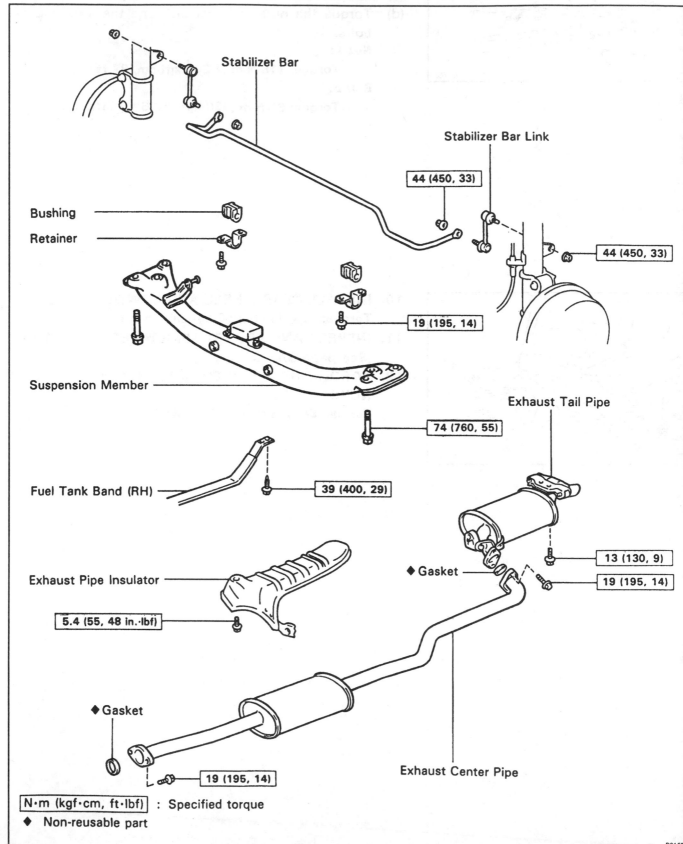

Stabilizer Bar

Stabilizer Bar Link

44 (450, 33)

Bushing

Retainer

44 (450, 33)

19 (195, 14)

Suspension Member

74 (760, 55)

Exhaust Tail Pipe

Fuel Tank Band (RH)

39 (400, 29)

13 (130, 9)

◆ Gasket

19 (195, 14)

Exhaust Pipe Insulator

5.4 (55, 48 in.·lbf)

◆ Gasket

Exhaust Center Pipe

19 (195, 14)

N·m (kgf·cm, ft·lbf) : Specified torque

◆ Non-reusable part

R01655

SA

STABILIZER BAR REMOVAL

SA09C-01

1. **JACK UP VEHICLE AND REMOVE LEFT AND RIGHT REAR WHEELS**
2. **REMOVE LEFT AND RIGHT STABILIZER BAR LINKS**

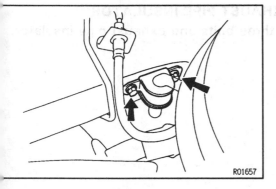

3. **REMOVE LEFT AND RIGHT STABILIZER BAR BUSHINGS**
   (a) Remove the left and right bushing retainers.
   (b) Remove the stabilizer bar bushings.

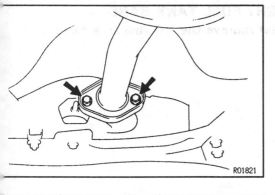

4. **REMOVE EXHAUST CENTER PIPE**
   (a) Remove the two bolts and gasket.

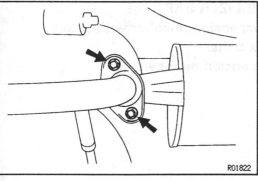

   (b) Remove the two bolts and exhaust center pipe.
   (c) Remove the gasket.

5. **REMOVE EXHAUST TAIL PIPE**
   (a) Remove the four bolts.

SA

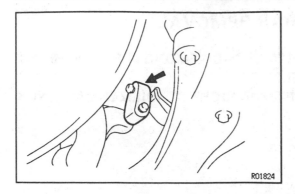

(b)   Disconnect the exhaust tail pipe from bracket.

6.   REMOVE EXHAUST PIPE INSULATOR
Remove the three bolts and exhaust pipe insulator.

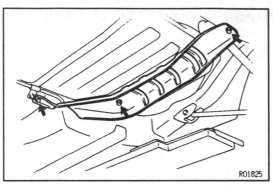

7.   REMOVE RIGHT FUEL TANK BAND
NOTICE: Do not remove the left fuel tank band.

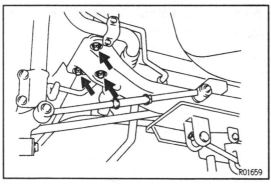

8.   REMOVE STABILIZER BAR
(a)   Support the suspension member with a jack.
(b)   Remove the six bolts.
(c)   Lower the suspension member.

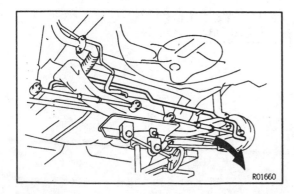

(d)   Remove the stabilizer bar.

SA

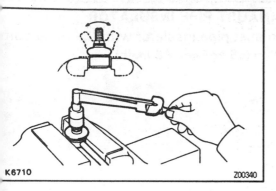

STABILIZER BAR LINK INSPECTION

INSPECT BALL JOINT FOR ROTATION CONDITION

(a) Flip the ball joint stud back and forth 5 times as shown in the figure, before installing the nut.

(b) Using a torque gauge, turn the nut continuously one turn each 2 , 4 seconds and take the torque reading on the fifth turn.

Turning torque:

0.05 — 1.0 N·m (0.5 — 10 kgf·cm, 0.4 — 8.7 in.·lbf)

If not within specification, replace the stabilizer bar link.

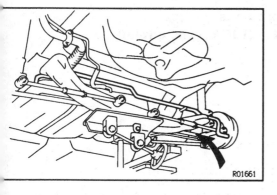

STABILIZER BAR INSTALLATION

1. **INSTALL STABILIZER BAR**

SA

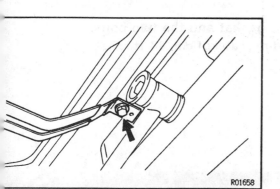

2. **INSTALL SUSPENSION MEMBER TO BODY**

(a) Jack up the suspension member.

(b) Install the six bolts.

Torque: 74 N·m (760 kgf·cm, 55 ft·lbf)

3. **INSTALL RIGHT FUEL TANK BAND**

Torque: 39 N·m (400 kgf·cm, 29 ft·lbf)

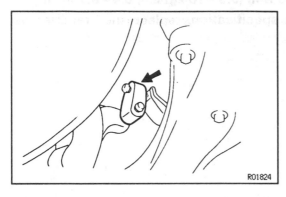

4. INSTALL EXHAUST PIPE INSULATOR
Install the exhaust pipe insulator with the three bolts
Torque: 5.4 N·m (55 kgf·cm, 48 in.·lbf)

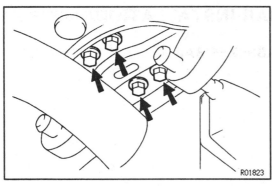

5. INSTALL EXHAUST TAIL PIPE
(a) Connect the exhaust tail pipe to the bracket.

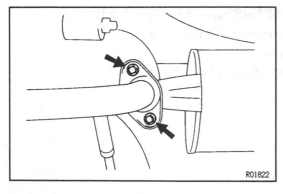

(b) Install the four bolts.
Torque: 13 N·m (130 kgf·cm, 9 ft·lbf)

6. INSTALL EXHAUST CENTER PIPE
(a) Install a new gasket and the exhaust center pipe wi⊦
the two bolts.
Torque: 19 N·m (195 kgf·cm, 14 ft·lbf)

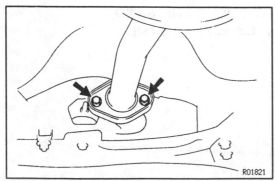

(b) Install a new gasket and the two bolts.
Torque: 19 N·m (195 kgf·cm, 14 ft·lbf)

SA

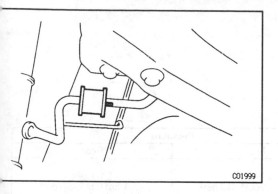

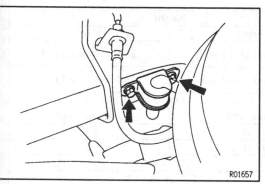

7. **INSTALL LEFT AND RIGHT STABILIZER BAR BUSHINGS**
(a) Align the marks and install the bushing as shown in the figure.

(b) Install the bushing retainers and bolts.
Torque: 19 N·m (195 kgf·cm, 14 ft·lbf)

8. **INSTALL LEFT AND RIGHT STABILIZER BAR LINKS**
Torque: 44 N·m (450 kgf·cm, 33 ft·lbf)
9. **INSTALL REAR WHEELS AND LOWER VEHICLE**
Torque: 103 N·m (1,050 kgf·cm, 76 ft·lbf)

SERVICE SPECIFICATIONS
SERVICE DATA

SA0J3—01

Cold tire inflation pressure	Tire size	Pressure	
		Front	Rear
	P175/65R14 81S 175/65R14 82S P185/65R14 85S 185/65R14 85S	210 kPa (2.1 kgf/cm², 30 psi)	210 kPa (2.1 kgf/cm², 30 psi)
Vehicle height	Tire size	Height	
		Front	Rear
	P175/65R14 81S 175/65R14 82S	185 mm (7.28 in.)	245 mm (9.65 in.)
	P185/65R14 85S 185/65R14 85S	190 mm (7.48 in.)	250 mm (9.84 in.)
Front wheel alignment	Toe-in (total)	0.1° ± 0.2° (1 ± 1 mm, 0.04 ± 0.04 in.)	
	Wheel angle	Inside wheel	Outside wheel
	Manual steering	39° ± 2°	33°
	Power steering	39° ± 2°	33°
	Camber	−10′ ± 30′	
	Cross camber	30′ or less	
	Caster	1°20′ ± 30′	
	Cross caster	30′ or less	
	Steering axis inclination	12°35′ ± 30′	
Rear wheel alignment	Toe-in (total)	0.3° ± 0.1° (3 ± 1 mm, 0.12 ± 0.04 in.)	
	Camber	−55′ ± 30′	
	Cross camber	30′ or less	
Front axle	Axle bearing backlash	0.05 mm (0.0020 in.) or less	
	Axle hub deviaton	0.07 mm (0.0028 in.) or less	
Front suspension	Lower ball joint turning torque	1.0 − 2.9 N·m (10 − 30 kgf·cm, 8.7 − 2.6 in.·lbf)	
	Stabilizer bar link turning torque	0.05 − 1.0 N·m (0.5 − 10 kgf·cm, 0.4 − 8.7 in.·lbf)	
Rear axle	Axle bearing backlash	0.05 mm (0.0020 in.) or less	
	Axle hub deviation	0.07 mm (0.0028 in.) or less	
Rear suspension	Stabilizer bar link turning torque	0.05 − 1.0 N·m (0.5 − 10 kgf·cm, 0.4 − 8.7 in.·lbf)	

SA

SA042-06

TORQUE SPECIFICATIONS
(FRONT)

Part tightened	N·m	kgf·cm	ft·lbf
Tie rod end lock nut	56	570	41
Steering knuckle x Shock absorber	275	2,800	203
Steering knuckle x Brake cylinder	88	900	65
Steering knuckle x Tie rod end	49	500	36
Axle hub nut	216	2,200	159
Ball joint x Lower arm	142	1,450	105
Ball joint x Steering knuckle	118	1,200	87
Steering knuckle x Disc brake dust cover	8.3	85	74 in.·lbf
Suspension upper support x Body	39	400	29
Suspension upper support x Piston rod	47	475	34
Brake hose x Shock absorber	29	300	22
Stabilizer bar link set nut	44	450	33
Suspension crossmember x Body	206	2,100	152
Suspension crossmember x Suspension centermember	61	620	45
Engine mount bracket x Suspension crossmember	48	490	35
Exhaust front pipe bracket x Suspension centermember	19	195	14
Exhaust front pipe x Exhaust center pipe	43	440	32
Lower arm bracket x Body (Front side)	147	1,500	108
Lower arm bracket x Body (Rear side)	50	510	37
Lower arm bracket x Body (Nut)	19	195	14
Lower arm bushing nut	137	1,400	101
Lower arm front bolt	218	2,220	161
ABS speed sensor x Axle carrier	7.8	80	69 in.·lbf
ABS wire harness x Shock absorber	5.4	55	48 in.·lbf

SA

(REAR)

Part tightened	N·m	kgf·cm	ft·lbf
Axle bearing set bolt	80	820	59
Bearing lock nut	123	1,250	90
Shock absorber x Rear axle carrier	142	1,450	105
Suspension upper support x Body	39	400	29
Suspension upper support x Piston rod	49	500	36
Lower suspension arm x Suspension member	118	1,200	87
Lower suspension arm x Rear axle carrier	118	1,200	87
Strut rod x Body	91	930	67
Strut rod x Rear axle carrier	91	930	67
Suspension member x Body	74	760	55
Stabilizer bar bushing retainer	19	195	14
Stabilizer bar link set nut	44	450	33
Suspension arm lock nut	56	570	41

Part tightened	N·m	kgf·cm	ft·lbf
Fuel tank band	39	400	29
Exhaust front pipe x Exhaust center pipe	19	195	14
Exhaust center pipe x Exhaust tail pipe	19	195	14
Exhaust tail pipe bracket	13	130	9
Exhaust pipe insulator	5.4	55	48 in.·lbf
ABS speed sensor x Axle carrier	7.8	80	69 in.·lbf
ABS wire harness x Shock absorber	5.4	55	48 in.·lbf
LSPV spring x No.2 lower suspension arm	25	260	19

BRAKE SYSTEM

GENERAL DESCRIPTION

1. Care must be taken to replace each part properly as it could affect the performance of the brake system and result in a driving hazard. Replace the parts with parts of the same part number or equivalent.

2. It is very important to keep parts and the area clean when repairing the brake system.

DESCRIPTION

The service brakes consist of a foot brake which changes rotational energy to thermal energy to stop the vehicle while it is being driven and a parking brake to keep the vehicle from moving while it is parked.

OPERATION
FOOT BRAKE

When the brake pedal is depressed, a vacuum builds up in the booster which amplifies the pedal force, pressing on the piston in the master cylinder. The piston raises the hydraulic pressure in the cylinder. This hydraulic pressure is then applied to each respective brake cylinder and wheel cylinder, and acts to press the brake pads and shoes against the rotating rotor discs and brake drum. The resulting friction converts the rotational energy to thermal energy, stopping the vehicle.

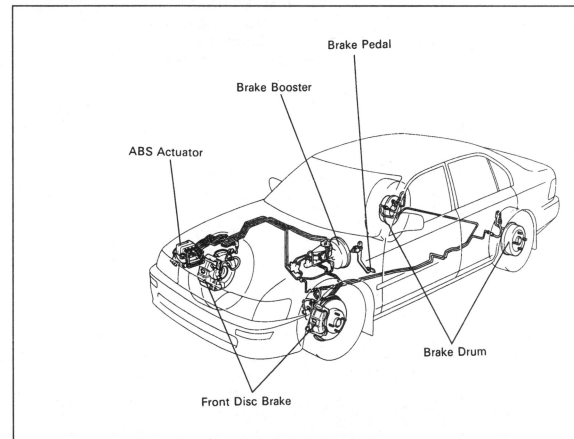

BR005-02

ARKING BRAKE

When the parking brake lever is pulled, the parking brake shoe lever is pulled via the parking brake wire. This causes the adjuster to push the front shoe, which expands and is pressed against the brake drum. If the parking brake lever continues to be pulled, the contact point of the parking brake shoe lever and adjuster then becomes the fulcrum so that the parking brake shoe lever causes the rear shoe to expand. This results in the brake drum being locked by the front shoe and rear shoe.

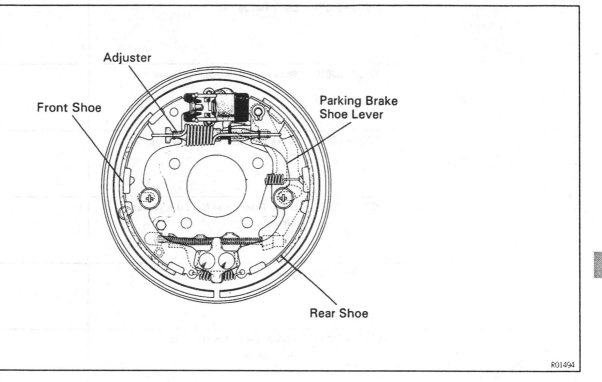

Adjuster

Front Shoe

Parking Brake
Shoe Lever

Rear Shoe

BR

R01494

PREPARATION
SST (SPECIAL SERVICE TOOLS)

	09023–00100	Union Nut Wrench 10 mm
	09703–30010	Brake Shoe Return Spring Tool
	09709–29017	LSPV Gauge Set
	09718–00010	Shoe Hold Down Spring Driver
	09737–00010	Brake Booster Push Rod Gauge
	09751–36011	Brake Tube Union Nut 10 x 12 mm Wrench
	09843–18020	Diagnosis Check Wire
	09990–00150	ABS Actuator Checker and Sub–harness
	09990–00163	ABS Actuator Checker Sheet "A"
	09990–00200	ABS Actuator Checker Sub–harness "C"
	09990–00300	ABS Actuator Checker Sub–harness "I"

BR

BRAKE SYSTEM BLEEDING

BR00C–05

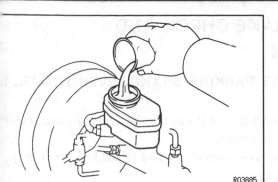

R03885

HINT: If any work is done on the brake system or if air in the brake lines is suspected, bleed the system of air.
NOTICE: Do not let brake fluid remain on a painted surface. Wash it off immediately.

1. **FILL BRAKE RESERVOIR WITH BRAKE FLUID**
    Fluid: SAEJ1703 or FMVSS No.116 DOT3

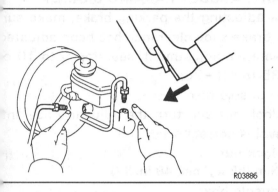

R03886

2. **BLEED MASTER CYLINDER**
    HINT: If the master cylinder has been disassembled or if the reservoir becomes empty, bleed the air from the master cylinder.
    (a) Disconnect the brake tubes from the master cylinder.
    (b) Slowly depress the brake pedal and hold it.

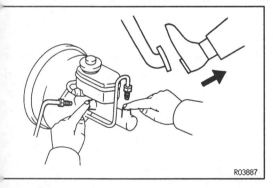

R03887

(c) Block off the outlet plug with your finger and release the brake pedal.
(d) Repeat (b) and (c) three or four times.

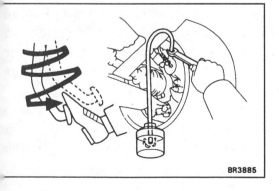

BR3885

3. **BLEED BRAKE LINE**
    (a) Connect the vinyl tube to the brake cylinder.
    (b) Depress the brake pedal several times, then loosen the bleeder plug with the pedal held down.
    (c) At the point when fluid stops coming out, tighten the bleeder plug, then release the brake pedal.
    (d) Repeat (b) and (c) until all the air in the fluid has been bled out.
    (e) Repeat the above procedure to bleed the air out of the brake line for each wheel.

4. **CHECK FLUID LEVEL IN RESERVOIR**
    Check the fluid level and add fluid if necessary.
    Fluid: SAEJ1703 or FMVSS No.116 DOT3

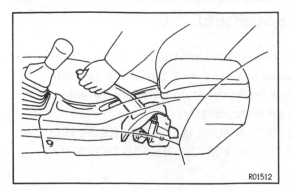

R01512

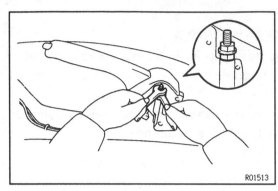

R01513

BROOD-0

PARKING BRAKE CHECK AND ADJUSTMENT

1. **CHECK THAT PARKING BRAKE LEVER TRAVEL I CORRECT**

   Pull the parking brake lever all the way up, and cour the number of clicks.

   Parking brake lever travel at 196 N (20 kgf, 44.1 lbf):
       4—7 clicks

   If incorrect, adjust the parking brake.

2. **IF NECESSARY, ADJUST PARKING BRAKE**

   HINT: Before adjusting the parking brake, make sur that the rear brake shoe clearance has been adjusted For shoe clearance adjustment, see step 9 to 10 o pages BR—35 to BR—36.

   (a)   Remove the console box.

   (b)   Loosen the lock nut and turn the adjusting nut un the lever travel is correct.

   (c)   Tighten the lock nut.
       Torque: 5.4 N·m (55 kgf·cm, 48 in.·lbf)

   (d)   Install the console box.

BR

MASTER CYLINDER
MASTER CYLINDER REMOVAL

BR00E–05

w/o ABS

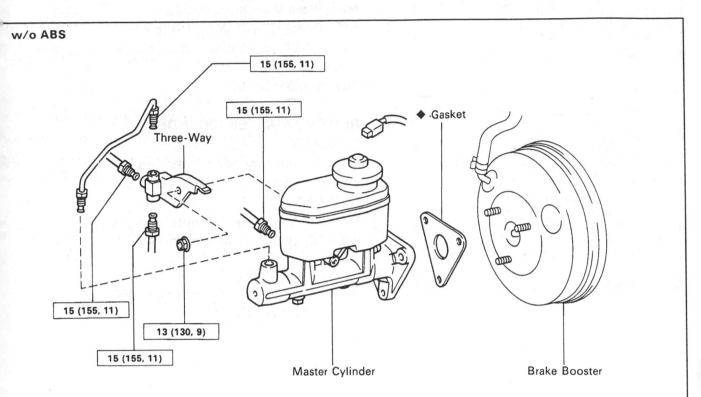

15 (155, 11)

15 (155, 11)

Three-Way

◆ Gasket

15 (155, 11)

13 (130, 9)

15 (155, 11)

Master Cylinder

Brake Booster

BR

w/ ABS

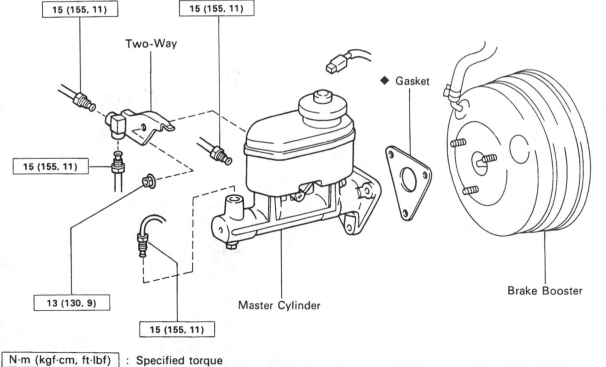

15 (155, 11)

15 (155, 11)

Two-Way

◆ Gasket

15 (155, 11)

13 (130, 9)

15 (155, 11)

Master Cylinder

Brake Booster

R04020
R04021

| N·m (kgf·cm, ft·lbf) | : Specified torque |

◆ Non-reusable part

Z03724

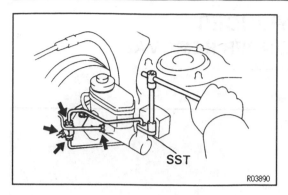

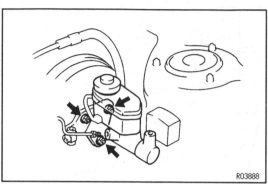

1. **DISCONNECT LEVEL WARNING SWITCH CON-NECTOR**

2. **DRAW OUT FLUID WITH SYRINGE**
   NOTICE: Do not let brake fluid remain on a painted sur-face. Wash it off immediately.

3. **DISCONNECT BRAKE TUBES**
   Using SST, disconnect the brake tubes from the master cylinder.
   SST 09023—00100

4. **REMOVE MASTER CYLINDER**
   (w/o ABS)
   Remove the mounting nuts and pull out the master cylinder, three — way and gasket.
   (w/ ABS)
   Remove the mounting nuts and pull out the master cylinder, two — way and gasket.

BR

COMPONENTS

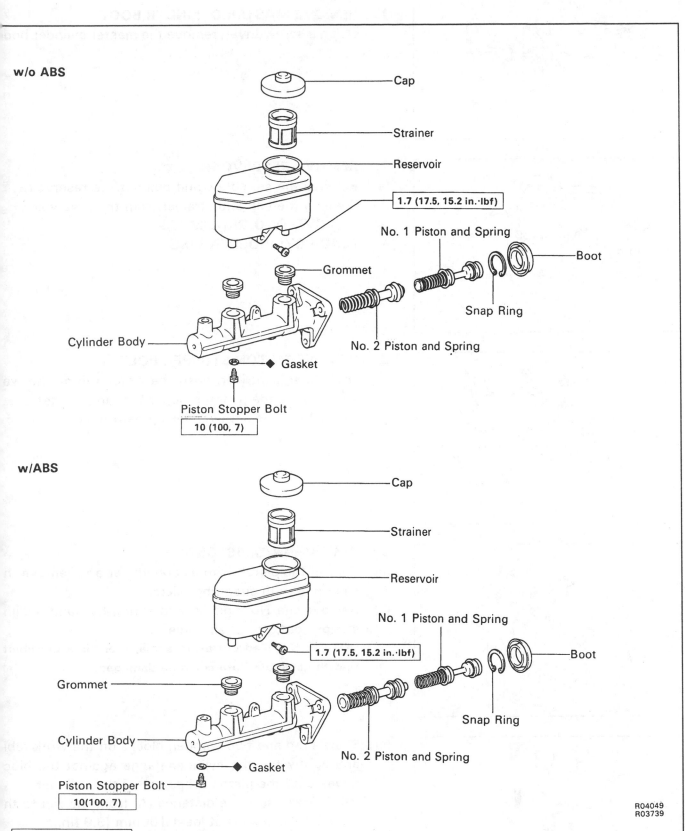

w/o ABS

Cap

Strainer

Reservoir

1.7 (17.5, 15.2 in.·lbf)

No. 1 Piston and Spring

Boot

Grommet

Snap Ring

Cylinder Body

No. 2 Piston and Spring

◆ Gasket

Piston Stopper Bolt

10 (100, 7)

w/ABS

Cap

Strainer

Reservoir

No. 1 Piston and Spring

1.7 (17.5, 15.2 in.·lbf)

Boot

Grommet

Snap Ring

Cylinder Body

No. 2 Piston and Spring

◆ Gasket

Piston Stopper Bolt

10(100, 7)

R04049
R03739

N·m (kgf·cm, ft·lbf) : Specified torque

◆ Non-reusable part

Z03725

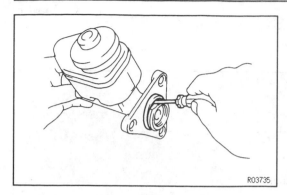

MASTER CYLINDER DISASSEMBLY

BR00G–0

1.   REMOVE MASTER CYLINDER BOOT
Using a screwdriver, remove the master cylinder boot

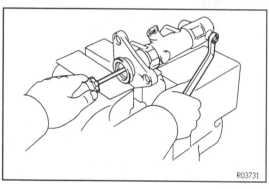

2.   REMOVE RESERVOIR
(a)   Remove the set screw and pull out the reservoir.
(b)   Remove the cap and strainer from the reservoir.
3.   REMOVE TWO GROMMETS
4.   PLACE CYLINDER IN VISE

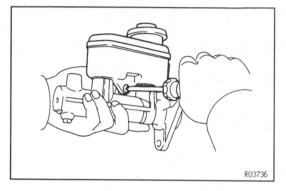

5.   REMOVE PISTON STOPPER BOLT
Using a screwdriver, push the pistons in all the wa
and remove the piston stopper bolt and gasket.
HINT: Tape the screwdriver tip before use.

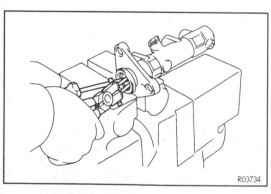

6.   REMOVE TWO PISTONS
(a)   Push in the piston with a screwdriver and remove th
snap ring with snap ring pliers.
(b)   Remove the No.1 piston and spring by hand, pullin
straight out, not at an angle.
**NOTICE: If pulled out at an angle, there is a possibilit
that the cylinder bore could be damaged.**

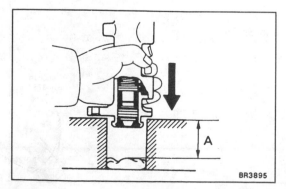

(c)   Place a rag and two wooden blocks on the work tabl
and lightly tap the cylinder flange against the bloc
edges until the piston drops out of the cylinder.
HINT: Make sure the distance (A) from the rag to th
top of the blocks is at least 100mm (3.94in.).

BROOH-03

MASTER CYLINDER COMPONENTS INSPECTION

HINT: Clean the disassembled parts with compressed air.

1. **INSPECT CYLINDER BORE FOR RUST OR SCORING**
2. **INSPECT CYLINDER FOR WEAR OR DAMAGE**
    If necessary, clean or replace the cylinder.

BROOJ-04

MASTER CYLINDER ASSEMBLY

1. **APPLY LITHIUM SOAP BASE GLYCOL GREASE TO RUBBER PARTS INDICATED BY ARROWS**

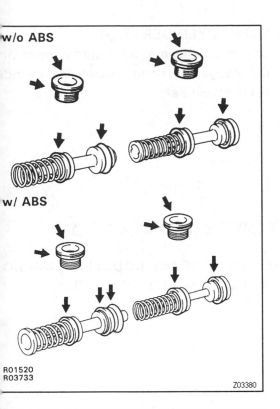

w/o ABS

w/ ABS

R01520
R03733

Z03380

BR

2. **INSTALL TWO PISTONS**
    NOTICE: Be careful not to damage the rubber lips on the pistons.
    (a) Insert the two pistons straight in, not at an angle.
    NOTICE: If inserted at an angle, there is a possibility that the cylinder bore could be damaged.
    (b) Push in the piston with a screwdriver and install the snap ring with snap ring pliers.
    HINT: Tape the screwdriver tip before use.

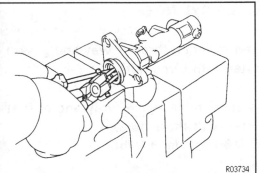

R03734

3. **INSTALL PISTON STOPPER BOLT**
    Using a screwdriver, push the piston in all the way and install the piston stopper bolt over the gasket. Torque the bolt.
    Torque: 10 N·m (100 kgf·cm, 7 ft·lbf)
4. **INSTALL TWO GROMMETS**

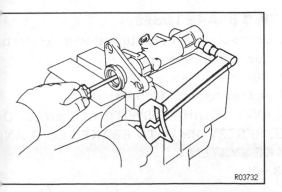

R03732

BR

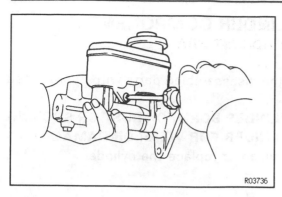

5. INSTALL RESERVOIR
(a) Install the cap and strainer to the reservoir.
(b) Push the reservoir onto the cylinder.
(c) Install the set screw while pushing on the reservoir.
Torque: 1.7 N·m (17.5 kgf·cm, 15.2 in.·lbf)

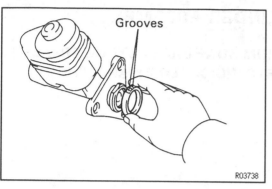

Grooves

6. INSTALL MASTER CYLINDER BOOT
Align the grooves on the master cylinder boot an
master cylinder flange as shown, install the cylind
boot on the master cylinder.

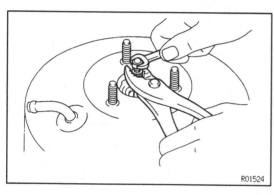

MASTER CYLINDER INSTALLATION

1. ADJUST LENGTH OF BRAKE BOOSTER PUSH RO
BEFORE INSTALLING MASTER CYLINDER
(See page BR−19)

2. INSTALL MASTER CYLINDER
(w/o ABS)
Install the master cylinder, three — way and gasket o
the brake booster with three nuts.
(w/ ABS)
Install the master cylinder, two — way and gasket o
the brake booster with three nuts.
Torque: 13 N·m (130 kgf·cm, 9 ft·lbf)

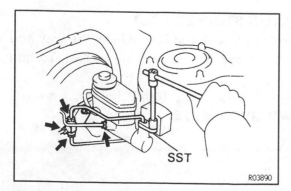

SST

3. CONNECT TWO BRAKE TUBES
Using SST, connect the brake tubes to the mast
cylinder. Torque the union nuts.
SST 09023−00100
Torque: 15 N·m (155 kgf·cm, 11 ft·lbf)
4. CONNECT LEVEL WARNING SWITCH CONNECTO
5. FILL BRAKE RESERVOIR WITH BRAKE FLUID AN
BLEED BRAKE SYSTEM
(See page BR−9)

6. **CHECK FOR LEAKS**
7. **CHECK AND ADJUST BRAKE PEDAL**
   (See page BR−7)

BRAKE BOOSTER
BRAKE BOOSTER REMOVAL

BR09M−

- Resonator

- Air Hose

- Charcoal Canister

w/o ABS

- Vacuum Hose

15 (155, 11)

Three-Way

15 (155, 11)

◆ Gasket

◆ Gasket   Clevis Pin   Clip

Return Spring

13 (130, 9)

15 (155, 11)

15 (155, 11)

Master Cylinder

Brake Booster

13 (130, 9)

w/ ABS

Vacuum Hose

15 (155, 11)

15 (155, 11)

Clevis Pin

Clip

Two-Way

◆ Gasket

◆ Gasket

15 (155, 11)

13 (130, 9)

Return Spring

15 (155, 11)

Master Cylinder

Brake Booster

13 (130, 9)

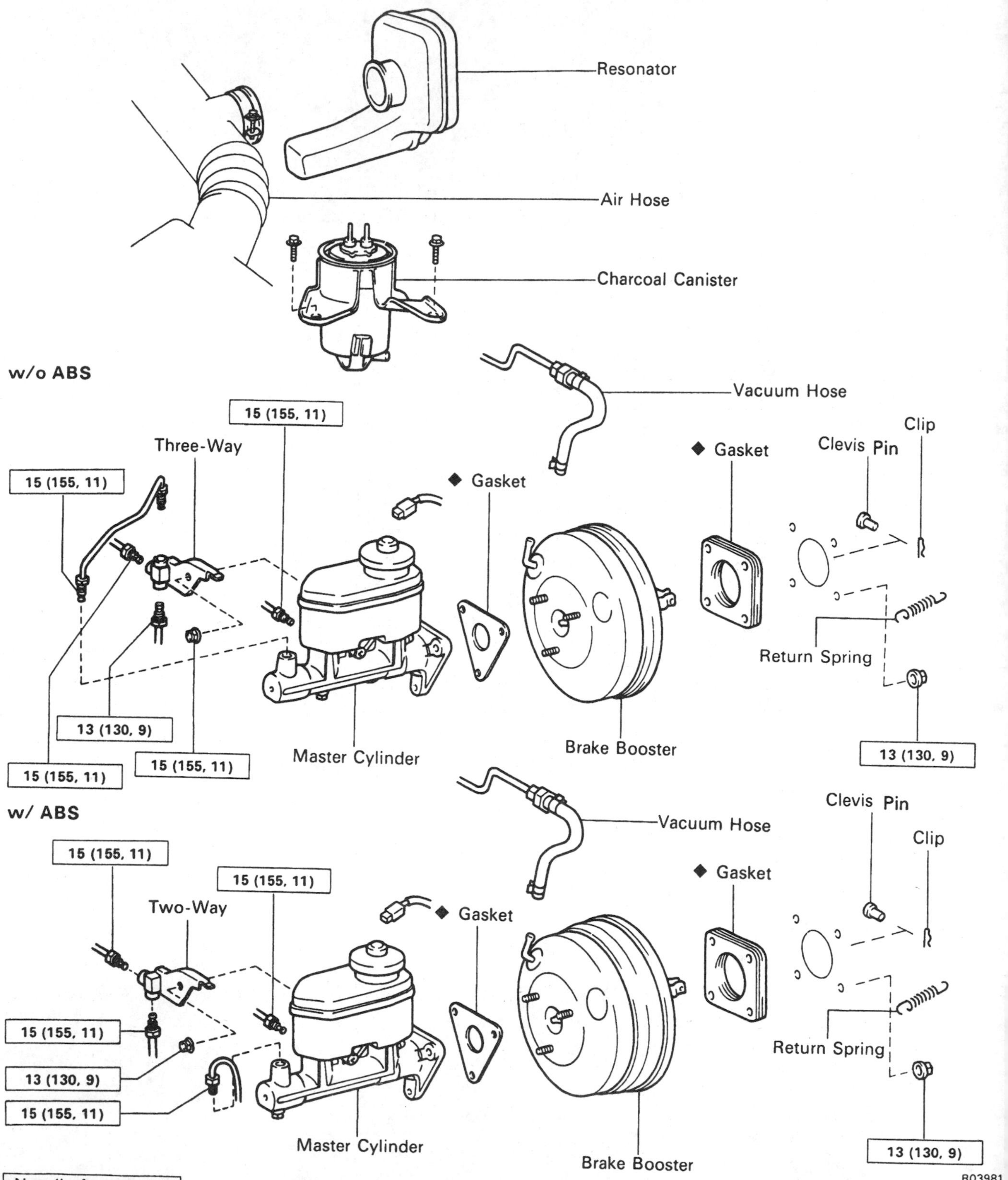

N·m (kgf·cm, ft·lbf) : Specified torque

◆ Non-reusable part

R03981

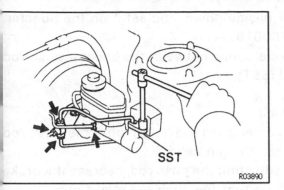

1. **REMOVE MASTER CYLINDER**
   (See page BR−11)
2. **DISCONNECT VACUUM HOSE FROM BRAKE BOO-STER**
3. **REMOVE PEDAL RETURN SPRING**
4. **REMOVE CLIP AND CLEVIS PIN**
5. **REMOVE RESONATOR FROM AIR HOSE**

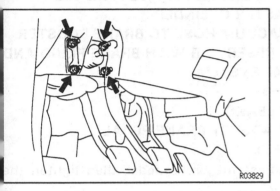

6. **REMOVE CHARCOAL CANISTER**
(a) Disconnect the two hoses.
(b) Remove the two bolts and charcoal canister.
7. **REMOVE BREKE BOOSTER**
(a) Remove the four nuts.
(b) Pull out the brake booster and gasket.

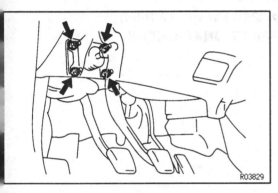

BRAKE BOOSTER INSTALLATION

BR04R−03

1. **INSTALL BRAKE BOOSTER**
(a) Install booster and new gasket.
(b) Install the two bolts and charcoal canister.
(c) Connect the two hoses.
(d) Install the clevis to the operating rod.
(e) Install the resonator to air hose.
(f) Install and torque the booster installation nuts.
   Torque: 13 N·m (130 kgf·cm, 9 ft·lbf)
(g) Insert the clevis pin into the clevis and brake pedal, and install the clip to the clevis pin.
(h) Install the pedal return spring.

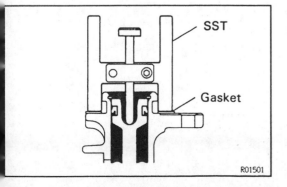

2. **ADJUST LENGTH OF BOOSTER PUSH ROD**
(a) Install the gasket on the master cylinder.
(b) Set the SST on the gasket, and lower the pin until its tip slightly touches the piston.
   SST 09737−00010

K5604   R01502

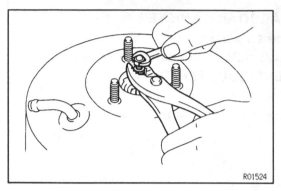

R01524

(c) Turn the SST upside down, and set it on the booster.
SST 09737−00010

(d) Measure the clearance between the booster push rod
and pin head (SST).
Clearance:

0 mm (0 in.)

(e) Adjust the booster push rod length until the push rod
slightly touches the pin head.
HINT: When adjusting the push rod, depress the brake
pedal enough so that the push rod sticks out.

3. **INSTALL MASTER CYLINDER**

4. **CONNECT VACUUM HOSE TO BRAKE BOOSTER**

5. **FILL BRAKE RESERVOIR WITH BRAKE FLUID AND**
BLEED BRAKE SYSTEM
(See page BR−9)

6. **CHECK FOR LEAKS**

7. **CHECK AND ADJUST BRAKE PEDAL**
(See page BR−7)

Check and adjust the brake pedal, then tighten the
clevis lock nut.
Torque: 25 N·m (260 kgf·cm, 19 ft·lbf)

8. **PERFORM OPERATIONAL CHECK**
(See page BR−8)

FRONT BRAKE
COMPONENTS

BROON—04

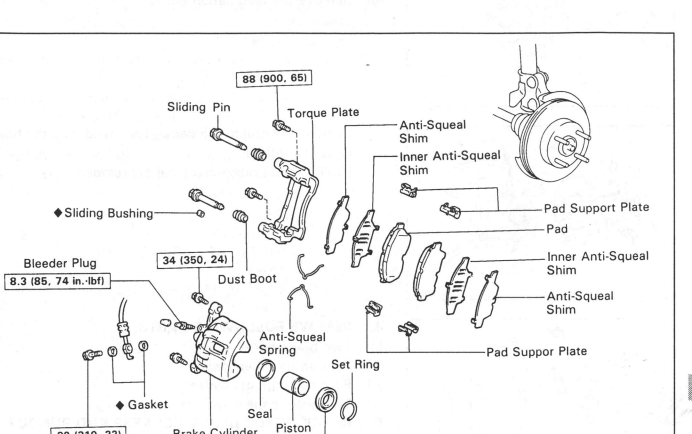

88 (900, 65)

Sliding Pin

Torque Plate

Anti-Squeal Shim

Inner Anti-Squeal Shim

Pad Support Plate

Pad

◆ Sliding Bushing

Inner Anti-Squeal Shim

Bleeder Plug

34 (350, 24)

Anti-Squeal Shim

8.3 (85, 74 in.·lbf)

Dust Boot

Anti-Squeal Spring

Pad Suppor Plate

Set Ring

◆ Gasket

Seal

Piston

Brake Cylinder

Cylinder Boot

30 (310. 22)

N·m (kgf·cm, ft·lbf) : Specified torque

◆ Non-reusable part

R04022

BRO9S—02

BRAKE PADS REPLACEMENT

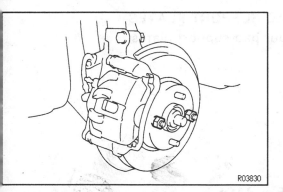

R03830

1. REMOVE FRONT WHEEL
Remove the wheel and temporarily fasten the rotor disc with the hub nuts.

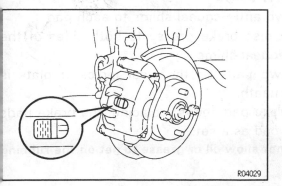

R04029

2. INSPECT PAD LINING THICKNESS
Check the pad thickness through the cylinder inspection hole and replace the pads if it is not within specification.
Minimum thickness:
 1.0 mm (0.039 in.)

BR

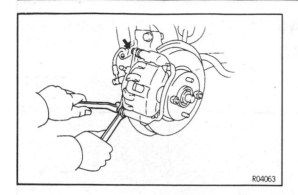

3. REMOVE CYLINDER FROM TORQUE PLATE
(a) Hold the sliding pin on the bottom and loosen the installation bolts.
(b) Remove the installation bolts.

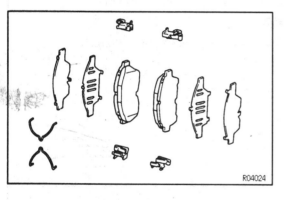

(c) Remove the brake cylinder and suspend it so the hose is not stretched.
HINT: Do not disconnect the brake hose.

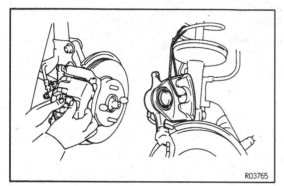

4. REMOVE FOLLOWING PARTS:
(a) Two brake pads
(b) Four anti—squeal shims
(c) Four pad support plates
(d) Two anti—squeal springs
5. CHECK ROTOR DISC THICKNESS AND RUNOUT
(See page BR—25)

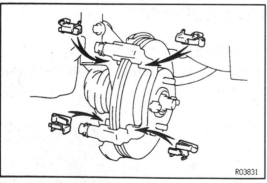

6. INSTALL PAD SUPPORT PLATES
Install the four pad support plates.

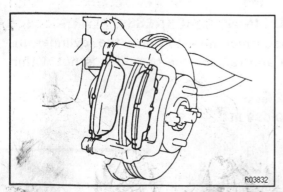

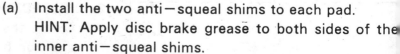

7. INSTALL NEW PADS
(a) Install the two anti—squeal shims to each pad.
HINT: Apply disc brake grease to both sides of the inner anti—squeal shims.
(b) Install the two pads so the wear indicator plate is facing underneath.
HINT: If a brake pad needs replacing, the brake pads must be replced as a set.
NOTICE: Do not allow oil or grease to get on the rubbing face.

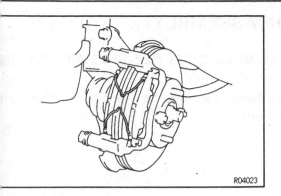

(c) Install two anti–squeal springs to the pad.

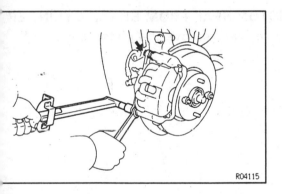

8. **INSTALL CYLINDER**
(a) Draw out a small amount of brake fluid from the reservoir.
(b) Press in the piston with a hammer handle or an equivalent.
HINT: If the piston is difficult to push in, loosen the bleeder plug and push in the piston while letting some brake fluid escape.

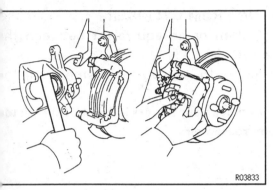

(c) Install the brake cylinder.
(d) Install and torque the two installation bolts.
Torque: 34 N·m (350 kgf·cm, 25 ft·lbf)
9. **INSTALL FRONT WHEEL**
10. **CHECK THAT FLUID LEVEL IS MAX LINE**

BR

BR00Q–04

CYLINDER REMOVAL

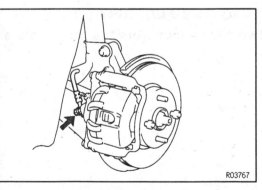

1. **DISCONNECT FLEXIBLE HOSE**
(a) Remove the union bolt and two gaskets from the brake cylinder, then disconnect the flexible hose from the brake cylinder.
(b) Use a container to catch the brake fluid as it drains out.

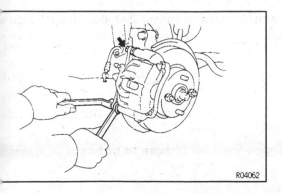

2. **REMOVE CYLINDER FROM TORQUE PLATE**
Hold the sliding pin, remove the two installation bolts and cylinder.
3. **REMOVE TWO BRAKE PADS**

BR

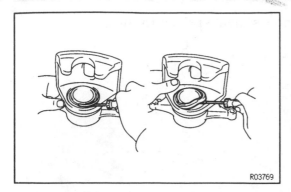

BR09T-02

CYLINDER DISASSEMBLY

1. REMOVE CYLINDER BOOT SET RING AND CYLIN-DER BOOT

Using a screwdriver, remove the cylinder boot set ring and cylinder boot.

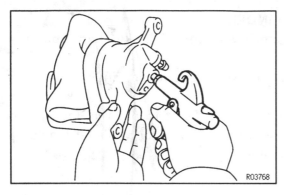

2. REMOVE PISTON FROM CYLINDER

(a) Put a piece of cloth or an equivalent between the piston and the cylinder.

(b) Use compressed air to remove the piston from the cylinder.

CAUTION: Do not place your fingers in front of the piston when using compressed air.

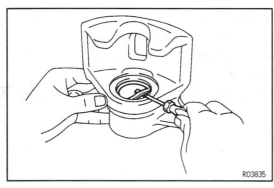

3. REMOVE PISTON SEAL FROM BRAKE CYLINDER

Using a screwdriver, remove the piston seal.

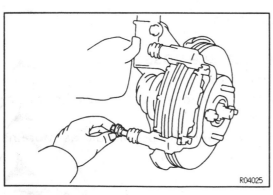

4. REMOVE SLIDING PINS AND DUST BOOTS

(a) Remove the two sliding pins from the torque plate.

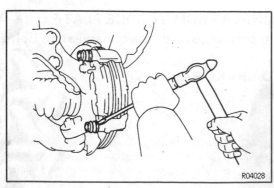

(b) Using a screwdriver and hammer, tap out the two dust boots.

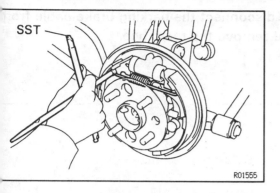

4.   REMOVE FRONT SHOE
(a)   Using SST, remove the return spring.
      SST 09703−30010

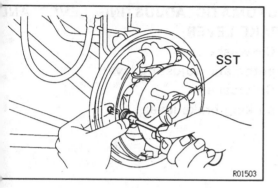

(b)   Using SST, remove the shoe hold−down spring, cups
      and pin.
      SST 09718−00010
(c)   Disconnect the anchor spring from the front shoe and
      remove the front shoe.
(d)   Remove the anchor spring from the rear shoe.

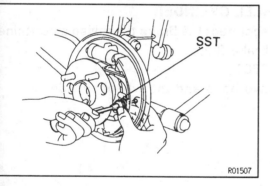

5.   REMOVE REAR SHOE
(a)   Using SST, remove the shoe hold−down spring, cups
      and pin.
      SST 09718−00010

BR

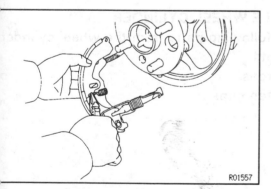

(b)   Using pliers, remove the adjusting lever spring.

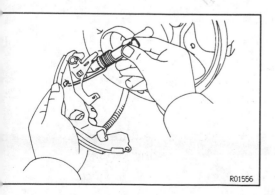

(c)   Remove the adjuster.

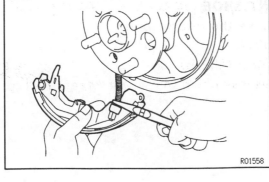

R01558

(d) Using pliers, disconnect the parking brake cable from the lever and remove the rear shoe.

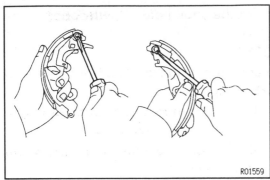

R01559

6. REMOVE AUTOMATIC ADJUSTING LEVER AND PARKING BRAKE LEVER

(a) Remove the C—washer.
(b) Remove the automatic adjusting lever.
(c) Remove the C—washer.
(d) Remove the parking brake lever.

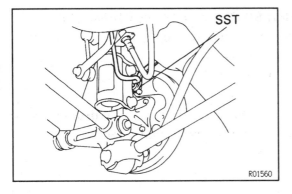

SST

R01560

7. REMOVE WHEEL CYLINDER

(a) Using SST, disconnect the brake tube. Use a container to catch the brake fluid.
   SST 09751—36011
(b) Remove the two bolts and the wheel cylinder.

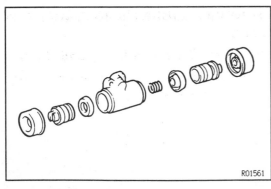

R01561

8. DISASSEMBLE WHEEL CYLINDER

Remove the following parts from the wheel cylinder
- Two boots
- Two pistons
- Two piston cups
- Spring

REAR BRAKE COMPONENTS INSPECTION AND REPAIR

1. **INSPECT DISASSEMBLED PARTS**
   Inspect the disassembled parts for wear, rust or damage.

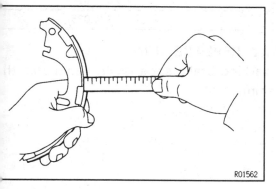

R01562

2. **MEASURE BRAKE SHOE LINING THICKNESS**
   Standard thickness:
   4.0 mm (0.157 in.)
   Minimum thickness:
   1.0 mm (0.039 in.)
   If the shoe lining is less than minimum or shows signs of uneven wear, replace the brake shoes.
   HINT: If a brake shoe needs replacing, the brake shoes must be replaced as a set.

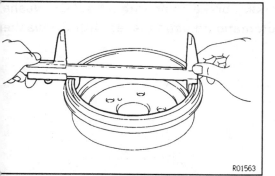

R01563

3. **MEASURE BRAKE DRUM INSIDE DIAMETER**
   Standard inside diameter:
   200.0 mm (7.874 in.)
   Maximum inside diameter:
   201.0 mm (7.913 in.)
   If the drum is scored or worn, the brake drum may be lathed to the maximum inside diameter.

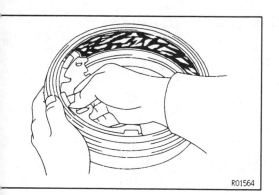

R01564

4. **INSPECT REAR BRAKE LINING AND DRUM FOR PROPER CONTACT**
   If the contact between the brake lining and drum is improper, repair the lining with a brake shoe grinder, or replace the brake shoe assembly.

BR

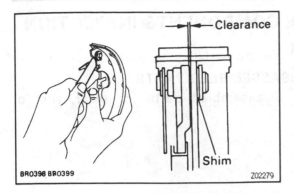

5.　MEASURE CLEARANCE BETWEEN BRAKE SHOE AND LEVER

Using a feeler gauge, measure the clearance.

Standard clearance:

　　Less than 0.35 mm (0.0138 in.)

If the clearance is not within specification, replace the shim with one of the correct size.

Shim thickness mm (in.)	Shim thickness mm (in.)
0.2 (0.008)	0.5 (0.020)
0.3 (0.012)	0.6 (0.024)
0.4 (0.016)	0.9 (0.035)

6.　IF NECESSARY, REPLACE SHIM

(a)　Remove the parking brake shoe lever, and install the correct size shim.

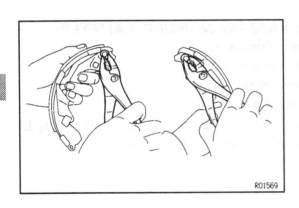

(b)　Install the parking brake lever with a new C—washer.

(c)　Install the automatic adjusting lever with C—washer.

BR0A0-02

REAR BRAKE INSTALLATION

HINT: Assemble the parts in the correct direction as shown.

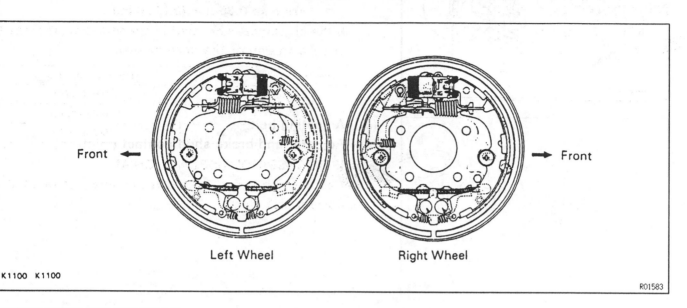

Front ←   → Front

Left Wheel   Right Wheel

K1100 K1100

R01583

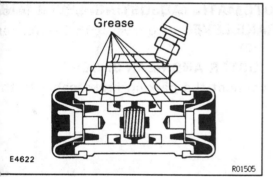

Grease

E4622   R01505

1. APPLY LITHIUM SOAP BASE GLYCOL GREASE TO FOLLOWING PARTS:

(a) Two piston cups

(b) Two pistons

(c) Two boots

BR

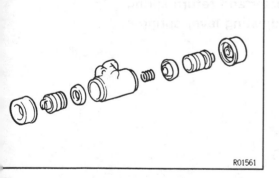

R01561

2. ASSEMBLE WHEEL CYLINDER

(a) Install two piston cups to the pistons.

(b) Install the spring and two pistons into the wheel cylinder. Check that the flanges of the piston are pointed inward.

(c) Install two boots.

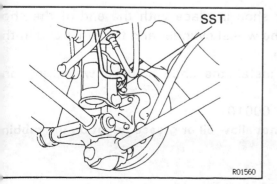

SST

R01560

3. INSTALL WHEEL CYLINDER

Install the wheel cylinder on the backing plate with the two bolts.

Torque: 10 N·m (100 kgf·cm, 7 ft·lbf)

4. CONNECT BRAKE TUBE TO WHEEL CYLINDER

Using SST, connect the brake tube.

SST 09751—36011

Torque: 15 N·m (155 kgf·cm, 11 ft·lbf)

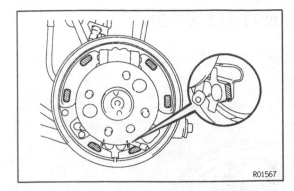

5. APPLY HIGH TEMPERATURE GREASE TO FOL-LOWING PARTS:
(a) Backing plate and brake shoe contact points
(b) Anchor plate and brake shoe contact points

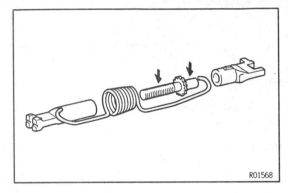

(c) Adjusting bolt
(d) Adjuster and brake shoe contact points

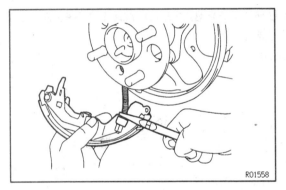

6. INSTALL AUTOMATIC ADJUSTING LEVER AND PARKING BRAKE LEVER
(See page BR-32)

7. INSTALL ADJUSTER AND REAR SHOE
(a) Using pliers, connect the parking brake cable to the lever.

(b) Set the adjuster and return spring.
(c) Install the adjusting lever spring.

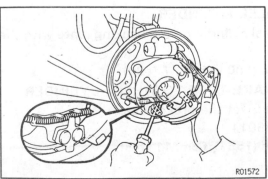

(d) Set the rear shoe in place with the end of the shoe inserted in the wheel cylinder and the other end in the anchor plate.
(e) Using SST, install the shoe hold-down spring and pin.
SST 09718-00010
NOTICE: Do not allow oil or grease to get on the rubbing face.

BR

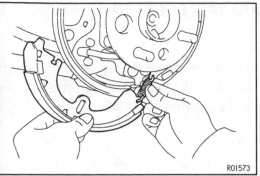

8.　INSTALL FRONT SHOE

(a)　Install the anchor spring between the front and rear shoes.

(b)　Set the front shoe in place with the end of the shoe inserted in the wheel cylinder and the adjuster in place.

NOTICE: Do not allow oil or grease to get on the rubbing face.

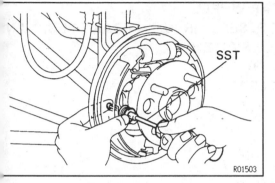

(c)　Using SST, install the shoe hold—down spring and pin.

SST 09718—00010

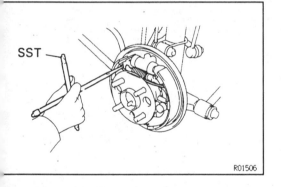

(d)　Using SST, install the return spring.

SST 09703—30010

BR

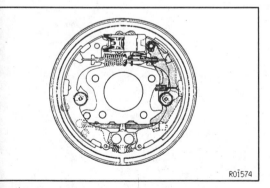

9.　CHECK OPERATION OF AUTOMATIC ADJUSTING MECHANISM

(a)　Move the parking brake lever of the rear shoe back and forth, as shown. Check that the adjuster turns.

If the adjuster does not turn, check for incorrect installation of the rear brake.

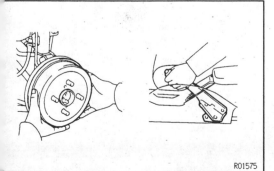

(b)　Adjust the adjuster length to the shortest possible amount.

(c)　Install the brake drum.

(d)　Pull the parking brake lever all the way up until a clicking sound can no longer be heard.

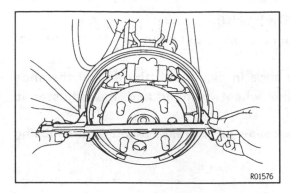

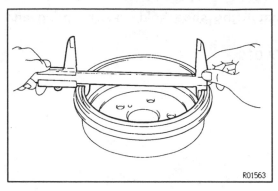

10. CHECK CLEARANCE BETWEEN BRAKE SHOE AND DRUM

(a) Remove the brake drum.

(b) Measure the brake drum inside diameter and diameter of the brake shoes. Check that the difference between the diameters is the correct shoe clearance.

Shoe clearance:

0.6 mm (0.024 in.)

If incorrect, check the parking brake system.

11. INSTALL BRAKE DRUM

12. INSTALL REAR WHEEL

13. FILL BRAKE RESERVOIR WITH BRAKE FLUID AND BLEED BRAKE SYSTEM

(See page BR—9)

14. CHECK FOR LEAKS

BR

PROPORTIONING VALVE (P VALVE)
FLUID PRESSURE CHECK

1. **INSTALL LSPV GAUGE (SST) AND BLEED AIR**
   SST 09709−29017

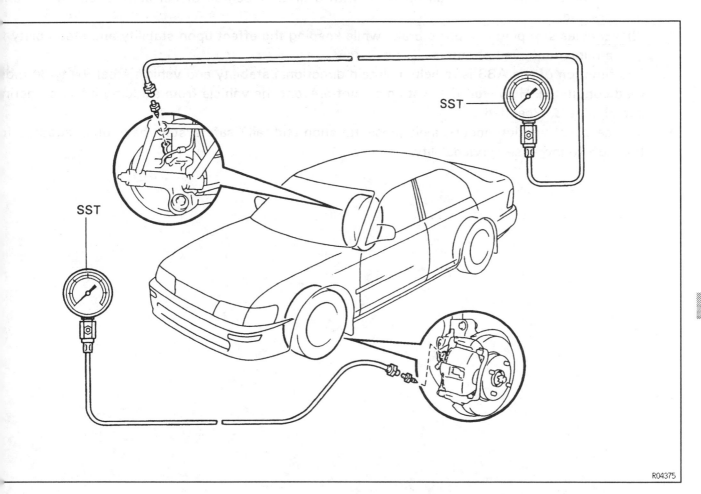

SST

SST

R04375

2. **BLEED AIR FROM FLUID PRESSURE GAUGE**
3. **RAISE MASTER CYLINDER PRESSURE AND CHECK REAR WHEEL CYLINDER PRESSURE**

Master cylinder pressure	Rear wheel cylinder
2,942 kPa (30 kgf/cm², 427 psi)	2,942 kPa (30 kgf/cm², 427 psi)
7,845 kPa (80 kgf/cm², 1,138 psi)	4,168 kPa (42.5 kgf/cm², 605 psi)

When inspecting the fluid pressure, inspect the left front and right rear together, and the right front and left rear together.

If the rear wheel cylinder pressure is incorrect, replace the P valve assembly.

4. **BLEED BRAKE SYSTEM**
5. **CHECK FOR LEAKS**

BR

ANTI—LOCK BRAKE SYSTEM (ABS)

DESCRIPTION

- The ABS is a brake system which controls the brake cylinder hydraulic pressure of all four wheels during sudden braking and braking on slippery road surfaces, preventing the wheels from locking. This ABS provides the following benefits:
  - (1) Enables steering round an obstacle with a greater degree of certainty even when panic braking.
  - (2) Enables stopping in a panic brake while keeping the effect upon stability and steerability to a minimum, even on curves.
- The function of the ABS is to help maintain directional stability and vehicle steerability on most road conditions. However, the system cannot prevent the vehicle from skidding if the cornering speed limit is exceeded.
- In case a malfunction occurs, a diagnosis function and fail—safe system have been adopted for the ABS to increase serviceability.

BR

BR02K-04

COMPONENTS FUNCTION

Component	Function
Front Vehicle Speed Sensor	Detect the wheel speed of each of the left and right front wheels.
Rear Vehicle Speed Sensor	Detect the wheel speed of each of the left and right rear wheels.
ABS Warning Light	Lights up to alert the driver when trouble has occured in the Anti-Lock Brake System.
Actuator	Controls the brake fluid pressure to each brake cylinder through signals from the ECU.
ABS ECU	From the wheel speed signals from each sensor, it caluclates acceleration, deceleration and slip values and sends signals to the actuator to control brake fluid pressure.

BR02L-03

SYSTEM PARTS LOCATION

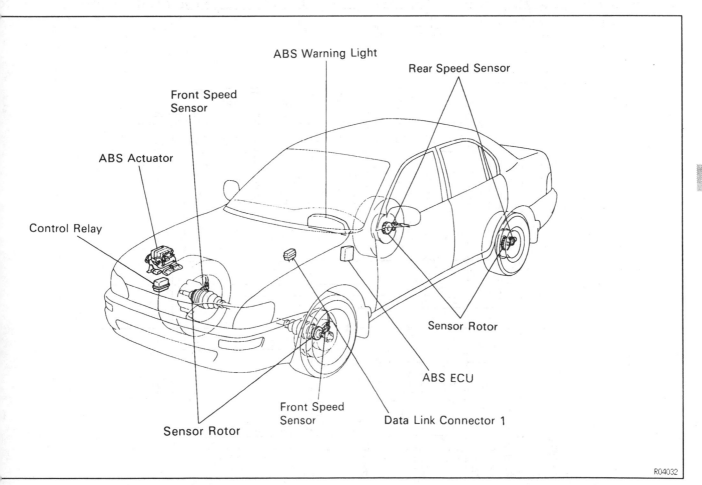

R04032

WIRING DIAGRAM

BR02M-04

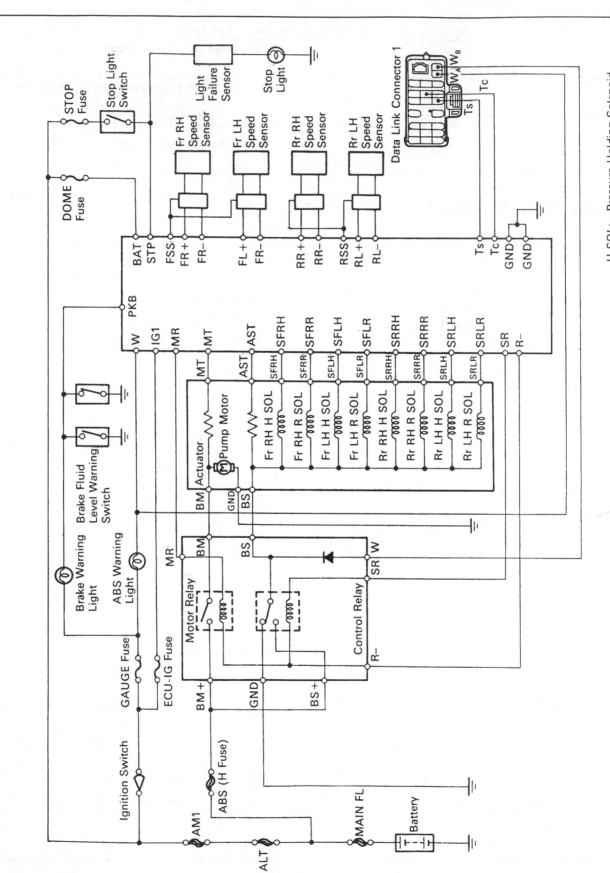

H SOL: Pressure Holding Solenoid
R SOL: Pressure Reduction Solenoid

BR

R03054

Z03911

CONNECTORS

ABS Actuator

CONNECTOR A

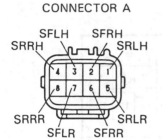

SFLH   SFRH
SRRH   SRLH

| 4 | 3 | 2 | 1 |
| 8 | 7 | 6 | 5 |

SRRR   SRLR
SFLR   SFRR

CONNECTOR B

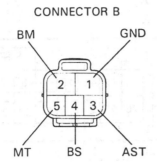

BM   GND

| 2 | 1 |
| 5 | 4 | 3 |

MT   BS   AST

Control Relay

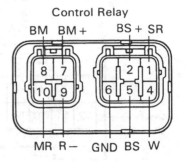

BM BM+   BS+ SR

| 8 | 7 | | 2 | 1 |
| 10 | 9 | | 6 | 5 | 4 |

MR R—   GND BS W

Front Speed Sensor (LH)

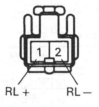

FL+   FL—

| 2 | 1 |

Front Speed Sensor (RH)

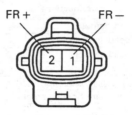

FR+   FR—

| 2 | 1 |

Rear Speed Sensor (LH)

RL+   RL—

| 1 | 2 |

Rear Speed Sensor (RH)

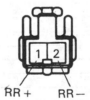

RR+   RR—

| 1 | 2 |

ABS ECU

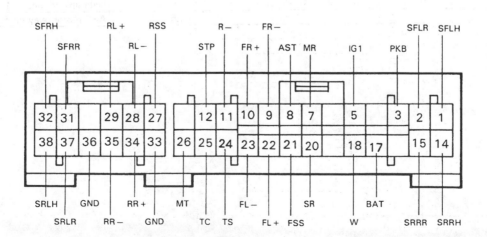

SFRH   RL+   RSS   R—   FR—   SFLR SFLH
      SFRR   RL—   STP   FR+   AST MR   IG1   PKB

| 32 | 31 | | 29 | 28 | 27 | | 12 | 11 | 10 | 9 | 8 | 7 | | 5 | | 3 | 2 | 1 |
| 38 | 37 | 36 | 35 | 34 | 33 | | 26 | 25 | 24 | 23 | 22 | 21 | 20 | | 18 | 17 | | 15 | 14 |

SRLH   GND   RR+   MT   FL—   SR   BAT   SRRR SRRH
    SRLR   RR—   GND   TC TS   FL+ FSS   W

le-8-2 RO4071 BR3999
le-2-2-T le-2-2-T
e-2-1-G e-2-1-G
R03953

Z03528

ECU TERMINALS

BROA4−0

R03953

Terminal No.	Symbol	Connection	Terminal No.	Symbol	Connection
A13 − 1	RSS	Sealed wiring harness	A14 − 1	SFLH	Front left pressure holding solenoid
2	RL−	Rear left speed sensor	2	SFLR	Front left pressure reduction solenoid
3	RL+	Rear left speed sensor	3	PKB	Parking brake switch
4	—		4	—	
5	SFRR	Front right pressure reduction solenoid	5	IG1	Ignition switch
6	SFRH	Front right pressure holding solenoid	6	—	
7	GND	Ground	7	MR	ABS motor relay
8	RR+	Rear right speed sensor	8	AST	ABS solenoid relay monitor
9	RR−	Rear right speed sensor	9	FR−	Front right speed sensor
10	GND	Ground	10	FR+	Front right speed sensor
11	SRLR	Rear left pressure reduction solenoid	11	R−	Relay ground
12	SRLH	Rear left pressure holding solenoid	12	STP	Stop light switch
			13	—	
			14	SRRH	Rear right pressure holding solenoid
			15	SRRR	Rear right pressure reduction solenoid
			16	—	
			17	BAT	Battery
			18	W	ABS warning light
			19	—	
			20	SR	ABS solenoid relay
			21	FSS	Sealed wiring harness
			22	FL+	Front left speed sensor
			23	FL−	Front left speed sensor
			24	TS	Data link connector 1
			25	TC	Data link connector 1
			26	MT	ABS motor relay monitor

V0169

BR

BROA5—01

ECU TERMINALS STANDATD VALUE

Symbols (Terminals No.)		STD Voltage (V)	Condition
BAT (A14 – 7)	GND (A13 – 7)	10 – 14	Always
IG1 (A14 – 5)	GND (A13 – 7)	10 – 14	IG switch ON
SR (A14 – 20)	R– (A14 – 11)	10 – 14	IG switch ON
MR (A14 – 7)	R– (A14 – 11)	Below 1.0	IG switch ON
SFRR (A13 – 5)	GND (A13 – 7)	10 – 14	IG switch ON, ABS warning light OFF
SFRH (A13 – 6)	GND (A13 – 7)	10 – 14	IG switch ON, ABS warning light OFF
SFLR (A14 – 2)	GND (A13 – 7)	10 – 14	IG switch ON, ABS warning light OFF
SFLH (A14 – 1)	GND (A13 – 7)	10 – 14	IG switch ON, ABS warning light OFF
SRRR (A14 – 5)	GND (A13 – 7)	10 – 14	IG switch ON, ABS warning light OFF
SRRH (A14 – 4)	GND (A13 – 7)	10 – 14	IG switch ON, ABS warning light OFF
SRLR (A13 – 11)	GND (A13 – 7)	10 – 14	IG switch ON, ABS warning light OFF
SRLH (A13 – 12)	GND (A13 – 7)	10 – 14	IG switch ON, ABS warning light OFF
AST (A14 – 8)	GND (A13 – 7)	10 – 14	IG switch ON, ABS warning light OFF
W (A14 – 18)	GND (A13 – 7)	Below 1.0	IG switch ON, ABS warning light ON
		10 – 14	IG switch ON, ABS warning light OFF
PKB (A14 – 3)	GND (A13 – 7)	Below 1.0	IG switch ON, PKB switch ON
		10 – 14	IG switch ON, PKB switch OFF
STP (A14 – 12)	GND (A13 – 7)	Below 1.0	Stop light switch OFF
		10 – 14	Stop light switch ON
Tc (A14 – 25)	GND (A13 – 7)	10 – 14	IG switch ON
Ts (A14 – 24)	GND (A13 – 7)	10 – 14	IG switch ON
FR+ (A14 – 10)	FR– (A14 – 9)	AC generation	IG switch ON Slowly turn front right wheel
FL+ (A14 – 22)	FL– (A14 – 23)	AC generation	IG switch ON Slowly turn front left wheel
RR+ (A13 – 8)	RR– (A13 – 9)	AC generation	IG switch ON Slowly turn rear right wheel
RL+ (A13 – 3)	RL– (A13 – 2)	AC generation	IG switch ON Slowly turn rear left wheel

BR

V01693

ABS ACTUATOR
ABS ACTUATOR REMOVAL AND INSTALLATION

BR09Y—03

Remove and install the parts as shown.

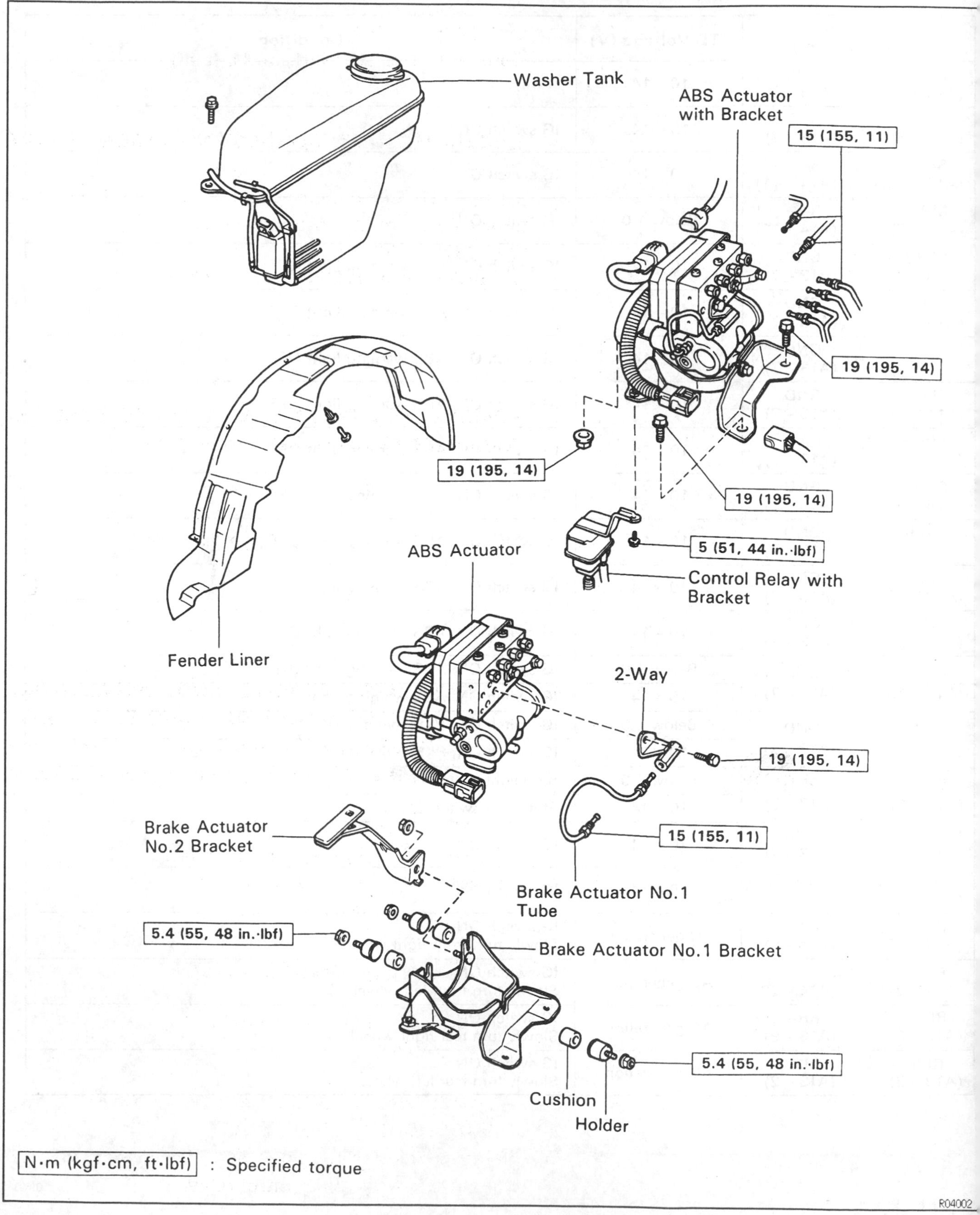

Washer Tank

ABS Actuator with Bracket

15 (155, 11)

19 (195, 14)

19 (195, 14)

19 (195, 14)

Fender Liner

ABS Actuator

5 (51, 44 in.·lbf)

Control Relay with Bracket

2-Way

19 (195, 14)

Brake Actuator No.2 Bracket

15 (155, 11)

Brake Actuator No.1 Tube

5.4 (55, 48 in.·lbf)

Brake Actuator No.1 Bracket

5.4 (55, 48 in.·lbf)

Cushion

Holder

BR

| N·m (kgf·cm, ft·lbf) | : Specified torque

R04002

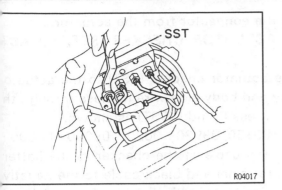

R04017

(MAIN POINT OF REMOVAL AND INSTALLATION)

1. **DISCONNECT AND CONNECT BRAKE TUBE**
   Using SST, disconnect and connect the brake tubes from/to the ABS actuator.
   SST 09751−36011
   Torque: 15 N·m (155 kgf·cm, 11 ft·lbf)

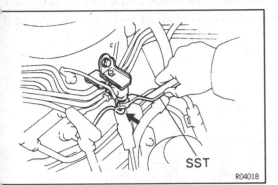

R04018

2. **DISCONNECT AND CONNECT NO.4 FRONT BRAKE TUBE**
   Using SST, disconnect and connect the No.4 front brake tube from/to the two−way.
   SST 09751−36011
   Torque: 15 N·m (155 kgf·cm, 11 ft·lbf)

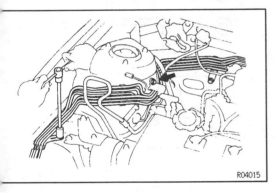

R04015

3. **REMOVE AND INSTALL NO.2 BRAKE TUBE W/ GROMMET CLAMP AND TWO−WAY**

BR

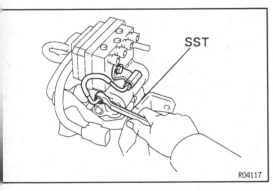

R04117

4. **IF NECESSARY, REMOVE AND INSTALLATION BRAKE ACTUATOR NO.1 TUBE AND TWO−WAY**
   Using SST, disconnect and connect the brake actuator No.1 tube and two−way from/to the ABS actuator.
   SST 09751−36011
   Torque: 15 N·m (155 kgf·cm, 11 ft·lbf)

5. **BLEED BRAKE SYSTEM**
   (See page BR−9)

BR02X−04

ABS ACTUATOR INSPECTION

1. **INSPECT BATTERY VOLTAGE**
   Battery voltage:
      10−14.5 V

2. **REMOVE WINDSHIELD WASHER TANK**

3. **DISCONNECT CONNECTORS**

(a) Remove the fender liner and disconnect the two connectors from the control relay.

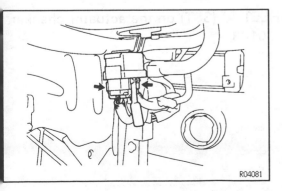

R04081

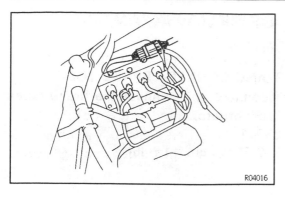

R04016

(b) Disconnect the connector from the actuator.

**4. CONNECT ACTUATOR CHECKER (SST) TO ACT
UATOR**

(a) Connect the actuator checker (SST) to the actuato
control relay and body side wire harness through th
sub—wire harness C and I (SST) as shown.
SST 09990—00150, 09990—00200, 09990—00300

(b) Connect the red cable of the checker to the batter
positive (+) terminal and black cable to the negativ
(—) terminal. Connect the black cable of the sub—wir
harness to the battery negative (—) terminal or bod
ground.

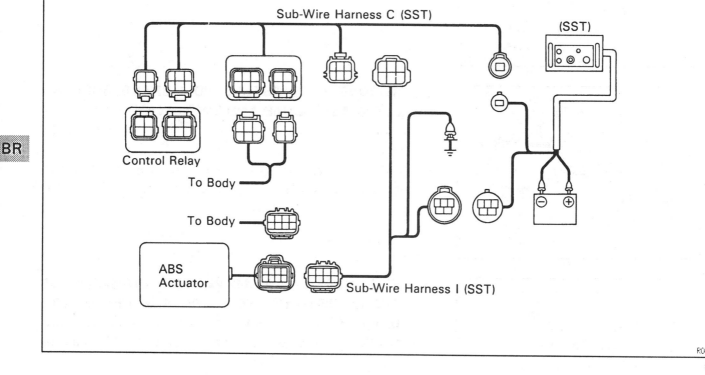

Sub-Wire Harness C (SST)

(SST)

Control Relay

To Body

To Body

ABS
Actuator

Sub-Wire Harness I (SST)

R04103

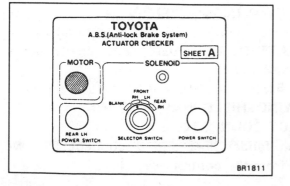

BR1811

(c) Place the "SHEET A" (SST) on the actuator checker.
SST 09990—00163

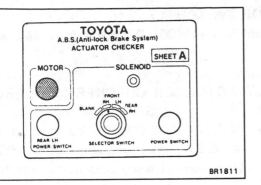

5.　INSPECT BRAKE ACTUATOR OPERATION

(a)　Start the engine, and run it at idle.

(b)　Turn the selector switch of the actuator checker to "FRONT RH" position.

(c)　Push and hold in the MOTOR switch for a few seconds. Make sure that you can hear the motor run.

(d)　Depress the brake pedal and hold it for about 15 seconds, and check that the pedal does not go down.

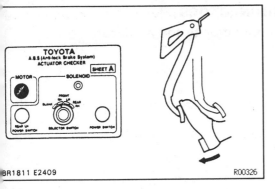

(e)　With your foot still applied onto the brake pedal, push MOTOR switch and check that the brake pedal does not pulsate.

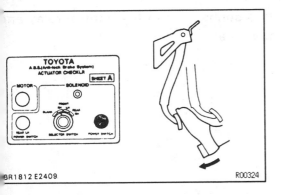

(f)　Depress the brake pedal and hold it. As you hold the pedal down, push and hold in the POWER SWITCH for a few seconds. Check that the pedal does not go down.

(g)　With your foot still applied onto the brake pedal, release the POWER SWITCH and check that the pedal go down.

BR

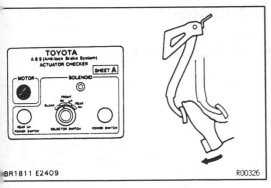

(h)　With your foot still applied onto the brake pedal, push the MOTOR switch and check that the brake pedal does pulsate.

(i)　Release the brake pedal.

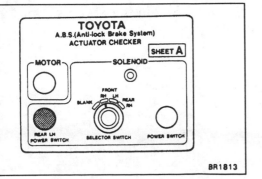

6.　(FOR OTHER WHEELS)

(a)　Turn the selector switch to "FRONT LH" position.

(b)　Repeating (c) to (i) to the step 5, check the actuator operation similarly.

(c)　Similarly, inspect "REAR RH" and "REAR LH" position.

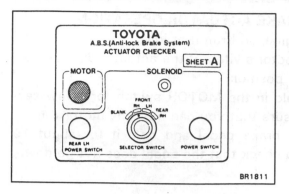

BR1811

7. **PUSH MOTOR SWITCH**
(a) Push and hold in the MOTOR switch for a few seconds.
(b) Stop the engine.

8. **DISCONNECT ACTUATOR CHECKER (SST) FROM ACTUATOR**
Remove the "SHEET A" (SST) and disconnect the actuator checker (SST) andsub—wire harness (SST) from the actuator, control relay and body side wire harness.

9. **CONNECT CONNECTORS**
(a) Connect the connector to the actuator.

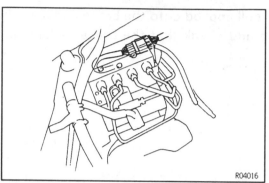

R04016

(b) Connect the two connectors to the control relay and install the fender liner.

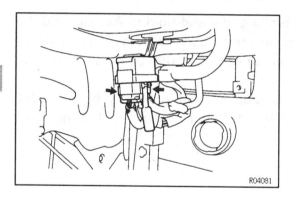

R04081

10. **CLEAR DIAGNOSTIC CODES**
(See page BR—57)
11. **INSTALL WINDSHIELD WASHER TANK**

FRONT SPEED SENSOR
COMPONENTS

BR02Z—03

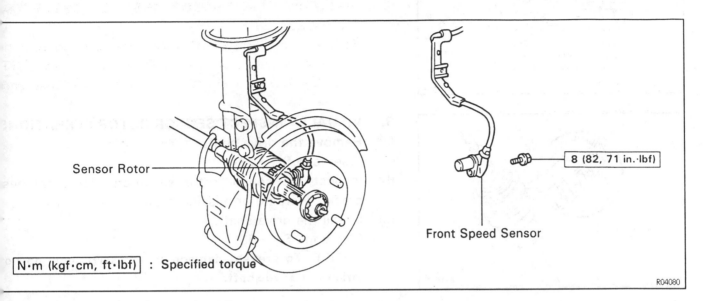

Sensor Rotor

8 (82, 71 in.·lbf)

Front Speed Sensor

N·m (kgf·cm, ft·lbf) : Specified torque

R04080

BR030—04

FRONT SPEED SENSOR INSPECTION

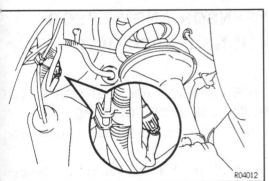

R04012

1. INSPECT SPEED SENSOR

(a) Remove the fendershield.

(b) Disconnect the speed sensor connector.

BR

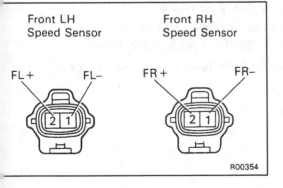

Front LH
Speed Sensor

Front RH
Speed Sensor

FL+   FL−   FR+   FR−

2 1   2 1

R00354

(c) Measure the resistance between terminals.
Resistance:

0.92—1.22 kΩ

If resistance value is not as specified, replace the sensor.

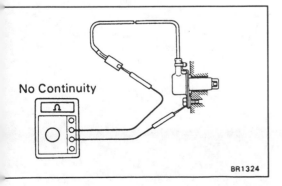

No Continuity

BR1324

(d) Check that there is no continuity between each terminal and sensor body.
If there is continuity, replace the sensor.

(e) Connect the speed sensor connector.

(f) Install the fendershield.

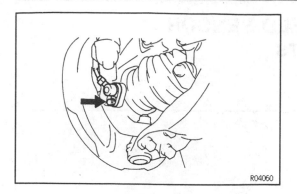

2. INSPECT SENSOR INSTALLATION
Check that the sensor installation bolt is tightened properly. If not, tighten the bolt.
Torque: 7.8 N·m (80 kgf·cm, 69 in.·lbf)

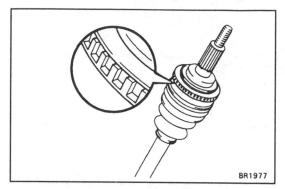

3. VISUALLY INSPECT SENSOR ROTOR SERRATIONS
(a) Remove the drive shaft.
(See page SA—23)
(b) Inspect the sensor rotor serrations for scratches, cracks, warping or missing teeth.
(c) Install the drive shaft.
(See page SA—33)
NOTICE: To prevent damage to the serrations, do no strike the drive shaft.

FRONT SPEED SENSOR AND SENSOR ROTOR SERRATIONS INSPECTION (REFERENCE)

INSPECT FRONT SPEED SENSOR AND SENSOR ROTOR SERRATIONS BY USING AN OSCILLOSCOPE
(a) Connect an oscilloscope to the speed sensor connector.
(b) Run the vehicle at 20 km/h (12.4 mph), and inspec speed sensor output wave.
(c) Check that C is 0.5 V or more.
If not as specified, replace the speed sensor.
(d) Check that B is 30 % or more of A.
If not as specified, replace the sensor rotor.

REAR SPEED SENSOR
COMPONENTS

BR034-03

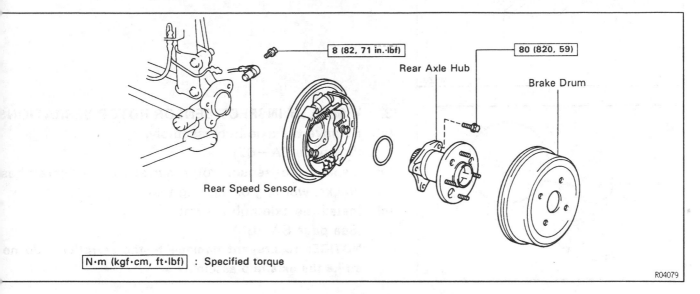

Rear Axle Hub

8 (82, 71 in.·lbf)

80 (820, 59)

Brake Drum

Rear Speed Sensor

N·m (kgf·cm, ft·lbf) : Specified torque

R04079

REAR SPEED SENSOR INSPECTION

BR035-05

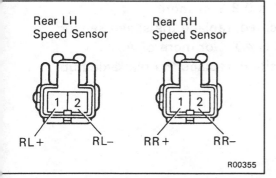

R04010

1.　INSPECT SPEED SENSOR

(a)　Remove the seat cushion and side seatback.

(b)　(Ex. Sedan)
　　　Remove the quarter trim panel.

(c)　Disconnect the speed sensor connector.

Rear LH
Speed Sensor

Rear RH
Speed Sensor

| 1 | 2 |

| 1 | 2 |

RL+　　　RL−　　　RR+　　　RR−

R00355

(d)　Measure the resistance between terminals.
　　　Resistance:
　　　　　1.05 − 1.45 kΩ

　　　If resistance value is not as specified, replace the sensor.

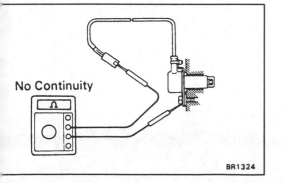

No Continuity

BR1324

(e)　Check that there is no continuity between each terminal and sensor body.
　　　If there is continuity, replace the sensor.

(f)　Connect the speed sensor connector.

(g)　Install the side seatback and the seat cushion.

BR

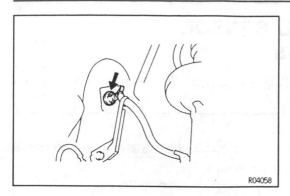

R04058

2. INSPECT SENSOR INSTALLATION
Check that the sensor installation bolt is tightened properly. If not, tighten the bolt.
Torque: 8.0 N·m (82 kgf·cm, 71 in.·lbf)

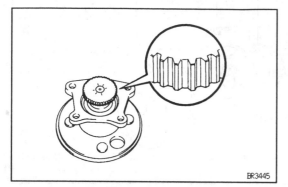

BR3445

3. VISUALLY INSPECT SENSOR ROTOR SERRATIONS
(a) Remove the axle hub assembly.
(See page SA—62)
(b) Inspect the sensor rotor serrations for scratches, cracks, warping or missing teeth.
(c) Install the axle hub assembly.
(See page SA—63)
NOTICE: To prevent damage to the serrations, do not strike the axle hub assembly.

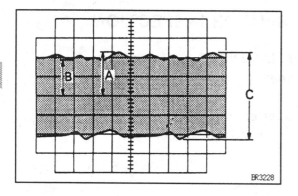

BR3228

BR036—04

REAR SPEED SENSOR AND SENSOR ROTOR SERRATIONS INSPECTION (REFERENCE)

INSPECT REAR SPEED SENSOR AND SENSOR ROTOR SERRATIONS BY USING AN OSCILLOSCOPE
(a) Connect an oscilloscope to the speed sensor connector.
(b) Run the vehicle at 20 km/h (12.4 mph), and inspect speed sensor output wave.
(c) Check that C is 0.8 V or more.
If not as specified, replace the speed sensor.
(d) Check that B is 40 % or more of A.
If not as specified, replace the rear axle hub.

TROUBLESHOOTING
HOW TO PROCEED WITH TROUBLESHOOTING
Perform troubleshooting in accordance with the procedure on the following pages.

1 CUSTOMER PROBLEM ANALYSIS

Using the customer problem analysis check sheet for reference, ask the customer in as much detail as possible about the problem.

2 CHECK AND CLEAR THE DIAGNOSTIC TROUBLE CODES (PRECHECK)

If the ABS warning light lights up, and the ABS does not operate, the ECU stores diagnostic trouble codes corresponding to the problem in memory.

Before confirming the trouble, first check the diagnostic trouble codes to see if there are any malfunction codes stored in memory. When there are malfunction codes, make a note of them, then clear them and proceed to " 3 Problem Symptom Confirmation".

3 PROBLEM SYMPTOM CONFIRMATION, 4 SYMPTOM SIMULATION

Confirm the problem symptoms. If the problem does not reoccur, be sure to simulate the problem by mainly checking the circuits indicated by the diagnostic trouble code in step 2 , using "Problem simulation method".

5 DIAGNOSTIC TROUBLE CODE CHECK

Check the diagnostic trouble codes.

If a malfunction code is output, proceed to " 6 Diagnostic Trouble Code Chart". If the normal code is output, proceed to " 7 Problem Symptoms Chart".

Be sure to proceed to " 6 Diagnostic Trouble Code Chart" after the steps 2 and 3 are completed.

If troubleshooting is attempted only by following the malfunction code stored in the memory, errors could be made in the diagnosis.

6 DIAGNOSTIC TROUBLE CODE CHART

If a malfunction code is confirmed in the diagnostic trouble code check, proceed to the inspection procedure indicated by the matrix chart for each diagnostic trouble code.

7 PROBLEM SYMPTOMS CHART

If the normal code is confirmed in the diagnostic trouble code check, perform inspection in accordance with the inspection order in the problem symptoms chart.

8 CIRCUIT INSPECTION

Proceed with diagnosis of each circuit in accordance with the inspection order confirmed in 6 and 7 . Determine whether the cause of the problem is in the sensor, actuators, wire harness and connectors, or the ECU.

9 SENSOR CHECK

Use the ABS warning light to check if each of the signals from the speed sensors are being input correctly to the ECU. Instructions for this check are given in the circuit inspection.

10 REPAIRS

After the cause of the problem is located, perform repairs by following the inspection and replacement procedures in this manual.

11 CONFIRMATION TEST

After completing repairs, confirm not only that the malfunction is eliminated, but also conduct a test drive, etc., to make sure the entire ABS system is operating correctly.

BR

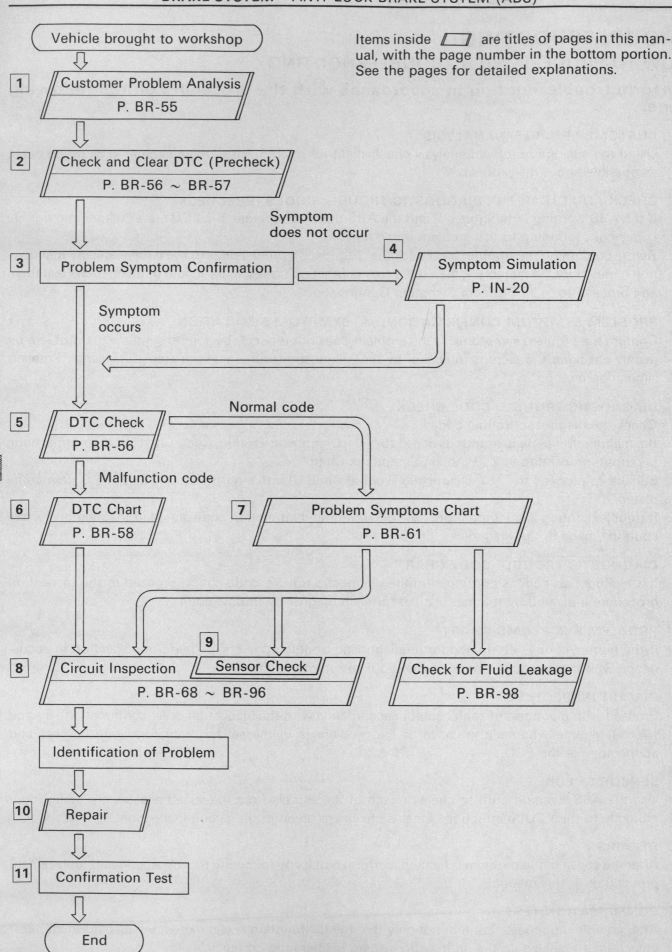

Vehicle brought to workshop

Items inside ⬜ are titles of pages in this manual, with the page number in the bottom portion. See the pages for detailed explanations.

1 Customer Problem Analysis
P. BR-55

2 Check and Clear DTC (Precheck)
P. BR-56 ~ BR-57

3 Problem Symptom Confirmation

Symptom does not occur

4 Symptom Simulation
P. IN-20

Symptom occurs

5 DTC Check
P. BR-56

Normal code

Malfunction code

6 DTC Chart
P. BR-58

7 Problem Symptoms Chart
P. BR-61

8 Circuit Inspection   **9** Sensor Check
P. BR-68 ~ BR-96

Check for Fluid Leakage
P. BR-98

Identification of Problem

10 Repair

11 Confirmation Test

End

BR

CUSTOMER PROBLEM ANALYSIS CHECK SHEET

ABS Check Sheet

Inspector's
Name

Customer's Name		Registration No.	
		Registration Year	/ /
		Frame No.	
Date Vehicle Brought In	/ /	Odometer Reading	km Mile

Condition of Problem Occurrence	Date of Problem Occurrence	/ /
	How Often Does Problem Occur?	☐ Continuous ☐ Intermittent (times a day)

Symptoms	☐ ABS does not operate.
	☐ ABS does not operate efficiently.
	ABS Warning Light Abnormal

	ABS Warning Light Abnormal	☐ Remain ON ☐ Does not Light UP

DTC Check	1st Time	☐ Normal Code ☐ Malfunction Code (Code)
	2nd Time	☐ Normal Code ☐ Malfunction Code (Code)

BR

R04042

DIAGNOSIS SYSTEM
INDICATOR CHECK

When the ignition switch is turned on, check that the ABS warning light goes on for 3 seconds.

HINT: If the indicator check result is not normal, proceed to troubleshooting (see BE-51) for the combination meter section.

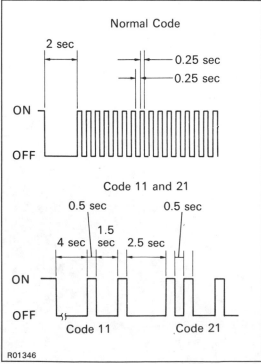

Short Pin

Data Link Connector 1

FI6443

DIAGNOSTIC TROUBLE CODE CHECK

1.   Turn the ignition switch to ON.
2.   Disconnect the Short Pin from the data link connector 1.

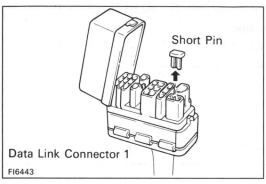

Data Link Connector 1

E1

Tc

Iei-23-1

3.   Using SST, connect terminals Tc and E1 of the data link connector 1.
     SST 09843-18020
4.   Read the diagnostic trouble code from the ABS warning light on the combination meter.
     HINT: If no code appears, inspect the diagnostic circuit (see page BR-94).

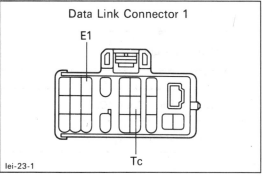

Normal Code

2 sec

0.25 sec

0.25 sec

ON

OFF

Code 11 and 21

0.5 sec   0.5 sec

1.5
sec

4 sec   2.5 sec

ON

OFF

Code 11   Code 21

R01346

As an example, the blinking patterns for normal code and codes 11 and 21 are shown on the left.
5.   Codes are explained in the code table on page BR-58.
6.   After completing the check, disconnect terminals Tc and E1, and turn off the display.
     If two or more malfunctions are indicated at the same time, the lowest numbered diagnostic trouble code will be displayed first.

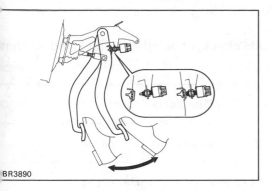

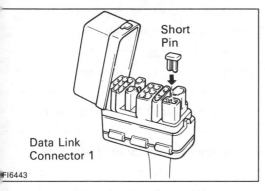

DIAGNOSTIC TROUBLE CODE CLEARANCE

1. Using SST, connect terminals Tc and E1 of the data link connector 1.
    SST 09843-18020
2. IG switch ON.
3. Clear the diagnostic trouble codes stored in ECU by depressing the brake pedal 8 or more times within 3 seconds.
4. Check that the warning light shows the normal code.
5. Remove the SST from the terminals of the data link connector 1.
6. Connect the Short Pin to the data link connector 1.

BR

DIAGNOSTIC TROUBLE CODE CHART

If a malfunction code is displayed during the diagnostic trouble code check, check the circuit listed for that code in the table below.

Code	ABS Warning Light Blinking Pattern	Diagnosis
11	ON OFF　BE3931	Open circuit in ABS control (solenoid) relay circuit
12	ON OFF　BE3931	Short circuit in ABS control (solenoid) relay circuit
13	ON OFF　BE3931	Open circuit in ABS control (pump motor) relay circuit
14	ON OFF　BE3931	Short circuit in ABS control (pump motor) relay circuit
21	ON OFF　BE3932	Open or short circuit in solenoid circuit for front right wheel
22	ON OFF　BE3932	Open or short circuit in solenoid circuit for front left wheel
23	ON OFF　BE3932	Open or short circuit in solenoid circuit for rear right wheel
24	ON OFF　BE3932	Open or short circuit in solenoid circuit for rear left wheel
31	ON OFF　BE3933	Front right wheel speed sensor signal malfunction
32	ON OFF　BE3933	Front left wheel speed sensor signal malfunction
33	ON OFF　BE3933	Rear right wheel speed sensor signal malfunction
34	ON OFF　BE3933	Rear left wheel speed sensor signal malfunction
35	ON OFF　BE3933	Open circuit in front left or rear right speed sensor circuit
36	ON OFF　BE3933	Open circuit in front right or rear left speed sensor circuit
37	ON OFF　BE3933	Faulty rear speed sensor rotor
41	ON OFF　BE3934	Low battery voltage or abnormally high battery voltage
51	ON OFF　BE3935	Pump motor is locked Open in pump motor ground
Always ON	ON OFF	Malfunction in ECU

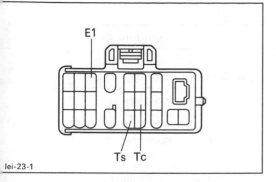

lei-23-1

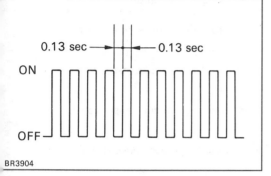

BR3904

SPEED SENSOR SIGNAL CHECK

1. Turn the ignition switch to OFF.
2. Using SST, connect terminals Ts and E1 of the data link connector 1.
    SST 09843-18020
3. Start the engine.

4. Check that the ABS warning light blinks.
    HINT: If the ABS warning light does not blink, inspect the ABS warning light circuit (see page BR-90).
5. Drive vehicle straight forward.
    HINT: Drive vehicle faster than 90 km/h (56 mph) for several seconds.
6. Stop the vehicle.
7. Using SST, connect terminals Tc and E1 of the data link connector 1.
    SST 09843-18020
8. Read the number of blinks of the ABS warning light.
    HINT: See the list of diagnostic trouble codes shown on the next page.
    If every sensor is normal, a normal code is output. (A cycle of 0.25 sec. ON and 0.25 sec. OFF is repeated)
    If two or more malfunctions are indicated at the same time, the lowest numbered code will be displayed first.

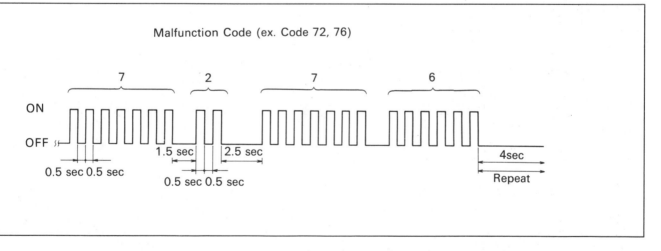

BR3893

9. After performing the check, disconnect terminals Ts and E1, Tc and E1 of the data link connector 1, and ignition switch turned off.

Diagnostic Trouble Code of Speed Sensor Check Function

Code No.	Diagnosis	Trouble Area
71	Low output voltage of front right speed sensor	• Front right speed sensor • Sensor installation
72	Low output voltage of front left speed sensor	• Front left speed sensor • Sensor installation
73	Low output voltage of rear right speed sensor	• Rear right speed sensor • Sensor installation
74	Low output voltage of rear left speed sensor	• Rear left speed sensor • Sensor installation
75	Abnormal change in output voltage of front right speed sensor	• Front right speed sensor rotor
76	Abnormal change in output voltage of front left speed sensor	• Front left speed sensor rotor
77	Abnormal change in output voltage of rear right speed sensor	• Rear right speed sensor rotor
78	Abnormal change in output voltage of rear left speed sensor	• Rear left speed sensor rotor

PROBLEM SYMPTOMS CHART

f a normal code is displayed during the diagnostic trouble code check but the problem still occurs, check he circuits for each problem symptom in the order given in the table below and proceed to the page for roubleshooting.

Symptoms	Inspection Circuit	See page
ABS does not operate.	1. Check the DTC, reconfirming that the normal code is output. 2. IG power source circuit. 3. Speed sensor circuit. 4. Check the ABS actuator with a checker. If abnormal, check the hydraulic circuit for leakage (see page BR-98). If 1. ~ 4. are all normal and the problem is still occuring, replace the ABS ECU.	BR-56 BR-83 BR-79 BR-45
ABS does not operate efficiently.	1. Check the DTC, reconfirming that the normal code is output. 2. Speed sensor circuit. 3. Stop light switch circuit. 4. Check the ABS actuator with a checker. If abnormal, check the hydraulic circuit for leakage (see page BR-98). If 1. ~ 4. are all normal and the problem is still occuring, replace the ABS ECU.	BR-56 BR-79 BR-88 BR-45
ABS warning light abnormal.	1. ABS warning light circuit. 2. ABS ECU.	BR-90
DTC check cannot be performed.	1. ABS warning light circuit. 2. Tc terminal circuit. 3. ABS ECU.	BR-90 BR-94
Speed sensor signal check cannot be performed.	1. Ts terminal circuit. 2. ABS ECU.	BR-96

BR

LOCATION OF CONNECTORS
Location of Connectors in Engine Compartment

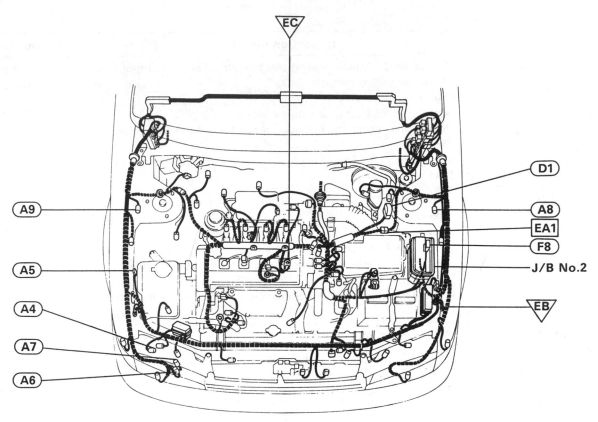

N05843

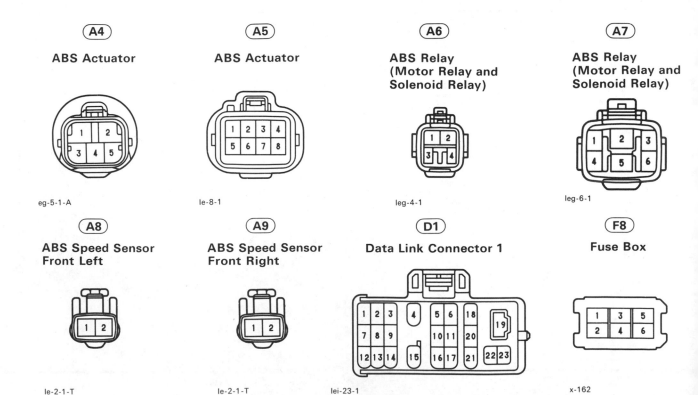

(A4)	(A5)	(A6)	(A7)
ABS Actuator	**ABS Actuator**	**ABS Relay (Motor Relay and Solenoid Relay)**	**ABS Relay (Motor Relay and Solenoid Relay)**
eg-5-1-A	le-8-1	leg-4-1	leg-6-1

(A8)	(A9)	(D1)	(F8)
ABS Speed Sensor Front Left	**ABS Speed Sensor Front Right**	**Data Link Connector 1**	**Fuse Box**
le-2-1-T	le-2-1-T	lei-23-1	x-162

Ifg-4-1

Ifg-4-2

J/B No.2

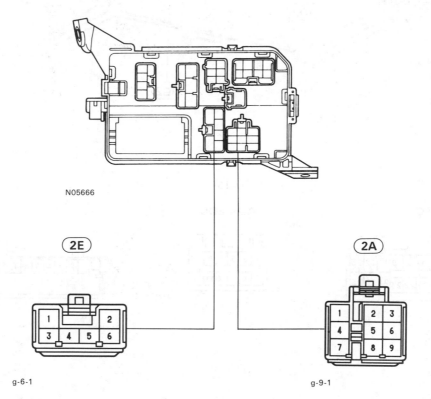

N05666

2E

2A

g-6-1

g-9-1

BR

Location of Connectors in Instrument Panel

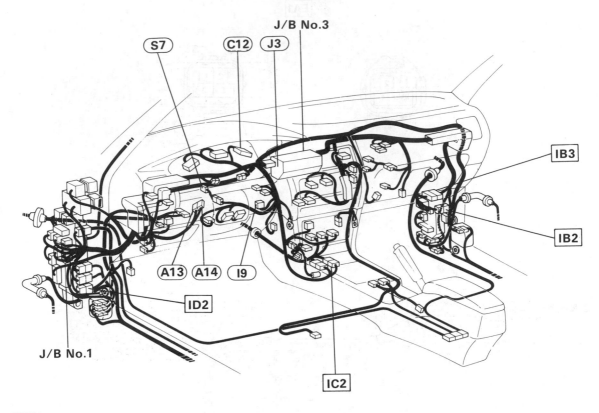

N05844

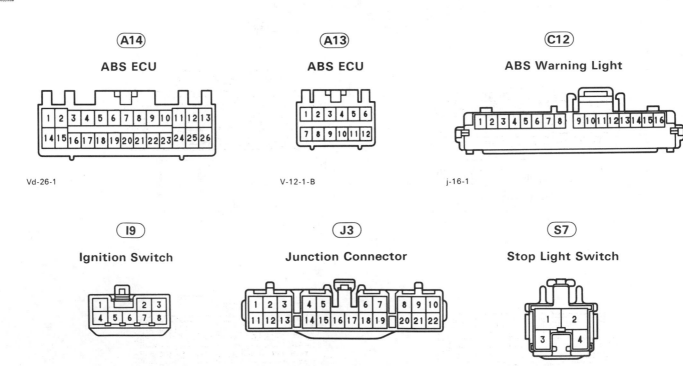

(A14) **ABS ECU**

Vd-26-1

(A13) **ABS ECU**

V-12-1-B

(C12) **ABS Warning Light**

j-16-1

(I9) **Ignition Switch**

g-8-1

(J3) **Junction Connector**

e-22-1-A

(S7) **Stop Light Switch**

eg-4-1

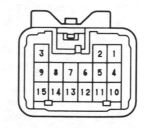

e-15-1

e-15-2

e-18-1

e-18-2

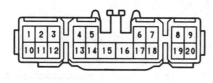

e-20-1

e-20-2

BR

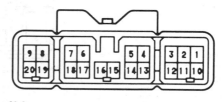

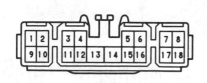

e-18-1

e-18-2

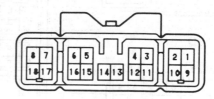
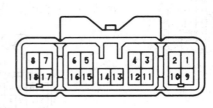

J/B No.1

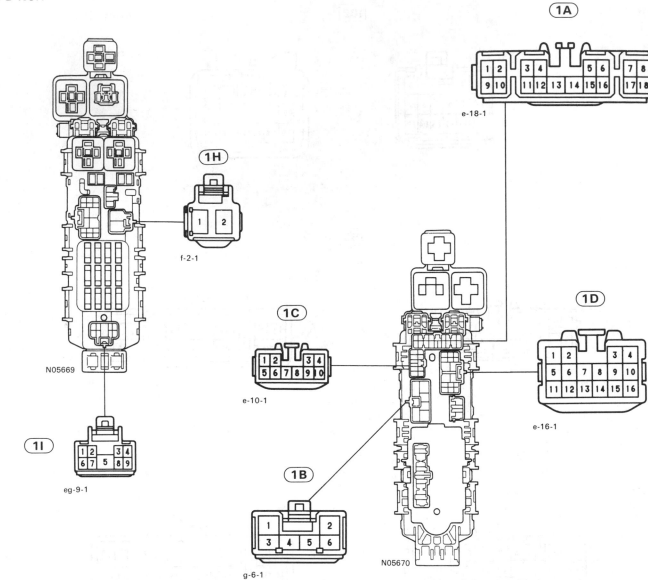

BR

J/B No.3

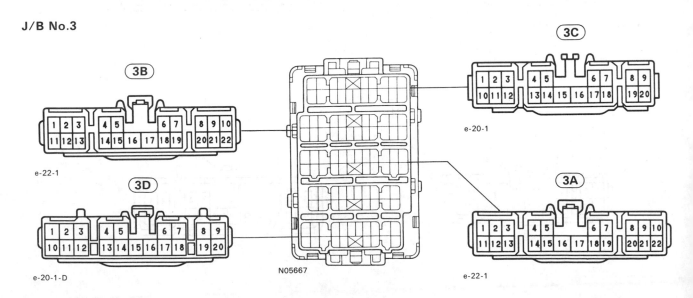

Location of Connectors in Body

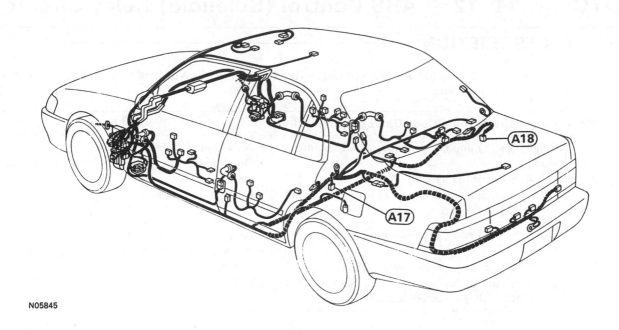

N05845

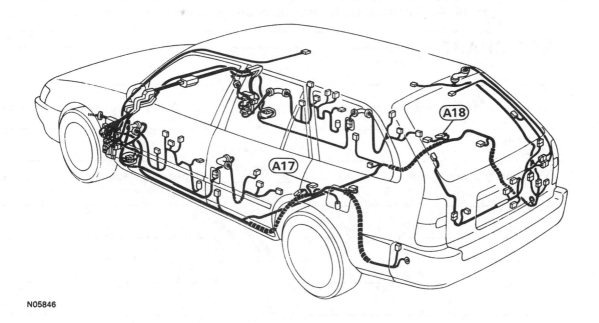

N05846

(A17)

**ABS Speed
Sensor Rear Left**

e-2-2-L

(A18)

**ABS Speed
Sensor Rear Right**

e-2-2-L

CIRCUIT INSPECTION

DTC	11, 12	ABS Control (Solenoid) Relay Circuit

CIRCUIT DESCRIPTION

This relay supplies power to each ABS solenoid. After the ignition switch is turned on, if the initial check is OK, the relay goes on.

DTC No.	Diagnostic Trouble Code Detecting Condition	Trouble Area
11	Conditions (1) and (2) continue for 0.2 sec. or more: (1) ABS control (solenoid) relay: ON (2) ABS control (solenoid) relay monitor terminal (AST) voltage: 0 V	• ABS control (solenoid) relay. • Open or short in ABS control (solenoid) relay circuit. • ECU.
12	Conditions (1) and (2) continue for 0.2 sec. or more: (1) ABS control (solenoid) relay: OFF (2) ABS control (solenoid) relay monitor terminal (AST) voltage: Battery voltage	• ABS control (solenoid) relay. • B+ short in ABS control (solenoid) relay circuit. • ECU.

Fail safe function: If trouble occurs in the control (solenoid) relay circuit, the ECU cuts off current to the ABS control (solenoid) relay and prohibits ABS control.

DIAGNOSTIC CHART

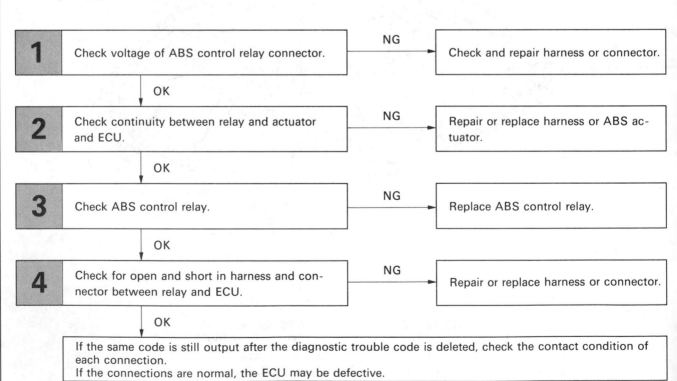

| 1 | Check voltage of ABS control relay connector. | NG→ | Check and repair harness or connector. |

OK↓

| 2 | Check continuity between relay and actuator and ECU. | NG→ | Repair or replace harness or ABS actuator. |

OK↓

| 3 | Check ABS control relay. | NG→ | Replace ABS control relay. |

OK↓

| 4 | Check for open and short in harness and connector between relay and ECU. | NG→ | Repair or replace harness or connector. |

OK↓

If the same code is still output after the diagnostic trouble code is deleted, check the contact condition of each connection.
If the connections are normal, the ECU may be defective.

WIRING DIAGRAM

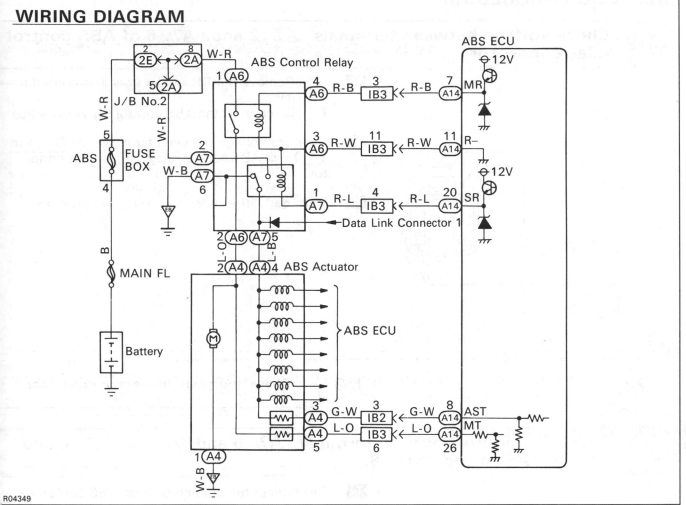

R04349

BR

INSPECTION PROCEDURE

1   Check voltage between terminals (A7) 2 and (A7) 6 of ABS control relay connector

OFF

⊘ IG OFF

(A7)

2

6

V

BE6653
R00892

OK

P
(1) Remove the RH fender liner and control relay.
(2) Disconnect the ABS control relay connector.

C Measure voltage between terminals (A7) 2 and (A7) 6 of ABS control relay harness side connector.

OK Voltage: 10 – 14 V

NG ⟩ Check and repair harness or connector.

BR

2   Check continuity between terminal (A7) 5 and (A4) 4, (A4) 4 and (A4) 3, (A4) 3 and (A14) 8.

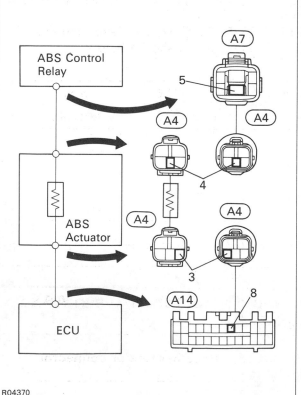

ABS Control Relay

(A7)

5

(A4)   (A4)

4

ABS Actuator   (A4)   (A4)

3

(A14)   8

ECU

R04370

P Disconnect the connector from ABS actuator.

C Check continuity terminal (A7) 5 and (A4) 4, (A4) 4 and (A4) 3, (A4) 3 and (A14) 8.

OK Continuity

Hint There is a resistance of 32 ~ 34 Ω between terminals (A4) 4 and (A4) 3.

OK

NG ⟩ Repair or replace harness or ABS actuator.

3   **Check ABS control relay.**

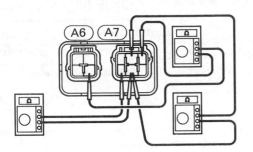

C Check continuity between each terminal of ABS control relay shown below.

OK

Terminals (A7) 1 and (A6) 3	Continuity (Reference value 80 Ω)
Terminals (A7) 5 and (A7) 6	Continuity
Terminals (A7) 2 and (A7) 5	Open

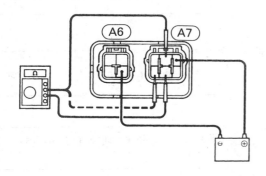

C (1) Apply battery voltage between terminals (A7) 1 and (A6) 3.
(2) Check continuity between each terminal of ABS control relay shown below.

OK

Terminals (A7) 5 and (A7) 6	Open
Terminals (A7) 2 and (A7) 5	Continuity

R00889
R00895

OK   **NG** ⟩ Replace ABS control relay.

BR

4   **Check for open and short in harness and connector between ABS control relay and ABS ECU (See page IN-27).**

OK   **NG** ⟩ Repair or replace harness or connector.

If the same code is still output after the diagnostic trouble code is deleted, check the contact condition of each connection.
If the connections are normal, the ECU may be defective.

DTC	13, 14	ABS Control (Motor) Relay Circuit

CIRCUIT DESCRIPTION

The ABS control (motor) relay supplies power to the ABS pump motor. If the accumulator pressure drops, the ECU switches the control (motor) relay ON and operates the ABS pump motor.

DTC No.	Diagnostic Trouble Code Detecting Condition	Trouble Area
13	Conditions (1) and (2) continue for 0.2 sec. or more: (1) ABS control (motor) relay: ON (2) ABS control (motor) relay monitor terminal (MT) voltage: 0 V	• ABS control (motor) relay. • Open or short in ABS control (motor) relay circuit. • ECU.
14	Conditions (1) and (2) continue for 4 sec. or more: (1) ABS control (motor) relay: OFF (2) ABS control (motor) relay monitor terminal (MT) voltage: Battery voltage	• ABS control (motor) relay. • B+ short in ABS control (motor) relay circuit. • ECU.

Fail safe function: If trouble occurs in the control (motor) relay circuit, the ECU cuts off the current to the ABS control (solenoid) relay and prohibits ABS control.

DIAGNOSTIC CHART

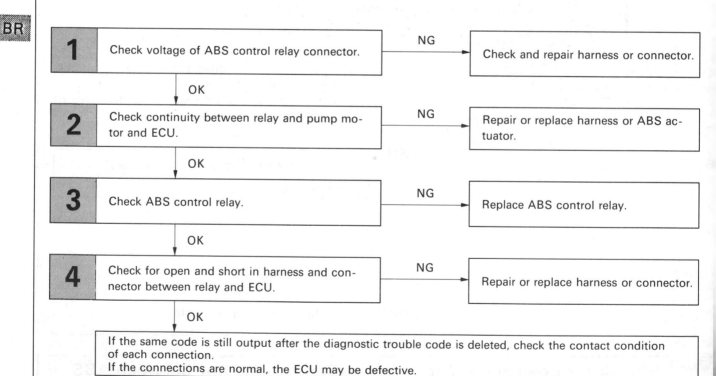

1   Check voltage of ABS control relay connector.   NG →   Check and repair harness or connector.

OK ↓

2   Check continuity between relay and pump motor and ECU.   NG →   Repair or replace harness or ABS actuator.

OK ↓

3   Check ABS control relay.   NG →   Replace ABS control relay.

OK ↓

4   Check for open and short in harness and connector between relay and ECU.   NG →   Repair or replace harness or connector.

OK ↓

If the same code is still output after the diagnostic trouble code is deleted, check the contact condition of each connection.
If the connections are normal, the ECU may be defective.

WIRING DIAGRAM

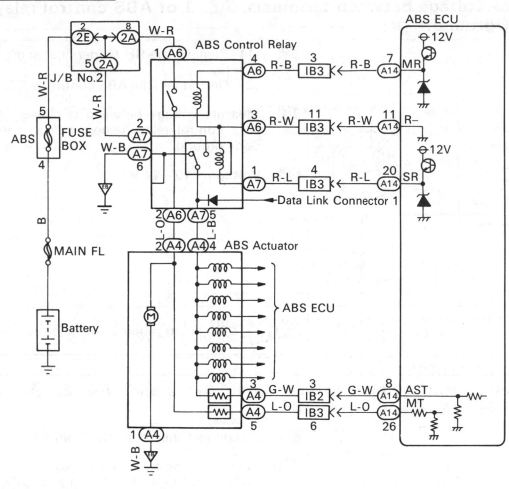

BR

INSPECTION PROCEDURE

1 Check voltage between terminals (A6) 1 of ABS control relay and body ground.

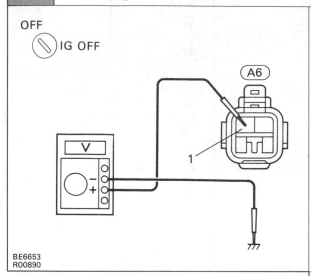

OFF
⊘ IG OFF

(A6)

1

BE6653
R00890

P (1) Remove the RH fender liner and control re-lay.
(2) Disconnect the ABS control relay connector.

C Measure voltage between terminals (A6) 1 of ABS control relay harness side connector and body ground.

OK Voltage: 10 – 14 V

⬡ OK

NG 〉 Check and repair harness or connector

2 Check continuity between terminal (A6) 2 and (A4) 2, (A4) 2 and (A4) 5, (A4) 5 and (A14) 26.

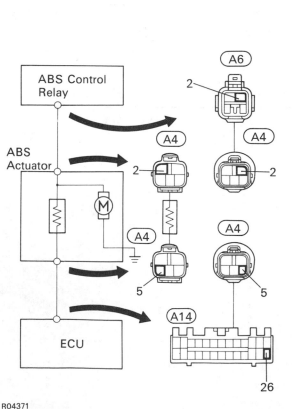

ABS Control Relay

ABS Actuator

M

(A6)
2

(A4)   (A4)

2   2

(A4)   (A4)

5   5

(A14)

ECU

26

R04371

P Disconnect the connector from ABS actuator.

C Check continuity terminal (A6) 2 and (A4) 2, (A4) 2 and (A4) 5, (A4) 5 and (A14) 26.

OK Continuity

Hint There is a resistance of $32 \sim 34\,\Omega$ between terminals (A4) 2 and (A4) 5.

⬡ OK

NG 〉 Repair or replace harness or ABS actuator.

BR

3	**Check ABS control relay.**

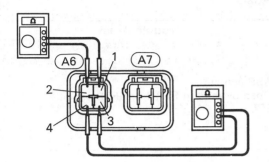

C Check continuity between each terminal of ABS control relay shown below.

OK

Terminals (A6) 3 and (A6) 4	Continuity (Reference value 62 Ω)
Terminals (A6) 1 and (A6) 2	Open

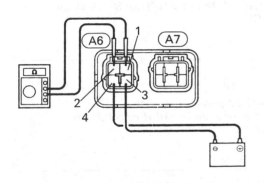

C (1) Apply battery voltage between terminals (A6) 3 and (A6) 4.
(2) Check continuity between each terminal of ABS control relay shown below.

OK

Terminals (A6) 1 and (A6) 2	Continuity

R00894
R00893

OK	**NG** ⟩ Replace ABS control relay

4	**Check for open and short in harness and connector between ABS control relay and ABS ECU (See page IN-27).**

OK	**NG** ⟩ Repair or replace harness or connector.

If the same code is still output after the diagnostic trouble code is deleted, check the contact condition of each connection.
If the connections are normal, the ECU may be defective.

BR

DTC	21, 22, 23, 24	ABS Actuator Solenoid Circuit

CIRCUIT DESCRIPTION

This solenoid goes on when signals are received from the ECU and controls the pressure acting on the wheel cylinders, thus controlling the turning of the wheels.

DTC No.	Diagnostic Trouble Code Detecting Condition	Trouble Area
21	Conditions (1) through (3) continue for 0.05 sec. or more: (1) ABS control (solenoid) relay: ON (2) Voltage of ABS ECU terminal AST: Battery voltage (3) When power transistor of ECU is ON, voltage of terminal SFRH or SFRR is 0 V or battery voltage.	• ABS actuator. • Open or short in SFRH or SFRR circuit. • ECU.
22	Conditions (1) through (3) continue for 0.05 sec. or more: (1) ABS control (solenoid) relay: ON (2) Voltage of ABS ECU terminal AST: Battery voltage (3) When power transistor of ECU is ON, voltage of terminal SFLH or SFLR is 0 V or battery voltage.	• ABS actuator. • Open or short in SFLH or SFLR circuit. • ECU.
23	Conditions (1) through (3) continue for 0.05 sec. or more: (1) ABS control (solenoid) relay: ON (2) Voltage of ABS ECU terminal AST: Battery voltage (3) When power transistor of ECU is ON, voltage of terminal SRRH or SRRR is 0 V or battery voltage.	• ABS actuator. • Open or short in SRRH or SRRR circuit. • ECU.
24	Conditions (1) through (3) continue for 0.05 sec. or more: (1) ABS control (solenoid) relay: ON (2) Voltage of ABS ECU terminal AST: Battery voltage (3) When power transistor of ECU is ON, voltage of terminal SRLH or SRLR is 0 V or battery voltage.	• ABS actuator. • Open or short in SRLH or SRLR circuit. • ECU.

Fail safe function: If trouble occurs in the actuator solenoid circuit, the ECU cuts off current to the control (solenoid) relay and prohibits ABS control.

DIAGNOSTIC CHART

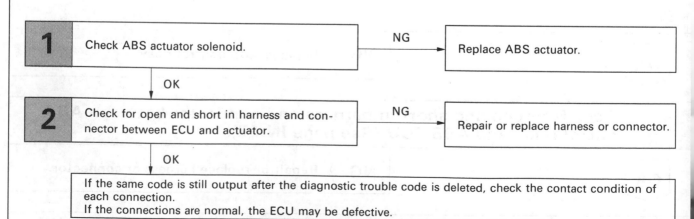

1 Check ABS actuator solenoid. —NG→ Replace ABS actuator.

↓ OK

2 Check for open and short in harness and connector between ECU and actuator. —NG→ Repair or replace harness or connector.

↓ OK

If the same code is still output after the diagnostic trouble code is deleted, check the contact condition of each connection.
If the connections are normal, the ECU may be defective.

WIRING DIAGRAM

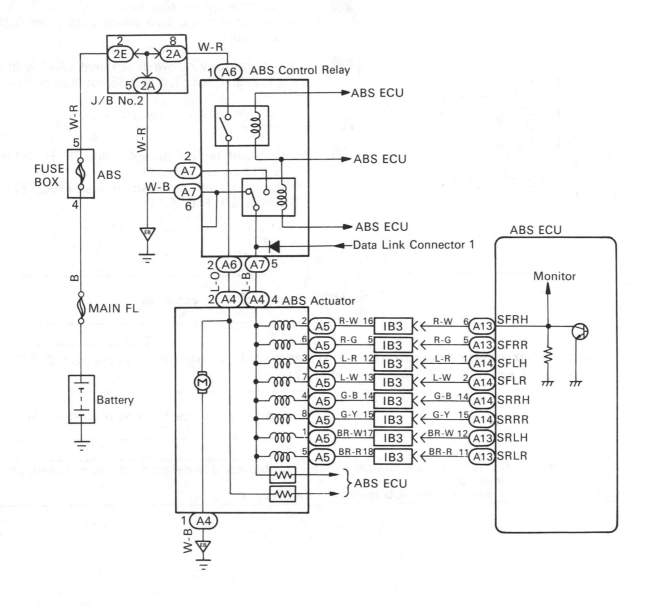

R04350

INSPECTION PROCEDURE

1	**Check ABS actuator solenoid.**

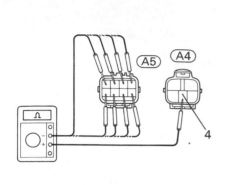

R04372

P   (1)   Remove the washer tank.
        (2)   Disconnect the two connectors from ABS actuator.

C   Check continuity between terminal (A4) 4 and (A5) 1, 2, 3, 4, 5, 6, 7, 8 of ABS actuator connector.

OK   **Continuity**

Hint   Resistance of each of the solenoids SFRH, SFLH, SRRH and SRLH is 5.0 Ω.
Resistance of each of the solenoids SFRR, SFLR, SRRR and SRLR is 2.2 Ω.

OK		**NG** ⟩ Replace ABS actuator.

BR	**2**	**Check for open and short in harness and connector between ABS ECU and actuator (See page IN-27).**

OK		**NG** ⟩ Repair or replace harness or connector.

If the same code is still output after the diagnostic trouble code is deleted, check the contact condition of each connection.
If the connections are normal, the ECU may be defective.

| DTC | 31, 32, 33, 34, 35, 36 | Speed Sensor Circuit |

CIRCUIT DESCRIPTION

The speed sensor detects the wheel speed and sends the appropriate signals to the ECU. These signals are used for control of the ABS system. The front rotor and rear rotor have 48 serrations. When the rotors rotate, the magnetic field emitted by the permanent magnet in the speed sensor generates an AC voltage. Since the frequency of this AC voltage changes in proportion to the speed of the rotors (wheels), the frequency is used by the ECU to detect the speed of each wheel.

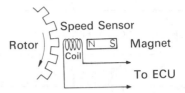

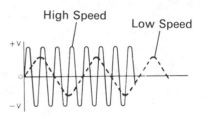

BR3583
BR3582

DTC No.	Diagnostic Trouble Code Detecting Condition	Trouble Area
31, 32, 33, 34	Detection of any of conditions (1) through (3): (1) At vehicle speed of 10 km/h (6 mph) or more, pulses are not input for 5 sec. (2) Momentary interruption of the vehicle speed sensor signal occurs at least 7 times in the time between switching the ignition switch ON and switching it OFF. (3) Abnormal fluctuation of speed sensor signals with the vehicle speed 20 km/h (12 mph) or more.	• Right front, left front, right rear and left rear speed sensor. • Open or short in each speed sensor circuit. • ECU.
35	Vehicle speed sensor signal is not input for about 1 sec. while the left front and right rear vehicle speed sensor signals are being checked with the IG switch is turned ON.	• Open in left front or right rear speed sensor circuit. • ECU.
36	Vehicle speed sensor signal is not input for about 1 sec. while the right front and left rear vehicle speed sensor signals are being checked with the IG switch is turned ON.	• Open in right front or left rear speed sensor circuit. • ECU.

HINT: DTC 31 is for the right front wheel speed sensor.
DTC 32 is for the left front wheel speed sensor.
DTC 33 is for the right rear wheel speed sensor.
DTC 34 is for the left rear wheel speed sensor.

Fail safe function: If trouble occurs in the speed sensor circuit, the ECU cuts off current to the ABS control (solenoid) relay and prohibits ABS control.

BR

DIAGNOSTIC CHART

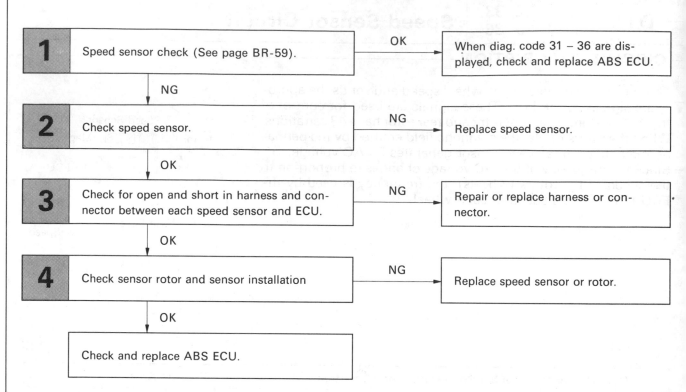

1 Speed sensor check (See page BR-59). — **OK** → When diag. code 31 – 36 are displayed, check and replace ABS ECU.

↓ **NG**

2 Check speed sensor. — **NG** → Replace speed sensor.

↓ **OK**

3 Check for open and short in harness and connector between each speed sensor and ECU. — **NG** → Repair or replace harness or connector.

↓ **OK**

4 Check sensor rotor and sensor installation — **NG** → Replace speed sensor or rotor.

↓ **OK**

Check and replace ABS ECU.

WIRING DIAGRAM

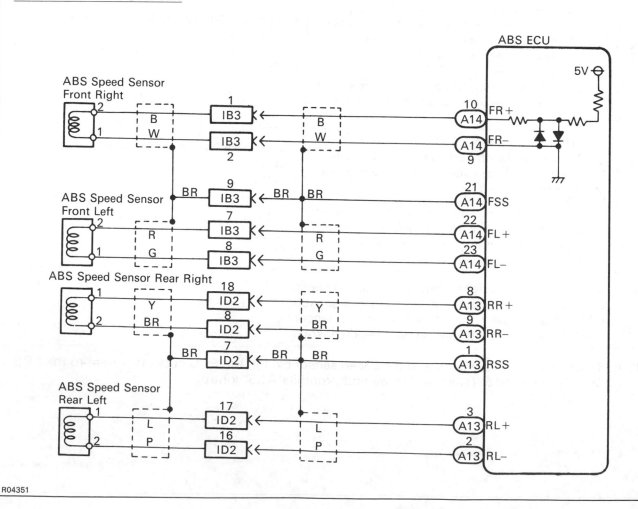

INSPECTION PROCEDURE

| **1** | **Speed sensor check.** |

P See speed sensor check on page BR-59.

| **NG** | | **OK** | When diag. Code 31 – 36 are displayed, check and replace ABS ECU. |

| **2** | **Check speed sensor.** |

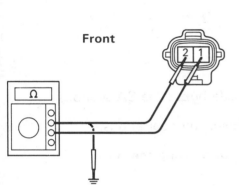

Front

Rear

BR5425
BR5424

Front

P (1) Remove front fender liner.
(2) Disconnect speed sensor connector.

C Measure resistance between terminals 1 and 2 of speed sensor connector.

OK Resistance: 0.92 – 1.22 kΩ

C Measure resistance between terminals 1 and 2 of speed sensor connector and body ground.

OK Resistance: 1 MΩ or higher

Rear

P (1) Remove the seat cushion and side seat back.
(2) Disconnect speed sensor connector.

C Measure resistance between terminals 1 and 2 of speed sensor connector.

OK Resistance: 1.05 – 1.45 kΩ

C Measure resistance between terminals 1 and 2 of speed sensor connector and body ground.

OK Resistance: 1 MΩ or higher

| **OK** | | **NG** | Replace speed sensor. |

| **3** | **Check for open and short in harness and connector between each speed sensor and ECU (See page IN-27).** |

| **OK** | | **NG** | Repair or replace harness or connector. |

BR

BR

4   Check sensor rotor and sensor installation.

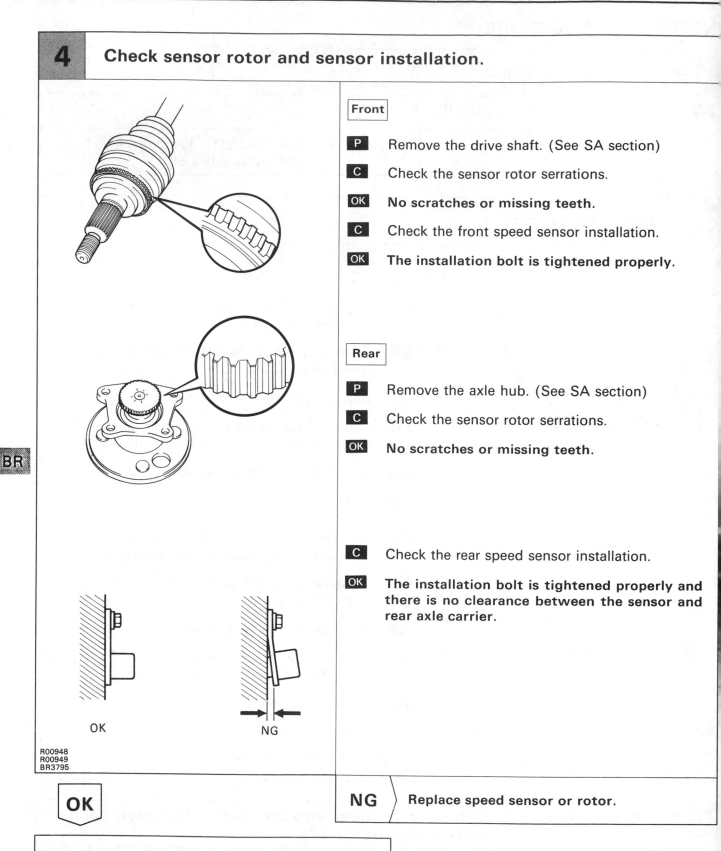

Front

P   Remove the drive shaft. (See SA section)

C   Check the sensor rotor serrations.

OK **No scratches or missing teeth.**

C   Check the front speed sensor installation.

OK **The installation bolt is tightened properly.**

Rear

P   Remove the axle hub. (See SA section)

C   Check the sensor rotor serrations.

OK **No scratches or missing teeth.**

C   Check the rear speed sensor installation.

OK **The installation bolt is tightened properly and there is no clearance between the sensor and rear axle carrier.**

OK   NG

R00948
R00949
BR3795

OK

NG 〉 Replace speed sensor or rotor.

Check and replace ABS ECU.

DTC	41	IG Power Source Circuit

CIRCUIT DESCRIPTION

This is the power source for the ECU and becomes power source for the CPU and actuators.

DTC No.	Diagnostic Trouble Code Detecting Condition	Trouble Area
41	Vehicle speed is 3 km/h (1.9 mph) or more and voltage of ECU terminal IG1 remains at more than 17 V or below 9.5 V for more than 10 sec.	• Battery. • IC regulator. • Open or short in power source circuit. • ECU.

Fail safe function: If trouble occurs in the power source circuit, the ECU cuts off current to the ABS control (solenoid) relay and prohibits ABS control.

DIAGNOSTIC CHART

First check battery voltage. If the voltage is not between 10 V and 14 V, check and repair the charging system.

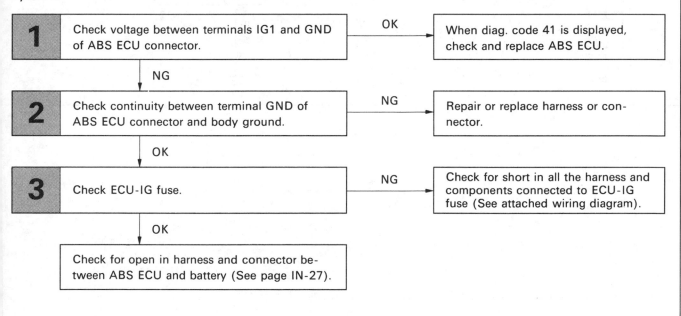

1 Check voltage between terminals IG1 and GND of ABS ECU connector. — **OK** → When diag. code 41 is displayed, check and replace ABS ECU.

↓ **NG**

2 Check continuity between terminal GND of ABS ECU connector and body ground. — **NG** → Repair or replace harness or connector.

↓ **OK**

3 Check ECU-IG fuse. — **NG** → Check for short in all the harness and components connected to ECU-IG fuse (See attached wiring diagram).

↓ **OK**

Check for open in harness and connector between ABS ECU and battery (See page IN-27).

BR

WIRING DIAGRAM

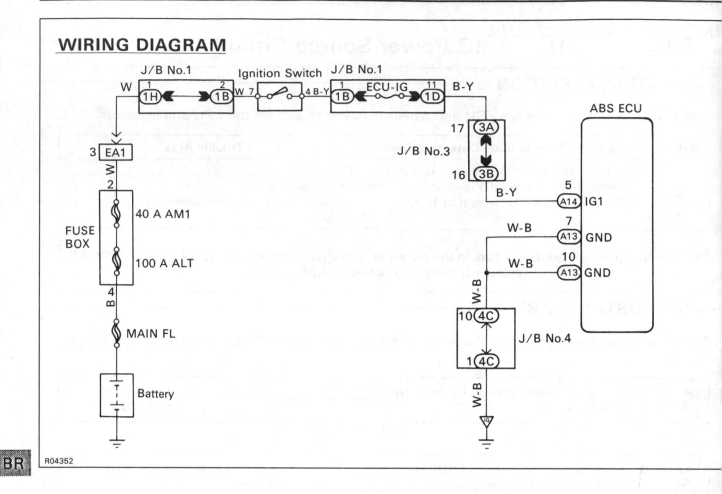

INSPECTION PROCEDURE

1 Check voltage between terminals IG1 and GND of ABS ECU connector.

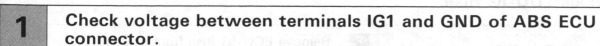

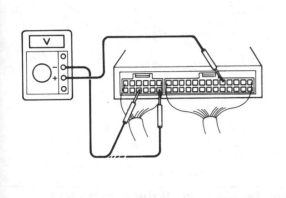

ON
IG ON

BE6653
R04170

P Remove ABS ECU with connectors still connected.

C (1) Turn ignition switch on.
(2) Measure voltage between terminals IG1 and GND of ABS ECU connector.

OK Voltage: 10 – 14 V

NG

OK ⟩ When diag. code 41 is displayed, check and replace ABS ECU.

BR

2 Check continuity between terminal GND of ECU connector and body ground.

OFF
IG OFF

BE6653
R04171

C Measure resistance between terminal GND of ABS ECU connector and body ground.

OK Resistance: 1Ω or less

OK

NG ⟩ Repair or replace harness or connector.

Go to step 3 .

3   **Check ECU-IG fuse.**

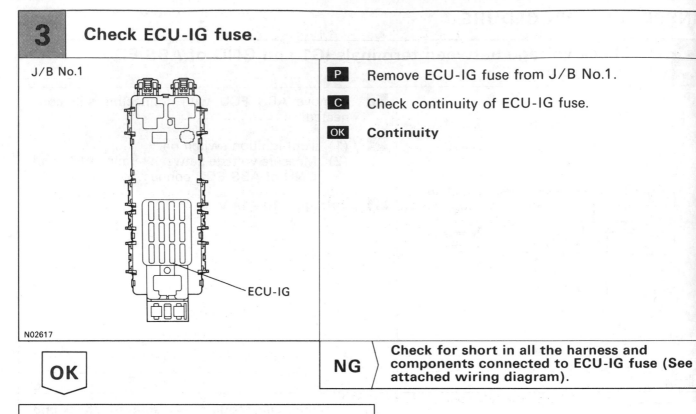

J/B No.1

ECU-IG

N02617

P   Remove ECU-IG fuse from J/B No.1.

C   Check continuity of ECU-IG fuse.

OK   **Continuity**

OK

NG   **Check for short in all the harness and components connected to ECU-IG fuse (See attached wiring diagram).**

Check for open in harness and connector between ABS ECU and battery.

BR

DTC	51	ABS Pump Motor Lock

CIRCUIT DESCRIPTION

DTC No.	Diagnostic Trouble Code Detecting Condition	Trouble Area
51	Pump motor is not operating normally during initial check.	• ABS pump motor.

Fail safe function: If trouble occurs in the ABS pump motor, the ECU cuts off the current to the control (solenoid) relay and prohibits ABS control.

DIAGNOSTIC CHART

See inspection of ABS actuator (See page BR-45)

WIRING DIAGRAM

(Reference)

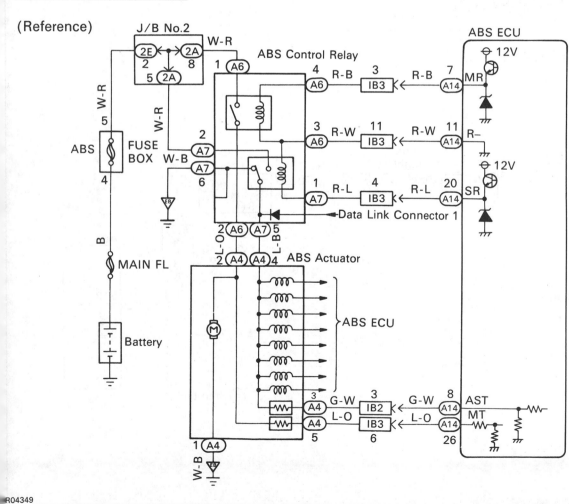

R04349

Stop Light Switch Circuit

CIRCUIT DESCRIPTION

This stop light switch senses whether the brake pedal is depressed or released, and send the signal to the ECU.

DIAGNOSTIC CHART

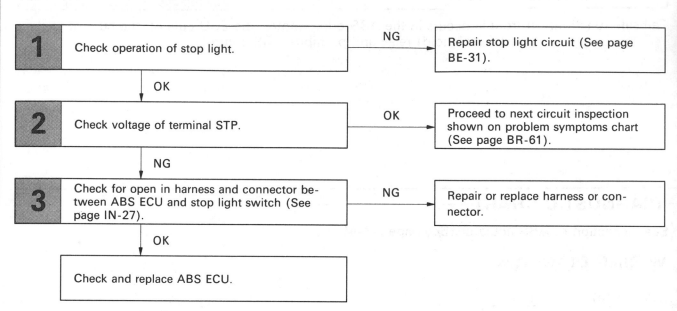

1   Check operation of stop light.   **NG** → Repair stop light circuit (See page BE-31).

↓ OK

2   Check voltage of terminal STP.   **OK** → Proceed to next circuit inspection shown on problem symptoms chart (See page BR-61).

↓ NG

3   Check for open in harness and connector between ABS ECU and stop light switch (See page IN-27).   **NG** → Repair or replace harness or connector.

↓ OK

Check and replace ABS ECU.

WIRING DIAGRAM

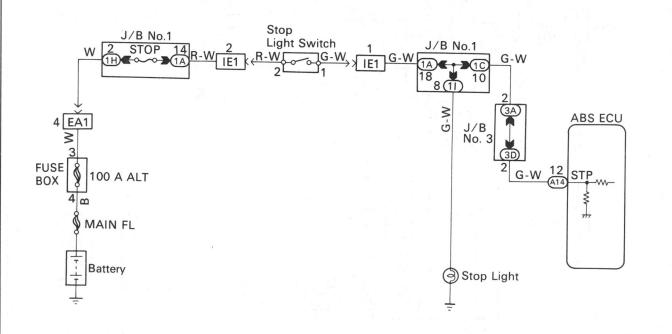

R04353

INSPECTION PROCEDURE

---

1   **Check operation of stop light.**

C   Check that stop light lights up when brake pedal is depressed and turns off when brake pedal is released.

| **OK** | **NG** > Repair stop light circuit (See page BE-31). |

---

2   **Check voltage between terminal STP of ABS ECU and body ground.**

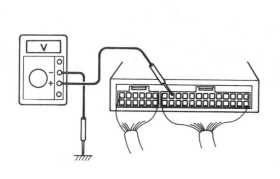

P   Remove ABS ECU with connectors still connected.

C   Measure voltage between terminal STP of ABS ECU and body ground when brake pedal is depressed.

OK   Voltage: 10 – 14 V

R04172

| **NG** | **OK** > Proceed to next circuit inspection shown on problem symptoms chart (See page BR-61). |

---

3   **Check for open in harness and connector between ABS ECU and stop light switch (See page IN-27).**

| **OK** | **NG** > Repair or replace harness or connector. |

Check and replace ABS ECU.

ABS Warning Light Circuit

CIRCUIT DESCRIPTION

If the ECU detects trouble, it lights the ABS warning light while at the same time prohibiting ABS control. At this time, the ECU records a diagnostic trouble code in memory.
After removing the short pin of the data link connector 1, connect between terminals Tc and E1 of the data link connector 1 to cause the ABS warning light to blink and output the diagnostic trouble code.

DIAGNOSTIC CHART

Perform troubleshooting in accordance with the chart below for each trouble symptom.

ABS warning light does not light up	Go to step 1
ABS warning light remains on	Go to step 3

WIRING DIAGRAM

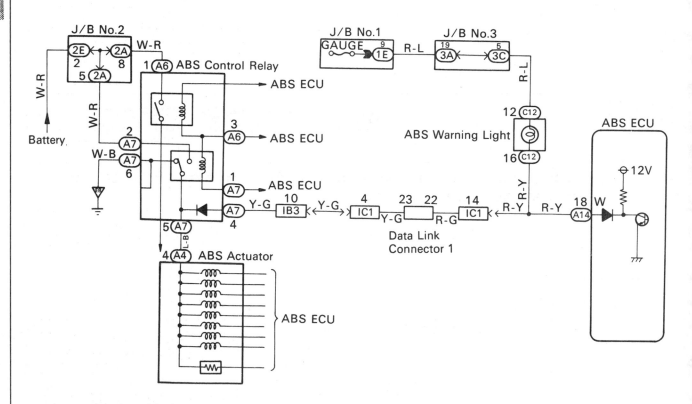

BR

R04354

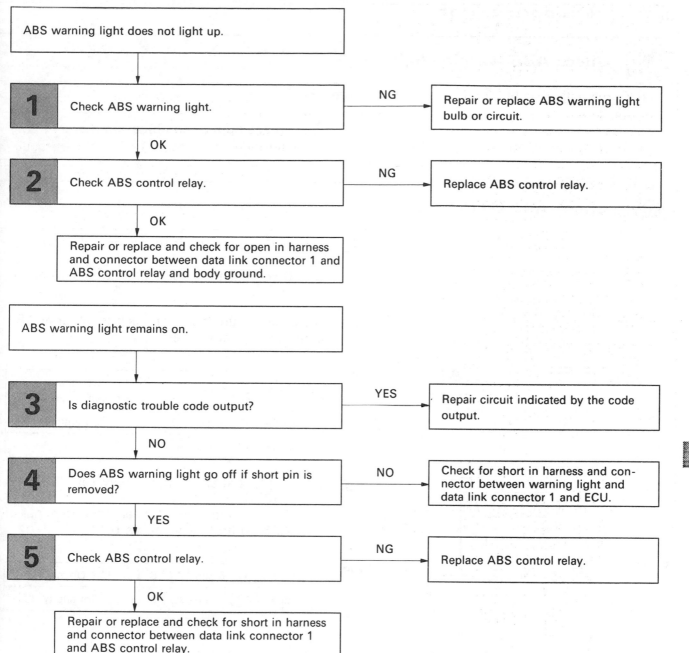

ABS warning light does not light up.

1 Check ABS warning light. —NG→ Repair or replace ABS warning light bulb or circuit.

↓ OK

2 Check ABS control relay. —NG→ Replace ABS control relay.

↓ OK

Repair or replace and check for open in harness and connector between data link connector 1 and ABS control relay and body ground.

ABS warning light remains on.

3 Is diagnostic trouble code output? —YES→ Repair circuit indicated by the code output.

↓ NO

4 Does ABS warning light go off if short pin is removed? —NO→ Check for short in harness and connector between warning light and data link connector 1 and ECU.

↓ YES

5 Check ABS control relay. —NG→ Replace ABS control relay.

↓ OK

Repair or replace and check for short in harness and connector between data link connector 1 and ABS control relay.

BR

INSPECTION PROCEDURE

1   **Check ABS warning light.**

See Combination Meter Troubleshooting on page BE-51.

| OK | NG > Replace bulb or combination meter assembly. |

2   **Check ABS control relay.**

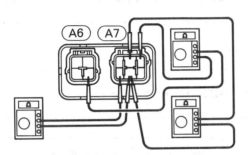

P (1) Remove the RH fender liner and control relay.
(2) Disconnect the connectors from control relay.

C Check continuity between each terminal of ABS control relay shown below.

OK

	Continuity
Terminals (A7) 1 and (A6) 3	Continuity (Reference value 80Ω)
Terminals (A7) 5 and (A7) 6	Continuity
Terminals (A7) 2 and (A7) 5	Open

C (1) Apply battery voltage between terminals (A7) 1 and (A6) 3.
(2) Check continuity between each terminal of ABS control relay shown below.

OK

Terminals (A7) 5 and (A7) 6	Open
Terminals (A7) 2 and (A7) 5	Continuity

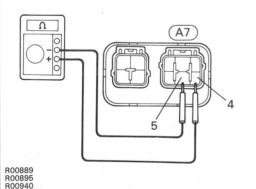

C Connect the ⊕ test lead to terminal 4 of (A7) and the ⊖ lead to terminal 5 of (A7). Check continuity between the terminals.

OK **Continuity**
If there is no continuity, connect the ⊖ test lead to terminal 4 of (A7) and the ⊕ lead to terminal 5 of (A7). Recheck continuity between terminals.

R00889
R00895
R00940

| OK | NG > Replace ABS control relay. |

Repair or replace and check for open in harness and connector between data link connector 1 and ABS control relay and body ground (See page IN-27).

3   **Is diagnostic trouble code output?**

Perform diagnostic trouble code check on page BR-56.

| NO | YES > Repair circuit indicated by the code output. |

4   **Does ABS warning light go off if short pin is removed?**

| YES | NO > Check for short in harness and connector between warning light and data link connector 1 and ECU (See page IN-27). |

5   **Check ABS control relay (See step No.2).**

| OK | NG > Replace ABS control relay. |

Repair or replace and check for short in harness and connector between data link connector 1 and ABS control relay (See page IN-27).

BR

Tc Terminal Circuit

CIRCUIT DESCRIPTION

Connecting between terminals Tc and E1 of the data link connector 1 causes the ECU to display the diagnostic trouble code by flashing the ABS warning light.

DIAGNOSTIC CHART

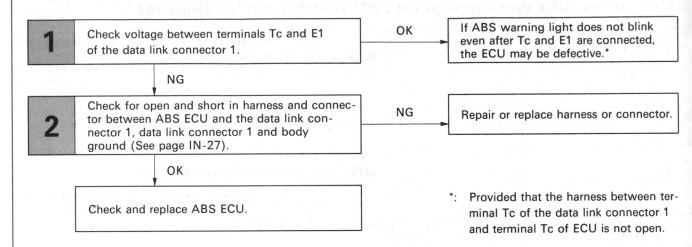

1   Check voltage between terminals Tc and E1 of the data link connector 1.

→ OK → If ABS warning light does not blink even after Tc and E1 are connected, the ECU may be defective.*

↓ NG

2   Check for open and short in harness and connector between ABS ECU and the data link connector 1, data link connector 1 and body ground (See page IN-27).

→ NG → Repair or replace harness or connector.

↓ OK

Check and replace ABS ECU.

*:   Provided that the harness between terminal Tc of the data link connector 1 and terminal Tc of ECU is not open.

BR

WIRING DIAGRAM

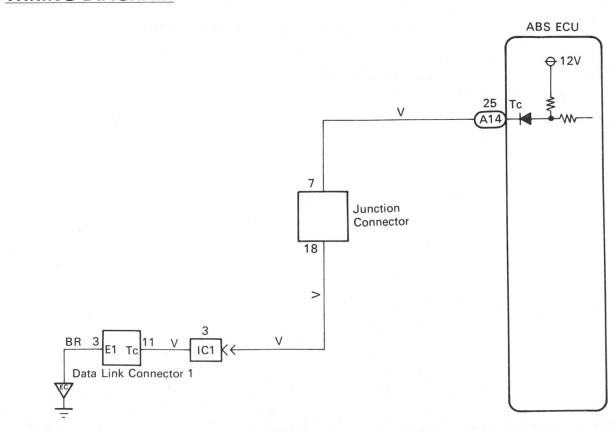

ABS ECU

12V

25   Tc
A14

V

7

Junction
Connector

18

>

BR   3   E1   Tc   11   V   3   IC1   ←   V

Data Link Connector 1

R04355

INSPECTION PROCEDURE

1 **Check voltage between terminals Tc and E1 of Data Link Connector 1.**

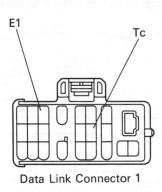

Data Link Connector 1

lei-23-1

C (1) Turn ignition switch ON.
(2) Measure voltage between terminals Tc and E1 of the data link connector 1.

OK Voltage: 10 – 14 V

NG

OK ⟩ If ABS warning light does not blink even after Tc and E1 are connected, the ECU may be defective.

---

2 Check for open and short in harness and connector between ABS ECU and data link connector 1, data link connector 1 and body ground (See page IN-27).

BR

OK

NG ⟩ Repair or replace harness or connector.

Check and replace ABS ECU.

Ts Terminal Circuit

CIRCUIT DESCRIPTION

The sensor check circuit detects abnormalities in the speed sensor signal which can not be detected with the diagnostic trouble code check.
Connecting terminals Ts and E1 of the data link connector 1 in the engine compartment starts the check.

DIAGNOSTIC CHART

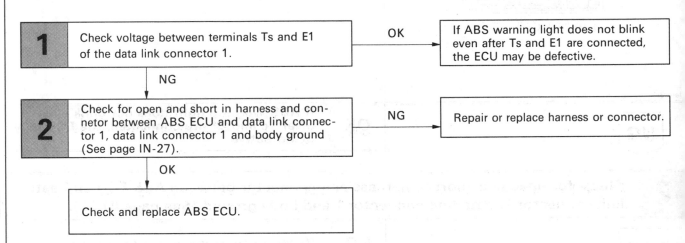

| **1** | Check voltage between terminals Ts and E1 of the data link connector 1. | OK → | If ABS warning light does not blink even after Ts and E1 are connected, the ECU may be defective. |

↓ NG

| **2** | Check for open and short in harness and connector between ABS ECU and data link connector 1, data link connector 1 and body ground (See page IN-27). | NG → | Repair or replace harness or connector. |

↓ OK

| Check and replace ABS ECU. |

WIRING DIAGRAM

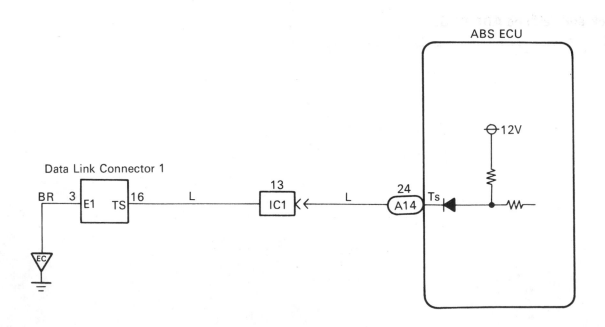

R04356

NSPECTION PROCEDURE

1   **Check voltage between terminals Ts and E1 of data link connector 1.**

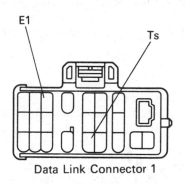

Data Link Connector 1

ei-23-1

C   (1)   Turn ignition switch ON.
      (2)   Measure voltage between terminals Ts and E1 of the data link connector 1.

OK   Voltage: **10 – 14 V**

| NG | | OK | If ABS warning light does not blink even after Ts and E1 are connected, the ECU may be defective. |

2   Check for open and short in harness and connector between ABS ECU and data link connector 1, data link connector 1 and body ground (See page IN-27).

BR

| OK | | NG | Repair or replace harness or connector. |

Check and replace **ABS ECU**.

Check for Fluid Leakage

Check for fluid leakage from actuator or hydraulic lines.

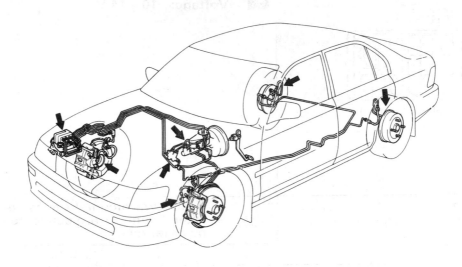

R04030

SERVICE SPECIFICATIONS
SERVICE DATA

BR03A-09

Brake pedal hight from asphalt sheet (LHD)		143.6 − 153.6 mm (5.65 − 6.05 in.)
Brake pedal freeplay		1 − 6 mm (0.04 − 0.24 in.)
Brake pedal reserve distance at 490 N (50 kgf, 110.2 lbf)		More than 70 mm (2.76 in.)
Brake booster push rod to piston clearance (W/ SST)		0 mm (0 in.)
Front brake pad thickness	STD	12.0 mm (0.472 in.)
Front brake pad thickness	Limit	1.0 mm (0.039 in.)
Front brake disc thickness	STD	22.0 mm (0.866 in.)
Front brake disc thickness	Limit	20.0 mm (0.787 in.)
Front brake disc runout	Limit	0.05 mm (0.0020 in.)
Rear brake drum inside diameter	STD	200.0 mm (7.874 in.)
Rear brake drum inside diameter	Limit	201.0 mm (7.913 in.)
Rear brake drum lining thickness	STD	4.0 mm (0.157 in.)
Rear brake drum lining thickness	Limit	1.0 mm (0.039 in.)
Parking brake adjusting shim thickness		0.2 mm (0.008 in.)
		0.3 mm (0.012 in.)
		0.4 mm (0.016 in.)
		0.5 mm (0.020 in.)
		0.6 mm (0.024 in.)
		0.9 mm (0.035 in.)

BR

BR03B-0A

TORQUE SPECIFICATIONS

Part tightened	N·m	kgf·cm	ft·lbf
Master cylinder x Piston stopper bolts	10	100	7
Master cylinder x Reserver	1.7	17.5	15.2 in.·lbf
Master cylinder x Brake booster	13	130	9
Brake tube union nut	15	155	11
Brake booster clevis lock nut	25	260	19
Brake booster x Pedal bracket	13	130	9
Front disc brake cylinder installation bolt	34	350	25
Bleeder pluge	8.3	85	74 in.·lbf
Front disc brake torque plate x Steering knuckle	88	900	65
Front disc brake cylinder x Flexible hose	30	310	22
Rear drum brake wheel cylinder x Backing plate	10	100	7
ABS actuator bracket x Body	19	195	14
Front speed sensor installation bolt	8	82	71 in.·lbf
Rear speed sensor installation bolt	8	82	71 in.·lbf
Control relay x ABS actuator bracket	5	51	44 in.·lbf
ABS ECU bracket x Body	13	130	9

BR

STEERING

SR

GENERAL DESCRIPTION

- Care must be taken to replace parts properly because they could affect the performance of the steering system and result in a driving hazard.
- The steering wheel pad has an airbag built in, so take all due precautions when handling it. For more details, see the SRS AIRBAG section.

TROUBLESHOOTING

You will find the cause of trouble more easily by properly using the table shown below. In the table, the numbers indicate the priority of the probable cause of trouble. Check each part in the order shown. If necessary, repair or replace the part.

See page	SA-3	SA-3	SR-39	SR-39	—	SA-52	—	—	—	SA-10
Parts Name / Trouble	Tires (Improperly inflated)	Front wheel alignment (Incorrect)	Fluid level (Low)	Drive belt (Loose)	Steering system joints (Worn)	Suspension arm ball joints (Worn)	Steering column (Binding)	Sliding yoke (Worn)	Steering gear housing	Front wheel bearing (Worn)
Hard steering	1	4	2	3	5	6	7		8	
Poor return	1	2					3		4	
Excessive play					1	2		3	5	4
Abnormal noise			1		2				3	

V000

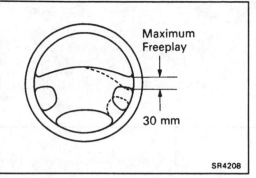

Maximum Freeplay

30 mm

SR4208

ON—VEHICLE INSPECTION

CHECK THAT STEERING WHEEL FREEPLAY IS CORRECT

With the vehicle stopped and tires pointed straight ahead, rock the steering wheel gently back and forth with light finger pressure.

Freeplay should not exceed the maximum.

Maximum freeplay:

    30 mm (1.18 in.)

If incorrect, repair.

SR

STEERING COLUMN

PREPARATION

SST (SPECIAL SERVICE TOOLS)

	09213−31021 Crankshaft Pulley Puller	

RECOMMENDED TOOLS

	09042−00010 Torx Socket T30	Steering wheel pad
	09904−00010 Expander Set	
	(09904−00050) No. 4 Claw	

EQUIPMENT

Torque wrench	

ASSEMBLY REMOVAL AND INSTALLATION

Remove and install the parts as shown.

SR0B3-01

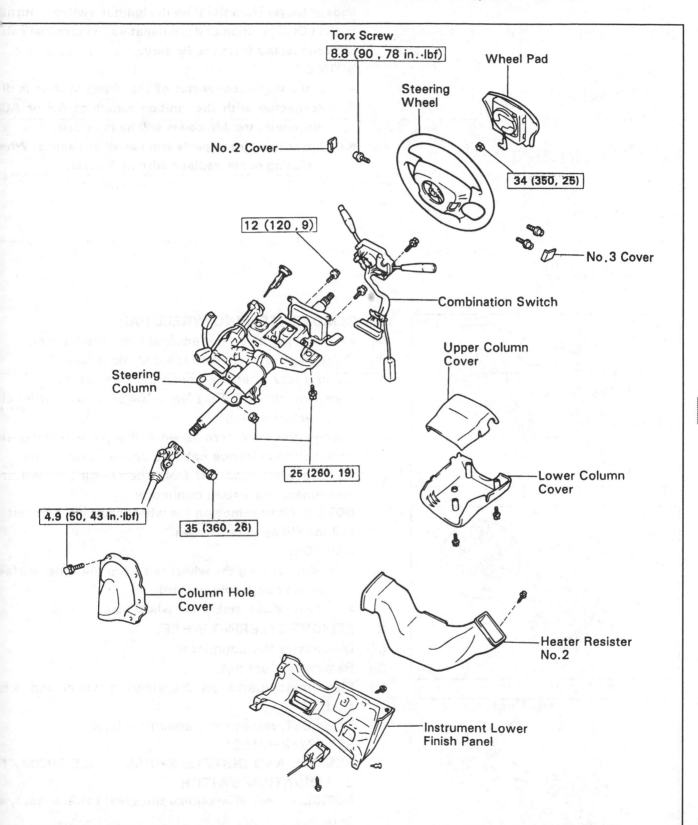

Torx Screw
8.8 (90 , 78 in.·lbf)

Wheel Pad

Steering Wheel

No.2 Cover

34 (350, 25)

12 (120 , 9)

No.3 Cover

Combination Switch

Upper Column Cover

Steering Column

Lower Column Cover

25 (260, 19)

4.9 (50, 43 in.·lbf)

35 (360, 26)

Column Hole Cover

Heater Resister No.2

Instrument Lower Finish Panel

SR

N·m (kgf·cm, ft·lbf) : Specified torque

R03947

(MAIN POINTS OF REMOVAL AND INSTALLATION)

CAUTION: Work must be started after approx. 90 se
onds or longer from the time the ignition switch is turne
to the LOCK position and the negative (−) terminal cab
is disconnected from the battery.

NOTICE:
- If the wiring coneector of the airbag system is di
  connected with the ignition switch at ON or AC
  diagnostic trouble codes will be recorded.
- Never use airbag parts from another vehicle. Whe
  replacing parts, replace with new parts.

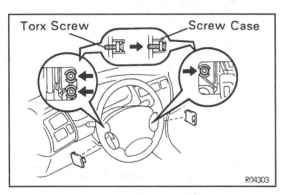

1. **REMOVE STEERING WHEEL PAD**
(a) Remove negative (−) terminal from the battery.
(b) Place the front wheels facing straight ahead.
(c) Using a torx wrench, loosen the three screws.
    Torx wrench: T30 (Part No. 09042−00010 or local
    manufactured tool)
(d) Loosen the torx screws until the groove along th
    screw circumference catches on the screw case.
(e) Pull the wheel pad out from the steering wheel ar
    disconnect the airbag connector.
    NOTICE: When removing the wheel pad, take care not
    pull the airbag wire harness.
    CAUTION:
    - When storing the wheel pad, keep the upper surfa
      of the pad facing upward.
    - Never disassemble the wheel pad.

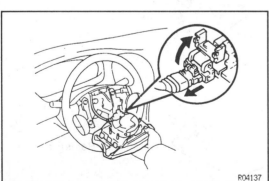

2. **REMOVE STEERING WHEEL**
(a) Disconnect the connector.
(b) Remove the set nut.
(c) Place matchmarks on the steering wheel and ma
    shaft.
(d) Using SST, remove the steering wheel.
    SST 09213−31021

3. **REMOVE AND INSTALL SPIRAL CABLE FROM/T
   COMBINATION SWITCH**
   NOTICE: Do not disassemble the spiral cable or apply
   to it.

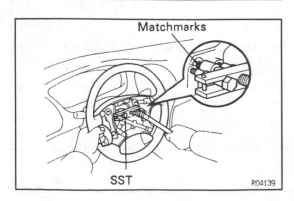

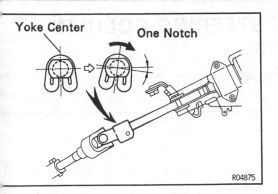

Yoke Center   One Notch

R04875

4. DISCONNECT AND CONNECT INTERMEDIATE SHAFT

(a) Place matchmarks on the intermediate shaft and main shaft, remove the bolt on the upper side and disconnect the main shaft.

(b) Install the intermediate shaft.

(c) Torque the bolt.

Torque: 27 N·m (280 kgf·cm, 20 ft·lbf)

HINT: Install the main shaft to the intermediate shaft, as shown.

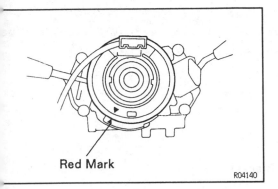

Red Mark

R04140

5. CENTER SPIRAL CABLE

(a) Check that the front wheels are facing straight ahead.

(b) Turn the spiral cable counterclockwise by hand until it becomes harder to turn the cable.

(c) Then rotate the spiral cable clockwise about 3 turns to align the red mark.

HINT: The spiral cable will rotate about 3 turns to either left or right of the cinter.

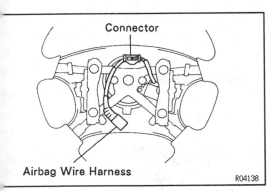

Connector

Airbag Wire Harness

R04138

6. INSTALL STEERING WHEEL

(a) Align matchmarks on the steering wheel and main shaft, and install the steering wheel to the main shaft.

(b) Install and torque the set nut.

Torque: 34 N·m (350 kgf·cm, 25 ft·lbf)

(c) Connect the connector.

SR

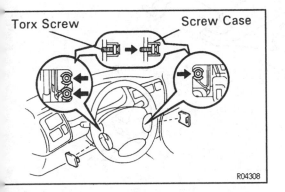

Torx Screw   Screw Case

R04308

7. INSTALL STEERING WHEEL PAD

(a) Connect the airbag connector.

(b) Install the wheel pad after confirming that the circumference groove of the torx screws is caught on the screw case.

(c) Using a torx wrench, tighten the three screws.

Torque: 8.8 N·m (90 kgf·cm, 78 in.·lbf)

NOTICE:

- **Make sure the wheel pad is installed to the specified torque.**

- **If the wheel pad has been dropped, or there are cracks, dents or other defects in the case or connector, replace the wheel pad with a new one.**

- **When installing the wheel pad, take care that the wirings do not interfere with other parts and are not pinched between other parts.**

8. CHECK STEERING WHEEL CENTER POINT

NON–TILT STEERING COLUMN
COMPONENTS
(NASTECH Type)

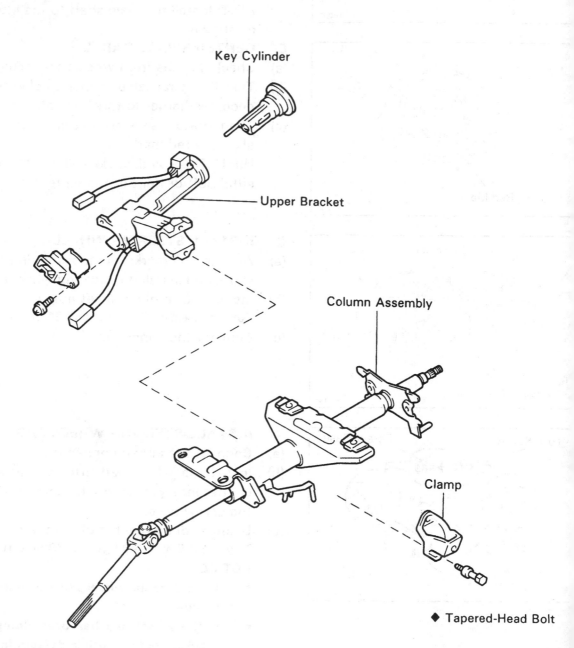

Key Cylinder

Upper Bracket

Column Assembly

Clamp

◆ Tapered-Head Bolt

◆ Non-reusable part

(TOYOTA Type)

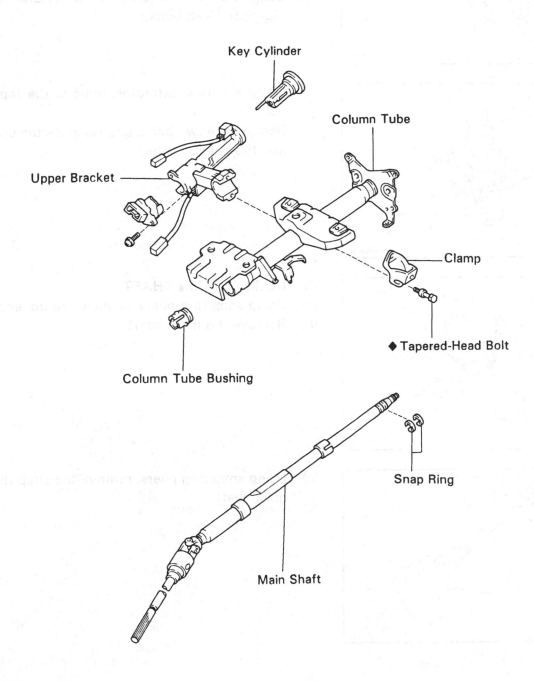

Key Cylinder

Column Tube

Upper Bracket

Clamp

Tapered-Head Bolt

Column Tube Bushing

Snap Ring

Main Shaft

SR

◆ Non-reusable part

R04224

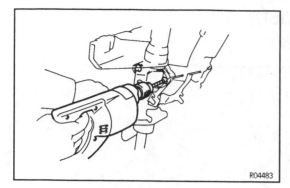

R04483

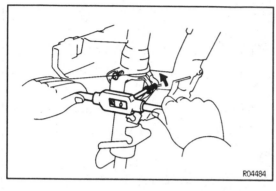

R04484

STEERING COLUMN DISASSEMBLY

SR03H—6

1. REMOVE UPPER BRACKET

(a) Using ventering punch, mark the center of the tapere —head bolts.

(b) Using a 3—4 mm (0.12—0.16 in.) drill, drill into th tapered—head bolts.

(c) Using a screw extractor, remove the tapered—hea bolts.

(d) Remove the two bolts, and separate the upper bracke and the column tube.

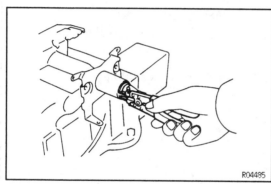

R04485

2. REMOVE MAIN SHAFT

(a) Using snap ring pliers, remove the upper snap ring.

(b) Remove the main shaft.

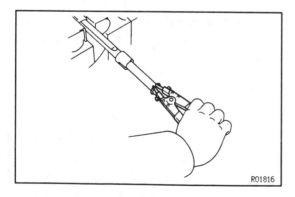

R01816

(c) Using snap ring pliers, remove the snap ring from th main shaft.

SR

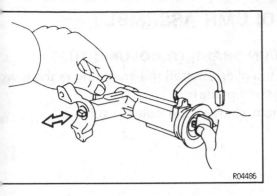

STEERING COLUMN INSPECTION AND REPLACEMENT

SR03J-02

1. INSPECT UPPER BRACKET

Check that the steering lock mechanism operates properly.

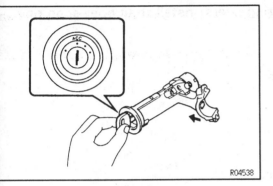

2. IF NECESSARY, REPLACE IGNITION KEY CYLINDER

(a) Place the ignition key at the ACC position.

(b) Push down the stop key with a thin rod, and pull out the key cylinder.

(c) Turn the ignition key plate to the ACC position, and install a new key cylinder into the upper bracket.

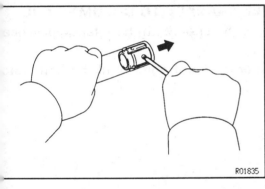

3. IF NECESSARY, REPLACE BUSHING

(a) Using a screwdriver, remove the bushing.

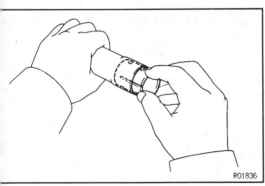

(b) Align the holes of the tube and the projections of new bushing, and install the bushing to the column tube.

SR

STEERING COLUMN ASSEMBLY

1. INSTALL MAIN SHAFT TO COLUMN TUBE

(a) Using snap ring pliers, install the snap ring in the lower groove of the main shaft.

(b) Install the main shaft in the column tube.

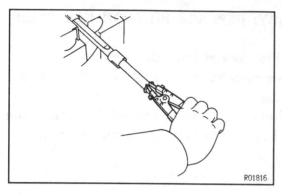

(c) Using snap ring pliers, install the upper snap ring.

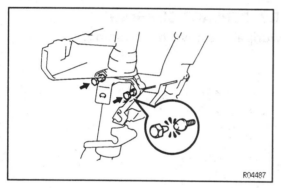

2. INSTALL UPPER BRACKET TO COLUMN TOBE

(a) Install the upper bracket with two tapered — head bolts.

(b) Tighten the tapered—head bolts until the bolt head break off.

SR

TILT STEERING COLUMN
COMPONENTS

SR03L—04

NOTICE: Do not disassemble the tilt steering column.

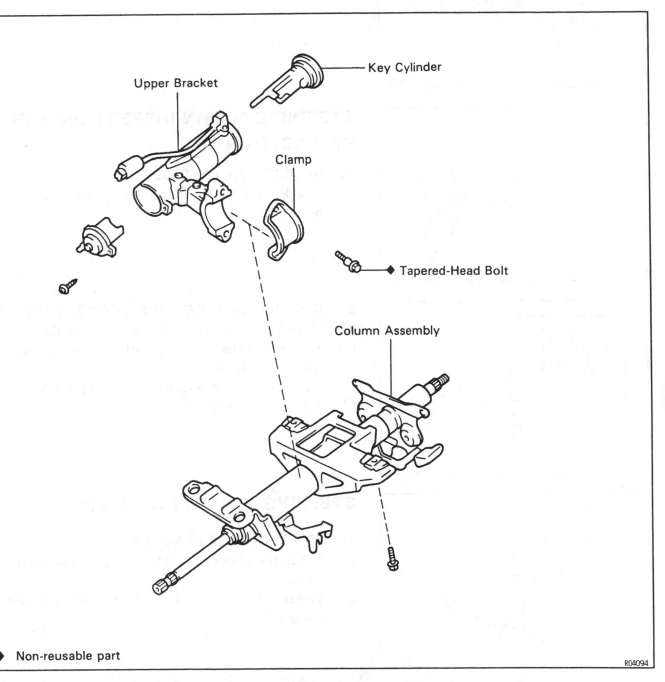

- Upper Bracket
- Key Cylinder
- Clamp
- ◆ Tapered-Head Bolt
- Column Assembly

◆ Non-reusable part

R04094

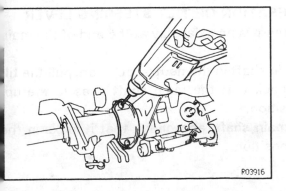

R03916

SR0AQ—01

STEERING COLUMN DISASSEMBLY

REMOVE UPPER BRACKET

(a) Using a centering punch, mark the center of the tapered—head bolts.

(b) Using a 3—4 mm (0.12—0.16 in.) drill, drill into the tapered—head bolts.

SR

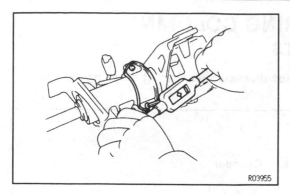

R03955

(c) Using a screw extractor, remove the taperd—hea
bolts.

(d) Remove the two bolts, and separate the upper bracke
and the column tube.

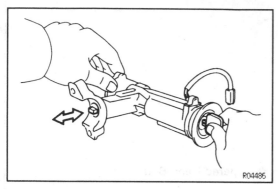

R04486

STEEING COLUMN INSPECTION AND REPLACEMENT

SROAR—01

1. INSPECT KEY CYLINDER
Check that the steering lock mechanism operate
properly.

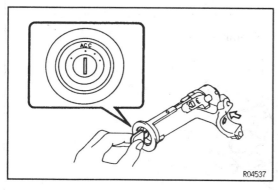

R04537

2. IF NECESSARY, REPLACE KEY CYLINDER
(a) Place the ignition key at the ACC position.
(b) Push down the stop key with a thin rod, and pull ou
the key cylinder.
(c) Make sure that the ignition key is at the ACC position
(d) Install a new key cylinder.

R03956

STEERING COLUMN ASSEMBLY

SROAS—01

1. INSTALL UPPER BRACKET
(a) Install the upper bracket with two new taperd—hea
bolts.
(b) Tighten the taperd—head bolts until the bolt head:
break off.

2. CHECK OPERATION OF TILT STEERING LEVER
(a) Check that there is no axial play at the end of the mair
shaft.
(b) With the main shaft in the neutral position, pull the til
lever and check that the main shaft rises to the up
permost position.
(c) Lower the main shaft, and check that it locks in the
lowermost position.

SR

MANUAL STEERING GEAR HOUSING

PREPARATION

SST (SPECIAL SERVICE TOOLS)

SR008-02

09612-00012	Rack & Pinion Steering Rack Housing Stand	
09612-10093	Steering Gear Housing Overhaul Tool Set	
(09617-10010)	Steering Pinion Bearing Adjusting Screw Lock Nut Wrench	
(09628-10020)	Ball Joint Lock Nut Wrench	
09612-24014	Steering Gear Housing Overhaul Tool Set	
(09612-10061)	Steering Pinion Bearing Replacer	
(09616-10010)	Steering Pinion Bearing Adjusting Socket	
(09616-10020)	Steering Pinion Bearing Adjusting Screw Wrench	
(09617-22030)	Steering Rack End Wrench	
(09617-24020)	Steering Pinion Bearing Adjusting Screw Lock Nut Wrench	
09628-62011	Ball Joint Puller	
09631-10010	Steering Rack Replacer "D"	

SR

	09631–12020	Handle	
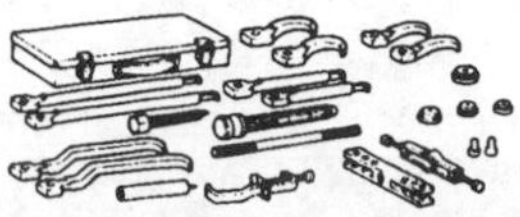	09950–20017	Universal Puller	

SR00T–01

RECOMMENDED TOOLS

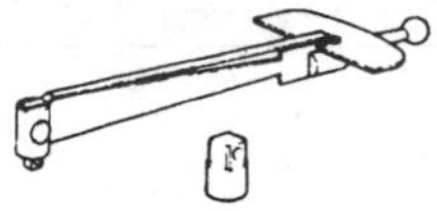	09025–00010	Small Torque Wrench	Total preload

SR00U–01

EQUIPMENT

Dial indicator	Steering rack
Torque wrench	

SR00V–03

SSM (SPECIAL SERVICE MATERIALS)

	08833–00080	Adhesive 1344, THREE BOND 1344, LOCTITE 242 or equivalent	Pinion bearing adjusting screw Pinion bearing adjusting screw lock nut Rack guide spring cap

SR

ASSEMBLY REMOVAL AND INSTALLATION

Remove and install the parts as shown.

SROAT—01

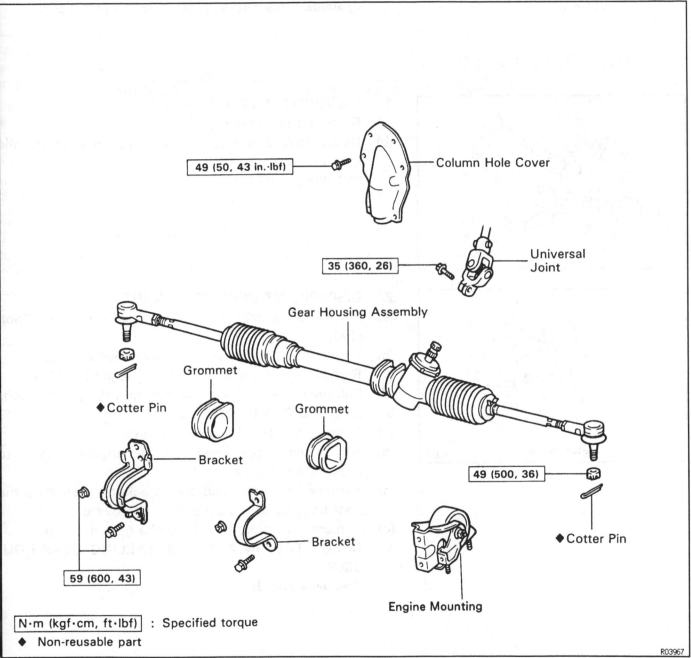

49 (50, 43 in.·lbf) — Column Hole Cover

35 (360, 26) — Universal Joint

Gear Housing Assembly

Grommet

♦ Cotter Pin

Grommet

Bracket

49 (500, 36) ♦ Cotter Pin

Bracket

59 (600, 43)

Engine Mounting

N·m (kgf·cm, ft·lbf) : Specified torque

♦ Non-reusable part

R03967

SR

(MAIN POINTS OF REMOVAL AND INSTALLATION)

NOTICE: When the steering wheel pad removed, always place it on a stable flat place with the pad surface facing upwards. Never place anything on top of the pad.

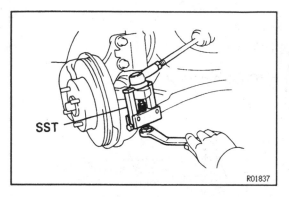

1. DISCONNECT TIE ROD ENDS

(a) Remove the cotter pins and nuts.

(b) Using SST, disconnect the tie rod ends from the knuckle arms.
SST 09628—62011

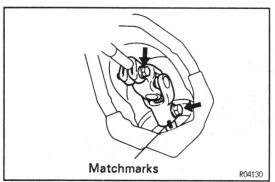

Matchmarks

2. DISCONNECT UNIVERSAL JOINT

(a) Place matchmarks on the universal joint and pinion shaft.

(b) Loosen the upper side of universal joint set bolt.

(c) Remove the lower side of universal joint set bolt.

(d) Pull the universal joint upward from the pinion shaft.

3. REMOVE GEAR HOUSING

(a) Remove the gear housing set nuts.

(b) Attach the engine hoist chain to engine hangers to support the engine.

(c) Remove two bolts and two brackets, then slide the gear housing to the LH side to remove it.

(d) Remove two grommets from the gear housing.

4. CHECK TOE—IN AFTER INSTALLING GEAR HOUSING

(See page SA—3)

COMPONENTS

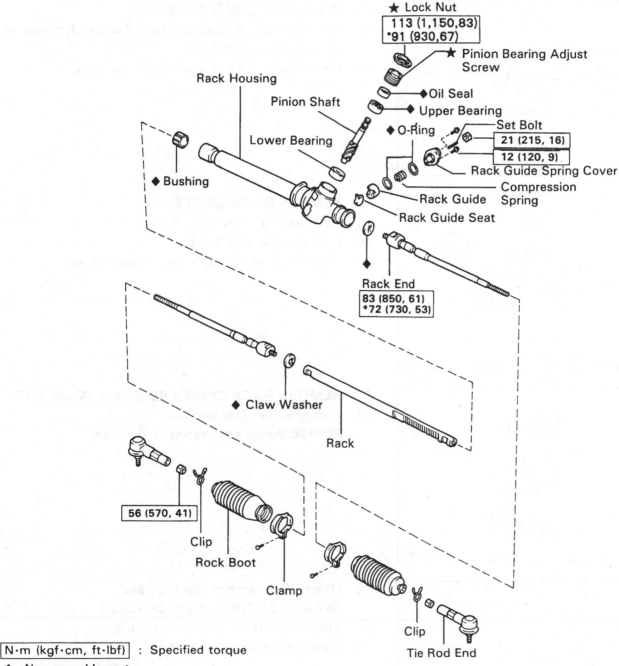

★ Lock Nut
113 (1,150, 83)
*91 (930, 67)

★ Pinion Bearing Adjust Screw

Rack Housing

Pinion Shaft

◆ Oil Seal

◆ Upper Bearing

Lower Bearing

◆ O-Ring

Set Bolt
21 (215, 16)
12 (120, 9)

◆ Bushing

Rack Guide Spring Cover

Compression Spring

Rack Guide

Rack Guide Seat

Rack End
83 (850, 61)
*72 (730, 53)

◆ Claw Washer

Rack

56 (570, 41)

Clip

Rock Boot

Clamp

Clip

Tie Rod End

N·m (kgf·cm, ft·lbf) : Specified torque

◆ Non-reusable part

★ Precoated part

* For use with SST

R04095

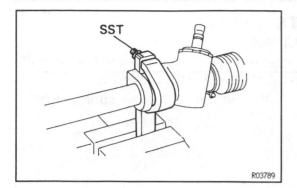

GEAR HOUSING DISASSEMBLY

1. CLAMP GEAR HOUSING IN VISE
Using SST, secure the steering gear housing in a vise
SST 09612—00012

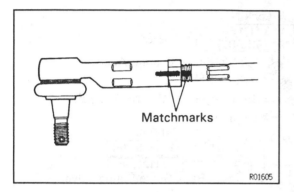

2. REMOVE TIE ROD ENDS
(a) Loosen the lock nut and place the matchmarks on the tie rod end and rack end.
(b) Remove the tie rod ends and lock nuts.

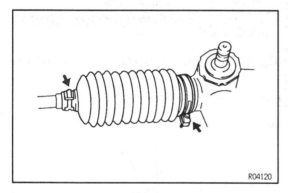

3. REMOVE RACK BOOTS
(a) Remove the clips and clamps.
(b) Remove the rack boots.
(c) Mark the left and right boots accordingly.

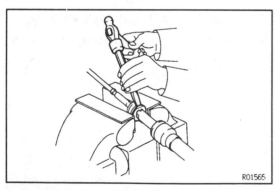

4. REMOVE RACK ENDS AND CLAW WASHERS
(a) Unstake the claw washer.
NOTICE: Avoid any impact to the rack.

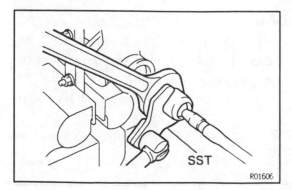

(b) Using SST, remove the rack end.
SST 09612—10093 (09628—10020)
(c) Mark the left and right rack ends.
(d) Remove the claw washer.

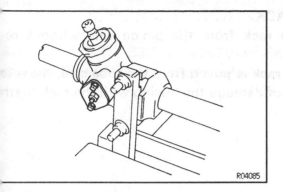

5. REMOVE HEXAGON NUT

6. REMOVE SET BOLT

Using a hexagon wrench 4 mm, remove the set bolt.

7. REMOVE RACK GUIDE SPRING COVER

Remove two bolts and the rack guide spring cover.

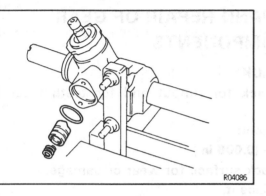

8. REMOVE O—RING

9. REMOVE COMPRESSION SPRING

10. REMOVE RACK GUIDE

11. REMOVE RACK GIDE SEAT

Remove rack guide seat from the rack guide.

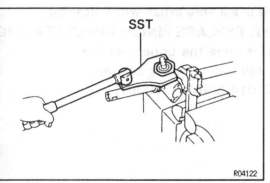

12. REMOVE PINION BEARING ADJUSTING SCREW LOCK NUT

Using SST, remove the pinion bearing adjusing screw lock nut.

SST 09612—10093 (09617—22030)

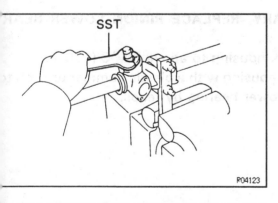

13. REMOVE PINION BEARING ADJUSTING SCREW

Using SST, remove the pinion bearing adjusting screw.

SST 09612—24014 (09616—10020)

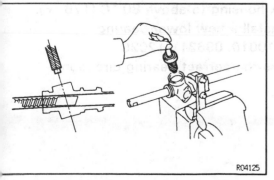

14. REMOVE PINION WITH UPPER BEARING

HINT: Becareful not to damage the serrations.

(a) Fully pull the rack from the housing side and align the rack notched portion with the pinion.

(b) Remove the pinion together with the upper bearing.

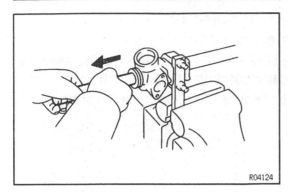

R04124

15. REMOVE RACK

Remove the rack from the pinion side without revolving it.

HINT: If the rack is pulled from the tube side, there is a possibility of damage the busing with the rack teeth surface.

INSPECTION AND REPAIR OF GEAR HOUSING COMPONENTS

SR0AV—01

1. INSPECT RACK

(a) Check the rack for runout and for teeth wear or damage.

  Maximum runout:

  0.15 mm (0.006 in.)

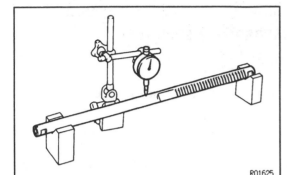

R01625

(b) Check the back surface for wear or damage.
  If faulty, replace it.
  NOTICE: Do not use a wire brush when cleaning.

2. IF NECESSARY, REPLACE PINION UPPER BEARING

(a) Using a press, remove the upper bearing.

(b) Using SST, install a new upper bearing.
  SST 09612—24014 (09612—10061)

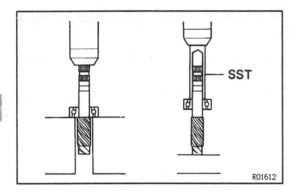

SST

R01612

3. IF NECESSARY, REPLACE PINION LOWER BEARING

(a) Heat the rack housing to above 80 °C (176°F).

(b) Tap the rack housing with a plastic hammer or such to remove the lower bearing by recoil.

R02659

(c) Heat the rack housing to above 80 °C (176 °F).

(d) Using SST, install a new lower bearing.
  SST 09631—10010, 09631—12020
  HINT: Observe the correct bearing direction.

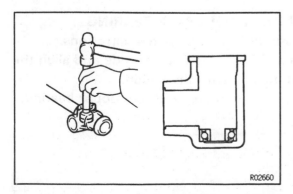

R02660

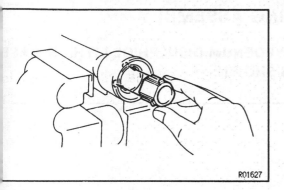

4. IF NECESSARY, REPLACE RACK BUSHING

(a) Using a screwdriver, loosen the three bushing claws and removethe rack bushing from the rack housing.

(b) Install a new bushing into the rack housing, making sure to align into the three holes.

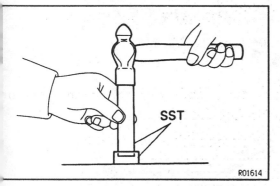

5. IF NECESSARY, REPLACE PINION OIL SEAL

(a) Using SST, remove the pinion oil seal.
SST 09631—10010, 09631—12020

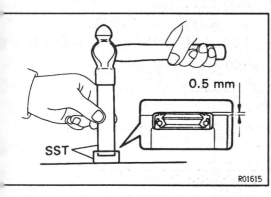

(b) Using SST, drive in a new oil seal until it is protruding 0.5 mm (0.020 in.).
SST 09631—10010, 09631—12020

SR

GEAR HOUSING ASSEMBLY

SR0AW—01

1. **PACK MOLYBDENUM DISULPHIDE LITHIUM BASE GREASE AS SHOWN:**

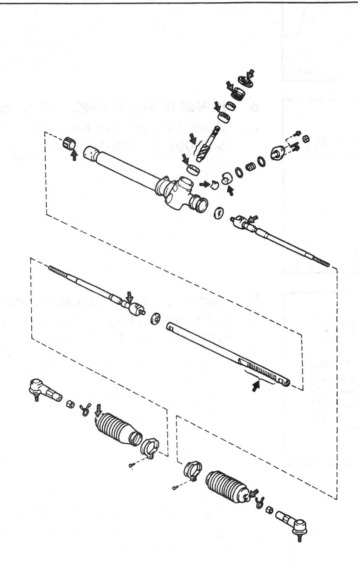

◄━ Molybdenum disulphide lithiun base grease

◄▭ Power steering fluid

R04096

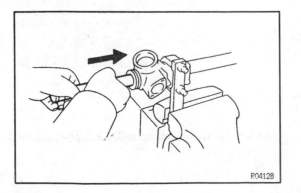

R04128

2. **INSTALL RACK INTO RACK HOUSING**
   - (a) From the pinion side, install the rack into the rack housing.
   - (b) Set the rack notched side so that the pinion can be positioned inside.

SR

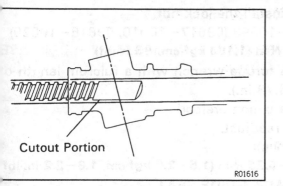

Cutout Portion

R01616

(c) Line up the cutout portion of the rack with the pinion.

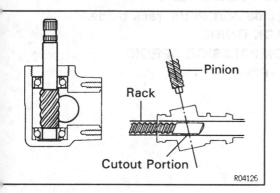

Pinion

Rack

Cutout Portion

R04126

3. INSTALL PINION INTO HOUSING

Insure that the pinion end is securely in the lower bearing.

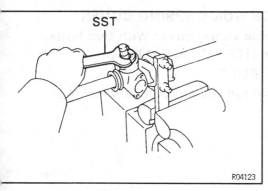

SST

R04123

4. INSTALL PINION BEARING ADJUSTING SCREW

(a) Apply sealant to 2 or 3 threads of the screw.
Sealant:
Part No.08833—00080, THREE BOND 1344, LOC-TITE 242 or epuivalent

(b) Using SST, install the pinion bearing adjusting screw.
SST 09612—24014 (09616—10020)

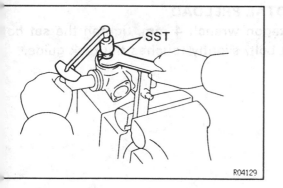

SST

R04129

5. ADJUST PINION PRELOAD

(a) Line up the cutout portion of the rack with the pinion.

(b) Using SST, tighten the pinion bearing adjusting screw to the point where the turning torque is 0.4 N·m (3.7 kgf·cm, 3.2 in.·lbf)
SST 09612—24014 (09616—10010, 09616—10020)

(c) Using SST, loosen the pinion bearing adjusting screw to the point where the turning torque of the pinion is 0.4 N·m (3.7 kgf·cm, 3.2 in.·lbf)
SST 09612—24014 (09616—10010, 09616—10020)
Preload (turning):
0.2—0.3 N·m (2.3—3.3 kgf·cm, 2.0—2.9 in.·lbf)

6. INSTALL PINION BEARING ADJUSTING SCREW LOCK NUT

(a) Apply sealant to 2 or 3 threads of the lock nut.
Sealant:
Part No. 08833—00080, THREE BOND 1344, LOC-TITE 242 or equivalent

SR

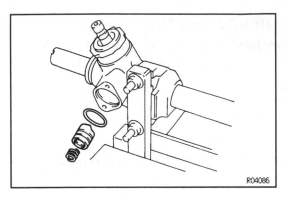

(b) Using SST, install the lock nut.
SST 09612—10093 (09617—10010, 09616—10020)
Torque: 113 N·m (1,150 kgf·cm, 83 ft·lbf)
HINT: Use a torque wrench with a fulcrum length o
425 mm (16.73 in.).

(c) Recheck the pinion preload.
If incorrect, readjust.
Preload (turning):
0.15—0.25 N·m (1.5—2.5 kgf·cm, 1.3—2.2 in.·lbf

7.   INSTALL RACK GUIDE SEAT
Install rack guide seat to the rack guide.

8.   INSTALL RACK GUIDE

9.   INSTALL COMPRESSION SPRING

10. INSTALL O—RING

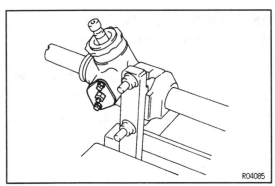

11. INSTALL RACK GUIDE SPRING COVER
Install rack guide spring cover with two bolts.
Torque: 12 N·m (120 kgf·cm, 9 ft·lbf)

12. INSTALL SET BOLT
Temporarily tighten the set bolt and lock nut.

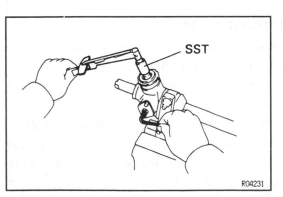

13. ADJUST TOTAL PRELOAD
(a) Using a hexagon wrench 4 mm, tighten the set bo
until the set bolt slightly touches the rack guide.

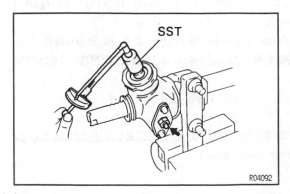

(b) Using SST and a torque meter, tighten the rack guid
spring cap until preload is within specification.
SST 09612—24014 (09616—10010)
Preload (Turning):
0.7—1.5 N·m (7—15 kgf·cm, 6.1—13.0 in.·lbf)

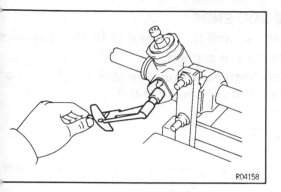

14. INSTALL HEXAGON NUT

(a) Install the hexagon nut.
Torque: 21 N·m (215 kgf·cm, 16 ft·lbf)

(b) Recheck the total preload.
If incorrect, readjust.
Preload (turning):
0.7 — 1.5 N·m (7 — 15 kgf·cm, 6.1 — 13.0 in.·lbf)

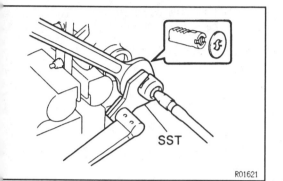

15. INSTALL RACK ENDS AND CLAW WASHERS

(a) Install new claw washers.
HINT: Align the claws of the claw washer with the rack grooves.

(b) Using SST, install and torque the rack ends.
SST 09612 — 10093 (09628 — 10020)
Torque: 83 N·m (850 kgf·cm, 61 ft·lbf)
HINT: Use a torque wrench with a fulcrum length of 340 mm (13.39 in.).

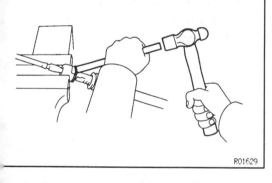

(c) Srake the claw washers.

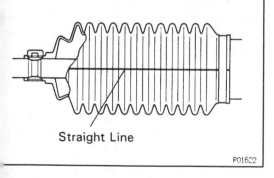

16. INSTALL RACK BOOTS

(a) Install the rack boots.
HINT: Be careful not to damage of twist the boot.

Straight Line

(b) Install the clamps and clips.
HINT: Face the open ends of the clip outward, as shown, to avoid damage to the boot.

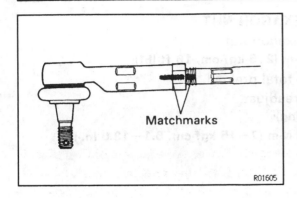

Matchmarks

R01605

17. INSTALL TIE ROD ENDS

(a) Screw the lock nut and tie rod end onto the rack end until matchmarks are aligned.

(b) After adjusting toe—in, torque the lock nut.
Torque: 56 N·m (570 kgf·cm, 41 ft·lbf)

POWER STEERING

DESCRIPTION

POWER STEERING PRINCIPLES

SR00Z—01

Power steering is one type of hydraulic device for utilizing engine power to reduce steering effort. Consequently, the engine is used to drive a pump to develop fluid pressure, and this pressure acts on a piston within the power cylinder so that the piston assists the rack effort. The amount of this assistance depends on the extent of pressure acting on the piston. Therefore, if more steering force is required, the pressure must be raised. The variation in the fluid pressure is accomplished by a control valve which is linked to the steering main shaft.

NEUTRAL (STRAIGHT—AHEAD) POSITION

Fluid from the pump is sent to the control valve. If the control valve is in the neutral position, all the fluid will flow through the control valve into the relief port and back to the pump. At this time, hardly any pressure is created and because the pressure on the cylinder piston equal on both sides, the piston will not move in either direction.

SR

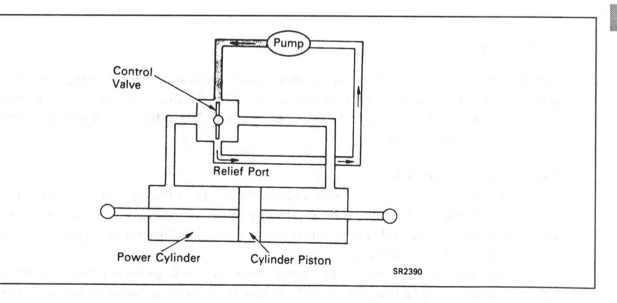

WHEN TURNING

When the steering main shaft is turned in either direction, the control valve also moves, closing one of the fluid passages. The other passage then opens wider, causing a change in fluid flow volume and, at the same time, pressure is created. Consequently, a pressure difference occurs between both sides of the piston and the piston moves in the direction of the lower pressure so that the fluid in the cylinder is forced back to the pump through the control valve.

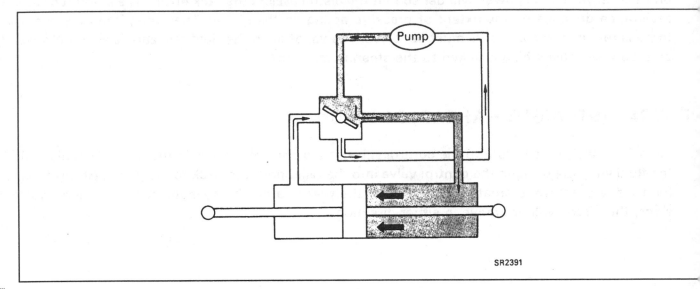

SR2391

SR

SR010—0

SERVICE HINT

Trouble with the power steering system usually involves hard steering resulting from lack of assist. In such cases, before attempting to make repairs, you should determine whether the trouble lies with the pump or with the gear housing. To do this, use a pressure gauge to perform an on—vehicle inspection.

ON—VEHICLE INSPECTION

Power steering is a hydraulic device and problems are normally due to insufficient fluid pressure acting on the piston. This could be caused by either the pump not producing the specified fluid pressure or the control valve in the gear housing not functioning properly so that the proper fluid pressure can not be obtained.

If the fault lies with the pump, the same symptoms will generally occur whether the steering wheel is turned fully to the right or left. On the other hand, if the fault lies with the control valve, there will generally be a difference between the amount of assist when the steering wheel is turned to the left and right, causing harder steering. However, if the piston seal of the power cylinder is worn, there will be a loss of fluid pressure whether the steering wheel is turned to the right or left and the symptoms will be the same for both.

Before performing an on—vehicle inspection, a check must first be made to confirm that the power steering system is completely free of any air. If there is any air in the system, the volume of this air will change when the fluid pressure is raised, causing a fluctuation in the fluid pressure so that the power steering will not function properly. To determine if there is any air in the system, check if there is a change of fluid level in the reservoir tank when the steering wheel turned fully to the right or left.

If there is air in the system, it will be compressed to a smaller volume when the steering wheel is turned, causing a considerable drop in the fluid level. If the system is free of air, there will be very little change in the level even when the fluid pressure is raised. This is because the fluid, being a liquid, does not change volume when compressed. The small change in the fluid level is due to expansion of the hoses between the pump and gear housing when pressure rises.

Also, air in the system sometimes causes abnormal noise in the pump or gear housing when the steering wheel is fully turned in either direction.

This on—vehicle inspection must be performed every time after overhauling or repairing the pump or gear housing to ensure that the power steering is working properly.

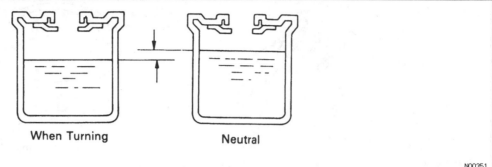

When Turning   Neutral

SR2392 SR2393   N00351

VANE PUMP

The main component parts of the vane pump, such as the cam ring, rotor, vanes and flow control valve are high precision parts and must be handled carefully. Also, because this pump produces a very high fluid pressure, O—rings are used for sealing each part. When reassembling the pump, always use new O—rings.

In the flow control valve, there is a relief valve which controls the maximum pressure of the pump. The amount of this maximum pressure is very important; if it is too low, there will be insufficient power steering assist and if too high, it will have an adverse effect on the pressure hoses, oil seals, etc. If the maximum pressure is either too high or too low due to a faulty relief valve, do not disassemble or adjust the relief valve, but replace the flow control valve as an assembly.

The clearance between the flow control valve and pump body installation hole is very important.

After manufacture, the factory measures the size of the installation hole and outer circumference of the flow control valve, and punches a mark accordingly. Therefore, when replacing the flow control valve, be sure to do so with one having the same mark in order to insure the proper clearance.

SR

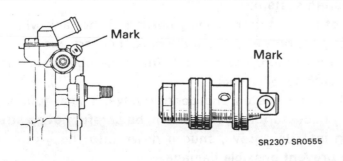

Mark   Mark

SR2307 SR0555

Z02076

The functional parts of the pump which produce fluid pressure are the cam ring, rotor and vane and these should be checked for wear. If the clearance between each is not within standard whe reassembling, any worn parts should be replaced.

In this case, the replaced cam ring and rotor should be of the same length (have the same mark and the vanes should be replaced with those having a length corresponding to that mar otherwise the proper thrust clearance cannot be obtained. If there is too much thrust clearanc there will be insufficient fluid pressure at low speeds. If there is too little thrust clearance, it ma result in seizure of the vanes.

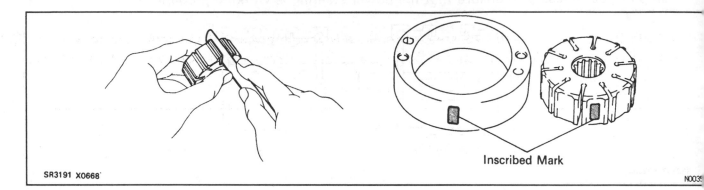

Inscribed Mark

SR3191 X0668

GEAR HOUSING

If the gear housing is secured directly in a vise during overhaul, there is danger of deforming so always first secure it in the SST provided (rack and pinion steering rack housing stand) befor placing it in the vise.

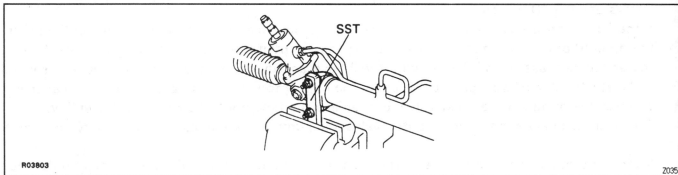

SST

R03803

The oil seals on both sides of the power cylinder are for the prevention of leakage of the hig pressure fluid which acts on the piston. Always use new oil seals when reassembling and be ve careful not to scratch or damage them.

Because of the high pressure, even the slightest scratch will cause fluid leakage, resulting in a inoperative power steering system.

Also, be very careful not to scratch the sliding portion of the rack which makes contact with th oil seals. When removing the rack ends from the rack, it is very easy to cause a burr when holdi the tip of the rack with a wrench. Therefore, before assembling the rack, first check the tip f burrs and remove any with an oil stone.

Teflon rings are used for the piston and control valve. These teflon rings are highly durab against wear, but if it is necessary to replace them, be careful not so stretch the new ones. Aft installing a teflon ring into its groove, snug it down into the groove before assembly of th cylinder or housing to prevent possible damage.

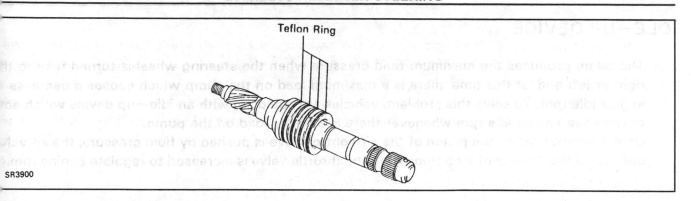

Teflon Ring

SR3900

As with the rack and pinion type steering, preload is very important. If the preload is not correct, it could result in such trouble as steering wheel play or shimmy or lack of durability, so always make sure that it is correct.

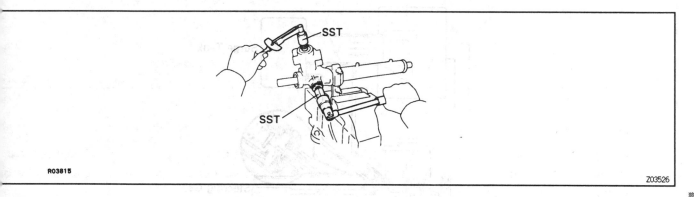

SST

SST

R03815

Z03526

SR

IDLE—UP DEVICE

The pump produces the maximum fluid pressure when the steering wheel is turned fully to th[e]
right or left and, at this time, there is a maximum load on the pump which causes a decrease [in]
engine idle rpm. To solve this problem, vehicles are equipped with an idle—up device which ac[ts]
to raise the engine idle rpm whenever there is a heavy load on the pump.
On EFI engines, when the piston of the air control valve is pushed by fluid pressure, the air valv[e]
opens and the volume of air by—passing the throttle valve is increased to regulate engine rpm.

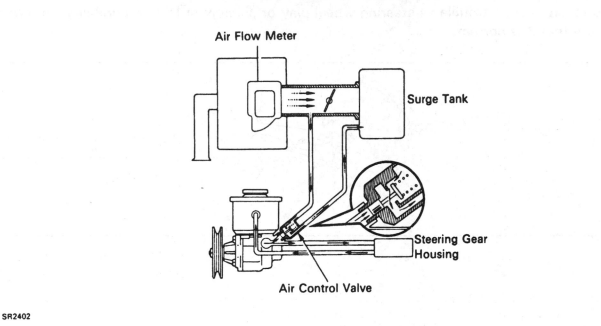

SR2402

PREPARATION

SST (SPECIAL SERVICE TOOLS)

SR012-06

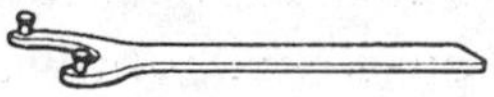	09278−54012	Drive Shaft Holding Tool
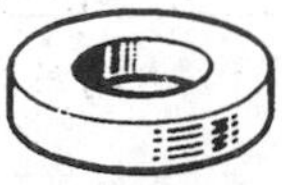	09515−21010	Rear Axle Shaft Bearing Replacer
	09608−30012	Front Hub & Drive Pinion Bearing Tool Set
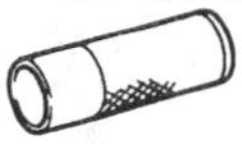	(09608−04030)	Front Hub Inner Bearing Cone Replacer
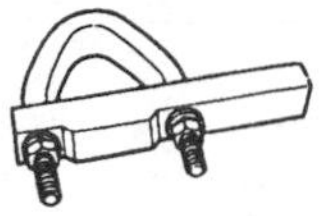	09612−00012	Rack & Pinion Steering Rack Housing Stand
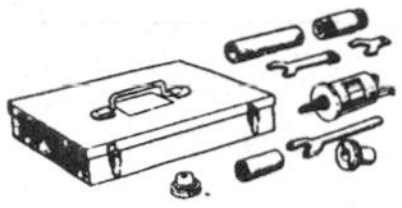	09612−10093	Steering Gear Housing Overhaul Tool Set
	(09616−10020)	Steering Pinion Bearing Adjusting Screw Wrench
	(09628−10020)	Ball Joint Lock Nut Wrench
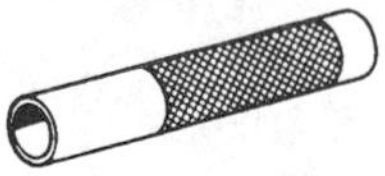	09612−22011	Tilt Handle Bearing Replacer
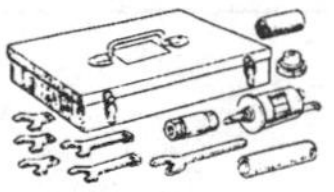	09612−24014	Steering Gear Housing Overhaul Tool Set
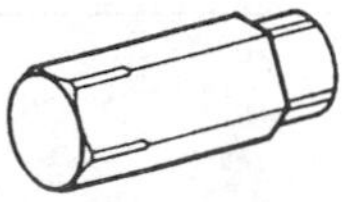	(09612−10022)	Hexagon Wrench
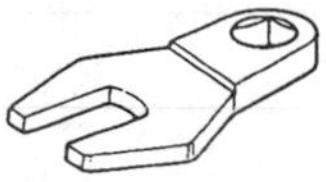	(09617−24011)	Steering Rack Wrench
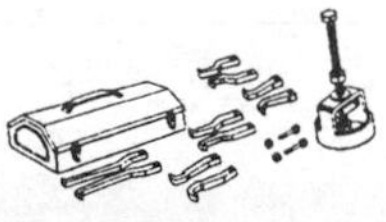	09612−65014	Steering Worm Bearing Puller

SR

SR

	(09612−01030)	Claw "C"
	09613−12010	Power Steering Control Valve Puller
	09613−12020	Control Valve Lock Nut Wrench
	09616−00010	Steering Worm Bearing Adjusting Socket
	09617−10020	Steering Rack End Wrench
	09617−12020	Rack Guide Cap Lock Nut Wrench
	09628−62011	Ball Joint Puller
	09631−12020	Handle
	09631−12031	Oil Seal "A" Remover
	09631−12040	Oil Seal "A" Replacer
	09631−12071	Steering Rack Oil Seal Test Tool
	09631−16020	Steering Rack Cover "A"
	09631−20070	Seal Ring Guide
	09631−20081	Seal Ring Tool

	09631—22020	Power Steering Hose Nut 14 x 17 mm Wrench Set	
	09633—00020	Power Steering Hose Nut Wrench	

SR

RECOMMENDED TOOLS

09025−00010 Small Torque Wrench		Total preload
09904−00010 Expander Set		
(09904−00050) No. 4 Claw		

EQUIPMENT

Dial indicator		Steering rack
Micrometer		Power steering pump
Oil pressure gauge		
Torque wrench		
Vacuum gauge		Gear housing

LUBRICANT

Item	Capacity	Classification
Power steering fluid Total	0.81 liters (0.86 US qts, 0.71 Imp.qts)	ATF DEXRON® II

SSM (SPECIAL SERVICE MATERIALS)

08833−00080 Adhesive 1344, THREE BOND 1344, LOCTITE 242 or equivalent		Rack housing cap Rack guide spring cap Rack guide spring cap lock nut

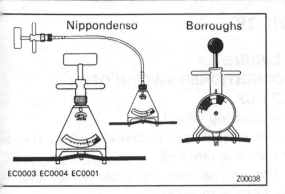

Nippondenso   Borroughs

EC0003 EC0004 EC0001   Z00038

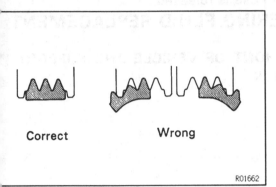

Correct   Wrong

R01662

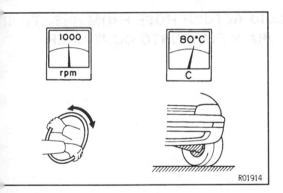

R01914

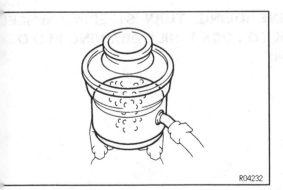

R04232

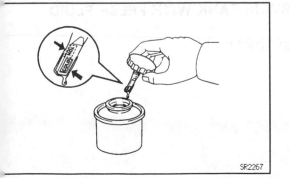

SR2267

ON—VEHICLE INSPECTION
DRIVE BELT TENSION CHECK

SR03W—02

Using a belt tension gauge, check the drive belt tension.

Belt tension gauge:
   Nippondenso BTG—20 (95506—00020) or
   Borroughs No.BT—33—73F
Drive belt tension:
   New belt
   441—539 N (45—55 kgf, 99—121 lbf)
   Used belt
   196—343 N (20—35 kgf, 44—77 lbf)

HINT:
- "New belt" refers to a belt which has been less than 5 minutes on a running engine.
- "Used belt" refers to a belt which has been used on a running engine for 5 minutes or more.
- After installing the drive belt, check that it fits properly in the ribbed grooves.

FLUID LEVEL CHECK

SR0AX—01

1. **KEEP VEHICLE LEVEL**
2. **BOOST FLUID TEMPERATURE**
   With the engine idling at 1,000 rpm or less, turn the steering wheel from lock to lock several times to boost fluid temperature.
   Fluid temperature:
   80°C (176°F)

3. **CHECK FOR FORMING OR EMULSIFICATION**
   HINT: Forming and emulsification indicate either the existence of air in the system or that the fluid level is too low.

4. **CHECK FLUID LEVEL IN RESERVOIR**
   Check the fluid level and add fluid if necessary.
   Fluid:
   ATF DEXRON® II
   HINT: Check that the fluid level is within the HOT LEVEL of the tank. If the fluid is cold, check that it is within the COLD LEVEL of the tank.

SR

SR017-0

IDLE—UP CHECK

1. **WARM UP ENGINE**
2. **TURN AIR CONDITIONER SWITCH OFF**
3. **CHECK IDLE—UP**
(a) Fully turn the steering wheel.
(b) Check that the engine rpm decreases when the ai
control valve hose is pinched.
(c) Check that the engine rpm increases when the ai
control valve hose is released.

POWER STEERING FLUID REPLACEMENT

SR018-0

1. **JACK UP FRONT OF VEHICLE AND SUPPORT IT
WITH STANDS**

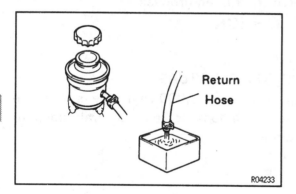

R01841

2. **REMOVE FLUID RETURN HOSE FROM RESERVOIR
TANK AND DRAIN FLUID INTO CONTAINER**

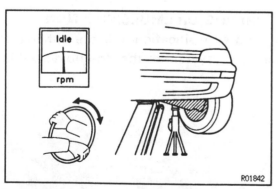

Return
Hose

R04233

3. **WITH ENGINE IDLING, TURN STEERING WHEEL
FROM LOCK TO LOCK WHILE DRAINING FLUID**
4. **STOP ENGINE**

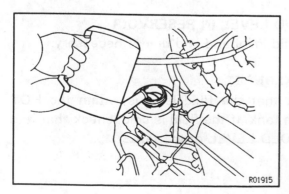

R01842

5. **FILL RESERVOIR TANK WITH FRESH FLUID**
Fluid:

   ATF DEXRON® II

R01915

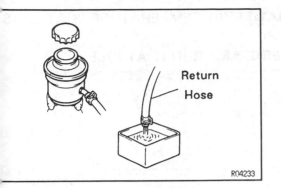

Return Hose

R04233

6. START ENGINE AND RUN IT AT 1,000 RPM

After 1 or 2 seconds, fluid will begin to discharge from the return hose. Stop the engine immediately at this time.

NOTICE: Take care that some fluid remains left in the reservoir tank.

7. REPEAT STEPS 5 AND 6 FOUR OR FIVE TIMES UNTIL THERE IS NO MORE AIR IN FLUID

8. CONNECT RETURN HOSE TO RESERVOIR TANK

9. BLEED POWER STEERING SYSTEM

POWER STEERING SYSTEM BLEEDING

SR00G–07

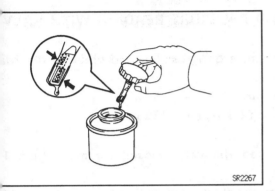

SR2267

1. CHECK FLUID LEVEL IN RESERVOIR TANK

Check the fluid level and add fluid if necessary.

Fluid:

ATF DEXRON® II

HINT: Check that the fluid level is within the HOT LEVEL of the tank. If the fluid is cold, check that it is within the COLD LEVEL of the tank.

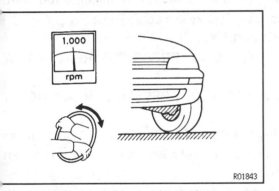

1,000 rpm

R01843

2. START ENGINE AND TURN STEERING WHEEL FROM LOCK TO LOCK THREE OR FOUR TIMES

With the engine speed below 1,000 rpm, turn the steering wheel to left or right full lock and keep it there for 2—3 seconds, then turn the wheel to the reverse full lock and keep it there for 2—3 seconds.

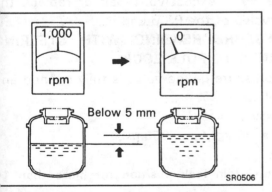

1,000 rpm → 0 rpm

Below 5 mm

SR0506

3. CHECK THAT FLUID IN RESERVOIR IS NOT FOAMY OR CLOUDY AND DOES NOT RISE OVER MAXIMUM WHEN ENGINE IS STOPPED

Measure the fluid level with the engine running. Stop the engine and measure the fluid level.

Maximum rise:

5 mm (0.20 in.)

If a problem is found, repeat steps 5 to 8 on page SR—40, 41. Repair the PS if the problem persists.

SR03Y–04

OIL PRESSURE CHECK

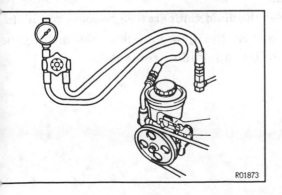

R01873

1. CONNECT PRESSURE GAUGE

(a) Disconnect the pressure line from the gear housing.

(b) Connect the gauge side of the pressure gauge to the PS pump and the valve side to the pressure line.

(c) Bleed the system. Start the engine and turn the steering wheel from lock to lock two or three times.

(d) Check that the fluid level is correct.

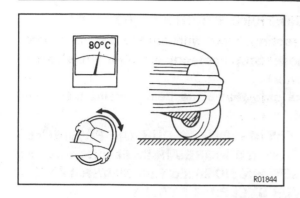

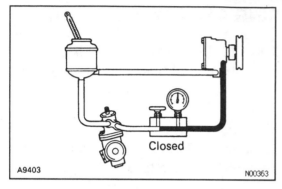

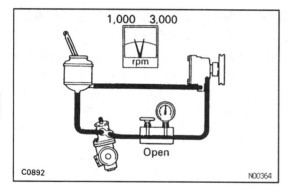

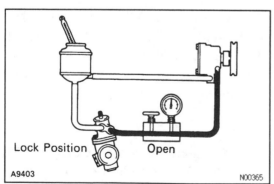

SR

2. **CHECK THAT FLUID TEMPERATURE IS AT LEAS**
   80°C (176°F)
3. **START ENGINE AND RUN IT AT IDLE**

4. **CHECK FLUID PRESSURE READING WITH VALV**
   CLOSED
   Close the pressure gauge valve and observe the rea
   ding on the gauge.
   Minimum pressure:
   　　5,884 kPa (60 kgf/cm² , 853 psi)
   NOTICE:
   - **Do not keep the valve closed for more than 1**
     seconds.
   - **Do not let the fluid temperature become too high.**
   If pressure is low, repair or replace the PS pump.
5. **OPEN VALVE FULLY**
6. **CHECK AND RECORD PRESSURE READING A**
   1,000 RPM
7. **CHECK AND RECORD PRESSURE READING A**
   3,000 RPM
   Check that there is 490 kPa (5 kgf/cm² , 71 psi) or les
   differencein pressure between the 1,000 rpm an
   3,000 rpm checks.
   If the difference is excessive, repair or replace th
   flow control valve of the PS pump.
8. **CHECK PRESSURE READING WITH STEERIN**
   WHEEL TURNED TO FULL LOCK
   Be sure the pressure gauge valve is fully opened an
   the engine idling.
   Minimum pressure:
   　　5,884 kPa (60 kgf/cm² , 853 psi)
   NOTICE:
   - **Do not maintain lock position for more than 1**
     seconds.
   - **Do not let the fluid temperature become too high.**
   If pressure is low, the gear housing has an interna
   leak and must be repaired or replaced.

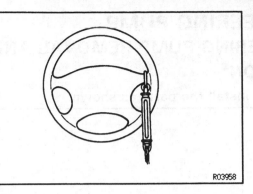

R03958

9. MEASURE STEERING EFFORT

(a) Center the steering wheel and run the engine at idle.

(b) Using a spring scale, measure the steering effort in both directions.

Maximum steering effort:
   50 N (5 kgf, 11 lbf)

If steering effort is excessive, repair the PS unit.

HINT: Be sure to consider the tire type, pressure and contact surface before making your diagnosis.

POWER STEERING PUMP
POWER STEERING PUMP REMOVAL AND INSTALLATION

Remove and install the parts as shown.

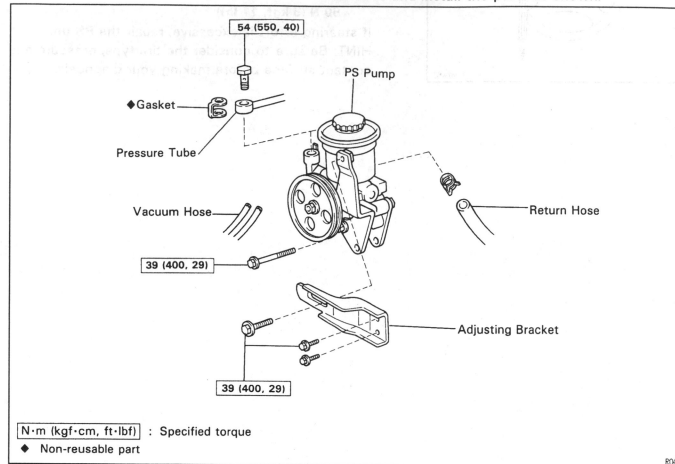

| 54 (550, 40) |
| PS Pump |
◆Gasket
Pressure Tube
Vacuum Hose
| 39 (400, 29) |
Return Hose
Adjusting Bracket
| 39 (400, 29) |

N·m (kgf·cm, ft·lbf) : Specified torque
◆ Non-reusable part

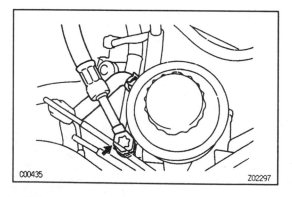

(MAIN POINTS OF REMOVAL AND INSTALLATION)

1. DISCONNECT AND CONNECT PRESSURE TUBE
Using SST, disconnect and connect the pressure tube from/to the PS pump.
SST 09631−22020
Torque: 54 N·m (550 kgf·cm, 40 ft·lbf)

2. ADJUST DRIVE BELT TENSION AFTER INSTALLING PS PUMP

COMPONENTS

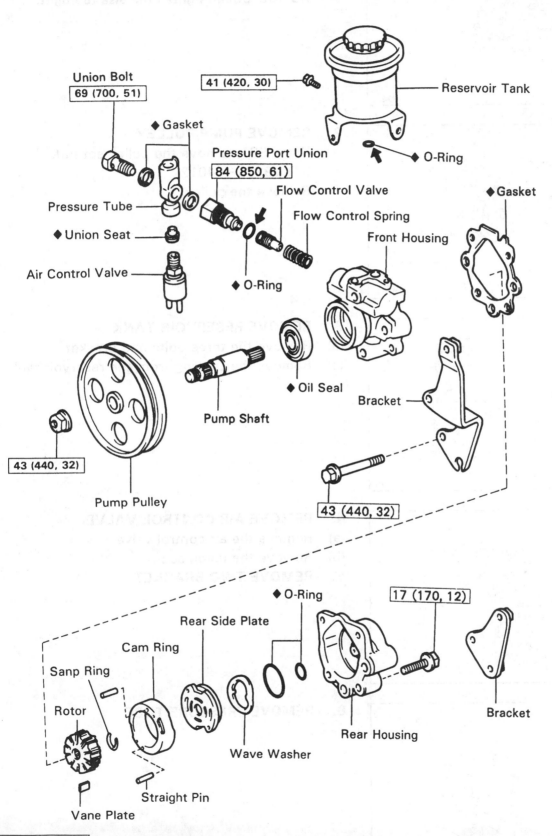

Union Bolt
69 (700, 51)

41 (420, 30)

Reservoir Tank

◆ Gasket

Pressure Port Union
84 (850, 61)

◆ O-Ring

Flow Control Valve

Pressure Tube

Flow Control Spring

◆ Gasket

◆ Union Seat

Front Housing

Air Control Valve

◆ O-Ring

◆ Oil Seal

Pump Shaft

Bracket

43 (440, 32)

Pump Pulley

43 (440, 32)

◆ O-Ring

17 (170, 12)

Rear Side Plate

Cam Ring

Sanp Ring

Rotor

Bracket

Rear Housing

Wave Washer

Straight Pin

Vane Plate

N·m (kgf·cm, ft·lbf) : Specified torque

R04226

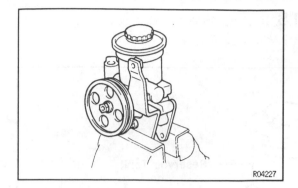

POWER STEERING PUMP DISASSEMBLY

1. **MOUNT PS PUMP IN VISE**
   NOTICE: Do not tighten the vise too tight.

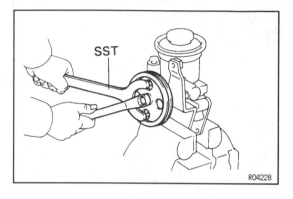

2. **REMOVE PUMP PULLEY**
   (a) Using SST, remove the pulley set nut.
       SST 09278—54012
   (b) Remove the pulley.

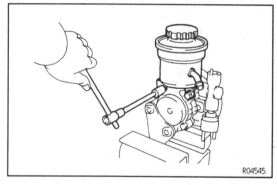

3. **REMOVE RESERVOIR TANK**
   (a) Remove the three bolts and bracket.
   (b) Remove the O—ring from the reservoir tank.

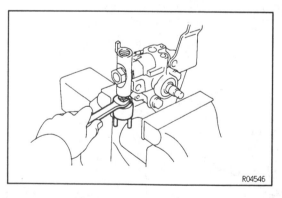

4. **REMOVE AIR CONTROL VALVE**
   (a) Remove the air control valve.
   (b) Remove the union seat.
5. **REMOVE TWO BRACKET**

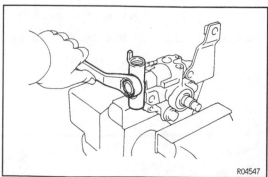

6. **REMOVE PRESSURE TUBE**

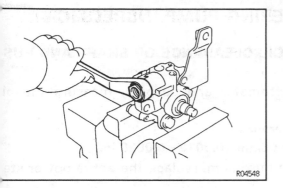

7. REMOVE PRESSURE PORT UNION, FLOW CONTROL VALVE AND SPRING

(a) Remove the pressure port union

(b) Remove the O—ring from the union.

(c) Remove the flow control valve and spring.

8. REMOVE REAR HOUSING

Remove the two bolts and rear housing.

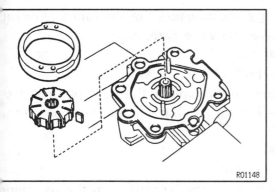

9. REMOVE CAM RING, ROTOR AND VANE PLATES
10. REMOVE STRAIGHT PINS
11. REMOVE GASKET

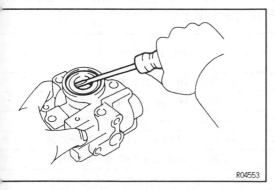

12. REMOVE VANE PUMP SHAFT WITH BEARING

Using a screwdriver, remove the bearing and pump shaft.

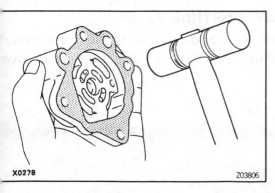

13. REMOVE REAR SIDE PLATE

(a) Using a plastic hammer, tap out the side plate and wave washer.

(b) Remove the two O—rings.

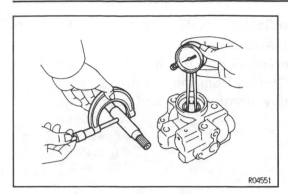

R04551

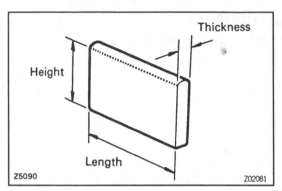

Z5090   Z02081

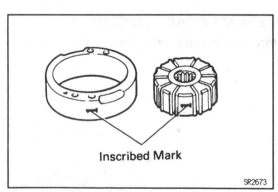

SR3191

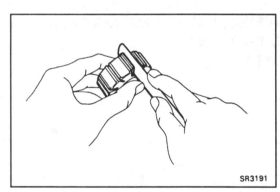

Inscribed Mark

SR2673

R04549

POWER STEERING PUMP INSPECTION   SR080-01

1. MEASURE OIL CLEARANCE OF SHAFT AND BUS-HING

Using a micrometer and calipers, measure the oil clearance.

Standard clearance:

0.03 – 0.05 mm (0.0012 – 0.0020 in.)

If more than maximum, replace the entire power steering pump.

2. INSPECT ROTOR AND VANE PLATES

(a) Using a micrometer, measure the height, thickness and length of the vane plates.

Minimum height:

8.6 mm (0.339 in.)

Minimum thickness:

1.397 mm (0.0550 in.)

Minimum length:

14.99 mm (0.5902 in.)

(b) Using a feeler gauge, measure the clearance between the rotor groove and vane plate.

Maximum clearance:

0.035 mm (0.0014 in.)

If more than maximum, replace the vane plate and/or rotor with one having the same mark stamped on the cam ring.

Inscribed mark:

1, 2, 3, 4 or None

HINT: There are five vane lengths with the following rotor and cam ring marks:

Rotor and cam ring mark	Vane length mm (in.)
None	14.999 – 15.001 (0.59051 – 0.59059)
1	14.997 – 14.999 (0.59043 – 0.59059)
2	14.995 – 14.997 (0.59035 – 0.59043)
3	14.993 – 14.995 (0.59027 – 0.59035)
4	14.991 – 14.993 (0.59002 – 0.59027)

3. INSPECT FLOW CONTROL VALVE

(a) Coat the valve with power steering fluid and check that it falls smoothly into the valve hole by its own weight.

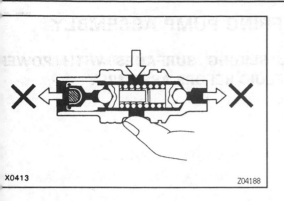

(b) Check the flow control valve for leakage. Close one of the holes and apply compressed air [392−490 kPa (4−5 kgf/cm², 57−71 psi)] into the opposite side, and confirm that air does not come out from the end hole.

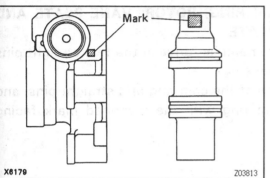

If necessary, replace the valve with one having the same letter as inscribed on the front housing.
Inscribed mark:
A, B, C, D, E or F

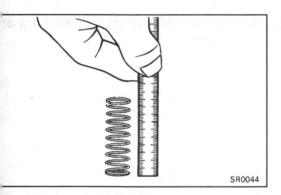

4. **INSPECT FLOW CONTROL SPRING**
Using a scale, measure the free length of the spring.
Spring length:
32.5−34.0 mm (1.28−1.34 in.)
If not within specification, replace the spring.

SR

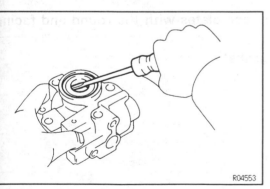

5. **IF NECESSARY, REPLACE OIL SEAL**
(a) Using a screwdriver, remove the oil seal.

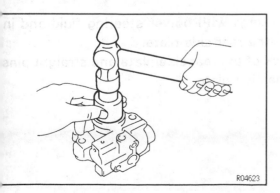

(b) Using a 24 mm socket wrench, press in a new oil seal.
(c) Coat the oil seal lip with power steering fluid.

POWER STEERING PUMP ASSEMBLY

SR081–01

1. **COAT ALL SLIDING SURFACES WITH POWER STEERING FLUID BEFORE ASSEMBLY**

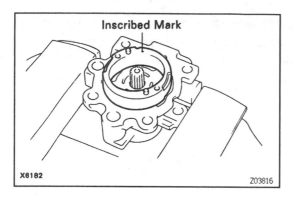

Inscribed Mark

X6182   Z03816

2. **INSTALL CAM RING, ROTOR, VANE PLATE AND REAR SIDE PLATE**
   (a) Using a plastic hammer, drive in the two straight pins to the front housing.
   (b) Align the holes of the cam ring and straight pins, and insert the cam ring with the inscribed mark facing outward.

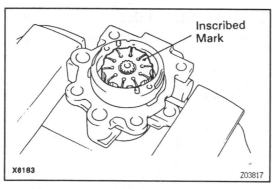

Inscribed Mark

X6183   Z03817

   (c) Install the rotor to the shaft with the inscribed mark on the rotor facing outward.

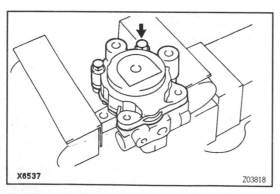

X6537   Z03818

   (d) Install the ten vane plates with the round end facing outward.
   (e) Install a new gasket.

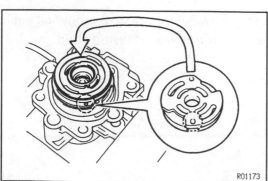

R01173

   (f) Coat new O—rings with power steering fluid and install them on the rear side plate.
   (g) Align the holes of the rear side plate and straight pins and install the side plate.

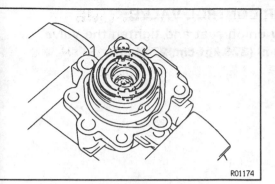

3. INSTALL WAVE WASHER

Install the wave washer so that its protursions fit into the slots in the rear side plate.

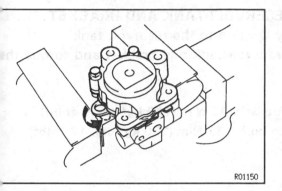

4. INSTALL REAR HOUSING

(a) Install the rear housing and tighten the two bolts.
Torque: 17 N·m (170 kgf·cm, 12 ft·lbf)

(b) Fold down in the direction of the front housing that part of the gasket indecated in the illustration.

5. MEASURE PUMP SHAFT PRELOAD

(a) Check that the shaft rotates smoothly without abnormal noise.

(b) Temporarily install the pulley nut and check that the rotating torque.
Rotating torque:
0.2 N·m (2.5 kgf·cm, 2.2 in.·lbf) or less

SR

6. INSTALL SPRING, FLOW CONTROL VALVE, O—RING AND PRESSURE PORT UNION

(a) Coat a new O—ring with power steering fluid and install it to the pressure port union.

(b) Install spring and valve to the housing.

(c) Install and torque the pressure port union.
Torque: 83 N·m (850 kgf·cm, 61 ft·lbf)

7. INSTALL TWO BRACKET

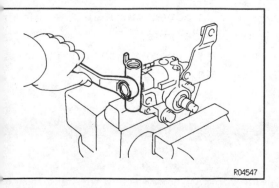

8. INSTALL PRESSURE TUBE

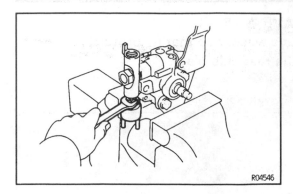

9. INSTALL AIR CONTROL VALVE

Install a new union seat and tighten the valve.

Torque: 36 N·m (370 kgf·cm, 27 ft·lbf)

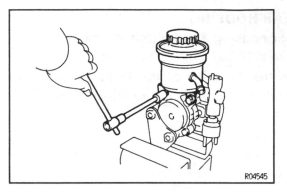

10. INSTALL RESERVOIR TANK AND BRACKET

(a) Install a new O—ring to the reservoir tank.

(b) Install the reservoir tank and bracket and torque the bolts.

Torque:

    Front side bolt 13 N·m (130 kgf·cm, 9 ft·lbf)

    Rear side bolt   17 N·m (170 kgf·cm, 12 ft·lbf)

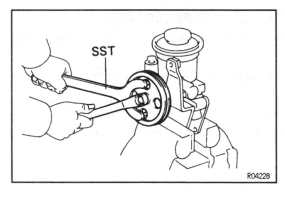

11. INSTALL PUMP PULLEY

(a) Install pully and nut to the shaft.

(b) Using SST to hold the pulley, torque the nut.

SST 09278—54012

Torque: 43 N·m (440 kgf·cm, 32 ft·lbf)

SR

GEAR HOUSING
STEERING GEAR HOUSING REMOVAL AND INSTALLATION

SR085-01

Remove and install the parts as shown.

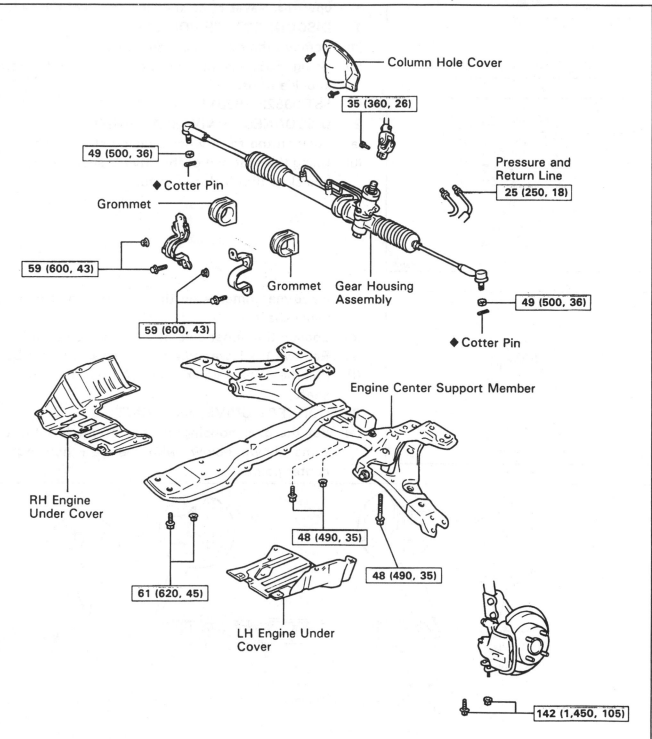

Column Hole Cover

35 (360, 26)

Pressure and Return Line

25 (250, 18)

49 (500, 36)

◆ Cotter Pin

Grommet

59 (600, 43)

Grommet

Gear Housing Assembly

59 (600, 43)

49 (500, 36)

◆ Cotter Pin

Engine Center Support Member

RH Engine Under Cover

48 (490, 35)

48 (490, 35)

61 (620, 45)

LH Engine Under Cover

142 (1,450, 105)

N·m (kgf·cm, ft·lbf) : Specified torque

◆ Non-reusable part

R03969

SR

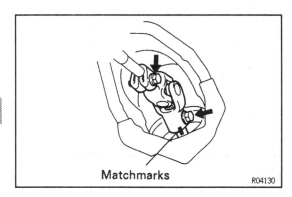

(MAIN POINTS OF REMOVAL AND INSTALLATION)

NOTICE: When the steering wheel pad removed, alway place it on a stable flat place with the pad surface facin upwards. **Never place anything on top of the pad.**

1. DISCONNECT TIE ROD ENDS

(a) Remove the cotter pins and nuts.

(b) Using SST, disconnect the tie rod ends from th knuckle arms.

SST 09628–62011

2. DISCONNECT UNIVERSAL JOINT

(a) Position the front wheels facing straight ahead.

(b) Using the seat belt of the driver's seat, fix the steerin wheel so that it does not turn.

(c) Place matchmarks on the universal joint and contr valve shaft.

(d) Loosen the upper side of universal joint set bolt.

(e) Remove the lower side of universal joint set bolt.

(f) Pull the universal joint upward from the control valv shaft.

3. CONNECT UNIVERSAL JOINT

(a) Set the gear housing so that it matches the dimer sions shown below, with the gear housing at th center point.

Matchmarks

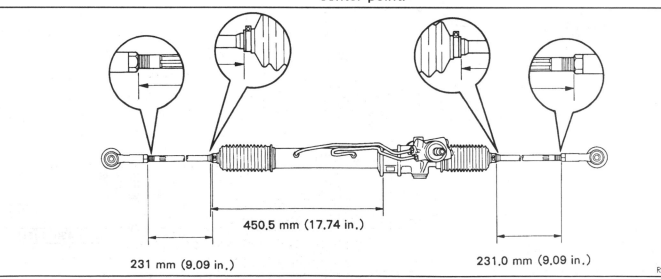

450.5 mm (17.74 in.)

231 mm (9.09 in.)   231.0 mm (9.09 in.)

SR

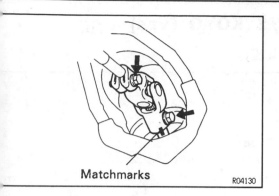

Matchmarks

R04130

(b) Align matchmarks on the universal joint and control valve shaft and connect them.

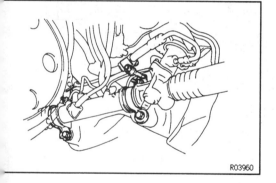

SST.

R03959

4. DISCONNECT PRESSURE AND RETURN TUBES

Using SST, disconnect and connect the pressure and return tubes.

SST 09631−22020

Torque: 25 N·m (250 kgf·cm, 18 ft·lbf)

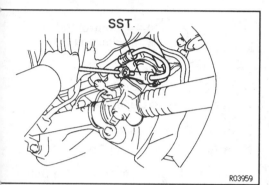

R03960

5. REMOVE GEAR HOUSING

Remove the two bolts, two nuts and two brackets.

6. CENTER SPIRAL CABLE

If the steering wheel has been removed, or the steering wheel may have moved during the operation, always perform centering of the spiral cable.

(See page AB−17)

7. CHECK STEERING WHEEL CENTER POINT

8. CHECK TOE−IN

(See page SA−3)

SR

COMPONENTS (KOYO Type)

SR047–03

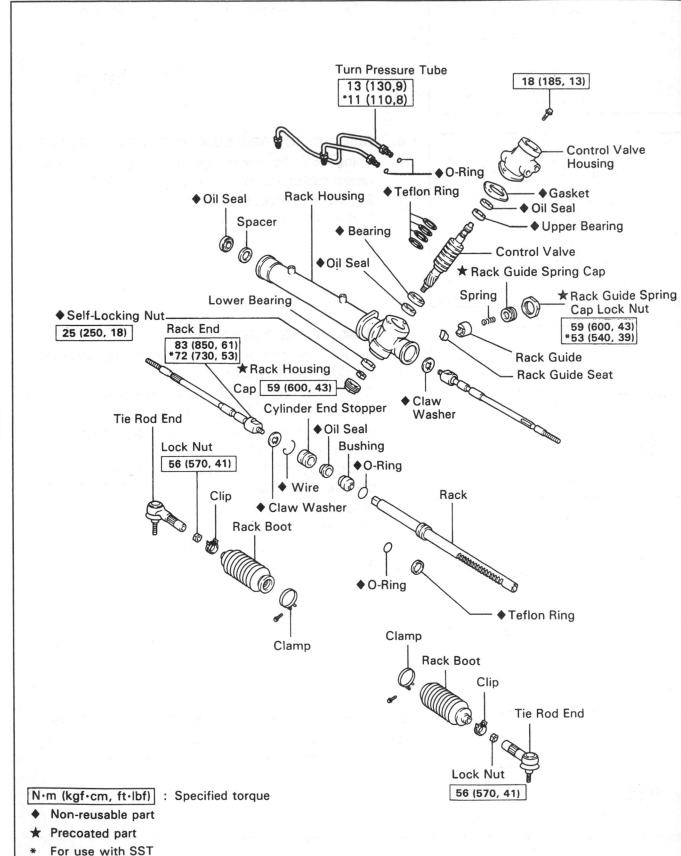

Turn Pressure Tube
13 (130,9)
*11 (110,8)

18 (185, 13)

Control Valve Housing

◆ O-Ring

◆ Oil Seal

◆ Teflon Ring

Rack Housing

◆ Gasket

◆ Oil Seal

◆ Upper Bearing

Spacer

◆ Bearing

Control Valve

◆ Oil Seal

★ Rack Guide Spring Cap

Lower Bearing

Spring

★ Rack Guide Spring Cap Lock Nut

◆ Self-Locking Nut
25 (250, 18)

Rack End
83 (850, 61)
*72 (730, 53)

59 (600, 43)
*53 (540, 39)

★ Rack Housing Cap **59 (600, 43)**

Rack Guide

Rack Guide Seat

Tie Rod End

Cylinder End Stopper

◆ Claw Washer

Lock Nut
56 (570, 41)

◆ Oil Seal

Bushing

◆ O-Ring

Clip

◆ Wire

◆ Claw Washer

Rack Boot

Rack

Clamp

◆ O-Ring

◆ Teflon Ring

Clamp

Rack Boot

Clip

Tie Rod End

Lock Nut
56 (570, 41)

| **N·m (kgf·cm, ft·lbf)** | : Specified torque |

◆　Non-reusable part

★　Precoated part

*　For use with SST

SR

R038

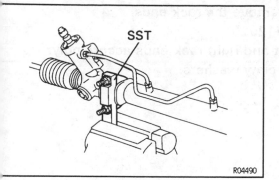

STEERING GEAR HOUSING DISASSEMBLY

1. CLAMP GEAR HOUSING IN VISE

Using SST, secure the steering gear in a vise.
SST 09612−00012

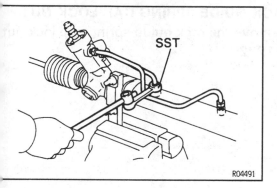

2. REMOVE RIGHT AND LEFT TURN PRESSURE TUBES

Using SST, remove the pressure tubes.
SST 09633−00020

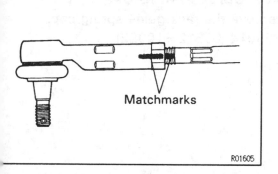

3. REMOVE TIE ROD ENDS

(a) Loosen the lock nut and place matchmarks on the tie rod end and rack end.

(b) Remove the tie rod ends and lock nuts.

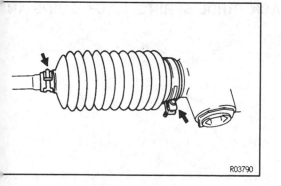

4. REMOVE RACK BOOTS

(a) Remove the clips and clamps.

(b) Remove the rack boots.

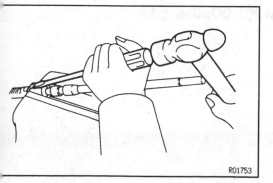

5. REMOVE RACK ENDS AND CLAW WASHERS

(a) Unstake the claw washers.

NOTICE: Avoid any impact to the rack.

SR

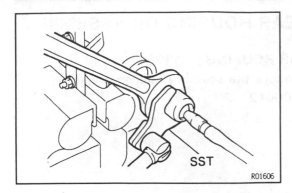

(b) Using SST, remove the rack ends.
SST 09617—12020

(c) Mark the left and right rack ends accordingly.

(d) Remove the claw washers.

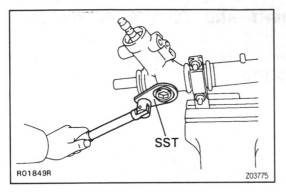

6. **REMOVE RACK GUIDE SPRING CAP LOCK NUT**
Using SST, remove the rack guide spring cap lock nut.
SST 09617—12020

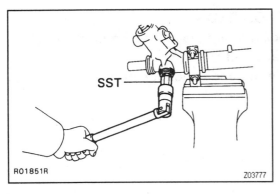

7. **REMOVE RACK GUIDE SPRING CAP**
Using SST, remove the rack guide spring cap.
SST 09612—24014 (09612—10022)

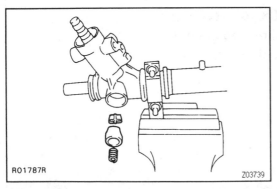

8. **REMOVE RACK GUIDE SPRING, RACK GUIDE AN**
SEAT

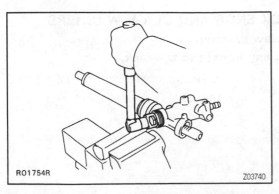

9. **REMOVE RACK HOUSING CAP**

SR

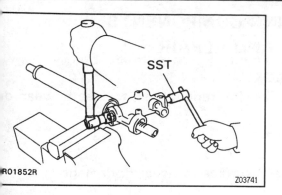

10. REMOVE SELF-LOCKING NUT AND LOWER BEARING

(a) Using SST to hold the control valve, remove the self-locking nut.
SST 09616—00010

(b) Remove the lower bearing and specer.

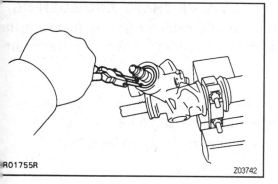

11. REMOVE CONTROL VALVE

(a) Using snap ring pliers, remove the snap ring.

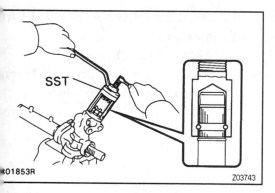

(b) Using SST, remove the control valve with the upper bearing and oil seal.
SST 09613—12010
NOTICE: Never attempt to tap out the control valve as this would damage it.

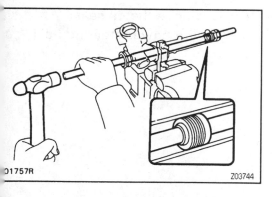

12. REMOVE RACK WITH OIL SEAL

Slighty tap the rack end with a brass bar hammer. Tap out the rack and the oil seal.

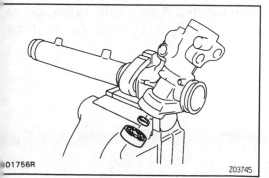

13. REMOVE CYLINDER OIL SEAL AND SPACER

Using SST, remove the oil seal with the spacer.
SST 09631—12020, 09631—12031
HINT: Extension may be required to the SST 09631—12020 to completely remove the seal from the housing.

SR

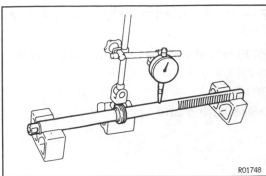

SR049-03

GEAR HOUSING COMPONENTS INSPECTION AND REPAIR

1. INSPECT RACK

(a) Check the rack for runout and for teeth wear or damage.

Maximum runout:
    0.15 mm (0.006 in.)

(b) Check the back surface for wear or damage.

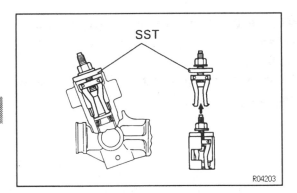

2. CHECK CONTROL VALVE SHAFT AND BUSHING

Using a micrometer and cylinder gauge, measure the outer diameter of the shaft and inner diameter of the bushing.

Limit:
    Shaft outer diameter   27.75 mm (1.0925 in.)
    Bushing inner diameter 28.20 mm (1.1102 in.)

If more than maximum, replace the bushing.

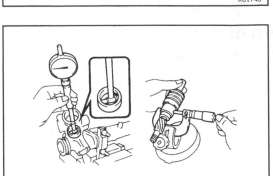

3. IF NECESSARY, REPLACE BUSHING AND OIL SEAL

(a) Using SST, remove the bushing.
SST 09612—65014 (09612—01030)
NOTICE: As shown, from the opposite side of SST confirm that its claw is firmly caught on the bushing.

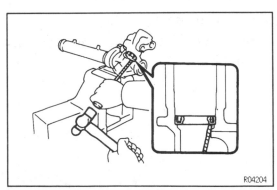

(b) Using a screwdriveer, remove the oil seal.
(c) Coat a new oil seal lip with power steering fluid.

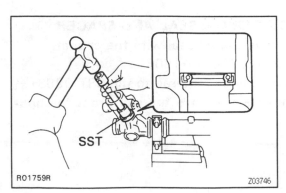

(d) Using SST, soket wrench (24 mm) and extension bar carefully press in a new bushing to a depth of 69. mm (2.736 in.).
SST 09515—21010

NOTICE: If the bushing is pushed in too far, it will cause deformation of the housing. If it is not pushed in far enough, it will interfare with the control valve.
Therfore, always use a press and install the bushing to the preperdepth. Then, install the control valve and insure that it rotates smoothly.

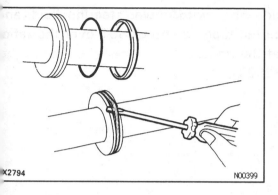

4. IF NECESSARY, REPLACE TEFLON RING AND O—RING
(a) Remove the teflon ring and O—ring.
NOTICE: Be careful not to damage the rack.
(b) Install a new O—ring.
(c) Expand a new teflon ring with your fingers.
NOTICE: Be careful no to over—expand the teflon ring.

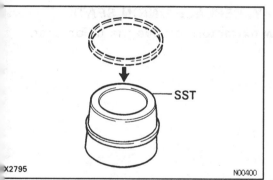

(d) Install the feflon ring to the steering rack.
(e) Coat the teflon ring with power steering fluid and snug it down with your fingers.

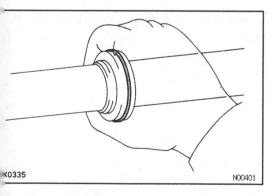

5. IF NECESSARY, REPLACE CONTROL VALVE TEFLON RINGS
(a) Using a screwdriver, remove the teflon rings.
NOTICE: Be careful not to damage the control valve.

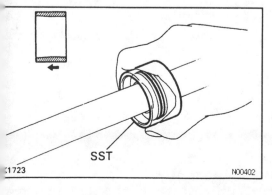

(b) Install new teflon rings to SST and expand them.
SST 09631—20070

SR

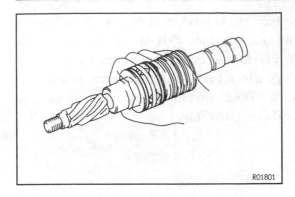

(c) Install the expanded teflon rings to the control valve and snug them down with your fingers.

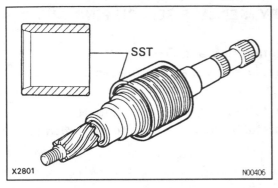

(d) Coat the teflon rings with power steering fluid, and carefully slide the tapered end of SST over the teflon rings to seat the rings.
SST 09631—20081

6. IF NECESSARY, REPLACE UNION SEAT

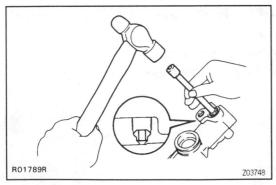

(a) Using a screw extractor, remove the union seat.

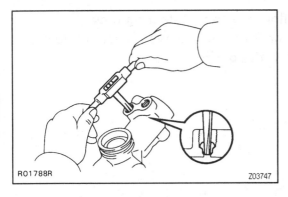

(b) Using a plastic hammer and extension bar, tap in new union seat.

SR

STEERING GEAR HOUSING ASSEMBLY

SR0AJ-02

1. COAT POWER STEERING FLUID OR GREASE ON FOLLOWING PARTS:

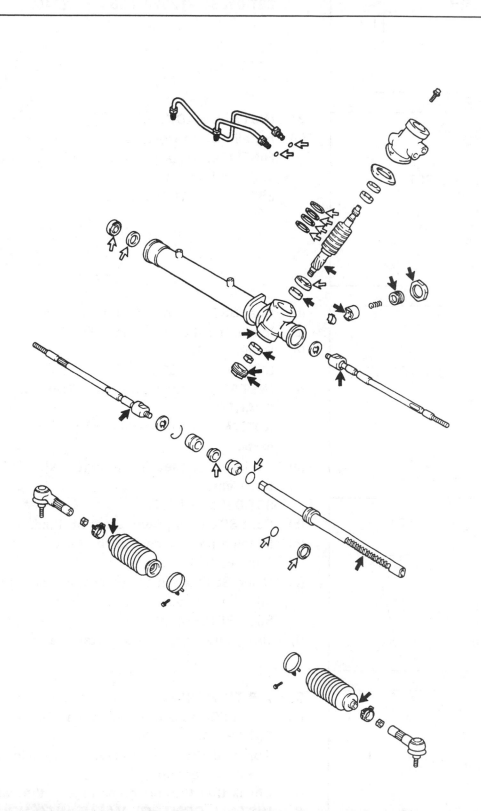

SR

◄━━ Molybdenum disulphide lithiun base grease

◁━━ Power steering fluid

R03823

SR

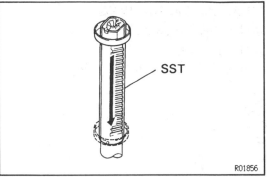

2. INSTALL CYLINDER HOUSING OIL SEAL AN
SPACER
Install a new oil seal and spacer to SST, and dri
them in with a plastic hammer.
SST 09631—12020, 09631—12040

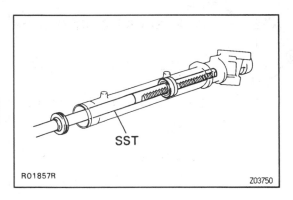

3. INSTALL RACK
(a) Install SST to the rack.
HINT: If necessary, scrape the burrs off the rack tee
end and burnish.
SST 09631—16020

(b) Coat SST with power steering fluid.
(c) Install the rack into the cylinder.
(d) Remove SST.
SST 09631—16020

4. INSTALL CYLINDER END STOPPER, OIL SEAL AN
SPACER
NOTICE: See illustration for proper installation of t
parts.

(a) To prevent oil seal lip damage, install SST to the rack
other end.
SST 09631—16020
(b) Coat SST with power steering fluid.
(c) Install a new oil seal to the rack.
(d) Remove SST.
(e) Using SST, tap in the oil seal, spacer and end stopp
into the cylinder.
SST 09612—22011
(f) Using snap ring pliers, install the snap ring.

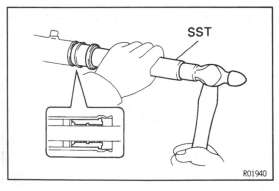

5. AIR TIGHTNESS TEST
(a) Install SST to the union of the cylinder housing.
SST 09631—12071
(b) Apply 53 kPa (400 mmHg, 15.75 in.Hg) of vacuum f
about 30 seconds.
(c) Check that there is no change in the vacuum.
6. INSTALL CONTROL VALVE INTO HOUSING

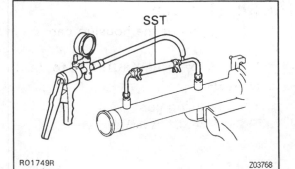

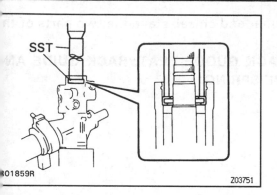

7. INSTALL UPPER BEARING
Using SST and a perss, install the upper bearing as shown.
SST 09515—21010, 09612—22011

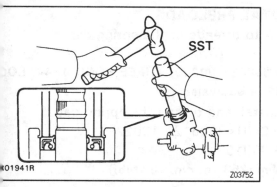

8. INSTALL OIL SEAL AND SNAP RING
(a) Using SST, install a new oil seal.
SST 09612—22011
(b) Using snap ring pliers, install the snap ring.

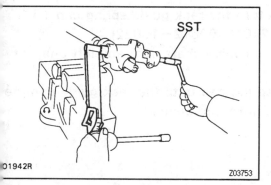

**9. INSTALL SPACER, LOWER BEARING AND CON-
TROL VALVE SHAFT**
(a) Install the spacer and bearing to the control valve shaft.
(b) Using SST to hold the control valve, install and torque a new self—locking nut.
SST 09616—00010
Torque: 12 N·m (125 kgf·cm, 9 ft·lbf)

SR

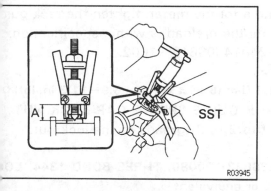

(c) Using SST, tighten the self locking nut until it touchs the spacer.
SST 09613—12020
Length A:
      16.5—17.0 mm (0.65—0.67 in.)
HINT: After adjusting the length A, stake the self—locking nut.

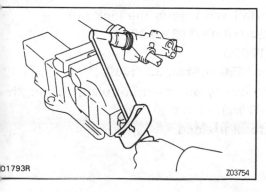

10. INSTALL RACK HOUSING CAP
(a) Apply sealant to the screws of the housing cap.
Sealant:
      **Part No.08833—00080, THREE BOND 1344, LOC-
      TITE 242 or equivalent**
(b) Install and torque the housing cap.
Torque: 69 N·m (700 kgf·cm, 51 ft·lbf)

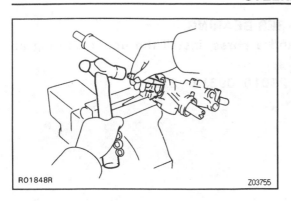

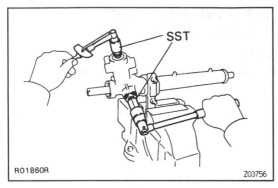

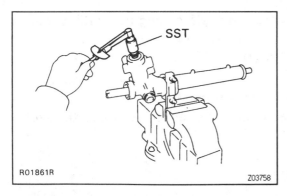

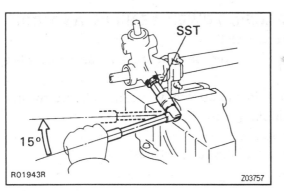

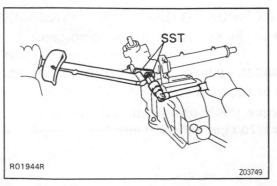

(c) Using a hammer and chisel, stake the two parts of the housing cap.

11. INSTALL RACK GUODE SEAT, RACK GUIDE ANI RACK GUIDE SPRING

12. ADJUST TOTAL PRELOAD
(a) Apply sealant to threads of the spring cap.
Sealant:
      Part No.08833−00080, THREE BOND 1344, LO(TITE 242 or equivalent
(b) Using SST, install and torque the spring cap.
      SST 09612−24014 (09612−10022)
           09616−00010
      Torque: 25 N·m (250 kgf·cm, 18 ft·lbf)

(c) Using SST, return the rack guide spring cap 15 °.
      SST 09612−24014 (09612−10022)
(d) Turn the control valve shaft right and left one or tw times.
(e) Loosen the spring cap until the rack guide compre sion spring is not functioning.

(f) Using SST and a torque meter, tighten the rack guid spring cap until the preload is within specification.
      SST 09612−24014 (09612−10022)
      Preload (turing):
           0.8−1.3 N·m (8−13 kgf·cm, 6.9−11.3 in.·lbf)

13. INSTALL RACK GUIDE SPRING CAP LOCK NUT
(a) Apply sealant to 2 to 3 tgreads of the lock nut.
Sealant:
      Part No.08833−00080, THREE BOND 1344, LO(TITE 242 or equivalent
(b) Using SST, install and torque the lock nut.
      SST 09612−24014 (09612−10022)
           09617−12020
      Torque: 44 N·m (450 kgf·cm, 33 ft·lbf)
      HINT: Use a torque wrench with a fulcrum length (300 mm (11.81 in.).
(c) Recheck the total preload.

SR

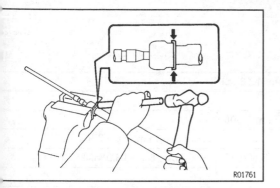

14. INSTALL CLAW WASHERS AND RACK ENDS

(a) Install a new claw washer.

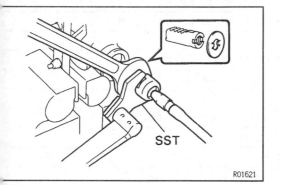

(b) Using SST, install and torque the rack ends.
SST 09612−10093 (09628−10020)
Torque: 83 N·m (850 kgf·cm, 61 ft·lbf)
HINT: Use a torque wrench with a fulcrum length of 340 mm (13.39 in.).

(c) Using a brass bar and hammer, stake the claw washers.

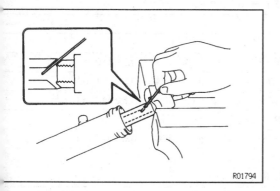

15. INSTALL RACK BOOTS, CLAMPS AND CLIPS

(a) Insure that the tube hole is not clogged with grease.
HINT: If the tube hole is clogged, the pressure inside the boot will change after it is assembled and the steering wheel turned.

(b) Install the boots.
HINT: Be careful not to damage or twist the boots.

(c) Install the clamps.

(d) Install the clips with the ends facing outward.

16. INSTALL TIE ROD ENDS

(a) Screw the lock nuts and tie rod ends onto the rack ends until the matchmarks are aligned.

(b) After adjusting toe−in, torque the lock nuts.
Torque: 56 N·m (570 kgf·cm, 41 ft·lbf)

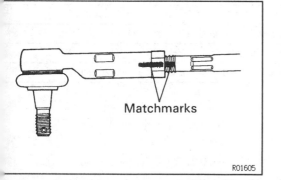

Matchmarks

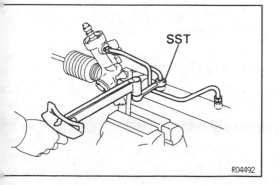

17. INSTALL RIGHT AND LEFT TURN PRESSURE TUBES

Using SST, install and torque the tubes.
SST 09633−00020
Torque: 13 N·m (130 kgf·cm, 9 ft·lbf)
HINT: Use a torque wrench a fulcrum length of 300 mm (11.81 in.).

SR

SERVICE SPECIFICATIONS
SERVICE DATA

SR01C—0A

Steering wheel freeplay (Maximum)	30 mm (1.18 in.)
MANUAL STEERING GEAR HOUSING	
Steering rack runout (Maximum)	0.15 mm (0.006 in.)
Pinion preload (Turning)	0.15—0.25 N·m (2.3—3.3 kgf·cm, 2.0—2.9 in.·lbf)
Total preload (Turning)	0.7—1.5 N·m (7—15 kgf·cm, 6.1—13.0 in.·lbf)
PS ON—VEHICLE INSPECTION	
Drive belt tension (New belt)	441—539 N (45—55 kgf, 99—121 lbf)
Drive belt tension (Used belt)	196—343 N (20—35 kgf, 44—77 lbf)
Maximum rise of oil level	5 mm (0.20 in.)
Oil pressure at idle speed with valve closed (Minimum)	5,883 kPa (60 kgf/cm², 853 psi)
Steering effort at idle speed (Maximum)	9.8 N·m (100 kgf·cm, 87 in.·lbf)
PS PUMP	
Rotor shaft bushing oil clearance (STD)	0.03—0.05 mm (0.0012—0.0020 in.)
Vane plate to rotor groove clearance (Maximum)	0.035 mm (0.0014 in.)
Vane plate length (Minimum)	14.99 mm (0.5902 in.)
Vane plate height (Minimum)	8.6 mm (0.339 in.)
Vane plate thickness (Minimum)	1.397 mm (0.0550 in.)
Vane plate length	
(Rotor and cam ring mark)	
None	14.999—15.001 mm (0.59051—0.59059 in.)
1	14.997—14.999 mm (0.59043—0.59051 in.)
2	14.995—14.997 mm (0.59035—0.59043 in.)
3	14.993—14.995 mm (0.59027—0.59035 in.)
4	14.991—14.993 mm (0.59002—0.59027 in.)
Flow control valve spring length (STD)	34.0 mm (1.34 in.)
Flow control valve spring length (Minimum)	32.5 mm (1.28 in.)
Pump rotating torque (Maximum)	0.3 N·m (2.8 kgf·cm, 2.4 in.·lbf)
PS GEAR HOUSING	
Steering rack runout (Maximum)	0.15 mm (0.006 in.)
Control valve shaft bushing oil clearance (Maximum)	0.125 mm (0.0049 in.)
Total preload (Turning)	0.8—1.4 N·m (8—14 kgf·cm, 6.9—12.2 in.·lbf)

SR

TORQUE SPECIFICATIONS

SR01D-07

Part tightened	N·m	kgf·cm	ft·lbf
STEERING COLUMN			
Steering main shaft x Universal joint	27	280	20
Column bracket x Body	25	260	19
Steering wheel	34	350	25
Column hole cover x Body	4.9	50	43 in.·lbf
Turn signal bracket x Upper column tube	7.8	80	69 in.·lbf
MANUAL STEERING GEAR HOUSING			
Pinion bearing adjusting screw lock nut	113	1,150	83
Rack guide spring cover	21	215	16
Rack x Rack end	83	850	61
Tie rod end lock nut	56	570	41
Gear housing bracket x Body	59	600	43
Pinion shaft x Universal joint	35	360	26
Tie rod end x Steering knuckle	49	500	36
POWER STEERING PUMP			
Reservpir tank installation bolt	41	420	30
Pressure port union x Pump housing	69	700	51
Suction port union x Pump housing	13	130	9
Pressure tube x Pressure port union	54	550	40
Drive pulley x Rotor shaft	43	440	32
PS pump installation bolt	43	440	32
POWER STEERING GEAR HOUSING			
Control valve self—locking nut	25	250	18
Rack housing cap	59	600	43
Rack guide spring cap lock nut	59	600	43
Rack x Rack end	83	850	61
Tie rod end lock nut	56	570	41
Turn pressure tube union nut	13	130	9
Gear housing bracket x Body	59	600	43
Column hole cover x Body	4.9	50	43 in.·lbf
Control valve shaft x Universal joint	35	360	26
Steering main shaft x Universal joint	35	360	26
Pressure and return tube x Gear housing	13	130	9
Pressure and return tube clamp x Gear housing	5.4	55	48 in.·lbf
Tie rod end x Steering knuckle	49	500	36

SR

SR

srs **AIRBAG**

AB

GENERAL DESCRIPTION

The 1993 COROLLA specifications is equipped with an SRS (Supplemental Restraint System) airbag. Failure to carry out service operations in the correct sequence could cause the airbag system to unexpectedly deploy during servicing, possibly leading to a serious accident.

Further, if a mistake is made in servicing the aribag system, it is possible the airbag may fail to operate when required.

Before performing servicing (including removal or installation of parts, inspection or replacement), be sure to read the following items carefully, then follow the correct procedure described in the repair manual.

1. Malfunction symptoms of the airbag system are difficult to confirm, so the diagnostic codes become the most important source of information when troubleshooting.
    When troubleshooting the airbag system, always inspect the diagnostic codes before disconnecting the battery (See page AB-26).

2. **Work must be started after 90 seconds from the time the ignition switch is turned to the LOCK position and the negative (–) terminal cable is disconnected from the battery.**
    (The airbag system is equipped with a back-up power source so that if work is started within 90 seconds of disconnecting the negative (–) terminal cable of the battery, the airbag may be deployed.)
    When the negative (–) terminal cable is disconnected from the battery, memory of the clock and audio systems will be cancelled. So before starting work, make a record of the contents memorized by the audio memory system. When work is finished, reset the audio system as before and adjust the clock. To avoid erasing the memory of each memory system, never use a back-up power supply from outside the vehicle.

3. Even in cases of a minor collision where the airbag does not deploy, the front airbag sensors and the steering wheel pad should be inspected (See page AB-11).

4. Never use airbag parts from another vehicle. When replacing parts, replace them with new parts.

5. Before repairs, remove the airbag sensors if shocks are likely to be applied to the sensors during repairs.

6. Never disassemble and repair the front airbag sensors, center airbag sensor assembly or steering wheel pad in order to reuse it.

7. If the front airbag sensors, center airbag sensor assembly or steering wheel pad have been dropped, or if there are cracks, dents or other defects in the case, bracket or connector, replace them with new ones.

8. Do not expose the front airbag senors, center airbag sensor assembly or steering wheel pad directly to hot air or flames.

9. Use a volt/ohmmeter with high impedance (10 kΩ/V minimum) for troubleshooting of the electrical circuit.

10. Information labels are attached to the periphery of the airbag components. Follow the instructions on the notices.

11. After work on the airbag system is completed, perform the airbag warning light check (See page AB-32).

FRONT AIRBAG SENSOR

1. Never reuse the front airbag sensors involved in a collision when the airbag has deployed. (Replace both the left and right airbag sensors.)
2. Install the front airbag sensor with the arrow on the sensor facing toward the front of the vehicle.
3. The front airbag sensor set bolts and nuts have been anti-rust treated.
   When the sensor is removed, always replace the set bolt and nut with new ones.
4. The front airbag sensor is equipped with an electrical connection check mechanism. Be sure to lock this mechanism securely when connecting the connector. If the connector is not securely locked, a malfunction code will be detected by the diagnosis system (See page AB-9).

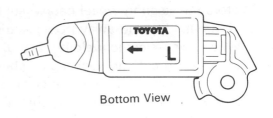

Bottom View

R04184

SPIRAL CABLE (in COMBINATION SWITCH)

The steering wheel must be fitted correctly to the steering column with the spiral cable at the neutral position, otherwise cable disconnection and other troubles may result. Refer to page AB-17 of this manual concerning correct steering wheel installation.

STEERING WHEEL PAD (with AIRBAG)

1. **When removing the steering wheel pad or handling a new steering wheel pad, it should be placed with the pad top surface facing up.**
   In this case, the twin-lock type connector lock lever should be in the locked state and care should be taken to place it so the connector will not be damaged. And do not store a steering wheel pad on top of another one. (Storing the pad with its metallic surface up may lead to a serious accident if the airbag inflates for some reason.)
2. **Never measured the resistance of the airbag squib. (This may cause the airbag to deploy, which is very dangerous).**

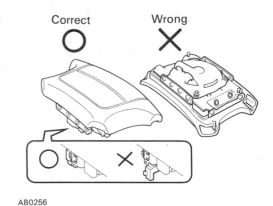

Correct   Wrong

AB0256

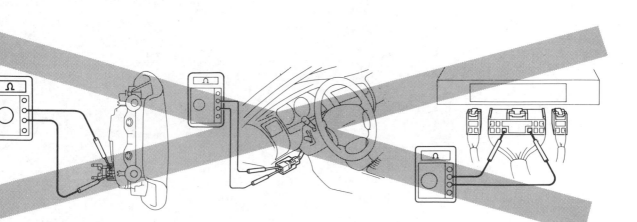

AB0014 R04185 AB0132

AB

3. Grease should not be applied to the steering wheel pad and the pad should not be cleaned with detergents of any kind.

4. Store the steering wheel pad where the ambient temperature remains below 93°C (200°F), without high humidity and away from electrical noise.

5. When using electric welding, first disconnect the airbag connector (yellow color and 2 pins) under the steering column near the combination switch connector before starting work.

6. When disposing of a vehicle or the steering wheel pad alone, the airbag should be deployed using an SST before disposal (See page AB-82). Perform the operation in a place away from electrical noise.

CENTER AIRBAG SENSOR ASSEMBLY

1. Never reuse the center airbag sensor assembly involved in a collision when the airbag has deployed.

2. The connectors to the center airbag sensor assembly should be connected or disconnected with the sensor mounted on the floor. If the connectors are connected or disconnected while the center airbag sensor assembly is not mounted to the floor, it could cause undesired ignition of the airbag system.

3. Work must be started after 90 seconds from the time the ignition switch is turned to the LOCK position and the negative (−) terminal cable is disconnected from the battery, even just loosing the set bolts of center airbag sensor assembly.

WIRE HARNESS AND CONNECTOR

The airbag system wire harness is integrated with the cowl wire harness assembly and luggage compartment wire harness assembly. The wires for the airbag wire harness are encased in a yellow corrugated tube. All the connectors for the system are also a standard yellow color. If the airbag system wire harness becomes disconnected or the connector becomes broken due to an accident, etc., repair or replace it as shown page AB-23.

AB

DESCRIPTION

The SRS (Supplemental Restraint System) airbag, together with the seat belt, is designed to help protect the driver. In a collision, the airbag sensors detect the shock, and if the front-to-rear shock is greater than a specified value, an airbag stored in the steering wheel pad is inflated instantaneously to help reduce the shock to the driver.

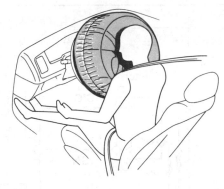

AB0279

LOCATION OF COMPONENTS

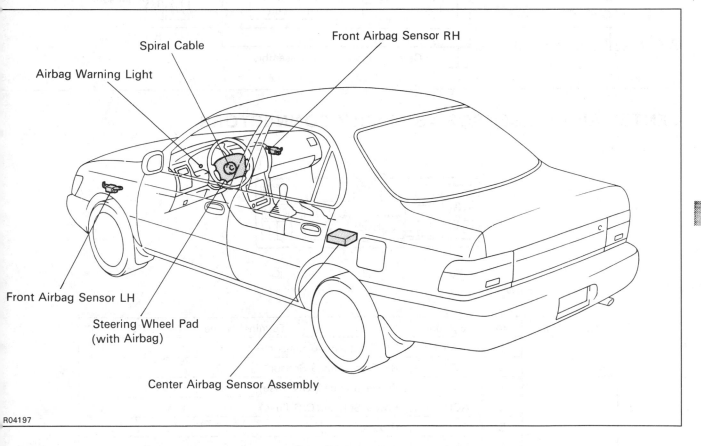

Spiral Cable

Front Airbag Sensor RH

Airbag Warning Light

Front Airbag Sensor LH

Steering Wheel Pad
(with Airbag)

Center Airbag Sensor Assembly

R04197

AB

WIRING DIAGRAM

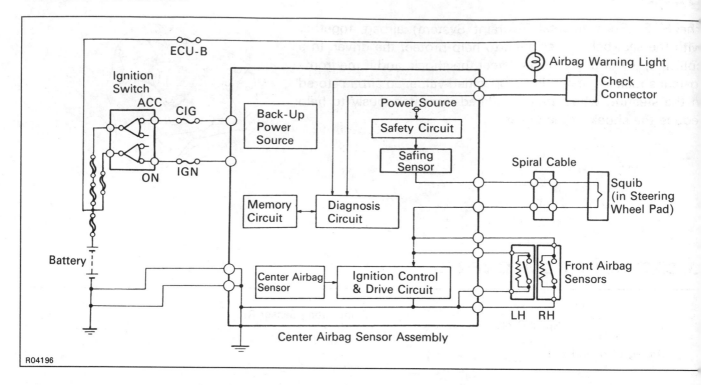

R04196

CENTER AIRBAG SENSOR ASSEMBLY CONNECTORS

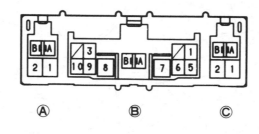

N02603

Connector	No.	Symbol	Terminal Name
Ⓐ	1	− SR	RH Front Airbag Sensor ⊖
	2	+ SR	RH Front Airbag Sensor ⊕
Ⓑ	1	IG_2	Power Source (IGN Fuse)
	3	ACC	Power Source (CIG Fuse)
	5	E_2	Ground
	6	LA	Airbag Warning Light
	7	D^-	Squib ⊖
	8	D^+	Squib ⊕
	9	Tc	Diagnosis
	10	E_1	Ground
Ⓒ	1	+ SL	LH Front Airbag Sensor ⊕
	2	− SL	LH Front Airbag Sensor ⊖
Ⓐ Ⓑ Ⓒ	A	−	Electrical Connection Check Mechanism
	B	−	Electrical Connection Check Mechanism

OPERATION
FUNCTION OF COMPONENTS

FRONT AIRBAG SENSOR

The front airbag sensors are mounted inside each of the front fenders. The sensor unit is a mechanical type. When the sensor detects deceleration force above a predetermined limit in a collision, the contacts in the sensor make contact, sending a signal to the center airbag sensor assembly.
The sensor cannot be disassembled.

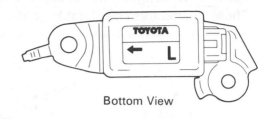

Bottom View

R04184

SPIRAL CABLE (in COMBINATION SWITCH)

A spiral cable is used as an electrical joint from the vehicle body side to the steering wheel.

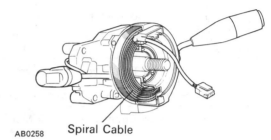

AB0258   Spiral Cable

STEERING WHEEL PAD (with AIRBAG)

The inflater and bag of the airbag system are stored in the steering wheel pad and cannot be disassembled.
The inflater contains a squib, igniter charge, gas generant, etc., and inflates the bag in case of a frontal collision.

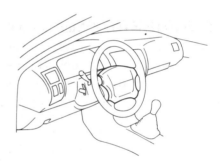

R04190

AB

AIRBAG WARNING LIGHT

The airbag warning light is located on the combination meter. If goes on to alert the driver of trouble in the system when a malfunction is detected in the center airbag sensor assembly self-diagnosis. In normal operating condition when the ignition switch is turned to the ACC or ON position, the light goes on for about 6 seconds and then goes off.

R04186

CENTER AIRBAG SENSOR ASSEMBLY

The center airbag sensor assembly is mounted on the floor inside the rear console box. The center airbag sensor assembly consists of a center airbag sensor, safing sensors, ignition control and drive circuit, diagnosis circuit, etc. It receives signals from the airbag sensors, judges whether the airbag must be activated or not and diagnoses system malfunctions.

Center Airbag Sensor Assembly

R04191

6. AIRBAG CONNECTORS

All connectors in the airbag system are colored yellow. Connectors having special functions and specifically designed for airbags are used in the locations shown below to ensure high reliability. These connectors use durable gold-plated terminals.

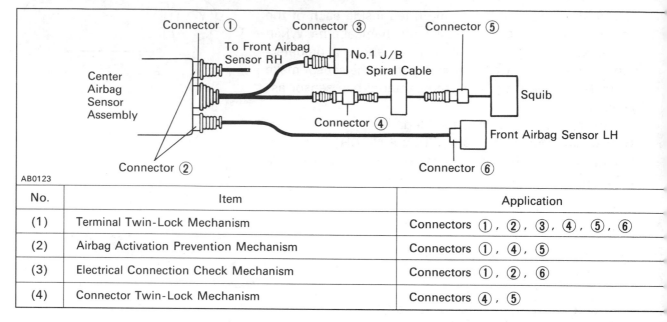

No.	Item	Application
(1)	Terminal Twin-Lock Mechanism	Connectors ①, ②, ③, ④, ⑤, ⑥
(2)	Airbag Activation Prevention Mechanism	Connectors ①, ④, ⑤
(3)	Electrical Connection Check Mechanism	Connectors ①, ②, ⑥
(4)	Connector Twin-Lock Mechanism	Connectors ④, ⑤

(1) **Terminal Twin-Lock Mechanism**
Each connector has a two-piece construction consisting of a housing and a spacer. This design secures the locking of the terminal by two locking devices (the spacer and the lane) to prevent terminals from coming out.

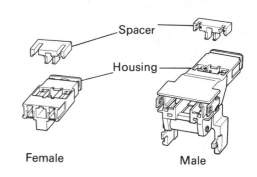

(2) **Airbag Activation Prevention Mechanism**
Each connector contains a short spring plate. When the connector is disconnected, the short spring plate automatically connects the power source and grounding terminals of the squib.

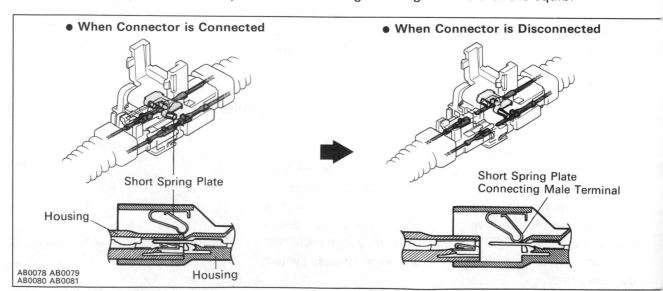

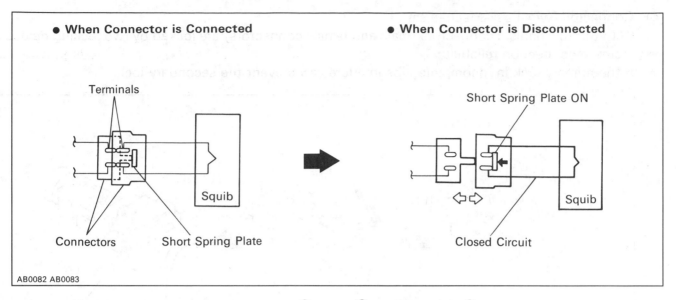

AB0082 AB0083

HINT: The illustration shows connectors ④ and ⑤ . Connector ① has a short spring plate on the female terminal side, but the operating principle is the same.

(3) Electrical Connection Check Mechanism
This mechanism is designed to electrically check if connectors are connected correctly and completely. The electrical connection check mechanism is designed so that the connection detection pin connects with the diagnosis terminals when the connector housing lock is in the locked condition.

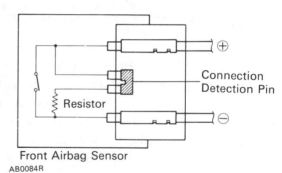

AB0084R

AB

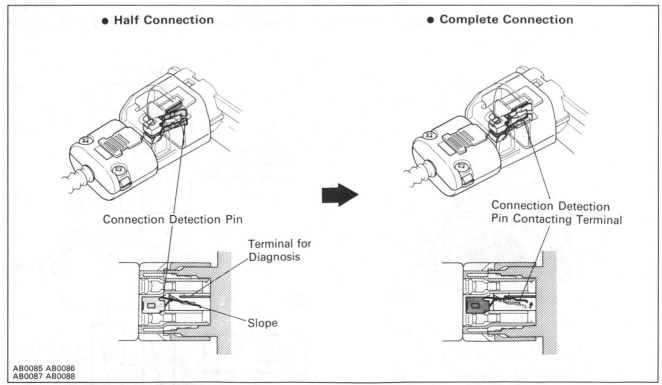

AB0085 AB0086
AB0087 AB0088

HINT: The illustration shows connector ⑥ . Connectors ① and ② also have the same operating principle.

(4) Connector Twin-Lock Mechanism
With this mechanism connectors (male and female connectors) are locked by two locking devices to increase connection reliability.
If the primary lock in incomplete, ribs interfere and prevent the secondary lock.

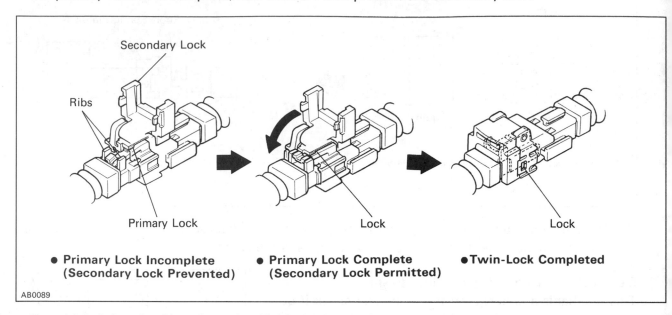

AB0089

When the vehicle is involved in a frontal collision in the hatched areas (Fig. 1) and the shock is larger than a predetermined level, the airbag is activated automatically. Safing sensors are designed to go on at a smaller deceleration rate than the front and center airbag sensors. As illustrated in Fig. 2 below, ignition is caused when current flows to the squib, which happens when a safing sensor and a front airbag sensor and/or the center airbag sensor go on simultaneously.

When a deceleration force acts on the sensors, it causes the squib to ignite. Gas is then generated, increasing the pressure inside the bag rapidly. The inflated bag breaks open the steering wheel pad. Bag inflation then ends, and the gas is discharged through discharge holes provided behind the bag. The bag becomes deflated as a result.

AB

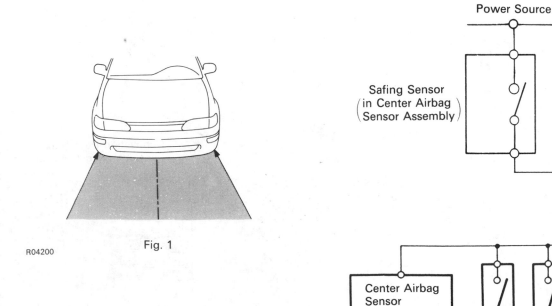

R04200   Fig. 1

N02881   Fig. 2

INSPECTION ITEMS AND REPLACEMENT REQUIREMENTS

If a vehicle is brought in for an airbag system inspection, or if a vehicle which has been involved in a collision is inspected, perform the inspection in accordance with the following procedure. If any problems are discovered, replace the affected part with a new one.

Steering Wheel Pad (with Airbag), Steering Wheel and Spiral Cable

INSPECTION ITEMS

1. **VEHICLES NOT INVOLVED IN A COLLISION**
(a) Perform a diagnostic system check (See page AB-32).
(b) Perform a visual check which includes the following items with the steering wheel pad (with airbag) installed in the vehicle.
  ● Check for cuts, minute cracks or marked discoloration of the steering wheel pad top surface and grooved portion.

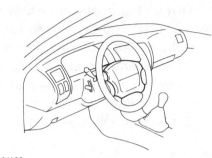

R04190

2. **VEHICLES INVOLVED IN A COLLISION**
   (IF THE AIRBAG IS NOT DEPLOYED)
(a) Perform a diagnostic system check (See page AB-32).
(b) Perform a visual check which includes the following items with the steering wheel pad (with airbag) removed from the vehicle.
  ● Check for cuts or cracks in, marked discoloration of the steering wheel pad top surface and grooved portion.
  ● Check for cuts and cracks in, or chipping of connectors and wire harnesses.
  ● Check for deformation of the horn button contact plate of the steering wheel.

R04175

HINT:
  ● If the horn button contact plate of the steering wheel is deformed, never repair it. Always replace the steering wheel with a new one.
  ● There should be no interference between the steering wheel pad and the steering wheel, and the clearance should be uniform all the way around when the new steering wheel pad is installed on the steering wheel.

CAUTION: For removal and installation of the steering wheel pad, see page AB-16, "REMOVAL AND INSTALLATION" and be sure to follow the correct procedure.

Horn Button Contact Plate

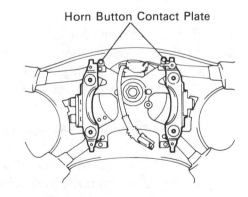

R04192

   (IF THE AIRBAG IS DEPLOYED)
(a) Perform a diagnostic system check (See page AB-32).
(b) Perform a visual check which includes the following items with the steering wheel pad (with airbag) removed from the vehicle.
  ● Check for deformation of the horn button contact plate of the steering wheel.
  ● Check for damage to the spiral cable connector and wire harness.

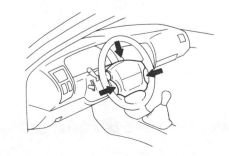

R04190

AB

HINT:

- If the horn button contact plate of the steering wheel is deformed, never repair it. Always replace the steering with a new one.
- There should be no interference between the steering wheel pad and the steering wheel, and the clearance should be uniform all the way around when the new steering wheel pad is installed on the steering wheel.

REPLACEMENT REQUIREMENTS

In the following cases, replace the steering wheel pad, steering wheel or spiral cable.

CAUTION:　For replacement of the steering wheel pad, see page AB-16, "REMOVAL AND IN-STALLATION" and be sure to follow the correct procedure.

- If the airbag has been deployed.
- If the steering wheel pad or spiral cable has been found to be faulty in troubleshooting.
- If the steering wheel pad, steering wheel or spiral cable has been found to be faulty during the check in item **1.** – (b) or **2.** – (b).
- If the steering wheel pad has been dropped.

Front Airbag Sensor
INSPECTION ITEMS

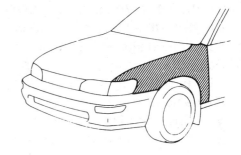

R04187

1.　**VEHICLES NOT INVOLVED IN A COLLISION**
- Perform a diagnostic system check (See page AB-32).

2.　**VEHICLES INVOLVED IN A COLLISION**
(a)　Perform a diagnostic system check (See page AB-32).
(b)　If the front bumper of the car or its periphery is damaged, perform visual check for damage to the front airbag sensor, which includes the following items even if the airbag was not deployed:

- Bracket deformation.
- Peeling of paint from the bracket.
- Cracks, dents or chips in the case.
- Cracks and dents in, or chipping and scratches of the connector.
- Peeling off of the label or damage to the series number.

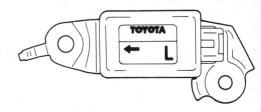

R04184

Also refer to the body dimension drawings on page BO-82 and check the dimensions and mounting surface angle of the body area where the front airbag sensors are mounted.

(The airbag may malfunction, or may not work, if the mounting angle or dimensions of the sensor mount are not correct.)

REPLACEMENT REQUIREMENTS

In the following cases, replace the front airbag sensor.
NOTICE: For replacement of the front airbag sensor, see page AB-19, "REMOVAL AND INSTAL-LATION".
- If the airbag has been deployed in a collision.
  (Replace both the left and right airbag sensors.)
- If the front airbag sensor has been found to be faulty in troubleshooting.
- If the front airbag sensor has been found to be faulty during the check in item **2. – (b)**.
- If the front airbag sensor has been dropped.

Center Airbag Sensor Assembly
INSPECTION ITEMS

1. **VEHICLES NOT INVOLVED IN A COLLISION**
   - Perform a diagnostic system check (See page AB-32).
2. **VEHICLES INVOLVED IN A COLLISION**
   (IF THE AIRBAG IS NOT DEPLOYED)
   - Perform a diagnostic system check (See page AB-32).
   (IF THE AIRBAG IS DEPLOYED)
   - Replace the center airbag sensor assembly certainly.

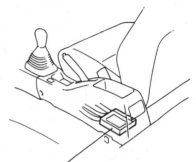

Center Airbag Sensor Assembly

R04191

REPLACEMENT REQUIREMENTS

In the following cases, replace the center airbag sensor assembly.
NOTICE: For replacement of the center airbag sensor assembly, see page AB-21, "REMOVAL AND INSTALLATION".
- If the airbag has been deployed in a collision.
- If the center airbag sensor assembly has been found to be faulty in troubleshooting.
- If the center airbag sensor assembly has been dropped.

AB

Wire Harness and Connector

HINT: The airbag system wire harness is integrated with instrument panel wire and engine room main wire. The wires for the airbag wire harness are encased in a yellow corrugated tube and all the connectors in the system are a standard yellow color.

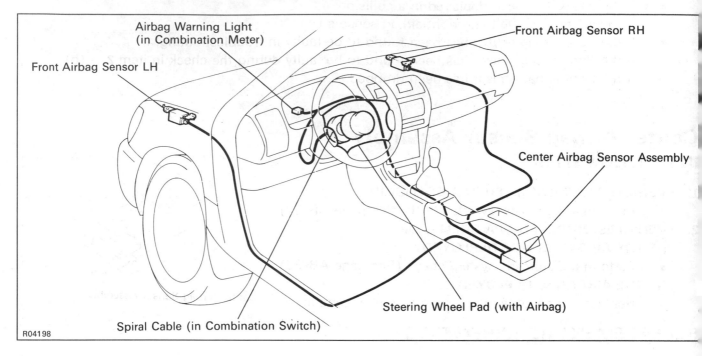

INSPECTION ITEMS

1. **VEHICLES NOT INVOLVED IN A COLLISION**
   - Perform a diagnostic system check (See page AB-32).
2. **VEHICLES INVOLVED IN A COLLISION**
(a) Perform a diagnostic system check (See page AB-32).
(b) If there is a brake in any of the wires in the airbag system wire harness, or if conductors are exposed.
(c) If the airbag system wire harness connectors are cracked or chipped.

REPLACEMENT REQUIREMENTS

In the following cases, replace the wire harness or connector.
   - If any part of the airbag system wire harness or any connector has been found to be faulty in troubleshooting.
   - If any part of the airbag system wire harness or any connector has been found to be faulty during the check in item **2. – (b)** or (c).

NOTICE: If the wire harness used in the airbag system is damaged replace the whole wire harness assembly.

When the connector to the front airbag sensors can be repaired alone (when there is no damage to the wire harness), use the repair wire specially designed for the purpose (See page AB-23).

PREPARATION

SST (SPECIAL SERVICE TOOLS)

09082-00700	SRS Airbag Deployment Tool	
09213-31021	Crankshaft Pulley Puller	Steering wheel
09843-18020	Diagnosis Check Wire	

RECOMMENDED TOOLS

09042-00010	Torx Socket T30	Steering wheel pad
09042-00020	Torx Socket T40	Center airbag sensor assembly
09082-00015	TOYOTA Electrical Tester	

EQUIPMENT

Torque wrench	

AB

COMPONENT PARTS REMOVAL AND INSTALLATION

STEERING WHEEL PAD AND SPIRAL CABLE

Remove and install the parts as shown.

AB00J-03

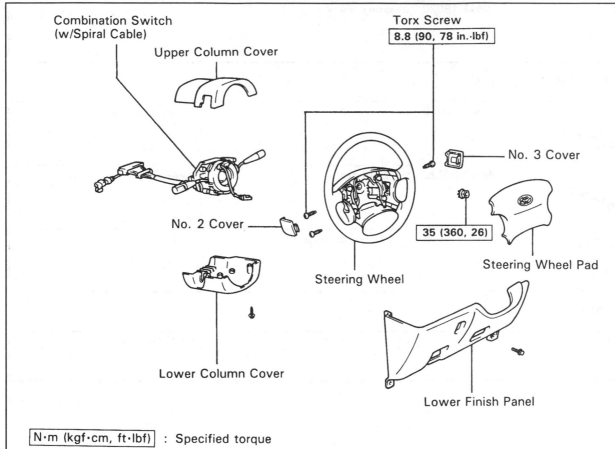

Combination Switch (w/Spiral Cable)
Upper Column Cover
Torx Screw
8.8 (90, 78 in.·lbf)
No. 3 Cover
No. 2 Cover
35 (360, 26)
Steering Wheel Pad
Steering Wheel
Lower Column Cover
Lower Finish Panel

N·m (kgf·cm, ft·lbf) : Specified torque

R04302

(MAIN POINTS OF REMOVAL AND INSTALLATION)

CAUTION: Work must be started after 90 seconds from the time the ignition switch is turned to the LOCK position and the negative (−) terminal cable is disconnected form the battery.

NOTICE:

- If the wiring connector of the airbag system is disconnected with the ignition switch at ON or ACC diagnostic trouble code will be recorded.

- Never use airbag parts from another vehicle. When replacing parts, replace with new parts.

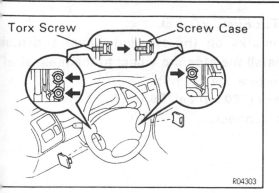

Torx Screw   Screw Case

R04303

1. REMOVE STEERING WHEEL PAD
(a) Remove negative terminal (−) from the battery.
(b) Place the front wheels facing straight ahead.
(c) Using a torx wrench, loosen the three screws.
    Torx wrench: T30 (Part No. 09042−00010 or locally
    manufactured tool)
(d) Loosen the torx screws until the groove along the
    screw circumfrerence catches on the screw case.

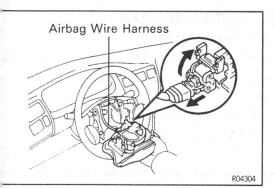

Airbag Wire Harness

R04304

(e) Pull the wheel pad out from the steering wheel and
    disconnect the airbag connector.
    **NOTICE: When removing the wheel pad, take care not to
    pull the airbag wire harness.**
    CAUTION:
    • **When storing the wheel pad, keep the upper surface
      of the pad facing upward.**
    • **Never disassemble the wheel pad.**

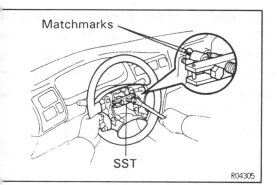

Matchmarks

SST

R04305

2. REMOVE STEERING WHEEL
(a) Disconnect the connector.
(b) Remove the set nut.
(c) Place matchmarks on the steering wheel and main
    shaft.
(d) Using SST, remove the steering wheel.
    SST 09213−31021

**3. REMOVE AND INSTALL SPIRAL CABLE FROM/TO
    COMBINATION SWITCH**
    (See page BE−21)
    **NOTICE: Do not disassemble the spiral cable or apply oil
    to it.**

AB

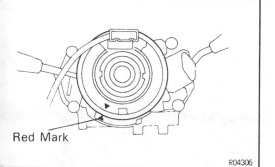

Red Mark

R04306

4. CENTER SPIRAL CABLE
(a) Check that the front wheels are facing straight ahead.
(b) Turn the spiral cable counterclockwise by hand until it
    becomes harder to turn the cable.
(c) Then rotate the spiral cable clockwise about 3 turns to
    align the red mark.
    HINT: The spiral cable will rotate about 3 turns to
    either left or right of the center.

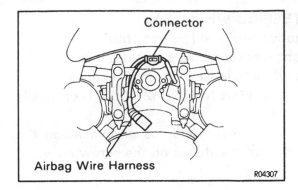

5.   INSTALL STEERING WHEEL
(a)   Align matchmarks on the steering wheel and main shaft, and install the steering wheel to the main shaft.
(b)   Install and torque the set nut.
     Torque: 35 N·m (360 kgf·cm, 26 ft·lbf)
(c)   Connect the connector.

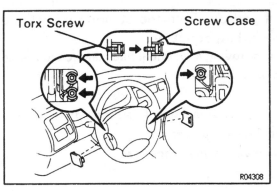

6.   INSTALL STEERING WHEEL PAD
(a)   Connect the airbag connector.
(b)   Install the wheel pad after confirming that the circumference groove of the torx screws is caught on the screw case.
(c)   Using a torx wrench, tighten the three screws.
     Torque: 8.8 N·m (90 kgf·cm, 78 in.·lbf)
     NOTICE:
     ●   Make sure the wheel pad is installed to the specified torque.
     ●   If the wheel pad has been dropped, or there are cracks, dents or other defects in the case or connector, replace the wheel pad with a new one.
     ●   When installing the wheel pad, take care that the wirings do not interfere with other parts and are not pinched between other parts.

7.   CHECK STEERING WHEEL CENTER POINT

FRONT AIRBAG SENSOR

Remove and install the parts as shown.

AB00N–01

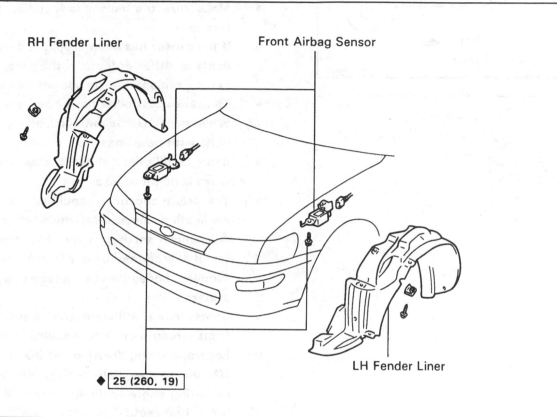

RH Fender Liner

Front Airbag Sensor

LH Fender Liner

◆ 25 (260, 19)

N·m (kgf·cm, ft·lbf) : Specified torque
◆ Non-reusable part

R04309

AB

(MAIN POINTS OF REMOVAL AND INSTALLATION)

CAUTION: Work must be started after 90 seconds from the time the ignition switch is turned to the LOCK position and the negative (−) terminal cable is disconnected from the battery.

NOTICE:

- If the wiring connector of the airbag system is disconnected with the ignition switch at ON or ACC, diagnostic trouble codes will be recorded.

- Never use airbag parts from another vehicle. When replacing parts, replace with new parts.

- Never reuse the sensor involved in a collision when the airbag has deployed.

- Never repair a sensor in order to reuse it.

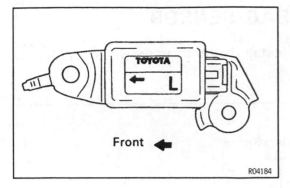

Front ◄

R04184

INSTALL FRONT AIRBAG SENSOR

Install the sensor with the arrow on the sensor facing toward the front of the vehicle.

Torque: 25 N·m (260 kgf·cm, 19 ft·lbf)

NOTICE:

- Make sure the sensor is installed to the specified torque.
- If the sensor has been dropped, or there are cracks, dents or other defects in the case, bracket or connector, replace the sensor with a new one.
- The sensor set bolts have been anti—rust treated. When the sensor is removed, always replace the set bolts with new ones.
- After installation, shake the sensor to check that there is no looseness.
- The front sensor is equipped with an electrical connection check mechanism. Be sure to lock this mechanism securely when connecting the connector. If the connector is not securely locked, a malfunction code will be detected by the diagnosis system.
- Check that the dimensions of the body where the front airbag sensor is installed match those in the body dimension drawings of BO section.

  (The airbag may malfunction, or may not work, if the mounting angle or dimensions of the sensor mount are not correct.)

AB

CENTER AIRBAG SENSOR ASSEMBLY

Remove and install the parts as shown.

AB00L-03

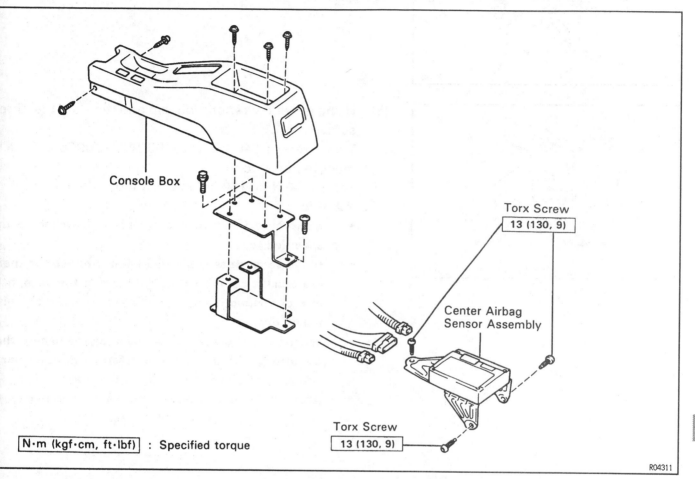

Console Box

Torx Screw
13 (130, 9)

Center Airbag
Sensor Assembly

Torx Screw
13 (130, 9)

N·m (kgf·cm, ft·lbf) : Specified torque

R04311

(MAIN POINTS OF REMOVAL AND INSTALLATION)

CAUTION: Work must be started after 90 seconds from the time the ignition switch is turned to LOCK position and the negative (−) terminal cable is disconnected from the battery.
NOTICE:

- **Do not open the cover or the case of the ECU and various computers unless absolutely necessary. (If the IC terminals are touched, the IC may be destroyed by static electricity.)**
- **Never use airbag parts from another vehicle. When replacing parts, replace with new parts.**
- **Never reuse the center airbag sensor assembly involved in a collision when the airbag has deployed.**
- **Never repair a sensor in order to reuse it.**

AB

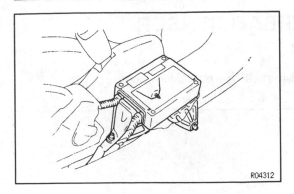

REMOVE AND INSTALL CENTER AIRBAG SENSOR ASSEMBLY

(a) Disconnect and connect the connectors.

NOTICE: Removal and installation of the connector is done with the sensor assembly installed.

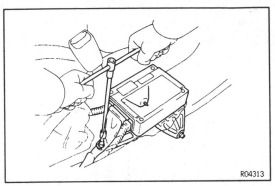

(b) Using a torx wrench, loosen and tighten the three screws.

Torx wrench: T40 (Part No. 09042—00020 or locally manufactured tool)

Torque: **13 N·m (130 kgf·cm, 9 ft·lbf)**

NOTICE:

- Make sure the sensor assembly is installed to the specified torque.
- If the sensor assembly has been dropped, or there are cracks, dents or other defects in the case, bracket or connector, replace the sensor assembly with a new one.
- When installing the sensor assembly, take care that the airbag wirings do not interfere with other parts and are not pinched between other parts.
- After installation, shake the sensor assembly to check that there is no looseness.

AB

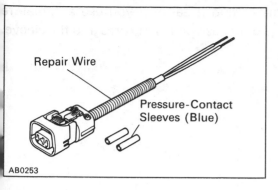

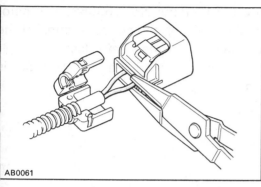

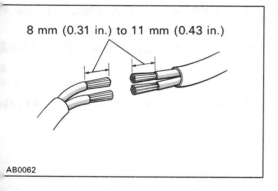

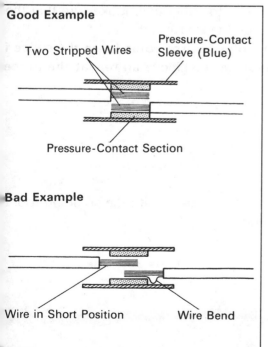

REPAIR WIRE FOR FRONT AIRBAG SENSOR REPLACEMENT

Repair wire with two pressure-contact sleeves (Part No. 82988-50010) has been prepared for exclusive use in repairing connector damage etc. caused by frontal collision of the vehicle.

When repairing the front airbag sensor connector on the wire harness side, always use the special repair wire.

NOTICE: Do not replace the connector housing or terminal only.

AIRBAG REPAIR WIRE REPLACEMENT

CAUTION: Work must be started after 90 seconds from the time the ignition switch is turned to the "LOCK" position and the negative (–) terminal cable is disconnected from the battery.

1. **DISCONNECT WIRE HARNESS AT VEHICLE SIDE**
(a) Remove the cover at the rear of the connector housing and expose the wire harness.
(b) Cut the wire harness behind the connector housing.
   HINT: The operation is performed more easily if the wire harness is left as long as possible.

2. **CONNECT FRONT AIRBAG SENSOR WIRE HARNESS AT VEHICLE SIDE AND REPAIR WIRE**
(a) Start strippig at least 8 mm (0.31 in.) to 11 mm (0.43 in.) away from the end of the existing harness at vehicle side and also from the end of the repair wire.
   NOTICE: Take care not to damage the wire when stripping the wire harness lead. After finishing the operation, visually inspect the wire. If there is any damage, perform the operation again.
(b) Overlap the two stripped wire ends inside of the pressure-contact sleeve as illustrated on the left.
   HINT: The blue pressure-contact sleeve (Part No. 82999-12020) is available individually.

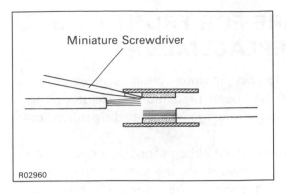

R02960

HINT: You might find it easier if you use a miniature screwdriver as a guide as you insert wires into the sleeve

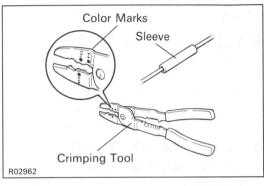

R02962

(c) The crimping tool (AMP Parts No. 169060) has color marks on it. Place the sleeve in the correct section of the tool according to the color of the sleeve itself.
HINT: As the crimping tool, AMP "Part No. 169060" is convenient to use.

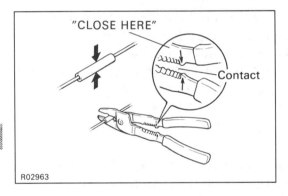

R02963

(d) With the center of the sleeve correctly placed between the crimping jaws, squeeze the crimping tool unitl either end comes into contact at the section marked by "CLOSE HERE".
HINT: Check to see that the sleeve and wires are still in the correct position before closing the crimping tool end with steady pressure.

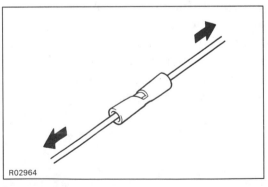

R02964

(e) Pull the joined wires to either end. Make sure that they are joined firmly by the sleeve.
NOTICE: If the joined wires come loose the splice is defective, so replace the sleeve an repeat the procedure.

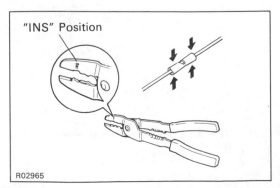

R02965

(f) Crimp both ends of the sleeve with the crimping tool at the "INS" position.

AB

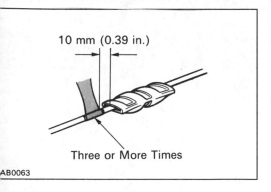

10 mm (0.39 in.)

Three or More Times

AB0063

3. **PROTECT JOINED SECTION**

Wrap silicon tape around the joins to protect them from water.

HINT:

- Before starting the operation, thoroughly wipe dirt and grease off the section to be joined.
- If the adhesive surfaces of two tapes come in contact they will stick together and will not come apart, so do not remove the backing film except when using the tape.
- Do not let oil and dust, etc. get on the tap surface.

(a) Ready about 100 mm (3.94 in.) of silicion tape (Part No. 08231-00045) and peel off the film.

(b) Stretch the silicion tape until its width is reduced by half.

(c) About 10 mm (0.39 in.) from the end of the pressure-contact sleeve, wrap the silicion tape around the sleeve three or more times while stretching the tape.

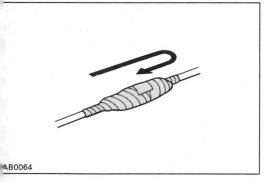

AB0064

(d) Wrap the remaining part of sleeve with half of the tape overlapping at each turn.

(e) Firmly wrap the tape two times or more about 10 mm (0.39 in.) from the other end of the pressure-contact sleeve, then wrap the tape back towards the start again and firmly finish winding the tape around the center of the sleeve.

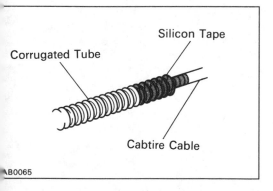

Silicon Tape

Corrugated Tube

Cabtire Cable

AB0065

(f) Fix the corrugated tube to the cabtire cable using silicon tape.

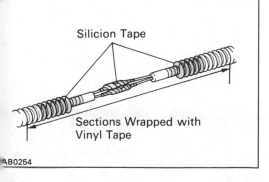

Silicion Tape

Sections Wrapped with Vinyl Tape

AB0254

(g) After applying the silicon tape, apply vinyl tape on the corrugated tube of repair wire side over to the corrugated tube of vehicle wire harness side.

MEMO

TROUBLESHOOTING

AB

How To Proceed With Troubleshooting

Malfunction symptoms of the airbag system are difficult to confirm, so the diagnostic trouble code become the most important source of information when troubleshooting.

Perform troubleshooting of the airbag system in accordance with the following procedure:

1. **CUSTOMER PROBLEM ANALYSIS**

   Using the CUSTOMER PROBLEM ANALYSIS CHECK SHEET (See page AB-31) for reference, as the customer in as much detail as possible about the problem.

2. **WARNING LIGHT CHECK**

   Check the airbag warning light. If the light remains on, a malfunction is stored in the center airba sensor assembly, so proceed to step 3. If the airbag warning light is not on, malfunction ha occurred in the airbag warning light circuit, so perform troubleshooting for code 22.

   HINT: Code 22 is recorded when a malfunction occurs in the airbag warning light system.

   If an open malfunction occurs in the airbag warning light system, the airbag warning light does no light up, so that until the malfunction is repaired, the diagnostic trouble codes (including code 22 cannot be confirmed.

3. **DIAGNOSTIC TROUBLE CODE CHECK AND RECORDING**

   Check the diagnostic trouble codes and make a note of any malfunction codes which ar output. If normal code is output, an abnormality in the power source circuit may have occurred, so perforr troubleshooting for source voltage in step 8.

   If code 22 is output, skip steps 4 and 5 and proceed to step 7.

4. **CLEARING OF MALFUNCTION CODE**

   Clear the malfunction code

   HINT: The malfunction code output in step 3 indicates that a malfunction has occurred in th circuit designated by the malfunction code, but does not indicate whether the malfunction is sti occurring or whether it was in the past.

   Accordingly, it is necessary to find out the present condition of the malfunction occurrence by clearin the malfunction code and performing the diagnostic trouble code check again. If this operation neglected and troubleshooting is performed using only the malfunction code confirmed in step 3 isolating the problem component becomes difficult and invites mistaken diagnosis.

5. **DIAGNOSTIC TROUBLE CODE CHECK AND RECORDING**   6. **SYMPTOM SIMULATION**

   After repeating ignition switch ON – OFF operation (ON: wait 20 secs., OFF: wait 20 secs.) 5 time check the diagnostic trouble code. If any malfunction code is output, the malfunction is still occurring so proceed to step 7.

   Bearing in mind that a malfunction code was registered in step 3, provided that the normal cod is presently output, use the methods described in step 6 to simulate the malfunction.

   NOTICE: When the battery has been reconnected, turn the ignition switch to ACC or ON positio after at least 2 seconds have elapsed.

   If the battery is reconnected with the ignition switch in ACC or ON position, or the ignition switc is turned to ACC or ON within 2 seconds of connecting the battery, it is possible that the diagnos system will not operate normally.

7. **DIAGNOSTIC TROUBLE CODE CHART**

   Proceed to the appropriate flow chart in step 8 in accordance with the malfunction code found i step 5 or 6.

8 CIRCUIT INSPECTION   9 REPAIR

Find out if the problem lies in a sensor, actuator or wire harness and connector, and repair the problem. After the problem part is repaired, reinstall the disassembled parts. Do not start work until at least 90 seconds after the ignition switch is turned to the LOCK position and the negative (–) terminal cable is disconnected.

CAUTION: If incorrect procedure is used, a malfunction may occur in the system or there is the danger that the airbag may be accidentally activated during the repair operation. Carefully read the GENERAL DESCRIPTION (See page AB-2) and the cautions for each operation, and perform repairs in the correct order using the correct methods.

HINT: The following illustration for the CIRCUIT INSPECTION shows each connector for the circuit from the center airbag sensor assembly to the steering wheel pad (squib).

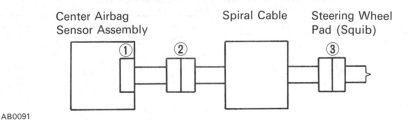

Center Airbag Sensor Assembly   Spiral Cable   Steering Wheel Pad (Squib)

AB0091

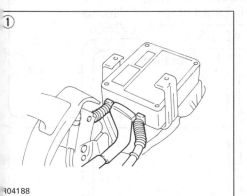

R04188

AB0270

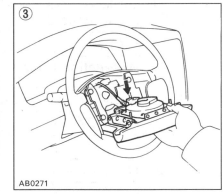

AB0271

AB

10 CLEARING OF MALFUNCTION CODE

When all the malfunction codes found in steps 5 and 6 have been repaired, clear the malfunction codes.

11 DIAGNOSTIC TROUBLE CODE CHECK

After repeating ignition switch ON – OFF operation (ON: wait 20 secs., OFF: wait 20 secs.) 5 times, check the diagnostic trouble codes. If a code is displayed, return to step 7 and troubleshoot the displayed malfunction code.

NOTICE: When connecting the battery after clearing the malfunction code, always of it with the ignition switch in LOCK position.

When the battery has been reconnected, turn the ignition switch to ACC or ON position after at least 2 seconds have elapsed.

If the battery is reconnected with the ignition switch in ACC or ON position, or the ignition switch is turned to ACC or ON within 2 seconds of connecting the battery, it is possible that the diagnosis system will not operate normally.

12 CONFIRMATION TEST

Check the warning light again and confirm that all the malfunctions have been repaired. If the warning light indicates and abnormally, repeat the operation again from step 2 .

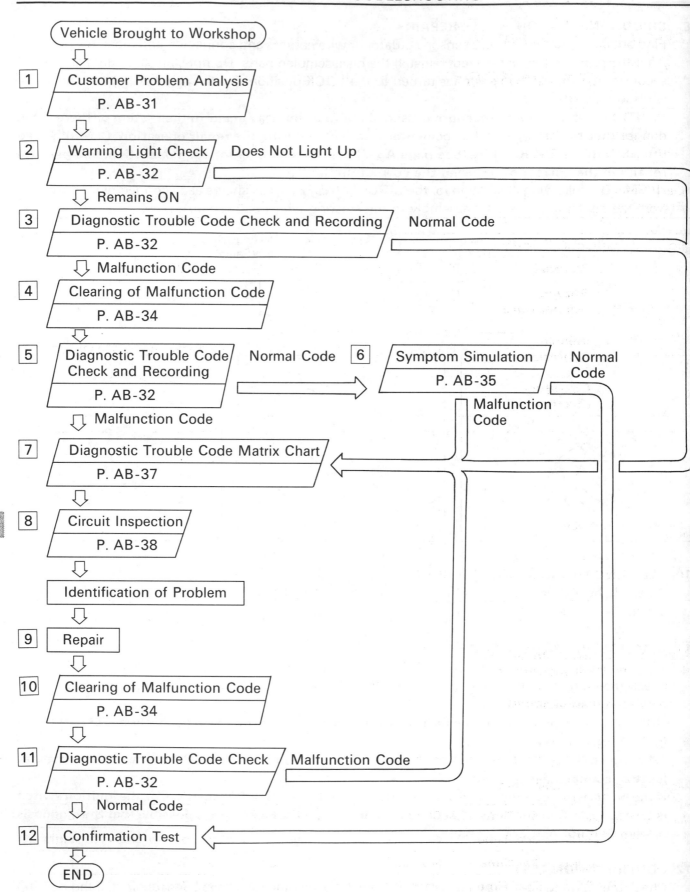

(Vehicle Brought to Workshop)

1   Customer Problem Analysis
    P. AB-31

2   Warning Light Check   Does Not Light Up
    P. AB-32

Remains ON

3   Diagnostic Trouble Code Check and Recording   Normal Code
    P. AB-32

Malfunction Code

4   Clearing of Malfunction Code
    P. AB-34

5   Diagnostic Trouble Code Check and Recording   Normal Code   6   Symptom Simulation   Normal Code
    P. AB-32   P. AB-35

Malfunction Code   Malfunction Code

7   Diagnostic Trouble Code Matrix Chart
    P. AB-37

AB

8   Circuit Inspection
    P. AB-38

Identification of Problem

9   Repair

10   Clearing of Malfunction Code
    P. AB-34

11   Diagnostic Trouble Code Check   Malfunction Code
    P. AB-32

Normal Code

12   Confirmation Test

(END)

Customer Problem Analysis Check Sheet

SRS **AIRBAG System Check Sheet**	Inspector's Name

Customer's Name		Registration No.	
		Registration Year	/ /
		Frame No.	
Date Vehicle Brought In	/ /	Odometer Reading	Miles

Date of Problem Occurrence		/ /
Conditions When Problem Occurs	Weather	☐ Fine ☐ Cloudy ☐ Rainy ☐ Snowy ☐ Various/Other ....
	Outdoor Temperature	☐ HOT ☐ Warm ☐ Cool ☐ Cold (Approx. °C (°F))
	Vehicle Operation	☐ Starting ☐ Idling ☐ Driving [☐ Constant speed ☐ Acceleration ☐ Deceleration ☐ Other ( )]
	Condition of road	

Details of Problem	
Vehicle Inspection, Repair History Prior to Occurrence of Malfunction (Including Airbag System)	

Diagnosis System Inspection

Airbag Warning Light Inspection	1st Time	☐ Remains ON ☐ Sometimes Lights Up ☐ Does Not Light Up
	2nd Time	☐ Remains ON ☐ Sometimes Lights Up ☐ Does Not Light Up
Diagnostic Trouble Code Inspection	1st Time	☐ Normal Code ☐ Malfunction Code [Code.]
	2nd Time	☐ Normal Code ☐ Malfunction Code [Code.]

AB

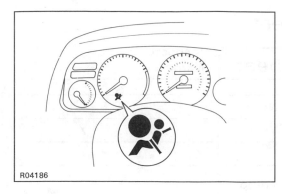

Diagnosis Inspection

AIRBAG WARNING LIGHT CHECK

(a) Turn the ignition switch to ACC or ON and check that the airbag warning light lights up.

(b) Check that the airbag warning light goes out after approx. 6 seconds.

HINT:
- When the ignition switch is at ACC or ON and the airbag warning light remains on, the center airbag sensor assembly has detected a malfunction code.
- If, after approx. 6 seconds have elapsed, the airbag warning light sometimes lights up or the airbag warning light lights up even when the ignition switch is OFF, a short in the airbag warning light circuit can be considered likely.
  Proceed to "Airbag warning light system (always lit up)" on page AB-76.

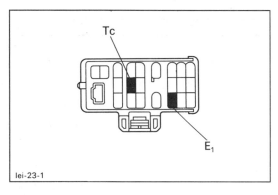

DIAGNOSTIC TROUBLE CODE CHECK

1. **OUTPUT DIAGNOSTIC TROUBLE CODE**

(a) Turn the ignition switch to ACC or ON position and wait approx. 20 seconds.

(b) Using SST, connect terminals Tc and E_1 of the DLC1.
SST 09843-18020
NOTICE: Never make a mistake with the terminal connection position as this will cause a malfunction.

2. **READ DIAGNOSTIC TROUBLE CODE**

Read the 2-digit diagnostic trouble code as indicated by the number of times the airbag warning light blinks. As an example, the blinking paterns; normal, 11 and 31 are as shown on the illustration.

- Normal code indication
  The light will blink 2 times per second.

- Malfunction code indication
  In the event of a malfunction, the light will blink. The number represented by the first blink code output indicates the first digit of a 2-digit diagnostic trouble code.
  After a 1.5 second pause, the second blink code will indicate the second digit.
  If there are two or more codes, there will be a 2.5 second pause between each.
  After all the codes have been output, there will be a 4.0 second pause and they will all be repeated.

HINT:
- In the event of a number of trouble codes, indication will begin from the smaller numbered code to the larger.
- If it does not output a diagnostic trouble code or outputs a diagnostic trouble code without terminal connection, proceed to the Tc terminal circuit inspection on page AB-76.

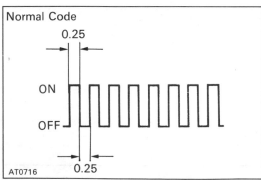

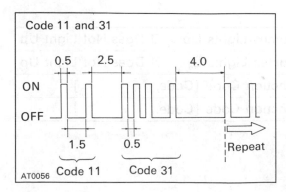

DIAGNOSTIC TROUBLE CODES

DTC No.	Blink Pattern	Diagnosis	Trouble Area	AIRBAG Warning Light
*1 (Normal) FI1401		● System normal	–	OFF
		● Source voltage drop	● Battery ● Center airbag sensor assembly	ON
11 AB0057		● Short in squib circuit (to ground) ● Front airbag sensor malfunction ● Floor sensor malfunction	● Steering wheel pad (squib) ● Front airbag sensor ● Spiral cable ● Center airbag sensor assembly ● Wire harness	ON
12 FI1389		● Short in squib circuit (to B+) ● Open in front airbag sensor circuit	● Steering wheel pad (squib) ● Front airbag sensor ● Spiral cable ● Center airbag sensor assembly ● Wire harness	ON
13 FI1390		● Short in squib circuit (between D^+ wire harness and D^- wire harness)	● Steering wheel pad (squib) ● Spiral cable ● Center airbag sensor assembly ● Wire harness	ON
14 FI1391		● Open in squib circuit	● Steering wheel pad (squib) ● Spiral cable ● Center airbag sensor assembly ● Wire harness	ON
15 AB0058		● Open in front airbag sensor circuit	● Front airbag sensor ● Center airbag sensor assembly ● Wire harness	ON
22 *2 FI1392		● Airbag warning light system malfunction	● Airbag warning light ● Center airbag sensor assembly ● Wire harness	ON
31 FI1394		● Center airbag sensor assembly malfunction	● Center airbag sensor assembly	ON

AB

HINT:

*1
● When the airbag warning light remains lit up and the diagnostic trouble code is the normal code, this means a source voltage drop.
This malfunction is not stored in memory by the center airbag sensor assembly and if the power source voltage returns to normal, the airbag warning light will automatically go out.

*2
● Code 22 is recorded when a malfunction occurs in the airbag warning light system.
If an open malfunction occurs in the airbag warning light system, the airbag warning light does not light up, so that until the malfunction is repaired, the diagnostic codes (including code 22) cannot be confirmed.

● When two or more codes are indicated, the lowest numbered code will appear first.

● If a code not listed on the chart is displayed, the center airbag sensor assembly is faulty.

CLEARING OF DIAGNOSTIC TROUBLE CODE

CLEARING OF MALFUNCTION CODE

(a) Connect service wires to terminals Tc and AB of the DLC1.

(b) Turn the ignition switch ACC or ON and wait approx. 6 seconds.

(c) Starting with the Tc terminal, apply body ground alternately to terminal Tc and terminal AB twice each in cycles of 1.0 ± 0.5 seconds. (Confirm that body grounds is absolute.)

Finally, keep applying body ground to terminal Tc.

HINT: When alternately grounding the terminals Tc and AB, release ground from one terminal and immediately apply it to the other terminal. This action must be done within the time limits shown below. If you are not within the time limits, repeat the procedure until you clear the codes.

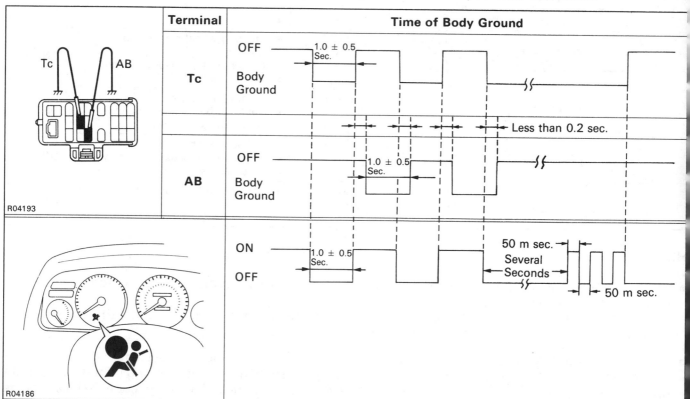

(d) Several seconds after performing the clearing procedure, the airbag warning light will blink in a 50 msec cycle to indicate the codes have been cleared.

Symptom Simulation

Intermittent troubles or problems" are the malfunctions about which the customer has a complaint, but which do not occur and can not be confirmed in the workshop. The intermittent problems also include complaints about the airbag warning light going on and off erratically.

The self-diagnostic system stores the circuit of the intermittent problem in memory even if the ignition switch is turned off.

And, for accurate diagnosis of the problems, ask the customer to obtain information as much as possible following the customer problem analysis check sheet (See page AB-31), and try to reproduce the intermittent problem.

The problem simulation methods described below are the effective ways for this nature of problem to produce the problem conditions by applying vibration, heat, and humidity.

---

1 | VIBRATION METHOD: When vibration seems to be the major cause.

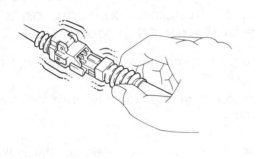

CONNECTORS

Slightly shake the connector vertically and horizontally.

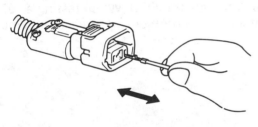

(Inspection of connectors)

(a) Does the wire harness connecting with its corresponding part have insufficient slack?

(b) Are the terminals dirty?

(c) Are the terminals making loose contact due to terminals spread?

AB0245
R02966

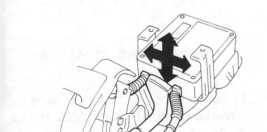

WIRE HARNESS

Slightly shake the wire harness vartically and horizontally. The connector joint, fulcrum of the vibration, and body through portion are the major areas to be checked thoroughly.

R04188

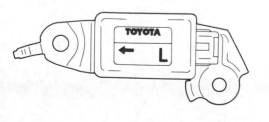

PARTS AND SENSORS

Apply vibration slightly by a finger to the part or sensor considered to be the problem cause and check if the malfunction will occur.

CAUTION: Do not apply vibration to the center airbag sensor.

R04184

AB

2　**HEAT METHOD:**　When the problem seems to occur when the suspect areas is heated.

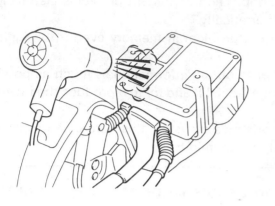

Heat the component that is likely the cause of the malfunction with a hair dryer or similar object. Check to see if the malfunction will occur.

NOTICE:
- **Do not heat to more than 60°C (140°F) (Temperature limit that the component can be touched with a hand.).**
- **Do not apply heat directly to part in the ECU.**

R04189

3　**WATER SPRINKLING METHOD:**　When the malfunction seems to occur on a rainy day or in a high-humidity condition.

Sprinkle water onto the vehicle and check to see if the malfunction will occur.

NOTICE: **Never apply water directly onto the electronic components.**

HINT:
- If a vehicle is subject to water leakage, the leaked water may contaminate the ECU. When testing a vehicle with a water leakage problem, special caution must be paid.

R04199

4　**OTHER:**　When a malfunction seems to occur when electrical load is excessive.

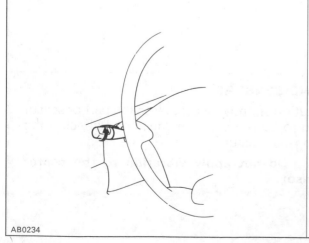

Turn on all electrical loads including the heater blower, headlights, rear window defogger, etc. and check to see if the malfunction will occur.

AB0234

AB

Diagnostic Trouble Code Matrix Chart

If a malfunction code is displayed during the diagnostic trouble code check, check the circuit listed for that code in the table below (Proceed to the page given for that circuit).

DTC No.	Diagnosis	Page
(Normal)*1	● Source voltage drop	AB-38
11	● Short in squib circuit (to ground) ● Front airbag sensor malfunction ● Floor sensor malfunction	AB-40
12	● Short in squib circuit (to B+) ● Open in front airbag sensor circuit	AB-46
13	● Short in squib circuit (between D^+ wire harness and D^- wire harness)	AB-51
14	● Open in squib circuit	AB-58
15	● Open in front airbag sensor circuit	AB-63
22*2	● Airbag warning light system malfunction	AB-68
31	● Center airbag sensor assembly malfunction	AB-74

HINT:
1   When the airbag warning light remains lit up and the diagnostic trouble code is the normal code, this means a source voltage drop.

2   Code 22 is recorded when a malfunction occurs in the airbag warning light system.
    If an open malfunction occurs in the airbag warning light system, the airbag warning light does not light up, so that until the malfunction is repaired, the diagnostic codes (including code 22) cannot be confirmed.

AB

Problem Symptom Chart

Proceed with troubleshooting of each circuit in the table below.

Problem Symptom	Inspection Item	Page
● With the ignition switch at ACC or ON, the airbag warning light sometimes lights up after approx. 6 seconds have elapsed. ● Airbag warning light lights up even when ignition switch is in the LOCK position.	● Airbag warning light system (Always lit up)	AB-76
● Diagnostic trouble code not displayed. ● Diagnostic trouble code displayed without Tc and E_1 terminal connection.	● Tc terminal circuit	AB-78

Circuit Inspection

DTC	(Normal)	Source Voltage Drop

CIRCUIT DESCRIPTION

The airbag system is equipped with a voltage-increase circuit (DC-DC converter) in the center airbag sensor assembly in case the source voltage drops.

When the battery voltage drops, the voltage-increase circuit (DC-DC converter) functions to increase the voltage of the airbag system to normal voltage.

The diagnosis system malfunction display for this circuit is different to other circuits – when the airbag warning light remains lit up and the diagnostic trouble code is a normal code, source voltage drop is indicated.

Malfunction in this circuit is not recorded in the center airbag sensor assembly, and the source voltage returns to normal, the airbag warning light automatically goes off.

DTC No.	Diagnosis
(Normal)	Source voltage drop.

DIAGNOSTIC CHART

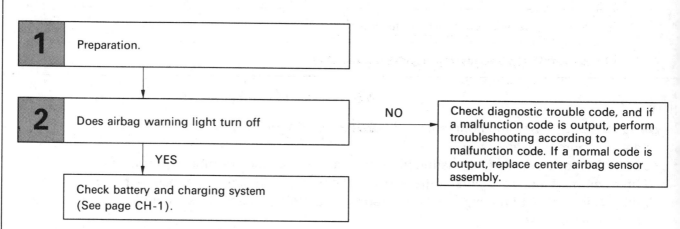

1 Preparation.

2 Does airbag warning light turn off

NO → Check diagnostic trouble code, and if a malfunction code is output, perform troubleshooting according to malfunction code. If a normal code is output, replace center airbag sensor assembly.

YES

Check battery and charging system (See page CH-1).

AB

INSPECTION PROCEDURES

P Preparation   C Check

1 Preparation.

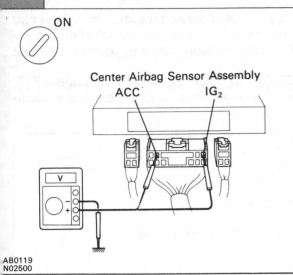

AB0119
N02500

P (1) Turn ignition switch LOCK.
(2) Disconnect center airbag sensor assembly connector.
(3) Turn ignition switch ON. But do not start engine.
(4) Measure voltage at IG₂ or ACC on connector wire harness side of center airbag sensor assembly and operate electric system (defogger, wiper, headlight, heater blower, etc.).
Voltage: 6 V – 11.5 V at IG₂ at ACC.
(5) Turn electric system switch OFF.
(6) Turn ignition switch LOCK.
(7) Remove voltmeter and connect center airbag sensor assembly connector.

2 Does airbag warning light turn off.

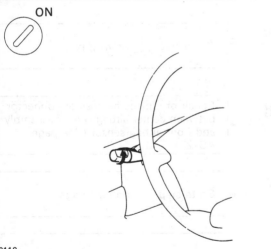

AB0119
AB0234

P Turn ignition switch ON.

C Operate electric system checked in 1 (4) and check that airbag warning light goes off.

AB

YES

NO Check diagnostic trouble code, and if a malfunction code is output, perform troubleshooting according to malfunction code. If a normal code is output, replace center airbag sensor assembly.

**Check battery and charging system
(See page CH-1).**

DTC	11	• **Short in Squib Circuit (to ground)** • **Front Airbag Sensor Malfunction** • **Floor Sensor Malfunction**

CIRCUIT DESCRIPTION

The squib circuit consists of the center airbag sensor assembly, spiral cable and the steering wheel pad (squib). It causes the airbag to deploy when the airbag deployment conditions are satisfied.

The front airbag sensor detects the deceleration force in a frontal collision and is located in the front fender on the left and right sides.

For details of the function of each component, see FUNCTION OF COMPONENTS on page AB-7.

Diagnostic trouble code 11 is recorded when occurrence of ground short is detected in the squib circuit or front airbag sensor circuit.

DTC No.	Diagnosis
11	• Short circuit in squib wire harness (to ground). • Squib malfunction. • Short circuit in front airbag sensor +S wire harness (to ground). • Front airbag sensor malfunction. • Short circuit between +S wire harness and –S wire harness of front airbag sensor. • Spiral cable malfunction. • Center airbag sensor assembly malfunction.

DIAGNOSTIC CHART

AB

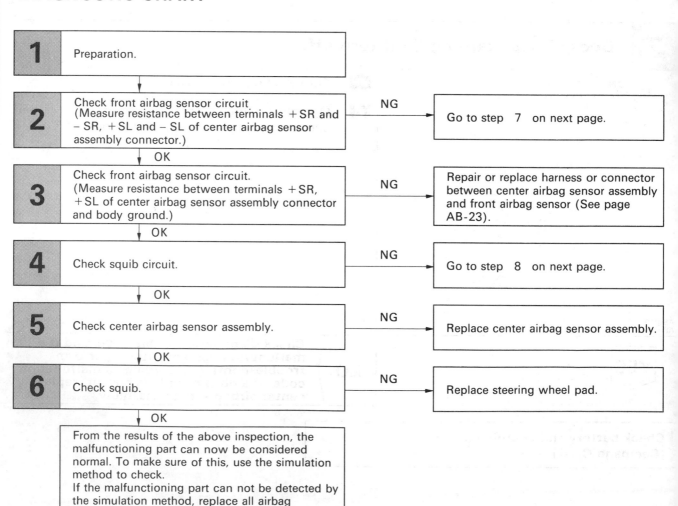

1 Preparation.

↓

2 Check front airbag sensor circuit.
(Measure resistance between terminals +SR and –SR, +SL and –SL of center airbag sensor assembly connector.) — NG → Go to step 7 on next page.

↓ OK

3 Check front airbag sensor circuit.
(Measure resistance between terminals +SR, +SL of center airbag sensor assembly connector and body ground.) — NG → Repair or replace harness or connector between center airbag sensor assembly and front airbag sensor (See page AB-23).

↓ OK

4 Check squib circuit. — NG → Go to step 8 on next page.

↓ OK

5 Check center airbag sensor assembly. — NG → Replace center airbag sensor assembly.

↓ OK

6 Check squib. — NG → Replace steering wheel pad.

↓ OK

From the results of the above inspection, the malfunctioning part can now be considered normal. To make sure of this, use the simulation method to check.
If the malfunctioning part can not be detected by the simulation method, replace all airbag components including the wire harness.

─ DIAGNOSTIC CHART (Cont'd) ─

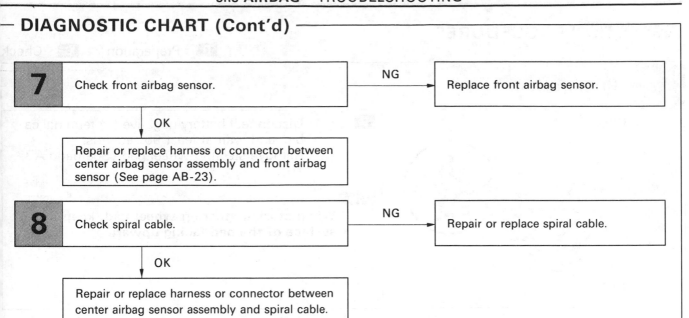

7 Check front airbag sensor.

NG → Replace front airbag sensor.

OK ↓

Repair or replace harness or connector between center airbag sensor assembly and front airbag sensor (See page AB-23).

8 Check spiral cable.

NG → Repair or replace spiral cable.

OK ↓

Repair or replace harness or connector between center airbag sensor assembly and spiral cable.

AB

INSPECTION PROCEDURES

P Preparation   **C** Check

---

1 **Preparation.**

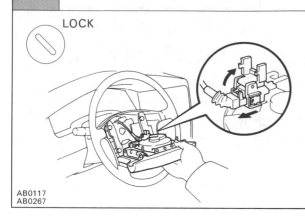

AB0117
AB0267

P (1) Disconnect battery negative (–) terminal cable, and wait at least 90 seconds.
(2) Remove steering wheel pad (See page AB-16).

Caution

When storing steering wheel pad, keep upper surface of the pad facing upward.

---

2 **Check front airbag sensor circuit. (Measure resistance between terminals +SR and –SR, +SL and –SL of center airbag sensor assembly connector.)**

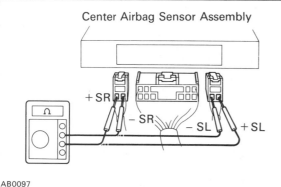

Center Airbag Sensor Assembly

+SR   –SR   –SL   +SL

AB0097

P Disconnect center airbag sensor assembly connectors.

C Measure resistance between terminals +SR and –SR, +SL and –SL of harness side connector of center airbag sensor assembly.

OK Resistance: 755 Ω – 885 Ω

OK

NG ⟩ Go to step **7** .

---

3 **Check front airbag sensor circuit. (Measure resistance between terminals +SR, +SL of center airbag sensor assembly connector and body ground.)**

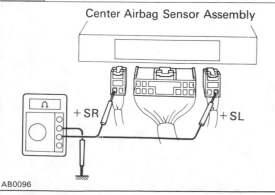

Center Airbag Sensor Assembly

+SR   +SL

AB0096

C Measure resistance between terminals +SR, +SL of harness side connector of center airbag sensor assembly and body ground.

OK Resistance: 1 MΩ or Higher

OK

NG ⟩ Repair or replace harness or connector between center airbag sensor assembly and front airbag sensor (See page AB-23).

4 | Check squib circuit.

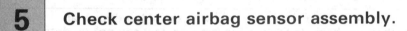

Center Airbag Sensor Assembly — **Spiral Cable** — **Steering Wheel Pad (Squib)**

D⁻   D⁺

AB0072
AB0070

C   Measure resistance between D⁺, D⁻ on spiral cable side of connector between spiral cable and steering wheel pad and body ground.

OK   **Resistance: 1 MΩ or Higher**

OK

NG ⟩ Go to step **8** .

---

5 | Check center airbag sensor assembly.

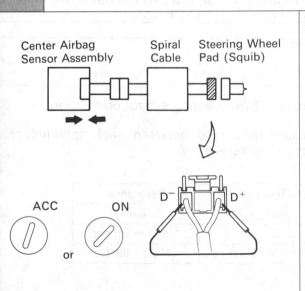

Center Airbag Sensor Assembly — **Spiral Cable** — **Steering Wheel Pad (Squib)**

ACC   ON   or

D⁻   D⁺

Tc   Code 11

E₁

AB0074
AB0069
AB0118 AB0119
lei-23-1 AB0057

P
(1) Connect connectors to center airbag sensor assembly.
(2) Using a service wire, connect D⁺ and D⁻ on spiral cable side of connector between spiral cable and steering wheel pad.
(3) Connect negative (–) terminal cable to battery, and wait at least 2 seconds.

C
(1) Turn ignition switch ACC or ON and wait at least 20 seconds.
(2) Using SST, connect terminals Tc and E₁ of DLC1.
SST 09843-18020
(3) Check diagnostic trouble code.

OK   **Diagnostic trouble code 11 is not output.**

Hint   Codes other than code 11 may be output at this time, but this is not relevant to this check.

OK

NG ⟩ Replace center airbag sensor assembly.

6 Check squib.

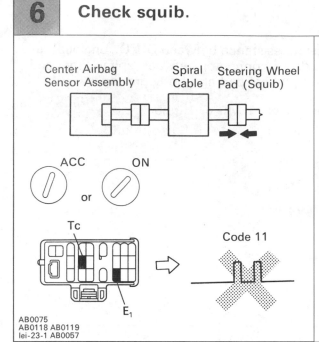

Center Airbag
Sensor Assembly

Spiral
Cable

Steering Wheel
Pad (Squib)

ACC   ON   or

Tc

Code 11

E₁

AB0075
AB0118 AB0119
lei-23-1 AB0057

P
(1) Turn ignition switch LOCK.
(2) Disconnect battery negative (–) terminal cable, and wait at least 90 seconds.
(3) Connect steering wheel pad (squib) connector.
(4) Connect negative (–) terminal cable to battery, and wait at least 2 seconds.

C
(1) Turn ignition switch ACC or ON, and wait at least 20 seconds.
(2) Using SST, connect terminals Tc and E_1 of DLC1.
SST 09843-18020
(3) Check diagnostic code.

OK Diagnostic trouble code 11 is not output.

Hint Codes other than code 11 may be output at this time, but this is not relevant to this check.

OK

NG ⟩ Replace steering wheel pad.

From the results of the above inspection, the malfunctioning part can now be considered normal.
To make sure of this, use the simulation method to check. If the malfunctioning part can not be detected by the simulation method, replace all airbag components including the wire harness.

AB

7 Check front airbag sensor.

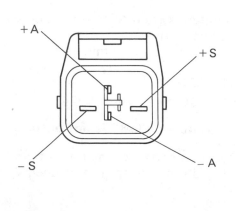

+A

+S

–S

–A

AB0034

P Disconnect front airbag sensor connector.

C Measure resistance between each terminal of front airbag sensor.

OK

Terminal	Resistance
$\oplus$S – $\oplus$A	Below 1Ω
$\oplus$S – $\ominus$S	1 MΩ or Higher
$\ominus$S – $\ominus$A	755Ω – 885Ω

Notice

• Do not touch ohmmeter probes strongly against terminals of front airbag sensor.
• Make sure the front airbag sensor connector is properly connected.

OK

NG ⟩ Replace front airbag sensor.

Repair or replace harness or connector between center airbag sensor assembly and front airbag sensor (See page AB-23).

8 **Check spiral cable.**

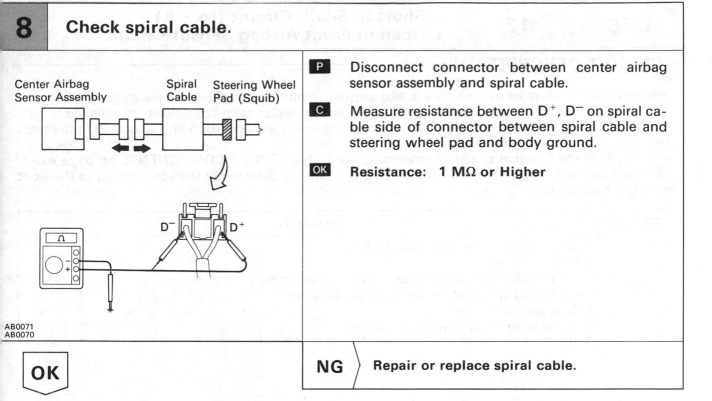

Center Airbag
Sensor Assembly

Spiral
Cable

Steering Wheel
Pad (Squib)

D^- D^+

AB0071
AB0070

P Disconnect connector between center airbag sensor assembly and spiral cable.

C Measure resistance between D^+, D^- on spiral cable side of connector between spiral cable and steering wheel pad and body ground.

OK Resistance: 1 MΩ or Higher

OK

NG Repair or replace spiral cable.

Repair or replace harness or connector between center airbag sensor assembly and spiral cable.

AB

DTC	12	• Short in Squib Circuit (to +B) • Open in Front Airbag Sensor Circuit

CIRCUIT DESCRIPTION

The squib circuit consists of the center airbag sensor assembly, spiral cable and the steering wheel pad (squib). It causes the airbag to deploy when the airbag deployment conditions are satisfied.

The front airbag sensor detects the deceleration force in a frontal collision and is located in the front fender on the left and right sides.

For details of the function of each component, see FUNCTION OF COMPONENTS on page AB-7.

Diagnostic trouble code 12 is recorded when a B+ short is detected in the squib circuit or the front airbag sensor circuit.

DTC No.	Diagnosis
12	• Short circuit in squib wire harness (to B+). • Squib malfunction. • Short circuit in front airbag sensor +S wire harness (to B+). • Open circuit in RH and LH front airbag sensor harness. • Spiral cable malfunction. • Center airbag sensor assembly malfunction.

AB

– DIAGNOSTIC CHART

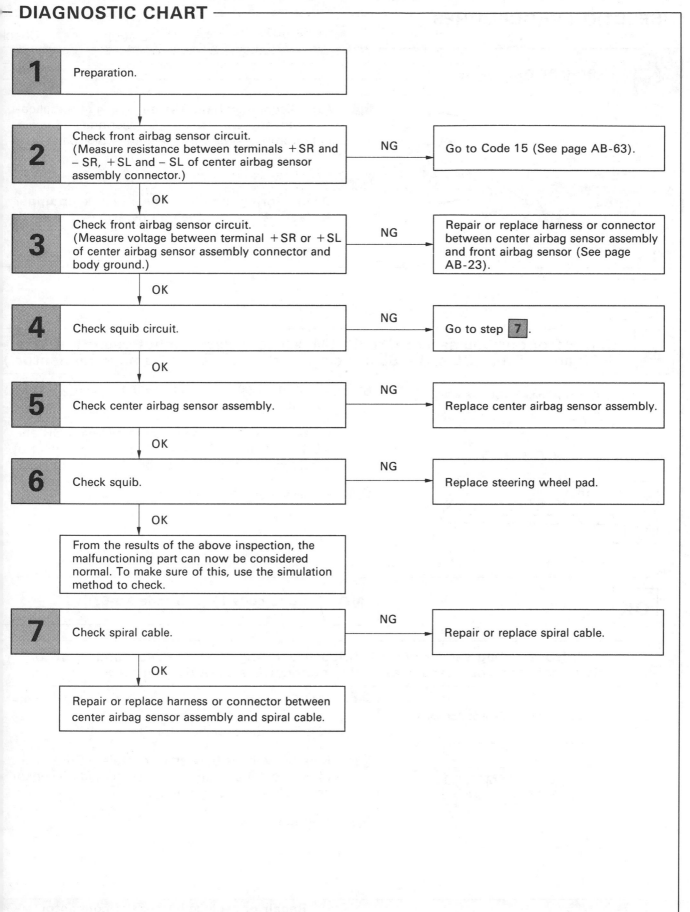

1 Preparation.

2 Check front airbag sensor circuit.
(Measure resistance between terminals +SR and – SR, +SL and – SL of center airbag sensor assembly connector.)

NG → Go to Code 15 (See page AB-63).

OK

3 Check front airbag sensor circuit.
(Measure voltage between terminal +SR or +SL of center airbag sensor assembly connector and body ground.)

NG → Repair or replace harness or connector between center airbag sensor assembly and front airbag sensor (See page AB-23).

OK

4 Check squib circuit.

NG → Go to step **7**.

OK

5 Check center airbag sensor assembly.

NG → Replace center airbag sensor assembly.

OK

6 Check squib.

NG → Replace steering wheel pad.

OK

From the results of the above inspection, the malfunctioning part can now be considered normal. To make sure of this, use the simulation method to check.

7 Check spiral cable.

NG → Repair or replace spiral cable.

OK

Repair or replace harness or connector between center airbag sensor assembly and spiral cable.

AB

INSPECTION PROCEDURES

P Preparation   **C** Check

1 Preparation.

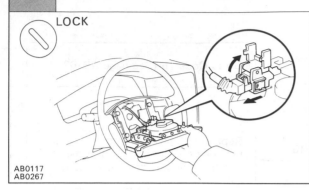

LOCK

AB0117
AB0267

P (1) Disconnect battery negative (–) terminal cable, and wait at least 90 seconds.
(2) Remove steering wheel pad (See page AB-16).

Caution

When storing steering wheel pad, keep upper surface of the pad facing upward.

2 Check front airbag sensor circuit. (Measure resistance between terminals +SR and –SR, +SL and –SL of center airbag sensor assembly connector.)

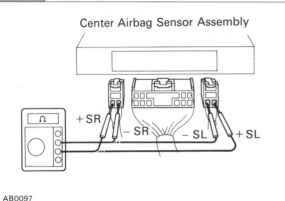

Center Airbag Sensor Assembly

+SR   –SR   –SL   +SL

AB0097

P Disconnect center airbag sensor assembly connectors.

C Measure resistance between terminals +SR and –SR, +SL and –SL of harness side connector of center airbag sensor assembly.

OK Resistance: 755Ω – 885Ω

OK

NG Go to code 15 (See page AB-63).

3 Check front airbag sensor circuit. (Measure voltage between terminal +SR or +SL of center airbag sensor assembly connector and body ground.)

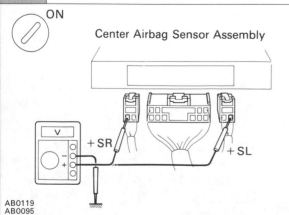

ON

Center Airbag Sensor Assembly

+SR   +SL

AB0119
AB0095

P (1) Connect negative (–) terminal cable to battery.
(2) Turn ignition switch ON.

C Measure voltage between terminals +SR or +SL of harness side connector of center airbag sensor assembly and body ground.

OK Voltage: 0 V

OK

NG Repair or replace harness or connector between center airbag sensor assembly and front airbag sensor (See page AB-23).

AB

4   Check squib circuit.

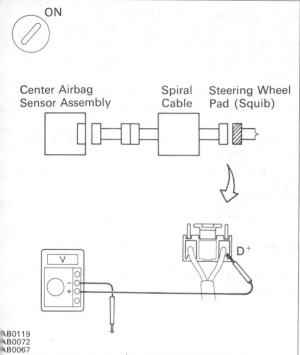

ON

Center Airbag
Sensor Assembly
Spiral
Cable
Steering Wheel
Pad (Squib)

AB0119
AB0072
AB0067

C   Measure voltage at D^+ on spiral cable side of connector between spiral cable and steering wheel pad.

OK   Voltage: 0 V

OK

NG ⟩ Go to step **7** .

5   Check center airbag sensor assembly.

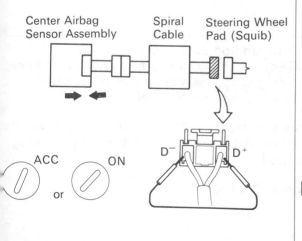

Center Airbag
Sensor Assembly
Spiral
Cable
Steering Wheel
Pad (Squib)

ACC   or   ON

D^- D^+

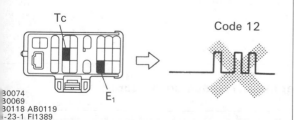

Tc

Code 12

E₁

30074
30069
30118 AB0119
-23-1 FI1389

P
(1) Turn ignition switch LOCK.
(2) Disconnect negative (–) terminal cable from battery.
(3) Connect connectors to center airbag sensor assembly.
(4) Using a service wire, connect D^+ and D^- on spiral cable side of connector between spiral cable and steering wheel pad.
(5) Connect negative (–) terminal cable to battery, and wait at least 2 seconds.

C
(1) Turn ignition switch ACC or ON, and wait at least 20 seconds.
(2) Using SST, connect terminals Tc and E_1 of DLC1.
SST 09843-18020
(3) Check diagnostic trouble code.

OK   Diagnostic trouble code 12 is not output.

Hint   Codes other than code 12 may be output at this time, but this is not relevant to this check.

OK

NG ⟩ Replace center airbag sensor assembly.

6   Check squib.

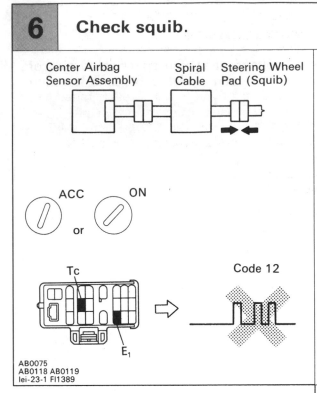

P
(1) Turn ignition switch LOCK.
(2) Disconnect battery negative (–) terminal cable, and wait at least 90 seconds.
(3) Connect steering wheel pad (squib) connector.
(4) Connect negative (–) terminal cable to battery, and wait at least 2 seconds.

C
(1) Turn ignition switch ACC or ON, and wait at least 20 seconds.
(2) Using SST, connect terminals Tc and E_1 of DLC1.
SST 09843-18020
(3) Check diagnostic trouble code.

OK   **Diagnostic trouble code 12 is not output.**

Hint   Codes other than code 12 may be output at this time, but this is not relevant to this check.

AB0075
AB0118 AB0119
Iei-23-1 FI1389

OK ⬡

NG ⟩   Replace steering wheel pad.

From the results of the above inspection, the malfunctioning part can now be considered normal. To make sure of this, use the simulation method to check.

---

7   Check spiral cable.

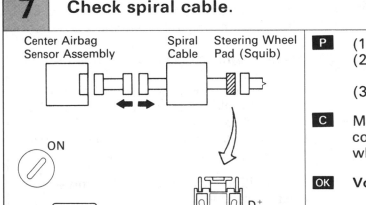

P
(1) Turn ignition switch LOCK.
(2) Disconnect connector between center airbag sensor assembly and spiral cable.
(3) Turn ignition switch ON.

C   Measure voltage at D^+ on spiral cable side of connector between spiral cable and steering wheel pad.

OK   **Voltage: 0 V**

AB0071
AB0119 AB0067

OK ⬡

NG ⟩   Repair or replace spiral cable.

Repair or replace harness or connector between center airbag sensor assembly and spiral cable.

DTC	13	Short in Squib Circuit (Between D⁺ Wire Harness and D⁻ Wire Harness)

CIRCUIT DESCRIPTION

The squib circuit consists of the center airbag sensor assembly, spiral cable and the steering wheel pad (squib). It causes the airbag to deploy when the airbag deployment conditions are satisfied.
For details of the function of each component, see FUNCTION OF COMPONENTS on page AB-7.
Diagnostic trouble code 13 is recorded when a short is detected in the D^+ wire harness and D^- wire harness of the squib circuit.

DTC No.	Diagnosis
13	• Short circuit between D^+ wire harness and D^- wire harness of squib. • Squib malfunction. • Spiral cable malfunction. • Center airbag sensor assembly malfunction.

DIAGNOSTIC CHART

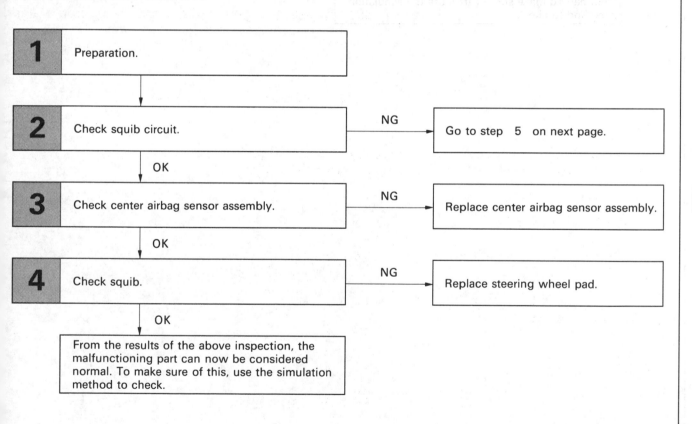

1 Preparation.

2 Check squib circuit. — NG → Go to step 5 on next page.

OK

3 Check center airbag sensor assembly. — NG → Replace center airbag sensor assembly.

OK

4 Check squib. — NG → Replace steering wheel pad.

OK

From the results of the above inspection, the malfunctioning part can now be considered normal. To make sure of this, use the simulation method to check.

AB

─ DIAGNOSTIC CHART (Cont'd) ─

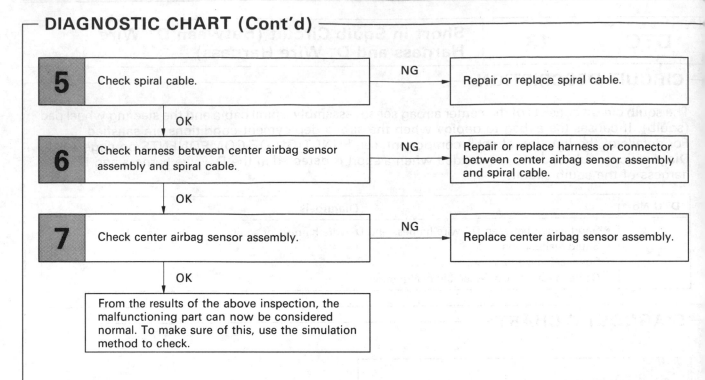

5 │ Check spiral cable. ──NG──▶ Repair or replace spiral cable.

│ OK

6 │ Check harness between center airbag sensor assembly and spiral cable. ──NG──▶ Repair or replace harness or connector between center airbag sensor assembly and spiral cable.

│ OK

7 │ Check center airbag sensor assembly. ──NG──▶ Replace center airbag sensor assembly.

│ OK

From the results of the above inspection, the malfunctioning part can now be considered normal. To make sure of this, use the simulation method to check.

AB

INSPECTION PROCEDURES

1	**Preparation.**

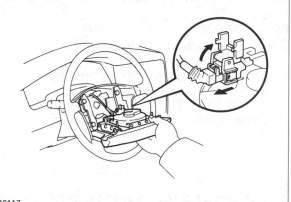

AB0117
AB0267

P (1) Disconnect battery negative (–) terminal cable, and wait at least 90 seconds.

(2) Remove steering wheel pad (See page AB-16).

Caution

When storing steering wheel pad, keep upper surface of the pad facing upward.

2	**Check squib circuit.**

Center Airbag   Spiral   Steering Wheel
Sensor Assembly   Cable   Pad (Squib)

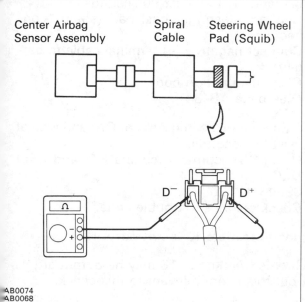

AB0074
AB0068

C Measure resistance between D⁺ and D⁻ on spiral cable side of connector between spiral cable and steering wheel pad.

OK Resistance: 1 kΩ or higher

OK	**NG** > Go to step **5** .

AB

3   **Check center airbag sensor assembly.**

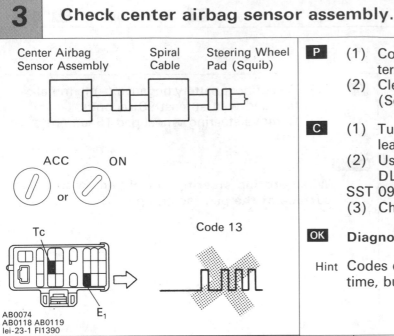

P (1) Connect negative (–) terminal cable to battery.
(2) Clear malfunction code
(See page AB-34).

C (1) Turn ignition switch ACC or ON, and wait at least 20 seconds.
(2) Using SST, connect terminals Tc and E_1 of DLC1.
SST 09843-18020
(3) Check diagnostic trouble code.

OK   **Diagnostic trouble code 13 is not output.**

Hint   Codes other than code 13 may be output at this time, but this is not relevant to this check.

OK

NG ❭ Replace center airbag sensor assembly.

---

4   **Check squib.**

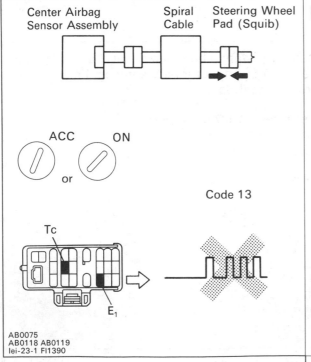

P (1) Turn ignition switch LOCK.
(2) Disconnect battery negative (–) terminal cable, and wait at least 90 seconds.
(3) Connect steering wheel pad (squib) connector.
(4) Connect negative (–) terminal cable to battery.
(5) Clear malfunction code
(See page AB-34).

C (1) Turn ignition switch ACC or ON, and wait at least 20 seconds.
(2) Using SST, connect terminals Tc and E_1 of DLC1.
SST 09843-18020
(3) Check diagnostic trouble code.

OK   **Diagnostic trouble 13 is not output.**

Hint   Codes other than code 13 may be output at this time, but this is not relevant to this check.

OK

NG ❭ Replace steering wheel pad.

From the results of the above inspection, the malfunctioning part can now be considered normal. To make sure of this, use the simulation method to check.

5   **Check spiral cable.**

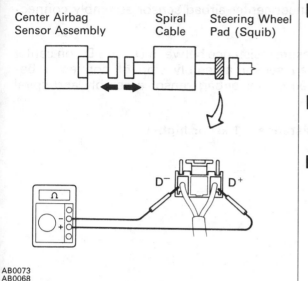

Center Airbag Sensor Assembly Spiral Cable Steering Wheel Pad (Squib)

D⁻ D⁺

AB0073
AB0068

P (1) Disconnect connector between center airbag sensor assembly and spiral cable.
(2) Release airbag activation prevention mechanism on center airbag sensor assembly side of spiral cable connector (See page AB-57).

C Measure resistance between D^+ and D^- on spiral cable side of connector between spiral cable and steering wheel pad.

OK Resistance: 1 MΩ or higher

OK

NG > Repair or replace spiral cable.

---

6   **Check harness between center airbag sensor assembly and spiral cable.**

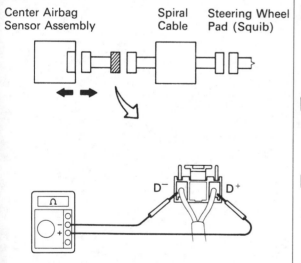

Center Airbag Sensor Assembly Spiral Cable Steering Wheel Pad (Squib)

D⁻ D⁺

AB0071
AB0068

P (1) Disconnect center airbag sensor assembly connector.
(2) Release airbag activation prevention mechanism on center airbag sensor assembly connector (See page AB-57).

C Measure resistance between D^+ and D^- on center airbag sensor assembly side of connector between center airbag sensor assembly and spiral cable.

OK Resistance: 1 MΩ or higher

OK

NG > Repair or replace harness or connector between center airbag sensor assembly and spiral cable.

7 | Check center airbag sensor assembly.

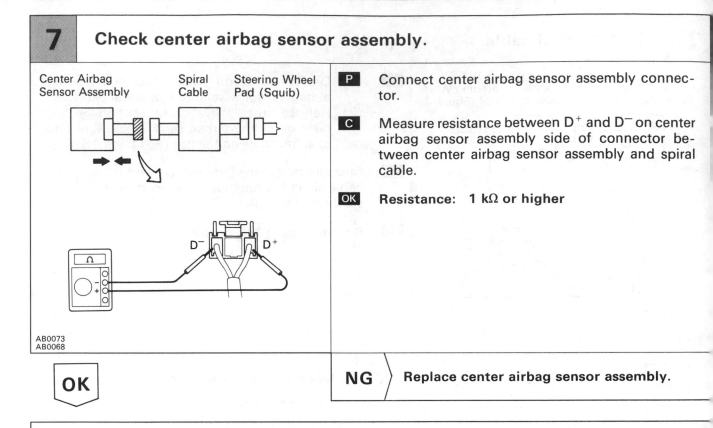

Center Airbag
Sensor Assembly   Spiral   Steering Wheel
                         Cable   Pad (Squib)

AB0073
AB0068

P   Connect center airbag sensor assembly connector.

C   Measure resistance between D$^+$ and D$^-$ on center airbag sensor assembly side of connector between center airbag sensor assembly and spiral cable.

OK   Resistance: 1 kΩ or higher

OK

NG ⟩ Replace center airbag sensor assembly.

From the results of the above inspection, the malfunctioning part can now be considered normal. To make sure of this, use the simulation method to check.

AB

RELEASE METHOD OF AIRBAG ACTIVATION PREVENTION MECHANISM

An airbag activation prevention mechanism is built into the connector for the squib circuit of the airbag system. When release of the airbag activation prevention mechanism is directed in the troubleshooting procedure, as shown in the illustration of the connectors 1 and 2 below, insert paper which is the same thickness as the terminal, between the terminal and the short spring.

CAUTION:

- **NEVER RELEASE** the airbag activation prevention mechanism on the steering wheel pad connector.

NOTICE:

- Do not release the airbag activation prevention mechanism unless specifically directed by the troubleshooting procedure.
- If the paper inserted is too thick the terminal and short spring may be damaged, so always use paper the same thickness as the male terminal.

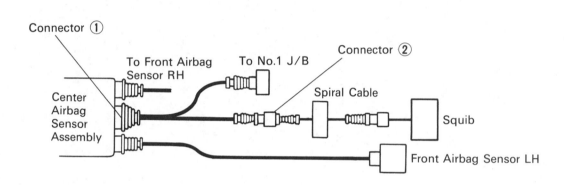

Connector 1
To Front Airbag Sensor RH
To No.1 J/B
Connector 2
Spiral Cable
Center Airbag Sensor Assembly
Squib
Front Airbag Sensor LH

Center Airbag Sensor Assembly Connector (Connector 1)

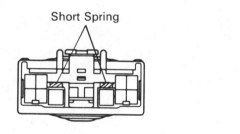

Short Spring

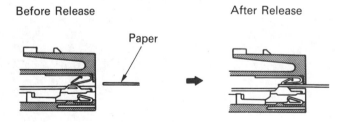

Before Release
Paper
After Release

Spiral Cable Connector (Connector 2)

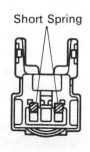

Short Spring

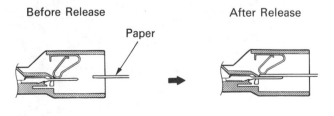

Before Release
Paper
After Release

AB0123
AB0129 AB0042 AB0043
AB0130 AB0045 AB0046

AB

DTC	14	Open in Squib Circuit

CIRCUIT DESCRIPTION

The squib circuit consists of the center airbag sensor assembly, spiral cable and the steering wheel pad (squib). It causes the airbag to deploy when the airbag deployment conditions are satisfied.
For details of the function of each component, see FUNCTION OF COMPONENTS on page AB-7.
Diagnostic trouble code 14 is recorded when an open is detected in the squib circuit.

DTC	Diagnosis
14	• Open circuit in D^+ wire harness or D^- wire harness of squib. • Squib malfunction. • Spiral cable malfunction. • Center airbag sensor assembly malfunction.

AB

– DIAGNOSTIC CHART

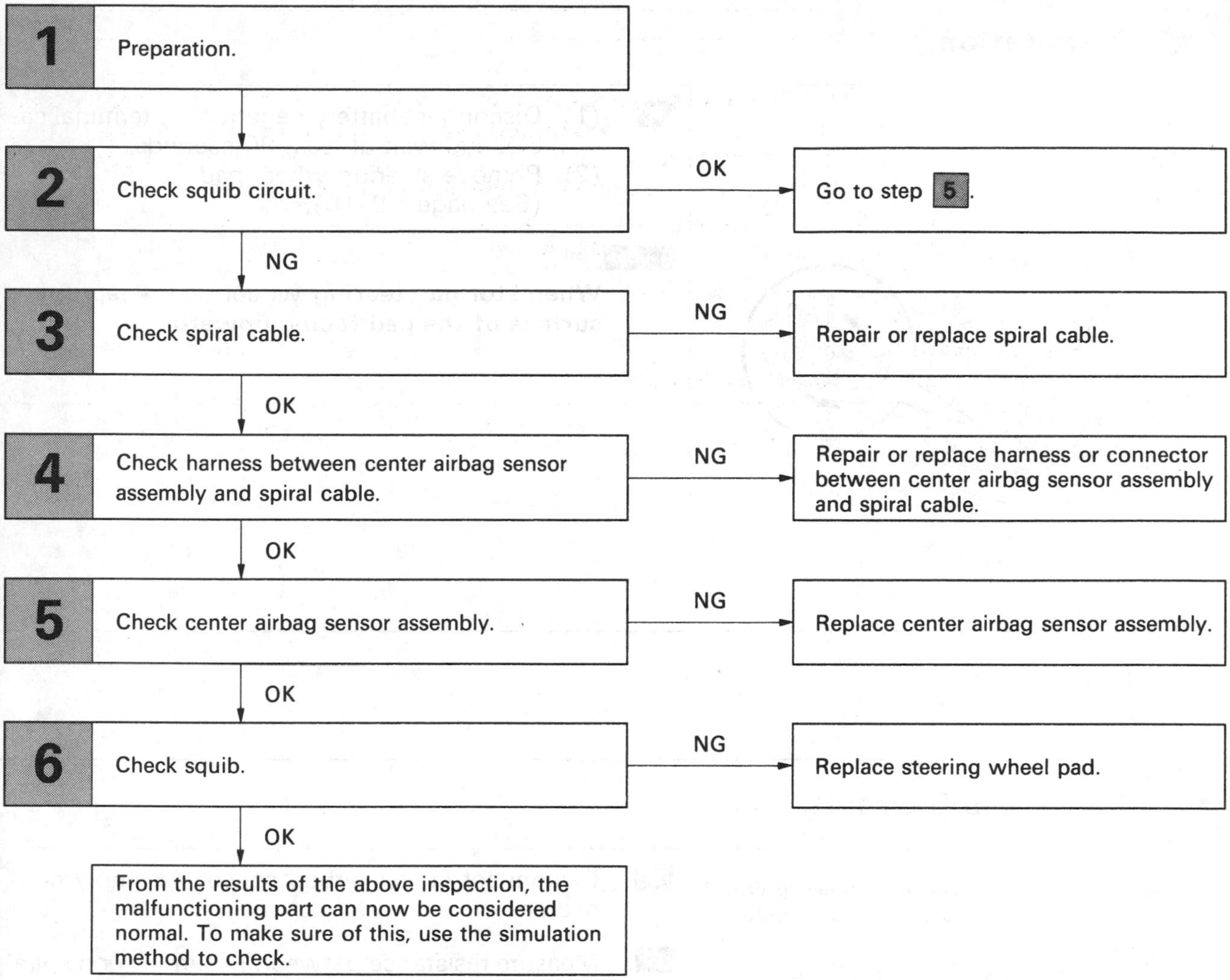

1 Preparation.

2 Check squib circuit. ──OK──> Go to step **5**.

│ NG

3 Check spiral cable. ──NG──> Repair or replace spiral cable.

│ OK

4 Check harness between center airbag sensor assembly and spiral cable. ──NG──> Repair or replace harness or connector between center airbag sensor assembly and spiral cable.

│ OK

5 Check center airbag sensor assembly. ──NG──> Replace center airbag sensor assembly.

│ OK

6 Check squib. ──NG──> Replace steering wheel pad.

│ OK

From the results of the above inspection, the malfunctioning part can now be considered normal. To make sure of this, use the simulation method to check.

AB

INSPECTION PROCEDURES

P Preparation   **C** Check

---

1   Preparation.

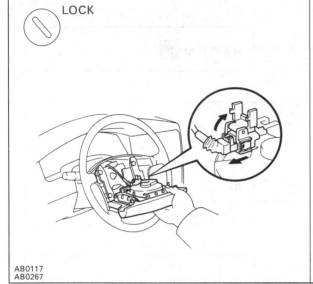

LOCK

AB0117
AB0267

P (1) Disconnect battery negative (−) terminal cable, and wait at least 90 seconds.
   (2) Remove steering wheel pad
     (See page AB-16).

Caution

When storing steering wheel pad, keep upper surface of the pad facing upward.

---

2   Check squib circuit.

Center Airbag   Spiral   Steering Wheel
Sensor Assembly Cable   Pad (Squib)

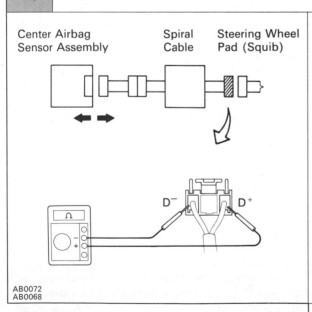

D^- D^+

AB0072
AB0068

P Disconnect center airbag sensor assembly connector.

C Measure resistance between D^+ and D^- on spiral cable side of connector between spiral cable and steering wheel pad.

OK **Resistance: Below 1 Ω**

NG

OK ⟩ Go to step **5** .

3 | Check spiral cable.

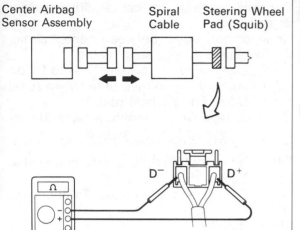

Center Airbag Sensor Assembly — Spiral Cable — Steering Wheel Pad (Squib)

D⁻   D⁺

AB0071
AB0068

P Disconnect connector between center airbag sensor assembly and spiral cable.

C Measure resistance between D⁺ and D⁻ on spiral cable side of connector between spiral cable and steering wheel pad.

OK Resistance: Below 1 Ω

OK

NG ⟩ Repair or replace spiral cable.

4 | Check harness between center airbag sensor assembly and spiral cable.

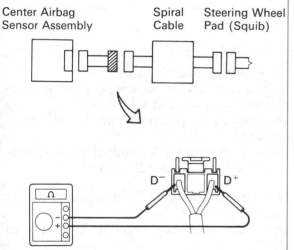

Center Airbag Sensor Assembly — Spiral Cable — Steering Wheel Pad (Squib)

D⁻   D⁺

B0071
B0068

C Measure resistance between D⁺ and D⁻ on center airbag sensor assembly side of connector between center airbag sensor assembly and spiral cable.

OK Resistance: Below 1 Ω

OK

NG ⟩ Repair or replace harness or connector between center airbag sensor assembly and spiral cable.

AB

5   Check center airbag sensor assembly.

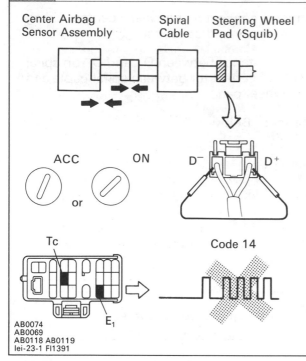

AB0074
AB0069
AB0118 AB0119
lei-23-1 FI1391

P
(1) Connect connector to center airbag sensor assembly.
(2) Connect connector between center airbag sensor assembly and spiral cable.
(3) Using a service wire, connect D^+ and D^- on spiral cable side of connector between spiral cable and steering wheel pad.
(4) Connect negative (–) terminal cable to battery, and wait at least 2 seconds.

C
(1) Turn ignition switch ACC or ON, and wait at least 20 seconds.
(2) Using SST, connect terminals Tc and E_1 of DLC1.
SST 09843-18020
(3) Check diagnostic trouble code.

OK   Diagnostic trouble code 14 is not output.

Hint Codes other than code 14 may be output at this time, but they are not relevant to this check.

OK

NG ⟩ Replace center airbag sensor assembly.

---

6   Check squib.

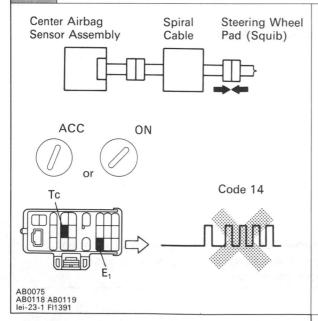

AB0075
AB0118 AB0119
lei-23-1 FI1391

P
(1) Turn ignition switch LOCK.
(2) Disconnect battery negative (–) terminal cable, and wait at least 90 seconds.
(3) Connect steering wheel pad (squib) connector.
(4) Connect negative (–) terminal cable to battery, and wait at least 2 seconds.

C
(1) Turn ignition switch ACC or ON, and wait at least 20 seconds.
(2) Using SST, connect terminals Tc and E_1 of DLC1.
SST 09843-18020
(3) Check diagnostic trouble code.

OK   Diagnostic trouble code 14 is not output.

Hint Codes other than code 14 may be output at this time, but they are not relevant to this check.

OK

NG ⟩ Replace steering wheel pad.

From the results of the above inspection, the malfunctioning part can now be considered normal. To make sure of this, use the simulation method to check.

DTC	15	Open in Front Airbag Sensor Circuit

— CIRCUIT DESCRIPTION

The front airbag sensor detects the deceleration force in a frontal collision and is located in the front fender on the left and right sides.

For details of the function of each component, see FUNCTION OF COMPONENTS on page AB-7.

Diagnostic trouble code 15 is recorded when an open is detected in the front airbag sensor circuit.

NOTICE: The front airbag sensor connector is equipped with an electrical connection check mechanism for the purpose of detecting an open in the front airbag sensor (See page AB-9). This mechanism is constructed so that when the terminals of the front airbag sensor have been connected (when the connector housing lock is in the locked condition), the connection detection pin on the wire harness side connects with the terminals for diagnosis use on the sensor side. If the connector is not properly connected, the diagnosis system may detect only a malfunction code, even though the airbag system is functioning normally.

When connecting the front airbag sensor connector, make sure it is connected properly. If diagnostic trouble code 15 is displayed after the front airbag sensor connector has been connected, check again that it is properly connected.

DTC No.	Diagnosis
15	• Open circuit in +S wire harness or –S wire harness of front airbag sensor. • Front airbag sensor malfunction. • Malfunction of electrical connection check mechanism of front airbag sensor. • Center airbag sensor assembly malfunction.

AB

DIAGNOSTIC CHART

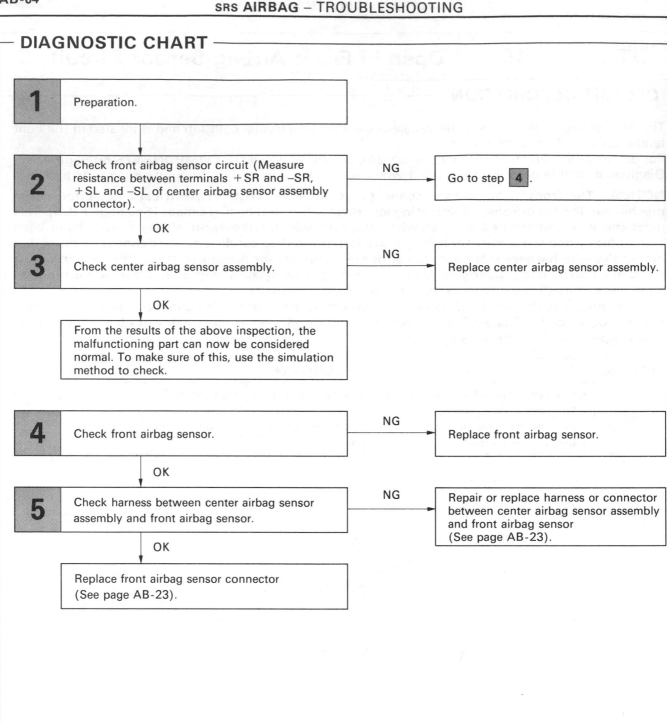

1 Preparation.

2 Check front airbag sensor circuit (Measure resistance between terminals +SR and −SR, +SL and −SL of center airbag sensor assembly connector). — NG → Go to step **4**.

OK

3 Check center airbag sensor assembly. — NG → Replace center airbag sensor assembly.

OK

From the results of the above inspection, the malfunctioning part can now be considered normal. To make sure of this, use the simulation method to check.

4 Check front airbag sensor. — NG → Replace front airbag sensor.

OK

5 Check harness between center airbag sensor assembly and front airbag sensor. — NG → Repair or replace harness or connector between center airbag sensor assembly and front airbag sensor (See page AB-23).

OK

Replace front airbag sensor connector (See page AB-23).

AB

INSPECTION PROCEDURES

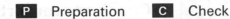 **P** Preparation   **C** Check

1   Preparation.

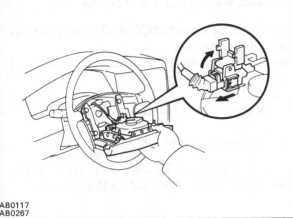

P (1) Disconnect battery negative (–) terminal cable, and wait at least 90 seconds.
(2) Remove steering wheel pad
(See page AB-16).

Caution

When storing steering wheel pad, keep upper surface of pad facing upward.

AB0117
AB0267

2   Check front airbag sensor circuit (Measure resistance between terminals +SR and –SR, +SL and –SL of center airbag sensor assembly connector.).

Center Airbag Sensor Assembly

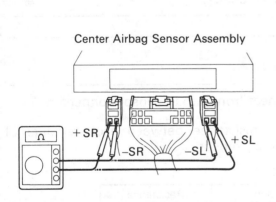

AB0097

P Disconnect center airbag sensor assembly connectors.

C Measure resistance between terminals +SR and –SR, +SL and –SL of harness side connector of center airbag sensor assembly.

OK Resistance: 755 Ω – 855 Ω

 OK

NG Go to step **4** .

3   Check center airbag sensor assembly.

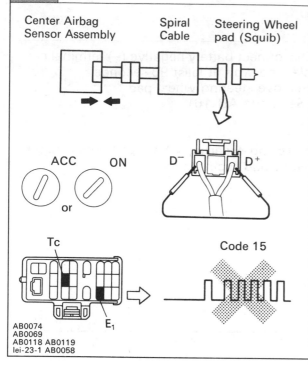

Center Airbag Sensor Assembly   Spiral Cable   Steering Wheel pad (Squib)

ACC   ON   or

D^- D^+

Tc   Code 15

E_1

AB0074
AB0069
AB0118 AB0119
lei-23-1 AB0058

P   (1) Connect connectors to center airbag sensor assembly.
(2) Using a service wire, connect D^+ and D^- on spiral cable side of connector between spiral cable and steering wheel pad.
(3) Connect negative (–) terminal cable to battery, and wait at least 2 seconds.

C   (1) Turn ignition switch ACC or ON, and wait at least 20 seconds.
(2) Using SST, connect terminals Tc and E_1 of DLC1.
SST 09843-18020
(3) Check diagnostic trouble code.

OK   **Diagnostic trouble code 15 is not output.**

Hint   Codes other than code 15 may be output at this time, but they are not relevant to this check.

OK

NG ⟩ Replace center airbag sensor assembly.

From the results of the above inspection, the malfunctioning part can now be considered normal. To make sure of this, use the simulation method to check.

AB

---

4   Check front airbag sensor.

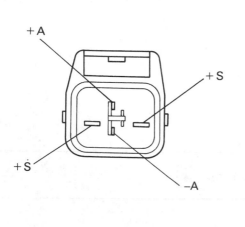

+A

+S

+S

–A

AB0034

P   Disconnect front airbag sensor connector.

C   Measure resistance between each terminal of front airbag sensor.

OK

Terminal	Resistance
$\oplus$ S – $\oplus$ A	Below 1 Ω
$\oplus$ S – $\ominus$ S	1 MΩ or Higher
$\ominus$ S – $\ominus$ A	755 Ω – 885 Ω

Notice

• Do not press ohmmeter probes too strongly against terminals of front airbag sensor.
• Make sure the front airbag sensor connector is properly connected.

OK

NG ⟩ Replace front airbag sensor.

5 | **Check harness between center airbag sensor assembly and front airbag sensor.**

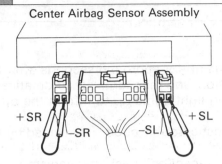

Center Airbag Sensor Assembly

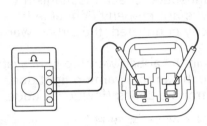

+SR −SR −SL +SL

AB0098
AB0039

P (1) Disconnect center airbag sensor assembly connectors.

(2) Using service wires, connect +SR and −SR, +SL and −SL on the wire harness side of the center airbag sensor assembly connectors.

C Measure resistance between terminals +SR and −SR, +SL and −SL of harness side connector of front airbag sensor.

OK **Resistance: Below 1 Ω**

Notice

- Lightly touch ohmmeter probes at position shown in illustration.
- Make sure the front airbag sensor connector is properly connected.

OK

NG ⟩ Repair or replace harness or connector between center airbag sensor assembly and front airbag sensor (See page AB-23).

Replace front airbag sensor connector (See page AB-23).

DTC	22	Airbag Warning Light System Malfunction

CIRCUIT DESCRIPTION

The airbag warning light is located on the combination meter.

When the airbag system is normal, the airbag warning light lights up for approx. 6 seconds after the ignition switch is turned from LOCK position to ACC or ON position, and then turns off automatically.

If there is a malfunction in the airbag system, the airbag warning light lights up to inform the driver of the abnormality.

When terminals Tc and E_1 of the DLC1 are connected, the diagnostic trouble code is displayed by the blinking of the airbag warning light.

The airbag warning light circuit is equipped with an electrical connection check mechanism which detects when the connector to the center airbag sensor assembly is not properly connected.

If the connector to the center airbag sensor assembly is not properly connected, the airbag warning light will not light up.

Diagnostic trouble code 22 is recorded when a malfunction occurs in the airbag warning light system.

If an OPEN malfunction occurs in the airbag warning light system, the airbag warning light does not light up, so that until the malfunction is repaired, the diagnostic trouble codes (including code 22) cannot be confirmed.

DTC No.	Diagnosis
22	• Open circuit in airbag warning light system. • Center airbag sensor assembly malfunction.

AB

─ DIAGNOSTIC CHART ─

Troubleshooting for this system is different for when the airbag warning light does not light up and for when diagnostic trouble code 22 is output. Confirm the problem symptoms first before selecting the appropriate troubleshooting procedure.

HINT: If airbag warning light does not light up, perform the following troubleshooting.

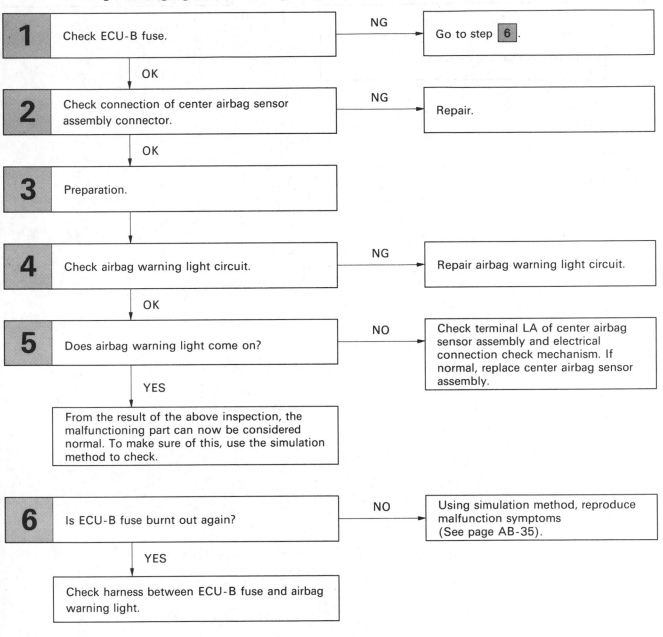

1 Check ECU-B fuse. ──NG──▶ Go to step **6**.

│ OK

2 Check connection of center airbag sensor assembly connector. ──NG──▶ Repair.

│ OK

3 Preparation.

│

4 Check airbag warning light circuit. ──NG──▶ Repair airbag warning light circuit.

│ OK

5 Does airbag warning light come on? ──NO──▶ Check terminal LA of center airbag sensor assembly and electrical connection check mechanism. If normal, replace center airbag sensor assembly.

│ YES

From the result of the above inspection, the malfunctioning part can now be considered normal. To make sure of this, use the simulation method to check.

6 Is ECU-B fuse burnt out again? ──NO──▶ Using simulation method, reproduce malfunction symptoms (See page AB-35).

│ YES

Check harness between ECU-B fuse and airbag warning light.

AB

DIAGNOSTIC CHART

HINT: If diagnostic trouble code 22 is output, perform the following troubleshooting:

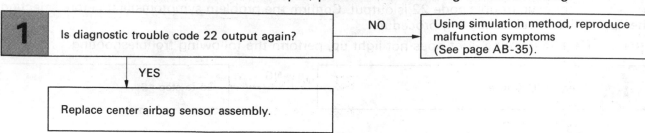

1 | Is diagnostic trouble code 22 output again? → NO → Using simulation method, reproduce malfunction symptoms (See page AB-35).

↓ YES

Replace center airbag sensor assembly.

INSPECTION PROCEDURES

P Preparation   C Check

HINT: If airbag warning light does not light up, perform the following troubleshooting:

1	**Check ECU-B fuse.**

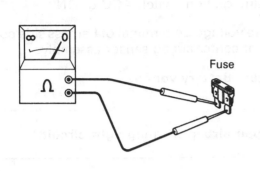

FI0044

P	Remove ECU-B fuse.
C	Check continuity of ECU-B fuse.
OK	**Continuity.**
Hint	• Fuse may be burnt out even if it appears to be OK during visual inspection. • If fuse is OK, install it.

OK

NG ⟩ Go to step **6**.

2	**Check connection of center airbag sensor assembly connector.**

OK

NG ⟩ Repair.

3	**Preparation.**

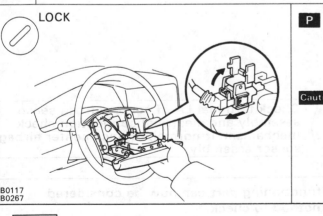

LOCK

AB0117
AB0267

P	(1) Disconnect battery negative (–) terminal cable, and wait at least 90 seconds. (2) Remove steering wheel pad (See page AB-16).

Caution

When storing steering wheel pad, keep upper surface of pad facing upward.

AB

4   Check airbag warning light circuit.

P (1) Disconnect center airbag sensor assembly connector.
(2) Connect negative (–) terminal cable to battery.
(3) Turn ignition switch ACC or ON.

C Measure voltage LA terminal of harness side connector of center airbag sensor assembly.

OK Voltage: Battery voltage.

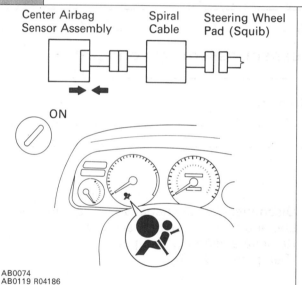

AB0119
AB0093

OK

NG ⟩ Repair airbag warning light circuit.

5   Does airbag warning light come on?

P (1) Disconnect negative (–) terminal cable from battery.
(2) Connect center airbag sensor assembly connector.
(3) Connect negative (–) terminal cable to battery.
(4) Turn ignition switch ACC or ON.

C Check operation of airbag warning light.

Center Airbag Sensor Assembly   Spiral Cable   Steering Wheel Pad (Squib)

AB0074
AB0119 R04186

YES

NO ⟩ Check terminal LA of center airbag sensor assembly and electrical connection check mechanism. If normal, replace center airbag sensor assembly.

From the results of the above inspection, the malfunctioning part can now be considered normal. To make sure of this, use the simulation method to check.

6   Is new ECU-B fuse burnt out again?

YES

NO ⟩ Using simulation method, reproduce malfunction symptoms (See page AB-35).

Check harness between ECU-B fuse and airbag warning light.

HINT: If diagnostic code 22 is output, perform the following troubleshooting:

1   **Is diagnostic trouble code 22 output again?**

ACC   ON
       or

Tc

Code 22

E₁

AB0118 AB0119
lei-23-1 FI1392

P   Clear malfunction code.
(See page AB-34).

C   (1)   Turn ignition switch LOCK, and wait at least
2 seconds.
(2)   Turn ignition switch ACC or ON, and wait at
least 20 seconds.
(3)   Using SST, connect terminals Tc and E_1 of
DLC1.
SST 09843-18020
(4)   Check diagnostic trouble code.

YES

NO   Using simulation method, reproduce
malfunction symptoms (See page AB-35).

Replace center airbag sensor assembly.

AB

DTC	31	**Center Airbag Sensor Assembly Malfunction**

CIRCUIT DESCRIPTION

The center airbag sensor assembly consists of a center a airbag sensor, safing sensors, ignition control and drive circuit, diagnosis circuit, etc.

It receives signals from the airbag sensors, judges whether or not the airbag must be activated, and diagnoses system malfunction.

Diagnostic trouble code 31 is recorded when occurrence of a malfunction in the center airbag sensor assembly is detected.

DTC No.	Diagnosis
31	• Center airbag sensor assembly malfunction.

DIAGNOSTIC CHART

HINT: When a malfunction code other than code 31 is displayed at the same time, first repair the malfunction indicated by the malfunction code other than code 31.

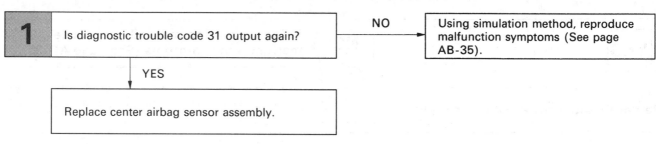

1 Is diagnostic trouble code 31 output again?

NO → Using simulation method, reproduce malfunction symptoms (See page AB-35).

YES ↓

Replace center airbag sensor assembly.

INSPECTION PROCEDURES

HINT: When a malfunction code other than code 31 is displayed at the same time, first repair the malfunction indicated by the malfunction code other than code 31.

P Preparation **C** Check

1	**Is diagnostic trouble code 31 output again?**

ACC or ON Tc Code 31 E₁ AB0118 AB0119 lei-23-1 FI1394	**P** Clear malfunction code. (See page AB-34). **C** (1) Turn ignition switch LOCK, and wait at least 20 seconds. (2) Turn ignition switch ACC or ON, and wait at least 20 seconds. (3) Repeat operation in step (1) and (2) at least 5 times. (4) Using SST, connect terminals Tc and E_1 of DLC1. SST 09843-18020 (5) Check diagnostic trouble code.
YES	**NO** Using simulation method, reproduce malfunction symptoms (See page AB-35).

Replace center airbag sensor assembly.

AB

Airbag Warning Light System (Always Lit Up)

CIRCUIT DESCRIPTION

The airbag warning light is located on the combination meter.
When the airbag system is normal, the airbag warning light lights up for approx. 6 seconds after the ignition switch is turned from LOCK position to ACC or ON position, and then turns off automatically.
If there is a malfunction in the airbag system, the airbag warning light lights up to inform the driver of the abnormality.
When terminals Tc and E_1 of the DLC1 are connected, the diagnostic trouble code is displayed by the blinking of the airbag warning light.

DIAGNOSTIC CHART

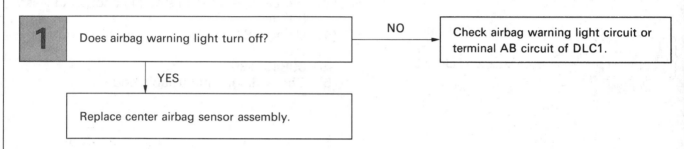

| **1** | Does airbag warning light turn off? | NO → | Check airbag warning light circuit or terminal AB circuit of DLC1. |

YES ↓

Replace center airbag sensor assembly.

AB

INSPECTION PROCEDURES

P Preparation   C Check

---

1 | **Does airbag warning light turn off?**

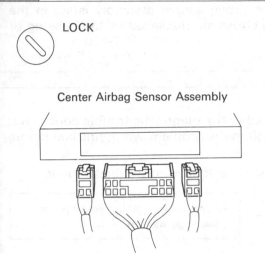

LOCK

Center Airbag Sensor Assembly

AB0117
AB0092

P (1) Turn ignition switch LOCK.
(2) Disconnect battery negative (–) terminal cable, and wait at least 90 seconds.
(3) Disconnect center airbag sensor assembly connector.
(4) Connect negative (–) terminal cable to battery.

C Check operation of airbag warning light.

YES

NO ⟩ **Check airbag warning light circuit or terminal AB circuit of DLC1.**

Replace center airbag sensor assembly.

AB

Tc Terminal Circuit

CIRCUIT DESCRIPTION

By connecting terminals Tc and E_1 of the DLC1, the center airbag sensor assembly is set in the diagnostic trouble code output mode. The diagnostic trouble codes are displayed by the blinking of the airbag warning light.

DIAGNOSTIC CHART

Troubleshooting for this system is different depending on whether the diagnostic trouble code is not displayed or is displayed without a DTC check procedure. Confirm the problem symptoms first before selecting the appropriate troubleshooting procedure.

HINT: If the diagnostic trouble code is not displayed, perform the following troubleshooting:

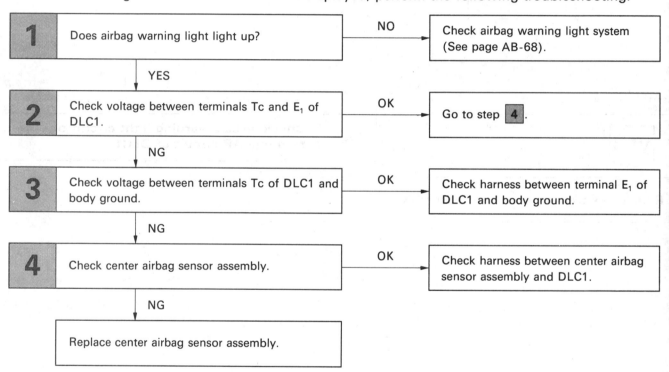

1 Does airbag warning light light up? — **NO** → Check airbag warning light system (See page AB-68).

↓ **YES**

2 Check voltage between terminals Tc and E_1 of DLC1. — **OK** → Go to step **4**.

↓ **NG**

3 Check voltage between terminals Tc of DLC1 and body ground. — **OK** → Check harness between terminal E_1 of DLC1 and body ground.

↓ **NG**

4 Check center airbag sensor assembly. — **OK** → Check harness between center airbag sensor assembly and DLC1.

↓ **NG**

Replace center airbag sensor assembly.

HINT: If the diagnostic trouble code is displayed without a DTC check procedure, perform the following troubleshooting:

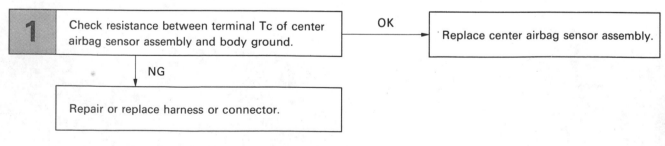

1 Check resistance between terminal Tc of center airbag sensor assembly and body ground. — **OK** → Replace center airbag sensor assembly.

↓ **NG**

Repair or replace harness or connector.

AB

INSPECTION PROCEDURES

P Preparation   C Check

HINT: If the diagnostic trouble code is not displayed, perform the following troubleshooting:

---

1 | **Does airbag warning light light up for approx. 6 seconds?**

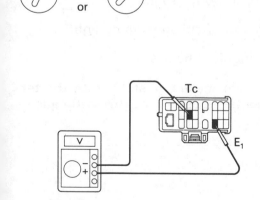

AB0117 AB0118 AB0119
R04186

C Check operation of airbag warning light after ignition switch turned from LOCK position to ACC or ON position.

YES

NO 〉 **Check airbag warning light system.** (See page AB-76).

---

2 | **Check voltage between terminals Tc and E₁ of DLC1.**

AB0118 AB0119
R04194

P Turn ignition switch ACC or ON.

C Measure voltage between terminals Tc and E₁ of DLC1.

OK **Voltage: Battery voltage**

NG

OK   Go to step **4** .

AB

3   Check voltage between terminals Tc of DLC1 and body ground.

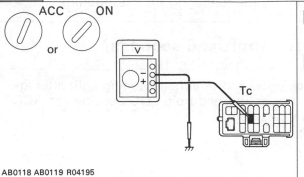

C   Measure voltage between terminals Tc of DLC1 and body ground.

OK   Voltage: Battery voltage

AB0118 AB0119 R04195

NG

OK ⟩ Check harness between terminal E₁ of DLC1 and body ground.

---

4   Check center airbag sensor assembly.

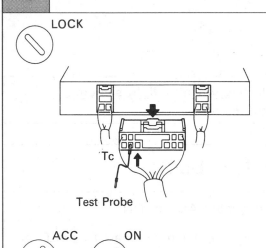

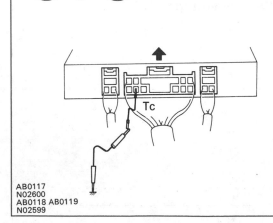

AB0117
N02600
AB0118 AB0119
N02599

P   (1) Turn ignition switch to lock.
(2) Disconnect battery negative (–) terminal cable, and wait at least 90 seconds.
(3) Disconnect center airbag sensor assembly connector.
(4) Insert test probe into terminal Tc from back side as shown.
(5) Connect center airbag sensor assembly connector with check pin.
(6) Connect battery negative (–) terminal cable.
(7) Turn ignition switch ACC or ON and wait at least 20 seconds.
(8) Using service wire, connect test probe of terminal Tc to body ground.

C   Check operation of airbag warning light.

OK   Airbag warning light comes on.

NOTICE: Never make a mistake with the terminal connection position as this will cause a malfunction.

NG

OK ⟩ Check harness between center airbag sensor assembly and DLC1.

Replace center airbag sensor assembly.

AB

HINT: If the diagnostic trouble code is displayed without a DTC check procedure, perform the following troubleshooting.

---

1 | **Check resistance between terminal Tc of center airbag sensor assembly and body ground.**

LOCK

Center Airbag Sensor Assembly

Tc

AB0117
AB0189

P
(1) Turn ignition switch LOCK.
(2) Disconnect battery negative (–) terminal cable, and wait at least 90 seconds.
(3) Disconnect center airbag sensor assembly connector.

C Check resistance between terminal Tc of center airbag sensor assembly connector and body ground.

OK **Resistance: 1 MΩ or Higher**

NG

OK ⟩ **Replace center airbag sensor assembly.**

Repair or replace harness or connector.

AB

AB0259

STEERING WHEEL PAD DISPOSAL (WITH AIRBAG)

When scrapping vehicles equipped with an airbag system or disposing of a steering wheel pad (with airbag), always first deploy the airbag in accordance with the procedure described below.

If any abnormality occurs with the airbag deployment, contact the SERVICE DEPT. of TOYOTA MOTOR SALES, U.S.A. INC.

Never dispose of a steering wheel pad which has an undeployed airbag.

When disposing of a steering wheel pad with an airbag deployed in a collision, follow the same procedure given under "AIRBAG DEPLOYMENT PROCEDURE (WHEN SCRAPPING THE VEHICLE), part 5, DISPOSAL OF STEERING WHEEL PAD (WITH AIRBAG)" (See page AB-84).

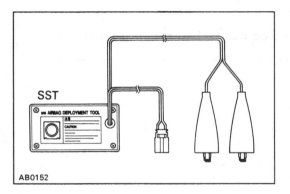

SST

AB0152

PRECAUTIONS FOR AIRBAG DEPLOYMENT

1. The airbag produces a sizeable exploding sound when it deploys, so perform the operation out-of-doors and where it will not create a nuisance to nearby residents.
2. When deploying the airbag, always use the specified SST: SRS AIRBAG DEPLOYMENT TOOL (SST 09082-00700). Perform the operation in a place away from electrical noise.
3. When deploying an airbag, perform the operation from at least 10 m (33 ft) away from the steering wheel pad.
4. The steering wheel pad is very hot when the airbag is deployed, so leave it alone for at least 30 minutes after deployment.
5. Use gloves and safety glasses when handling a steering wheel pad with deployed airbag.
6. Always wash your hands with water after completing the operation.
7. Do not apply water, etc. to a steering wheel pad with deployed airbag.

AIRBAG DEPLOYMENT PROCEDURE (WHEN SCRAPPING VEHICLE)

HINT: Have a battery ready as the power source to deploy the airbag.

LOCK

AB0117
FI1066

1. **DISCONNECT NEGATIVE (–) TERMINAL CABLE FROM BATTERY**
   CAUTION: Work must be started after approx. 90 seconds or longer from the time the ignition switch is turned to the LOCK position and the negative (–) terminal cable is disconnected from the battery (See page AB-2).

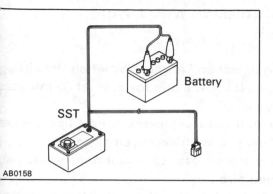

2. **CONFIRM FUNCTIONING OF SST (SEE PAGE AB-88)**
   SST 09082-00700

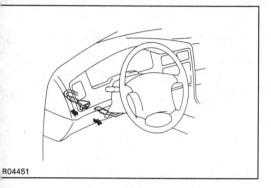

3. **INSTALL SST**
   CAUTION: Check that there is no looseness in the steering wheel and steering wheel pad.
   (a) Remove the instrument panel lower finish panel.
   (b) Disconnect the airbag connector of the spiral cable.

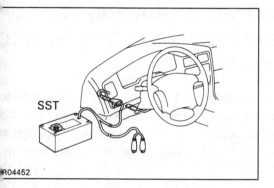

(c) Connect the SST connector to the airbag connector of the spiral cable.
   SST 09082-00700
(d) Move the SST to at least 10 m (33 ft) from the front of the vehicle.
(e) Close all the doors and windows of the vehicle.
   NOTICE: Take care not to damage the SST wire harness.
(f) Connect the SST red clip to the battery positive (+) terminal and the black clip to the battery negative (–) terminal.

AB

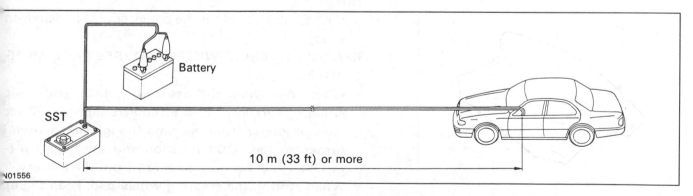

10 m (33 ft) or more

4. **DEPLOY AIRBAG**
   (a) Confirm that no-one is inside the vehicle or within 10 m (33 ft) of the vehicle.
   (b) Press the SST activation switch and deploy the airbag.
   HINT: The airbag deploys simultaneously as the LED of the SST activation switch lights up.

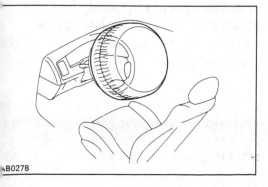

5. **DISPOSAL OF STEERING WHEEL PAD (WITH AIRBAG)**
   CAUTION:
   - **The steering wheel pad is very hot when the airbag is deployed, so leave it alone for at least 30 minutes after deployment.**
   - **Use gloves and safety glasses when handling a steering wheel pad with deployed airbag.**
   - **Do not apply water, etc. to a steering wheel pad with deployed airbag.**
   - **Always wash your hands with water after completing the operation.**

(a) When scrapping a vehicle, deploy the airbag and scrap the vehicle with the steering wheel pad still installed.

(b) When moving a vehicle for scrapping which has a steering wheel pad with deployed airbag, use gloves and safety glasses.

AIRBAG DEPLOYMENT PROCEDURE (PROCEDURE FOR DISPOSAL OF STEERING WHEEL PAD ONLY)

When disposing of the steering wheel pad (with airbag) only, never use the customer's vehicle to deploy the airbag. Remove the steering wheel pad from the vehicle and be sure to follow the procedure given below when deploying the airbag.

   HINT:
   - Have a battery ready as the power source to deploy the airbag.

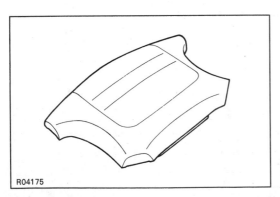

R04175

1. **REMOVE STEERING WHEEL PAD (SEE PAGE AB-16)**
   CAUTION:
   - **When removing the steering wheel pad (with airbag), work must be started after approx. 90 seconds or longer from the time the ignition switch is turned to the LOCK position and the negative (–) terminal cable is disconnected from the battery.**
   - **When storing the steering wheel pad, keep the upper surface of the pad facing upward.**

2. **REMOVE STEERING WHEEL PAD CONNECTOR**
   Remove the connector on the steering wheel pad rear surface from the inflater cover.

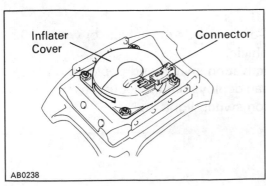

Inflater Cover   Connector

AB0238

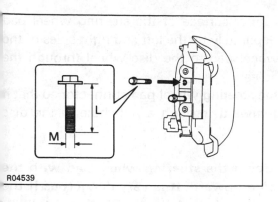

R04539

3.   FIX STEERING WHEEL PAD TO DISC WHEEL WITH TIRE

(a) Install bolts with washers in the three bolt holes in the steering wheel pad.

Bolt: L   35.0 mm (1.378 in.)
          M   6.0 mm
          Pitch 1.0 mm

NOTICE: Tighten the bolts by hand until the bolts become difficult to turn.

Do not tighten the bolts too much.

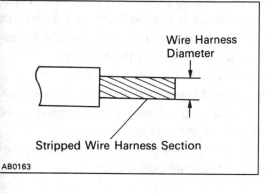

Wire Harness Diameter

Stripped Wire Harness Section

AB0163

(b) Using a service-purpose wire harness for vehicle, tie down the steering wheel pad to the disc wheel.

Wire harness: Stripped wire harness section 1.25 mm^2 or more (0.002 in.^{2} or more)

HINT: To calculate the square of the stripped wire harness section –

$$\text{Square} = \frac{3.14 \times (\text{Diameter})^2}{4}$$

CAUTION: If a wire harness which is too thin or some other thing is used to tie down the steering wheel pad, it may be snapped by the shock when the airbag is deployed, this is highly dangerous.

Always use a wire harness for vehicle use which is at least 1.25 mm^2 (0.002 in.^{2}).

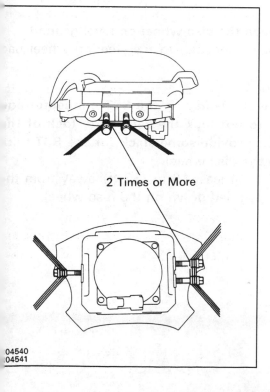

2 Times or More

04540
04541

(1) Using 3 wire harnesses, wrap the wire harnesses at least 2 times each around the bolts installed on the left and right sides of the steering wheel pad.

CAUTION: Tightly wind the wire harness around the bolts so that there is no slack.

If there is slackness in the wire harness, the steering wheel pad may come loose due to the shock when the airbag is deployed, this is highly dangerous.

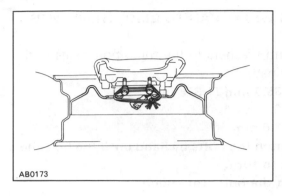

AB0173

(2) Face the upper surface of the steering wheel pad upward. Separately tie the left and right sides of the steering wheel pad to the disc wheel through the hub nut holes.

Position the steering wheel pad connector so that it hangs downward through a hub hole in the disc wheel.

CAUTION:

- **Always tie down the steering wheel pad with the pad side facing upward. It is very dangerous if the steering wheel pad is tied down with the metal surface facing upward, as the wire harness will be cut by the shock of the airbag deploying and the steering wheel pad will be thrown into the air.**
- **Make sure that the wire harness is tight.**
  It is very dangerous if looseness in the wire harness results in the steering wheel pad coming free through the shock of the airbag deploying.

NOTICE: The disc wheel will be marked by airbag deployment, so use a redundant disc wheel.

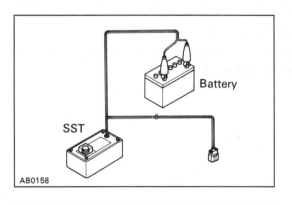

AB0158

4. CONFIRM FUNCTIONING OF SST (SEE PAGE AB-88)
   SST 09082-00700

AB

AB0175

5. INSTALL SST
   CAUTION: Place the disc wheel on level ground.
   (a) Connect the SST connector to the steering wheel pad connector.
   SST 09082-00700
   NOTICE: To avoid damaging the SST connector and wire harness, do not lock the secondary lock of the twin lock. Also, provide some slack for the SST wire harness inside the disc wheel.
   (b) Move the SST to at least 10 m (33 ft) away from the steering wheel pad tied down on the disc wheel.

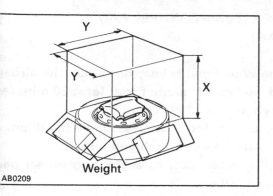

AB0209

6. COVER STEERING WHEEL PAD WITH CARDBOARD BOX OR TIRES
(Covering Method Using Cardboard Box)
Cover the steering wheel pad with the cardboard box and weigh the cardboard box down in four places with a at least 196 N (20 kgf, 44 lbf).

Size of cardboard box: Must exceed the following dimensions –

X = 460 mm (18.11 in.)

When dimension Y of the cardboard box exceeds the diameter of the disc wheel with tire the steering wheel pad is ties to –

X = 460 mm (18.11 in.) + width of tire

Y = 650 mm (25.59 in.)

NOTICE: If a cardboard box smaller than the size specified is used, the cardboard box will be broken by the shock of the airbag deployment.

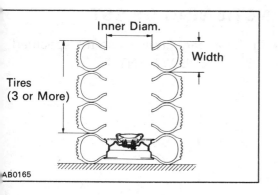

AB0165

(Covering Method Using Tires)
Place at least three tires without disc wheel on top of the disc wheel with tire to which the steering wheel pad is tied.

Tire size: Must exceed the following dimensions –
   Width   185 mm (7.28 in.)
   Inner diam.   360 mm (14.17 in.)

CAUTION: Do not use tires with disc wheels.
NOTICE: The tires may be marked by the airbag deployment, so use redundant tires.

7. AIRBAG DEPLOYMENT

(a) Connect the SST red clip to the battery positive (+) terminal and the black clip to the battery negative (−) terminal.

(b) Confirm that no-one is within 10 m (33 ft) of the disc wheel the steering wheel pad is tied to.

(c) Press the SST activation switch and deploy the airbag.
   HINT: The airbag deploys simultaneously at the LED of the SST activation switch lights up.

AB

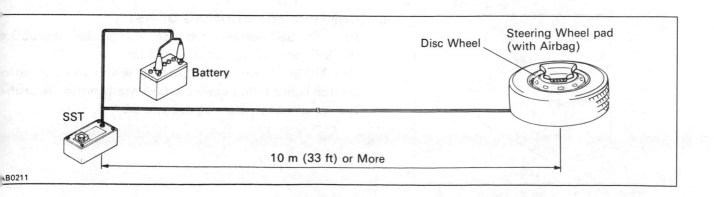

AB0211

**8. DISPOSAL OF STEERING WHEEL PAD
(WITH AIRBAG)**

CAUTION:
- The steering wheel pad is very hot when the airbag is deployed, so leave it alone for at least **30 minutes** after deployment.
- Use gloves and safety glasses when handling a steering wheel pad with deployed airbag.
- Do not apply water, etc. to a steering wheel pad with deployed airbag.
- Always wash your hands with water after completing the operation.

(a) Remove the steering wheel pad from the disc wheel.

(b) Place the steering wheel pad in a vinyl bag, tie the end tightly and dispose of it the same way as other general parts.

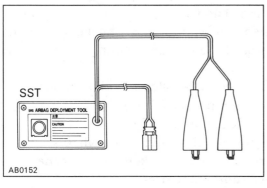

AB0166

CONFIRM FUNCTIONING OF SST

When deploying the airbag, always use the specified SST: SRS AIRBAG DEPLOYMENT TOOL.
SST 09082-00700

SST

AB0152

AB

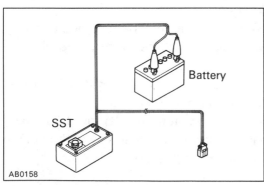

SST

Battery

SST

AB0158

1. CONNECT SST TO BATTERY

Connect the red clip of the SST to the battery positive (+) terminal and the black clip to the battery negative (–) terminal.

HINT: Do not connect the yellow connector which connects with the airbag system.

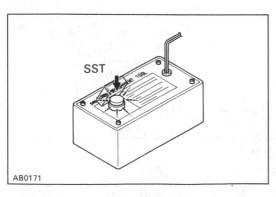

SST

AB0171

2. CONFIRM FUNCTIONING OF SST

Press the SST activation switch, and confirm the LED of the SST activation switch lights up.

CAUTION: If the LES lights up when the activation switch is not being pressed, SST malfunction is probable, so difinitely do not use the SST.

SERVICE SPECIFICATIONS
SERVICE DATA

Terminal	Front airbag sensor resistance
$\oplus$ S – $\oplus$ A	Less than 1 Ω
$\oplus$ S – $\ominus$ S	∞
$\ominus$ S – $\ominus$ A	755 – 885 Ω

TORQUE SPECIFICATIONS

Part tightened	N·m	kgf·cm	ft·lbf
Steering wheel	35	360	26
Steering wheel pad	8.8	90	78 in.·lbf
Front airbag sensor	25	260	19
Center airbag sensor assembly	13	130	9

AB

AB

BODY ELECTRICAL SYSTEM

Example:

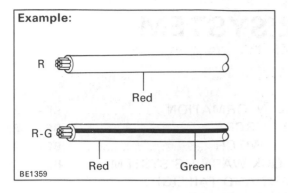

R — Red

R-G — Red — Green

BE1359

GENERAL INFORMATION

WIRING COLOR CODE

Wire Colors are indicated by an alphabetical code.

B = Black   L = Blue   R = Red
BR = Brown   LG = Light Green   V = Violet
G = Green   O = Orange   W = White
GR = Gray   P = Pink   Y = Yellow

The first letter indicates the basic wire color and th
second letter indicates the color of the stripe.

CONNECTOR

1.   PIN NUMBER OF FEMALE CONNECTOR

Numbered in order from upper left to lower right.

2.   PIN NUMBER OF MALE CONNECTOR

Numbered in order from upper right to lower left.

HINT: When connectors with different or the sam
number of terminals are used with the same parts, eac
connector name (letter of the alphabet) and pin numbe
is specified.

Example:

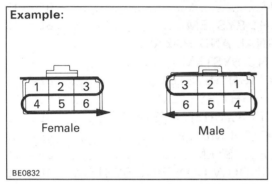

Female   Male

BE0832

e.g. A-7 = No.7 pin of connector "A"

Example:

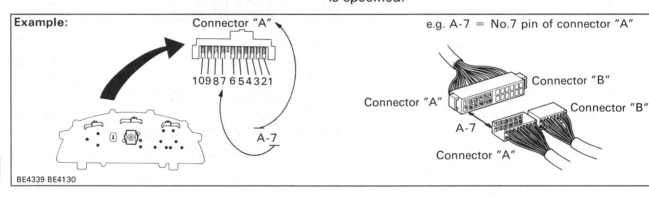

BE4339 BE4130

3.   DISTINCTION OF MALE AND FEMALE CONNECTOR

Male and female connectors are distinguished by shap
of their internal pins.

(a)   All connectors are shown from the open end, and th
lock is on top.

(b)   To pull apart the connectors, pull on the connector itsel
not the wires.

HINT: Check to see what kind of connector you ar
disconnecting before pulling apart.

Example:

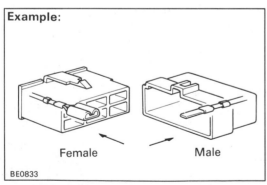

Female   Male

BE0833

Example:

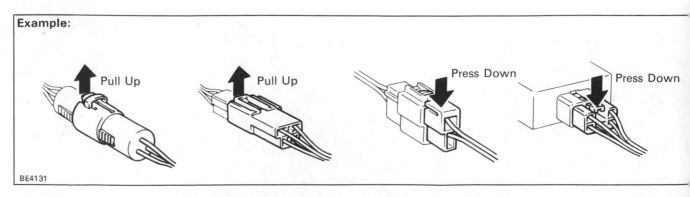

BE4131

Reference:

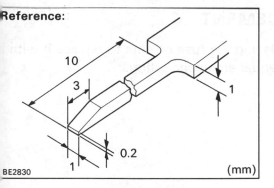

BE2830 (mm)

HOW TO REPLACE TERMINAL
(With Terminal Retainer Type)

HINT: To remove the terminal for this type of connector, please construct and use the special tool or like object shown on the left.

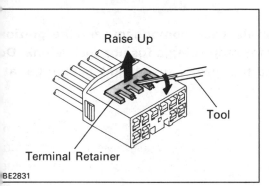

BE2831

1. **DISCONNECT CONNECTOR**

Disconnect the connector according to the instructions on BE-2.

2. **DISCONNECT TERMINAL FROM CONNECTOR**

(a) Using the special tool, raise the retainer up to the temporary lock position.

HINT: The needle insertion position varies according to the connector's shape (number of terminals, etc.), so check the position before inserting it.

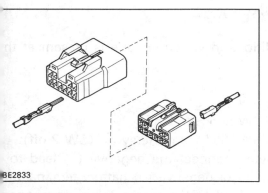

BE2832

(b) Using the special tool, release the locking lug and pull the terminal out from rear.

BE

3. **INSTALL TERMINAL TO CONNECTOR**

(a) Insert the terminal.

HINT:

1. Make sure the terminal is positioned correctly.
2. Insert the terminal until the locking lug locks firmly.
3. Insert the terminal with retainer in the temporary lock position.

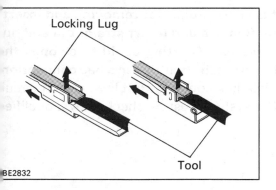

BE2833

(b) Push the retainer in as far as the full lock position.

4. **CONNECT CONNECTOR**

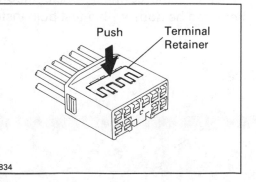

BE2834

Equal Amperage Rating

BE1366

Medium Current Fuse and High Current
Fuse Equal Amperage Rating

BE1367

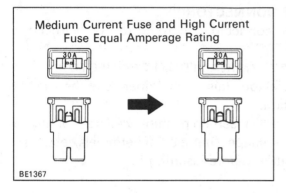

Puller

BE1365

FUSE REPLACEMENT

HINT: If replacing the fuse be sure to replace it with a fuse with an equal amperage rating.

NOTICE:
- **Turn off all electrical components and the ignition switch before replacing a fuse or fusible link. Do not exceed the fuse or fusible link amperage rating.**

- **Always fuse a use puller for removing and inserting a fuse. Remove and insert straight in and out without twisting. Twisting could force open the terminals too much, resulting in a bad connection.**

If a fuse or fusible link continues to blow, a short circuit is indicated. The system must be checked by a qualified technician.

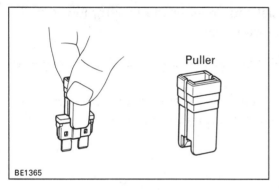

To Ignition Switch
IG Terminal

Fuse

Ⓐ

SW1   Voltmeter

Ⓑ

Relay

Ⓒ

SW2   Solenoid

BE0819

CHECK FOR VOLTAGE

(a) Establish conditions in which voltage is present at the check point.
Example:
Ⓐ – Ignition SW on
Ⓑ – Ignition SW and SW 1 on
Ⓒ – Ignition SW, SW 1 and Relay on (SW 2 off)

(b) Using a voltmeter, connect the negative (–) lead to good ground point or negative (–) battery terminal and the positive (+) lead to the connector or component terminal. This check can be done with a test bulb instead of a voltmeter.

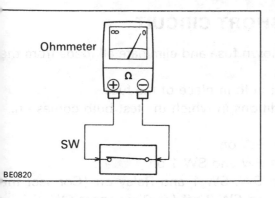

BE0820

CHECK FOR CONTINUITY AND RESISTANCE

(a) Disconnect the battery terminal or wire so there is no voltage between the check points.

(b) Contact the two leads of an ohmmeter to each of the check points.

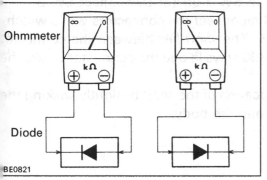

BE0821

If the circuit diodes, reverse the two leads and check again.

When contacting the negative (–) lead to the diode positive (+) side and the positive (+) lead to the negative (–) side, there should be continuity. When contacting the two leads in reverse, there should be no continuity.

HINT: Specifications may very depending on the type of tester, so refer to the tester's instruction manual before performing the inspection.

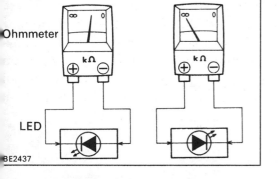

BE2437

Check LED (Light Emitting Diode) in the same manner as that for diodes.

HINT:
● Use a tester with a power source of 3 V or greater to overcome the circuit resistance.
● If a suitable tester is not available, apply battery positive voltage and check that the LED lights up.

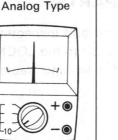

FI0889

(c) Use a volt/ohmmeter with high impedance (10 k/V minimum) for troubleshooting of the electrical circuit.

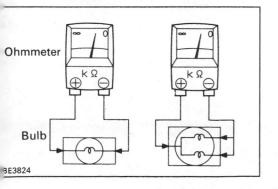

BE3824

CHECK THE BULB

(a) Remove the bulb.

(b) There should be continuity between the respectire terminals of the bulb together with a certain amount of resistance.

(c) Apply the two leads of the ohmmeter to each of the terminals.

(d) Apply battery voltage and check that the bulb light up.

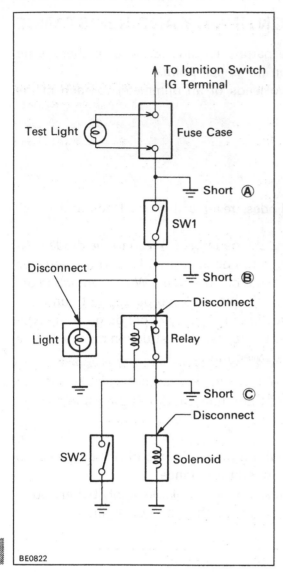

BE0822

CHECK FOR SHORT CIRCUIT

(a) Remove the blown fuse and eliminate all loads from the fuse.

(b) Connect a test bulb in place of the fuse.

(c) Establish conditions in which the test bulb comes on. Example:

    Ⓐ – Ignition SW on

    Ⓑ – Ignition SW and SW 1 on

    Ⓒ – Ignition SW, SW 1 and Relay on (Connect the Relay) and SW 2 off (or Disconnect SW 2)

(d) Disconnect and reconnect the connectors while watching the test bulb. The short lies between the connector where the test bulb stays lit and the connector where the bulb goes out.

(e) Find the exact location of the short by lightly shaking the problem wire along the body.

ELECTRICAL PARTS

Before removing and inspecting the electrical parts, set the ignition switch to the LOCK position and disconnect the negative (–) terminal cable from the battery.

HOW TO INSPECT FOR SYSTEM INSPECTION

This inspection precedure is a simple troubleshooting which should be carried out on the vehicle during system operation and is based on the assumption of system component trouble (except for the wires and connectors, etc.).

Always inspect the trouble taking the following items into consideration.

- Ground point fault
- Open or short circuit of the wire harness
- Connector or terminal connection fault
- Fuse or fusible link fault

NOTICE:

- **This is an on-vehicle inspection during system operation. Therefore, inspect the trouble with due regard for safety.**
- **If connecting the battery directly, be careful not to short circuit, and select the applicable voltage.**

POWER SOURCE
PARTS LOCATION

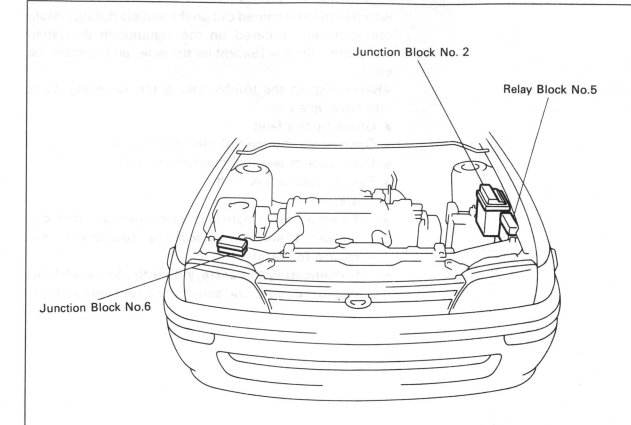

Junction Block No. 2

Relay Block No.5

Junction Block No.6

BE

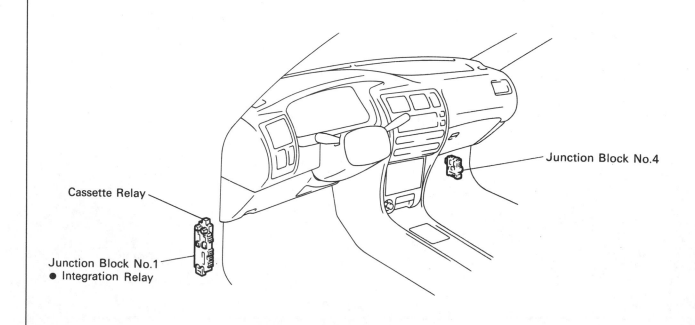

Junction Block No.4

Cassette Relay

Junction Block No.1
● Integration Relay

N05741
N05742

● Junction Block No.1
(Front Side)

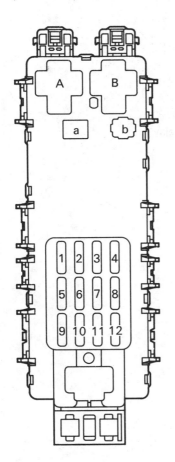

RELAYS
A. DEFOG
B. TAIL

FUSES
Medium Current Fuses
a. Power   30A
b. DEFOG   30A

Fuses
2. IGN   10A
3. STOP   15A
5. CIG & RADIO   20A
6. ECU-B   20A
7. TURN   10A
8. GAUGE   10A
9. TAIL   15A
10. DEF-I/UP   7.5A
11. ECU-IG   15A
12. WIPER   20A

BE

● Junction Relay No.1
  (Rear Side)

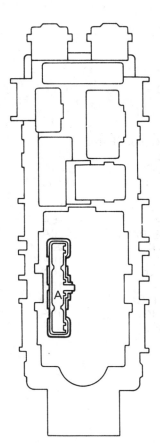

RELAY
A. Integration Relay

BE

● Junction Block No.2

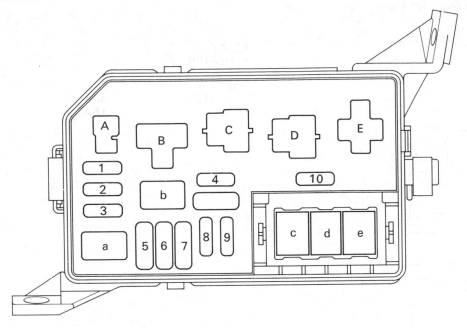

RELAYS
A. HORN
B. FAN
C. E/G-MAIN
D. HEAD
E. EFI

FUSES
High Current Fuses
c. GLOW
d. ALT   100A (4A-FE)
   AM1   40A (7A-FE)

Medium Current Fuses
a. AM2   30A
b. FAN   30A
c. AM1   40A (4A-FE)
e. ABS   50A (w/ABS)

Fuses
1. DOME   20A
2. HAZ-HORN   20A
3. ———   –
4. ALT-S   7.5A
5. SPARE   7.5A
6. SPARE   15A
7. SPARE   20A
8. HEAD (LH)   15A (for USA)
   D.R.L.   15A (for CANADA)
9. HEAD (RH)   15A (for USA)
10. EFI F-HTR

● Junction Block No.4

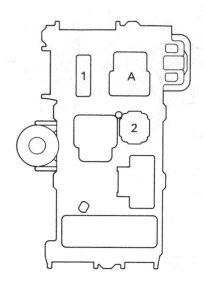

RELAY
A. HEATER

FUSES
1. HEATER   40A
2. A/C   15A

● Relay Block No.5

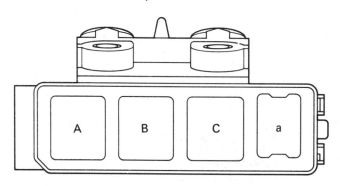

RELAYS
A. A/C FAN No.2
B. A/C FAN No.3
C. A/C MG

FUSE
Medium Current Fuse
a. CDS   30A

● Cassette Relay

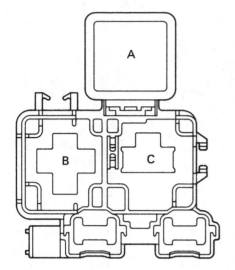

RELAYS
A. P/W
B. ———
C. FLASHER

● Junction Block No.6 (for **CANADA**)

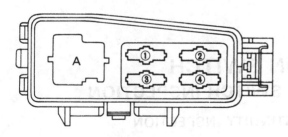

RELAY
A. D.R.L. Relay No.2

FUSES
1. HEAD LH-UPR   10A
2. HEAD LH-LWR   10A
3. HEAD RH-UPR   10A
4. HEAD RH-LWR   10A

D.R.L. : Daytime Running Light

IGNITION SWITCH
PARTS LOCATION

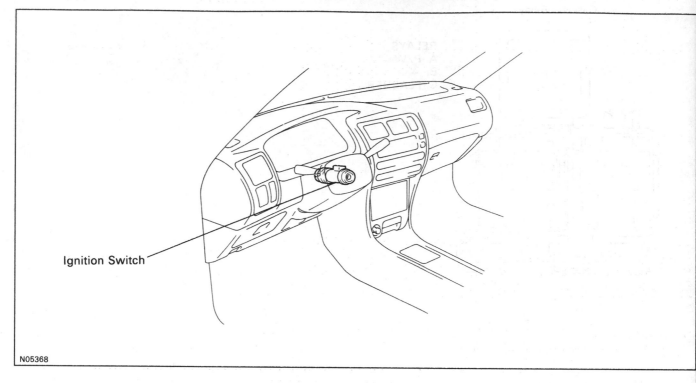

Ignition Switch

N05368

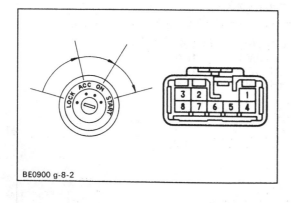

BE0900 g-8-2

IGNITION SWITCH
IGNITION SWITCH INSPECTION

O—O: CONTINUITY INSPECTION

Terminal Switch position	1	2	3	4	5	7	8
LOCK							
ACC					O—O		
ON		O—O		O—O—O			
START	O—O—O		O—	—O—O		

If continuity is not as specified, replace the switch.

KEY UNLOCK WARNING SYSTEM
PARTS LOCATION

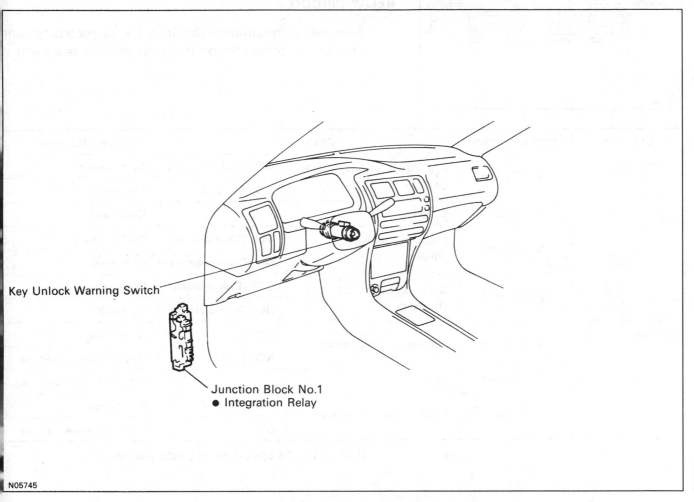

Key Unlock Warning Switch

Junction Block No.1
● Integration Relay

N05745

KEY UNLOCK WARNING SWITCH
KEY UNLOCK WARNING SWITCH
INSPECTION
CONTINUITY

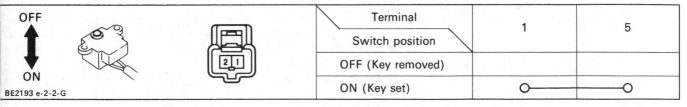

Terminal Switch position	1	5
OFF (Key removed)		
ON (Key set)	o———————————o	

BE2193 e-2-2-G

If continuity is not as specified, replace the switch.

DOOR COURTESY SWITCH

See page BE-37

If continuity is not as specified, replace the switch.

Junction Block side

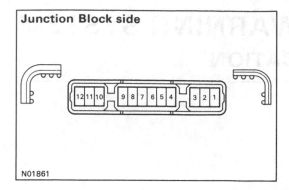

N01861

INTEGRATION RELAY
INTEGRATION RELAY INSPECTION
RELAY CIRCUIT

Remove the integration relay from the junction block and inspect the connector on the junction side as shown.

Check for	Tester connection	Condition		Specified value
Continuity	4 – Ground	Key unlock warning switch position	OFF (Key removed)	No continuity
			ON (Key set)	Continuity
	7 – Ground	Constant		Continuity
	8 – Ground	Door courtesy switch (Driver's)	OFF (Door closed)	No continuity
			ON (Door opened)	Continuity
	12 – Ground	Door courtesy switch (Passenger's)	OFF (Door closed)	No continuity
			ON (Door opened)	Continuity
Voltage	1 – Ground	Ignition switch position	LOCK	No voltage
			ACC or ON	Battery positive voltage
	3 – Ground	Constant		Battery positive voltage
	9 – Ground	Ignition switch position	LOCK or ACC	No voltage
			ON	Battery positive voltage

If circuit is as specified, replace the relay.

BE

HEADLIGHT AND TAILLIGHT SYSTEM
PARTS LOCATION

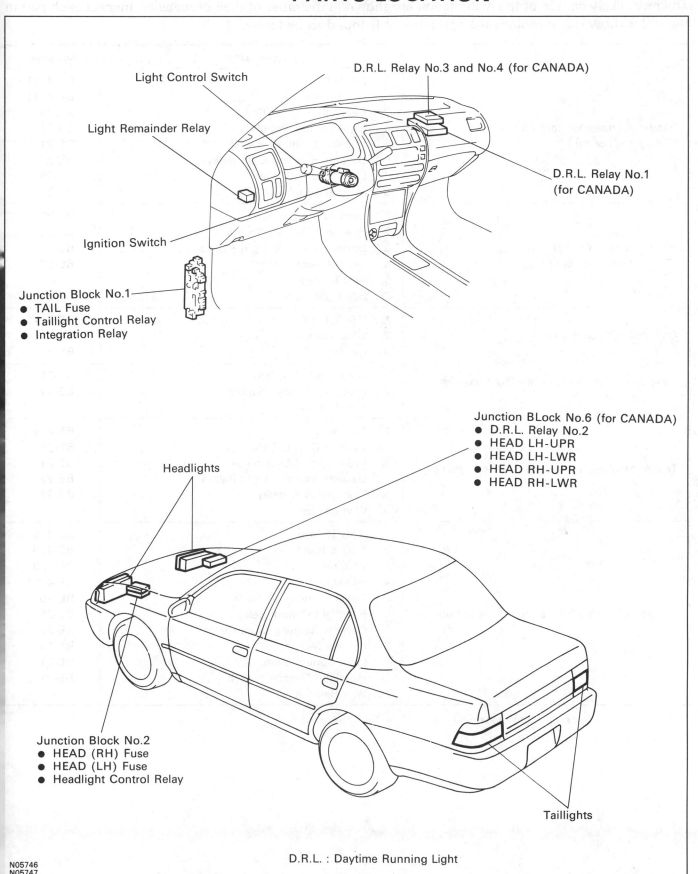

Light Control Switch

D.R.L. Relay No.3 and No.4 (for CANADA)

Light Remainder Relay

D.R.L. Relay No.1
(for CANADA)

Ignition Switch

Junction Block No.1
- TAIL Fuse
- Taillight Control Relay
- Integration Relay

Junction BLock No.6 (for CANADA)
- D.R.L. Relay No.2
- HEAD LH-UPR
- HEAD LH-LWR
- HEAD RH-UPR
- HEAD RH-LWR

Headlights

Junction Block No.2
- HEAD (RH) Fuse
- HEAD (LH) Fuse
- Headlight Control Relay

Taillights

D.R.L. : Daytime Running Light

BE

TROUBLESHOOTING

The table below will be useful for you in troubleshooting these electrical problems.
The most likely causes of the malfunction are shown in the order of their probability. Inspect each part in the order shown, and replace the part when it is found to be faulty.

Trouble	Part name	See page
Headlights does not light up. (Taillight is normal.)	1. MAIN FL 2. HEAD Fuse 3. Headlight Control Relay 4. Light Control Switch 5. Headlight Dimmer Switch 6.*1 Daytime Running Light Relays 7.*2 Light Retainer Relay 8. Headlight Bulb	BE-4, 11 BE-4, 11 BE-25 BE-21 BE-21 BE-27 BE-26 BE-5
Headlight does not light up. (Taillight does not light up.)	1. Light Control Switch 2. Headlight Dimmer Switch 3.*1 Daytime Running Light Relays 4.*2 Light Retainer Relay 5. Wire Harness 6. Headlight Bulb	BE-21 BE-21 BE-27 BE-26 – BE-5
Only one light comes on.	1. HEAD Fuse 2. Wire Harness 3. Headlight Bulb	BE-4, 11 – BE-5
Head beam headlights or headlight flashers do not operate.	1. Light Control Switch 2. Headlight Dimmer Switch 3. Wire Harness	BE-21 BE-21 –
Tail, parking and license light do not light up.	1. TAIL fuse 2. Taillight Control Relay 3. Light Control Switch 4.*1 Daytime Running Light Relays 5.*2 Light Retainer Relay 6. Wire Harness	BE-4, 9 BE-25 BE-21 BE-27 BE-26 –
*1Daytime running light system does not operate.	1. GAUGE fuse 2. ECU-B fuse 3. TAIL fuse 4. HEAD fuse 5. Taillight Control Relay 6. Headlight Control Relay 7.*1 Daytime Running Light Relays 8. Ignition Switch 9. Light Control Switch 10. Headlight Dimmer Switch 11. Wire Harness	BE-4, 9 BE-4, 9 BE-4, 9 BE-4, 11 BE-25 BE-25 BE-27 BE-14 BE-21 BE-21 –

*1: w/ Daytime Running Light System, D.R.L. No.1 ~ No.4 Relay
*2: w/ Light Auto Turn Off System

Trouble	Part name	See page
*2Light auto turn off system does not operate.	1. ECU-B Fuse 2. Taillight Control Relay 3. Door Courtesy Switch 4.*2 Light Retainer Relay 5. Wire Harness	BE-4, 9 BE-25 BE-37 BE-26 –
Combination meter lights do not light up. (Taillight light up)	1. Light control rheostat 2. Wire Harness	BE-60 –

*2: w/ Light Auto Turn Off System

HEADLIGHT
HEADLIGHT AIMING ADJUSTMENT

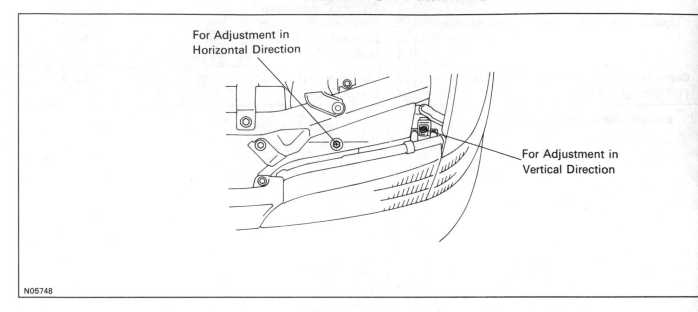

For Adjustment in Horizontal Direction

For Adjustment in Vertical Direction

N05748

COMBINATION SWITCH
COMPONENTS

(Combination Switch with Intermittent Wiper or Mist Wiper)

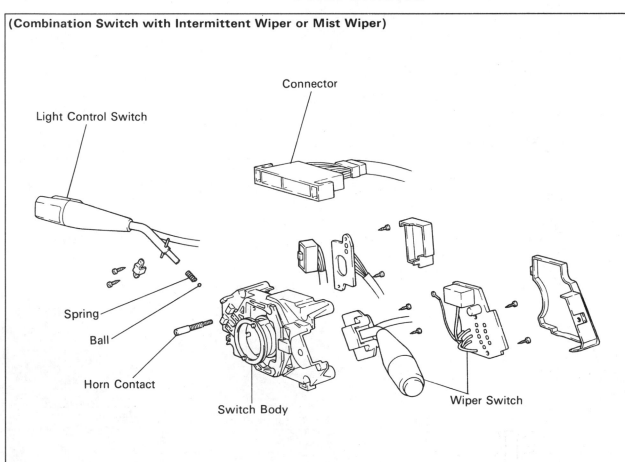

Connector

Light Control Switch

Spring

Ball

Horn Contact

Switch Body

Wiper Switch

N05375

(Combination Switch with Intermittent Wiper and Mist Wiper)

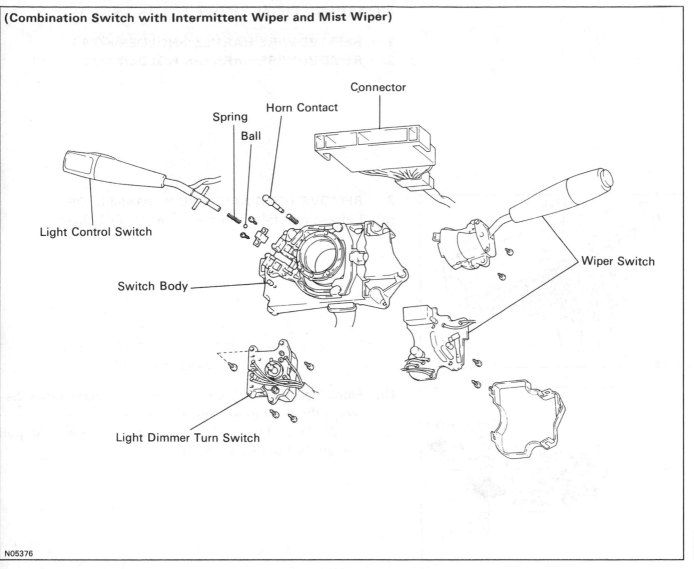

N05376

BE

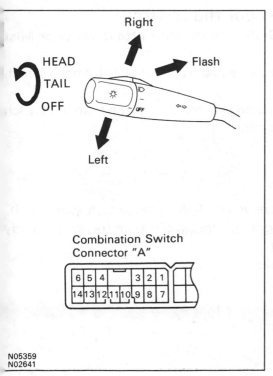

N05359
N02641

COMBINATION SWITCH INSPECTION

LIGHT CONTROL SWITCH AND DIMMER SWITCH/ CONTINUITY

O—O : CONTINUITY INSPECTION

Terminal		2	3	9	11	12	13	14
Switch position								
Light control SW	Dimmer SW							
OFF	Low beam							
	High beam							
	Flash			O		O		O
TAIL	Low beam	O			O			
	High beam	O			O			
	Flash	O			O			
				O				O
HEAD	Low beam	O			O		O	
			O	O				
	High beam	O			O			O
	Flash	O			O			O

COMBINATION SWITCH DISASSEMBLY

1. **REMOVE WIRE HARNESS HOLDER NO.1**
2. **REMOVE WIRE HARNESS HOLDER NO.2**

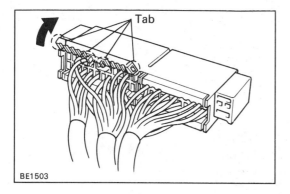

BE1503

3. **REMOVE TERMINALS FROM CONNECTOR**
(a) Release four tabs and open the terminal cover.

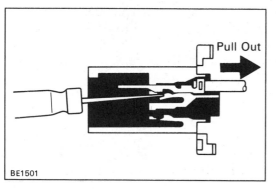

BE1501

(b) From the open end, insert a miniature screwdriver between the locking lug and terminal.
(c) Pry down the locking lug with the screwdriver and pull the terminal out from the rear.

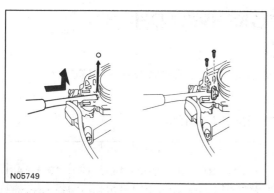

N05749

4. **REMOVE LIGHT CONTROL SWITCH**
Combination Switch with Intermittent Wiper or Mist Wiper
(a) Remove two screws and the ball set plate from the switch body.
(b) Remove the ball and side out the switch from the switch body with the spring.

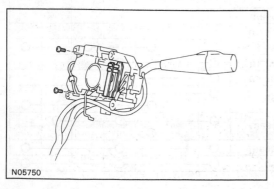

N05750

(c) Remove two screws and light dimmer turn switch unit.
(d) Slide out the light control switch from the switch body with the spring.
(e) Remove the roller.

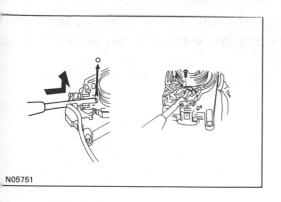

Combination Switch with Intermittent and Mist Wiper

(a) Remove one screw and the ball set plate from the switch body.

(b) Remove the ball and side out the switch from the switch body with the spring.

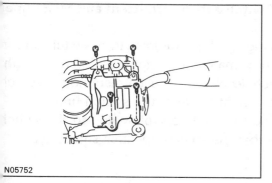

(c) Remove four screws and light dimmer turn switch unit.

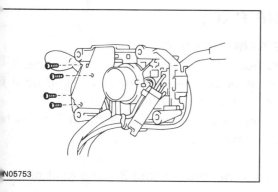

5. **REMOVE WIPER AND WASHERS SWITCH**
Combination Switch with Intermittent Wiper or Mist Wiper
Remove four screws and the switch from the switch body.

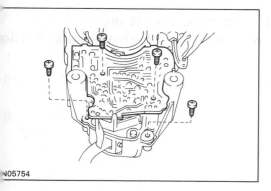

Combination Switch with Intermittent and Mist Wiper
Remove four screws and the switch from the switch body.

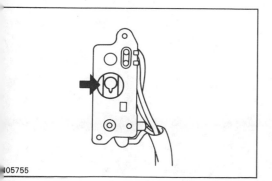

COMBINATION SWITCH ASSEMBLY

INSTALL PARTS OF COMBINATION SWITCH IN REVERSE SEQUENCE OF REMOVAL

Combination Switch with Intermittent Wiper or Mist Wiper
HINT:
- When installing the light dimmer turn switch unit in the switch body, match up switch position of the light control switch lever with the corresponding switch position of the light dimmer turn switch unit.

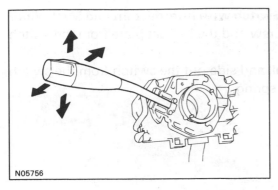

N05756

- After installing the light control switch to the switch body, insure that the switch operates smoothly.

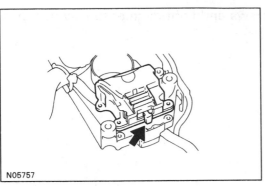

N05757

Combination Switch with Intermittent and Mist Wiper
HINT:
- When installing the light dimmer turn switch unit in the switch body, match up switch position of the light control switch level with the corresponding switch position of the light dimmer turn switch unit.
- After installing the light control switch to the switch body, insure that the switch operates smoothly.

NOTICE (w/AIR BAG)

ADJUSTMENT OF SPIRAL CABLE
(a) Check that the front wheels are facing straight ahead.
(b) Turn the spiral cable counterclockwise by hand until it becomes harder to turn the cable.
(c) Then rotate the spiral cable clockwise about 3 turns to align the matchmarks.
   HINT:
   - The spiral cable will rotate about 3 turns to either left or right of the center.
   - The connector should be straight up.
(d) Install the steering wheel so that the matchmarks will not be misaligned.

(b)

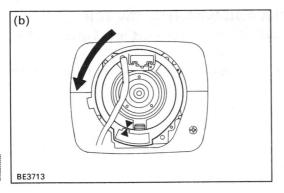

BE3713

(c)

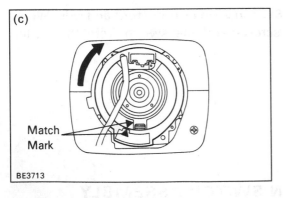

Match Mark

BE3713

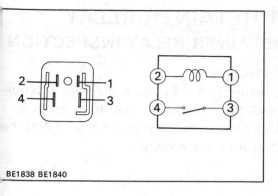

BE1838 BE1840

HEADLIGHT CONTROL RELAY
HEADLIGHT CONTROL RELAY INSPECTION

O——O: CONTINUITY INSPECTION

Terminal / Condition	1	2	3	4
Constant	O—⸺⸺—O			
Apply battery positive voltage to terminals 1 and 2.			O——O	

If continuity is not as specified, replace the relay.

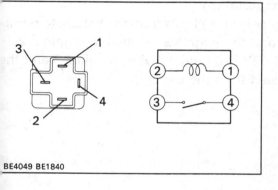

BE4049 BE1840

TAILLIGHT CONTROL RELAY
TAILLIGHT CONTROL RELAY INSPECTION

O——O: CONTINUITY INSPECTION

Terminal / Condition	1	2	3	4
Constant	O—⸺⸺—O			
Apply battery positive voltage to terminals 1 and 2.			O——O	

If continuity is not as specified, replace the relay.

BE

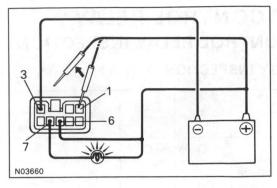

N03660

HEADLIGHT RETAINER RELAY
HEADLIGHT RETAINER RELAY INSPECTION

(Headlight Circuit/Operation)

(a) Connect the positive (+) leads from the battery termi-
    nals 1 and 6, and the negative (–) lead to terminal 3.

(b) Connect the 3.4 W test bulb between terminal 7 and the
    positive (+) lead from the battery.

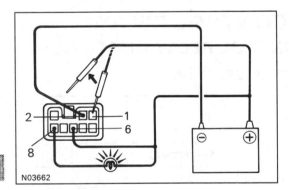

N03661

(c) Disconnect the positive (+) lead from terminal 1, check
    that the test bulb is lighting.

(d) Connect the negative (–) lead to terminal 5, check that
    the test bulb goes out.
    If operation is not as specified, replace the relay.

(Taillight Circuit/Operation)

(a) Connect the positive (+) leads from the battery to termi-
    nals 1 and 6, and the negative (–) lead to terminal 2.

(b) Connect the 3.4 W test bulb between terminal 8 and the
    positive (+) lead from the battery.

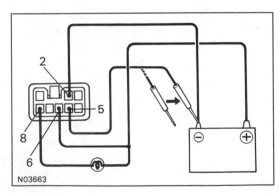

N03662

(c) Disconnect the positive (+) lead from terminal 1, check
    that the test bulb is lighting.

(d) Connect the negative (–) lead to terminal 5, check that
    the test bulb goes out.
    If operation is not as specified, replace the relay.

N03663

Wire Harness Side

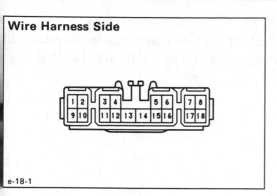

e-18-1

DAYTIME RUNNING LIGHT RELAY NO.1
DAYTIME RUNNING LIGHT RELAY NO.1 INSPECTION

RELAY CIRCUIT

Disconnect the connector from relay and inspect the connector on the wire harness side as shown in the chart.

Check for	Tester connection	Condition		Specified value
Continuity	3 – Ground	Light control switch position	OFF	No continuity
			TAIL or HEAD	Continuity
	5 – Ground	Light control switch position	OFF or TAIL	No continuity
			HEAD	Continuity
		Headlight dimmer switch position	Low beam or High beam	No continuity
			Flash	Continuity
	16 – Ground	Headlight dimmer switch position	Low beam	No continuity
			Flash or High beam	Continuity
	8 – Ground	Parking brake switch position	OFF (Parking brake lever released)	No continuity
			ON (Parking brake lever pulled up)	Continuity
	13 – Ground	Constant		Continuity
Voltage	2 – Ground 18 – Ground	Ignition switch position	LOCK or ACC	No voltage
			ON or START	Battery positive voltage
	4 – Ground 15 – Ground 17 – Ground	Constant		Battery positive voltage
	11 – Ground	Engine	Stop	No voltage
			Running	Battery positive voltage

If circuit is as specified, replace the relay.

BE

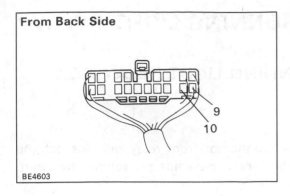

From Back Side

BE4603

RELAY CIRCUIT (CONNECTOR CONNECTED)

Connect the wire harness side connector to the relay and inspect wire harness side connector from the back side as shown.

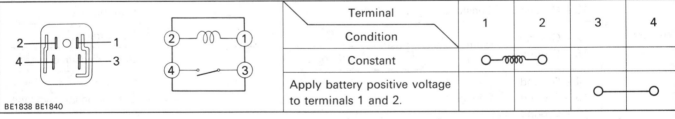

Check for	Tester connection	Condition		Specified value
Voltage	9 – Ground	Light control switch position	OFF	No voltage
			TAIL or HEAD	Battery positive voltage
	10 – Ground	Light control switch position	OFF	No voltage
			TAIL or HEAD	Battery positive voltage

If circuit is as specified, trying replacing the relay with a new one.

If circuit is not specified, refer to BE-16 wiring diagram and inspect the circuits connected to other parts.

DAYTIME RUNNING LIGHT RELAY NO.2
DAYTIME RUNNING LIGHT RELAY NO.2 INSPECTION

CONTINUITY

Terminal / Condition	1	2	3	4
Constant	O—៣៣៣—O			
Apply battery positive voltage to terminals 1 and 2.			O——O	

BE1838 BE1840

If continuity is not as specified, replace the relay.

DAYTIME RUNNING LIGHT RELAY NO.3 AND NO.4
DAYTIME RUNNING LIGHT RELAY NO.3 AND NO.4 INSPECTION

CONTINUITY

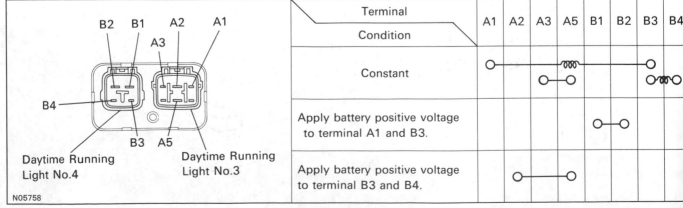

Terminal / Condition	A1	A2	A3	A5	B1	B2	B3	B4
Constant	O		O—៣៣—O	O——O			O	O—៣៣—O
Apply battery positive voltage to terminal A1 and B3.					O——O			
Apply battery positive voltage to terminal B3 and B4.		O——O						

B2 B1 A2 A1
A3
B4
B3 A5
Daytime Running Light No.4
Daytime Running Light No.3
N05758

If continuity is not as specified, replace the relay.

STOP LIGHT SYSTEM
PARTS LOCATION

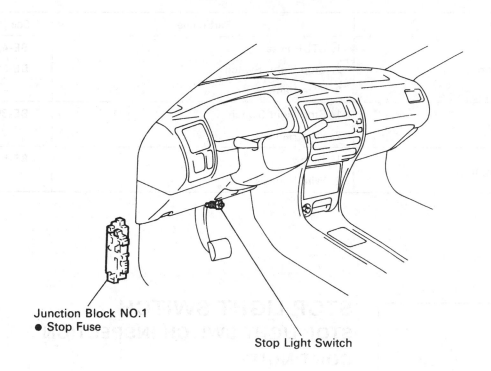

Junction Block NO.1
● Stop Fuse

Stop Light Switch

Stop Lights

BE

TROUBLESHOOTING

The table below will be useful for you in troubleshooting these electrical problems. The most likely causes of the malfunction are shown in the order of their probability. Inspect each part in the order shown, and replace the part when it is found to be faulty.

Trouble	Part name	See Page
Stop light does not light up	1. STOP Fuse	BE-4, 9
	2. Stop Light Switch	BE-30
	3. Wire Harness	–
Stop light always light up	1. Stop Light Switch	BE-30
	2. Wire Harness	–
Only one light does not light	1. Bulb	BE-5
	2. Wire Harness	–

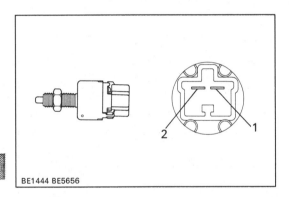

BE1444 BE5656

STOP LIGHT SWITCH
STOP LIGHT SWITCH INSPECTION
CONTINUITY

○——○: CONTINUITY INSPECTION

Terminal Switch position	1	2
Switch pin free (Brake pedal depressed	○——————○	
Switch pin pushed in (Brake pedal released)		

If continuity is not as specified, replace the switch.

BE

TURN SIGNAL AND HAZARD WARNING SYSTEM
PARTS LOCATION

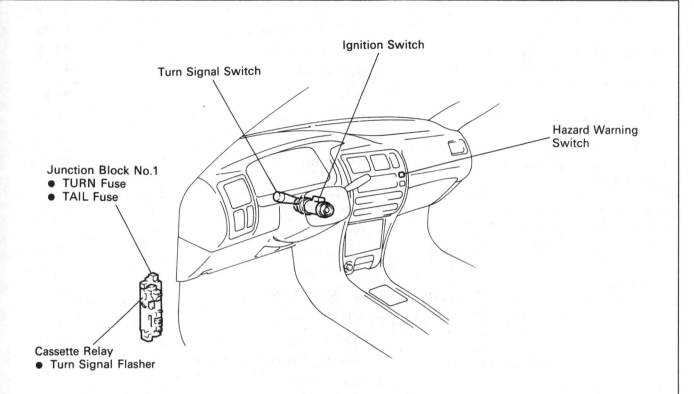

Turn Signal Switch

Ignition Switch

Hazard Warning Switch

Junction Block No.1
- TURN Fuse
- TAIL Fuse

Cassette Relay
- Turn Signal Flasher

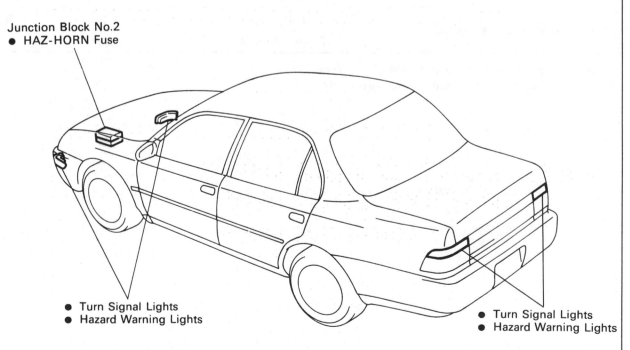

Junction Block No.2
- HAZ-HORN Fuse

- Turn Signal Lights
- Hazard Warning Lights

- Turn Signal Lights
- Hazard Warning Lights

BE

TROUBLESHOOTING

The table below will be useful for you in troubleshooting these electrical problems. The most likely causes of the malfunction are shown in the order of their probability. Inspect each part in the order shown, and replace the part when it is found to be faulty.

Trouble	Part name	See Page
"Hazard" and "Turn" do not light up.	1. Hazard Warning Switch	BE-33
	2. Turn Signal Flasher	BE-33
	3. Wire Harness	–
The flashing frequency is abnormal	1. Bulb	BE-6
	2. Turn Signal Switch	BE-33
	3. Wire Harness	–
Hazard warning light does not light up (Turn is normal)	1. HAZ-HORN Fuse	BE-4, 11
	2. Wire Harness	–
Hazard warning light does not light up in one direction	1. Hazard Warning Switch	BE-33
	2. Wire Harness	–
*1 Turn signal does not light up	1. Ignition Switch	BE-14
	2. TURN Fuse	BE-4, 9
	3. Turn Signal Switch	BE-33
	4. Wire Harness	–
*2 Turn signal does not light up	1. TURN Fuse	BE-4, 9
	2. Turn Signal Switch	BE-33
	3. Wire Harness	–
Turn signal does not light up in one direction	1. Turn Signal Switch	BE-33
	2. Wire harness	–
Only one bulb does not light up	1. Bulb	BE-6
	2. Wire Harness	–

*1: Combination Meter, Wiper and Washer do not operate.
*2: Combination Meter, Wiper and Washer are normal.

BE

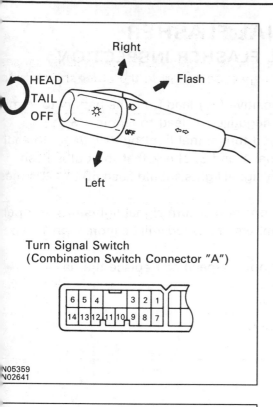

Turn Signal Switch
(Combination Switch Connector "A")

N05359
N02641

TURN SIGNAL SWITCH
TURN SIGNAL SWITCH INSPECTION

○——○: CONTINUITY INSPECTION

Terminal / Switch position	5	1	8
Left turn	○——	——○	
Neutral			
Right turn		○——	——○

If continuity is not as specified, replace the switch.

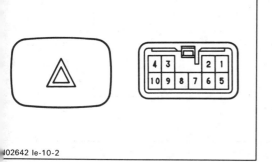

N02642 le-10-2

HAZARD WARNING SWITCH
HAZARD WARNING SWITCH INSPECTION

○——○: CONTINUITY INSPECTION

Terminal / Switch position	4	5	6	7	8	9	10	Illumination 2	Illumination 3
OFF				○——	——	——○			
ON	○——	——○——	——○			○			○——	——○
				○——	——○				

If continuity is not as specified, replace the switch.

BE

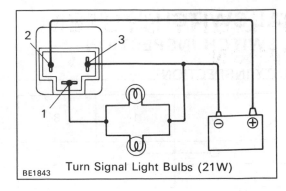

Turn Signal Light Bulbs (21W)

BE1843

TURN SIGNAL FLASHER
TURN SIGNAL FLASHER INSPECTION

OPERATION

(a) Connect the positive (+) lead from the battery to terminal 2 and the negative (−) lead to terminal 3.

(b) Connect the two turn signal light bulbs parallel to each
other to terminal 1 and 3, check that the bulbs flash.

HINT: The turn signal lights should flash 60 to 120 times
par minute.

If one of the front or rear turn signal lights has an oper
circuit, the numbers of flashed will be more than 140 pa
minutes.

If operation is not as specified, replace the flasher.

INTERIOR LIGHT SYSTEM
PARTS LOCATION

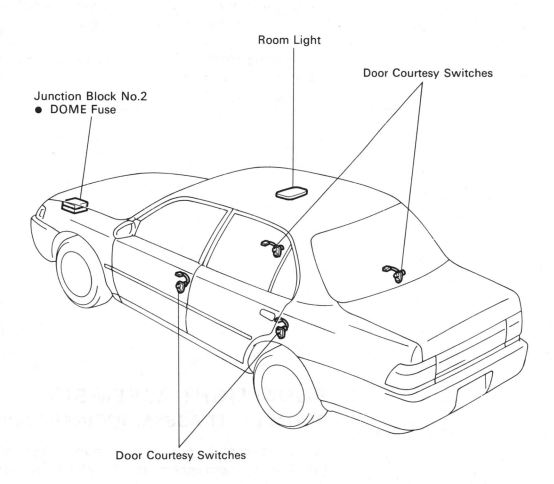

Room Light

Door Courtesy Switches

Junction Block No.2
● DOME Fuse

Door Courtesy Switches

BE

TROUBLESHOOTING

The table below will be useful for you in troubleshooting these electrical problems. The most likely causes of the malfunction are shown in the order of their probability. Inspect each part in the order shown, and replace the part when it is found to be faulty.

Trouble	Parts name	See page
Room light does not light up	1. DOME Fuse	BE-4, 11
	2. Room Light Switch	BE-36
	3. Door Courtesy Switch	BE-37
	4. Wire Harness	–
	5. Bulb	BE-6
Room light remains always on	1. Room Light Switch	BE-36
	2. Door Courtesy Switch	BE-37
	3. Wire Harness	–

BE

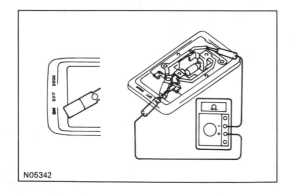

N05342

ROOM LIGHT ASSEMBLY
ROOM LIGHT ASSEMBLY INSPECTION

(a) Disconnect the connector from room light assembly.
(b) Turn the room light switch ON, check that there is continuity between terminal 2 and body ground.

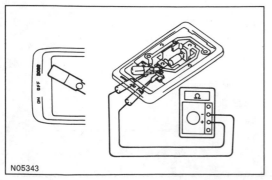

N05343

(c) Turn the room light switch DOOR, check that there is continuity between terminal 1 and 2.
If operation is not as specified, replace the switch.

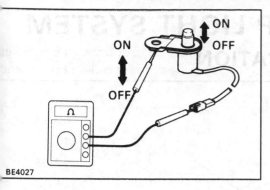

BE4027

DOOR COURTESY SWITCH
DOOR COURTESY SWITCH INSPECTION

(a) Check that there is continuity between terminal and the switch body with the switch ON (switch pin released).

(b) Check that there is no continuity between terminal and the switch body with the switch OFF (switch pin pushed in).

If operation is not as specified, replace the switch.

BACK-UP LIGHT SYSTEM
PARTS LOCATION

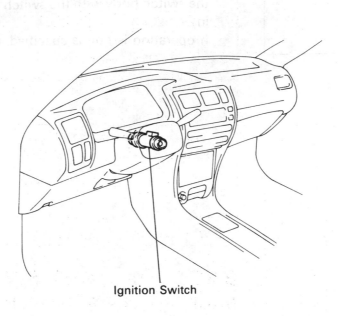

Ignition Switch

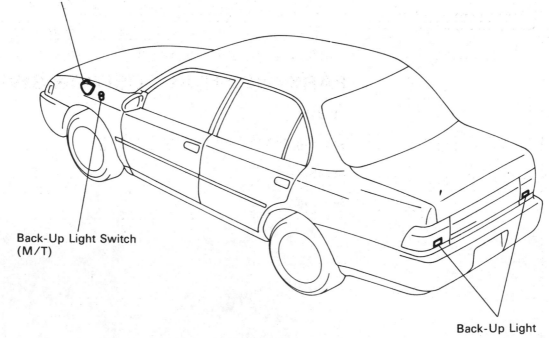

Park/Neutral Position Switch (A/T)

Back-Up Light Switch
(M/T)

Back-Up Light

BE

TROUBLESHOOTING

The table below will be useful for you in troubleshooting these electrical problems. The most likely causes of the malfunction are shown in the order of their probability. Inspect each part in the order shown, and replace the part when it is found to be faulty.

Trouble	Parts name	See page
Back-Up Light does not light up.	1. GAUGE Fuse	BE-4, 9
	2. Ignition Switch	BE-14
	3. Back-Up Light Switch (M/T)	BE-39
	4. Park/Neutral Position Switch (A/T)	AX-31 (A131L)
		AX-20 (A245E)
	5. Wire Harness	–
Back-Up light always light up	1. Back-Up Light Switch (M/T)	BE-39
	2. Park/Neutral Position Switch (A/T)	AX-31 (A131L)
		AX-20 (A245E)
	3. Wire Harness	–
Only one light does not light	1. Bulb	
	2. Wire Harness	

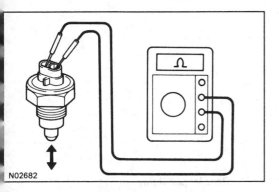

N02682

BACK- UP LIGHT SWITCH
BACK -UP LIGHT SWITCH INSPECTION

Check that there is continuity between terminals as shown.

Switch position	Specified
Push	Continuity
Free	No continuity

If operation is not as specified, replace the switch.

PARK/NEUTRAL POSITION SWITCH

(A131L)

See page AX-31

(A245E)

See page AX-20

BE

WIPER AND WASHER SYSTEM
PARTS LOCATION

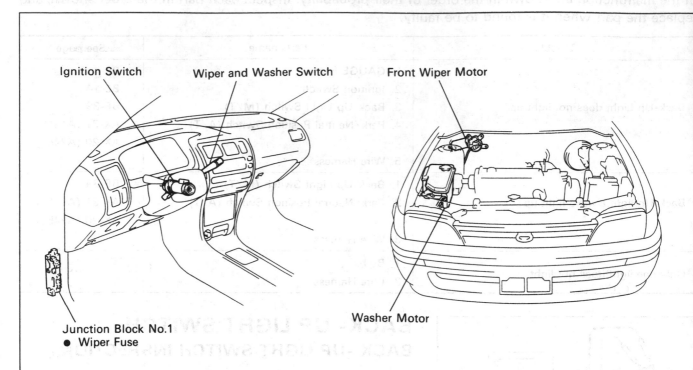

Ignition Switch

Wiper and Washer Switch

Front Wiper Motor

Washer Motor

Junction Block No.1
● Wiper Fuse

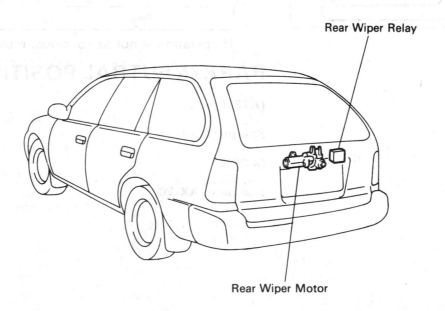

Rear Wiper Relay

Rear Wiper Motor

TROUBLESHOOTING

The table below will be useful for you in troubleshooting these electrical problems. The most likely causes of the malfunction are shown in the order of their probability. Inspect each part in the order shown, and replace the part when it is found to be faulty.

Trouble	Parts name	See page	
		Front	Rear
Wipers do not operate are or return to off position	1. WIPER Fuse	BE-4, 9	BE-4, 9
	2. Wiper Motor	BE-44	BE-45
	3. Wiper Switch	BE-42	BE-43
	4. Wire Harness	–	–
Wiper do not operate in Mist position	1. Wiper Switch	BE-42	–
	2. Wiper Motor	BE-44	–
	3. Wire Harness	–	–
Wiper do not operate in intermittent (INT) position	1. Wiper Relay	–	BE-44
	2. Wiper Switch	BE-42	BE-43
	3. Wiper Motor	BE-44	BE-45
	4. Wire Harness	–	–
Washer do not operate	1. Washer hose or nozzle clogged	–	–
	2. Washer Motor	BE-45	BE-45
	3. Washer Switch	BE-42	BE-43
	4. Wire Harness	–	–

COMBINATION SWITCH
COMBINATION SWITCH REMOVAL

See Headlight and Taillight System on page BE-20.

COMBINATION SWITCH DISASSEMBLY

See Headlight and Taillight System on page BE-20.

COMBINATION SWITCH ASSEMBLY

See Headlight and Taillight System on page BE-20.

COMBINATION SWITCH INSTALLATION

See Headlight and Taillight System on page BE-20.

BE

Reference

w/Mist Wiper Switch

w/Intermittent Wiper Switch

w/Mist Wiper Switch and
Intermittent Wiper Switch

Combination Switch
Connector "B"

N05365
N05366
N05367
N02620

COMBINATION SWITCH INSPECTION

INSPECT WIPER AND WASHER SWITCH

○——○ : CONTINUITY INSPECTION

w/Mist Wiper

Terminal Switch position		4	7	13	18	8	16
Wiper	MIST		○—	—	—○		
	OFF	○—	—○				
	LO		○—	—○			
	HI			○—	—○		
Washer	OFF						
	ON					○—	—○

w/Intermittent Wiper

Terminal Switch position		4	7	13	18	8	16
Wiper	MIST	○—	—○				
	OFF	○—	—○				
	LO		○—	—○			
	HI			○—	—○		
Washer	OFF						
	ON					○—	—○

w/Mist Wiper and Intermittent Wiper

Terminal Switch position	Mist switch position		4	7	13	18	8	16
Wiper	OFF	OFF	○—	—○				
		MIST		○—	—	—○		
	INT	OFF	○—	—○				
		MIST		○—	—	—○		
	LO	OFF		○—	—○			
		MIST		○—	—	—○		
	HI	OFF			○—	—○		
		MIST		○—	—○—	—○		
Washer	OFF							
	ON						○—	—○

If continuity is not as specified, replace the switch.

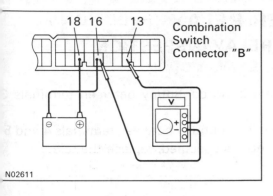

N02611

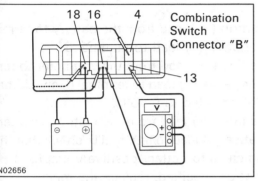

N02656

OPERATION (WIPER AND WASHER SWITCH/ INTERMITTENT WIPER)

(a) Turn the wiper switch to INT position.

(b) Connect the positive (+) lead from the battery to terminal 18 and the negative (–) lead to terminal 16.

(c) Connect the positive (+) lead from the voltmeter to terminal 13 and the negative (–) lead to terminal 14, check that the meter needle indicates battery positive voltage.

(d) After connecting terminal 4 and terminal 16, connect to terminal 4 and terminal 18.

Then, check that the voltage rises from 0 V to battery positive voltage within the times as shown in the table.

Switch position	Voltage
INT	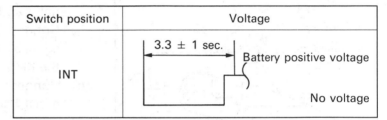

If operation is not as specified, replace the switch.

BE

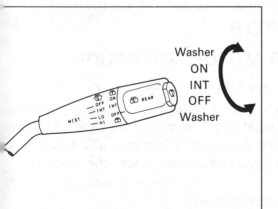

Washer
ON
INT
OFF
Washer

Combination Switch
Connector "B"

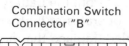

N05362
N02620

INSPECT REAR WIPER AND WASHER SWITCH
O——O: CONTINUITY INSPECTION

Terminal / Switch position		1	2	10	16
Washer 1			O—	———	—O
Wiper	OFF				
	INT			O—	—O
	ON	O—	———	———	—O
Washer 2		O—	—O—	———	—O

If continuity is not specified, replace the switch.

Relay Side

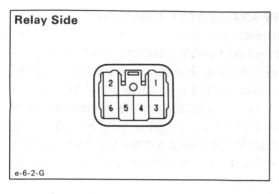

e-6-2-G

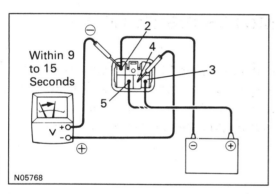

N05767

Within 9 to 15 Seconds

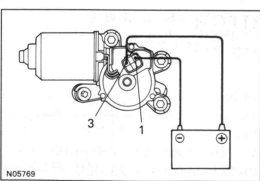

N05768

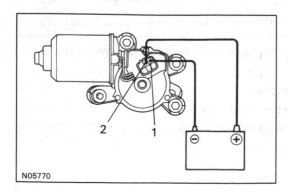

N05769

N05770

REAR WIPER RELAY
REAR WIPER RELAY INSPECTION

CONTINUITY

(a) Check that there is no continuity between terminals 3 and 4.

(b) Check that there is continuity between terminals 4 and 5. If continuity is not as specified, replace the relay.

OPERATION

(a) Connect the position (+) lead from the battery to terminal 3 and the negative (−) lead to terminal 6.

(b) Connect the positive (+) lead from the voltmeter to terminal 5 and the negative (−) lead to terminal 6, check that the meter needle indicated to 0 volts.

(c) Connect the positive (+) lead from the voltmeter to terminal 4 and negative (−) lead to terminal 6, check that the meter needle indicates to battery positive voltage. If operation is not as specified, replace the relay.

INTERMITTENT OPERATION

(a) Connect the positive (+) lead from the battery to terminal 5 and the negative (−) lead to terminal 2 more than 2 seconds.

(b) Connect the positive (+) lead from the voltmeter to terminal 4 and the negative (−) lead to terminal 2.

(c) After disconnecting the positive (+) lead from terminal 5 connect it to terminal 3, and then, check that the meter needle rises from 0 volts to battery positive voltage within 9 to 15 seconds.
   If operation is not as specified, replace the relay.

WIPER MOTOR
FRONT WIPER MOTOR INSPECTION

OPERATION (AT LOW SPEED)

Connect the positive (+) lead from the battery to terminal 3 and the negative (−) lead from the battery to terminal 1, check that the motor operates at low speed.
If operation is not as specified, replace the motor.

OPERATION (AT HIGH SPEED)

Connect the positive (+) lead from the battery to terminal 2 and the negative (−) lead from the battery to terminal 1, check that the motor operates at high speed.
If operation is not as specified, replace the motor.

BE

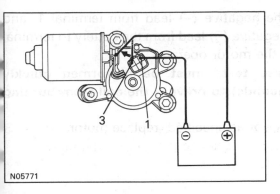

OPERATION (STOPPING AT STOP POSITION)

(a) Operate the motor at low speed and stop the motor operation anywhere except at the stop position by disconnecting positive (+) lead from terminal 3.

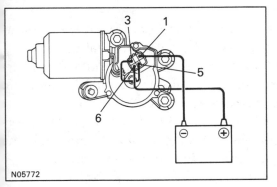

(b) Connect terminals 3 and 5.

(c) Connect the positive (+) lead from the battery to terminal 6 and the negative (–) lead from the battery to terminal 1, check that the motor stops running at the stop position after the motor operates again.

If operation is not as specified, replace the motor.

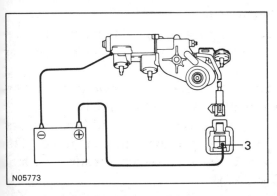

REAR WIPER MOTOR INSPECTION

OPERATION

Connect the positive (+) lead from the battery to terminal 3 and the negative (–) lead from the battery to the motor body, check that the motor operates.

If operation is not as specified, replace the motor.

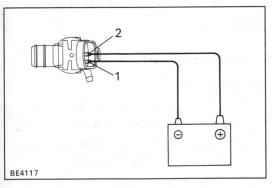

WASHER MOTOR
WASHER MOTOR INSPECTION

(w/o REAR WIPER)

Connect the positive (+) lead from the battery to terminal 2 and the negative (–) lead to terminal 1, check that the motor operates.

NOTICE: These tests must be performed quickly (within 20 seconds) to prevent the coil from burning out.

If operation is not as specified, replace the motor.

(w/REAR WIPER)

(a) Connect the positive (+) lead from the battery to terminal 2 and the negative (–) lead to terminal 1, check that the motor operates.

NOTICE: These tests must be performed quickly (within 20 seconds) to prevent the coil from burning out.

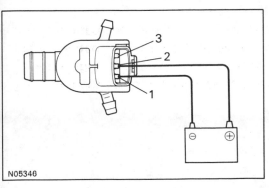

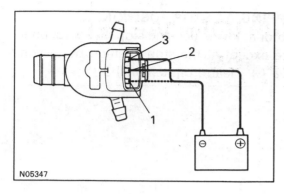

N05347

(b)   Disconnect the negative (−) lead from terminal 1, and connect the negative (−) lead from the battery to terminal 3, check that the motor operates.

NOTICE: These tests must be performed quickly (within 20 seconds) to prevent the coil from burning out.

If operation is not as specified, replace motor.

COMBINATION METER
PARTS LOCATION

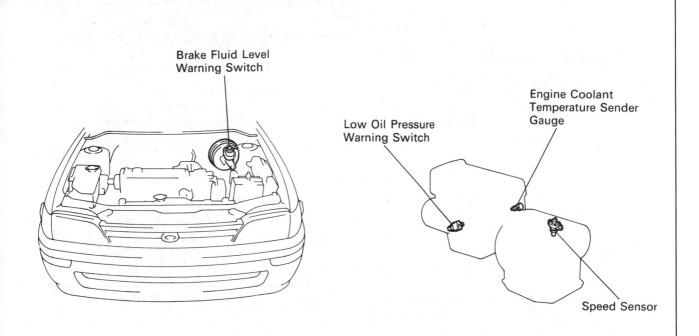

Brake Fluid Level Warning Switch

Low Oil Pressure Warning Switch

Engine Coolant Temperature Sender Gauge

Speed Sensor

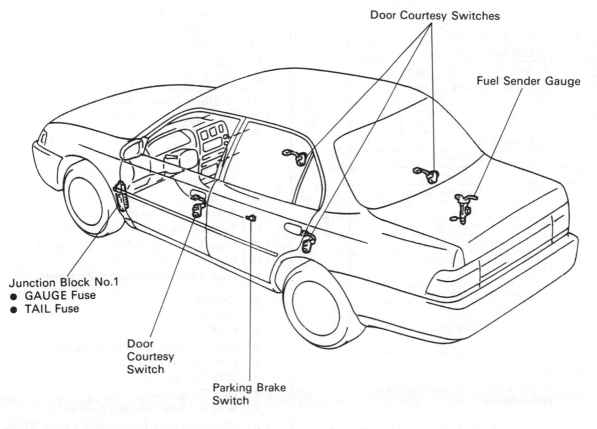

Door Courtesy Switches

Fuel Sender Gauge

Junction Block No.1
● GAUGE Fuse
● TAIL Fuse

Door Courtesy Switch

Parking Brake Switch

BE

METER CIRCUIT
(w/TACHOMETER)

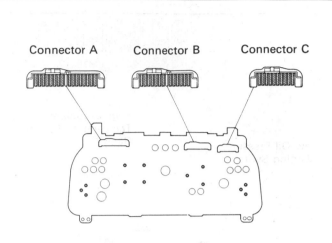

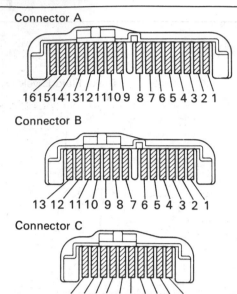

Connector A

16 15 14 13 12 11 10 9 8 7 6 5 4 3 2 1

Connector B

13 12 11 10 9 8 7 6 5 4 3 2 1

Connector C

10 9 8 7 6 5 4 3 2 1

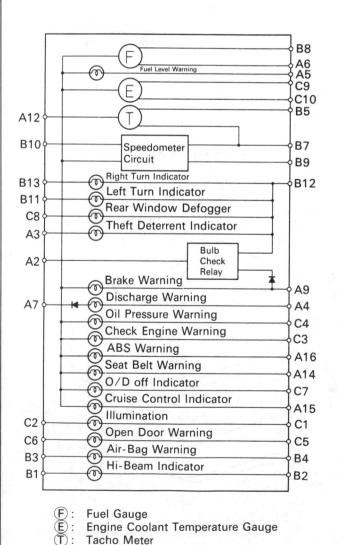

No.		Wiring Connector Side
A	2	Starter Relay
	3	Theft Deterrent ECU
	4	ALT – Terminal L
	5	Fuel Sender Gauge – Terminal 3
	6	Fuel Sender Gauge – Terminal 2
	7	IGN Fuse
	9	Brake Fluid Level Warning Switch
	12	GAUGE Fuse
	14	Buckle Switch
	15	Cruise Control ECU
	16	ABS ECU
B	1	Headlight Dimmer Switch
	2	Headlights
	3	ECU + B Fuse
	4	Air-bag ECU
	5	Ignitor
	7	Speed Sensor – Terminal 1
	8	Ground
	9	Speed Control Unit
	10	Speed Sensor – Terminal 3
	11	Hazard Warning Switch – Terminal 5
	12	Ground
	13	Hazard Warning Switch – Terminal 6
C	1	Ground
	2	TAIL Fuse
	3	ECM
	4	Low Oil Pressure Warning Switch
	5	Door Courtesy Switch
	6	DOME Fuse
	7	O/D Off Switch
	8	Rear Window Defogger Switch
	9	Engine Coolant Temperature Sender Gauge
	10	Ground

(F) : Fuel Gauge
(E) : Engine Coolant Temperature Gauge
(T) : Tacho Meter

N06103
N06102 N05406
N05775 N05407

BE

(w/o TACHOMETER)

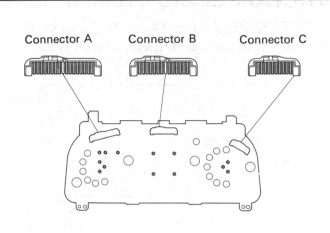

Connector A

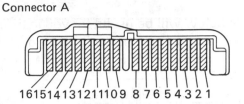

16 15 14 13 12 11 10 9 8 7 6 5 4 3 2 1

Connector B

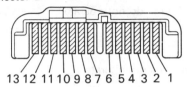

13 12 11 10 9 8 7 6 5 4 3 2 1

Connector C

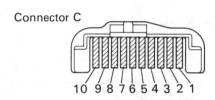

10 9 8 7 6 5 4 3 2 1

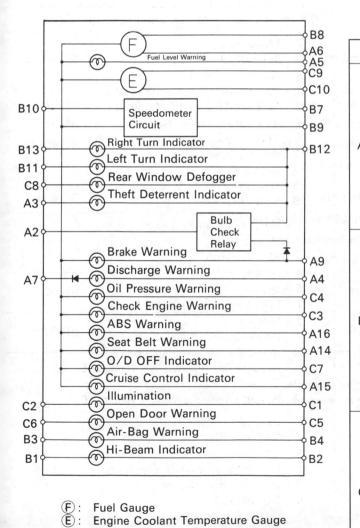

F : Fuel Gauge
E : Engine Coolant Temperature Gauge

No.		Wiring Connector Side
A	2	Starter Relay
	3	Theft Deterrent ECU
	4	ALT – Terminal L
	5	Fuel Sender Gauge – Terminal 3
	6	Fuel Sender Gauge – Terminal 2
	7	IGN Fuse
	9	Brake Fluid Level Warning Switch
	14	Buckle Switch
	15	Cruise Control ECU
	16	ABS ECU
B	1	Headlight Dimmer Switch
	2	Headlights
	3	ECU +B Fuse
	4	Air-bag ECU
	7	Speed Sensor – Terminal 1
	8	Ground
	9	Speed Control Unit
	10	Speed Sensor – Terminal 3
	11	Hazard Warning Switch – Terminal 5
	12	Ground
	13	Hazard Warning Switch – Terminal 6
C	1	Ground
	2	TAIL Fuse
	3	ECM
	4	Low Oil Pressure Warning Switch
	5	Door Courtesy Switch
	6	DOME Fuse
	7	O/D Off Switch
	8	Rear Window Defogger Switch
	9	Engine Coolant Temperature Sender Gauge
	10	Ground

BE

N06103
N05409 N05406
N05776 N05407

TROUBLESHOOTING
METERS, GAUGES AND ILLUMINATIONS

The table below will be useful for you in troubleshooting these electrical problems. The most likely causes of the malfunction are shown in the order of their probability. Inspect each part in the order shown, and replace the part when it is found to be faulty.

Trouble	Parts name	See page
Tachometer, Fuel Gauge and engine coolant temperature Gauge do not operate	1. GAUGE Fuse	BE-4, 9
	2. Combination Meter Wiring Circuit	BE-48, 49
	3. Wire Harness	–
	4. Other Parts*1	–
Speedometer does not operate	1. Speedometer Cable	–
	2. Other Parts*2	–
Tachometer does not operate	1. Combination Meter Wiring Circuit	BE-48, 49
	2. Wire Harness	–
	3. Igniter	–
	4. Other Parts*3	–
Fuel Gauge does not operate or abnormal operation	1. Fuel Receiver Gauge	BE-55
	2. Fuel Sender Gauge	BE-55
	3. Combination Meter Wiring Circuit	BE-48, 49
	4. Wire Harness	–
Engine Coolant Temperature Gauge does not operate or abnormal operation	1. Engine Coolant Temperature Receiver Gauge	BE-57
	2. Engine Coolant Temperature Sender Gauge	BE-57
	3. Combination Meter Wiring Circuit	BE-48, 49
	4. Wire Harness	–
All illumination lights do not light up	1. TAIL Fuse	BE-4, 9
	2. Light Control Rheostat	BE-60
	3. Wire Harness	–
	4. Other Parts	–
Brightness does not change even when rheostat turned	1. Light Control Rheostat	BE-60
Only one illumination light does not light up	1. Bulb	BE-60

*1 Refer to BE-48 inspect the meter circuit plate.
*2 Inspect the speedometer driven and drive gear or try another speedometer.
*3 Refer to BE-48 inspect the meter circuit plate or try another tachometer.

WARNING LIGHTS AND INDICATOR LIGHTS

Trouble	Parts name	See page
Warning lights do not light up (Except Discharge, Airbag, Door)	1. GAUGE Fuse	BE-4, 9
	2. Combination Meter Wiring Circuit	BE-48, 49
	3. Wire Harness	–
Low oil pressure warning warning light does not light up	1. Bulb	BE-5
	2. Combination Meter Wiring Circuit	BE-48, 49
	3. Low Oil Pressure Warning Switch	BE-58
	4. Wire Harness	–
Fuel level warning light does not light up	1. Bulb	BE-5
	2. Combination Meter Wiring Circuit	BE-48, 49
	3. Fuel Level Warning Switch	BE-56
Brake warning light does not light up	1. Bulb	BE-5
	2. Combination Meter Wiring Circuit	BE-48, 49
	3. Parking Brake Switch	BE-59
	4. Brake Fluid Level Warning Switch	BE-58
	5. Other Parts	–
ABS warning light does not light up	1. Bulb	BE-5
	2. Combination Meter Wiring Circuit	BE-48, 49
	3. ABS ECU	–
	4. Other Parts	–

BE

WARNING LIGHTS AND INDICATOR LIGHT (Cont'd)

Trouble	Part name	See page
Check engine warning light does not light up	1. Bulb	BE-5
	2. Other Parts *1	–
	3. Wire Harness	–
Discharge warning light does not light up	1. Bulb	BE-5
	2. Wire Harness	–
	3. Other Parts*2	–
Open door warning light does not light up	1. DOME Fuse	BE-11
	2. Combination Meter Wiring Circuit	BE-48, 49
	3. Door Courtesy Switch	BE-59
High beam indicator light does not light up	1. Bulb	BE-5
	2. Combination Meter Wiring Circuit	BE-48, 49
	3. Wire Harness	–
	4. Other Parts*3	–
Turn indicator light does not light up	1. Bulb	BE-5
	2. Combination Meter Wiring Circuit	BE-48, 49
	3. Wire harness	–
	4. Other Parts*4	–
Seat belt warning light does not light up	1. Bulb	BE-5
	2. Combination Meter Wiring Circuit	BE48, 49
	3. Buckle Switch	BE-59
	4. Seat Belt Warning Relay	BE-60
	5. Wire Harness	–

*1 Inspect ECM.
*2 Inspect "Alternator"
*3 Refer to BE-17 inspect the "Headlight System"
*4 Refer to BE-31 inspect "Turn Signal and Hazard Warning System"

BE

SPEEDOMETER SYSTEM
SPEEDOMETER INSPECTION

(a) Using a speedometer tester, inspect the speedometer for allowable indication error and check the operation of the odometer.
   HINT: Tire wear and tire over or under inflation will increase the indication error.
   If error is excessive, replace the speedometer.
(b) Check the speedometer for pointer vibration and abnormal noise.
   HINT: Pointer vibration can be cause by a loose speedometer cable.

w/Tachometer

km/h

for USA

Standard indication	Allowable range
20	20 – 30
40	40 – 43.5
60	60 – 64
80	80 – 84.5
100	100 – 105

for CANADA

Standard indication	Allowable range
20	18 – 23
40	40 – 44
60	60 – 64.5
80	80 – 85
100	100 – 105
120	120 – 125.5
140	140 – 146
160	160 – 167

w/o Tachometer

km/h

for USA

Standard indication	Allowable range
20	20 – 23
40	40 – 43.5
60	60 – 64
80	80 – 84.5
100	100 – 105

for CANADA

Standard indication	Allowable range
20	18 – 23
40	40 – 44
60	60 – 64.5
80	80 – 85
100	100 – 105
120	120 – 125.5
140	140 – 146
160	160 – 167

BE

SPEED SENSOR INSPECTION

(a) Connect the positive (+) lead from battery to terminal 1 and negative (–) lead to terminal 2.

(b) Connect the positive (+) lead from tester to terminal 3 and negative (–) lead to terminal 2.

(c) Revolve shaft.

(d) Check that there is voltage changer from approx. 0 V to 11 V or more between terminal 3 and 2.

HINT: The voltage change should be 20 times per each revolution of the speed sensor shaft.

If operation is not as specified, replace the sensor.

• M/T

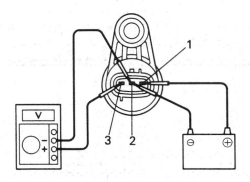

• A/T

4A-FE Engine

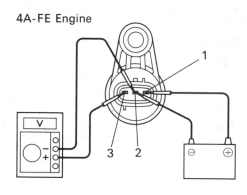

7A-FE Engine

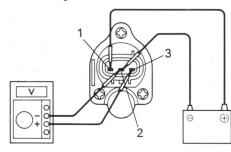

N05373 N05373
N05374

DC 13.5 V 25°C (77°F) rpm	
Standard indication	Allowable range
700	630 – 700
3,000	2,800 – 3,200
5,000	4,800 – 5,200
7,000	6,700 – 7,300

TACHOMETER SYSTEM
TACHOMETER INSPECTION

(ON-VEHICLE)

(a) Connect a tune-up test tachometer, and start the engine.

NOTICE:

- **Reversing the connection of the will damage the transistors and diodes inside.**

- **When removing or installing the tachometer, be careful not to drop or subject it to heavy shocks.**

(b) Compare the tester and tachometer indications.

If error is excessive, replace the tachometer.

BE

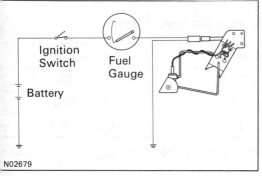

N02679

FUEL GAUGE SYSTEM
FUEL RECEIVER GAUGE INSPECTION
OPERATION
(a) Disconnect the connector from the sender gauge.
(b) Turn the ignition switch ON, check that the receiver gauge needle indicates EMPTY.

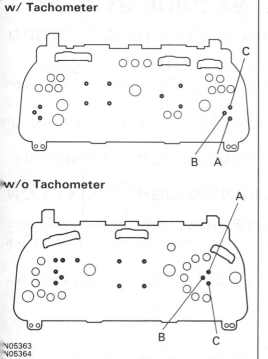

BE1206 e-3-1-B

(c) Connect terminals 1 and 3 on the wire harness side connector through a 3.4 watts test bulb.
(d) Turn the ignition switch ON, check that the bulb lights up and the receiver gauge needle moves towards the full side.
HINT: Because of the silicon oil in the gauge, it will take a short time for needle stabilize.
If operation is not as specified, inspect the receiver gauge resistance.

RESISTANCE
w/Tachometer

Between terminals	Resistance (Ω)
A – B	Approx. 154.3
A – C	Approx. 107.2
B – C	Approx. 261.5

w/o Tachometer

Between terminals	Resistance (Ω)
A – B	Approx. 280.5
A – C	Approx. 126.2
B – C	Approx. 154.3

If resistance value is not as specified, replace the receiver gauge.

w/ Tachometer

w/o Tachometer

N05363
N05364

BE

FUEL SENDER GAUGE INSPECTION
OPERATION
(a) Connect a series of three 1.5 volts dry cell batteries.
(b) Connect the positive (+) lead from the dry cell batteries to terminal 2 through a 3.4 watts test bulb and the negative (–) lead to terminal 1.
(c) Connect the positive (+) lead from the voltmeter to terminal and combination negative (–) lead to terminal.
(d) Check that the voltage rises as the float is moved from the full to empty position.

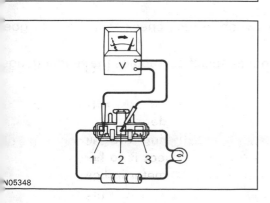

N05348

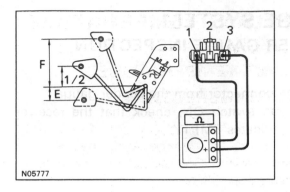

N05777

RESISTANCE

Measure the terminals between 1 and 3.

Float Position		Resistance (Ω)
F	Approx. 73.9	Approx. 3.0
1/2	Approx. 26.1	Approx. 30.8
E	Approx. 20.7	Approx. 110.0

If resistance value is not as specified, replace the sender gauge.

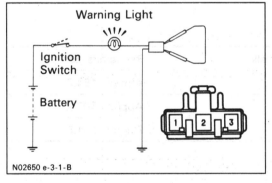

Warning Light

Ignition Switch

Battery

N02650 e-3-1-B

BE

FUEL LEVEL WARNING SYSTEM
FUEL LEVEL WARNING LIGHT INSPECTION

(a) Disconnect the connector from the sender gauge.
(b) Connect terminals 1 and 3 on the wire harness side connector.
(c) Turn the ignition switch ON, check that the warning light lights up.
     If the warning light does not light up, test the bulb.

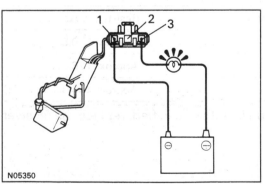

N05350

FUEL LEVEL WARNING LIGHT INSPECTION

(a) Apply battery positive voltage between terminals 1 and and through a 3.4 watts test bulb, check that the bulb lights up.
     HINT: It will take a short time for the bulb to light up.

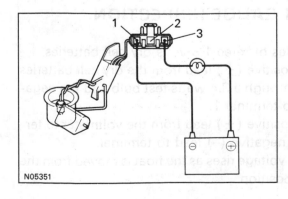

N05351

(b) Submerge the switch in fuel, check that the bulb goes out.
     If operation is not as specified, replace the sender gauge.

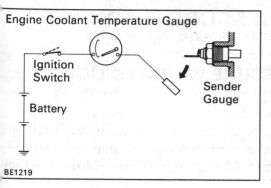

Engine Coolant Temperature Gauge

Ignition Switch

Battery

Sender Gauge

BE1219

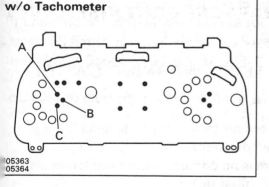

Engine Coolant Temperature gauge

Ignition Switch

Battery

Test Bulb (3.4 W)

BE0144

ENGINE COOLANT TEMPERATURE GAUGE SYSTEM
ENGINE COOLANT TEMPERATURE RECEIVER GAUGE INSPECTION

OPERATION

(a) Disconnect the connector from the sender gauge.

(b) Turn the ignition switch ON, check that the receiver gauge needle indicates COOL.

(c) Ground terminal on the wire harness side connector through a 3.4 watts test bulb.

(d) Turn the ignition switch ON, check that the bulb lights up and the receiver gauge needle moves to the hot side.
If operation is as specified, replace the sender gauge. Then, recheck the system.
If operation is not as specified, measure the receiver gauge resistance.

w/Tachometer

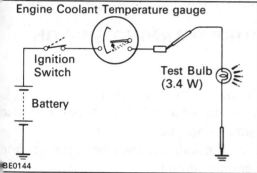

w/o Tachometer

05363
05364

RESISTANCE
w/ Tachometer

Between terminals	Resistance (Ω)
A – B	Approx. 175.7
A – C	Approx. 54.0
B – C	Approx. 229.7

w/o Tachometer

Between terminals	Resistance (Ω)
A – B	Approx. 229.7
A – C	Approx. 54.0
B – C	Approx. 175.7

If resistance value is not as specified, replace the receiver gauge.

BE

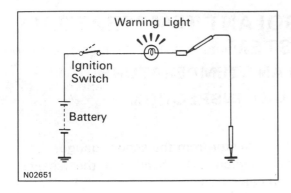

N02651

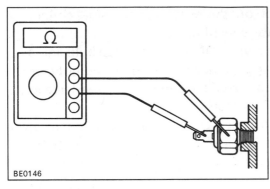

BE0146

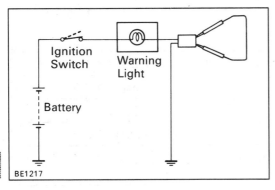

BE1217

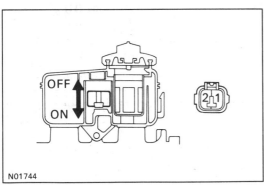

N01744

LOW OIL PRESSURE WARNING SYSTEM

LOW OIL PRESSURE WARNING LIGHT INSPECTION

(a) Disconnect the connector from the warning switch and ground terminal on the wire harness side connector.

(b) Turn the ignition switch ON, check that the warning light lights up.

   If the warning light does not light up, test the bulb.

LOW OIL PRESSURE WARNING SWITCH INSPECTION

(a) Disconnect the connector from the switch.

(b) Check that there is continuity between terminal and ground with the engine stopped.

(c) Check that there is no continuity between terminal and ground with the engine running.

   HINT: Oil pressure should be over 49 kPa (0.5 kgf/cm² 7.1 psi).

   If operation is not as specified, replace the switch.

BRAKE WARNING SYSTEM

BRAKE WARNING LIGHT INSPECTION

(a) Disconnect connector from the brake fluid level warning switch and the parking brake switch.

(b) Turn the ignition switch to START, check that the warning light lights up.

(c) Start the engine, check that the warning light goes out.

   If operation is not as specified, inspect the bulb and the bulb check relay.

BRAKE FLUID LEVEL WARNING SWITCH INSPECTION

(a) Remove the reservoir tank cap and strainer.

(b) Disconnect the connector.

(c) Check that there is no continuity between terminals with the switch OFF (float up).

(d) Use syphon, etc. to take fluid out of the reservoir tank.

(e) Check that there is continuity between terminals with the switch ON (float down).

(f) Pour the fluid back in the reservoir tank.

   If operation is not as specified, replace the switch.

BE

PARKING BRAKE SWITCH INSPECTION

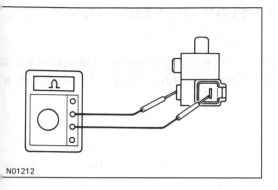

(a) Check that there is continuity between terminals with the switch ON. (switch pin released).

(b) Check that there is no continuity between terminals with the switch OFF (switch pin pushed in).

OPEN DOOR WARNING SYSTEM
OPEN DOOR WARNING LIGHT INSPECTION

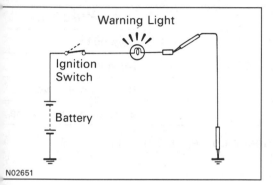

(a) Disconnect the connector from the door courtesy switch and ground terminal on the wire harness side connector.

(b) Turn the ignition switch ON, check that the warning light lights up.

If the warning light does not light up, test the bulb.

DOOR COURTESY SWITCH INSPECTION

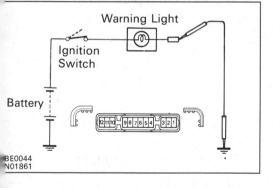

(a) Check that there is continuity between terminal and the switch body with the ON (switch pin released: opened door).

(b) Check that there is no continuity between terminal and the switch body with the OFF (switch pin pushed in: closed door).

If operation is not as specified, replace the switch.

SEAT BELT WARNING SYSTEM
SEAT BELT WARNING LIGHT INSPECTION

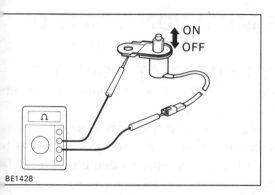

(a) Remove the integration relay from the junction block.

(b) Ground terminal 5 on the junction block side connector.

(c) Turn the ignition switch ON, check that the warning light lights up.

If the warning lights does not light up, test the bulb.

BUCKLE SWITCH INSPECTION

INSPECT SWITCH

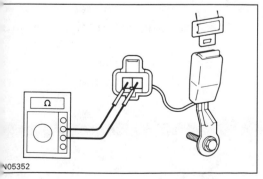

(a) Check that there is continuity between terminals on the switch side connector with the switch ON (belt fastened).

(b) Check that there is no continuity between terminals on the switch side connector with the switch OFF (belt unfastened).

If operation is not as specified, replace the seat belt inner.

Junction Block Side

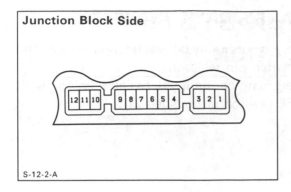

S-12-2-A

INTEGRATION RELAY INSPECTION

RELAY CIRCUIT

Remove the integration relay from the junction block and inspect the connector on the junction side as shown in the chart.

Check for	Tester connection	Condition		Specified valve
Continuity	7 – Ground	Constant		Continuity
Voltage	9 – Ground	Ignition switch position	LOCK or ACC	No voltage
			ON	Battery positive voltage
	3 – Ground	Constant		Battery positive voltage

If circuit is as specified, replace the relay.

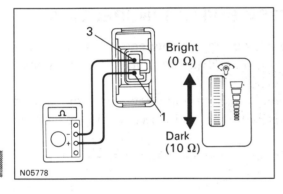

N05778

METER ILLUMINATION CONTROL SYSTEM

LIGHT CONTROL RHEOSTAT INSPECTION

(a) Turn the rheostat knob OFF check that there is continuity between terminals 1 and 3.
(Rheostat knob turned to counter clockwise)

(b) Gradually, turn the rheostat knob from the dark side to bright side, check that the resistance decreases from 1 to 0 Ω. (Rheostat knob turned to clockwise)
If operation is not as specified, replace the rheostat.

BE

DEFOGGER SYSTEM
PARTS LOCATION

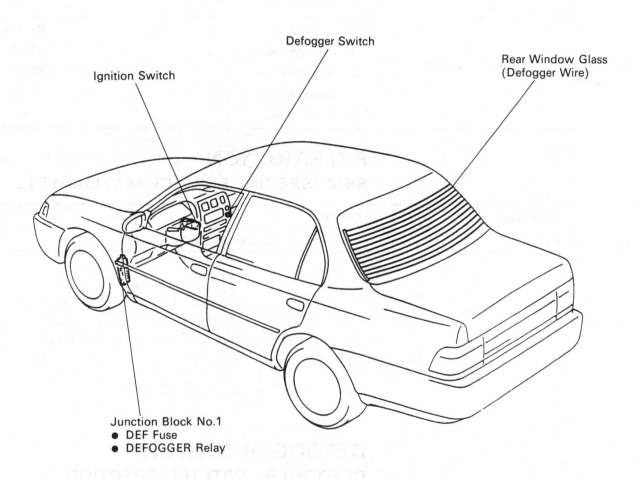

Defogger Switch

Ignition Switch

Rear Window Glass
(Defogger Wire)

Junction Block No.1
● DEF Fuse
● DEFOGGER Relay

05415

TROUBLESHOOTING

The table below will be useful for you in troubleshooting these electrical problems. The most likely causes of the malfunction are shown in the order of their probability. Inspect each part in the order shown, and replace the part when it is found to be faulty.

Trouble	Parts name	See page
Rear window defogger does not operate (w/ Timer)	1. DEFOG Fuse	BE-4, 9
	2. GAUGE Fuse	BE-4, 9
	3. Defogger Switch	BE-63
	4. Defogger Relay	BE-64
	5. Defogger Wire	BE-64
	6. Wire Harness	—
Rear window defogger does not operate (w/o Timer)	1. DEFOG Fuse	BE-4, 9
	2. Defogger Switch	BE-62
	3. Defogger Relay	BE-64
	4. Defogger Wire	BE-64
	5. Wire Harness	—

PREPARATION
SSM (SPECIAL SERVICE MATERIALS)

Part Name	Part No.	Use etc.
Dupont Paste No.4817	–	Rear window defogger wire.

DEFOGGER SWITCH
DEFOGGER SWITCH INSPECTION

w/o Timer

O——O: CONTINUITY INSPECTION

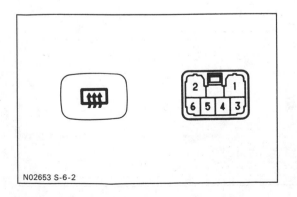

Terminal / Switch position	4	6	Illumination	
			1	3
OFF			O—⊗—O	
ON	O—O			

N02653 S-6-2

If continuity is not as specified, replace the switch.

Switch Side

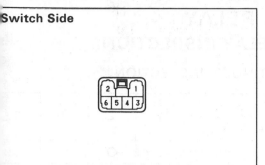

6-6-2

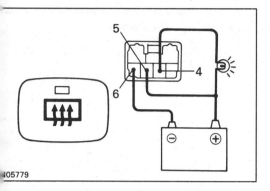

J05779

Wire Harness Side

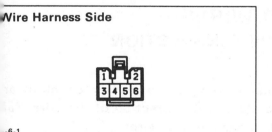

-6-1

W/ Timer
CONTINUITY

Check that there is continuity between terminals 1 and 3. If continuity is not as specified, check the bulb.

TIMER OPERATION

(a) Connect the positive (+) lead from the battery to terminals 5 and the negative (–) lead to terminal 6.

(b) Connect the positive (+) lead from the battery to terminal 4 through a 3.4 watts test bulb.

(c) Push the defogger switch ON, check that the indicator light and test bulb lights up for 12 to 18 minutes, then the indicator light and test bulb lights goes out.

If operation is not as specified, replace the switch.

TIMER CIRCUIT

Disconnect the connector from the switch and inspect the connector on the wire harness side as shown in the chart.

Check for	Tester connection	Condition		Specified value
Continuity	6 – Ground	Constant		Continuity
Voltage	2 – Ground	Ignition switch position	LOCK or ACC	No voltage
			ON	Battery positive voltage
	4 – Ground	Ignition switch position	LOCK or ACC	No voltage
			ON	Battery positive voltage
Operation	–	Connect terminals 4 and 6.		Defogger system operation is normal

If the circuit is as specified, replace the switch.

BE

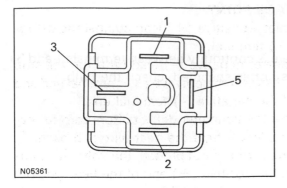

N05361

DEFOGGER RELAY
DEFOGGER RELAY INSPECTION

○———○ : CONTINUITY INSPECTION.

Terminal Condition	1	2	3	5
Constant	○—〰〰—○			
Apply battery positive voltage to terminal 1 and 2.			○——○	

If continuity is not as specified, replace the relay.

DEFOGGER WIRES
DEFOGGER WIRE INSPECTION

NOTICE:
- **When cleaning the glass, use a soft, dry cloth, an** **wipe the glass in the direction of the wire. Ta** **care not to damage the wires.**
- **Do not use detergents or glass cleaners with abra** **sive ingredients.**
- **When measuring voltage, wind a piece of tin fo** **around the top of the negative (–) probe and pre** **the foil against the wire with your finger** **shown.**

1. **WIRE BREAKAGE**
(a) Turn the ignition switch ON.
(b) Push in the defogger switch.
(c) Inspect the voltage at the center of each heat wire shown.

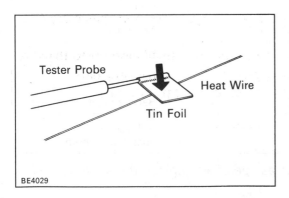

Tester Probe   Heat Wire

Tin Foil

BE4029

Voltage	Criteria
approx. 5 V	Okey (No break in wire)
approx. 10 V or 0 V	Broken wire

HINT: If there is 10 V, the wire is broken between t center of the wire and positive (+) end. If there is voltage, the wire is broken between the center of the w and ground.

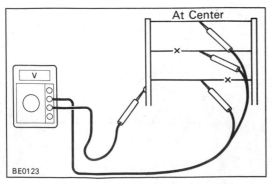

At Center

BE0123

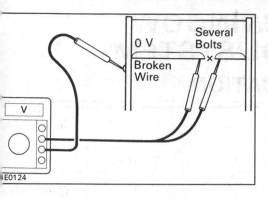

2.   WIRE BREAKAGE POINT

(a)   Place the boltmeter positive (+) lead against the defogger positive (+) terminal.

(b)   Place the boltmeter negative (–) lead with the foil strip against the heat wire at the positive (+) terminal end and slide it toward the negative (–) terminal end.

(c)   The point where the voltmeter deflects from zero to several volts is the place where the heat wire is broken.

HINT: If the heat wire is not broken, the voltmeter indicates 0 volts at the positive (+) end of the heat wire but gradually increases to about 12 V as the meter probe is moved to the other end.

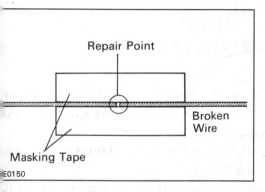

3.   DEFOGGER WIRES REPAIR

(a)   Clean the broken wire tips with a grease, wax and silicone remover.

(b)   Please the masking tape along both sides of the wire to be repaired.

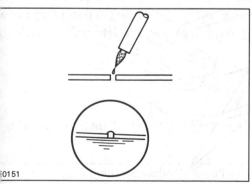

(c)   Throughly mix the repair agent (Dupont paste No.4817 or equivalent).

(d)   Using a fine tip brush, apply a small amount to the wire.

(e)   After a few minutes, remove the masking tape.

(f)   Allow the repair to stand at least 24 hours.

POWER WINDOW CONTROL SYSTEM
PARTS LOCATION

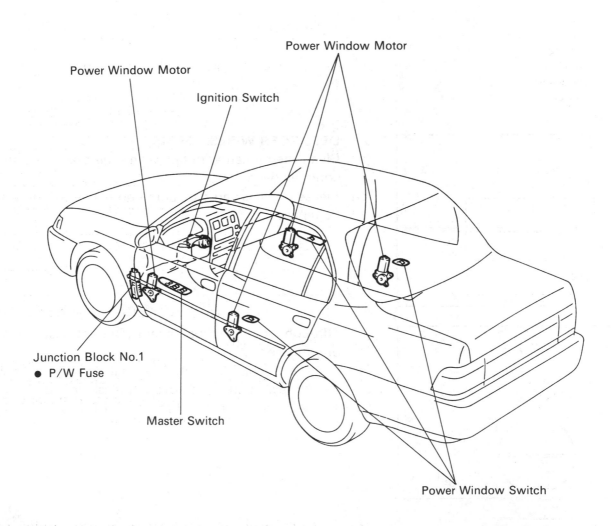

Power Window Motor

Power Window Motor

Ignition Switch

Junction Block No.1
● P/W Fuse

Master Switch

Power Window Switch

N05416

MASTER SWITCH
MASTER SWITCH INSPECTION

CONTINUITY

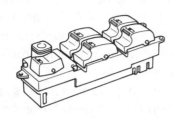

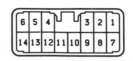

BE2594 S-14-2-B

Window operation	Front								Rear							
	Driver's				Passenger's				Left				Right			
Terminal	1 and 2	6	7 and 8	13	1 and 2	5	7 and 8	12	1 and 2	7 and 8	9	10	1 and 2	7 and 8	11	14
Window lock — UP	○a	○b	○b	○a	○a	○b	○b	○a	○a	○b	○b	○a	○a	○b	○b	○a
Window lock — OFF	○a	○a	○b	○b	○a	○a	○b	○b	○a	○a	○b	○b	○a	○a	○b	○b
Window lock — DOWN	○a	○b	○a	○b	○a	○b	○a	○b	○a	○b	○a	○b	○a	○b	○a	○b
Window unlock — UP	○a	○b	○b	○a			○a	○a		○a		○a		○a	○a	
Window unlock — OFF	○a	○a	○b	○b	○a	○a					○a	○a			○a	○a
Window unlock — DOWN	○a	○b	○a	○b		○a		○a		○a		○a		○a		○a

(○a and ○b indicate the terminals joined by each continuity bar — dots sharing the same letter are connected.)

If continuity is not as specified, replace the master switch.

ILLUMINATION LIGHT
(a) Set the window lock switch to the unlock position.
(b) Connect the positive (+) lead from the battery to terminal 7 and the negative (–) lead to terminal 1, check that all the illuminations light up.

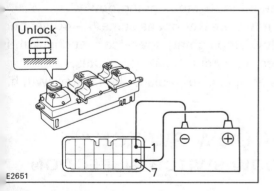

E2651

(c) Set the window lock switch to the lock position, check that all the passenger's power window switch illuminations go out.
If operation is not as specified, replace the master switch.

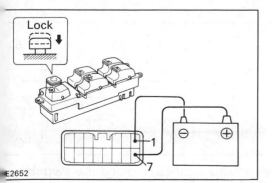

E2652

BE

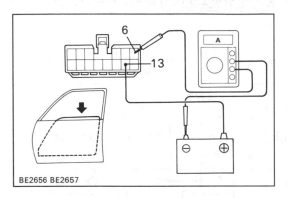

BE2654 BE2657

BE2656 BE2657

ONE TOUCH POWER WINDOW SYSTEM
(Inspection using an ammeter)
(a) Disconnect the connector from the master switch.
(b) Connect the positive (+) lead from the ammeter to terminal 6 on the wire harness side connector and the negative (–) lead to negative terminal of the battery.
(c) Connect the positive (+) lead from the battery to terminal 13 on the wire harness side connector.
(d) As the window goes down, check that the current flow approximately 7 A.
(e) Check that the current increases approximately 14.5 A or more when the window stops going down.
HINT: The circuit breaker opens some 4 – 40 second after the window stops going down, so that check must be made before the circuit breaker operates.
If the operation is as specified, replace the master switch.

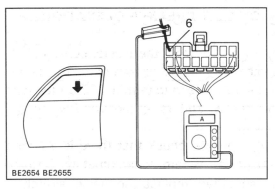

BE2654 BE2655

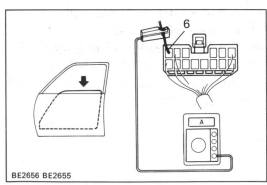

BE2656 BE2655

(Inspection using an ammeter with a current-measuring probe.)
(a) Remove the master switch with connector connected.
(b) Attach a current-measuring probe to terminal 6 of the wire harness.
(c) Turn the ignition switch ON and set a the power window switch in the down position.
(d) As the window goes down, check that the current flow approximately 7 A.
(e) Check that the current increases approximately 14.5 A or more when the window stops going down.
HINT: The circuit breaker opens some 4 – 40 second after the window stops going down, so that check must be made before the circuit breaker operates.
If operation is as specified, replace the master switch.

POWER WINDOW SWITCH
POWER WINDOW SWITCH INSPECTION

CONTINUITY

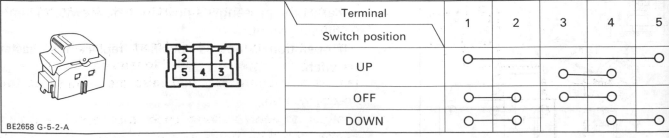

Terminal / Switch position	1	2	3	4	5
UP	O——————————————————————O			O——————O	
			O——————O		
OFF	O——————O		O——————O		
DOWN	O——————O			O——————O	

If continuity is not as specified, replace the switch.

● **FRONT DOOR**

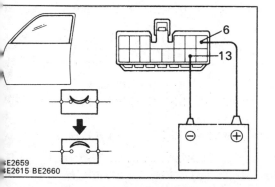

● **REAR DOOR**

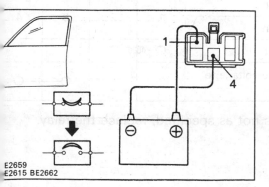

N05780
N05781

POWER WINDOW MOTOR
POWER WINDOW MOTOR INSPECTION
LEFT SIDE DOOR MOTOR (OPERATION)
(a) Connect the positive (+) lead from the battery to terminal 1 and the negative (–) lead to terminal 2, check that the motor turns counterclockwise.

(b) Reverse the polartiy, check that the motor turns clockwise.

    If operation is not as specified, replace the motor.

LEFT SIDE MOTOR (CIRCUIT BREAKER OPERATION)
Driver's Door:

(a) Disconnect the connector from the master switch.

(b) Connect the positive (+) lead from the battery to terminal 6 and the negative (–) lead to terminal 13 on the wire harness side connector and raise the window to full closed position.

(c) Continue to apply voltage, check that there is a circuit breaker operation noise within approximately 4 to 40 seconds.

(d) Reverse the polarity, check that window begins to descend within approximately 60 seconds.

    If operation is not as specified, replace the motor.

E2659
E2615 BE2660

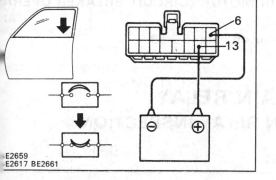

E2659
E2617 BE2661

Passenger's Door:

(a) Disconnect the connector from the power window switch.

(b) Connect the positive (+) lead from the battery to terminal 1 and the negative (–) lead to terminal 4 on the wire harness side connector, and raise the window to full closed position.

(c) Continue to apply voltage, check that there is a circuit breaker operation noise within approximately 4 to 40 seconds.

E2659
E2615 BE2662

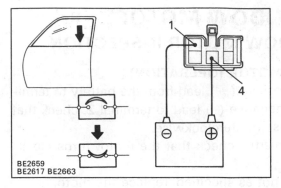

BE2659
BE2617 BE2663

(d) Reverse the polarity, check that the window begins to descend within approximately 60 seconds.
If operation is not as specified, replace the motor.

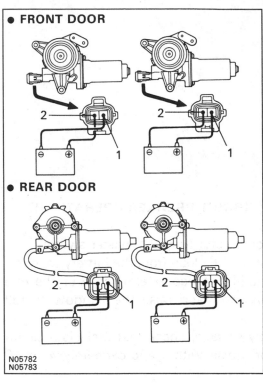

● **FRONT DOOR**

● **REAR DOOR**

N05782
N05783

RIGHT SIDE DOOR MOTOR (MOTOR OPERATION)

(a) Connect the positive (+) lead from the battery to terminal 1 and the negative (–) lead to terminal 2, check that the motor turns clockwise.

(b) Reverse the polarity, check that the motor turns counter clockwise.
If operation is not as specified, replace the motor.

RIGHT SIDE DOOR MOTOR (CIRCUIT BREAKER OPERATION)
See Left Side Motor on page BE-69.

POWER MAIN RELAY
POWER MAIN RELAY INSPECTION

CONTINUITY

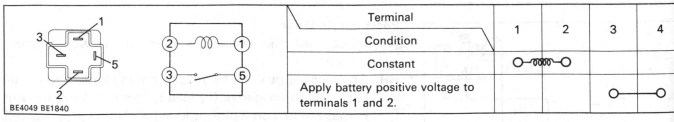

BE4049 BE1840

Terminal Condition	1	2	3	4
Constant	O—‿‿‿—O			
Apply battery positive voltage to terminals 1 and 2.			O—————O	

If continuity is not as specified, replace the relay.

BE

SLIDING ROOF SYSTEM
PARTS LOCATION

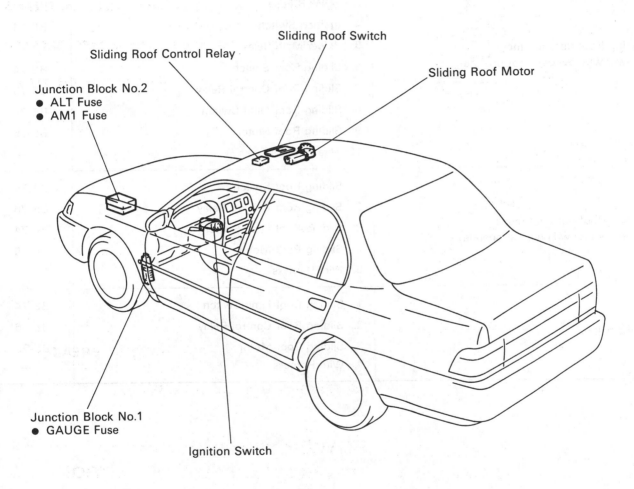

Sliding Roof Switch

Sliding Roof Control Relay

Sliding Roof Motor

Junction Block No.2
● ALT Fuse
● AM1 Fuse

Junction Block No.1
● GAUGE Fuse

Ignition Switch

TROUBLESHOOTING

The table below will be useful for you in troubleshooting these electrical problems. The most likely causes of the malfunction are shown in the order of their probability. Inspect each part in the order shown, and replace the part when it is found to be faulty.

[OPEN]

Trouble	Parts name	See page
Sliding Roof does not move (Power window does not operate)	1. DOME Fuse	BE-4, 9
	2. GAUGE Fuse	BE-4, 9
	3. POWER Fuse	BE-4, 9
	4. Ignition Switch	BE-14
	5. Power Main Relay	—
	6. Sliding Roof Switch	BE-74
	7. Sliding Roof Control Relay	BE-76
	8. Sliding Roof Limit Switch	BE-74
	9. Sliding Roof Motor	BE-75
	10. Wire Harness	—
Sliding Roof does not move (Power window is normal operate)	1. Sliding Roof Switch	BE-74
	2. Sliding Roof Control Relay	BE-76
	3. Sliding Roof Limit Switch	BE-74
	4. Sliding Roof Motor	BE-75
	5. Wire Harness	—
Stops halfway	1. Sliding Roof Limit Switch	BE-74
	2. Sliding Roof Control Relay	BE-76
	3. Sliding Roof Motor	BE-75
	4. Wire Harness	—

BE

[CLOSE]

Trouble	Parts name	See page
Sliding Roof does not move (Power window does not operate)	1. DOME Fuse	BE-4, 9
	2. GAUGE Fuse	BE-4, 9
	3. POWER Fuse	BE-4, 9
	4. Ignition Switch	BE-14
	5. Power Main Relay	BE-70
	6. Sliding Roof Switch	BE-74
	7. Sliding Roof Control Relay	BE-76
	8. Sliding Roof Limit Switch	BE-74
	9. Sliding Roof Motor	BE-75
	10. Wire Harness	—
Sliding Roof does not move (Power window is normal operate)	1. Sliding Roof Switch	BE-74
	2. Sliding Roof Control Relay	BE-76
	3. Sliding Roof Limit Switch	BE-74
	4. Sliding Roof Motor	BE-75
	5. Wire Harness	—
Stops halfway	1. Sliding Roof Limit Switch	BE-74
	2. Sliding Roof Control Relay	BE-76
	3. Sliding Roof Motor	BE-75
	4. Wire Harness	—
Sliding roof does not stop at the stopping position.	1. Sliding Roof Limit Switch	BE-74
	2. Sliding Roof Control Relay	BE-76
Returns and stops	1. Sliding Roof Limit Switch	BE-74
	2. Sliding Roof Control Relay	BE-76

BE

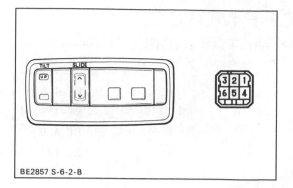

BE2857 S-6-2-B

SLIDING ROOF SWITCH
SLIDING ROOF SWITCH INSPECTION

O———O : CONTINUITY INSPECTION

Terminal Switch position		2	3	4	5	6
SLIDE	OPEN		O——O			
	OFF					
	CLOSE				O——O	
TILT	DOWN	O——O				
	OFF					
	UP				O——O	

If continuity is not as specified, replace the switch.

LIMIT SWITCH
LIMIT SWITCH INSPECTION

O———O : CONTINUITY INSPECTION

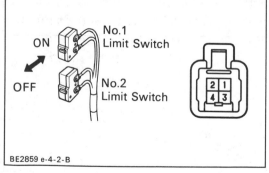

BE2859 e-4-2-B

Terminal Switch position		1	2	4
No.1 Limit switch	OFF (SW pin released)			
	ON (SW pin pushed in)	O——————O		
No.2 Limit switch	OFF (SW pin released)			
	ON (SW pin pushed in)		O——O	

If continuity is not specified, replace the switch.

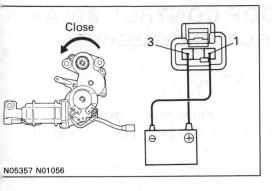

N05357 N01056

SLIDING ROOF MOTOR
SLIDING ROOF MOTOR INSPECTION

OPERATION

(a) Connect the positive (+) lead from the battery to terminal 3 and the negative (−) lead to terminal 1, check that the motor turns to counterclockwise (moves to the close side).

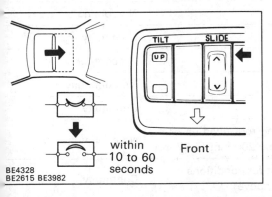

N05357 N01057

(b) Reverse the polarity, check that the motor turns to clockwise (moves to the open side).
   If operation is not as specified, replace the motor.

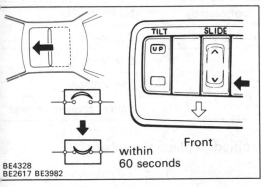

BE4328
BE2615 BE3982

CIRCUIT BREAKER OPERATION

(a) With the sliding roof in the fully opened position, hold the sliding roof switch in "OPEN" position and check that there is a circuit breaker operation noise within 10 to 60 seconds.

(b) With the sliding roof in fully opened position, hold the sliding roof switch in "CLOSE" position and check that the sliding roof begins to close within 60 seconds.
   If operation is not as specified, replace the motor.

BE4328
BE2617 BE3982

BE

Wire Harness Side

1	2	3		4	5
6	7	8	9	10	11	12

S-12-1

SLIDING ROOF CONTROL RELAY
SLIDING ROOF CONTROL RELAY INSPECTION

RELAY CIRCUIT
Disconnect the relay connector and inspect the connector on the wire harness side as shown in the chart.

Check for	Tester connection	Condition		Specified value
Continuity	8 – ground	Sliding roof control switch position (SLIDE)	OFF or CLOSE	No continuity
			OPEN	Continuity
	7 – ground	Sliding roof control switch position (SLIDE)	OFF or OPEN	No continuity
			CLOSE	Continuity
	2 – ground	Sliding roof control switch position (TILT)	OFF or DOWN	No continuity
			UP	Continuity
	5 – ground	Constant		No continuity
	1 – 5	Constant		Continuity
	1 – ground	Constant		No continuity
	11 – ground	Sliding roof control switch position (TILT)	OFF or UP	No continuity
			DOWN	Continuity
	10 – ground	No.1 limit switch position	OFF (Sliding roof tilted up or open approx. 200 mm (7.87 in.)	No continuity
			ON (Except for conditions mentioned above)	Continuity
	4 – ground	No.2 limit switch position	OFF (Sliding roof closed)	No continuity
			ON (Sliding roof open)	Continuity
	12 – ground	Constant		Continuity
Voltage	6 – Ground	Ignition switch position	LOCK or ACC	*No voltage
			ON	Battery positive voltage

If circuit is as specified, replace the relay.

POWER MAIN RELAY
POWER MAIN RELAY INSPECTION

See Taillight Control Relay on page BE-25.

POWER MIRROR CONTROL SYSTEM
PARTS LOCATION

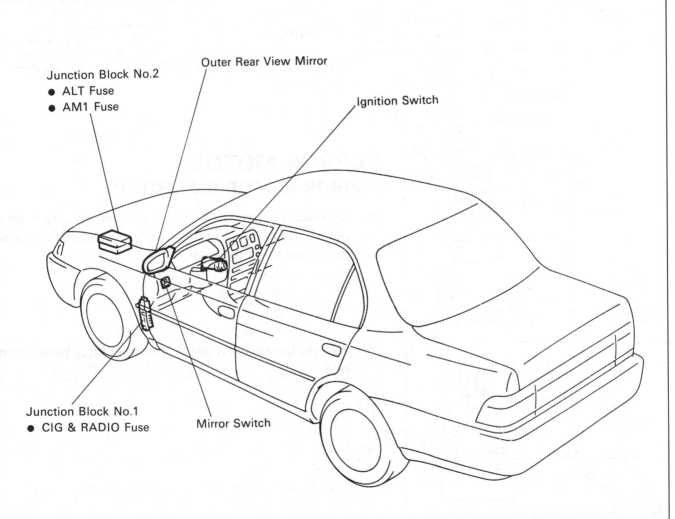

Outer Rear View Mirror

Junction Block No.2
- ALT Fuse
- AM1 Fuse

Ignition Switch

Junction Block No.1
- CIG & RADIO Fuse

Mirror Switch

N05419

MIRROR SWITCH
MIRROR SWITCH INSPECTION

O————O : CONTINUITY INSPECTION

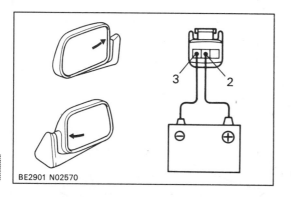

Left/Right Adjustment

N01992 S-8-2

Mirror	Left					Right				
Terminal	1	4	8	3	7	7	3	8	6	5
Switch position										
UP		O—	—O	O—	—O	O—	—O	O—	—O	
DOWN		O—	O—	—O	—O		O—	O—	—O	—O
LEFT	O—		—O	O—	—O	O—	—O	O—		—O
RIGHT		O—	O—	—O	—O		O—	O—	—O	—O

If continuity is not as specified, replace the switch.

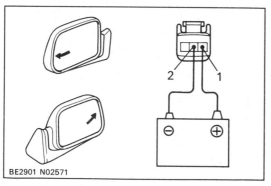

MIRROR MOTOR
MIRROR MOTOR INSPECTION

(a) Connect the positive (+) lead from the battery to terminal 3 and the negative (–) lead to terminal 2, check that the mirror turns to left side.

BE2901 N02570

(b) Reverse the polarity, check that the mirror turns to right side.

BE2901 N02571

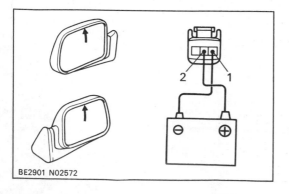

(c) Connect the positive (+) lead from the battery to terminal 1 and the negative (–) lead to terminal 2, check that the mirror turns upward.

BE2901 N02572

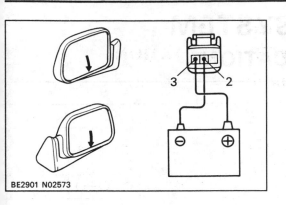

BE2901 N02573

(d) Reverse the polarity, check that the mirror turns downward.
If operation is not as specified, replace the mirror assembly.

AUDIO SYSTEM
PARTS LOCATION

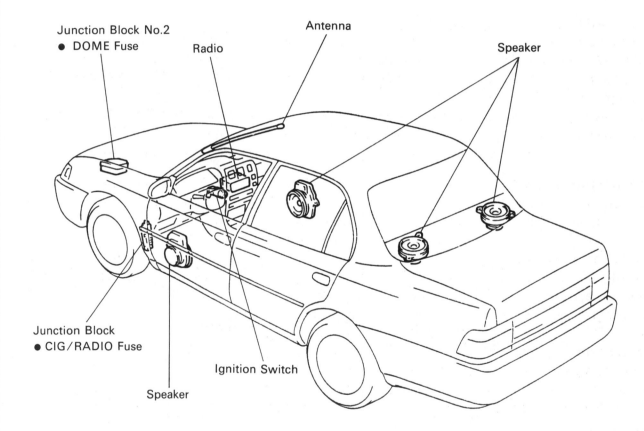

Junction Block No.2
● DOME Fuse

Radio

Antenna

Speaker

Junction Block
● CIG/RADIO Fuse

Speaker

Ignition Switch

BE

DESCRIPTION

RADIO WAVE BAND

The radio wave bends in radio broadcasting are as follows:

Frequency	30kHz		300kHz		3MHz		30MHz		300MHz
Designation		LF		MF		HF		VHF	
Radio wave			AM				FM		
Modulation method			Amplitude modulation				Frequency modulation		

LF: Low Frequency MF: Medium Frequency HF: High Frequency VHF: Very High Frequency

HINT: In this section, the term "AM" includes LW, MW and SW, and the term "FM" includes UKW.

SERVICE AREA

There is great difference in the size of the service area for AM, FM monaural, and FM stereo broadcasting. Thus it may happen that FM broadcast cannot be received even though AM comes in very clearly.

Not only does FM stereo have the smallest service area, but it also picks up static and other types of interference ("noise") the most easily.

RECEPTION PROBLEMS

Besides the problem of static, there are also the problems called "fading", "multipath" and "fade out". These problems are caused not by electrical noise but by the nature of the radio waves themselves.

Fading

Besides electrical interference. AM broadcasts are also susceptible to other types of interference, especially at night. This is because AM radio waves bounce off the ionosphere at night. These radio waves then interfere with the signals from the same transmitter that reach the vehicle's antenna directly. This type of interference is called "fading".

Multipath

One type of interference caused by the bouncing of radio waves off of obstructions is called "multipath". Multipath occurs when a signal from the broadcast transmitter antenna bounces off of buildings and mountains and interferes with the signal that is received directly.

Fade Out

Because FM radio waves are of higher frequencies than AM radio waves, they bounce off of buildings, mountains, and other obstructions. For this reason, FM signals often seem to gradually disappear or fade away as the vehicle goes behind a building or other obstruction. This is called "fade out".

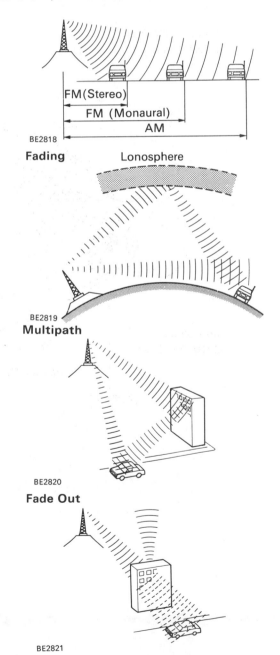

BE2818
Fading   Lonosphere

BE2819
Multipath

BE2820
Fade Out

BE2821

BE

MAINTENANCE

(TAPE PLAYER)

Head Cleaning

(a) Raise the cassette door with your finger. Next using a pencil or like object, push in the guide.

(b) Using a cleaning pen or cotton applicator soaked in cleaner, clean the head surface, pinch rollers and capstans.

Example:

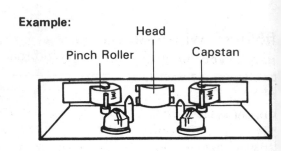

C0192

TROUBLESHOOTING

NOTICE: When replacing the internal mechanism (ECU part) of the audio system, be careful that no part of your body or clothing comes in contact with the terminals of the leads from the IC etc. of the replacement part (spare part).

HINT: This inspection procedure is a simple troubleshooting which should be carried out on the vehicle during system operation and was prepared on the assumption of system component troubles (except for the wires and connectors, etc.).

Always inspect the trouble taking the following items into consideration.

- Open or short circuit of the wire harness
- Connector or terminal connection fault

	Problem	No.
Radio	No power coming in.	1
	Power coming in, but radio not operating.	2
	Noise present, but AM-FM not operating.	3
	Either speaker does not work.	4
	Either AM or FM does not work.	5
	Reception poor (Volume faint).	5
	Few preset tuning bands.	5
	Sound quality poor.	6
	Cannot set station select button.	7
	Preset memory disappears.	7
Tape Player	Cassette tape cannot be inserted.	8
	Cassette tape inserts, but no power.	9
	Power coming in, but tape player not operating.	10
	Either speaker does not work.	11
	Sound quality poor (Volume faint).	12
	Tape jammed, malfunction with tape speed or auto-reverse.	13
	APS, SKIP, RPT buttons not operating.	14
	Cassette tape will not eject.	15
Antenna	Antenna-related.	16
Noise	Noise produced by vibration or shock while driving.	17
	Noise produced when engine starts.	18

BE

HOW TO USE DIAGNOSTIC CHART

Reference:

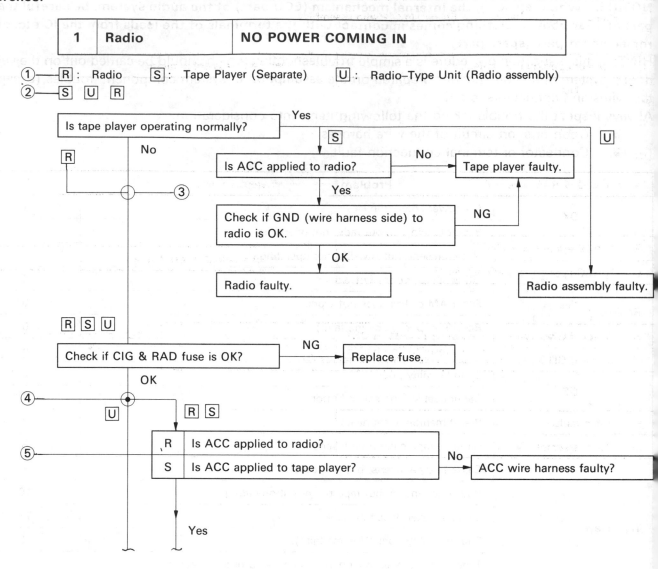

1	Radio	**NO POWER COMING IN**

① — R : Radio　　S : Tape Player (Separate)　　U : Radio–Type Unit (Radio assembly)

② — S　U　R

Is tape player operating normally? — Yes

R — No

③

S — Is ACC applied to radio? — No → Tape player faulty.

Yes

Check if GND (wire harness side) to radio is OK. — NG

OK

Radio faulty.

U — Radio assembly faulty.

R S U

Check if CIG & RAD fuse is OK? — NG → Replace fuse.

OK

④

U — R S

R — Is ACC applied to radio?
S — Is ACC applied to tape player? — No → ACC wire harness faulty?

⑤

Yes

---

① Audio system type and symbol used.

　HINT: Confirm the applicable type of audio system.

② Symbol for type of audio system the question applies to.

　HINT: If the audio system type is not applicable, proceed to next question below.

③ Junction without black circle.

　HINT: Proceed to next question below.

④ Junction with black circle.

　HINT: Proceed to question for applicable audio system type.

⑤ HINT: Select question for applicable audio system type.

1	Radio	**NO POWER COMING IN**

R : Radio   U : Radio-Tape Player Unit (Radio assembly)

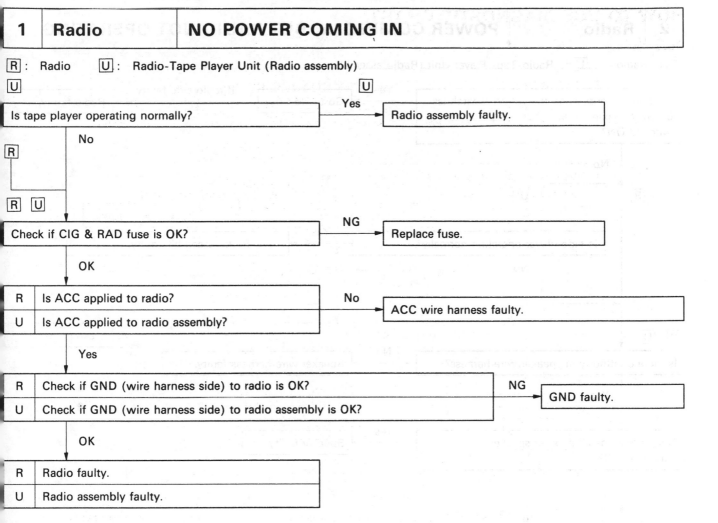

U

| U Is tape player operating normally? | Yes → | Radio assembly faulty. |

No

R

R U

| Check if CIG & RAD fuse is OK? | NG → | Replace fuse. |

OK

| R Is ACC applied to radio? | No → | ACC wire harness faulty. |
| U Is ACC applied to radio assembly? | | |

Yes

| R Check if GND (wire harness side) to radio is OK? | NG → | GND faulty. |
| U Check if GND (wire harness side) to radio assembly is OK? | | |

OK

| R Radio faulty. |
| U Radio assembly faulty. |

BE

| 2 | Radio | **POWER COMING IN, BUT RADIO NOT OPERATING** |

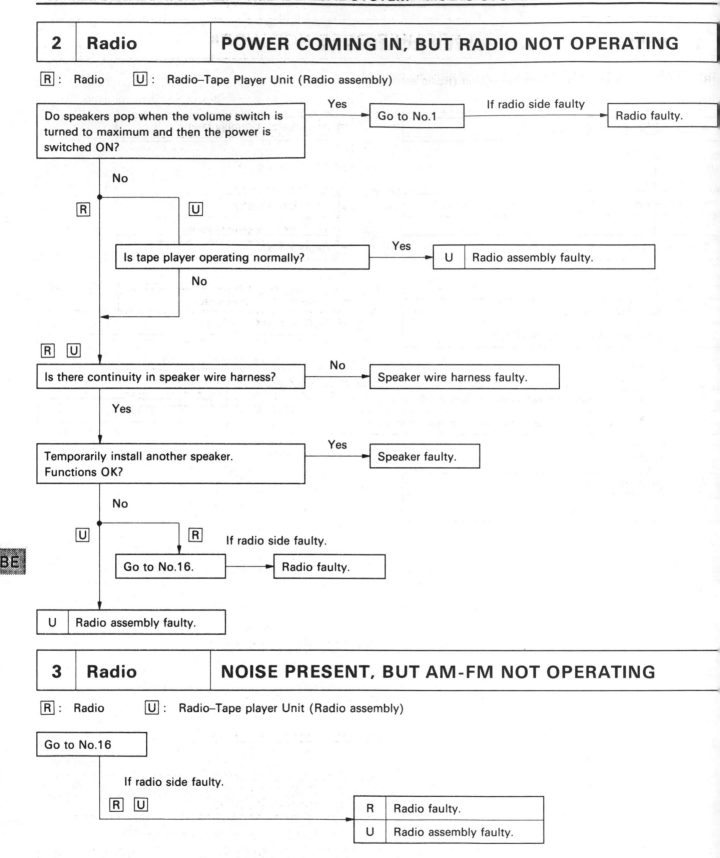

R : Radio   U : Radio–Tape Player Unit (Radio assembly)

Do speakers pop when the volume switch is turned to maximum and then the power is switched ON?
— Yes → Go to No.1 — If radio side faulty → Radio faulty.

No

R   U

Is tape player operating normally? — Yes → U | Radio assembly faulty.

No

R   U

Is there continuity in speaker wire harness? — No → Speaker wire harness faulty.

Yes

Temporarily install another speaker. Functions OK? — Yes → Speaker faulty.

No

U   R

Go to No.16. — If radio side faulty. → Radio faulty.

U | Radio assembly faulty.

| 3 | Radio | **NOISE PRESENT, BUT AM-FM NOT OPERATING** |

R : Radio   U : Radio–Tape player Unit (Radio assembly)

Go to No.16

If radio side faulty.

R   U

| R | Radio faulty. |
| U | Radio assembly faulty. |

BE

4	Radio	**EITHER SPEAKER DOES NOT WORK**

R : Radio   U : Radio–Tape Player Unit (Radio assembly)

U

Is tape player operating normally? ──Yes──▶ | U | Radio assembly faulty. |

│ No

R U

Is hiss noise produced by non-functioning speaker? ──Yes──▶

| R | Radio faulty. |
| U | Radio assembly faulty. |

│ No

Is there continuity in speaker wire harness? ──No──▶ Speaker wire harness faulty.

│ Yes

Temporarily install another speaker. Functions OK? ──Yes──▶ Speaker faulty.

│ No

| R | Radio faulty. |
| U | Radio assembly faulty. |

BE

| 5 | Radio | **EITHER AM OR FM DOES NOT WORK, RECEPTION POOR (VOLUME FAINT), FEW PRESET TUNING BANDS** |

R : Radio   U : Radio–Tape Player Unit (Radio assembly)

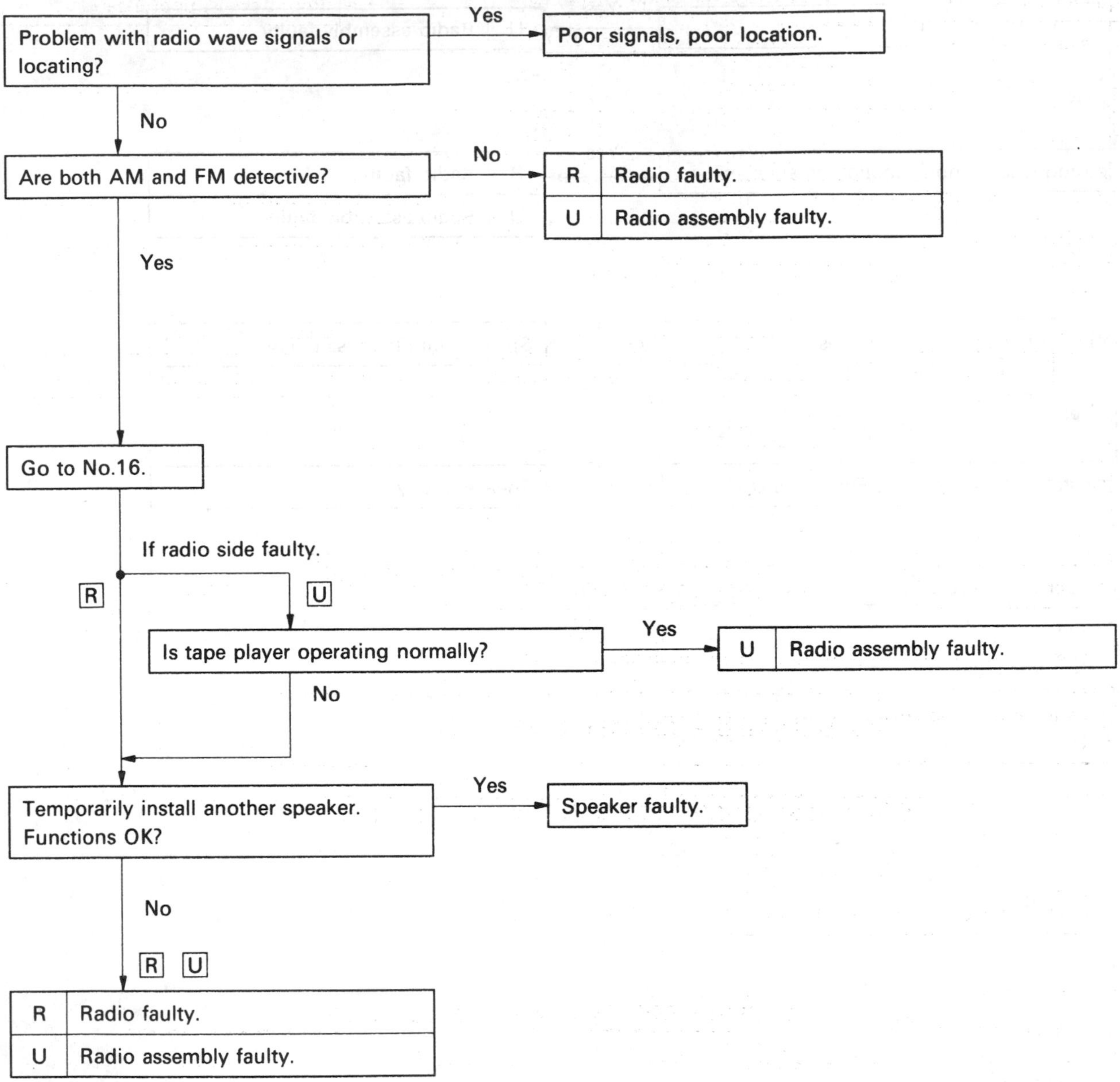

Problem with radio wave signals or locating? —— Yes ——> Poor signals, poor location.

No

Are both AM and FM detective? —— No ——>

| R | Radio faulty. |
| U | Radio assembly faulty. |

Yes

Go to No.16.

If radio side faulty.

R

U

Is tape player operating normally? —— Yes ——> | U | Radio assembly faulty. |

No

Temporarily install another speaker. Functions OK? —— Yes ——> Speaker faulty.

No

R U

| R | Radio faulty. |
| U | Radio assembly faulty. |

| 6 | Radio | **SOUND QUALITY POOR** |

R : Radio   U : Radio–Tape Player Unit (Radio assembly)

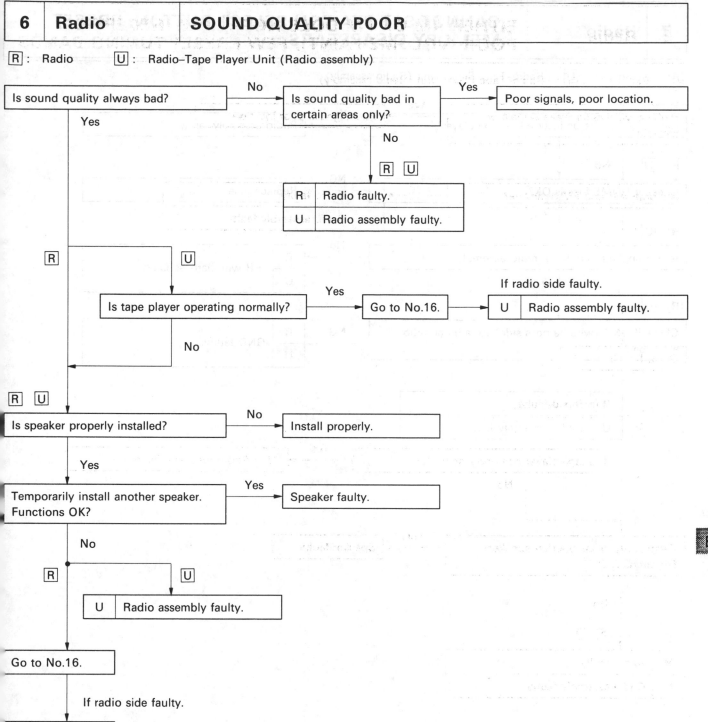

7	Radio	**CANNOT SET STATION SELECT BUTTON, PRESET MEMORY DISAPPEARS**

R : Radio   U : Radio–Tape Player Unit (Radio assemly)

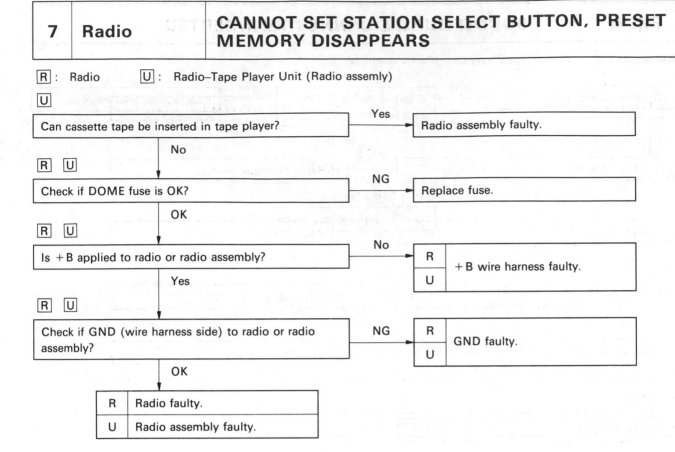

R	Radio faulty.
U	Radio assembly faulty.

8	Tape Player	CASSETTE TAPE CANNOT BE INSERTED

Only for Radio–Tape Player Unit (Radio assembly)

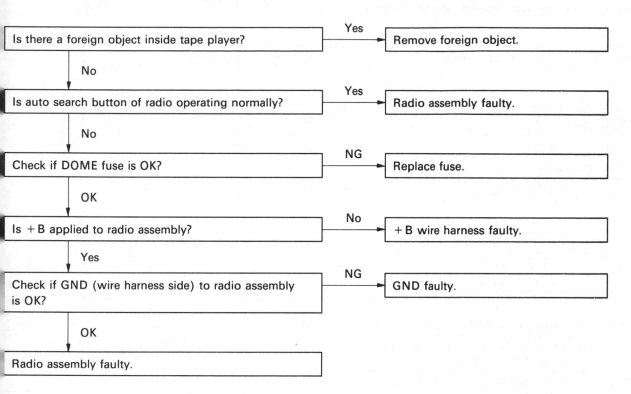

Is there a foreign object inside tape player? — Yes → Remove foreign object.

No ↓

Is auto search button of radio operating normally? — Yes → Radio assembly faulty.

No ↓

Check if DOME fuse is OK? — NG → Replace fuse.

OK ↓

Is +B applied to radio assembly? — No → +B wire harness faulty.

Yes ↓

Check if GND (wire harness side) to radio assembly is OK? — NG → GND faulty.

OK ↓

Radio assembly faulty.

9	Tape Player	CASSETTE TAPE INSERTS, BUT NO POWER

Only for Radio–Tape Player Unit (Radio assembly)

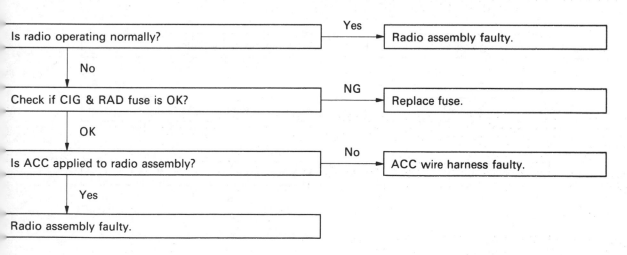

Is radio operating normally? — Yes → Radio assembly faulty.

No ↓

Check if CIG & RAD fuse is OK? — NG → Replace fuse.

OK ↓

Is ACC applied to radio assembly? — No → ACC wire harness faulty.

Yes ↓

Radio assembly faulty.

10	Tape Player	POWER COMING IN, BUT TAPE PLAYER NOT OPERATING

Only for Radio – Tape Player Unit (Radio assembly)

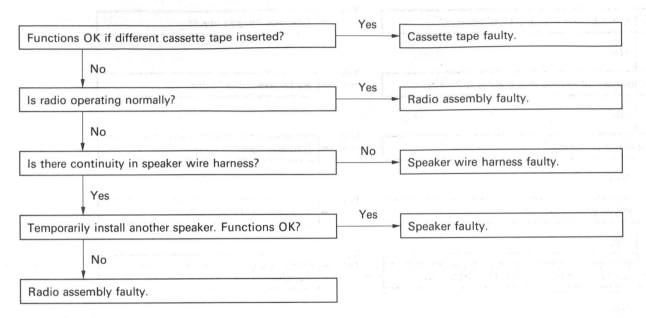

Functions OK if different cassette tape inserted?	—Yes→	Cassette tape faulty.

↓ No

Is radio operating normally?	—Yes→	Radio assembly faulty.

↓ No

Is there continuity in speaker wire harness?	—No→	Speaker wire harness faulty.

↓ Yes

Temporarily install another speaker. Functions OK?	—Yes→	Speaker faulty.

↓ No

Radio assembly faulty.

11	Tape Player	EITHER SPEAKER DOES NOT WORK

Only for Radio – Tape Player Unit (Radio assembly)

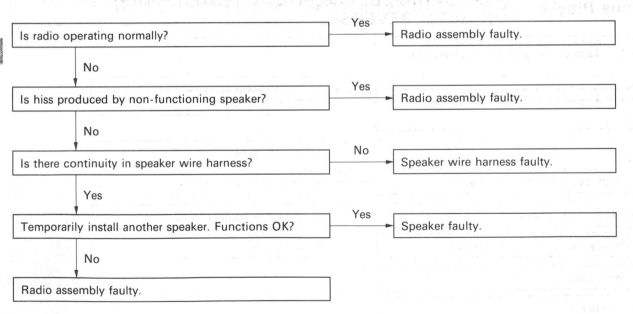

Is radio operating normally?	—Yes→	Radio assembly faulty.

↓ No

Is hiss produced by non-functioning speaker?	—Yes→	Radio assembly faulty.

↓ No

Is there continuity in speaker wire harness?	—No→	Speaker wire harness faulty.

↓ Yes

Temporarily install another speaker. Functions OK?	—Yes→	Speaker faulty.

↓ No

Radio assembly faulty.

BE

| 12 | Tape Player | **SOUND QUALITY POOR (VOLUME FAINT)** |

Only for Radio – Tape Player Unit (Radio assembly)

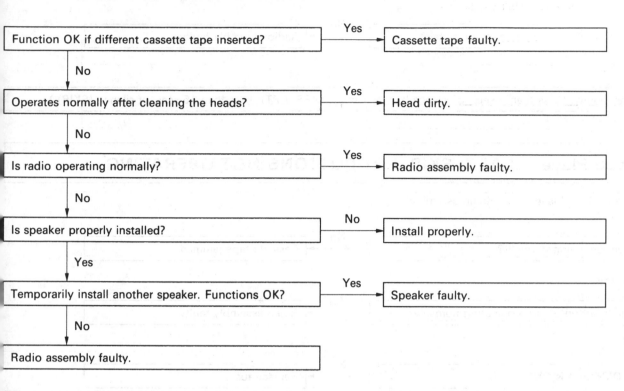

	Yes	
Function OK if different cassette tape inserted?	→	Cassette tape faulty.

No ↓

	Yes	
Operates normally after cleaning the heads?	→	Head dirty.

No ↓

	Yes	
Is radio operating normally?	→	Radio assembly faulty.

No ↓

	No	
Is speaker properly installed?	→	Install properly.

Yes ↓

	Yes	
Temporarily install another speaker. Functions OK?	→	Speaker faulty.

No ↓

Radio assembly faulty.

| 13 | Tape Player | **TAPE JAMMED, MALFUNCTION WITH TAPE SPEED OR AUTO-REVERSE** |

Only for Radio – Tape Player Unit (Radio assembly)

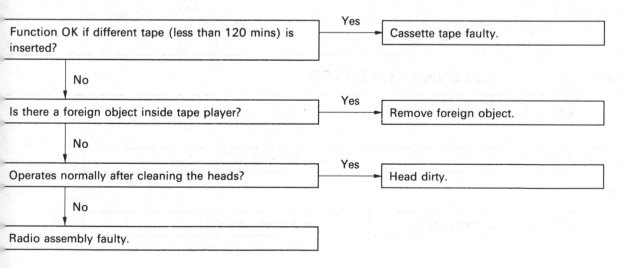

	Yes	
Function OK if different tape (less than 120 mins) is inserted?	→	Cassette tape faulty.

No ↓

	Yes	
Is there a foreign object inside tape player?	→	Remove foreign object.

No ↓

	Yes	
Operates normally after cleaning the heads?	→	Head dirty.

No ↓

Radio assembly faulty.

BE

| 14 | Tape Player | **APS, SKIP RPT BUTTONS NOT OPERATING** |

Only for Radio – Tape Player Unit (Radio assembly)

Functions OK if different cassette tape inserted? — **No** → Radio assembly faulty.

↓ **Yes**

Cassette tape faulty. (Less than 3 secs. of silence between songs (APS, RPT). Less than 15 secs. of silence (SKIP).)

| 15 | Tape Player | **APS, SKIP, RPT BUTTONS NOT OPERATING** |

Only for Radio – Tape Player Unit (Radio assembly)

Is tape player operating normally? — **No** → Cassette tape jammed.

↓ **Tape**

Is auto search button of radio operating normally? — **Yes** → Radio assembly faulty.

↓ **No**

Check if DOME fuse is OK? — **NG** → Replace fuse.

↓ **OK**

Is +B applied to radio assembly? — **No** → +B wire harness faulty.

↓ **Yes**

Radio assembly faulty.

| 16 | Antenna | **ANTENNA-RELEATED** |

Only for Radio – Tape Unit (Radio assembly)

Is antenna extended? — **No** → Extend fully.

↓ **Yes**

Temporarily install another antenna. Functions OK? — **Yes** → Antenna faulty.

↓ **No**

Radio side faulty.

17	Noise	**NOISE PRODUCED BY VIBRATION OR SHOCK WHILE DRIVING**

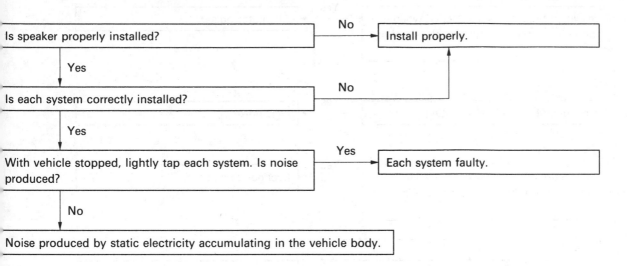

Is speaker properly installed? ──No──→ Install properly.

　│
　Yes
　↓

Is each system correctly installed? ──No──→ Install properly.

　│
　Yes
　↓

With vehicle stopped, lightly tap each system. Is noise produced? ──Yes──→ Each system faulty.

　│
　No
　↓

Noise produced by static electricity accumulating in the vehicle body.

BE

| 18 | Noise | **NOISE PRODUCED WHEN ENGINE STARTS** |

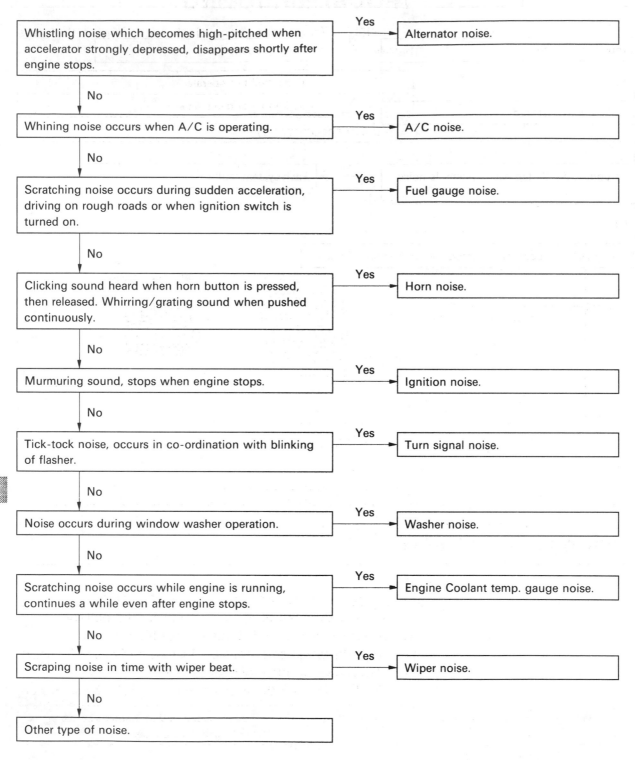

Whistling noise which becomes high-pitched when accelerator strongly depressed, disappears shortly after engine stops. → Yes → Alternator noise.

No ↓

Whining noise occurs when A/C is operating. → Yes → A/C noise.

No ↓

Scratching noise occurs during sudden acceleration, driving on rough roads or when ignition switch is turned on. → Yes → Fuel gauge noise.

No ↓

Clicking sound heard when horn button is pressed, then released. Whirring/grating sound when pushed continuously. → Yes → Horn noise.

No ↓

Murmuring sound, stops when engine stops. → Yes → Ignition noise.

No ↓

Tick-tock noise, occurs in co-ordination with blinking of flasher. → Yes → Turn signal noise.

No ↓

Noise occurs during window washer operation. → Yes → Washer noise.

No ↓

Scratching noise occurs while engine is running, continues a while even after engine stops. → Yes → Engine Coolant temp. gauge noise.

No ↓

Scraping noise in time with wiper beat. → Yes → Wiper noise.

No ↓

Other type of noise.

CLOCK
TROUBLESHOOTING

HINT: Troubleshoot the clock according to the table below.

Clock will not operate	1
Clock loses or gains time	2

±1.5 seconds/day

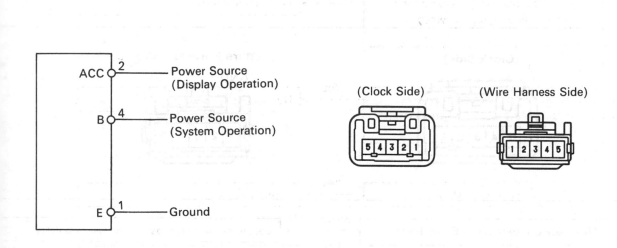

ACC 2 ── Power Source
(Display Operation)

B 4 ── Power Source
(System Operation)

(Clock Side)   (Wire Harness Side)

E 1 ── Ground

E5540 e-5-2 e-5-1

BE

---

1 | CLOCK WILL NOT OPERATE

(a) Check that the battery voltage is 10 – 16 V.
If voltage is not as specified, replace the battery.
(b) Check that the DOME fuse is not blown.
If the fuse is blown, replace the fuse and check for short.
(c) Troubleshoot the clock as follows.
HINT: Inspect the connector on the wire harness side.

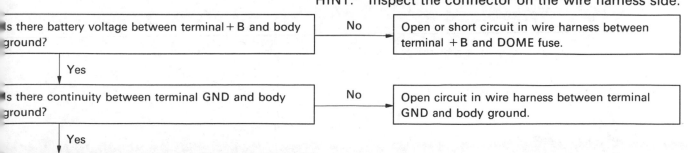

Is there battery voltage between terminal +B and body ground? — No → Open or short circuit in wire harness between terminal +B and DOME fuse.

Yes

Is there continuity between terminal GND and body ground? — No → Open circuit in wire harness between terminal GND and body ground.

Yes

Replace clock.

2 | CLOCK LOSES OR GAINS TIME

(a) Check that the battery voltage is 10 – 16 V.
   If voltage is not as specified, replace the battery.

(b) Inspect the error of the clock.
   Allowable error (per day): ±1.5 seconds
   If the error exceeds the allowable error, replace the clock

(c) Check that the clock adjusting button is sticking in posi‐
   tion and has failed to return.
   If the button is not returned, repair or replace the clock

(d) Troubleshoot the clock as follows.
   HINT: Inspect the connector on the wire harness side

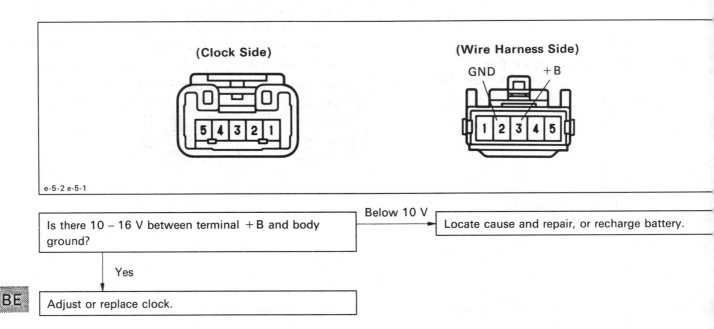

(Clock Side)

(Wire Harness Side)

GND   +B

5 4 3 2 1

1 2 3 4 5

e-5-2 e-5-1

| Is there 10 – 16 V between terminal +B and body ground? | Below 10 V | → | Locate cause and repair, or recharge battery. |

Yes
↓

Adjust or replace clock.

POWER DOOR LOCK CONTROL SYSTEM

BE

HOW TO PROCEED WITH TROUBLESHOOTING

Perform troubleshooting in accordance with the procedure on the following page.

1 **CUSTOMER PROBLEM ANALYSIS**

Using the customer problem analysis check sheet for reference, ask the customer in as much deta
as possible about the problem.

2 **PROBLEM SYMPTOM CONFIRMATION,** **3** **SYMPTOM SIMULATION**

Confirm the problem symptoms. If the problem does not reappear, be sure to simulate the problem
using "Problem Simulation Method".

For example, if the malfunction involves failure of the door to lock or unlock during operation of th
Door Lock Control Switch, check if lock and unlock operation of the door using the key is normal o
abnormal, and also check if key confinement prevention function and luggage compartment doc
opener function are normal or not. And having fully checked the extent of the malfunction.

4 **MATRIX CHART OF PROBLEM SYMPTOMS**

Confirm the order of inspection for each applicable problem symptom on the matrix chart.

5 **CIRCUIT INSPECTION**

Proceed with diagnosis of each circuit in accordance with the inspection order confirmed in **4**
Judge whether the cause of the problem is in the sensor, wire harness and connectors, or the EC
(relay).

6 **REPAIR**

When the cause of the problem is found in **5** , perform repairs.

7 **CONFIRMATION TEST**

After completing repairs, confirm that the problem is eliminated and that all functions of the door loc
control system are normal.

BE

CUSTOMER PROBLEM ANALYSIS CHECK SHEET

DOOR LOCK CONTROL System Check Sheet

Inspector's
Name

Customer's Name		Registration No.	
		Registration Year	/ /
		Frame No.	
Date Vehicle Brought In	/ /	Odometer Reading	Km Miles

Date of Problem Occurrence		/ /
Frequency of Problem Occurrence		☐ Constant ☐ Sometimes (times per day, month) ☐ Once only
Conditions at Time of Problem Occurrence	Weather	☐ Fine ☐ Cloudy ☐ Rainy ☐ Snowy ☐ Various/Others
	Outdoor Temperature	☐ Hot ☐ Warm ☐ Cool ☐ Cold (Approx. °C (°F))

Problem Symptom

☐ Malfunction in Door Lock/Unlock Operation Using Door Lock Control Switch.	☐ Driver's door lock control switch	☐ Driver's door ☐ Passenger's door ☐ Rear RH door ☐ Rear LH door
	☐ Passenger's door lock control switch	☐ Driver's door ☐ Passenger's door ☐ Rear RH door ☐ Rear LH door
☐ Malfunction in Door Lock/Unlock Operation Using Key.	☐ Driver's door key operated switch	☐ Driver's door ☐ Passenger's door ☐ Rear RH door ☐ Rear LH door
	☐ Passenger's door key operated switch	☐ Driver's key ☐ Passenger's door ☐ Rear RH door ☐ Rear LH door
☐ Fault in Key Confinement Prevention Function.		
☐ Fault in Luggage Compartment Door Opener Function.		
☐ Fault in security function of door lock control system.		
☐ Others		

BE

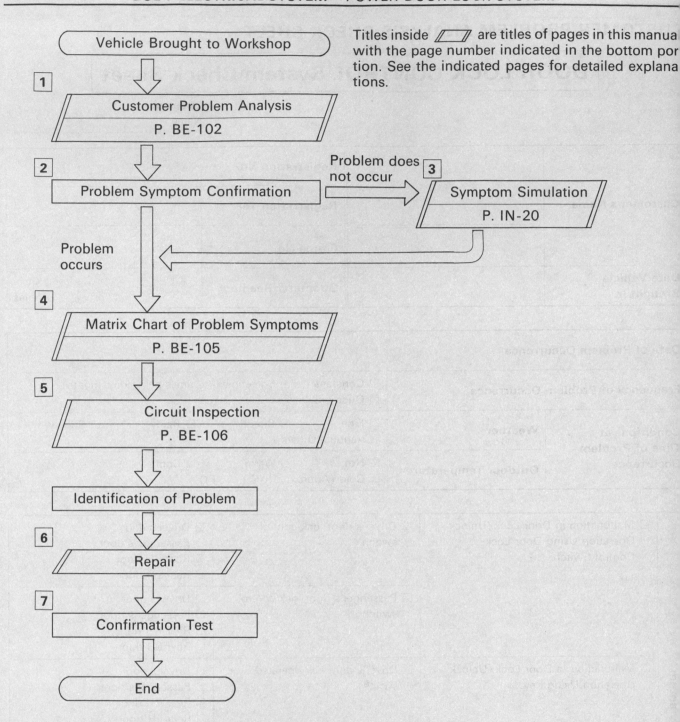

Titles inside ▱ are titles of pages in this manual with the page number indicated in the bottom portion. See the indicated pages for detailed explanations.

Vehicle Brought to Workshop

1 | Customer Problem Analysis
P. BE-102

2 | Problem Symptom Confirmation → Problem does not occur → 3 | Symptom Simulation
P. IN-20

Problem occurs

4 | Matrix Chart of Problem Symptoms
P. BE-105

5 | Circuit Inspection
P. BE-106

Identification of Problem

6 | Repair

7 | Confirmation Test

End

DESCRIPTION

The door lock control system has a key-interlocked door lock and unlock function and a key-confine prevention function. All doors can be locked and unlocked simultaneously by key operation at the front right or left door. If the door lock operation is performed when one of the front doors is open and the ignition key inserted in the key cylinder, doors are unlocked automatically to prevent the ignition key from being left inside the vehicle.

For the function of component parts of this system, refer to the circuit description in the troubleshooting section.

PARTS LOCATION

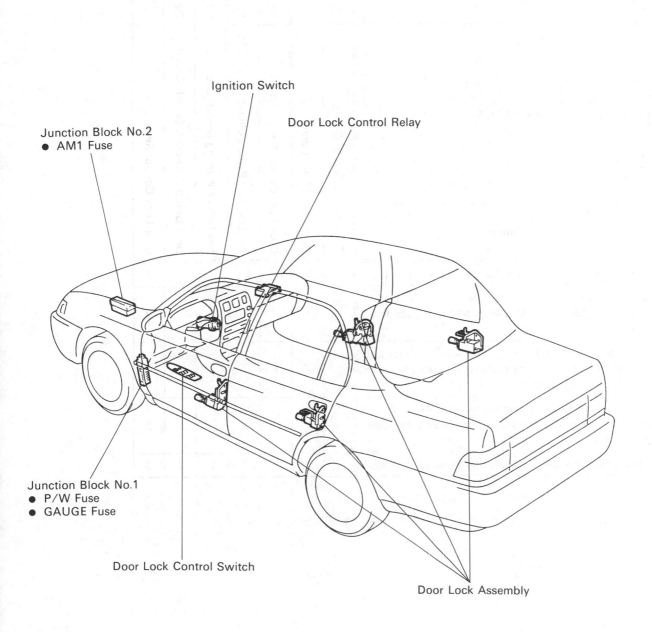

Ignition Switch

Door Lock Control Relay

Junction Block No.2
● AM1 Fuse

Junction Block No.1
● P/W Fuse
● GAUGE Fuse

Door Lock Control Switch

Door Lock Assembly

BE

MATRIX CHART OF PROBLEM SYMPTOMS

Perform troubleshooting of the circuits for the applicable problem symptom in the order given in the char below.
Proceed to the page given for each circuit.
HINT:
- If the instruction "Proceed to next circuit inspection shown on matrix chart" is given in the flow char for each circuit, proceed to the circuit with the next highest number in the table to continue the check
- If the trouble still reappears even though there are no abnormalities in any of the other circuits, ther check and replace the Door Lock Control Relay as the last step.

See Page / Symptom	BE-106 Relay Power Source Circuit	BE-108 Door Lock Motor Circuit	BE-110 Door Lock Control Switch Circuit	BE-112 Key Operated Switch Circuit	BE-113 Key Unlock Warning Switch Circuit	BE-114 Door Unlock Detection Switch Circuit	– Door Lock Control Relay
No functions of the door lock control system operate.	1	2					3
All doors or some doors are not locked and unlocked with the Door Lock Control Switch and Key Operated Switch.		1					2
Doors cannot be locked or unlocked with the Door Lock Control Switch. (Doors lock and unlock normally with the Key Operated Switch.)			1				2
Doors are not locked or unlocked with the KeyOperated Switch. (Doors lock and unlock normally with the Door Lock Control Switch).				1			2
Key confinement prevention function does not operate.					1	2	3

BE

CIRCUIT INSPECTION

Relay Power Source Circuit

CIRCUIT DESCRIPTION

This circuit provides power to operate the door lock control relay.

DIAGNOSTIC CHART

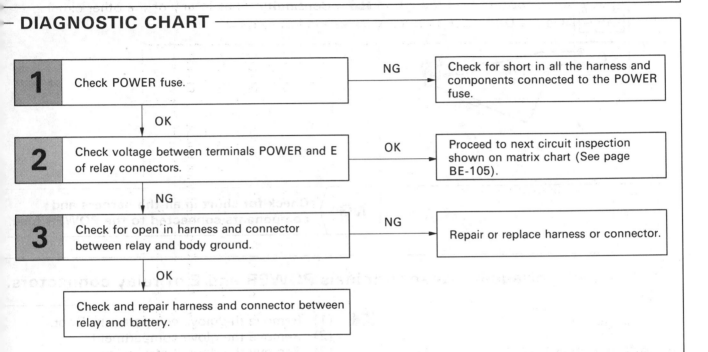

1 Check POWER fuse. ——— NG ——→ Check for short in all the harness and components connected to the POWER fuse.

OK

2 Check voltage between terminals POWER and E of relay connectors. ——— OK ——→ Proceed to next circuit inspection shown on matrix chart (See page BE-105).

NG

3 Check for open in harness and connector between relay and body ground. ——— NG ——→ Repair or replace harness or connector.

OK

Check and repair harness and connector between relay and battery.

BE

INSPECTION PROCEDURE

1   Check POWER fuse.

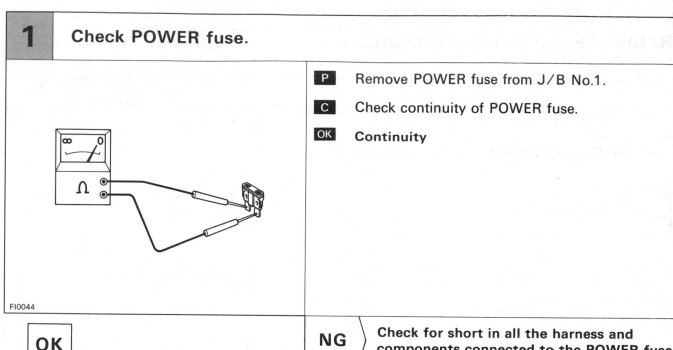

P Remove POWER fuse from J/B No.1.

C Check continuity of POWER fuse.

OK Continuity

FI0044

OK

NG > Check for short in all the harness and components connected to the POWER fuse.

2   Check voltage between terminals POWER and E of relay connectors.

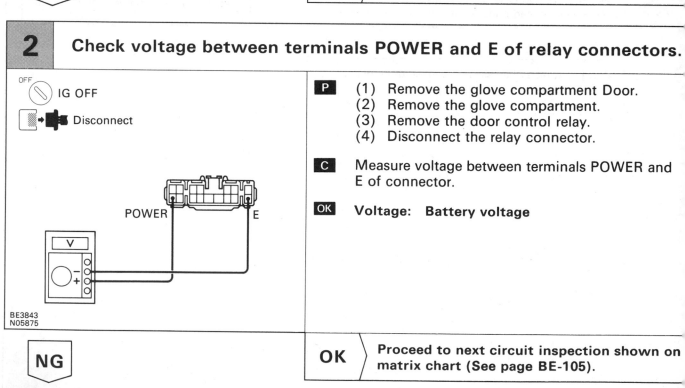

OFF ⊘ IG OFF

▉→▉ Disconnect

POWER   E

P (1) Remove the glove compartment Door.
    (2) Remove the glove compartment.
    (3) Remove the door control relay.
    (4) Disconnect the relay connector.

C Measure voltage between terminals POWER and E of connector.

OK Voltage: Battery voltage

BE3843
N05875

NG

OK > Proceed to next circuit inspection shown on matrix chart (See page BE-105).

3   Check for open in harness and connector between relay and body ground.

OK

NG > Repair or replace harness or connector.

Check and repair harness and connector between relay and battery.

Door Lock Motor Circuit

CIRCUIT DESCRIPTION

The door lock motor locks and unlocks the door in accordance with signals from the relay.

DIAGNOSTIC CHART

HINT: Inspect the door which is malfunctioning.

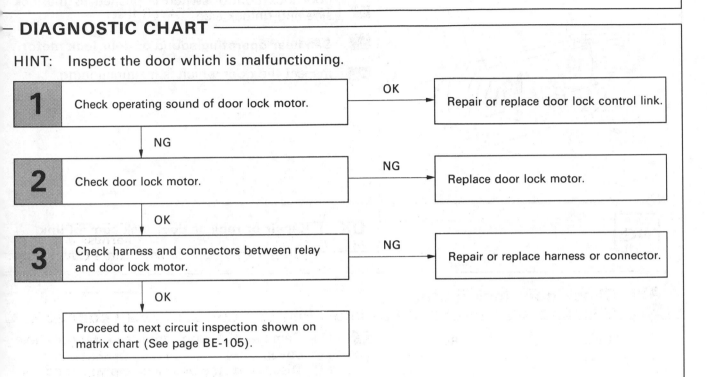

1 Check operating sound of door lock motor.	OK →	Repair or replace door lock control link.
↓ NG		
2 Check door lock motor.	NG →	Replace door lock motor.
↓ OK		
3 Check harness and connectors between relay and door lock motor.	NG →	Repair or replace harness or connector.
↓ OK		
Proceed to next circuit inspection shown on matrix chart (See page BE-105).		

INSPECTION PROCEDURE

1 Check operating sound of door lock motor.

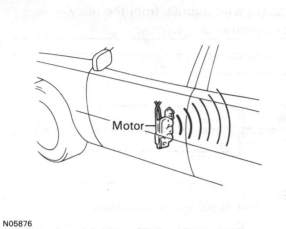

N05876

C Check operating sound of door lock motor, when door lock control switch is pushed to the lock side and unlock side.

OK **Can hear operating sound of door lock motor.**

Hint Inspect the door which is malfunctioning.

| NG | | OK | Repair or replace door lock control link. |

---

2 Check door lock motor.

Front   Rear

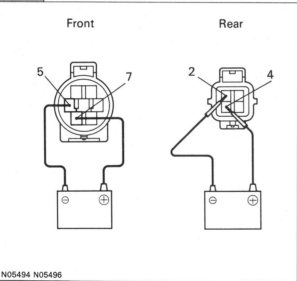

N05494 N05496

P (1) Remove the door trim and service hole cover.
(2) Disconnect the door lock motor connector.

C (1) Connect positive lead to terminal 7 (Front) and 4 (Rear) and negative lead to terminal 5 (Front) and 2 (Rear) of door lock motor connector.
(2) Connect positive lead to terminal 5 (Front) and 2 (Rear) and negative lead to terminal 7 (Front) and 4 (Rear) of door lock motor connector.

OK (1) **Door lock motor locks door.**
(2) **Door lock motor unlocks door.**

Hint Perform inspection in a short time (within 2 seconds).

| OK | | NG | Replace door lock motor. |

---

3 Check harness and connectors between relay and door lock motor.

| OK | | NG | Repair or replace harness or connector. |

Proceed to next circuit inspection shown on matrix chart (See page BE-105).

Door Lock Control Switch Circuit

CIRCUIT DESCRIPTION

When the door lock control switch is pushed to the lock side, Lock terminal of the switch is grounded, and when the switch is pushed to the unlock side, Unlock terminal is grounded.

DIAGNOSTIC CHART

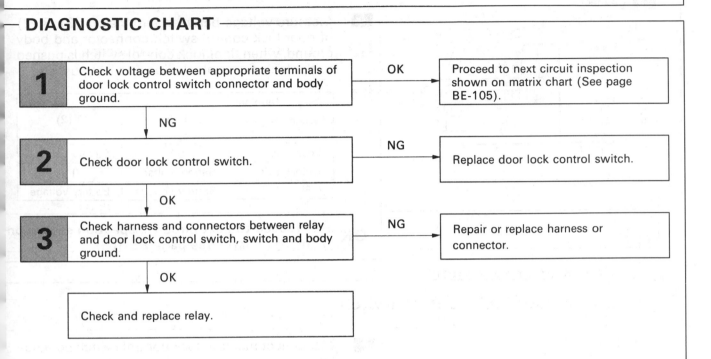

1	Check voltage between appropriate terminals of door lock control switch connector and body ground.	OK →	Proceed to next circuit inspection shown on matrix chart (See page BE-105).

NG ↓

2	Check door lock control switch.	NG →	Replace door lock control switch.

OK ↓

3	Check harness and connectors between relay and door lock control switch, switch and body ground.	NG →	Repair or replace harness or connector.

OK ↓

Check and replace relay.

BE

INSPECTION PROCEDURE

1 Check voltage between appropriate terminals of door lock control switch connector and body ground.

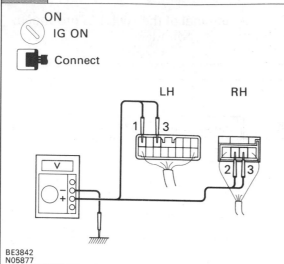

BE3842
N05877

P (1) Remove the door trim and service hole cover.
(2) Turn ignition switch on.

C Measure voltage between terminals 1 (3), 3 (2) of door lock control switch connector and body ground, when door lock control switch is pushed to the lock side, unlock side and not pushed.

OK

Terminal / Switch position	1 (3)	3 (2)
Lock side	0 V	Battery voltage
Unlock side	Battery voltage	0 V
OFF	Battery voltage	Battery voltage

NG

OK ⟩ Proceed to next circuit inspection shown on matrix chart (See page BE-105).

---

2 Check door lock control switch.

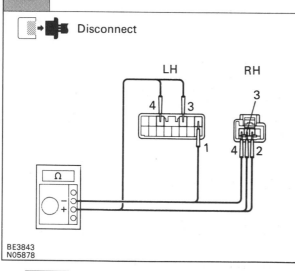

BE3843
N05878

P Disconnect the door lock control switch connector.

C Check continuity between terminals 4 (3), 3 (2) and 1 (4) of door lock control switch connector, when door lock control switch is pressed to the lock side, and unlock side and not pressed.

OK

○——○ Continuity

Terminal / Switch position	4 (3)	3 (2)	1 (4)
Lock side	○—————————————○		○
Unlock side		○————————○	
OFF			

OK

NG ⟩ Replace door lock control switch.

---

3 Check harness and connectors between relay and door lock control switch, switch and body ground.

OK

NG ⟩ Repair or replace harness or connector.

Check and replace relay.

Key Operated Switch Circuit

CIRCUIT DESCRIPTION

The key operated switch is built into the door key cylinder.
When the key is turned to the unlock side, terminal 1 of the switch is grounded.

DIAGNOSTIC CHART

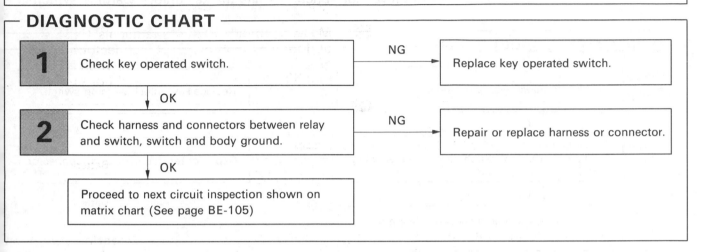

| 1 | Check key operated switch. | NG → | Replace key operated switch. |

OK ↓

| 2 | Check harness and connectors between relay and switch, switch and body ground. | NG → | Repair or replace harness or connector. |

OK ↓

Proceed to next circuit inspection shown on matrix chart (See page BE-105)

INSPECTION PROCEDURE

1 Check key operated switch.

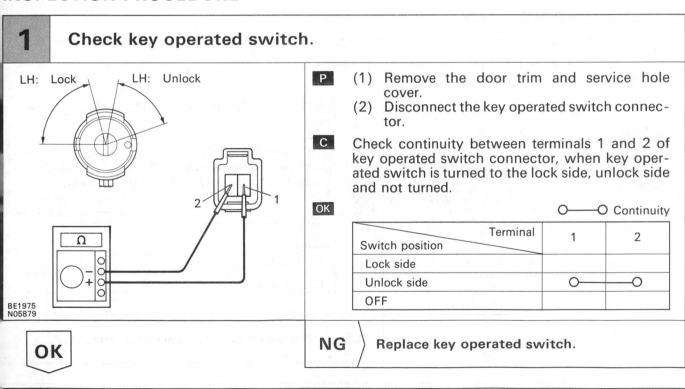

LH: Lock   LH: Unlock

P
(1) Remove the door trim and service hole cover.
(2) Disconnect the key operated switch connector.

C Check continuity between terminals 1 and 2 of key operated switch connector, when key operated switch is turned to the lock side, unlock side and not turned.

OK

○——○ Continuity

Switch position	Terminal	1	2
Lock side			
Unlock side		○	○
OFF			

BE1975
N05879

OK

NG ⟩ Replace key operated switch.

2 Check harness and connectors between relay and switch, switch and body ground.

OK

NG ⟩ Repair or replace harness or connector.

Proceed to next circuit inspection shown on matrix chart (See page BE-105).

Key Unlock Warning Switch Circuit

CIRCUIT DESCRIPTION

The key unlock warning switch goes on when the ignition key is inserted in the key cylinder and goes off when the ignition key is removed.

The relay operates the key confinement prevention function while the key unlock warning switch is on.

DIAGNOSTIC CHART

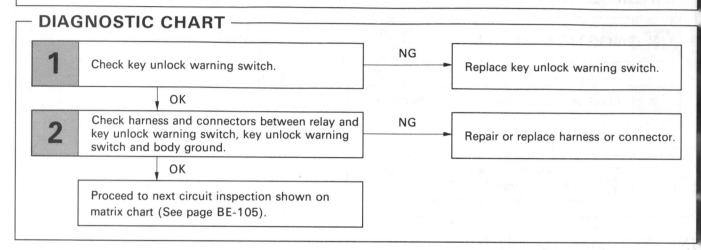

| 1 | Check key unlock warning switch. | NG → | Replace key unlock warning switch. |

OK ↓

| 2 | Check harness and connectors between relay and key unlock warning switch, key unlock warning switch and body ground. | NG → | Repair or replace harness or connector. |

OK ↓

Proceed to next circuit inspection shown on matrix chart (See page BE-105).

INSPECTION PROCEDURE

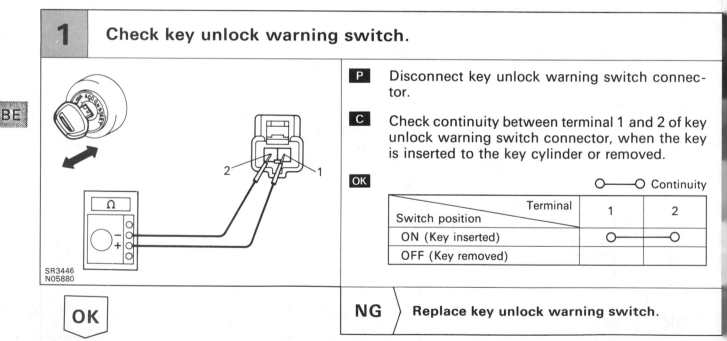

1   Check key unlock warning switch.

P Disconnect key unlock warning switch connector.

C Check continuity between terminal 1 and 2 of key unlock warning switch connector, when the key is inserted to the key cylinder or removed.

OK

○——○ Continuity

Switch position \ Terminal	1	2
ON (Key inserted)	○——○	
OFF (Key removed)		

SR3446
N05880

OK

NG ⟩ Replace key unlock warning switch.

2   Check harness and connectors between relay and key unlock warning switch, key unlock warning switch and body ground.

OK

NG ⟩ Repair or replace harness or connector.

Proceed to next circuit inspection shown on matrix chart (See page BE-105).

Door Unlock Detection Switch Circuit

CIRCUIT DESCRIPTION

The door unlock detection switch is built in the door lock motor assembly. This switch is on when the door lock knob is in the unlock position and off when the lock knob is in the lock position.
The relay detects the front door lock knob conditions in this circuit. It is used as one of the operating conditions for the key confinement prevention function.

DIAGNOSTIC CHART

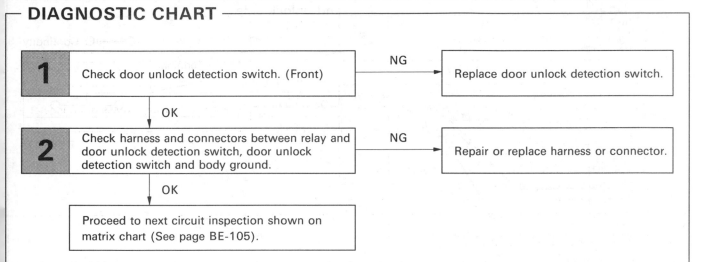

INSPECTION PROCEDURE

1   Check Door Unlock Detection Switch.

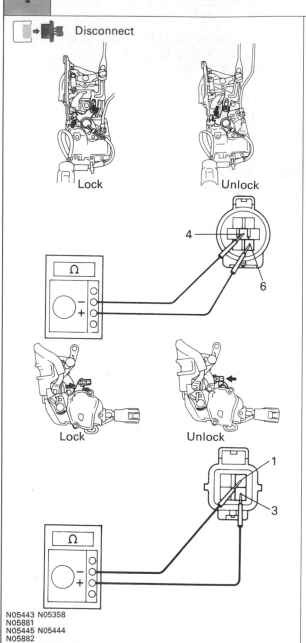

P
(1) Remove the door trim
(2) Remove the door lock

C Check continuity between terminals 4 (1) and 6 (3) of door unlock detection switch connector, when the door lock is operated to the lock side and unlock side.

OK

O———O Continuity

Switch condition	Terminal	4 (1)	6 (3)
Door unlock		O———————O	
Door lock			

OK

NG ⟩ Replace door unlock detection switch.

2   Check harness and connectors between relay and door unlock detection switch, door unlock detection switch and body ground.

OK

NG ⟩ Repair or replace harness or connector.

Proceed to next circuit inspection shown on matrix chart (See page BE-105).

N05443 N05358
N05881
N05445 N05444
N05882

BE

THEFT DETERRENT SYSTEM

BE

HOW TO PROCEED WITH TROUBLESHOOTING

HINT: Troubleshooting of the theft deterrent system is based on the premise that the door lock control system is operating normally. Accordingly, before troubleshooting the theft deterrent system, first make certain that the door lock control system is operating normally.

For troubleshooting using a volt/ohm meter, see pages BE-117, 118.

For troubleshooting using both volt/ohm meter and Theft Deterrent System (TDS) checker, see page BE-119.

Be sure to use troubleshooting procedure appropriate to the diagnostic tool being used.

Perform troubleshooting in accordance with the procedure on the following page.

How to Proceed with Troubleshooting Using Volt/Ohm Meter

1 CUSTOMER PROBLEM ANALYSIS

Using the customer problem analysis check sheet for reference, ask the customer in as much detail as possible about the problem.

2 PROBLEM SYMPTOM CONFIRMATION, 3 SYMPTOM SIMULATION

Confirm the problem symptoms referring to the system inspection on page BE-122. If the problem does not reappear, be sure to simulate the problem, using the "Problem Simulation Method".

4 MATRIX CHART OF PROBLEM SYMPTOMS

Confirm the order of inspection for each applicable problem symptom on the Matrix Chart.

5 CIRCUIT INSPECTION

Proceed with diagnosis of each circuit in accordance with the inspection order confirmed in 4 . Judge whether the cause of the problem is in the sensor, actuators, wire harness and connectors, or the ECU.

6 REPAIR

If the cause of the problem is found in 5 , perform repairs.

7 CONFIRMATION TEST

After completing repairs, confirm not only that the problem is eliminated but also make sure the theft deterrent system is operating normally in accordance with the system inspection on page BE-   .

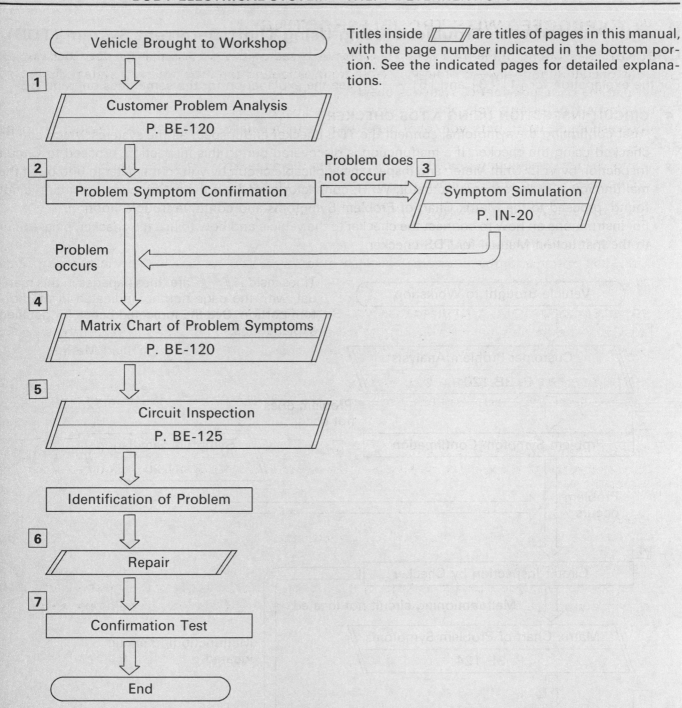

Titles inside ⟍⟋ are titles of pages in this manual, with the page number indicated in the bottom portion. See the indicated pages for detailed explanations.

Vehicle Brought to Workshop

1 Customer Problem Analysis
P. BE-120

2 Problem Symptom Confirmation   Problem does not occur → **3** Symptom Simulation
P. IN-20

Problem occurs

4 Matrix Chart of Problem Symptoms
P. BE-120

5 Circuit Inspection
P. BE-125

Identification of Problem

6 Repair

7 Confirmation Test

End

How to Proceed with Troubleshooting Using Theft Deterrent System (TDS) Checker

For the explanation for $\boxed{1}$ $\boxed{3}$ and $\boxed{5}$ ~ $\boxed{8}$, see the explanation for the same titles on page BE-

$\boxed{4}$ **CIRCUIT INSPECTION USING A TDS CHECKER**

After confirming the symptoms, connect the TDS checker and inspect all the systems which can be checked using the checker. If a malfunction is discovered during this inspection, proceed to Circuit Inspection by Volt/Ohm Meter, and inspect the applicable circuit by volt/ohm meter to find out if the malfunction is in the sensors, actuator, W/H, connector or ECU. If the malfunctioning circuit is not found, proceed to the Matrix Chart of Problem Symptoms and continue troubleshooting.

For instructions on how to connect the checker to the vehicle and how to use the checker, please refer to the Instruction Manual for TDS checker.

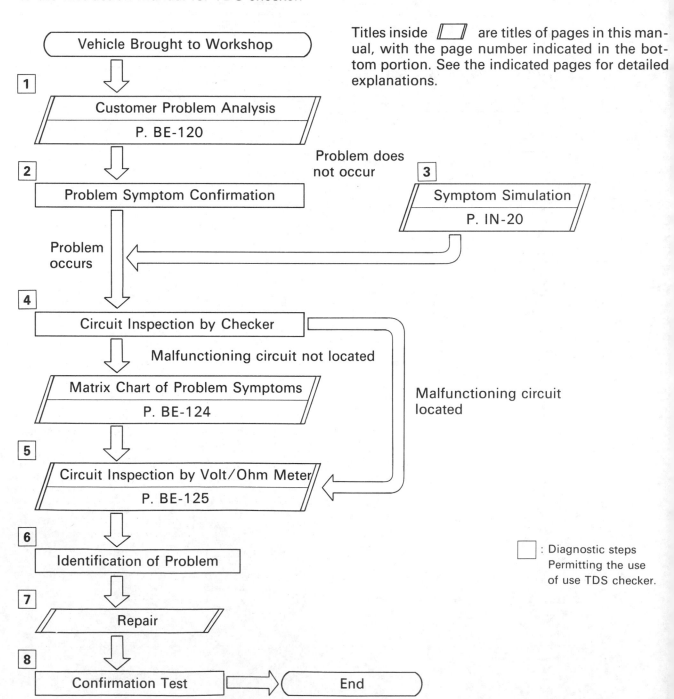

Titles inside ▱ are titles of pages in this manual, with the page number indicated in the bottom portion. See the indicated pages for detailed explanations.

BE

▢ : Diagnostic steps Permitting the use of use TDS checker.

CUSTOMER PROBLEM ANALYSIS CHECK SHEET

THEFT DETERRENT System Check Sheet

Inspector's
Name

Customer's Name		Registration No.	
		Registration Year	/ /
		Frame No.	
Date Vehicle Brought In	/ /	Odometer Reading	Km Miles

Date of Problem Occurrence		/ /
Frequency of Problem Occurrence		☐ Constant ☐ Sometimes (times per day, month) ☐ Once only
Conditions at Time of Problem Occurrence	Weather	☐ Fine ☐ Cloudy ☐ Rainy ☐ Snowy ☐ Various/Others
	Outdoor Temperature	☐ Hot ☐ Warm ☐ Cool ☐ Cold (Approx. °F (°C))

Problem Symptom

☐ Theft deterrent system cannot be set.

☐ Indicator light does not flash when the theft deterrent system is set. (It stays on or does not light at all.)

☐ Theft deterrent system does not operate.	☐ When unlocked using the door lock knob. ☐ When the engine hood is opened.	Malfunction ☐ Horns only ☐ Theft deterrent horn only ☐ Headlights only ☐ Taillights only ☐ Starter cut only ☐ Door lock operation only
☐ System cannot be canceled once set.	☐ When door is unlocked using key or wireless door lock control system. ☐ When the key is inserted in the ignition key cylinder and turned to ACC or ON position. (However, only when the system has never operated) ☐ When the luggage compartment door is opened with the key.	
☐ System cannot be canceled during warning operation.	☐ When door is unlocked using key or wireless door lock control system. ☐ When the key is inserted in the ignition key cylinder and turned to ACC or ON position.	

☐ Warning operation starts when the system is set and the door or luggage compartment door is opened with the key.

☐ Others

BE

DESCRIPTION

The theft deterrent system uses the door lock control system components and some other parts. When somebody attempts to forcibly enter the vehicle or open the engine hood or luggage compartment door without a key, or when the battery terminals are removed and reconnected, the theft deterrent system sounds the horns and flashes the headlights and taillights for about one minute as an alert. At the same time, it locks all the doors and electrically disconnects the starter.

For the function of component parts of this system, refer to the circuit description in troubleshooting section.

PARTS LOCATION

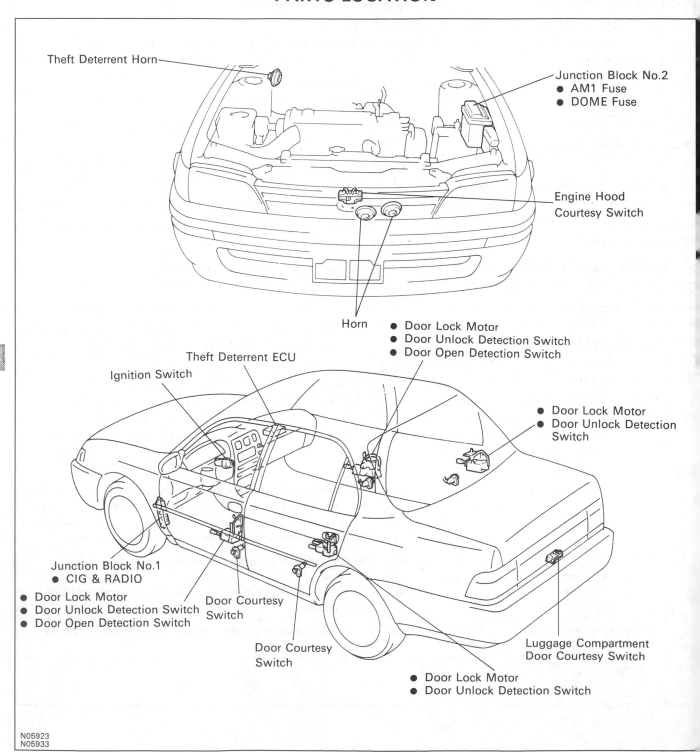

Theft Deterrent Horn

Junction Block No.2
● AM1 Fuse
● DOME Fuse

Engine Hood
Courtesy Switch

Horn

● Door Lock Motor
● Door Unlock Detection Switch
● Door Open Detection Switch

Theft Deterrent ECU

Ignition Switch

● Door Lock Motor
● Door Unlock Detection Switch

Junction Block No.1
● CIG & RADIO

● Door Lock Motor
● Door Unlock Detection Switch
● Door Open Detection Switch

Door Courtesy Switch

Door Courtesy Switch

Luggage Compartment
Door Courtesy Switch

● Door Lock Motor
● Door Unlock Detection Switch

BE

SYSTEM INSPECTION

1. SETTING OF THE THEFT DETERRENT SYSTEM
Setting Conditions
(a) Close all the doors.
(b) Close the engine hood and luggage compartment door.
(c) Remove the ignition key out of the ignition key cylinder.

Setting Operation
When any of the following operations (a) or (b) is performed, the theft deterrent indicator light will light up as shown below.
(a) Lock the left or right front door using the key.
   (All doors are locked by key-interlinked lock operation)
(b) With the rear doors locked and with one of the front doors locked, lock the other front door without using the key.

Elapsed time after operation	Indicator light
Within about 30 seconds	Lights up
After about 30 seconds	Blinks*1

*1: 1 sec. on, 1 sec. off

HINT: When the theft deterrent system is set, doors cannot be locked or unlocked with the door lock control switch and the luggage compartment door cannot be unlocked with the luggage compartment door opener switch.

2. CANCELING OF THE THEFT DETERRENT SYSTEM IN THE SET CONDITION
Check if the theft deterrent indicator light is blinking.
Canceling Operation
When any of the following operations (a), (b) or (c) is performed, the theft deterrent system is canceled and indicator light will go off.
(a) Unlock the left or right front door using the key.
(b) Insert the ignition key in the ignition key cylinder and turn it to the ACC or ON position.
   (This is operative only when the theft deterrent system has never operated.)
(c) Unlock the luggage compartment door with the key.*1
   *1: The theft deterrent system is temporarily canceled only while the luggage compartment door is open. Approximately 2 seconds after the luggage compartment door is closed, the theft deterrent system is reset.

BE

3. CHECK OF THE THEFT DETERRENT SYSTEM OPERATION

Check if the theft deterrent indicator light is blinking.

When any of the following operation (a) or (b) is performed, the system sounds the horns and theft deterrent horn and flashes the headlights and taillights for about one minute to alert. At the same time, the system disconnects the starter motor circuit and locks all doors (If all doors are not locked, the system repeats door locking operation every 2 seconds during the one minute alert time).

(a) Open the engine hood using the engine hood opener lever.

(b) Unlock any of the front of rear doors without key operation.

4. CANCELING OF THE THEFT DETERRENT SYSTEM IN OPERATING CONDITION

The theft deterrent operation can be canceled when any of the following conditions is met:

No.	Condition	Canceling Operation
1	Unlock left or right door with the key.	○
2	Unlock doors with wireless door lock control system.	○
3	Insert key into ignition key cylinder and turn it to ACC or ON position.	○
4	About 1 minute passes after theft deterrent operation begins.	Automatic stop[1]

[1]: In this case, the theft deterrent system resets in about 2 seconds after if all doors are closed.

BE

MATRIX CHART OF PROBLEM SYMPTOMS

Proceed to the reference page shown in the matrix chart below for each malfunction symptom and troubleshoot for each circuit.

HINT: Troubleshooting of the theft deterrent system is based on the premise that the door lock control system is operating normally. Accordingly, before troubleshooting the theft deterrent system, first make certain that the door lock control system is operating normally.

Details of Problem			Inspecting Circuit*¹	See Page
The theft deterrent system cannot be set			1. Indicator light circuit	BE-125
			2. Luggage compartment door key operated switch circuit	BE-134
			3. Luggage compartment door courtesy switch circuit	BE-136
			4. Door unlock detection switch circuit	BE-138
			5. Engine hood courtesy switch circuit	BE-140
The indicator light does not blink when system is set			Indicator light circuit	BE-125
When the system is set	When the rear door is unlocked	The system does not operate	Door unlock detection switch circuit (Rear)	BE-138
	When the luggage compartment door is opened by a method other than the key		Luggage compartment door courtesy switch circuit	BE-136
	When the engine hood is opened		Engine hood courtesy switch circuit	BE-140
While the system is in warning operation	Horns do not sound		Horn relay circuit	BE-127
	Theft deterrent horn does not sound		Theft deterrent horn circuit	BE-128
	Headlights do not flash		Headlight control relay circuit	BE-130
	Taillights do not flash		Taillight control relay circuit	BE-131
	The starter cut is not cut off		Starter relay circuit	BE-126
	The rear door lock is not locked in unlock condition		Door unlock detection switch circuit	BE-138
When the system is set	It is not canceled when the ignition key is turned to ACC or ON position		Ignition switch circuit	BE-125
	It still operates when the luggage compartment door is opened with the key		Luggage compartment door key operated switch circuit	BE-134
Even when the system is not set	Horns sound		Horn relay circuit	BE-127
	Theft deterrent horn sounds		Theft deterrent horn circuit	BE-128
	Headlights stay on		Headlight control relay circuit	BE-130
	Taillights stay on		Taillight control relay circuit	BE-131

¹: If numbers are given to the circuit proceed with troubleshooting in the order indicated by those numbers.

CIRCUIT INSPECTION

Indicator Light Circuit

CIRCUIT DESCRIPTION

When the theft deterrent system is preparing to set, this circuit lights up the indicator light. When the system has been set, it continually turns the indicator light on for 1 second and turns it off for 1 second, thus blinking the indicator light.

DIAGNOSTIC CHART

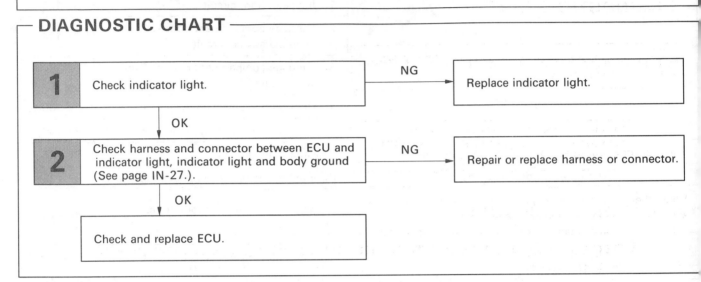

| 1 | Check indicator light. | NG → | Replace indicator light. |

↓ OK

| 2 | Check harness and connector between ECU and indicator light, indicator light and body ground (See page IN-27.). | NG → | Repair or replace harness or connector. |

↓ OK

Check and replace ECU.

INSPECTION PROCEDURE

1   Check indicator light.

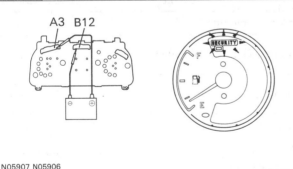

A3 B12

N05907 N05906

P (1) Remove meter cluster finish panel.
(2) Remove combination meter.

C Connect positive ⊕ lead to terminal A3 and negative ⊖ lead to terminal B12 of combination meter connector. (See page BE-52)

OK Indicator light comes on.

OK ▽

NG ⟩ Replace indicator light.

2   Check harness and connector between ECU and indicator light, indicator light and body ground (See page IN-27).

OK ▽

NG ⟩ Repair or replace harness or connector.

Check and replace ECU.

Starter Relay Circuit

CIRCUIT DESCRIPTION

When the theft deterrent system is activated, creating an open circuit in terminal ST circuit and making the starter inoperative (starter cut).
In this condition, if one of the following operations in done, thus canceling the starter cut.
- Unlock the front LH or RH door with key.

DIAGNOSTIC CHART

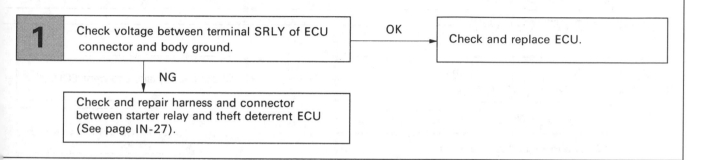

1 Check voltage between terminal SRLY of ECU connector and body ground. ──OK──▶ Check and replace ECU.

│ NG
▼

Check and repair harness and connector between starter relay and theft deterrent ECU (See page IN-27).

INSPECTION PROCEDURE

1 **Check voltage between terminal SRLY of ECU connector and body ground.**

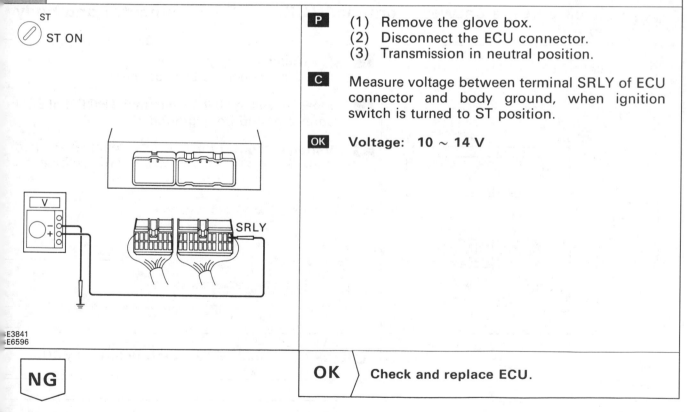

ST
ST ON

P
(1) Remove the glove box.
(2) Disconnect the ECU connector.
(3) Transmission in neutral position.

C
Measure voltage between terminal SRLY of ECU connector and body ground, when ignition switch is turned to ST position.

OK Voltage: 10 ~ 14 V

E3841
E6596

NG

OK ⟩ Check and replace ECU.

Check and repair harness and connector between starter relay and ECU (See page IN-27).

Horn Relay Circuit

CIRCUIT DESCRIPTION

When the theft deterrent system is activated, it causes the ECU to switch on and off in approximately 0.4 sec. cycles. This switches the horn relay on and off, thus the horns blow.
In this condition, if any of the following operations is done, the ECU goes off and the horn relay switches off, thus stopping the horns blow:
① Unlock the front LH or RH door with key.
② Turn the ignition switch to ACC or ON position.
③ Wait for approximately 1 minute.

DIAGNOSTIC CHART

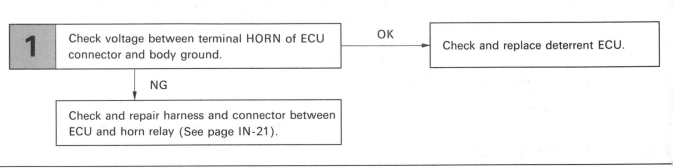

| 1 | Check voltage between terminal HORN of ECU connector and body ground. | OK → | Check and replace deterrent ECU. |

NG ↓

Check and repair harness and connector between ECU and horn relay (See page IN-21).

INSPECTION PROCEDURE

1   Check voltage between terminal HORN of ECU connector and body ground.

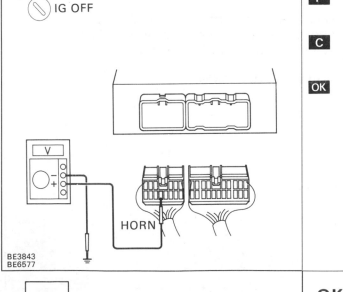

P (1) Remove the glove box.
(2) Disconnect the ECU connector.

C Measure voltage between terminal HORN of ECU connector and body ground.

OK Voltage: 10 ~ 14 V

OFF / IG OFF

BE3843
BE6577

NG

OK ⟩ Check and replace theft deterrent ECU.

Check and repair harness and connector between ECU and horn relay (See page IN-27).

Theft Deterrent Horn Circuit

– CIRCUIT DESCRIPTION

When the theft deterrent system is activated, causing the theft deterrent horn to blow.
In this condition, if any of the following operations is done, thus stopping the theft deterrent horn blow:
①   Unlock the front LH or RH door with key.
②   Turn the ignition switch to ACC or ON position.
③   Wait for approximately 1 minute.

– DIAGNOSTIC CHART

| **1** Check voltage between terminal 2 of theft deterrent horn connector and body ground. | NG → | Check and repair harness and connector between HAZ-HORN Fuse and theft deterrent horn. (See page IN-27) |

OK ↓

| **2** Check theft deterrent horn. | NG → | Replace theft deterrent horn. |

OK ↓

| **3** Check harness and connector between ECU and theft deterrent horn (See page IN-27). | NG → | Check and repair harness or connector. |

OK ↓

Check and replace ECU.

BE

INSPECTION PROCEDURES

1 Check voltage between terminal 2 of theft deterrent horn connector and body ground.

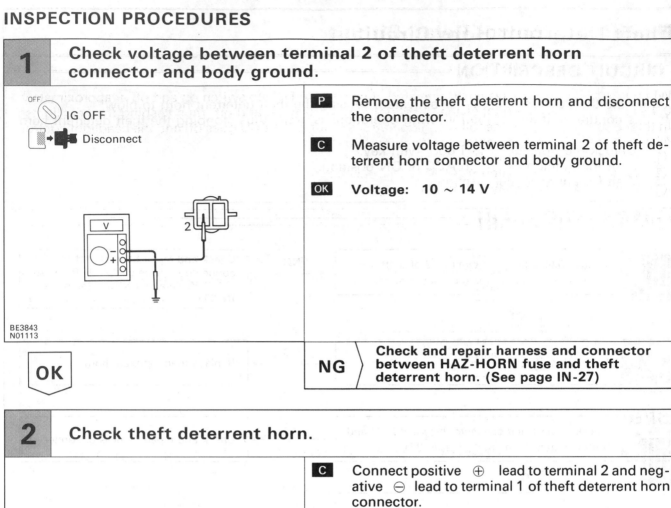

P Remove the theft deterrent horn and disconnect the connector.

C Measure voltage between terminal 2 of theft deterrent horn connector and body ground.

OK **Voltage: 10 ~ 14 V**

BE3843
N01113

OK

NG > Check and repair harness and connector between HAZ-HORN fuse and theft deterrent horn. (See page IN-27)

2 Check theft deterrent horn.

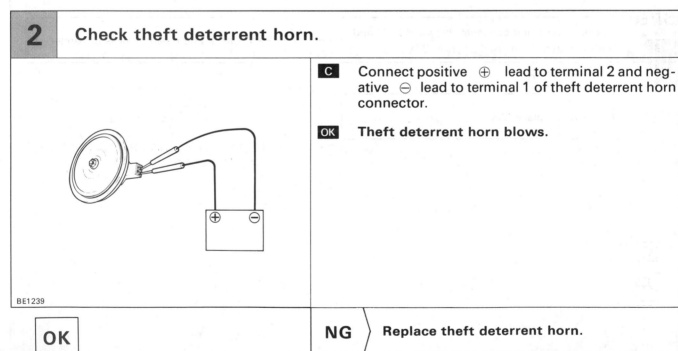

C Connect positive ⊕ lead to terminal 2 and negative ⊖ lead to terminal 1 of theft deterrent horn connector.

OK **Theft deterrent horn blows.**

BE1239

OK

NG > Replace theft deterrent horn.

3 Check harness and connector between ECU and theft deterrent horn (See page IN-27).

OK

NG > Check and repair harness or connector.

Check and replace ECU.

Headlight Control Relay Circuit

CIRCUIT DESCRIPTION

When the theft deterrent system is activated, it causes the ECU to switch on and off at approximately 0.4 sec. intervals. This switches the headlight control relay on and off, thus flashing the headlights. In this condition, if any of the following operations is done, the ECU goes off and the headlight control relay switches off, thus stopping the headlights flashing:
1. Unlock the front LH or RH door with key.
2. Turn the ignition switch to ACC or ON position.
3. Wait for approximately 1 minute.

DIAGNOSTIC CHART

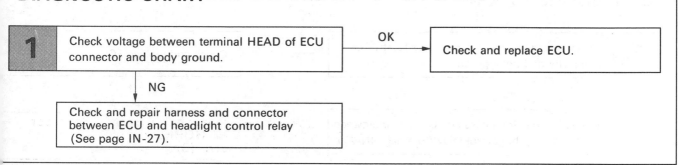

1   Check voltage between terminal HEAD of ECU connector and body ground. — OK → Check and replace ECU.

NG ↓

Check and repair harness and connector between ECU and headlight control relay (See page IN-27).

INSPECTION PROCEDURE

1   **Check voltage between terminal HEAD of ECU connector and body ground.**

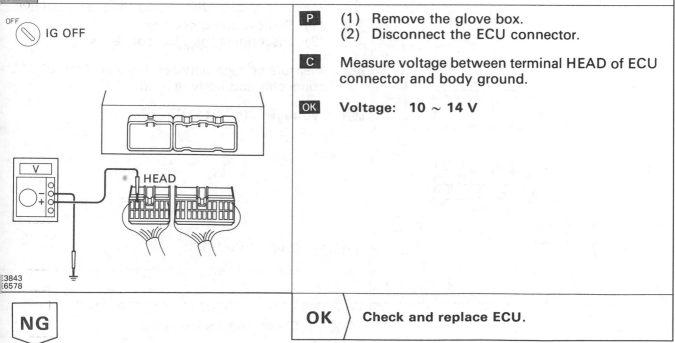

P
(1) Remove the glove box.
(2) Disconnect the ECU connector.

C Measure voltage between terminal HEAD of ECU connector and body ground.

OK Voltage: **10 ~ 14 V**

NG

OK ⟩ Check and replace ECU.

Check and repair harness and connector between ECU and headlight control relay (See page IN-27).

Taillight Control Relay Circuit

CIRCUIT DESCRIPTION

When the theft deterrent system is activated, it causes the ECU to switch on and off at approximately 0.4 sec. intervals. This switches the taillight control relay on and off, thus flashing the taillights.
In this condition, if any of the following operations is done, the ECU goes off and the taillight control relay switches off, thus stopping the taillights flashing:
① Unlock the front LH or RH door with key.
② Turn the ignition switch to ACC or ON position.
③ Wait for approximately 1 minute.

DIAGNOSTIC CHART

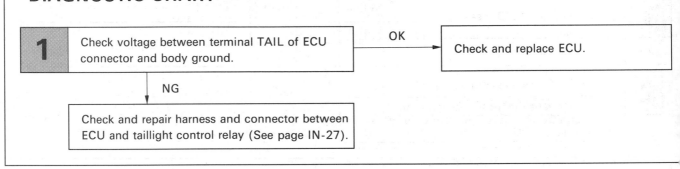

1 Check voltage between terminal TAIL of ECU connector and body ground. ──OK──▸ Check and replace ECU.

│ NG

Check and repair harness and connector between ECU and taillight control relay (See page IN-27).

INSPECTION PROCEDURE

1 **Check voltage between terminal TAIL of ECU connector and body ground.**

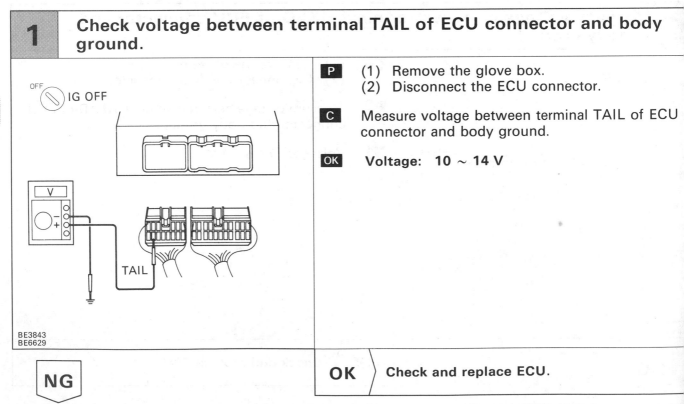

P (1) Remove the glove box.
(2) Disconnect the ECU connector.

C Measure voltage between terminal TAIL of ECU connector and body ground.

OK Voltage: 10 ~ 14 V

BE3843
BE6629

NG

OK ⟩ **Check and replace ECU.**

Check and repair harness and connector between ECU and taillight control relay (See page IN-27).

Ignition Switch Circuit

CIRCUIT DESCRIPTION

When the ignition switch is turned to the ACC position, battery voltage is applied to the terminal ACC of the ECU. Also, if the ignition switch is turned to the ON position, battery voltage is applied to the terminals ACC of the ECU. When the battery voltage is applied to the terminal ACC of the ECU while the theft deterrent system is activated, the warning stops. Furthermore, power supplied from the terminals ACC of the ECU is used as power for the door open detection switch, etc.

DIAGNOSTIC CHART

| **1** Check CIG & RADIO fuses. | NG → | Check for short in all the harness and components connected to the CIG & RADIO fuses. |

OK ↓

| **2** Check voltage between terminals ACC of ECU connector and body ground. | OK → | Check and replace ECU. |

NG ↓

Check and repair harness and connector between ECU and battery (See page IN-27).

BE

INSPECTION PROCEDURE

1   Check RADIO & CIG and ECU-IG fuses

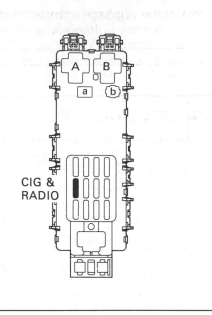

N02617

P (1) Remove the front lower panel.
(2) Remove CIG & RADIO fuses from J/B No.1.

C Check continuity of CIG & RADIO fuses.

OK **Continuity**

OK

NG ⟩ Check for short in all the harness and components connected to the CIG & RADIO fuses.

2   Check voltage between terminals ACC of ECU and body ground.

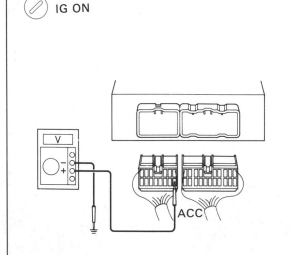

BE3841
N05908

P (1) Remove the glove box.
(2) Disconnect the ECU connectors.
(3) Turn ignition switch on.

C Measure voltage between terminals ACC of ECU connector and body ground.

OK **Voltage: 10 ~ 14 V**

NG

OK ⟩ Check and replace ECU.

Check and repair harness and connector between ECU and battery (See page IN-27).

Luggage Compartment Door Key Operated Switch Circuit

CIRCUIT DESCRIPTION

The luggage compartment door key operated switch goes on when the luggage compartment door key cylinder is turned to the unlock side with the key.

DIAGNOSTIC CHART

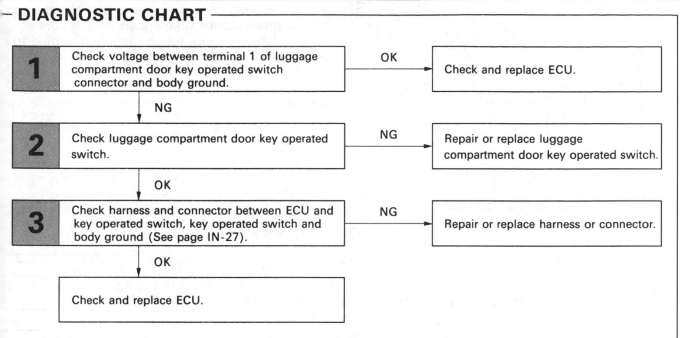

1 Check voltage between terminal 1 of luggage compartment door key operated switch connector and body ground.	OK →	Check and replace ECU.

NG ↓

2 Check luggage compartment door key operated switch.	NG →	Repair or replace luggage compartment door key operated switch.

OK ↓

3 Check harness and connector between ECU and key operated switch, key operated switch and body ground (See page IN-27).	NG →	Repair or replace harness or connector.

OK ↓

Check and replace ECU.

BE

INSPECTION PROCEDURE

1 Check voltage between terminal 1 of luggage compartment door key operated switch connector and body ground.

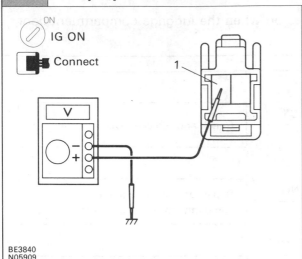

P (1) Remove luggage compartment door trim.
   (2) Turn ignition switch on.

C Measure voltage between terminal 1 of luggage compartment door key operated switch connector and body ground, when the key is turned to the unlock side and not turned.

OK

Key operation	Voltage
Turned to the unlock side	Below 1 V
Not turned	10 ~ 14 V

BE3840
N05909

NG

OK ⟩ Check and replace ECU.

---

2 Check luggage compartment door key operated switch.

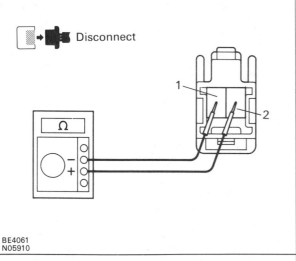

P Disconnect luggage compartment door key operated switch connector.

C Check continuity between terminals 1 and 2, when the key is turned to the unlock side and not turned.

OK   ○——○ Continuity

Key operation	1	2
Turned to unlock side	○——	——○
Not turned		

BE4061
N05910

OK

NG ⟩ Repair or replace luggage compartment door key operated switch.

---

3 Check harness and connector between ECU and key operated switch, key operated switch and body ground (See page IN-27).

OK

NG ⟩ Repair or replace harness or connector.

Check and replace ECU.

Luggage Compartment Door Courtesy Switch Circuit

CIRCUIT DESCRIPTION

The luggage compartment door courtesy switch goes on when the luggage compartment door is opened and goes off when the luggage compartment door is closed.

DIAGNOSTIC CHART

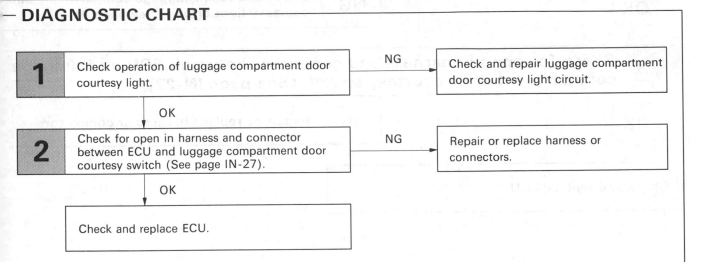

| **1** | Check operation of luggage compartment door courtesy light. | → NG → | Check and repair luggage compartment door courtesy light circuit. |

OK ↓

| **2** | Check for open in harness and connector between ECU and luggage compartment door courtesy switch (See page IN-27). | → NG → | Repair or replace harness or connectors. |

OK ↓

Check and replace ECU.

INSPECTION PROCEDURE

1 **Check operation of luggage compartment door courtesy light.**

c Check that luggage compartment door courtesy light goes off when luggage compartment door courtesy switch is pushed, and comes on when switch is not pushed.

OK

NG > Check and repair luggage compartment door courtesy light circuit (See page BE-37).

2 **Check for open in harness and connector between ECU and luggage compartment door courtesy switch (See page IN-27).**

OK

NG > Repair or replace harness or connectors.

Check and replace ECU.

Door Unlock Detection Switch Circuit

CIRCUIT DESCRIPTION

The door unlock detection switch is built in the door lock motor assembly. This switch is on when the door lock knob is in the unlock position and off when the lock knob is in the lock position. The ECU detects the front door lock knob conditions in this circuit. It is used as one of the operating conditions for the key confinement prevention function.

DIAGNOSTIC CHART

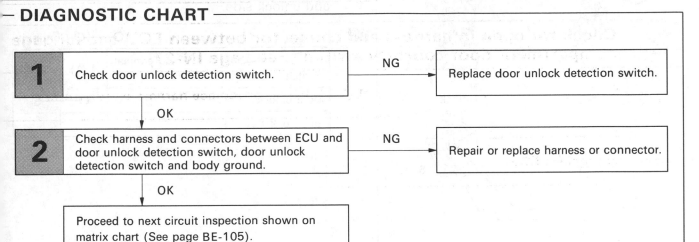

1 Check door unlock detection switch.

→ NG → Replace door unlock detection switch.

↓ OK

2 Check harness and connectors between ECU and door unlock detection switch, door unlock detection switch and body ground.

→ NG → Repair or replace harness or connector.

↓ OK

Proceed to next circuit inspection shown on matrix chart (See page BE-105).

BE

INSPECTION PROCEDURE

1 | **Check Door Unlock Detection Switch.**

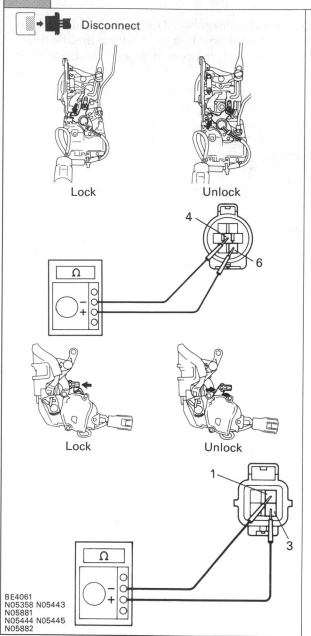

P   Remove the door

C   Check continuity between terminals 4 (1) and 6 (3) of door unlock detection switch connector, when the door lock is operated to the lock side and unlock side.

OK

Switch condition \ Terminal	4 (1)	6 (3)
Door unlock	○———————○	
Door lock		

○———○ Continuity

BE4061
N05358 N05443
N05881
N05444 N05445
N05882

OK

NG ⟩ Replace door unlock detection switch.

2 | **Check harness and connectors between relay and door unlock detection switch, door unlock detection switch and body ground.**

OK

NG ⟩ Repair or replace harness or connector.

Proceed to next circuit inspection shown on matrix chart (See page BE-105).

BE

Engine Hood Courtesy Switch Circuit

CIRCUIT DESCRIPTION

The engine hood courtesy switch is built into the engine hood lock assembly and goes on when the engine hood is opened and goes off when the engine hood is closed.

DIAGNOSTIC CHART

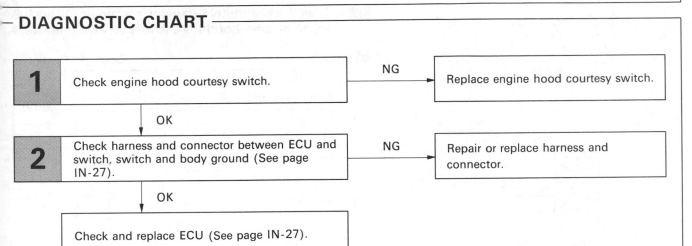

1 Check engine hood courtesy switch. ――NG――> Replace engine hood courtesy switch.

│ OK

2 Check harness and connector between ECU and switch, switch and body ground (See page IN-27). ――NG――> Repair or replace harness and connector.

│ OK

Check and replace ECU (See page IN-27).

BE

INSPECTION PROCEDURE

1   Check engine hood courtesy switch.

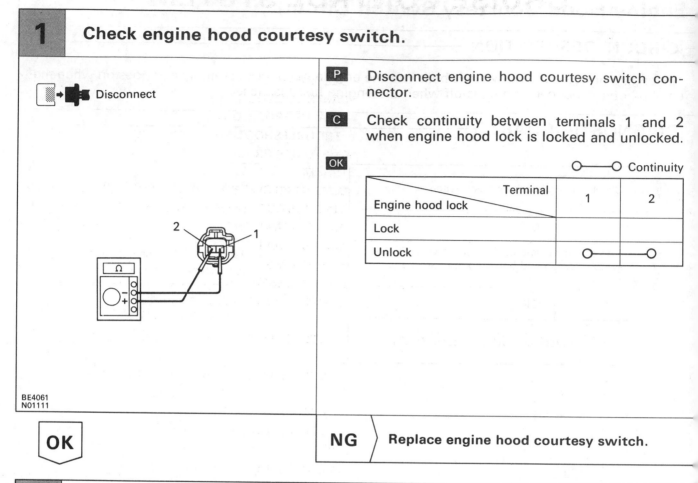

P   Disconnect engine hood courtesy switch connector.

C   Check continuity between terminals 1 and 2 when engine hood lock is locked and unlocked.

OK

Terminal Engine hood lock	1	2
Lock		
Unlock	○—	—○

○——○ Continuity

BE4061
N01111

OK

NG   Replace engine hood courtesy switch.

2   Check harness and connector between ECU and switch, switch and body ground (See page IN-27).

OK

NG   Repair or replace harness or connector.

Check and replace ECU (See page IN-27).

BE

CRUISE CONTROL SYSTEM

BE

DESCRIPTION

The cruise control system is standard, which is convenient when driving continuously at a constant speed.
The cruise control ECM controls all cruise control functions.
A diagnosis function is built in. In the unlikely event of a malfunction in the system, the problem area is
detected by the cruise control ECM and it causes the power indicator light on the combination meter to
blink, warning the driver that there is an abnormality as well as storing a malfunction code in the Cruise
Control ECM memory for the service technician to retrieve.

PARTS LOCATION

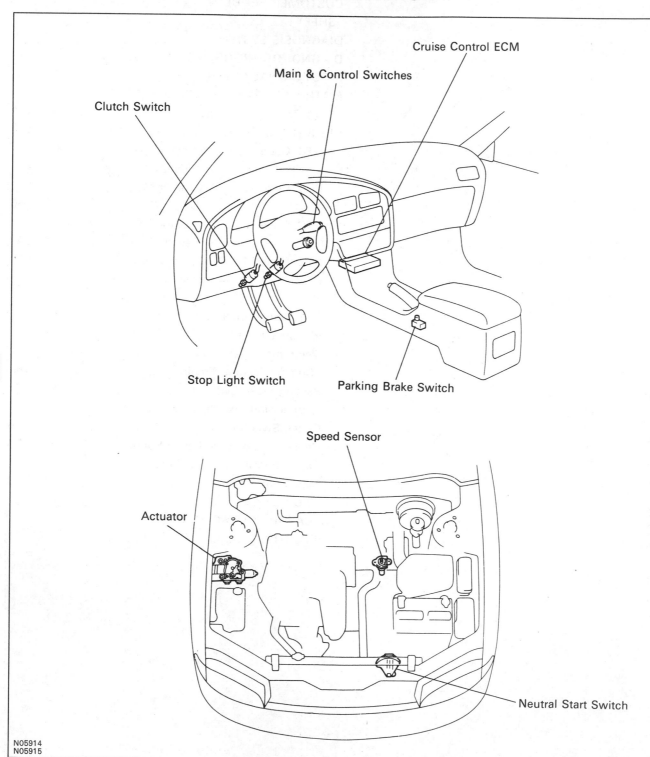

HOW TO PROCEED WITH TROUBLESHOOTING

Perform troubleshooting in accordance with the procedure on the following page.

1 **CUSTOMER PROBLEM ANALYSIS**

Using the customer problem analysis check sheet for reference, ask the customer in as much detail as possible about the problem.

2 **CHECK AND CLEAR THE DIAGNOSTIC TROUBLE CODES (PRECHECK)**

When there is a problem with the cruise control being canceled or failing to set, first check the diagnostic trouble code if there are any trouble codes stored in memory. If there are trouble codes, make a note of them, then clear them and proceed to " **3** Problem Symptom Confirmation".

3 **PROBLEM SYMPTOM CONFIRMATION,** **4** **SYMPTOM SIMULATION**

Confirm the problem symptoms. If the problem does not reappear, be sure to simulate the problem by mainly checking the circuits indicated by the diagnostic trouble code in step **2**, using "Problem Simulation Method".

5 **DIAGNOSTIC TROUBLE CODE CHART**

Check the diagnostic trouble codes. Determine if the problem is in the sensors or the wire harness. If a malfunction code is present, proceed to " **6** Diagnostic trouble Code Chart". If the normal code is output, proceed to " **7** Matrix Chart of Problem Symptoms".
Be sure to proceed to " **6** Diagnostic trouble Code Chart" after **2** and **3**.
If troubleshooting is attempted after only the first malfunction code in the memory is output, errors could be made in the diagnosis.

6 **DIAGNOSTIC TROUBLE CODE CHART**

If a trouble code is confirmed in the diagnostic trouble code check, proceed to the check procedure indicated by the matrix chart for each diagnostic trouble code.

7 **MATRIX CHART OF PROBLEM SYMPTOMS**

If the normal code is confirmed in the diagnostic trouble code check, perform inspection in accordance with the inspection order in the matrix chart of problem symptoms.

BE

8 **CIRCUIT INSPECTION**

Proceed with diagnosis of each circuit in accordance with the inspection order in **6** and **7**.
Determine whether the cause of the problem is in the sensor, actuators, wire harness and connectors, or the ECM.

9 **INPUT SIGNAL CHECK**

Check whether signals from the stop light switch and neutral start switch, etc. are input normally to the cruise control ECM. This check is indicated in the flow chart for each circuit.

10 **CONFIRMATION TEST**

After completing repairs, confirm not only that the malfunction is eliminated, but also perform a drive test, etc. to make sure the entire cruise control system is operating correctly.

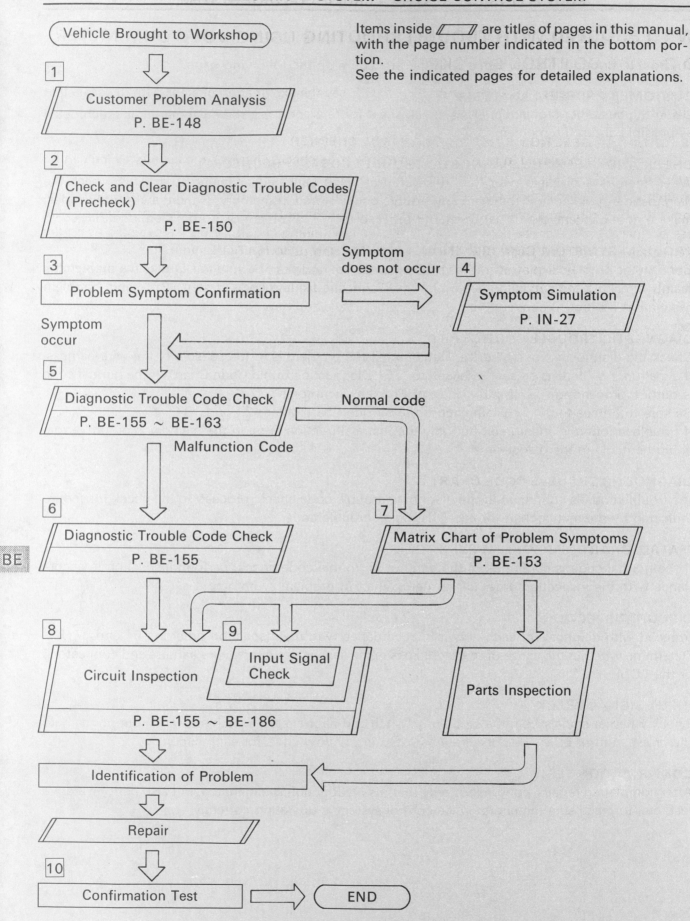

Vehicle Brought to Workshop

Items inside ⟋▱⟋ are titles of pages in this manual, with the page number indicated in the bottom portion.
See the indicated pages for detailed explanations.

1 Customer Problem Analysis
P. BE-148

2 Check and Clear Diagnostic Trouble Codes (Precheck)
P. BE-150

3 Problem Symptom Confirmation

Symptom does not occur

4 Symptom Simulation
P. IN-27

Symptom occur

5 Diagnostic Trouble Code Check
P. BE-155 ~ BE-163

Normal code

Malfunction Code

6 Diagnostic Trouble Code Check
P. BE-155

7 Matrix Chart of Problem Symptoms
P. BE-153

8 Circuit Inspection   **9** Input Signal Check
P. BE-155 ~ BE-186

Parts Inspection

Identification of Problem

Repair

10 Confirmation Test   END

HOW TO PROCEED WITH TROUBLESHOOTING USING VOLT/OHM METER AND CRUISE CONTROL CHECKER

For the explanation of steps ☐1 ~ ☐6 and ☐9 ~ ☐12 , see the explanation of steps with the same title on page BE-143.

☐7 ☐8 CIRCUIT INSPECTION BY CRUISE CONTROL CHECKER

If the Normal code is displayed in the diagnostic trouble code check, check all the circuits which can be inspected using the checker.

If a malfunctioning circuit is then detected, proceed to "Circuit Inspection by Volt/Ohm Meter" and check the applicable circuit using a volt/ohm meter. Determine if the malfunction is in the sensor, actuator, wire harness, connector or the cruise control ECM. If the malfunctioning circuit cannot be detected using the checker, proceed to "Matrix Chart of Problem Symptoms" and perform troubleshooting.

If a malfunction code is displayed in the diagnostic trouble code check, use the checker to inspect the circuit indicated by the diagnostic trouble code chart for the displayed code.

For instructions on how to connect the checker to the vehicle and how to use the checker, please refer to the Instruction Manual for Cruise Control.

BE

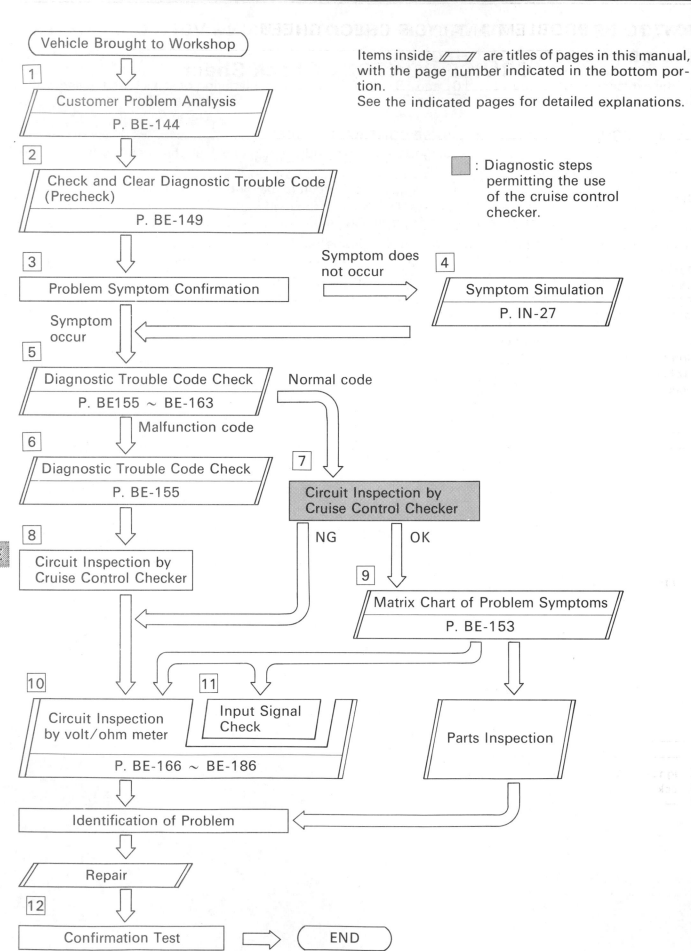

Vehicle Brought to Workshop

Items inside ▱ are titles of pages in this manual, with the page number indicated in the bottom portion.
See the indicated pages for detailed explanations.

1
Customer Problem Analysis
P. BE-144

▨ : Diagnostic steps permitting the use of the cruise control checker.

2
Check and Clear Diagnostic Trouble Code (Precheck)
P. BE-149

3
Problem Symptom Confirmation → Symptom does not occur → 4 Symptom Simulation P. IN-27

Symptom occur

5
Diagnostic Trouble Code Check
P. BE155 ~ BE-163

Normal code

Malfunction code

6
Diagnostic Trouble Code Check
P. BE-155

7
Circuit Inspection by Cruise Control Checker

NG   OK

8
Circuit Inspection by Cruise Control Checker

9
Matrix Chart of Problem Symptoms
P. BE-153

10
Circuit Inspection by volt/ohm meter

11
Input Signal Check

P. BE-166 ~ BE-186

Parts Inspection

Identification of Problem

Repair

12
Confirmation Test ⟹ END

BE

CUSTOMER PROBLEM ANALYSIS CHECK SHEET

CRUISE CONTROL Check Sheet

Inspector's Name :

Customer's Name		Registration No.	
		Registration Year	/ /
		Frame No.	
Date of Vehicle Brought In	/ /	Odometer Reading	Km Miles

Condition of Problem Occurrence	Date of Problem Occurrence	/ /
	How Often Does Problem Occur?	☐ Continuous ☐ Intermittent (Times a day)
	Vehicle Speed when Problem Occurred	km/h mile/h

Symptoms	☐ Auto cancel occurs	• Driving condition ☐ City driving ☐ Freeway ☐ Up hill ☐ Down hill • After cancel occurred, did the driver activate cruise control again? ☐ Yes ☐ No
	☐ Cancel does not occur	☐ With brake ON ☐ With parking brake ON ☐ With clutch ON ☐ During N range shift ☐ At 40 km/h (25 mph) or less ☐ When control SW turns to CANCEL position
	☐ Cruise control malfunction	☐ Slip to acceleration side ☐ Slip to acceleration side ☐ Hunting occurs ☐ O/D cut off does not occur ☐ O/D does not return
	☐ Switch malfunction	☐ SET ☐ ACCEL. ☐ COAST ☐ RESUME ☐ CANCEL
	☐ Faulty CRUISE MAIN indicator light	☐ Remains ON ☐ Does not light up ☐ Blinking

Diagnostic Code Check	1st Time	☐ Normal Code ☐ Malfunction Code (Code)
	2nd Time	☐ Normal Code ☐ Malfunction Code (Code)

BE

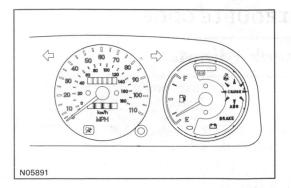

N05891

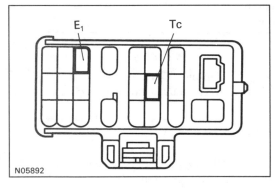

Warning

1.5 sec   0.5 sec

ON

OFF

5 times

BE4034

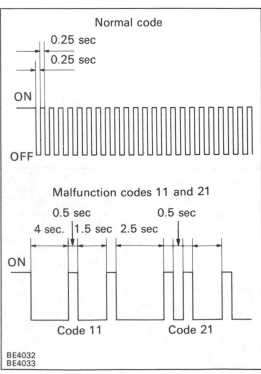

DIAGNOSIS SYSTEM
INDICATOR CHECK

1. Turn the ignition switch to ON.
2. Check that the CRUISE MAIN indicator light comes on when the cruise control main switch is turned on, and that the indicator light goes off when the main switch is turned OFF.

   HINT: If the indicator check result is not normal, proceed to troubleshooting (See page BE-50) for the combination meter section.

DIAGNOSTIC TROUBLE CODE CHECK

HINT: If a malfunction occurs in the speed sensors or actuator, etc. during cruise control driving, the Cruise Control ECM actuates AUTO CANCEL of the cruise control and blinks the CRUISE MAIN indicator light 5 times to inform the driver of a malfunction. At the same time, the malfunction is stored in memory as a diagnostic trouble code.

Output of Diagnostic Trouble Code

1. Turn the ignition switch ON.
2. Using SST, connect terminals Tc and E1 of DLC 1.
   SST 09843-18020
3. Read the diagnostic trouble code on the CRUISE MAIN indicator light.

   HINT: If the diagnostic trouble code is not output, inspect the Tc circuit (See page BE-47).

As an example, the blinking patterns for codes; normal, 11 and 21 are shown in the illustration.

4. Check for the problem using the diagnostic trouble code table on the next page.
5. After completing the check, disconnect terminals Tc and E1, and turn off the display.

Normal code

0.25 sec
0.25 sec

ON

OFF

Malfunction codes 11 and 21

0.5 sec   0.5 sec
4 sec. 1.5 sec 2.5 sec

ON

Code 11   Code 21

BE4032
BE4033

DIAGNOSTIC TROUBLE CODE

Code No.	CRUISE MAIN Indicator Light Blinking Pattern	Diagnosis
–	ON / OFF (BE3931)	Normal
11	ON / OFF (BE3931)	• Continuous output to motor acceleration side. • Overcurrent (short) in motor circuit.
12	ON / OFF (BE3931)	• Overcurrent (short) in magnet clutch circuit. • Open in magnet clutch circuit.
13	ON / OFF (BE3931)	• Open in actuator motor circuit. • Position sensor detects abnormal voltage. • Position sensor signal value does not change when the motor operates.
21	ON / OFF (BE3932)	• Speed signal is not input to the cruise control ECM.
*23	ON / OFF (BE3932)	• Actual vehicle speed has dropped by 16 km/h (10 mph) or more below the set speed during crusing.
32	ON / OFF (BE3933)	• Short in control switch circuit.
34	ON / OFF (BE3933)	• Voltage abnormality in control switch circuit.

HINT: When two or more codes are indicated, the lowest numbered code will be displayed first.
(*) When the vehicle speed is reduced on uphill roads, the speed can be set again and driving continued. (This is not a malfunction.)

BE

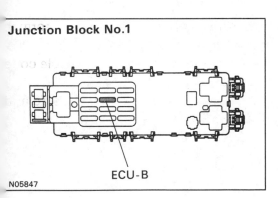

Junction Block No.1

ECU-B

N05847

Diagnostic Trouble Code Clearance
1. After completing repairs the diagnostic trouble code retained in memory can be cleared by removing the ECU-B fuse for 10 seconds or more, with the ignition switch off.
2. Check that the normal code is displayed after connecting the fuse.

DIAGNOSTIC TROUBLE CODE CHART

If a malfunction code is displayed during the diagnostic trouble code check, check the circuit listed for that code in the table below and proceed to the page given.

The circuits indicated by ※ on the matrix chart can be inspected using the cruise control checker.

Code No.	Circuit Inspection	Page
11	• ※ Actuator Motor Circuit	BE-155
12	• ※ Actuator Magnet Clutch Circuit	BE-157
13	• ※ Actuator Motor Circuit • ※ Actuator Position Sensor Circuit	BE-155 BE-159
21	• ※ Speed Sensor Circuit	BE-161
23	• ※ Actuator Control Cable • ※ Speed Sensor Circuit • ※ Actuator Motor Circuit	BE-188 BE-161 BE-155
32, 34	• ※ Control switch circuit. (cruise control switch)	BE-163

HINT:
1. If the instruction "Proceed to next circuit inspection shown on matrix chart" is given in the flow chart for each circuit, proceed to the circuit with the next highest number in the table to continue the check.
2. If the trouble still reappears even though there are no abnormalities in any of the other circuits, then check or replace the cruise control ECM as the last step.

BE

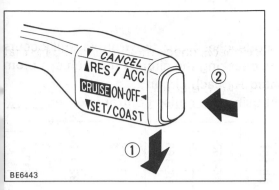

BE6443

INPUT SIGNAL CHECK

Output Code

1. (a) For check No.1 ~ No.2
      Turn the ignition switch on.
   (b) For check No.3 ~ No.4
      Jack up the vehicle.
      Start the engine.
2. Turn the control switch to SET/COAST position and hold it down ①.
3. Push the main switch on ②.
4. Check that the CRUISE MAIN indicator light blinks twice repeatedly.
5. Turn the SET/COAST switch off.
6. Operate each switch as listed in the table below.
7. Read the blinking pattern of the CRUISE MAIN indicator light.
8. After performing the check, turn the main switch off.
   HINT: When two or more signals are input to the cruise control ECM, only the lowest-numbered code is displayed.

No.	Operation Method	CRUISE MAIN Indicator Light Blinking Pattern		Diagnosis
1	Turn SET/COAST switch ON.	Light ON — 0.25⟷0.25 ⊓ ⊓ ⊓ OFF (BE4006)		SET/COAST switch circuit is normal.
2	Turn RES/ACC switch ON.	Light ON ⊓ ⊓ ⊓ ⊓ ⊓ OFF (BE4006)		RES/ACC switch circuit is normal.
3	Turn CANCEL switch ON.	Light ON — Switch OFF ⎤ OFF ------- ⎦ Switch ON (BE4006)		CANCEL switch circuit is normal.
	Turn stop light switch ON. (Depress brake pedal)			Stop light switch circuit is normal.
	Turn parking brake switch ON. (Release parking brake)			Parking brake switch circuit is normal.
	Turn neutral start switch ON. (Shift to N or P range)			Park/Neutral Position Switch is normal.
4	Drive at 40 km/h (25 mph) or higher.	Light ON ⊓⊓⊓⊓⊓⊓⊓ OFF (BE4006)		Vehicle speed sensor is normal.
	Drive at 40 km/h (25 mph) or below.	Light ON —————— OFF ------------ (BE4006)		

MATRIX CHART OF PROBLEM SYMPTOMS

If a normal code is displayed during the diagnostic trouble code check but the trouble still occurs (reappears), perform troubleshooting for each problem symptom, checking the circuits for each symptom in the order given in the table below. Proceed to the page located for each circuit.
The circuits indicated by ※ on the matrix chart can be inspected using the cruise control checker.

See Page / Symptom \ Suspect Area	BE-155 BE-157 BE-159 — ※ Actuator	BE-161 — ※ Vehicle Speed Sensor Circuit	BE-163 — ※ Control Switch Circuit (Cruise Control Switch)	BE-166 — ※ Stop Light Switch Circuit	BE-168 — ※ Idle Switch Circuit (main throttle position sensor)	BE-170 — ※ Electronic Controlled Transmission Communication Circuit	BE173 — ※ Parking Brake Switch Surcuit
SET not occurring or CANCEL occurring. (Diagnostic Trouble Code is normal)	8	2	3	4			7
SET not occurring or CANCEL occurring. (Diagnostic Trouble Code does not output.)							
Actual vehicle speed deviates above or below the set speed.	4	2			5	3	
Gear shifting is frequent between 3rd and OD when driving on uphill road. (Hunting)						1	
Cruise control not cancelled, even when parking brake pedal is depressed.	3			1			
Cruise control not cancelled, even when parking brake is operating.	3						1
Cruise control not cancelled, even when clutch pedal is depressed.	3						
Cruise control not cancelled, even when transmission is shifted to "N" range.	3						
Control switch does not operate. (SET/COAST, ACC/RES, CANCEL not possible)	3		1				
SET possible at 40 km/h (25 mph) or less, or CANCEL does not operate at 40 km/h (25 mph) or less.	3	1					
Poor response in ACCEL and RESUME modes.	3					2	
O/D does not Resume, even though the road is not uphill.						1	
Diagnostic trouble code memory is erased.							
Diagnostic trouble code is not output, or is output when it should not be.							
Cruise MAIN indicator light remains ON or fall to light up.	Combination meter troubleshooting on page BE-50.						

BE

HINT:
1. If the instruction "Proceed to next circuit inspection shown on matrix chart" is given in the flow chart for each circuit, proceed to the circuit with the next highest number in the table to continue the check.
2. If the trouble still reappears even though there are no abnormalities in any of the other circuits, then check or replace the cruise control ECM as the last step.

Symptom / Suspect Area	※Neutral Start Switch Circuit (BE-175)	Clutch Switch Circuit (BE-177)	※Cruise Control ECM Power Source Circuit (BE-179)	※Back-up Power Source Circuit (BE-182)	※Main Switch Circuit (Cruise Control Switch) (BE-184)	TC Terminal Circuit (BE-186)	Actuator Control Cable (BE-188)	Cruise Control ECM (IN-32)
SET not occurring or CANCEL occurring. (Diagnostic trouble code is normal)	5	6			1			9
SET not occurring or CANCEL occurring. Diagnostic trouble code does not output.			1					2
Actual vehicle speed deviates above or below the set speed.							1	6
Gear shifting is frequent between 3rd and OD when driving on uphill road. (Hunting)								3
Cruise control not cancelled, even when parking brake pedal is depressed.								2
Cruise control not cancelled, even when parking brake is operating.		1						2
Cruise control not cancelled, even when clutch pedal is depressed.		1						2
Cruise control not cancelled, even when transmission is shifted to "N" range.	1							2
Control switch does not operate. (SET/COAST, ACC/RES, CANCEL not possible)								2
SET possible at 40 km/h (25 mph) or less, or CANCEL does not operate at 40 km/h (25 mph) or less.								2
Poor response in ACCEL and RESUME modes.							1	4
O/D does not Resume, even though the road is not uphill.								2
Diagnostic trouble code memory is erased.				1				2
Diagnostic trouble code is not output, or is output when it should not be.							1	2
Cruise MAIN indicator light remains ON or fall to light up.	Combination meter troubleshooting on page BE-50							

BE

CIRCUIT INSPECTION

DTC	11, 13	Actuator Motor Circuit

CIRCUIT DESCRIPTION

The actuator motor is operated by signals from the cruise control ECM. Acceleration and deceleration signals are transmitted by changes in the Duty Ratio (See note below).

Duty Ratio
The duty ratio is the ratio of the period of continuity in one cycle. For example, if A is the period of continuity in one cycle, and B is the period of non-continuity, then

$$\text{Duty Ratio} = \frac{A}{A + B} \times 100 \ (\%)$$

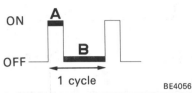

DTC No.	Diagnosis	Trouble Area
11	• Continuous output to motor acceleration side. • Overcurrent (short) in motor circuit.	• Cruise control actuator motor. • Harness or connector between actuator motor and Cruise Control ECM. • Cruise Control ECM.
13	• Open in actuator motor circuit.	

DIAGNOSTIC CHART

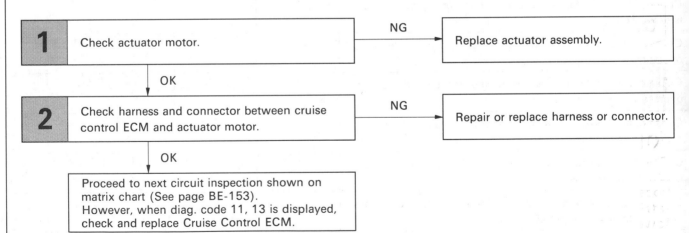

INSPECTION PROCEDURE

| **1** | Check actuator motor. |

Acceleration side

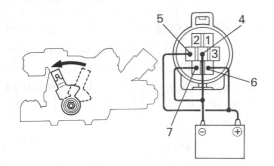

Deceleration side

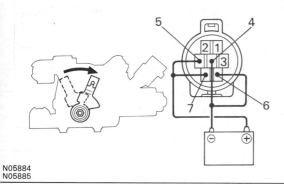

N05884
N05885

P
(1) Remove cruise control actuator.
(2) Disconnect actuator connector.

C
(1) Connect positive ⊕ lead to terminal 5 and negative ⊖ lead to terminal 4 of actuator connector. (Magnet clutch ON)
(2) When battery voltage is applied to each terminals of actuator connector, check that the control plate moves smoothly without hesitating.

○——○ Connect

Terminal Moving direction	Positive ⊕	Negative ⊖	6	7
Acceleration side	○——————○		○	
		○————————○		○
Deceleration side	○		○————————○	
		○—————○		

OK ▽

NG ⟩ Replace actuator assembly.

| **2** | Check harness and connector between cruise control ECM and actuator motor. (See page IN-27) |

OK ▽

NG ⟩ Repair or replace harness or connector.

Proceed to next circuit inspection shown on matrix chart (See page BE-153).
However, when diag. code 11, 13 is displayed, check and replace Cruise Control ECM.

| DTC | 12 | Actuator Magnet Clutch Circuit |

CIRCUIT DESCRIPTION

This circuit turns on the magnet clutch inside the actuator during cruise control operation according to the signal from the cruise control ECM. If a malfunction occurs in the actuator or speed sensor, etc. during cruise control, the rotor shaft between the motor and control plate is released.

When the brake pedal is depressed, the stoplight switch turns on supplying electrical power to the stoplight. Power supply to the magnet clutch is mechanically cut and the magnet clutch is turned OFF.

When driving downhill, if the vehicle speed exceeds the set speed by 15 km/h (9 mph), the cruise control ECM turns the magnet clutch OFF. If the vehicle speed later drops to within 10 km/h (6 mph) above the set speed, then cruise control at the set speed is resumed.

DTC No.	Diagnosis	Trouble Area
12	• Overcurrent (short) in magnet clutch circuit. • Open in magnet clutch circuit.	• Cruise control magnet clutch. • Harness or connector between Cruise Control ECM and magnet clutch, magnet clutch and body ground. • Stop light switch. • Cruise Control ECM.

DIAGNOSTIC CHART

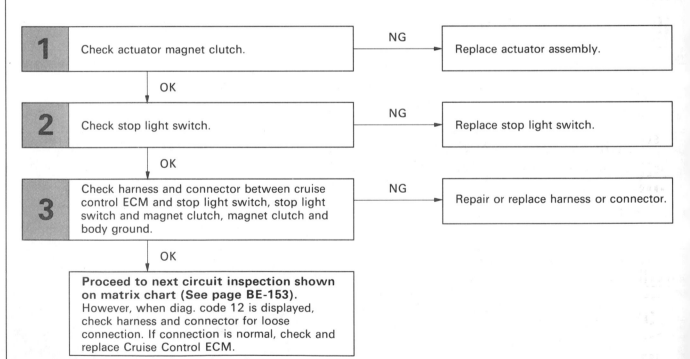

1 Check actuator magnet clutch. —NG→ Replace actuator assembly.

OK

2 Check stop light switch. —NG→ Replace stop light switch.

OK

3 Check harness and connector between cruise control ECM and stop light switch, stop light switch and magnet clutch, magnet clutch and body ground. —NG→ Repair or replace harness or connector.

OK

Proceed to next circuit inspection shown on matrix chart (See page BE-153). However, when diag. code 12 is displayed, check harness and connector for loose connection. If connection is normal, check and replace Cruise Control ECM.

INSPECTION PROCEDURE

1 **Check actuator magnet clutch.**

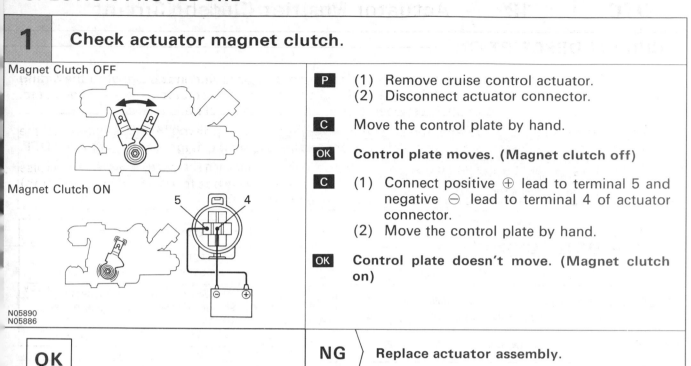

Magnet Clutch OFF

Magnet Clutch ON

N05890
N05886

P   (1) Remove cruise control actuator.
      (2) Disconnect actuator connector.

C   Move the control plate by hand.

OK   **Control plate moves. (Magnet clutch off)**

C   (1) Connect positive ⊕ lead to terminal 5 and negative ⊖ lead to terminal 4 of actuator connector.
      (2) Move the control plate by hand.

OK   **Control plate doesn't move. (Magnet clutch on)**

OK

NG ⟩ Replace actuator assembly.

2 **Check stop light switch.**

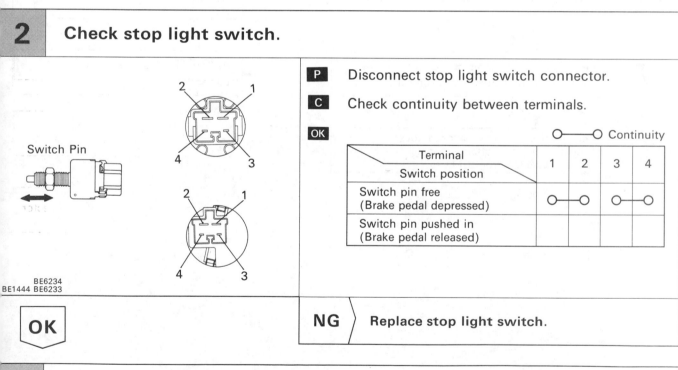

Switch Pin

BE6234
BE1444 BE6233

P   Disconnect stop light switch connector.

C   Check continuity between terminals.

OK   O——O Continuity

Terminal Switch position	1	2	3	4
Switch pin free (Brake pedal depressed)	O—	—O	O—	—O
Switch pin pushed in (Brake pedal released)				

OK

NG ⟩ Replace stop light switch.

3   **Check harness and connectors between cruise control ECM and stop light switch, stop light switch and magnet clutch, magnet clutch and body ground. (See page IN-27).**

OK

NG ⟩ Repair or replace harness or connector.

Proceed to next circuit inspection shown on matrix chart (See page BE-153). However, when diag code 12 is displayed, check harness and connector for loose connection. If connection is normal, check and replace Cruise Control ECM.

BE

DTC	13	Actuator Position Sensor Circuit

CIRCUIT DESCRIPTION

This circuit detects the rotation position of the actuator control plate and sends signal to the Cruise Control ECM.

DTC No.	Diagnosis	Trouble Area
13	• Position sensor detects abnormal voltage. • Position sensor signal value does not change when the motor operates.	• Cruise control actuator Position sensor. • Harness or connector between actuator position sensor and body ground. • Cruise Control ECM.

DIAGNOSTIC CHART

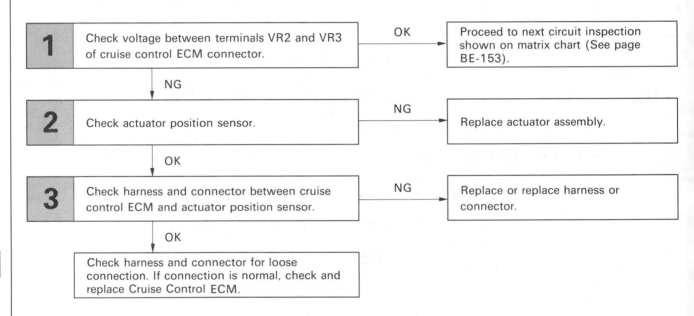

1 Check voltage between terminals VR2 and VR3 of cruise control ECM connector. — OK → Proceed to next circuit inspection shown on matrix chart (See page BE-153).

↓ NG

2 Check actuator position sensor. — NG → Replace actuator assembly.

↓ OK

3 Check harness and connector between cruise control ECM and actuator position sensor. — NG → Replace or replace harness or connector.

↓ OK

Check harness and connector for loose connection. If connection is normal, check and replace Cruise Control ECM.

BE

INSPECTION PROCEDURE

1 Check voltage between terminals VR2 and VR3 of cruise control ECM connector.

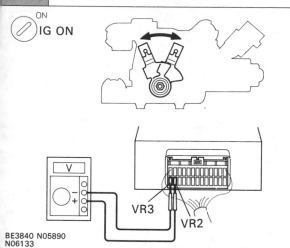

BE3840 N05890
N06133

P Remove cruise control ECM with connectors still connected.

C (1) Turn ignition switch on.
(2) Measure voltage between terminals VR2 and VR3 of cruise control ECM connector while turning control plate slowly by hand from the deceleration side to the acceleration side.

OK Voltage:
Fully closed: 1.1 – 1.4 V
Fully opened: 3.8 – 4.5 V
In addition, as the control plate is turned, the voltage should increase gradually without interruption.

NG

OK Proceed to next circuit inspection shown on matrix chart (See page BE-153).

2 Check actuator position sensor.

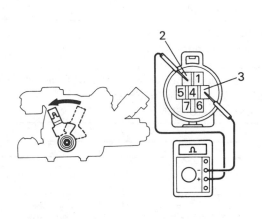

N05889

P (1) Remove cruise control actuator.
(2) Disconnect the actuator connector.

C Measure resistance between actuator terminals 1 and 3 actuator connector.

OK Resistance: Approx. 2 kΩ

C Measure resistance between terminals 2 and 3 of actuator connector, while turning the control plate slowly by hand from the deceleration side to the acceleration side.

OK Resistance:
Fully closed: Approx. 0.5 Ω
Fully opened: Approx. 1.8 kΩ
In addition, as the control plate turns, the resistance should increase gradually without interruption.

OK

NG Replace actuator assembly.

BE

3 Check harness and connector between cruise control ECM and actuator position sensor. (See page IN-27)

OK

NG Repair or replace harness or connector.

Check harness and connector for loose connection. If connection is normal check and replace cruise control ECM.

DTC	21, 23	Speed Sensor Circuit

CIRCUIT DESCRIPTION

The speed sensor signal is sent to cruise control ECM as vehicle speed signal.

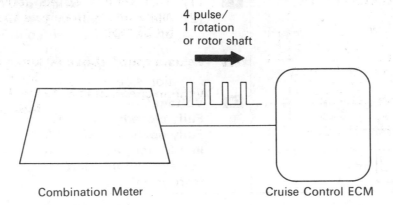

4 pulse/
1 rotation
or rotor shaft

Combination Meter   Cruise Control ECM

N02163

DTC No.	Diagnosis	Trouble Area
21	Speed signal is not input to the cruise control ECM.	• Speed sensor. • Combination meter. • Harness or connector between speed sensor and combination meter, combination meter and Cruise Control ECM. • Cruise Control ECM.
23	Actual vehicle speed has dropped by 16 km/h (10 mph) or more below the set speed during cruising. HINT: When speed sensor circuit is opened intermittently (Below 0.2 sec), code 23 is output.	• Actuator. • Actuator control cable. • Speed sensor. • Harness or connector in OD and SPD circuit. (Open or short intermittently) • Cruise Control ECM.

DIAGNOSTIC CHART

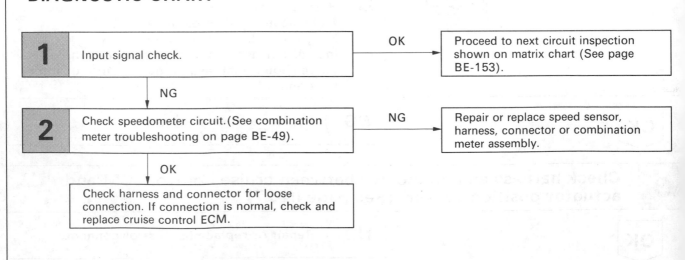

1 Input signal check. — OK → Proceed to next circuit inspection shown on matrix chart (See page BE-153).

↓ NG

2 Check speedometer circuit. (See combination meter troubleshooting on page BE-49). — NG → Repair or replace speed sensor, harness, connector or combination meter assembly.

↓ OK

Check harness and connector for loose connection. If connection is normal, check and replace cruise control ECM.

BE

NSPECTION PROCEDURE

1   Input signal check.

Vehicle speed	Indicator light blinking pattern
Above 40 km/h (25 mph)	ON ⎤ ⎡⎤⎡⎤⎡⎤⎡ Blinks OFF ⎦ ⎣⎦⎣⎦⎣⎦⎣ 0.25 sec →‖←0.25 sec
Below 40 km/h (25 mph)	ON ———— Stays ON OFF — — — — — —

BE4006

C (1) See input signal check on page BE-54.
(2) Check indicator light operation when driving with vehicle speed above 40 km/h (25 mph), and with vehicle speed below 40 km/h (25 mph).

OK Vehicle speed above 40 km/h (25 mph)
: Indicator light blinks
Vehicle speed below 40 km/h (25 mph)
: Indicator light stays on

NG

OK ⟩ Proceed to next circuit inspection shown on matrix chart (See page BE-153).

2   Check speedometer circuit. (See combination meter troubleshooting on page BE-49).

OK

NG ⟩ Repair or replace speed sensor, harness, connector or combination meter assembly.

Check harness and connector for loose connection.
If connection is normal, check and replace cruise control ECM.

BE

DTC	32, 34	Control Switch Circuit (Cruise Control Switch)

CIRCUIT DESCRIPTION

This circuit carries the SET/COAST, RESUME/ACCEL and CANCEL signals (each voltage) to the cruise control ECM.

DTC No.	Diagnosis	Trouble Area
32	Short in, control switch circuit.	• Cruise control switch.
34	Voltage abnormality in control switch circuit.	• Harness or connector between control switch and Cruise Control ECM. • Cruise Control ECM.

DIAGNOSTIC CHART

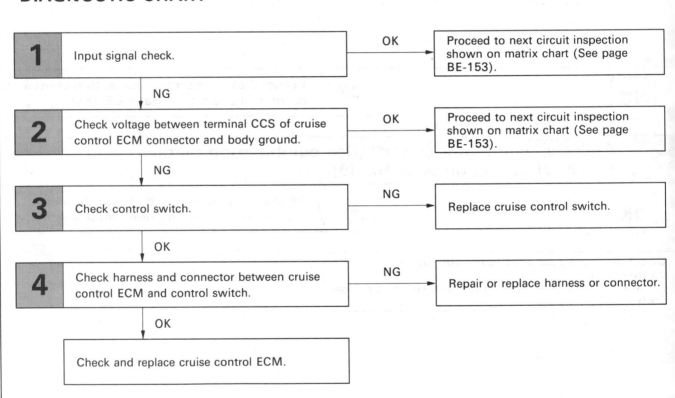

1	Input signal check.	OK →	Proceed to next circuit inspection shown on matrix chart (See page BE-153).

↓ NG

2	Check voltage between terminal CCS of cruise control ECM connector and body ground.	OK →	Proceed to next circuit inspection shown on matrix chart (See page BE-153).

↓ NG

3	Check control switch.	NG →	Replace cruise control switch.

↓ OK

4	Check harness and connector between cruise control ECM and control switch.	NG →	Repair or replace harness or connector.

↓ OK

Check and replace cruise control ECM.

BE

NSPECTION PROCEDURE

1   Input signal check.

Input signal	Indicator light blinking pattern
SET/COAST SWITCH	ON ⎯ ⎤ ⎡⎤⎡⎤ 2 Pulse OFF
RESUME/ACCEL SWITCH	ON ⎯ ⎤ ⎡⎤⎡⎤⎡⎤ 3 Pulse OFF
CANCEL SWITCH	ON ⎯ switch OFF ⎤ OFF ⎦ switch ON

3E4006

C (1) See input signal check on page BE-152.
(2) Check the indicator light operation when each of the SET/COAST, RESUME/ACCEL and CANCEL is turned ON.

OK SET/COAST, RESUME/ACCEL switch
The signals shown in the table on the left should be output when each switch is ON. The signal should disappear when the switch is turned OFF.
CANCEL switch
The indicator light goes off when the cancel switch is turned ON.

NG

OK ⟩ Proceed to next circuit inspection shown on matrix chart (See page BE-153).

2   Check voltage between terminal CCS of cruise control ECM connector and body ground.

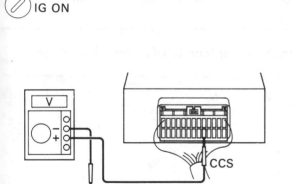

IG ON

CCS

P Remove cruise control ECM with connectors still connected.

C (1) Turn ignition switch ON.
(2) Measure voltage between terminal CCS of cruise control ECM connector and body ground, when each of the SET/COAST, RESUME/ACCEL and CANCEL is turned ON.

OK

Switch position	Voltage
Neutral	10 – 14 V
RES/ACC	0.7 – 2.5 V
SET/COAST	2.4 – 4.6 V
CANCEL	4.1 – 7.2 V

E3840
E6616

NG

OK ⟩ Proceed to next circuit inspection shown on matrix chart (See page BE-153).

BE

3   Check control switch.

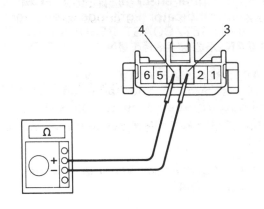

N05887

P   (1) Remove steering wheel center pad.
(2) Disconnect control switch connector (See page AB-16).

C   Measure resistance between terminals 3 and 4 of control switch connector when control switch is operated.

OK

Switch position	Resistance
Neutral	∞ (No continuity)
RES/ACC	Approx. 68 Ω
SET/COAST	Approx. 198 Ω
CANCEL	Approx. 418 Ω

Hint   When diagnostic code 34 is displayed, carefully check that resistance is always 1 MΩ or higher in neutral position, particularly when switching between REC/ACC and SET/COAST.

OK

NG ⟩ Replace cruise control switch.

---

4   Check harness and connector between cruise control ECM and control switch. (See page IN-27)

OK

NG ⟩ Repair or replace harness or connector.

Check and replace cruise control ECM.

BE

Stop Light Switch Circuit

CIRCUIT DESCRIPTION

When the brake is on, battery voltage normally applies through the stop fuse and stop switch to terminal STP– of the cruise control ECM, and the cruise control ECM turns the cruise control off.

A fail-safe function is provided so that the cancel functions normally, even if there is a malfunction in the stop light signal circuit.

1   If the harness connected to terminal STP– has an open, terminal STP– will have battery voltage and the cruise control will be turned off, also SET not occurring.

2   If the stop fuse is open, terminal STP+ becomes approx. 0 V when the brake is turned on, so the cruise control ECM performs cancel function normally.

Also, shown the brake is on, the magnet clutch circuit is cut mechanically by the stop light switch, turning the cruise control off.

DIAGNOSTIC CHART

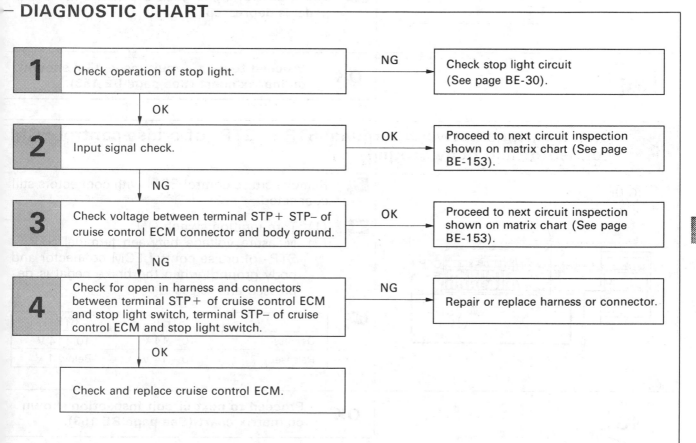

1   Check operation of stop light. — NG → Check stop light circuit (See page BE-30).

↓ OK

2   Input signal check. — OK → Proceed to next circuit inspection shown on matrix chart (See page BE-153).

↓ NG

3   Check voltage between terminal STP+ STP– of cruise control ECM connector and body ground. — OK → Proceed to next circuit inspection shown on matrix chart (See page BE-153).

↓ NG

4   Check for open in harness and connectors between terminal STP+ of cruise control ECM and stop light switch, terminal STP– of cruise control ECM and stop light switch. — NG → Repair or replace harness or connector.

↓ OK

Check and replace cruise control ECM.

BE

INSPECTION PROCEDURE

1 **Check operation of stop light.**

C   Check that stop light comes on when brake pedal is depressed, and turns off when brake pedal is released.

OK

NG ⟩ Check stop light circuit (See page BE-30).

---

2 **Input signal check.**

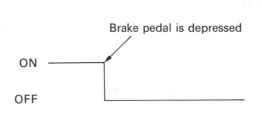

Brake pedal is depressed

ON

OFF

C   (1) See input signal check on page BE-54.
     (2) Check the indicator light when the brake pedal is depressed.

OK **The indicator light goes off when the brake pedal is depressed.**

NG

OK ⟩ Proceed to next circuit inspection shown on matrix chart (See page BE-153).

---

3 **Check voltage between terminal STP+, STP– of cruise control ECM connector and body ground.**

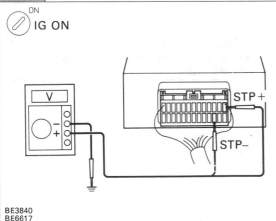

ON
IG ON

P   Remove cruise control ECM with connectors still connected.

C   (1) Turn ignition switch ON.
     (2) Measure voltage between terminal STP+, STP– of cruise control ECM connector and body ground, when the brake pedal is depressed and released.

OK

	STP+	STP–
Depressed	10 – 14 V	10 – 14 V
Released	10 – 14 V	Below 1 V

STP+
STP–

BE3840
BE6617

NG

OK ⟩ Proceed to next circuit inspection shown on matrix chart (See page BE-153).

---

4 Check for open in harness and connectors between terminal STP+ of cruise control ECM and stop light switch, terminal STP– of cruise control ECM and stop light switch. (See page IN-27)

OK

NG ⟩ Repair or replace harness or connector.

Check and replace cruise control ECM.

Idle Switch Circuit

CIRCUIT DESCRIPTION

When the idle switch is turned ON, a signal is sent to the cruise control ECM. The cruise control ECM uses this signal to enable accurate cruise control at the set speed quickly. If the idle switch is malfunctioning, problem symptoms also occur in the engine, so also inspect the engine.

DIAGNOSTIC CHART

1 Check voltage between terminal IDL of cruise control ECM connector and body ground.

→ OK → Proceed to next circuit inspection shown on matrix chart (See page BE-153).

↓ NG

2 Check throttle position sensor.

→ NG → Replace throttle position sensor.

↓ OK

3 Check harness and connector between cruise control ECM and throttle position sensor, throttle position sensor and body ground.

→ NG → Repair or replace harness or connector.

↓ OK

Check and replace cruise control ECM.

BE

INSPECTION PROCEDURE

1 Check voltage between terminal IDL of cruise control ECM connector and body ground.

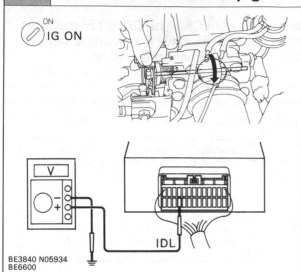

BE3840 N05934
BE6600

P (1) Remove cruise control ECM with connectors still connected.
(2) Disconnect PCM and ABS & TRAC ECM connector.

C (1) Turn ignition switch ON.
(2) Measure voltage between terminal IDL of cruise control ECM connector and body ground, when the throttle valve is fully closed and fully opened.

OK

Throttle valve position	Voltage
Fully opened	10 – 14 V
Fully closed	Below 1 V

NG

OK > Proceed to next circuit inspection shown on matrix chart (See page BE-153).

---

2 Check throttle position sensor.

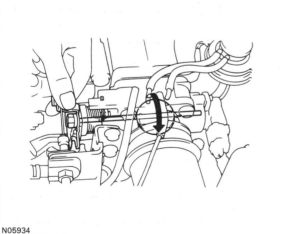

N05934

P Disconnect throttle position sensor connector.

C Measure resistance between terminals 1 and 2 of throttle position sensor connector, when the throttle valve is fully closed and fully opened.

OK

Throttle valve position	Resistance
Fully opened	1 MΩ or higher
Fully closed	Below 2 V

OK

NG > Replace throttle position sensor.

---

3 Check harness and connector between cruise control ECM and throttle position sensor, throttle position sensor and body ground. (See page IN-27)

OK

NG > Repair or replace harness or connector.

Check and replace cruise control ECM.

Electronic Controlled Transmission Communication Circuit

CIRCUIT DESCRIPTION

When driving uphill under cruise control, in order to reduce shifting due to ON-OFF overdrive operation and to provide smooth driving, when down shifting in the ECT occurs, a signal to prevent upshift until the end of the uphill slope is sent from the cruise control ECM to the ECM.

Terminal ECT of the cruise control ECM detects the shift change signal (output to Electronic Controlled Transmission No.2 solenoid) from the ECM.

If vehicle speed down and terminal ECT of the cruise control ECM receives down shifting signal, it sends a signal from terminal OD to ECM to cut overdrive until the end of the uphill slope, and the gear shifts are reduced.

DIAGNOSTIC CHART

1 Check operation of overdrive. — NG → Check and repair Electronic Controlled Transmission.

OK

2 Check voltage between terminal OD of harness side connector of cruise control ECM and body ground. — NG →

OK

3 Check voltage between terminal ECT of cruise control ECM connector and body ground (ON test drive). — OK → Proceed to next circuit inspection shown on matrix chart. (See page BE-153)

NG

4 Check harness and connector between terminal ECT of cruise control ECM and ECT No.2 solenoid. (See page IN-27) — NG → Repair or replace harness or connector.

OK

Check and repair cruise control ECM.

5 Check harness and connector between terminal OD of cruise control ECM and terminal OD 1 of ECM. — NG → Repair or replace harness or connector.

OK

Check and replace ECM.

BE

INSPECTION PROCEDURE

1   **Check operation of overdrive.**

P   Test drive after engine warm up.

C   Check that overdrive ON ↔ OFF occurs with operation of OD switch ON-OFF.

| OK | NG | **Check and Repair Electronic Controlled Transmission (See AX section).** |

2   **Check voltage between terminal OD of harness side connector of cruise control ECM and body ground.**

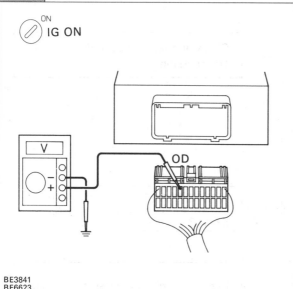

P   Remove cruise control ECM with connectors still connected.

C   (1)   Disconnect cruise control ECM connector.
       (2)   Turn ignition switch ON.
       (3)   Measure voltage between terminal OD of harness side connector of cruise control ECM and body ground.

OK   Voltage: 10 – 14 V

BE3841
BE6623

| OK | NG | Go to step **5** . |

Go to step **3** .

3 Check voltage between terminal ECT of cruise control ECM connector and body ground (On test drive).

P
(1) Connect cruise control ECM connector.
(2) Test drive after engine warm up.

C
Check voltage between terminal ECT of cruise control ECM connector and body ground when OD switch is on and off.

OK

Gear Position	Voltage
O/D	Below 1 V
3rd	10 – 14 V

ECT

BE6618

NG

OK Proceed to next circuit inspection shown on matrix chart (See page BE-153).

4 Check harness and connector between terminal ECT of cruise control ECM and Electronic Controlled Transmission solenoid. (See page IN-27)

OK

NG Repair or replace harness or connector.

Check and repair cruise control ECM.

5 Check harness and connector between terminal OD of cruise control ECM and terminal OD1 of ECM. (See page IN-27)

OK

NG Repair or replace harness or connector.

Check and replace ECM.

BE

Parking Brake Switch Circuit

CIRCUIT DESCRIPTION

When the parking brake is operating, the parking brake switch sends a signal to the cruise control ECM. When this signal is input to the cruise control ECM during cruise control driving, the cruise control ECM cancels cruise control.

DIAGNOSTIC CHART

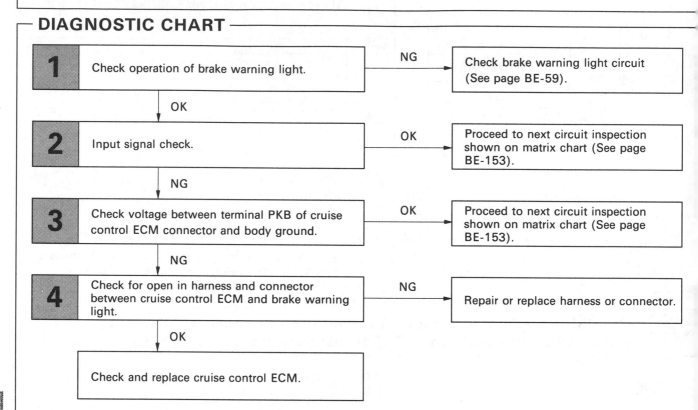

1 Check operation of brake warning light. — NG → Check brake warning light circuit (See page BE-59).

OK

2 Input signal check. — OK → Proceed to next circuit inspection shown on matrix chart (See page BE-153).

NG

3 Check voltage between terminal PKB of cruise control ECM connector and body ground. — OK → Proceed to next circuit inspection shown on matrix chart (See page BE-153).

NG

4 Check for open in harness and connector between cruise control ECM and brake warning light. — NG → Repair or replace harness or connector.

OK

Check and replace cruise control ECM.

BE

INSPECTION PROCEDURE

1   Check operation of brake warning light.

C   Check that the brake warning light in the instrument panel comes on when the parking brake is operating with the engine running, and the light goes off when the parking brake is not operating.

OK   **NG** ❯ Check brake warning light circuit (See page BE-59).

---

2   Input signal check.

Parking brake is operating

ON

OFF

C   (1) See input signal check on page BE-152.
     (2) Check the indicator light when the parking brake is operating.

OK The indicator light goes off when the parking brake is operating.

NG   **OK** ❯ Proceed to next circuit inspection shown on matrix chart (See page BE-153).

---

3   Check voltage between terminal PKB of cruise control ECM connector and body ground.

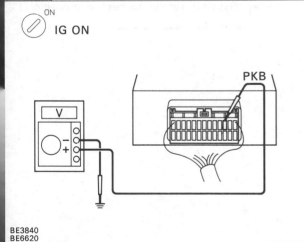

IG ON

PKB

BE3840
BE6620

P   Remove cruise control ECM with connectors still connected.

C   (1) Turn ignition switch ON.
     (2) Measure voltage between terminal PKB of cruise control ECM connector and body ground, when the parking brake lever is operating.

OK

Switch Position	Voltage
ON (lever pulled)	Below 1 V
OFF (lever released)	10 – 14 V

NG   **OK** ❯ Proceed to next circuit inspection shown on matrix chart (See page BE-153).

---

4   Check for open in harness and connector between cruise control ECM and brake warning light. (See page IN-27)

OK   **NG** ❯ Repair or replace harness or connector.

Check and replace cruise control ECM.

Neutral Start Switch Circuit

CIRCUIT DESCRIPTION

When the shift position is put in P or N, a signal is sent from the neutral start switch to the cruise control ECM.
When this signal is input during cruise control driving, the cruise control ECM cancels the cruise control.

DIAGNOSTIC CHART

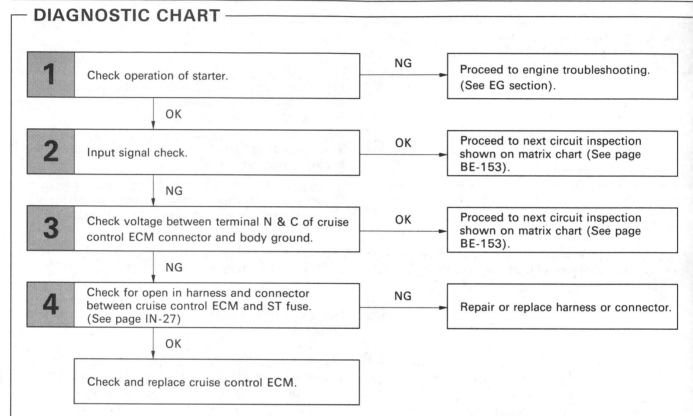

1 Check operation of starter.
— NG → Proceed to engine troubleshooting. (See EG section).

↓ OK

2 Input signal check.
— OK → Proceed to next circuit inspection shown on matrix chart (See page BE-153).

↓ NG

3 Check voltage between terminal N & C of cruise control ECM connector and body ground.
— OK → Proceed to next circuit inspection shown on matrix chart (See page BE-153).

↓ NG

4 Check for open in harness and connector between cruise control ECM and ST fuse. (See page IN-27)
— NG → Repair or replace harness or connector.

↓ OK

Check and replace cruise control ECM.

BE

INSPECTION PROCEDURE

1   Check operation of starter.

C   Check that the starter operates normally and that the engine starts.

OK	NG	Proceed to engine troubleshooting (See EG section).

2   Input signal check.

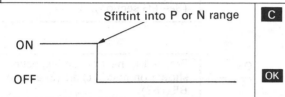

C   (1) See input signal check on page BE- .
      (2) Check the indicator light when shifting into P range or N range.

OK   **The indicator light goes off when shifting into P range or N range.**

NG	OK	Proceed to next circuit inspection shown on matrix chart (See page BE-153).

3   Check voltage between terminal N & C of cruise control ECM connector and body ground.

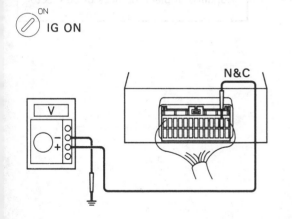

BE3840
BE6621

P   Remove cruise control ECM with connectors still connected.

C   (1) Turn ignition switch ON.
      (2) Measure voltage between terminal N & C of cruise control ECM connector and body ground, when shifting into P, N range and other ranges.

OK

Switch Position	Voltage
P or N range	Below 1 V
Other ranges	10 – 14 V

NG	OK	Proceed to next circuit inspection shown on matrix chart (See page BE-153).

4   Check for open in harness and connector between cruise control ECM and ST fuse. (See page IN-27).

OK	NG	Repair or replace harness or connector.

Check and replace cruise control ECM.

BE

Clutch Switch Circuit

CIRCUIT DESCRIPTION

When the clutch pedal is depressed, the clutch switch sends a signal to the cruise control ECM, when this signal is input to the cruise control ECM during cruise control driving, the cruise control ECM cancels cruise control.

DIAGNOSTIC CHART

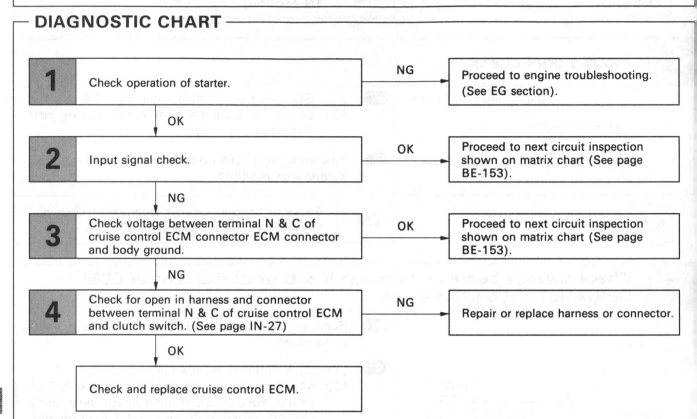

1 Check operation of starter. — NG → Proceed to engine troubleshooting. (See EG section).

OK

2 Input signal check. — OK → Proceed to next circuit inspection shown on matrix chart (See page BE-153).

NG

3 Check voltage between terminal N & C of cruise control ECM connector ECM connector and body ground. — OK → Proceed to next circuit inspection shown on matrix chart (See page BE-153).

NG

4 Check for open in harness and connector between terminal N & C of cruise control ECM and clutch switch. (See page IN-27) — NG → Repair or replace harness or connector.

OK

Check and replace cruise control ECM.

BE

INSPECTION PROCEDURE

1   Check operation of starter.

C   Check that the starter operates normally and that the engine starts.

OK   **NG** ⟩ Proceed to engine troubleshooting (See EG section).

2   Input signal check.

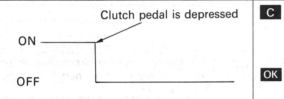

Clutch pedal is depressed

ON

OFF

C
(1) See input signal check on page BE-54.
(2) Check the indicator light when shifting into P range or N range.

OK   **The indicator light goes off when the clutch pedal is depressed.**

NG   **OK** ⟩ Proceed to next circuit inspection shown on matrix chart (See page BE-153).

3   Check voltage between terminal N & C of cruise control ECM connector and body ground.

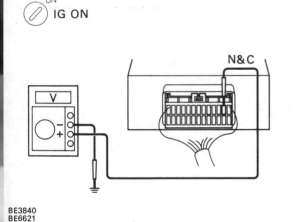

IG ON

N&C

BE3840
BE6621

P   Remove cruise control ECM with connectors still connected.

C
(1) Turn ignition switch ON.
(2) Measure voltage between terminal N & C of cruise control ECM connector and body ground, when the clutch pedal is depressed.

OK

Switch Position	Voltage
ON (pedal depressed)	Below 1 V
OFF	10 – 14 V

NG   **OK** ⟩ Proceed to next circuit inspection shown on matrix chart (See page BE-153).

4   Check for open in harness and connector between cruise control ECM and fuse.

OK   **NG** ⟩ Repair or replace harness or connector.

Check and replace cruise control ECM.

BE

Cruise Control ECM Power Source Circuit

CIRCUIT DESCRIPTION

The cruise control ECM power source supplies power to the actuator. Terminal GND and the cruise control ECM case are grounded.

DIAGNOSTIC CHART

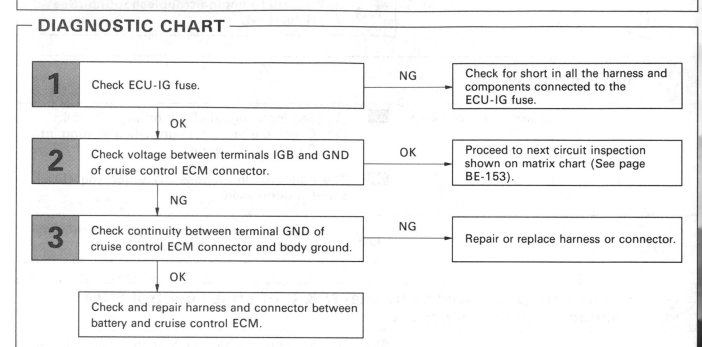

1 Check ECU-IG fuse. — NG → Check for short in all the harness and components connected to the ECU-IG fuse.

OK

2 Check voltage between terminals IGB and GND of cruise control ECM connector. — OK → Proceed to next circuit inspection shown on matrix chart (See page BE-153).

NG

3 Check continuity between terminal GND of cruise control ECM connector and body ground. — NG → Repair or replace harness or connector.

OK

Check and repair harness and connector between battery and cruise control ECM.

BE

INSPECTION PROCEDURE

1 Check ECU-IG fuse.

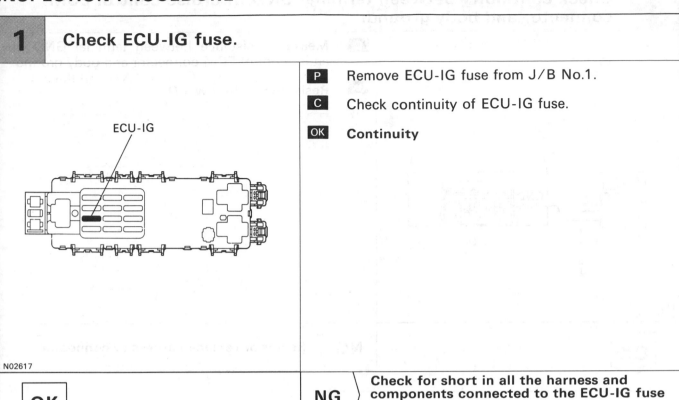

P Remove ECU-IG fuse from J/B No.1.

C Check continuity of ECU-IG fuse.

OK **Continuity**

ECU-IG

N02617

OK

NG ⟩ **Check for short in all the harness and components connected to the ECU-IG fuse (See attached wiring diagram).**

2 Check voltage between terminals IGB and GND of cruise control ECM connector.

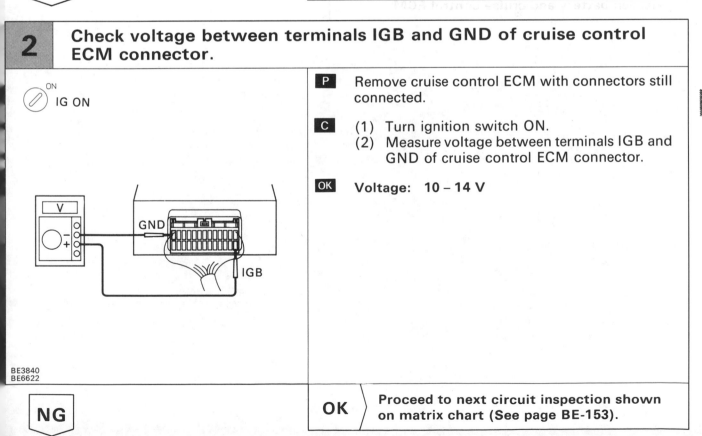

P Remove cruise control ECM with connectors still connected.

C (1) Turn ignition switch ON.
(2) Measure voltage between terminals IGB and GND of cruise control ECM connector.

OK **Voltage: 10 – 14 V**

IG ON

GND

IGB

BE3840
BE6622

NG

OK ⟩ **Proceed to next circuit inspection shown on matrix chart (See page BE-153).**

Go to step **3**.

BE

3 **Check continuity between terminal GND of cruise control ECM connector and body ground.**

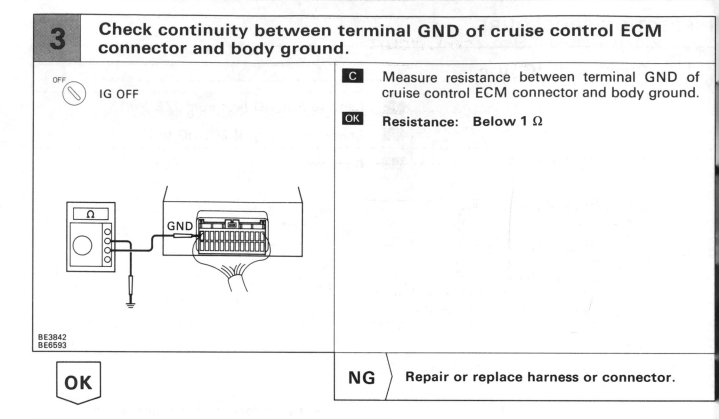

OFF
IG OFF

Ω

GND

BE3842
BE6593

C Measure resistance between terminal GND of cruise control ECM connector and body ground.

OK **Resistance: Below 1 Ω**

OK

NG Repair or replace harness or connector.

Check and repair harness and connector between battery and cruise control ECM.

Back-up Power Source Circuit

─ CIRCUIT DESCRIPTION ─

The cruise control ECM back-up power source provides power even when the ignition switch is off and is used for diagnostic code memory, etc.

─ DIAGNOSTIC CHART ─

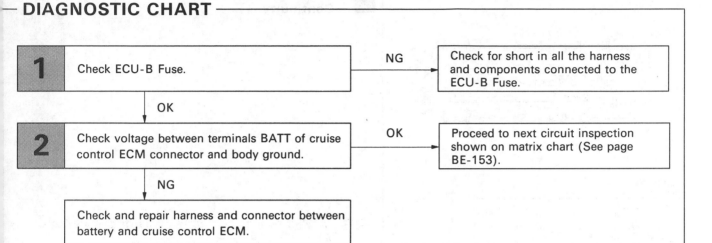

1 Check ECU-B Fuse. ──NG──▶ Check for short in all the harness and components connected to the ECU-B Fuse.

│OK

2 Check voltage between terminals BATT of cruise control ECM connector and body ground. ──OK──▶ Proceed to next circuit inspection shown on matrix chart (See page BE-153).

│NG

Check and repair harness and connector between battery and cruise control ECM.

BE

INSPECTION PROCEDURE

1   Check ECU-B.

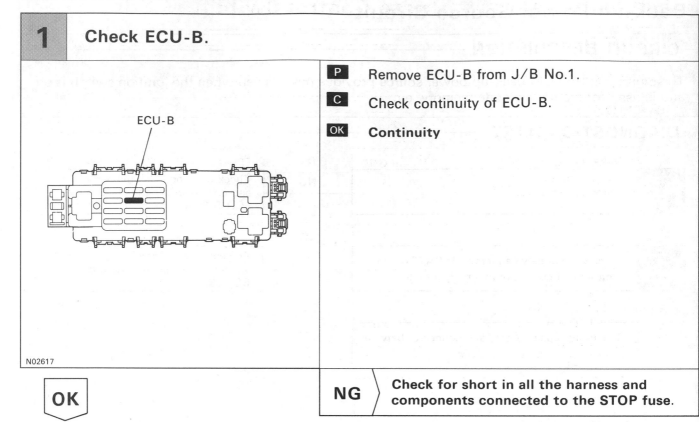

ECU-B

N02617

P   Remove ECU-B from J/B No.1.

C   Check continuity of ECU-B.

OK   **Continuity**

OK ⬇

NG ⟩ Check for short in all the harness and components connected to the STOP fuse.

2   Check voltage between terminals BATT of cruise control ECM connector and body ground.

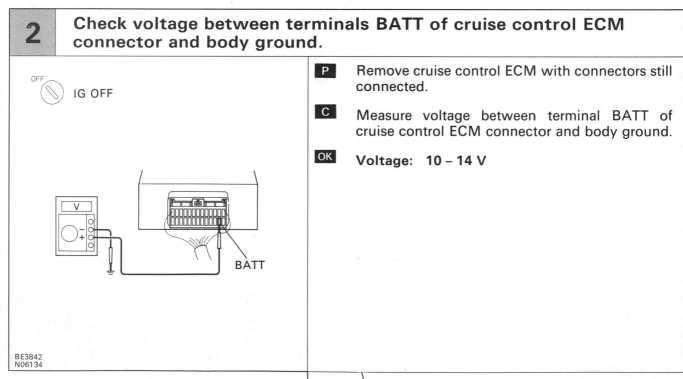

OFF   IG OFF

BATT

BE3842
N06134

P   Remove cruise control ECM with connectors still connected.

C   Measure voltage between terminal BATT of cruise control ECM connector and body ground.

OK   **Voltage: 10 – 14 V**

NG ⬇

OK ⟩ Proceed to next circuit inspection shown on matrix chart (See page BE-153).

Check and repair harness and connector between battery and cruise control ECM.

BE

Main Switch Circuit (Cruise Control Switch)

CIRCUIT DESCRIPTION

When the cruise control main switch is turned off, the cruise control does not operate.

DIAGNOSTIC CHART

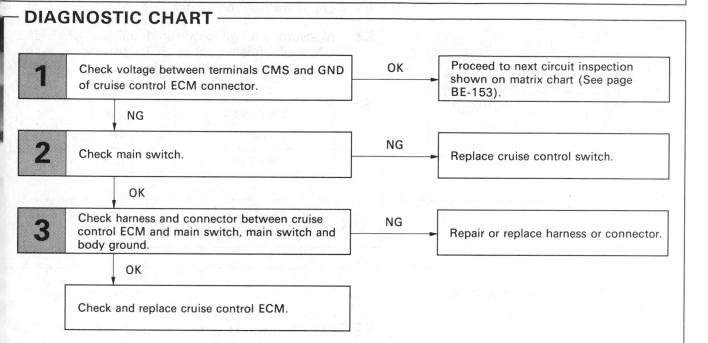

1 Check voltage between terminals CMS and GND of cruise control ECM connector. — OK → Proceed to next circuit inspection shown on matrix chart (See page BE-153).

NG

2 Check main switch. — NG → Replace cruise control switch.

OK

3 Check harness and connector between cruise control ECM and main switch, main switch and body ground. — NG → Repair or replace harness or connector.

OK

Check and replace cruise control ECM.

BE

INSPECTION PROCEDURE

1 **Check voltage between terminals CMS and GND of cruise control ECM connector.**

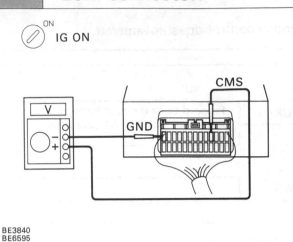

P
(1) Remove cruise control ECM with connectors still connected.
(2) Turn ignition switch ON.

C Measure voltage between terminals CMS and GND of cruise control ECM connector when main switch is hold on and off.

OK

Main switch	Voltage
OFF	10 – 14 V
Hold on	Below 1 V

BE3840
BE6595

NG   **OK** ⟩ **Proceed to next circuit inspection shown on matrix chart (See page BE-153).**

---

2 **Check main switch.**

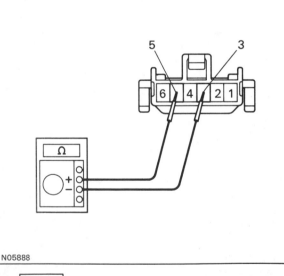

P
(1) Remove steering wheel center pad (See page AB-16).
(2) Disconnect cruise control switch connector.

C Check continuity between terminals 3 and 5 of cruise control switch connector when main switch is hold on and off.

OK   O————O Continuity

Terminal / Main switch	3	5
OFF		
Hold on	O	O

N05888

OK   **NG** ⟩ **Replace control switch.**

---

3 **Check harness and connector between cruise control ECM and main switch, main switch and body ground.**

OK   **NG** ⟩ **Repair or replace harness or connector.**

Check and replace cruise control ECM.

TC Circuit

CIRCUIT DESCRIPTION

This circuit sends a signal to the ECM that diagnostic trouble code output is required.

DIAGNOSTIC CHART

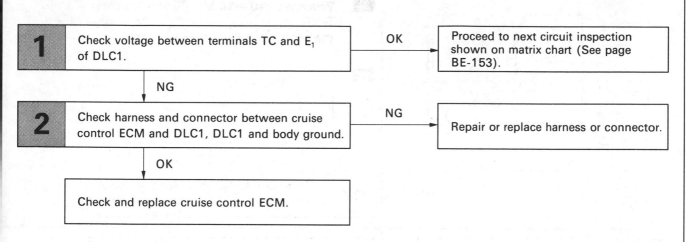

1 Check voltage between terminals TC and E_1 of DLC1.

→ OK → Proceed to next circuit inspection shown on matrix chart (See page BE-153).

↓ NG

2 Check harness and connector between cruise control ECM and DLC1, DLC1 and body ground.

→ NG → Repair or replace harness or connector.

↓ OK

Check and replace cruise control ECM.

BE

INSPECTION PROCEDURE

1 Check voltage between terminals TC and E1 of DLC1.

E₁   Tc

V

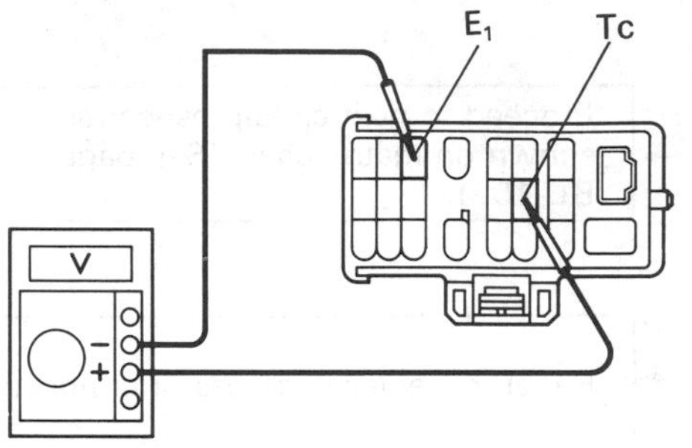

N05912

C (1) Turn ignition switch ON.
(2) Measure voltage between terminals TC and E₁ of DLC1.

OK Voltage: 10 – 14 V

NG

OK > Proceed to next circuit inspection shown on matrix chart (See page BE-153).

2 Check harness and connector between cruise control ECM and DLC1, DLC1 and body ground. (See page IN-27)

OK

NG > Repair or replace harness or connector.

BE

Check and replace cruise control ECM.

Actuator Control Cable Inspection

C (1) Check that the actuator, control cable and throttle link are properly installed and that the cable and link are connected correctly.
(2) Check that the actuator and throttle link are operating smoothly.
(3) Check that the cable is not loose or too tight.

Hint (1) If the control cable is very loose, the vehicle's loss of speed going uphill will be large.
(2) If the control cable is too tight, the idle rpm will become high.

BE

BE

BE

BODY

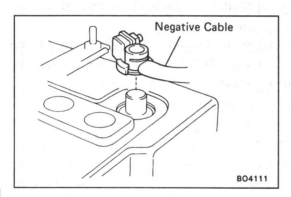

Example

Protection Tape

Protection Tape

BO4110
BO2488

Z00167

Negative Cable

BO4111

GENERAL INFORMATION
HANDLING PRECAUTIONS

BO01M—

Taping

When it is possible that the body or parts may b
scratched during the operation, apply protection tap
before starting work.

Example:

1. Before starting work, apply protection tape t
   body surfaces around parts to be removed an
   installed.

2. Before prying parts loose with a screwdriver c
   scraper etc., apply protection tape to the tip c
   the tool to avoid scratching parts or painte
   surfaces of the body.

Battery

In order to prevent a short circuit while doing work c
the electrical circuit such as disconnecting a co
nector, first turn off the ignition switch and disco
nect the negative cable from the battery termin
before starting work.

HINT: When battery voltage is required for operatic
of a functioning part, connect the cable to the batte
when needed, and promptly disconnect it when r
longer necessary.

CAUTION:

- **Work must be started after approx. 90 seconds
  longer from the time the ignition switch is turned
  the "LOCK" position and the negative (−) termin
  cable is disconnected from the battery.**

- **To avoid erasing the memory of each memo
  system, never use a back−up power supply fro
  outside the vehicle.**

Fitting Adjustments

When removing and installing body panels which ha
a preload value, after the installation refer to the pag
containing the installation adjustment methods, ar
make adjustments according to the required speci
cations.

HINT: When making adjustments, do not complete
loosen the bolts and nuts of the part being adjuste
Tighten them appropriately, and move the panels l
hand to align them.

Example

Peeling

Cracks

Body Sealer

BO2489
BO4112   Z00168

ANTI—RUST TREATMENT

Anti—rust treatment used on the vehicle body includes body sealer, undercoat, rust inhibitor and paint.
HINT: Refer to the Body Collision Damage Repair Manual for details of which parts have received anti—rust treatment.
Body Sealer
If the body sealer is damaged (peeling, cracks, etc.) during the operation, replace it with new body sealer.

HINT: If body sealer gets on other parts, promptly wipe it off with a clean cloth dipped in a grease, wax and silicone remover.
Undercoat
If the undercoat is damaged during the operation, apply new undercoat.
HINT:
- Cover the surrounding area with masking paper to avoid applying undercoat where it is not needed.
- Do not apply undercoat to high temperature parts such as the tailpipe, or to drive parts such as the drive shaft.

Example

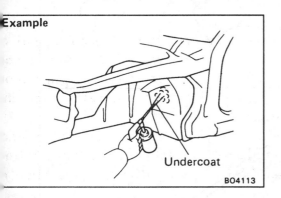

Undercoat

BO4113

Rust Inhibitor

After removing and re—installing hinges and outer panel parts, apply rust inhibitor to the parts.
HINT: If rust inhibitor gets spilled on other parts, promptly wipe it off with a clean cloth dipped in a grease, wax and silicon remover.

BO

Example

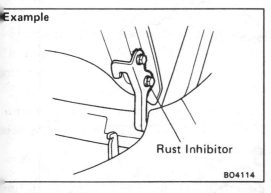

Rust Inhibitor

BO4114

Example

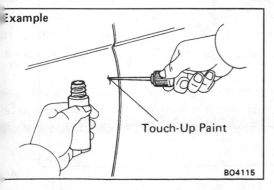

Touch-Up Paint

BO4115

Touch—Up Paint

If a small scratch is made in the body surface, correct the scratch using touch—up paint the same color as the body color.

BO01P-01

CLIPS

The removal and installation methods of typical clips used in body parts are shown in the table below.
HINT: If the clip is damaged during the operation, always replace it with a new clip.

BO

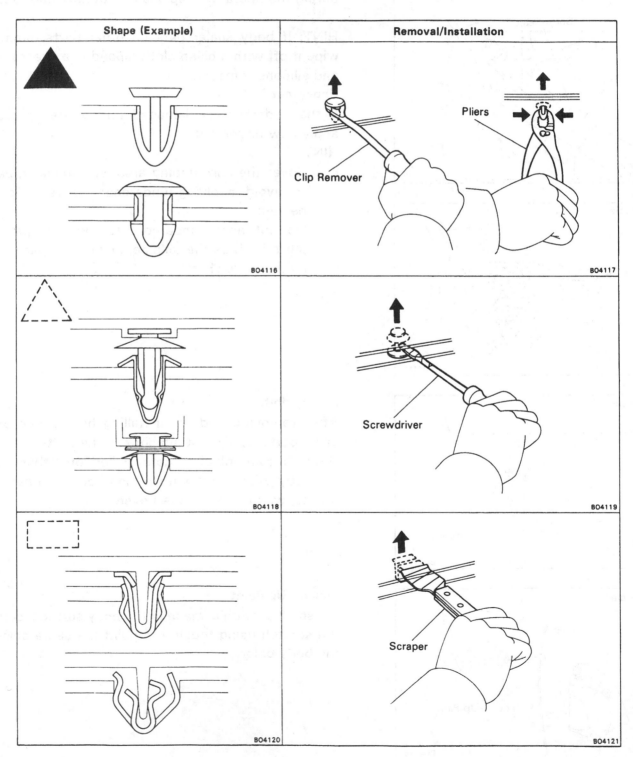

Shape (Example)	Removal/Installation
BO4116	Clip Remover — Pliers — BO4117
BO4118	Screwdriver — BO4119
BO4120	Scraper — BO4121

V0000I

CLIPS (Cont'd)

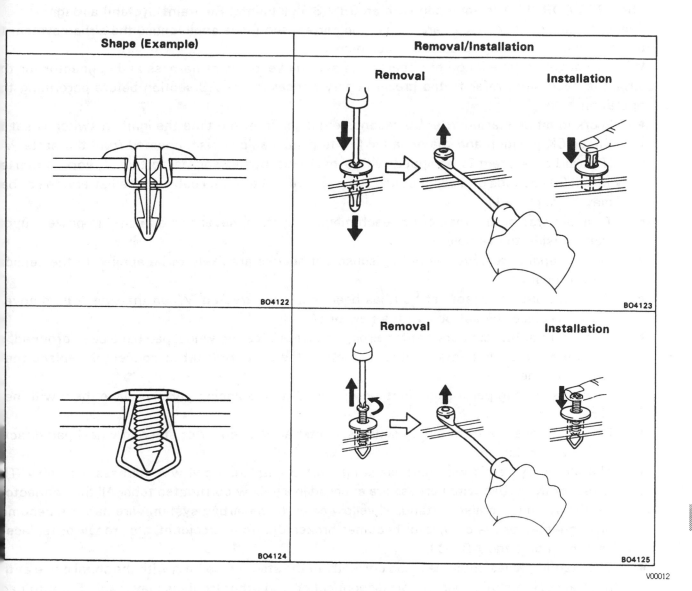

Shape (Example)	Removal/Installation

BO4122

BO4123

BO4124

BO4125

V00012

SRS AIRBAG

B001Q-

(See page AB—2)

The 1993 COROLLA is equipped with an SRS (Supplemental Restraint System) airbag.

Failure to carry out service operations in the correct sequence could cause the airbag system t deploy, possibly leading to a serious accident.

When removal or installation of airbag parts and the yellow wire harness and connector for th airbag is necessary, refer to the precautionary notices in the AB section before perorming th operation.

- Work must be started after 90 seconds or longer from the time the ignition switch is set t the LOCK position and the negative (−) terminal cable is disconnected from the battery. (The airbag system is equipped with a back—up power source so that if work is starte within 90 seconds of disconnecting the negative (−) terminal cable of the battery, the airba may be deployed.)
- To avoid erasing the memory of each memory system, never use a back—up power suppl from outside the vehicle.
- Before repairs, remove the airbag sensors if shocks are likely to be applied to the senso during repaires.
- The front airbag sensor set bolt has been anti—rust treated. When the sensor is remove always replace the set bolt with a new one.
- If the front airbag sensors, center airbag sensor or steering wheel pad have been dropped, if there are cracks, dents or other defects in the case, bracket or connector, replace the with new ones.
- Never use airbag parts from another vehicle. When replacing parts, replace them with ne parts.
- Do not expose the front airbag sensors, center airbag sensor or steering wheel pad direct to hot air or flames.
- The airbag system's wire harness is integrated with the cowl wire harness assembly. Th wires for the airbag wire harness are encased in a yellow corrugated tube. All the connecto for the system are also a standard yellow color. If the airbag system wire harness become disconnected or the connector becomes broken due to an accident, etc., repair or replace as shown on page AB—23.
- The steering wheel must be fitted correctly to the steering column with the spiral cable at th neutral position; otherwise, cable disconnection and other troubles may result. Refer to pag AB—18 of this manual concerning correct steering wheel installation.
- When removing the steering wheel pad or handling a new steering wheel pad, it should b placed with the pad top surface facing up. In this case, the twin—lock type connector loc lever should be in the locked state and care should be taken to place it so the connector w not be damaged. (Storing the pad with its metallic surface up may lead to a serious accide if the airbag inflates for some reason.)
- Grease should not be applied to the steering wheel pad and the pad should not be cleane with detergents of any kind.
- Store the steering wheel pad where the ambient temperature remains below 93°C (200°F without high humidity and away from electrical noise.
- Information labels are attached to the periphery of the airbag components. Follow th notices.
- When the ignition switch is at ACC or ON and the airbag warning light remains on, the cent airbag sensor assembly has detected a malfunction code. (See page AB—31)

PREPARATION
SST (SPECIAL SERVICE TOOLS)

09812—00010	Door Hinge Set Bolt Wrench	
09804—24010	Luggage Compartment Door Torsion Bar Tool	
09806—30010	Windshield Moulding Remover	

LUBRICANT

Item	Capacity	Classification
MP grease	—	—

SSM (SPECIAL SERVICE MATERIALS)

08833—00070	Adhesive 1324, THREE BOND 1324 or equivalent	Front Door Rear Door
08850—00070	Windshield glass adhesive set No.15 or equivalent	Windshield Back Window Glass (0—15°C or 32—59°F)
08850—00080	Windshield glass adhesive set No.35 or equivalent	Windshield Back Window Glass (15—35°C or 59—95°F)
08850—00090	Windshield glass adhesive set No.45 or equivalent	Windshield Back Window Glass (35—45°C or 95—113°F)
08833—00030	Auto glass sealer or equivalent	Windshield Moulding Back Window Moulding Windshield Back Window Glass
08850—00051	Adhesive (Super Special) or equivalent	Side Protection Moulding

BO

Ambient temperature	Part No.	Part Name
0 – 15°C (32 – 59°F)	08850-00070	Windshield glass adhesive set No. 15
15 – 35°C (59 – 95°F)	08850-00080	Windshield glass adhesive set No. 35
35 – 45°C (95 – 113°F)	08850-00090	Windshield glass adhesive set No. 45

V00250

1. CHOOSE SUITABLE ADHESIVE SET

Use an adhesive set suitable for the ambient temperature.

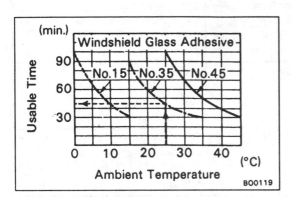

2. CHECK ADHESIVE USABLE TIME

After mixing main and hardening agents, finish glass installation within the specified time as shown.

Example: For glass installation in an ambient temperature of 25°C (77°F), apply adhesive set No.35 within 45 minutes.

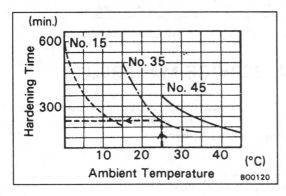

3. CHECK ADHESIVE HARDENING TIME

After main and hardening agents are mixed, leak test should be made only after the hardening time has elapsed.

Example: The hardening time for adhesive set No.3 with and ambient temperature of 25°C (77°F) is 2 1 2 hours.

NOTICE: Do not drive the vehicle until at least double the hardening time has elapsed.

BO

FRONT BUMPER
COMPONENTS

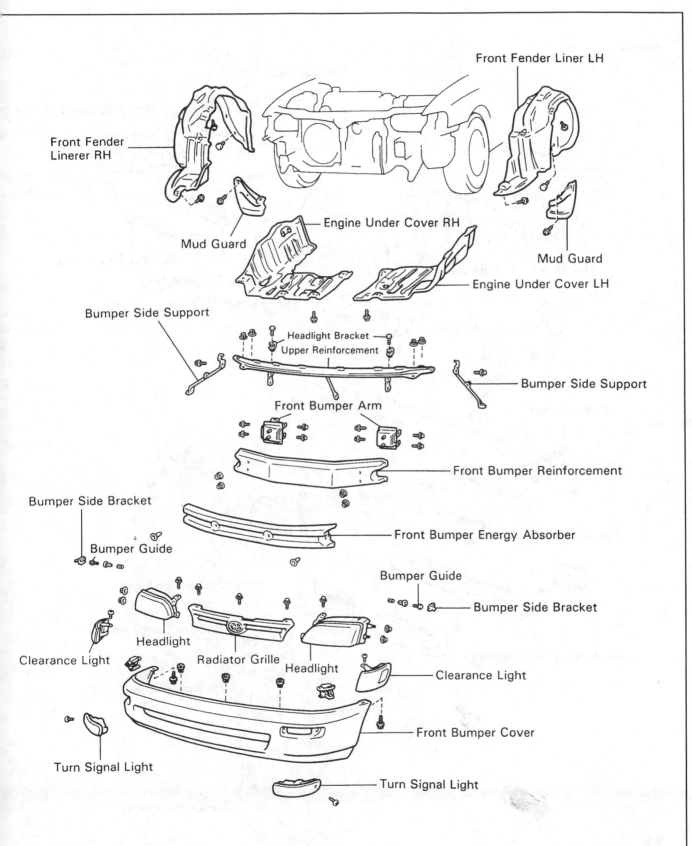

Front Fender Liner LH

Front Fender Linerer RH

Mud Guard

Engine Under Cover RH

Mud Guard

Engine Under Cover LH

Bumper Side Support

Headlight Bracket
Upper Reinforcement

Bumper Side Support

Front Bumper Arm

Front Bumper Reinforcement

Bumper Side Bracket

Bumper Guide

Front Bumper Energy Absorber

Bumper Guide

Bumper Side Bracket

Headlight

Clearance Light

Radiator Grille

Headlight

Clearance Light

Front Bumper Cover

Turn Signal Light

Turn Signal Light

REAR BUMPER
COMPONENTS

BOOHP−0

Sedan

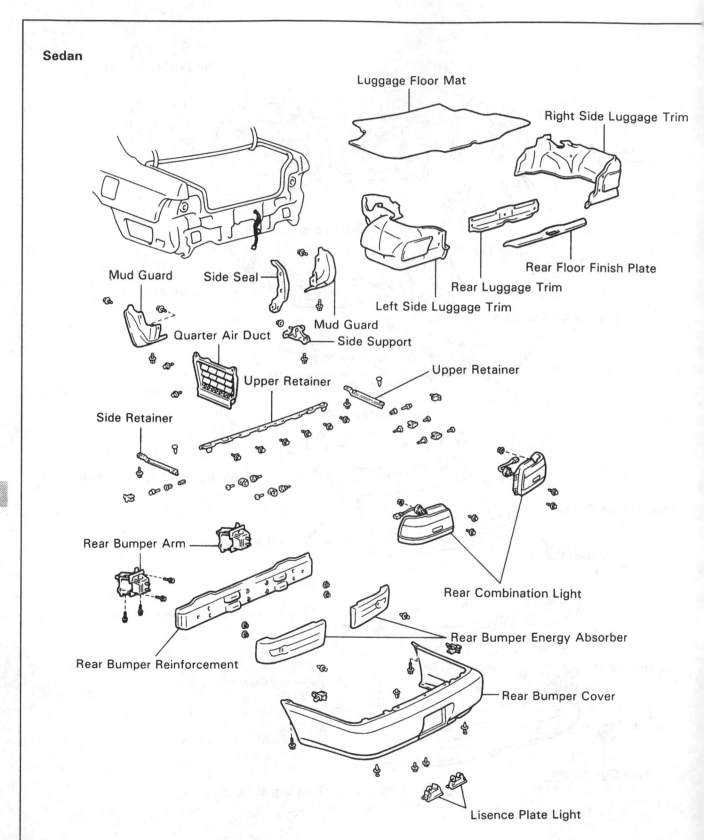

Luggage Floor Mat

Right Side Luggage Trim

Rear Floor Finish Plate

Rear Luggage Trim

Left Side Luggage Trim

Mud Guard

Side Seal

Mud Guard

Side Support

Quarter Air Duct

Upper Retainer

Upper Retainer

Side Retainer

Rear Bumper Arm

Rear Combination Light

Rear Bumper Reinforcement

Rear Bumper Energy Absorber

Rear Bumper Cover

Lisence Plate Light

N05452

COMPONENTS (Cont'd)

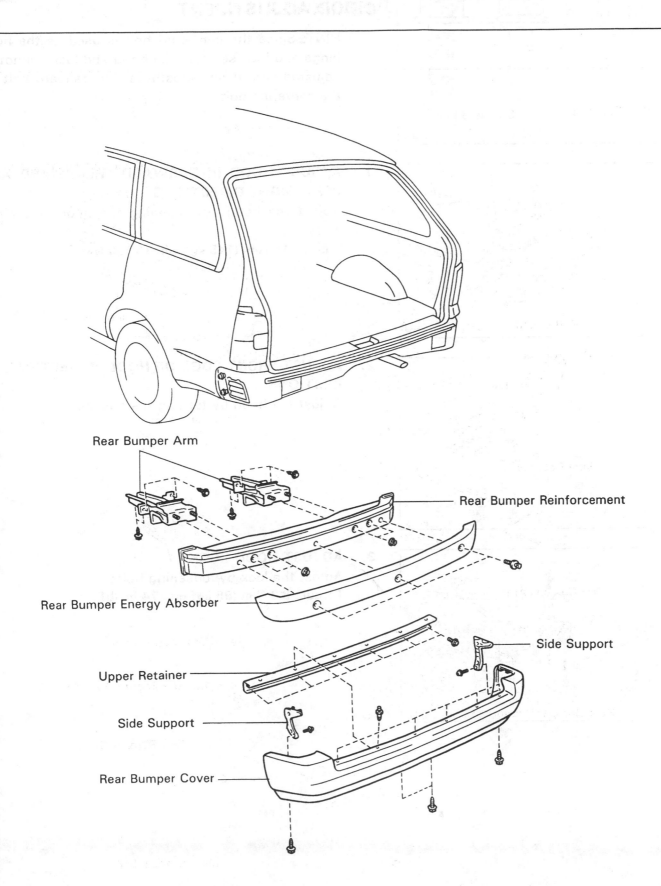

Rear Bumper Arm

Rear Bumper Reinforcement

Rear Bumper Energy Absorber

Side Support

Upper Retainer

Side Support

Rear Bumper Cover

N05895

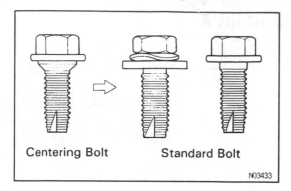

Centering Bolt   Standard Bolt

N03433

HOOD
HOOD ADJUSTMENT

HINT: Since the centering bolt is used as the hoo[d] hinge and lock set bolt, the hood and lock cannot b[e] adjusted with it on. Substitute the standard bolt f[or] the centering bolt.

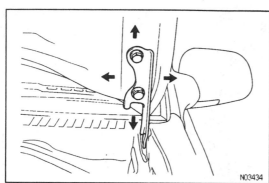

N03434

1. ADJUST HOOD IN FORWARD / REARWARD AN[D] LEFT/RIGHT DIRECTIONS
Adjust the hood by loosening the hood side hing[e] bolts.
Torque: 14 N·m (145 kgf·cm, 10 ft·lbf)

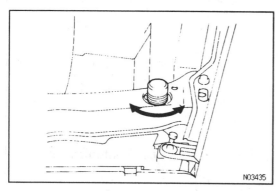

N03435

2. ADJUST FRONT EDGE OF HOOD IN VERTICAL D[I] RECTIONS
Adjust the hood by turning the cushions.

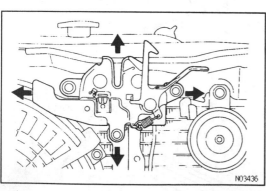

N03436

3. ADJUST HOOD LOCK
Adjust the lock by loosening bolts.
Torque: 8.3 N·m (85 kgf·cm, 74 in.·lbf)

BO

FRONT DOOR
COMPONENTS

BO021-02

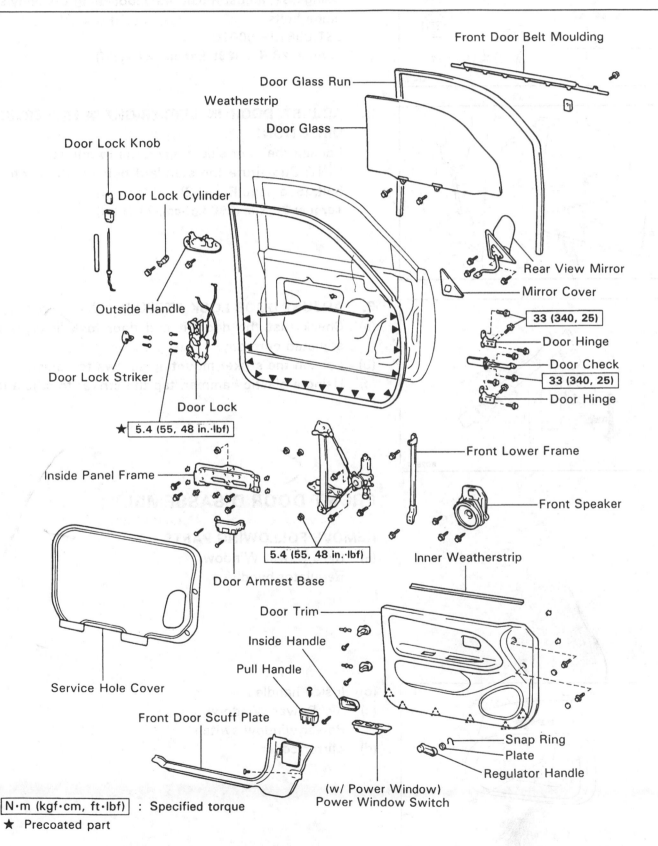

Front Door Belt Moulding

Door Glass Run

Weatherstrip

Door Glass

Door Lock Knob

Door Lock Cylinder

Rear View Mirror

Mirror Cover

Outside Handle

33 (340, 25)

Door Hinge

Door Check

Door Lock Striker

33 (340, 25)

Door Hinge

Door Lock

★ 5.4 (55, 48 in.·lbf)

Front Lower Frame

Inside Panel Frame

Front Speaker

5.4 (55, 48 in.·lbf)

Inner Weatherstrip

Door Armrest Base

Door Trim

Inside Handle

Service Hole Cover

Pull Handle

Snap Ring

Front Door Scuff Plate

Plate

Regulator Handle

(w/ Power Window)
Power Window Switch

N·m (kgf·cm, ft·lbf) : Specified torque

★ Precoated part

N05454

BO

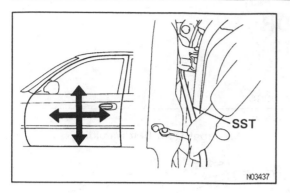

N03437

FRONT DOOR ADJUSTMENT

BO022-06

1. **ADJUST DOOR IN FORWARD / REARWARD AND VERTICAL DIRECTIONS**
   Using SST, adjust the door by loosening the body side hinge bolts.
   SST 09812−00010
   Torque: 28 N·m (290 kgf·cm, 21 ft·lbf)

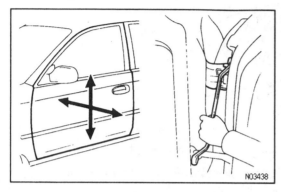

N03438

2. **ADJUST DOOR IN LEFT/RIGHT AND VERTICAL DIRECTIONS**
   Loosen the door side hinge bolts to adjust.
   HINT: Substitute the standard bolt for the centering bolt. (See page BO−12)
   Torque: 28 N·m (290 kgf·cm, 21 ft·lbf)

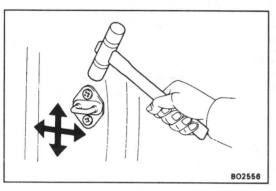

BO2556

3. **ADJUST DOOR LOCK STRIKER**
   (a) Check that the door fit and door lock linkages are adjusted correctly.
   (b) Loosen the striker mounting screws to adjust.
   (c) Using a plastic hammer, tap the striker to adjust it.

BO

FRONT DOOR DISASSEMBLY

BO08P-03

REMOVE FOLLOWING PARTS:
(a) (w/o Power Window)
    Regulator handle

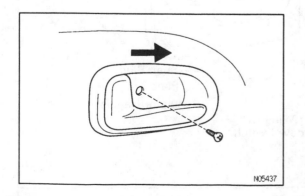

N05437

(b) Inside handle
(c) (w/ Power Window)
    Power window switch
(d) Mirror cover

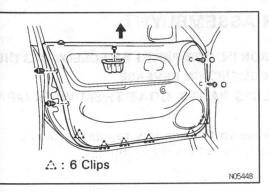

△ : 6 Clips

N05448

(e) Pull handle
(f) Door trim
(g) Speaker
(h) Rear view mirror
(i) Door armrest base
(j) Service hole cover

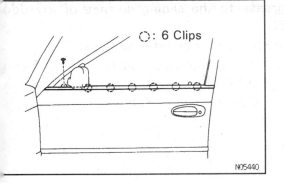

○ : 6 Clips

N05440

(k) Door belt moulding
(l) Door glass
(m) Inside panel flame
(n) Door glass
(o) Window regulator
(p) Door glass run
(q) Weatherstrip
(r) Front lower frame
(s) Door lock remote control link
(t) Door lock knob
(u) Door lock
(v) Outside handle
(w) Door lock cylinder

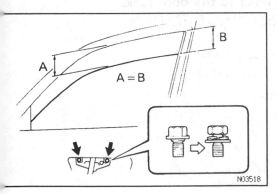

N03518

BO08R-01

BO

FRONT DOOR GLASS ADJUSTMENT

ADJUST FRONT DOOR GLASS ADJUSTMENT

Adjust the glass and tighten if where dimension A and B, as shown are equal.

HINT: Substitute the standard bolt for the centering bolt.

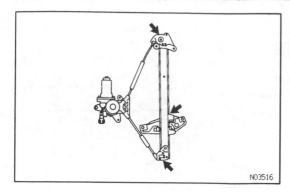

FRONT DOOR ASSEMBLY

ASSEMBLE FRONT DOOR PARTS BY FOLLOWING DIS
ASSEMBLY SEQUENCE IN REVERSE
BEFORE INSTALLING PARTS, COAT THEM WITH MP
GREASE

(a) Apply MP grease to the window regulator rollers.

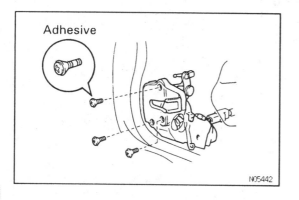

(b) Apply MP grease to the sliding surface of the doo
     lock.

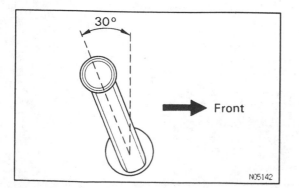

Adhesive

INSTALL DOOR LOCK

(a) Apply adhesive to three screws.
     Part No.08833—00070,THREE BOND 1324 or equivalen
(b) Install the door lock with three screws.
     Torque: 5.4 N·m (55 kgf·cm, 48 in.·lbf)
(c) (w/ Power Door Lock)
     Connect the connector.
(d) Connect two links to the outside handle and the doo
     lock cylinder.
(e) Connect two links to the door lock.
(f) Install the clip.

30°

Front

(w/o Power Window)
INSTALL REGULATOR HANDLE

With door window fully closed, install the plate and
the regulator handle with the snap ring as shown.

REAR DOOR
COMPONENTS

BO025-02

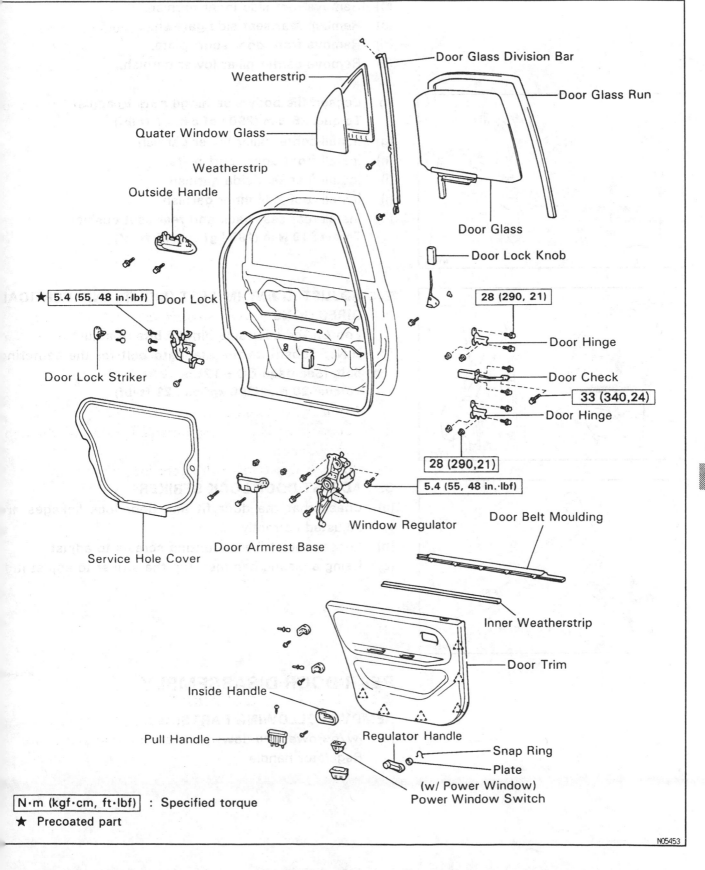

Door Glass Division Bar

Weatherstrip

Door Glass Run

Quater Window Glass

Weatherstrip

Outside Handle

Door Glass

Door Lock Knob

★ 5.4 (55, 48 in.·lbf) Door Lock

28 (290, 21)

Door Hinge

Door Lock Striker

Door Check

33 (340, 24)

Door Hinge

28 (290, 21)

5.4 (55, 48 in.·lbf)

Service Hole Cover

Door Armrest Base

Window Regulator

Door Belt Moulding

Inner Weatherstrip

Door Trim

Inside Handle

Pull Handle

Regulator Handle

Snap Ring

Plate

(w/ Power Window)
Power Window Switch

N·m (kgf·cm, ft·lbf) : Specified torque

★ Precoated part

N05453

BO

REAR DOOR ADJUSTMENT

1. **ADJUST DOOR IN FORWARD / REARWARD AND VERTICAL DIRECTIONS**
(a) Remove rear seat cushion and rear seat back.
(b) Remove roof side inner garnish.
(c) Remove rear seat side garnish.
(d) Remove front door scuff plate.
(e) Remove center pillar lower garnish.

(f) Loosen the body side hinge nuts to adjust.
Torque: 28 N·m (290 kgf·cm, 21 ft·lbf)
(g) Install center pillar lower garnish.
(h) Install front door scuff plate.
(i) Install rear seat side garnish.
(j) Install roof side inner garnish.
(k) Install rear seat back and rear seat cushion.
Torque: 19 N·m (195 kgf·cm, 14 ft·lbf)

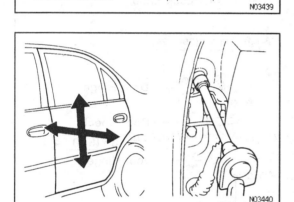

2. **ADJUST DOOR IN LEFT/RIGHT AND VERTICAL DIRECTIONS**
Loosen the door side hinge bolts to adjust.
HINT: Substitute the standard bolt for the centering bolt. (See page BO−12)
Torque: 28 N·m (290 kgf·cm, 21 ft·lbf)

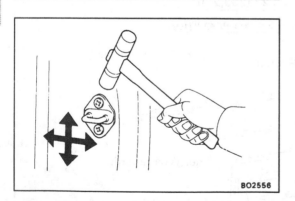

3. **ADJUST DOOR LOCK STRIKER**
(a) Check that the door fit and door lock linkages are adjusted correctly.
(b) Loosen the striker mounting screws to adjust.
(c) Using a plastic hammer, tap the striker to adjust it.

REAR DOOR DISASSEMBLY

REMOVE FOLLOWING PARTS:
(a) (w/o Power Window)
Regulator handle

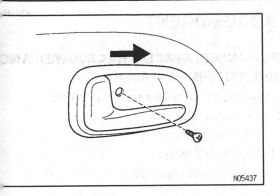

(b) Inside handle
(c) (w/ Power Window)
Power window switch

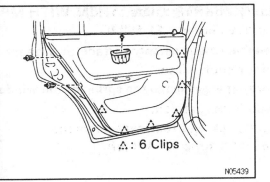

(d) Pull handle
(e) Door trim
(f) Door armrest base
(g) Service hole cover

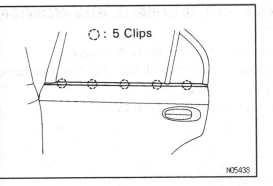

(h) Door belt moulding
(i) Division bar
(j) Door glass
(k) Door glass run
(l) Weatherstrip
(m) Quarter window glass with weatherstrip
(n) Window regulator
(o) Door lock remote control link
(p) Door locking link
(q) Door lock knob
(r) Child protector lock lever knob
(s) Door lock
(t) Outside handle

REAR DOOR ASSEMBLY

**ASSEMBLE REAR DOOR PARTS BY FOLLOWING DIS[...]
ASSEMBLY SEQUENCE IN REVERSE**

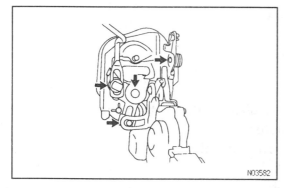

**BEFORE INSTALLING PARTS, COAT THEM WITH MP[...]
GREASE**

(a) Apply MP grease to the sliding surface and gears o[...]
the window regulator.
**NOTICE: Do not apply grease to the spring of the windov[...]
regulator.**

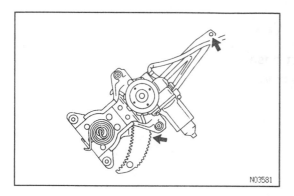

(b) Apply MP grease to the sliding surface of the doc[...]
lock.

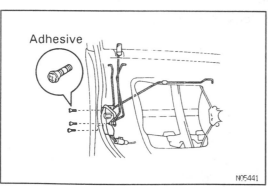

INSTALL DOOR LOCK

(a) Apply adhesive to three screws.
Part No.08833—00070,THREE BOND 1324 or equivalen[...]
(b) Install the door lock with three screws.
Torque: 5.4 N·m (55 kgf·cm, 48 in.·lbf)
(c) (w/ Power Door Lock)
Connect the connector.
(d) Connect two links to the door lock.
(e) install the clip.

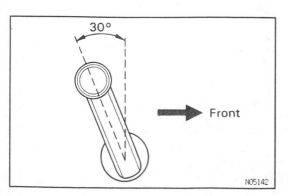

30°

Front

(w/o Power Window)
INSTALL REGULATOR HANDLE

With door window fully closed, install the plate an[...]
the regulator handle with the snap ring as shown.

BACK DOOR
COMPONENTS

BO0HQ—01

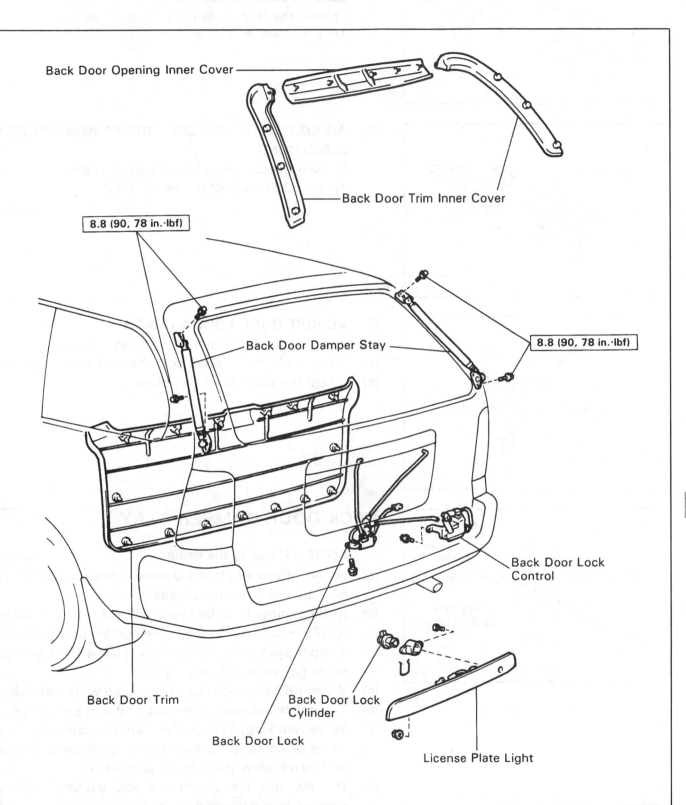

Back Door Opening Inner Cover

Back Door Trim Inner Cover

8.8 (90, 78 in.·lbf)

Back Door Damper Stay

8.8 (90, 78 in.·lbf)

Back Door Lock Control

Back Door Trim

Back Door Lock Cylinder

Back Door Lock

License Plate Light

N05583

| N·m (kgf·cm, ft·lbf) | : Specified torque

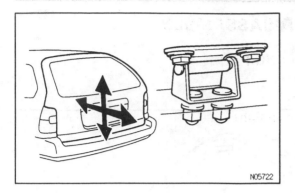

BACK DOOR ADJUSTMENT

1. ADJUST DOOR IN FORWARD /REARWARD AND LEFT /RIGHT DIRECTIONS
Loosen the body side hinge nuts to adjust.
Torque : 13 N·m (130 kgf·cm, 9 ft·lbf)

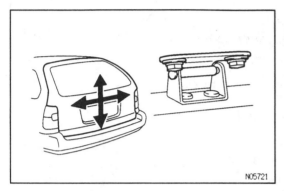

2. ADJUST DOOR IN LEFT /RIGHT AND VERTICAL DIRECTIONS
Loosen the door side hinge bolts to adjust.
Torque : 13 N·m (130 kgf·cm, 9 ft·lbf)

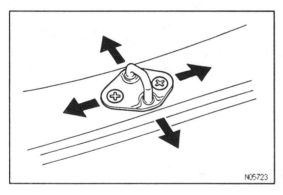

3. ADJUST DOOR LOCK STRIKER
(a) Loosen the striker mounting screws to adjust.
(b) Using a plastic hammer, tap the striker to adjust it.
(c) Install the rear floor finsh plate.

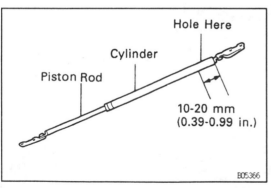

Hole Here
Cylinder
Piston Rod
10-20 mm
(0.39-0.99 in.)

BACK DOOR DAMPER STAY

NOTICE: Handling the damper.
(a) Do not disassemble the damper because the cylinder is filled with pressurized gas.
(b) If the damper is to be replaced, drill a 2.0 — 3.0 mm (0.079 — 0.118 in.) hole in the bottom of the removed damper cylinder to completely release the high—pressure gas before disposing of it.
(c) When drilling, chips may fly out, so work carefully.
(d) The gas is colorless, odorless and non poisonous.
(e) When working, handle the damper carefully. Never score or scratch the exposed part of the piston rod and never allow paint or oil to get on it.
(f) Do not turn the piston rod and cylinder with the damper fully extended.

BO0HT—01

BACK DOOR DISASSEMBLY

REMOVE FOLLOWING PARIS
(a) (w/ Rear wiper)
   Rear wiper arm
(b) High mount stop light

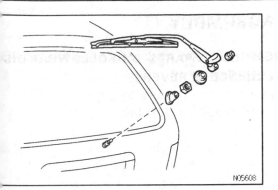
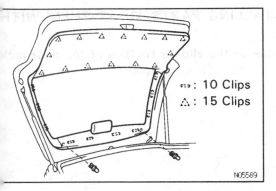

N05608

(c) Back door trim
(d) Back door trim inner cover
(e) Back door opening inner cover
(f) Service hole cover
(g) (w/ Rear wiper)
   Wiper motor and link

⇨ : 10 Clips
△ : 15 Clips

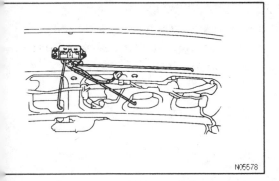

N05589

(h) Back door lock

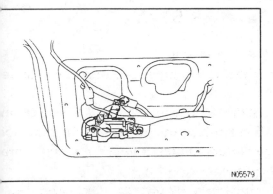

N05578

(i) Back door lock control

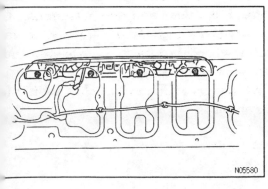

N05579

(j) License plate light
(k) Back Door lock cylinder

N05580

BO

BACK DOOR ASSEMBLY

ASSEMBLE REAR DOOR PARTS BY FOLLOWING DIS

ASSEMBLY SEQUENCE IN REVERSE

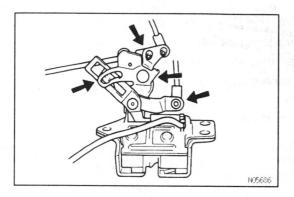

BEFORE INSTALLING PARTS, COAT THEM WITH

MP GREASE

Apply MP grease to the sliding surface of the door lock

control

LUGGAGE COMPARTMENT
COMPONENTS

BO04P—01

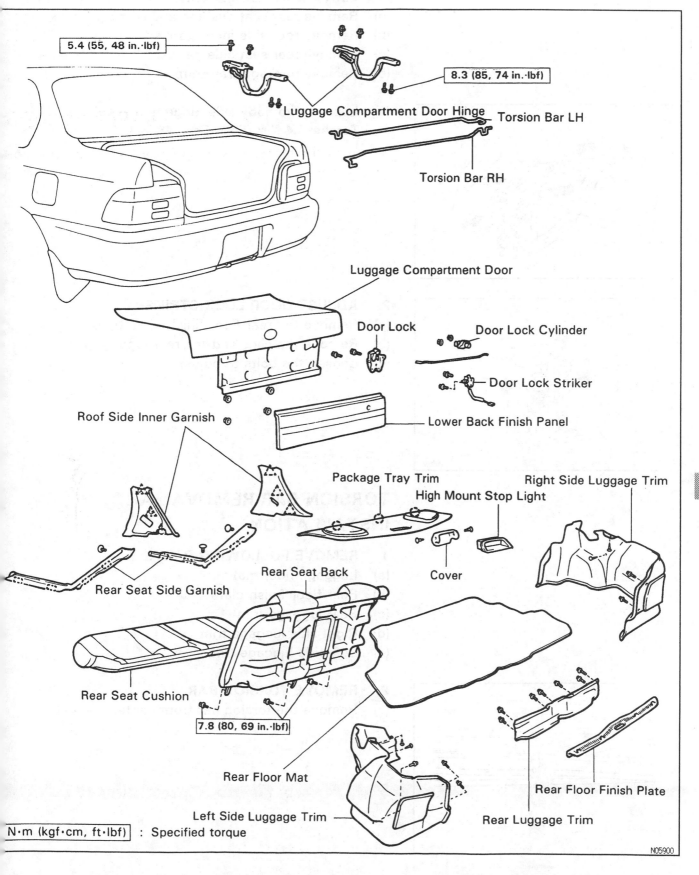

5.4 (55, 48 in.·lbf)

8.3 (85, 74 in.·lbf)

Luggage Compartment Door Hinge

Torsion Bar LH

Torsion Bar RH

Luggage Compartment Door

Door Lock

Door Lock Cylinder

Door Lock Striker

Roof Side Inner Garnish

Lower Back Finish Panel

Package Tray Trim

High Mount Stop Light

Right Side Luggage Trim

Rear Seat Side Garnish

Rear Seat Back

Cover

Rear Seat Cushion

7.8 (80, 69 in.·lbf)

Rear Floor Mat

Left Side Luggage Trim

Rear Floor Finish Plate

Rear Luggage Trim

N·m (kgf·cm, ft·lbf) : Specified torque

BO

N05900

LUGGAGE COMPARTMENT DOOR ADJUSTMENT

1. ADJUST DOOR IN FORWARD / REARWARD AND LEFT/RIGHT DIRECTIONS

(a) Remove rear seat cushion and rear seat back.

(b) Remove roof side inner garnish.

(c) Remove rear seat side garnish.

(d) Remove package tray trim.

(e) Loosen two body side hinge bolt to adjust.
Torque: 5.4 N·m (55 kgf·cm, 48 in.·lbf)

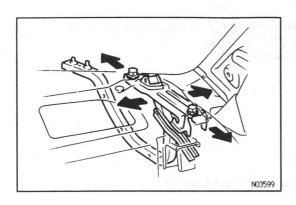

2. ADJUST DOOR LOCK STRIKER

(a) Remove the rear floor finish plate by pulling.

(b) Remove the clips and the rear luggage trim.

(c) Loosen the bolts to adjust.

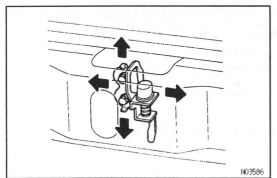

TORSION BAR REMOVAL AND INSTALLATION

1. REMOVE FOLLOWING PARTS:

(a) Luggage floor mat

(b) Rear floor finish plate

(c) Rear luggage trim

(d) Right side luggage trim

(e) Left side luggage trim

2. REMOVE TORSION BAR

(a) Remove the torsion bar from center bracket.

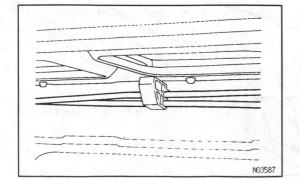

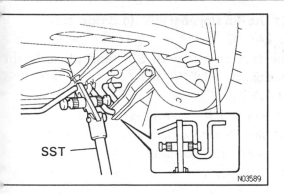

(b) Install SST to the torsion bar on the hinge side.
SST 09804−24010

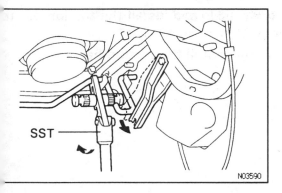

(c) Push down on SST, and pull the luggage compartment
door hinge from the torsion bor.

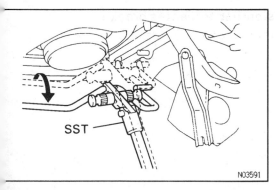

(d) Slowly lift SST, and remove the torsion bar from the
torsion bar bracket with SST.
(e) Remove the torsion bar.
(f) Do the same for the other side.

BO

3. INSTALL TORSION BAR

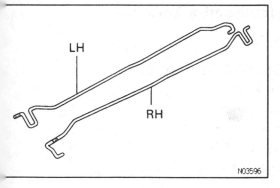

(a) Insert the torsion bar into the bracket as shown.

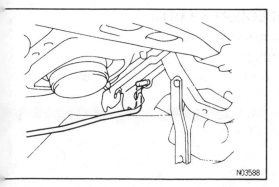

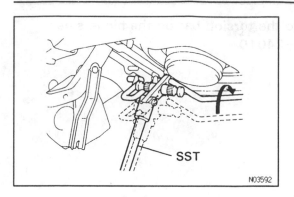

(b) Install SST to the torsion bar of the hinge side.
SST 09804—24010

(c) Slowly lift the torsion bar with SST and place in the torsion bar bracket.

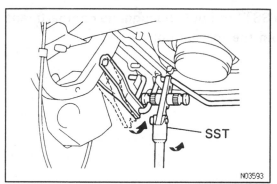

(d) Slowly push down SST, and install the torsion bar to the hinge.

(e) Slowly lift SST, and install the torsion bar.

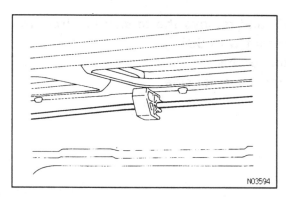

(f) Install the torsion bar to center bracket.

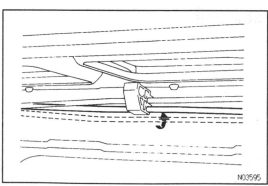

(g) Do the same for the other side.

4. INSTALL FOLLOWING PARTS:
(a) Left side luggage trim
(b) Right side luggage trim
(c) Rear luggage trim
(d) Rear floor finish plate

WIPER AND WASHER
COMPONENTS

BO0HV—01

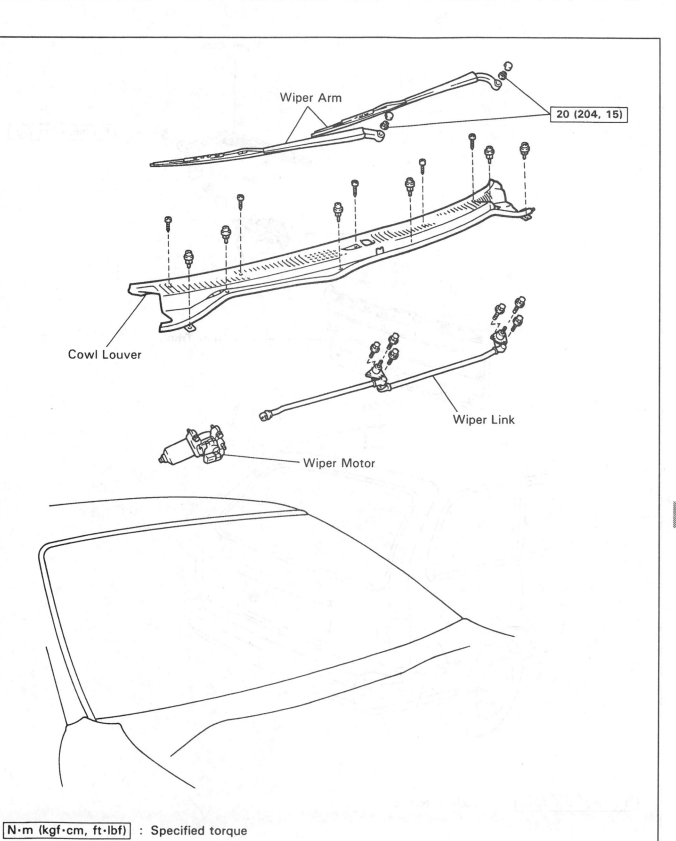

Wiper Arm

20 (204, 15)

Cowl Louver

Wiper Link

Wiper Motor

N·m (kgf·cm, ft·lbf) : Specified torque

N05084

COMPONENTS (Con'd)

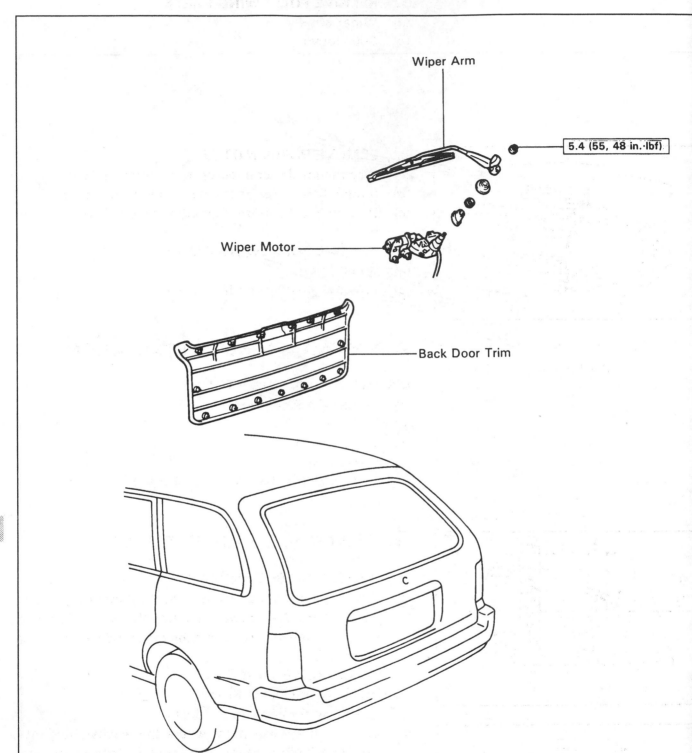

Wiper Arm

5.4 (55, 48 in.·lbf)

Wiper Motor

Back Door Trim

N·m (kgf·cm, ft·lbf) : Specified torque

BO008Y—03

WIPER AND WASHER REMOVAL

1. REMOVE FOLLOWING PARTS:
(a) Wiper arms
(b) Cowl louver

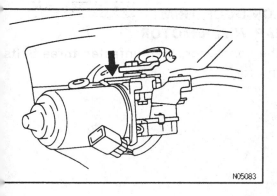

2. REMOVE WIPER MOTOR
(a) Disconnect the connector, then unfasten four bolts.
(b) Connect the claw of the wiper link to the panel.
(c) Disconnect the motor from the wiper link and remove it.

3. REMOVE FOLLOWING PARTS:
(a) Wiper link
(b) Window washer nozzle

BO008Z—01

WIPER AND WASHER INSTALLATION

INSTALL FOLLOWING PARTS:
(a) Window washer nozzle
(b) Wiper link
(c) Wiper motor
(d) Wiper arms
Torque: 20 N·m (204 kgf·cm, 15 ft·lbf)

BO007S—05

BO

WASHER NOZZLE ADJUSTMENT

1. INSPECT WASHER NOZZLE
(a) While operating the washer, check whether the upper point where the washer fluid hits the windshield and the up surge area are within the range indicated by the hatched line.
Ⓐ Approx. 150 mm (5.91 in.)
Ⓑ Approx. 50 mm (1.99 in.)
Ⓒ Approx. 0—50 mm (0—1.99 in.)

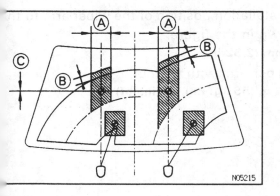

(b) Check if the lower point where the washer fluid hits the windshield is within the range of the wiping pattern (the area of the glass which is wiped by the wiper blades.

2. ADJUST WASHER NOZZLE
Using a tool like that shown in the figure, change the direction of the nozzle hole to adjust the point where washer fluid strikes the windshield.

2 — 2.5 mm
(0.079 — 0.098 in.)

0.7 — 0.75 mm
(0.028 — 0.030 in.)

BOOHW-01

REAR WIPER REMOVAL

1. REMOVE REAR WIPER ARM

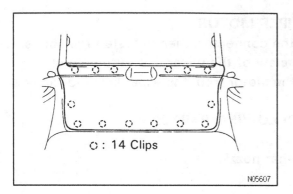

○ : 14 Clips

N05607

2. REMOVE BACK DOOR TRIM
3. REMOVE REAR WIPER MOTOR
(a) Disconnect the connector, then unfasten three bolts
(b) Remove the motor.

BOOHX-0

REAR WIPER INSTALLATION

1. INSTALL REAR WIPER MOTOR
2. INSTALL BACK DOOR TRIM
3. INSTALL REAR WIPER ARM
(a) Install the wiper arm and operate the wiper once an
turn the wiper switch OFF.

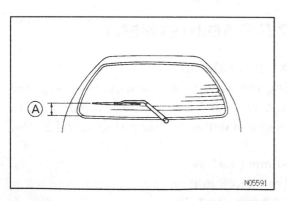

N05591

(b) Adjust the installation position of the wiper arm to th
position shown in the figure.
Approx. 59 mm (2.32 in.)
(c) Install the wiper arm with the nut.
Torque: 5.4 N·m (55 kgf·cm, 48 in.·lbf)

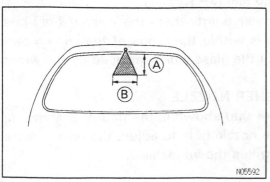

N05592

BOOHY-0

REAR WASHER NOZZLE ADJUSTMENT

1. INSPECT REAR WASHER NOZZLE
While operating the washer, check whether the uppe
point where the washer fluid hits the windshield an
the up surge area are within the range indicated by th
hatched line.
● **Approx. 130 mm (5.12 in.)**
● **Approx. 150 mm (5.91 in.)**

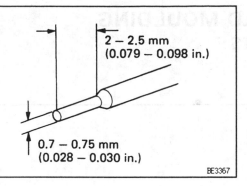

2 — 2.5 mm
(0.079 — 0.098 in.)

0.7 — 0.75 mm
(0.028 — 0.030 in.)

BE3367

2. **ADJUST WASHER NOZZLE**

Using a tool like that shown in the figure, change the direction of the nozzle hole to adjust the point where washer fluid strikes the windshield.

BO

WINDSHIELD MOULDING
COMPONENTS

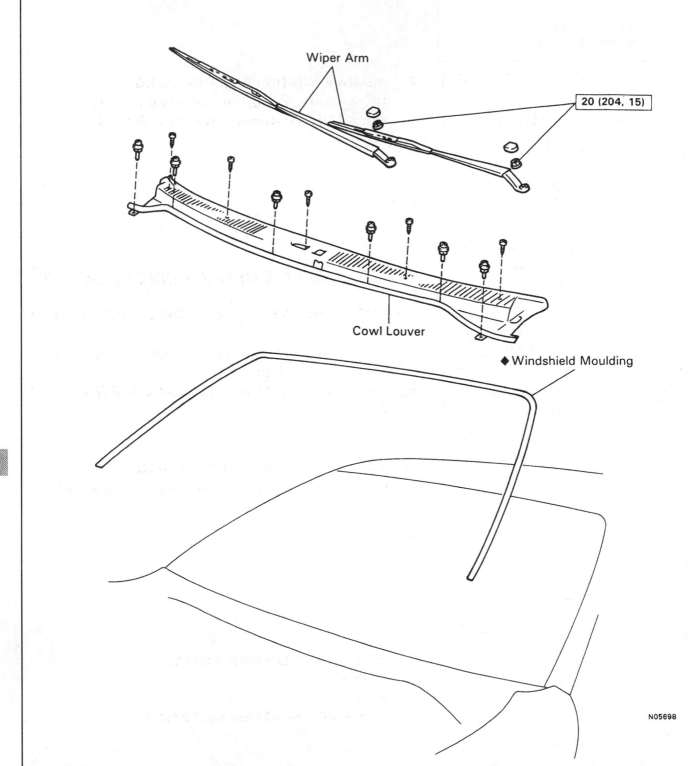

Wiper Arm

20 (204, 15)

Cowl Louver

◆ Windshield Moulding

N05698

| N·m (kgf·cm, ft·lbf) | : Specified torque
◆ Non-reusable part

WINDSHIELD MOULDING REMOVAL

BO099-02

1. REMOVE FOLLOWING PARTS:
(a) Wiper arms
(b) Cowl louver

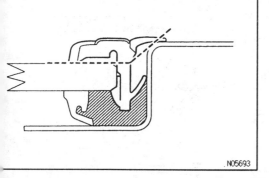

2. REMOVE WINDSHIELD MOULDING
Using a knife, cut off the moulding as shown.
NOTICE: Do not damage the body with the knife.

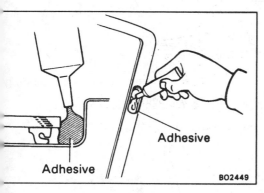

WINDSHIELD MOULDING INSTALLATION

BO019-04

1. CUT ADHESIVE AT MOULDING INSTALLATION AREA
Using the knife, cut off the adhesive around the moulding installation area.

2. APPLY ADHESIVE AT MOULDING INSTALLATION AREA

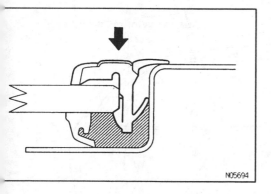

3. INSTALL WINDSHIELD MOULDING
Place the moulding onto the body and tap it by hand.

BO

4. INSTALL FOLLOWING PARTS:
(a) Cowl louver
(b) Wiper arms
Torque: 20 N·m (204 kgf·cm, 15 ft·lbf)

BODY OUTSIDE MOULDING
COMPONENTS

BO02K —

Sedan

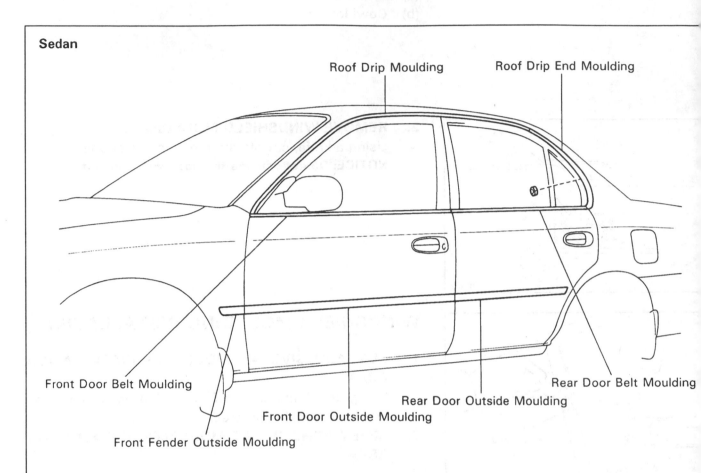

Roof Drip Moulding

Roof Drip End Moulding

Front Door Belt Moulding

Front Fender Outside Moulding

Front Door Outside Moulding

Rear Door Outside Moulding

Rear Door Belt Moulding

Wagon

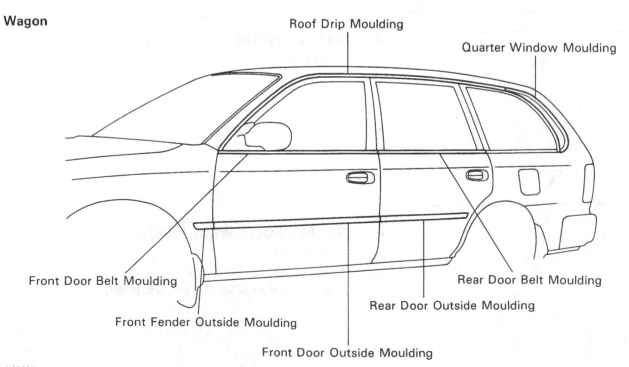

Roof Drip Moulding

Quarter Window Moulding

Front Door Belt Moulding

Front Fender Outside Moulding

Front Door Outside Moulding

Rear Door Outside Moulding

Rear Door Belt Moulding

BO

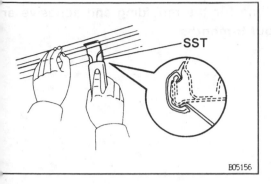

ROOF DRIP MOULDING REMOVAL

1. **REMOVE ROOF DRIP MOULDING**
   Using SST, pull off the roof drip moulding from front ends.
   SST 09806−30010
2. **REMOVE ROOF DRIP END MOULDING**

ROOF DRIP MOULDING INSTALLATION

1. **INSTALL ROOF DRIP END MOULDING**
2. **INSTALL ROOF DRIP MOULDING**
   Attach the upper edge of the moulding to the body flange. Tap on the moulding by hand.

FRONT DOOR BELT MOULDING REMOVAL AND INSTALLATION

1. **REMOVE FRONT DOOR COMPONENTS PARTS**
   (See page BO−13)
2. **REMOVE FRONT DOOR BELT MOULDING**
3. **INSTALL FRONT DOOR BELT MOULDING**
4. **INSTALL FRONT DOOR COMPONENTS PARTS**

REAR DOOR BELT MOULDING REMOVAL AND INSTALLATION

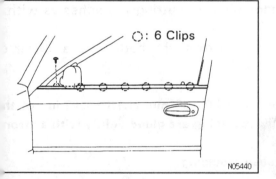

1. **REMOVE REAR DOOR COMPONENTS PARTS**
   (See page BO−17)
2. **REMOVE REAR DOOR BELT MOULDING**
3. **INSTALL REAR DOOR BELT MOULDING**
4. **INSTALL REAR DOOR COMPONENTS PARTS**

SIDE PROTECTION MOULDING REMOVAL

Precautions for storing moulding material:
- Store in a cool place, avoiding direct sunlight, high temperature and dust.
- The moulding is of polyvinyl chloride, so do not allow it to come in contact with thinner or other solvent, open flame, or boiling water.

BO

● The storage time for the moulding and adhesive ar
limited to about 9 months.

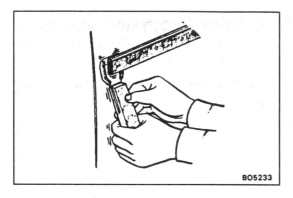

1. REMOVE ENDS OF MOULDING
Using a scraper, pry the moulding loose about 30 mr
(1.18 in.) from the ends.
HINT: Tape the scraper tip before use.

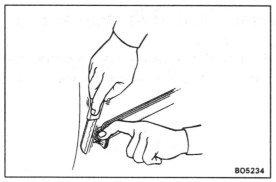

2. REMOVE MOULDING AND ADHESIVE
(a) Pull off the moulding by cutting the adhesive with
knife.
(b) Scrape off adhesive from the body with a cutter c
sandpaper.
NOTICE:
● **Remember that 30–80 mm (1.18–3.15 in.) of th
ends of the moulding are glued tightly with a stro
adhesive.**
● **Do not reuse moulding.**

**SIDE PROTECTION MOULDING
INSTALLATION**

1. CLEAN MOULDING MOUNTING SURFACE
Wipe off stains with cleaner.

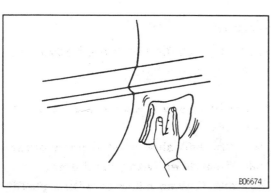

2. HEAT BODY MOUNTING SURFACE
Using a heat light, heat the body mounting surface t
40–60°C (104–140°F).
**NOTICE: When the moulding is installed, the temperatu
of the mounting surface should be 20°C (68°F) or highe**

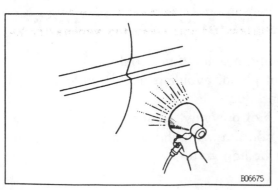

BO

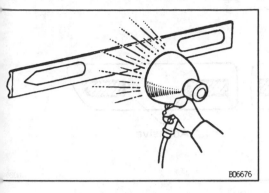

3. HEAT MOULDING

Using a heat light, heat the moulding to 20—30°C (68 —86°F).

NOTICE: Do not heat moulding excessively.

The temperature should not be higher than 80°C (176°F).

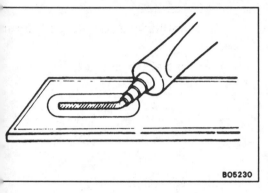

4. APPLY ADHESIVE TO DOOR OUTSIDE MOULDING

Apply adhesive to both punched out ends of the moulding.

NOTICE: Install the moulding within 30 minutes after applying the adhesive.

Part No. 08850—00051

5. LIFT MOULDING RELEASE SHEET FROM FACE OF MOULDING

NOTICE: When the moulding release sheet is removed, be sure that no dirt or dust can get onto the uncoated area.

BO

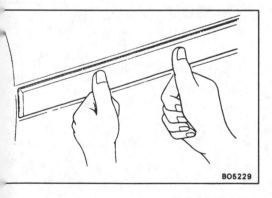

6. INSTALL MOULDING

Align the bosses an the moulding with the body holes, and push the moulding to the body.

NOTICE:

- **Be sure that the body and moulding are heated to the proper temperature.**
- **Do not depress the adhesive—coated parts excessively just hold them down with your thumb.**
- **Scrape off any overflowing adhesive with a plastic spatula and clean the surface with a dry rang.**
- **After installation, do not wash the vehicle for 24 hours.**

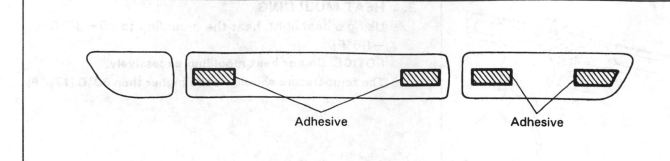

Adhesive   Adhesive

N0364

BACK WINDOW MOULDING
COMPONENTS

BO093—01

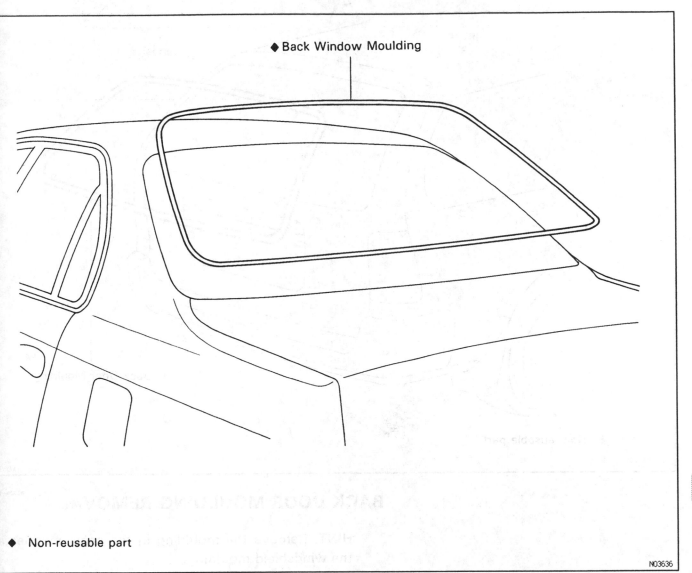

◆ Back Window Moulding

◆ Non-reusable part

N03636

BO094—01

BACK WINDOW MOULDING REMOVAL

HINT: Remove the moulding in the same manner as the windshield moulding.

BACK WINDOW MOULDING INSTALLATION

HINT: Install the moulding in the same manner as the windshield moulding.

BO

BACK DOOR MOULDING
COMPONENTS

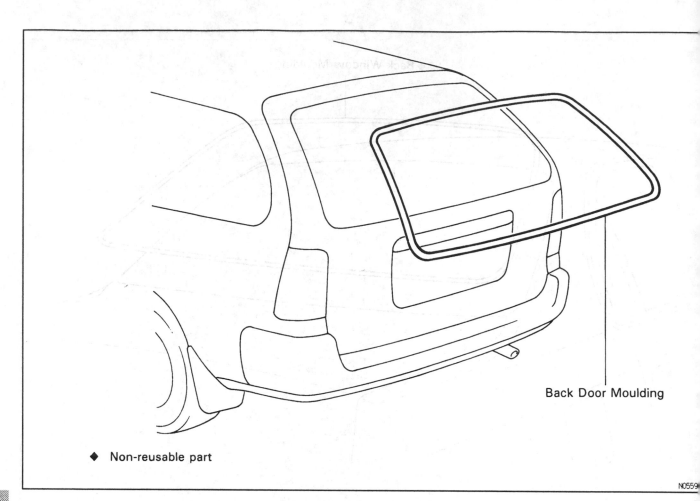

Back Door Moulding

◆ Non-reusable part

BACK DOOR MOULDING REMOVAL

HINT: Remove the moulding in the same manner a
the windshield moulding.

BACK DOOR MOULDING INSTALLATION

HINT: Install the moulding in the same manner as th
windshield moulding.

WINDSHIELD
COMPONENTS

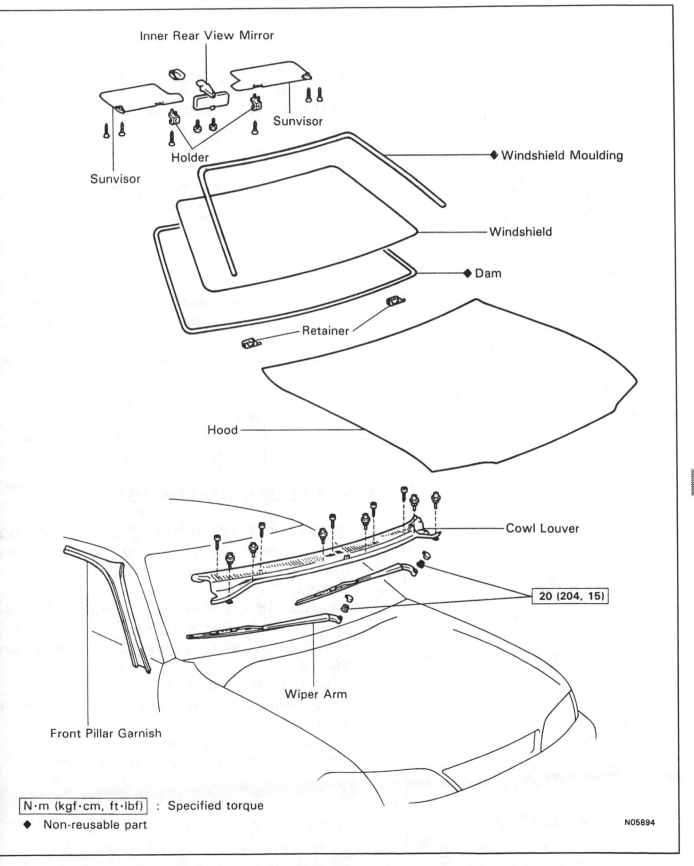

Inner Rear View Mirror

Sunvisor

Holder

Sunvisor

◆ Windshield Moulding

Windshield

◆ Dam

Retainer

Hood

Cowl Louver

20 (204, 15)

Wiper Arm

Front Pillar Garnish

N·m (kgf·cm, ft·lbf) : Specified torque

◆ Non-reusable part

BO

N05894

BO095-0

WINDSHIELD REMOVAL

1. **REMOVE FOLLOWING PARTS:**
(a) Inner rear view mirror
(b) Sunvisors and holders
(c) Front assist grip
(d) Front pillar garnish
(e) Hood
(f) Wiper arms
(g) Cowl louver
2. **REMOVE WINDSHIELD MOULDING**
3. **REMOVE WINDSHIELD GLASS**
(a) Push piano wire through from the interior.
(b) Tie both wire ends to a wooden block or like object
HINT: Apply adhesive tape to the outer surface t
keep the surface from being scratched.

NOTICE: When separating the glass, take care not t
damage the paint and interior and exterior ornaments. T
prevent scratching the safety pad when removing th
windshield, place a plastic sheet between the piano wi
eand safety pad.
(c) Cut the adhesive by pulling the piano wire around it
(d) Remove the glass.
NOTICE: Leave as much of the adhesive on the body a
possible when cutting off the glass.

WINDSHIELD INSTALLATION

BO096-0

1. **CLEAN AND SHAPE CONTACT SURFACE OF BOD**
(a) Using a knife, cut away any rough areas on the bod
HINT: Leave as much of the adhesive on the body a
possible.
(b) Clean the cutting surface of the adhesive with a piec
of shop rag saturated in cleaner.
HINT: Even if all the adhesive has been removed, clea
the body.
2. **CLEAN REMOVED GLASS**
(a) Using a scraper, remove the adhesive sticking to th
glass.
(b) Clean the glass with cleaner.
NOTICE: Do not touch the glass after cleaning it.

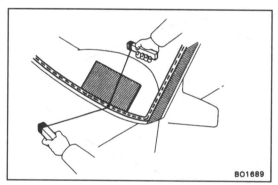

Adhesive

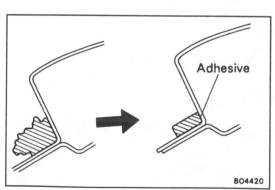

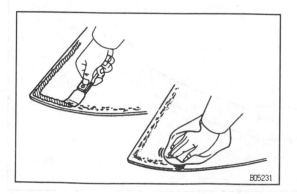

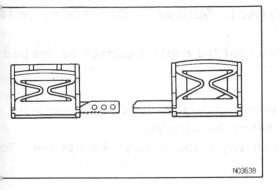

3. REPLACE AND ADJUST RETAINERS
(a) Removce old retainers.

(b) Install new retainers.

(c) Place the windshield glass to the body.

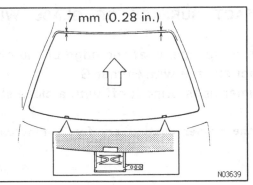

(d) Adjust the retainer as shown.
   Clearance: 7 mm (0.28 in.)

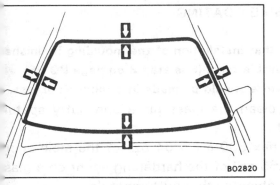

4. POSITION GLASS
(a) Place glass in correct position.

(b) Check that all contacting parts of the glass rim are perfectly even and do not make contact with the fasteners.

(c) Place reference marks between the glass and body.

(d) Remove the glass.

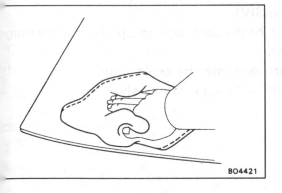

5. CLEAN CONTACT SURFACE OF GLASS
Using a cleaner, clean the contact surface black—colored area around the entire glass rim.
NOTICE: Do not touch the glass face after cleaning it.

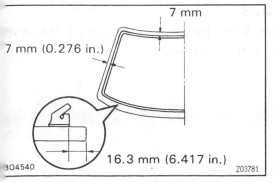

6. INSTALL DAM
Install the dam with double—stick tape as shown in the drawing.
NOTICE: Do not touch the glass face after cleaning it.

BO

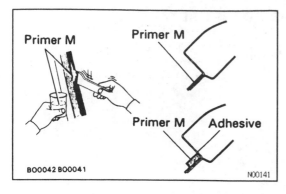

BO0042 BO0041   N00141

7. COAT CONTACT SURFACE OF BODY WITH PRIMER "M"

Using a brush, coat the contact surface on the body with Primer M.

NOTICE:
- **Let the primer coating dry for 3 minutes or more.**
- **Do not coat to the adhesive.**
- **Do not keep any of the opened primer M and G for later use.**

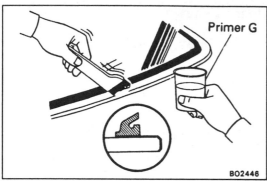

BO2446

8. COAT CONTACT SURFACE OF GLASS WITH PRIMER "G"

(a) Using a brush or sponge, coat the edge of the glass and the contact surface with Primer G.

(b) Before the Primer dries, wipe it off with a clean short rag.

NOTICE: Let the primer coating cry for 3 minutes or more.

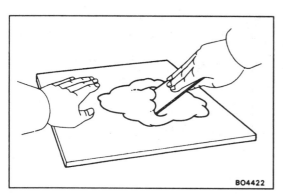

BO4422

9. MIX ADHESIVE COATING

NOTICE:
- **Be sure that installation of the moulding is finished within usable time. (See step 3 on page BO—8)**
- **The mixture should be made in 5 minutes or less.**

(a) Thoroughly clean the glass plate and putty spatula with solvent.

(b) Thoroughly mix 500 g (17.64 oz.) of the main agent and 75 g (2.65 oz.) of the hardening agent on a glass plate or like object with a putty spatula.

10. APPLY ADHESIVE

(a) Cut off the tip of the cartridge nozzle. Fill the cartridge with adhesive.

(b) Load the cartridge into the sealer gun.

(c) Coat the glass with adhesive as shown.

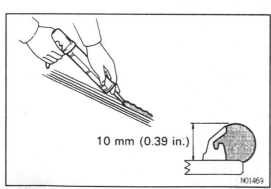

10 mm (0.39 in.)

N01469

11. INSTALL GLASS

HINT: Confirm that the dam is attached the body panel as shown in the drawing.

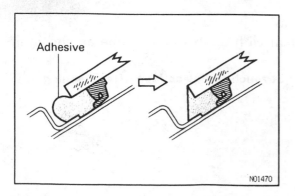

N01470

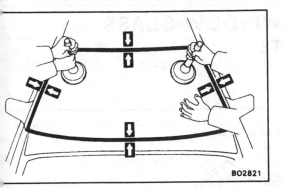

(a) Position the glass so that the reference marks are lined up, and press in gently along the rim.

(b) Using a spatula, apply adhesive on the glass rim.

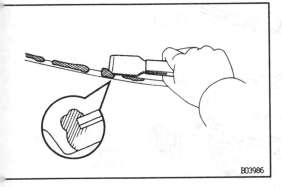

(c) Use a scraper to remove any excess or protruding adhesive.

(d) Fasten glass securely until the adhesive sets.

12. INSPECT FOR LEAKS AND REPAIR

(a) Perform a leak test after the hardening time has elapsed.

(b) Seal any leak with auto glass sealer.
Part No. 08833—00030

13. INSTALL WINDSHIELD MOULDING

14. INSTALL FOLLOWING PARTS:

(a) Cowl louver

(b) Wiper arms

(c) Hood

(d) Front pillar garnish

(e) Front assist grip

(f) Sunvisors and holders

(g) Inner rear view mirror

BO

QUARTER WINDOW GLASS
COMPONENTS

BO0J1—01

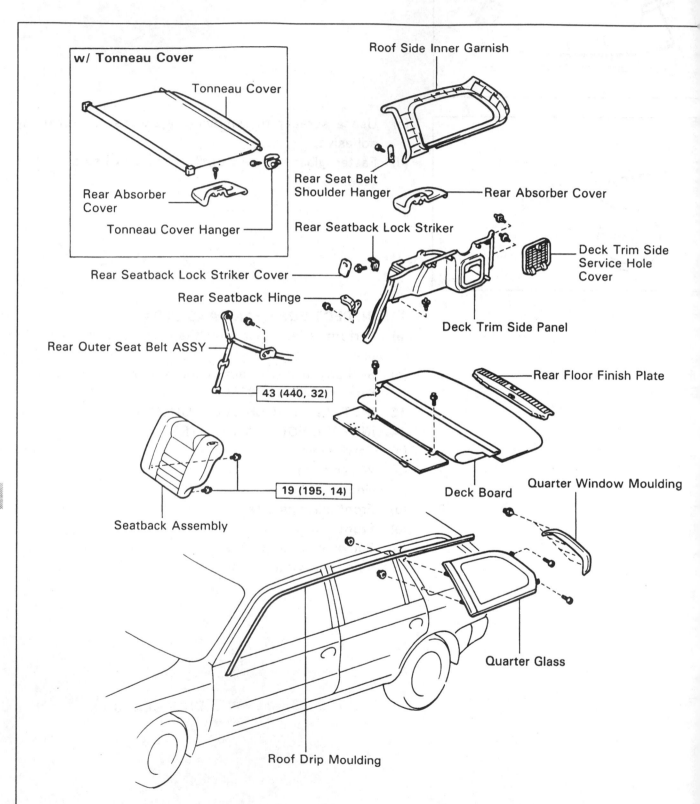

w/ Tonneau Cover

Tonneau Cover

Rear Absorber Cover

Tonneau Cover Hanger

Roof Side Inner Garnish

Rear Seat Belt Shoulder Hanger

Rear Absorber Cover

Rear Seatback Lock Striker

Rear Seatback Lock Striker Cover

Deck Trim Side Service Hole Cover

Rear Seatback Hinge

Deck Trim Side Panel

Rear Outer Seat Belt ASSY

Rear Floor Finish Plate

43 (440, 32)

19 (195, 14)

Seatback Assembly

Deck Board

Quarter Window Moulding

Quarter Glass

Roof Drip Moulding

N·m (kgf·cm, ft·lbf) : Specified torque

N05585

QUARTER WINDOW GLASS REMOVAL

BO0J2-01

1. **(w/ TONNEAU COVER)**
   REMOVE TONNEAU COVER

2. **REMOVE FOLLOWING PARTS:**

(a) Rear floor finish plate

(b) Deck board

(c) Rear seatback

(d) Rear absorber cover

(e) Rear seatback hinge

(f) Rear seatback lock striker

(g) Rear seat belt guide

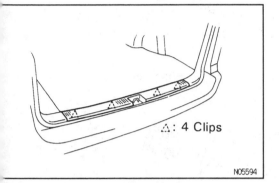

△: 4 Clips

N05594

(h) Deck trim side panel

(i) Rear seat belt

(j) Rear seat belt Shoulder hanger

(k) (w/ Tonneau cover)
   Tonneau cover hanger

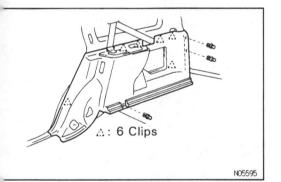

△: 6 Clips

N05595

(l) Roof side inner garnish

(m) Roof drip moulding

(n) Quarter window moulding

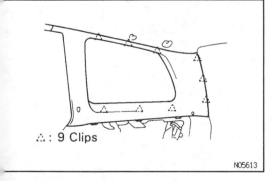

△: 9 Clips

N05613

3. **REMOVE QUARTER WINDOW GLASS**

(a) Remove two screws.

(b) Remove two nuts.

(c) Remove glass.
   NOTICE: Do not damage the body.

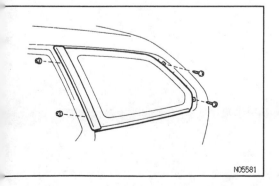

N05581

BO

QUARTER WINDOW INSTALLATION

BO0J3—01

INSTALL QUARTER WINDOW PARTS BY FOLLOWING REMOVAL SEQUENCE IN REVERSE

(a) Rear side of roof headlining
(b) Package tray trim
(c) High mount stop light
(d) Rear seat side garnish
(e) Roof side inner garnish
(f) Rear seat cushion and rear seat back
Torque: 19 N·m (195 kgf·cm, 14 ft·lbf)

BACK DOOR GLASS
COMPONENTS

BO0J4-01

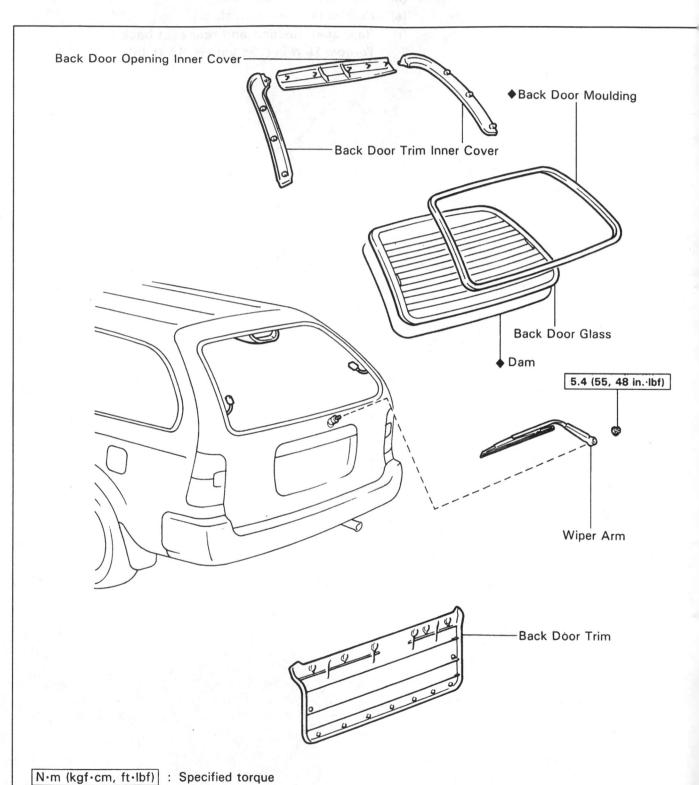

Back Door Opening Inner Cover

◆Back Door Moulding

Back Door Trim Inner Cover

Back Door Glass

◆Dam

5.4 (55, 48 in.·lbf)

Wiper Arm

Back Door Trim

N·m (kgf·cm, ft·lbf) : Specified torque

◆ Non-reusable part

BO

N05584

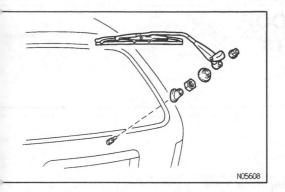

BO0J5-01

BACK DOOR GLASS REMOVAL

1. **REMOVE FOLLOWING PARTS:**
(a) Rear wiper arm
(b) High mount stop light and cover

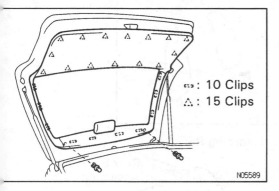

⊏⊐ : 10 Clips
△ : 15 Clips

(c) Back door trim
(d) Back door trim inner cover
(e) Back door opening inner cover
2. **DEFOGGER WIRE CONNECTOR**
3. **REMOVE BACK DOOR MOULDING**
   (See pege BO–42)
4. **REMOVE BACK DOOR GLASS**
   Remove the glass in the same manner as windshield.

BO0J6-01

BACK DOOR GLASS INSTALLATION

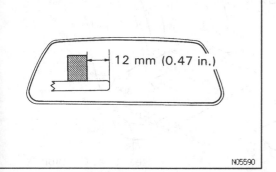

12 mm (0.47 in.)

HINT: Install the glass in the same manner as the windshield.
1. **CLEAN AND SHAPE CONTACT SURFACE OF BODY**
2. **CLEAN REMOVED GLASS**
3. **POSITION GLASS**
4. **CLEAN CONTACT SURFACE OF GLASS**
5. **INSTALL DAM**
   Install the dam with double–stick tape as shown in the drawing.
   NOTICE: Do not touch the glass face after ceaning it.
6. **COAT CONTACT SURFACE OF BODY WITH PRIMER"M"**
7. **COAT CONTACT SURFACE OF GLASS WITH PRIMER"G"**
8. **MIX ADHESIVE COATING**
9. **APPLY ADHESIVE**
10. **INSTALL GLASS**
11. **INSTALL BACK WINDOW MOULDING**
12. **INSPECT FOR LEAKS AND REPAIR**
13. **CONNECT DEFOGGER WIRE CONNECTORS**
14. **INSTALL FOLLWING PARTS:**
(a) Back door opening inner cover
(b) Back door trim inner cover
(c) Back door trim
(d) Hight mount stop light
(e) Rear wiper arm

BO

SLIDING ROOF
COMPONENTS

BO0J7–01

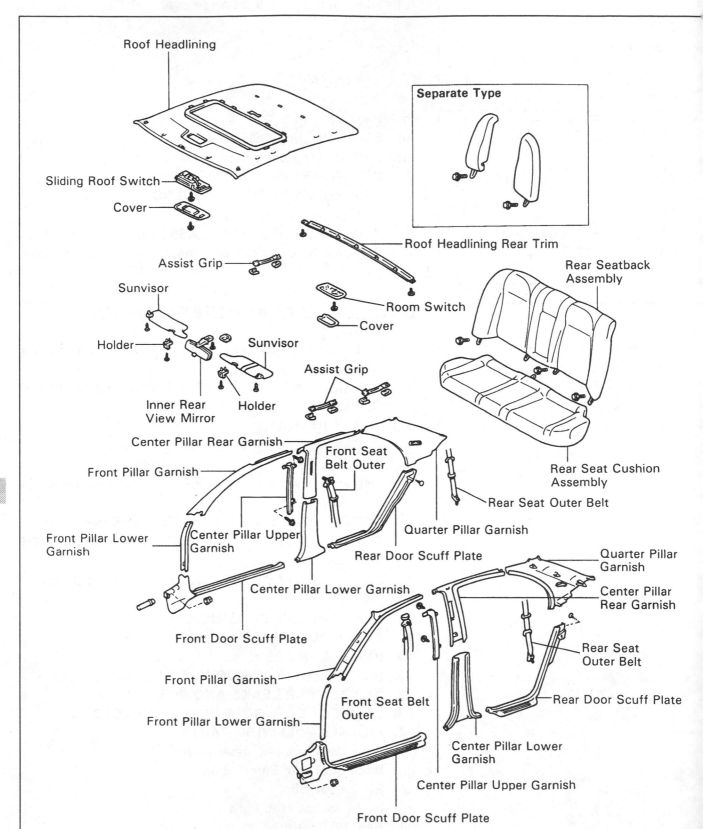

Roof Headlining

Separate Type

Sliding Roof Switch

Cover

Roof Headlining Rear Trim

Assist Grip

Sunvisor

Room Switch

Cover

Rear Seatback Assembly

Holder

Sunvisor

Assist Grip

Inner Rear View Mirror

Holder

Center Pillar Rear Garnish

Front Pillar Garnish

Front Seat Belt Outer

Rear Seat Cushion Assembly

Rear Seat Outer Belt

Front Pillar Lower Garnish

Center Pillar Upper Garnish

Quarter Pillar Garnish

Rear Door Scuff Plate

Quarter Pillar Garnish

Center Pillar Lower Garnish

Center Pillar Rear Garnish

Front Door Scuff Plate

Rear Seat Outer Belt

Front Pillar Garnish

Front Seat Belt Outer

Rear Door Scuff Plate

Front Pillar Lower Garnish

Center Pillar Lower Garnish

Center Pillar Upper Garnish

Front Door Scuff Plate

BO

N05684

CONPONENTS (Cont'd)

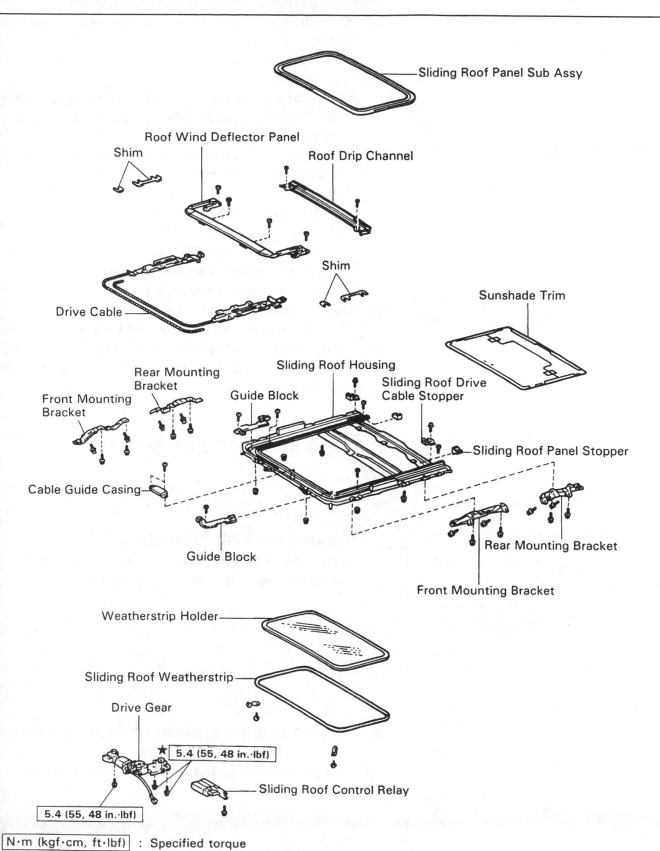

Sliding Roof Panel Sub Assy

Roof Wind Deflector Panel

Shim

Roof Drip Channel

Shim

Drive Cable

Sunshade Trim

Rear Mounting Bracket

Sliding Roof Housing

Front Mounting Bracket

Guide Block

Sliding Roof Drive Cable Stopper

Sliding Roof Panel Stopper

Cable Guide Casing

Guide Block

Rear Mounting Bracket

Front Mounting Bracket

Weatherstrip Holder

Sliding Roof Weatherstrip

Drive Gear

★ 5.4 (55, 48 in.·lbf)

Sliding Roof Control Relay

5.4 (55, 48 in.·lbf)

N·m (kgf·cm, ft·lbf) : Specified torque
★ Precoated part

N05796

BO

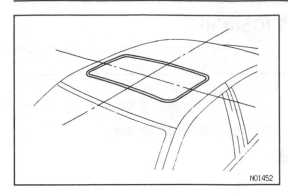

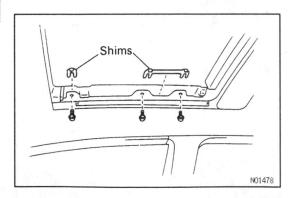

ON−VEHICLE INSPECTION

B00J8−01

INSPECT SLIDING ROOF GRASS ALIGNMENT

(a) Start the engine and check the operation time of the sliding roof.

   Operation time:

   Approx. 6 secs.

(b) Check for abnormal noise or binding during operation

(c) With the sliding roof fully closed, check for water leakage.

(d) Check for a difference in level between the sliding roof weatherstrip and roof panel.

   Front end:

   1 ± 1 mm (0.039 ± 0.039 in.)

   Rear end:

   0 ± 1 mm (0 ± 0.039 in.)

   If the sliding roof does not operate:

(e) Remove the control switch cover.

(f) Remove the large screw inside.

   NOTICE: Be careful not to lose the spring washer or shim

(g) Manually operate the moon roof by inserting a special crank−shaped screwdriver into the hole and turning the drive shaft.

SLIDING ROOF ADJUSTMENT

B00J9−01

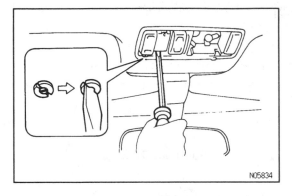

Shims

1. TO ADJUST LEVEL DIFFERENCE

Adjust by increasing or decreasing the number of shims between the bracket and sliding roof.

2. ADJUST SLIDING ROOF IN FOWARD/REARWARD AND VERTICAL DERECTIONS

Loosen the sliding roof installtion bolts to adjust.

SLIDING ROOF REMOVAL

BOOJA-01

1. DISCONNECT BATTERY CABLE FROM NEGATIVE TERMINAL

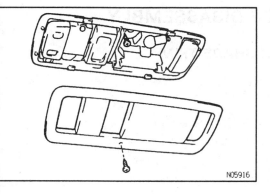

2. REMOVE SLIDING ROOF SWITCH
(a) Remove the screw.
(b) Using a screwdriver, remove the cover.
HINT: Tape the screwdriver tip before use.
(c) Remove the screws and the switch, then disconnect the connectors.

3. REMOVE FOLLOWING PARTS:
(a) Inner rear view mirror
(b) Sunvisors and holders
(c) Assist grips
(d) Interior light

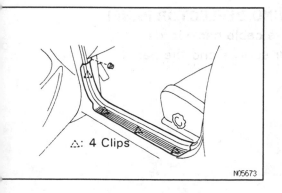

△: 4 Clips

N05673

(e) Front door scuff plates
(f) Front pillar lower garnishes

BO

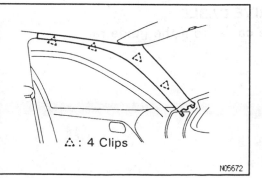

△: 4 Clips

N05672

(g) Front piller garnishes
(h) Center piller lower garnishes
(i) Rear door scuff plates
(j) Rear seat cushions
(k) Rear seatback
(l) Roof headlining rear trim

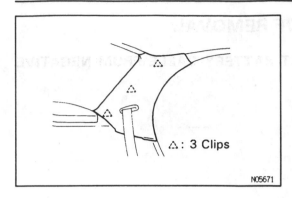

△ : 3 Clips

N05671

(m) Quarter piller garnishes
(n) Rear seat belts outer belt anchor
(o) Front seat belts shoulder anchor
(p) Center piller rear garnishes
(q) Center piller upper garnishes
(r) Roof headlining
(s) Sliding roof control relay
(t) Drive motor
(u) Cable guide casing assembly

BO0JB—01

SLIDING ROOF DISASSEMBLY

1. REMOVE SUNSHADE TRIM

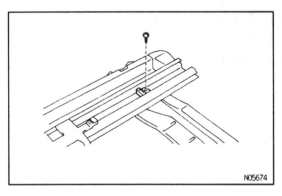

N05674

2. REMOVE ROOF DRIP CHANNEL
Remove two screws and the channel.

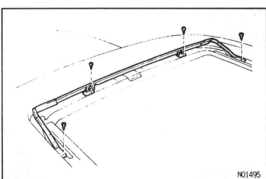

N01495

3. REMOVE WIND DEFLECTOR PANEL
(a) Side the drive cable backwards.
(b) Remove four screws and the panel.

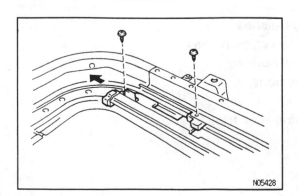

N05428

4. REMOVE DRIVE CABLE
Pull the drive cable from the guide rail.

SLIDING ROOF ASSEMBLY

B00JC−01

ASSEMBLE SLIDING ROOF PARTS BY FOLLOWING DISASSEMBLY SEQUENCE IN REVERSE

SLIDING ROOF INSTALLATION

B00JD−01

INSTALL SLIDING ROOF PARTS BY FOLLOWING RE-MOVAL SEQUENCE IN REVERSE

ADJUST DRIVE RAIL
(a) Operate the drive rail to tilted up and down again.
(b) Operate the drive rail to opened and closed again.
(c) Using a screwdriver, slide the rail forwards or rearwards to align the marks as shown.

N05569

BO

INSTRUMENT PANEL
COMPONENTS

B004Q-02

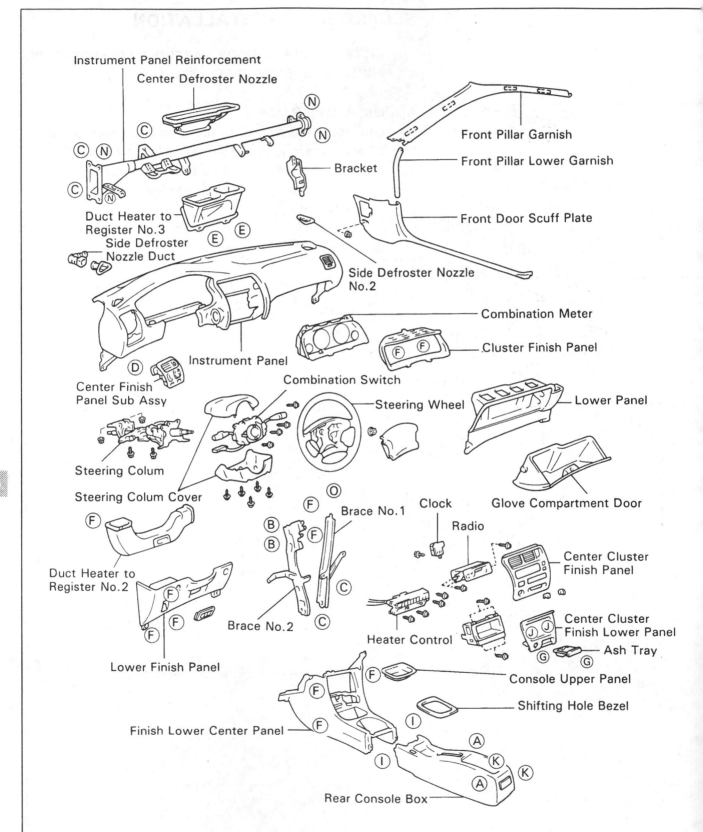

Instrument Panel Reinforcement
Center Defroster Nozzle
Bracket
Front Pillar Garnish
Front Pillar Lower Garnish
Duct Heater to Register No.3
Side Defroster Nozzle Duct
Front Door Scuff Plate
Side Defroster Nozzle No.2
Combination Meter
Instrument Panel
Cluster Finish Panel
Center Finish Panel Sub Assy
Combination Switch
Steering Wheel
Lower Panel
Steering Colum
Steering Colum Cover
Clock
Radio
Glove Compartment Door
Duct Heater to Register No.2
Brace No.1
Center Cluster Finish Panel
Lower Finish Panel
Brace No.2
Heater Control
Center Cluster Finish Lower Panel
Ash Tray
Console Upper Panel
Shifting Hole Bezel
Finish Lower Center Panel
Rear Console Box

BO

N0590C

COMPONENTS (Cont'd)

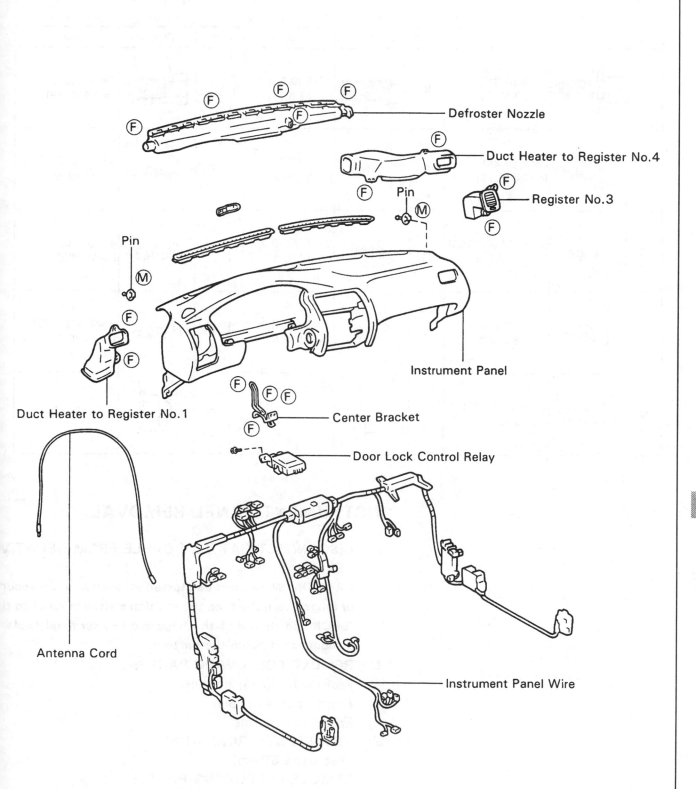

Defroster Nozzle

Duct Heater to Register No.4

Pin

Register No.3

Pin

Instrument Panel

Duct Heater to Register No.1

Center Bracket

Door Lock Control Relay

Antenna Cord

Instrument Panel Wire

BO

N05901

HINT: Screw in the illustration on the previous page are indicated using the code below for removal and installation of instrument panel.

Code	Shape	Size	Code	Shape	Size	Code	Shape	Size
A		$\phi = 8\ (0.31)$ $L = 20\ (0.79)$	B		$\phi = 8\ (0.31)$ $L = 17\ (0.67)$	C		$\phi = 8\ (0.31)$ $L = 15\ (0.59)$
D		$\phi = 6\ (0.24)$ $L = 20\ (0.79)$	E		$\phi = 6\ (0.24)$ $L = 20\ (0.79)$	F		$\phi = 5.22\ (0.2055)$ $L = 14\ (0.55)$
G		$\phi = 5.22\ (0.2055)$ $L = 14\ (0.55)$	H		$\phi = 5.22\ (0.2055)$ $L = 12\ (0.47)$	I		$\phi\ 5\ (0.20)$ $L = 16\ (0.63)$
J		$\phi = 5\ (0.20)$ $L = 16\ (0.63)$	K		$\phi = 5\ (0.20)$ $L = 14\ (0.55)$	L		$\phi = 4.5\ (0.177)$ $L = 14\ (0.55)$
M		$\phi = 4.5\ (0.177)$ $L = 12\ (0.47)$	N		—	O		—

V0064

BO09A—

INSTRUMENT PANEL REMOVAL

1. **DISCONNECT BATTERY CABLE FROM NEGATIVE TERMINAL**
   CAUTION: Work must be started after approx. 90 seconds or longer from the time the ignition switch is tured to the "LOCK" position and the negative (−) terminal cable disconnected from the battery.

2. **REMOVE FOLLOWING PARTS:**
   (a) Front pillar lower garnish
   (b) Front door scuff plate
   (c) Front pillar garnish

3. **REMOVE STEERING WHEEL**
   (See page SR−5)

4. **REMOVE FOLLOWING PARTS:**
   (a) Steering column cover
   (b) Shifting hole bezel
   (c) Rear console box
   (d) Hood lock release lever

(e) Lower finish panel
(f) Combination switch
(g) Glove compartment door
(h) Lower panel

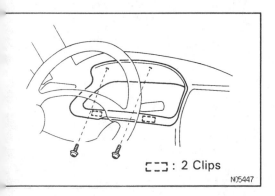

**: 2 Clips

N05446

5. REMOVE CENTER CLUSTER FINISH LOWER PANEL
(a) Remove two screws.
(b) Using a screwdriver, remove the panel, then disconnect the connector.
HINT: Tape the screwdriver tip before use.
(c) Remove the stereo opening cover.

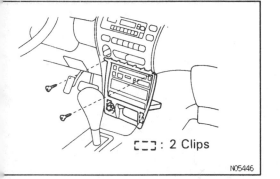

**: 4 Clips

N05455

6. REMOVE CENTER CLUSTER FINISH PANEL
(a) Remove the heater control knobs.
(b) Using a screwdriver, remove the panel.
HINT: Tape the screwdriver tip before use.
(c) Remove the radio.
(d) Remove the heater control.

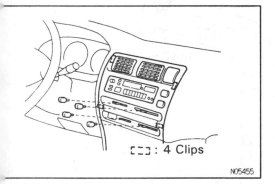

**: 2 Clips

N05447

7. REMOVE CLUSTER FINISH PANEL
(a) Remove two screws.
(b) Using a screwdriver, remove the panel.
HINT: Tape the screwdriver tip before use.
(c) Remove the combination meter.

8. REMOVE FOLLOWING PARTS:
(a) Finish lower center panel
(b) Cluster finish panel sub assy
(c) Duct heater to register No.2
(d) Side defroster nozzle No.2

BO

9. REMOVE INSTRUMENT PANEL
(a) Disconnect the connectors.
(b) Remove five bolts.
(c) Remove two bolts, J/B No.1 and J/B No.4.
(d) Remove eight bolts, the screw and the instrumer
panel.

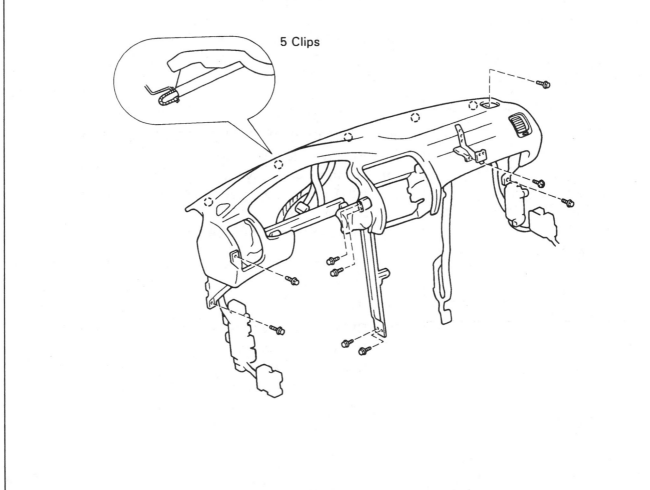

5 Clips

N059

10. REMOVE INSTRUMENT PANEL REINFORCEMENT
(a) Remove four nuts, three bolts and the reinforcemer
(b) Remove the nuts, two bolts and the bracket.

INSTRUMENT PANEL DISASSEMBLY

BO09B—01

1. REMOVE FOLLOWING PARTS FROM INSTRUMENT PANEL

(a) Brace No.1 and No.2

(b) Duct heater to register No.1

(c) Duct heater to register No.4

(d) Defroster nozzle

(e) Defroster nozzle No.1 and No.2

(f) Register No.3

(g) Center bracket

(h) Mounting bracket No.1

(i) Side defroster nozzle No.1

(j) Side defroster nozzle duct

2. REMOVE FOLLOWING PARTS:

(a) Duct heater to register No.3

(b) Center defroster nozzle

3. REMOVE INSTRUMENT PANEL WIRE
Remove ten screws and the wire.

INSTRUMENT PANEL ASSEMBLY

BO03B—02

ASSEMBLE INSTRUMENT PANEL PARTS BY FOLLOW-
ING DISASSEMBLY SEQUENCE IN REVERSE

INSTRUMENT PANEL INSTALLATION

BO03C—02

INSTALL INSTRUMENT PANEL PARTS BY FOLLOWING
REMOVAL SEQUENCE IN REVERSE

BO

FRONT SEAT
COMPONENTS

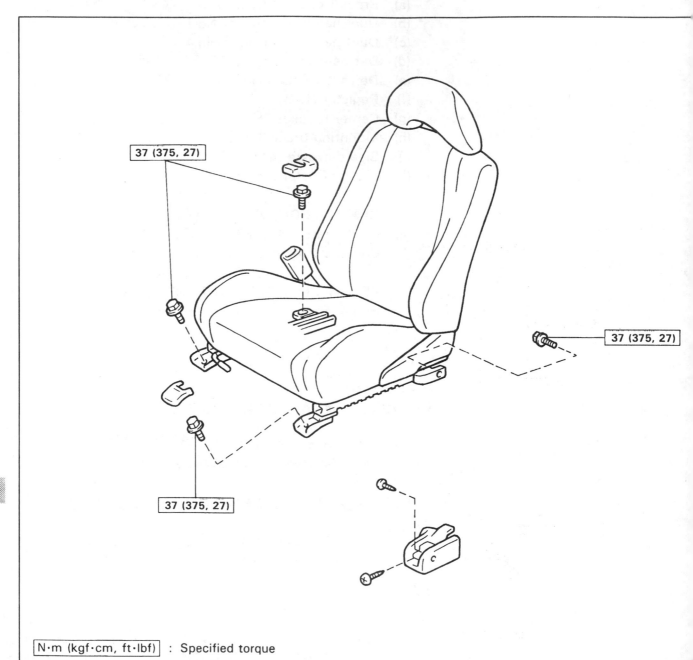

37 (375, 27)

37 (375, 27)

37 (375, 27)

N·m (kgf·cm, ft·lbf) : Specified torque

COMPONENTS (Cont'd)

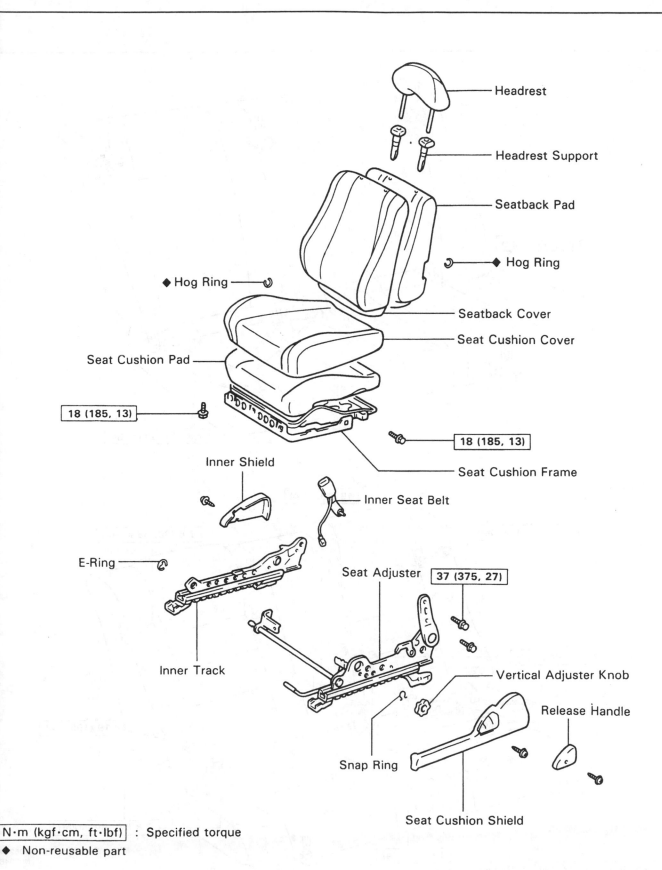

Headrest

Headrest Support

Seatback Pad

◆ Hog Ring

Seatback Cover

Seat Cushion Cover

◆ Hog Ring

Seat Cushion Pad

18 (185, 13)

Seat Cushion Frame

Inner Shield

Inner Seat Belt

E-Ring

Seat Adjuster 37 (375, 27)

Inner Track

Vertical Adjuster Knob

Release Handle

Snap Ring

Seat Cushion Shield

N·m (kgf·cm, ft·lbf) : Specified torque

◆ Non-reusable part

BO

N05932

REAR SEAT
COMPONENTS

BO0JE-0

Fixed

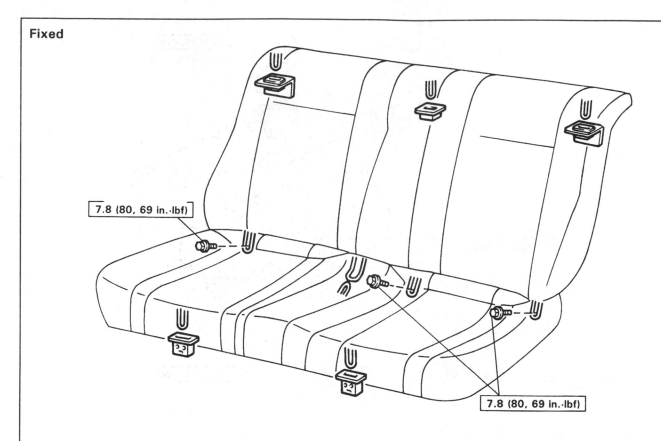

7.8 (80, 69 in.·lbf)

7.8 (80, 69 in.·lbf)

Separate

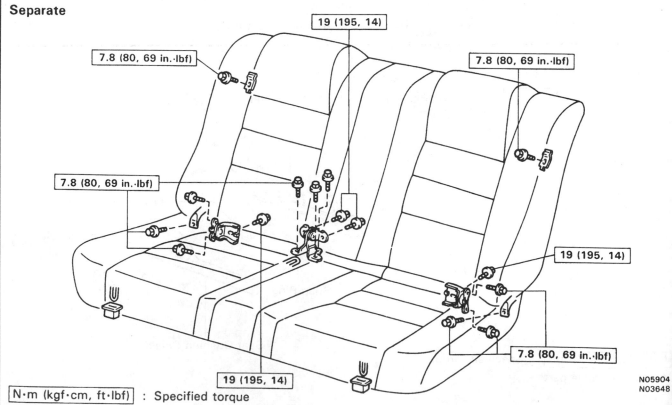

19 (195, 14)

7.8 (80, 69 in.·lbf)

7.8 (80, 69 in.·lbf)

7.8 (80, 69 in.·lbf)

19 (195, 14)

7.8 (80, 69 in.·lbf)

19 (195, 14)

N·m (kgf·cm, ft·lbf) : Specified torque

N05904
N03648

Z03979

BO

COMPONENTS (Cont'd)

Wagon

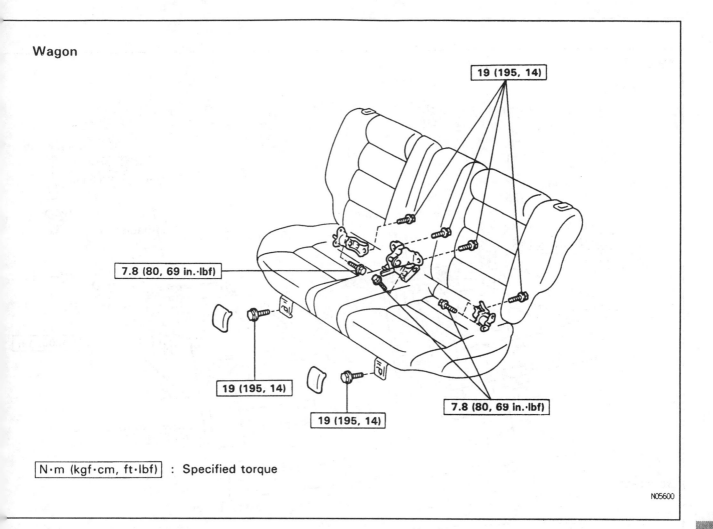

19 (195, 14)

7.8 (80, 69 in.·lbf)

19 (195, 14)

19 (195, 14)

7.8 (80, 69 in.·lbf)

N·m (kgf·cm, ft·lbf) : Specified torque

N05600

BO

COMPONENTS (Cont'd)

Separate

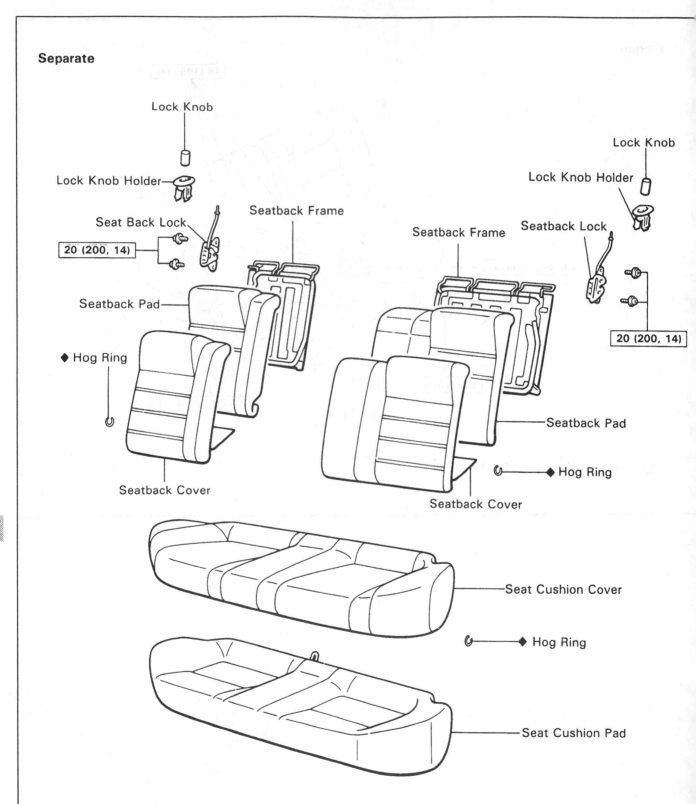

Lock Knob

Lock Knob Holder

Seat Back Lock

20 (200, 14)

Seatback Frame

Seatback Pad

◆ Hog Ring

Seatback Cover

Lock Knob

Lock Knob Holder

Seatback Lock

Seatback Frame

20 (200, 14)

Seatback Pad

◆ Hog Ring

Seatback Cover

Seat Cushion Cover

◆ Hog Ring

Seat Cushion Pad

N·m (kgf·cm, ft·lbf) : Specified torque

◆ Non-reusable part

N0360

COMPONENTS (Cont'd)

Wagon

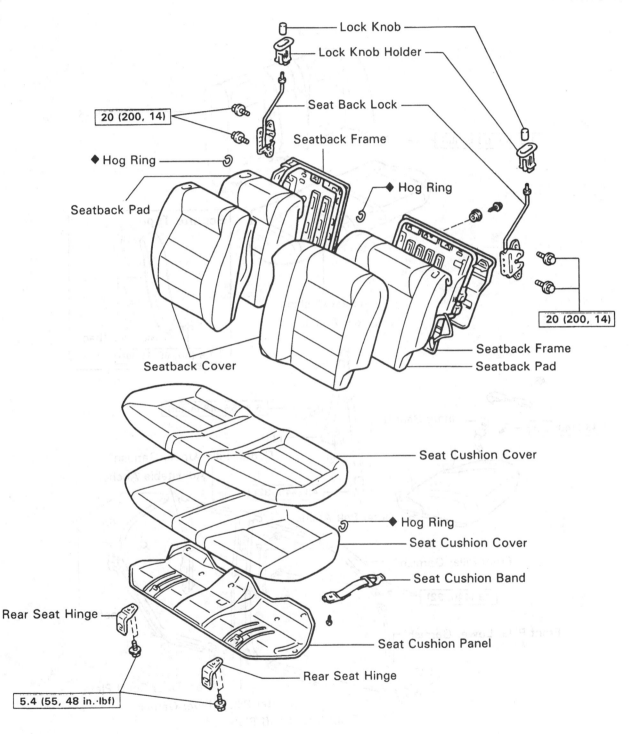

Lock Knob
Lock Knob Holder
Seat Back Lock
20 (200, 14)
Seatback Frame
◆ Hog Ring
◆ Hog Ring
Seatback Pad
20 (200, 14)
Seatback Cover
Seatback Frame
Seatback Pad
Seat Cushion Cover
◆ Hog Ring
Seat Cushion Cover
Seat Cushion Band
Rear Seat Hinge
Seat Cushion Panel
Rear Seat Hinge
5.4 (55, 48 in.·lbf)

N·m (kgf·cm, ft·lbf) : Specified torque

◆ Non-reusable part

N05586

SEAT BELT
COMPONENTS

BOOJF—0

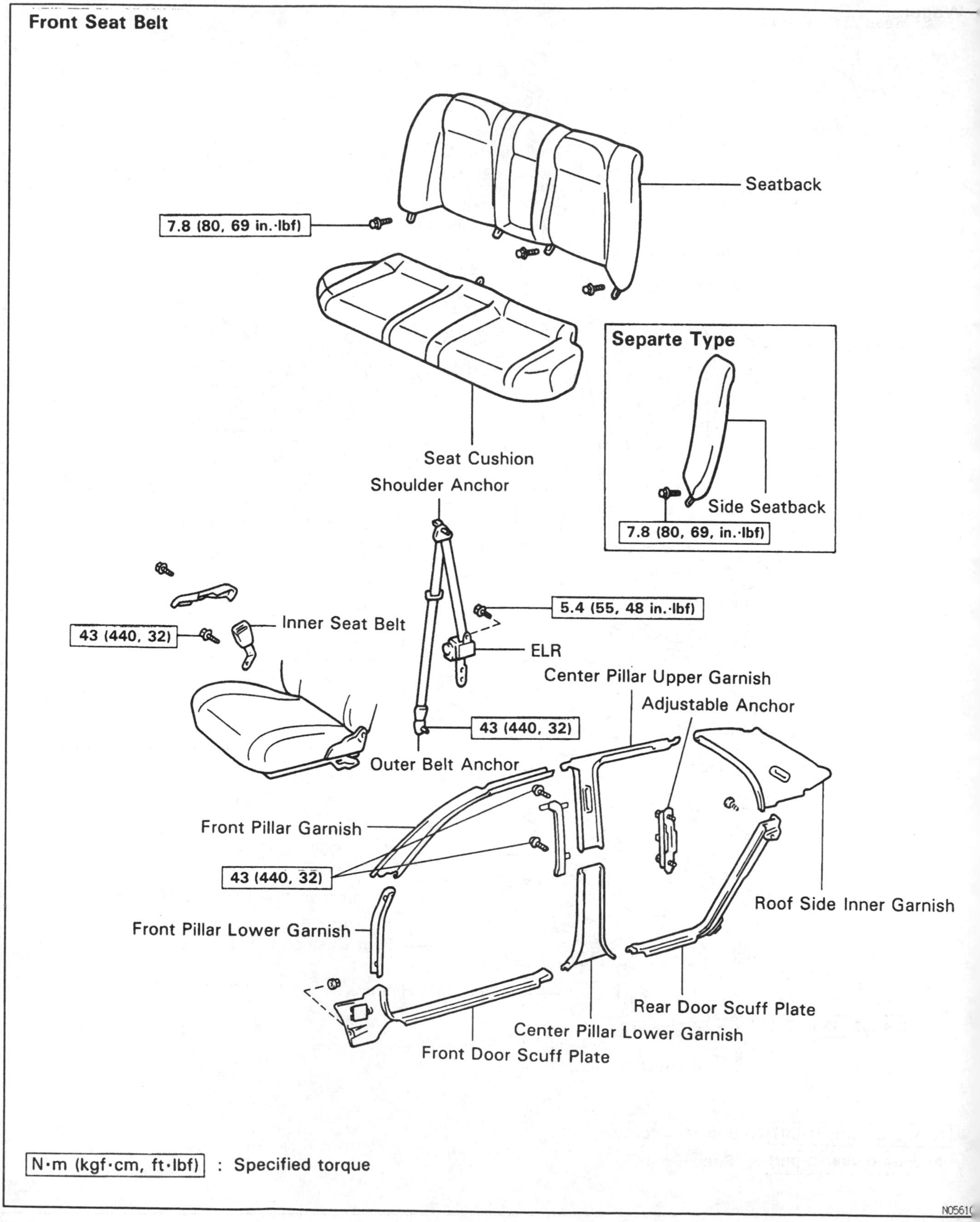

Front Seat Belt

7.8 (80, 69 in.·lbf)

Seatback

Seat Cushion

Shoulder Anchor

Separte Type

Side Seatback

7.8 (80, 69, in.·lbf)

5.4 (55, 48 in.·lbf)

ELR

Inner Seat Belt

43 (440, 32)

Center Pillar Upper Garnish

Adjustable Anchor

43 (440, 32)

Outer Belt Anchor

Front Pillar Garnish

43 (440, 32)

Roof Side Inner Garnish

Front Pillar Lower Garnish

Rear Door Scuff Plate

Center Pillar Lower Garnish

Front Door Scuff Plate

N·m (kgf·cm, ft·lbf) : Specified torque

N0561C

COMPONENTS (Cont'd)

Rear Seat Belt (Sedan)

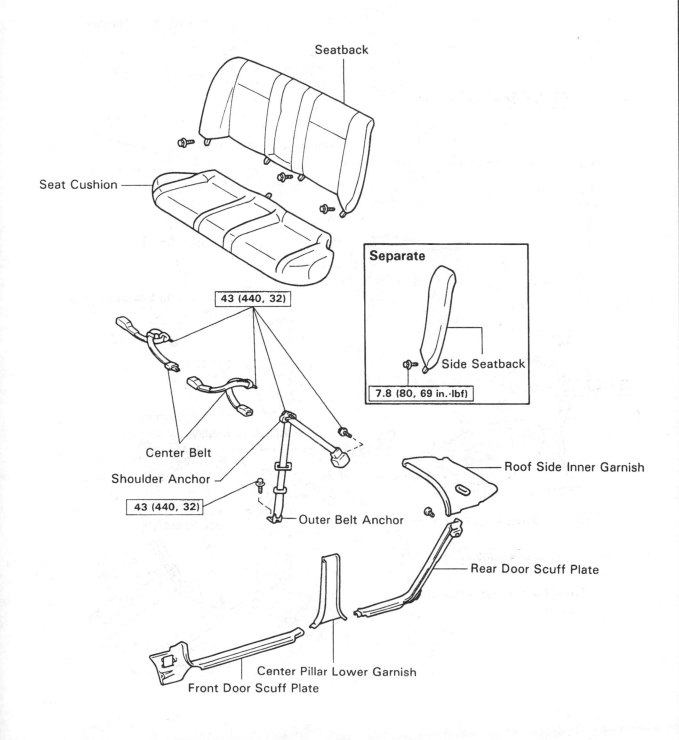

Seatback

Seat Cushion

Separate

Side Seatback

7.8 (80, 69 in.·lbf)

43 (440, 32)

Center Belt

Shoulder Anchor

43 (440, 32)

Outer Belt Anchor

Roof Side Inner Garnish

Rear Door Scuff Plate

Center Pillar Lower Garnish

Front Door Scuff Plate

N·m (kgf·cm, ft·lbf) : Specified torque

COMPONENTS (Cont'd)

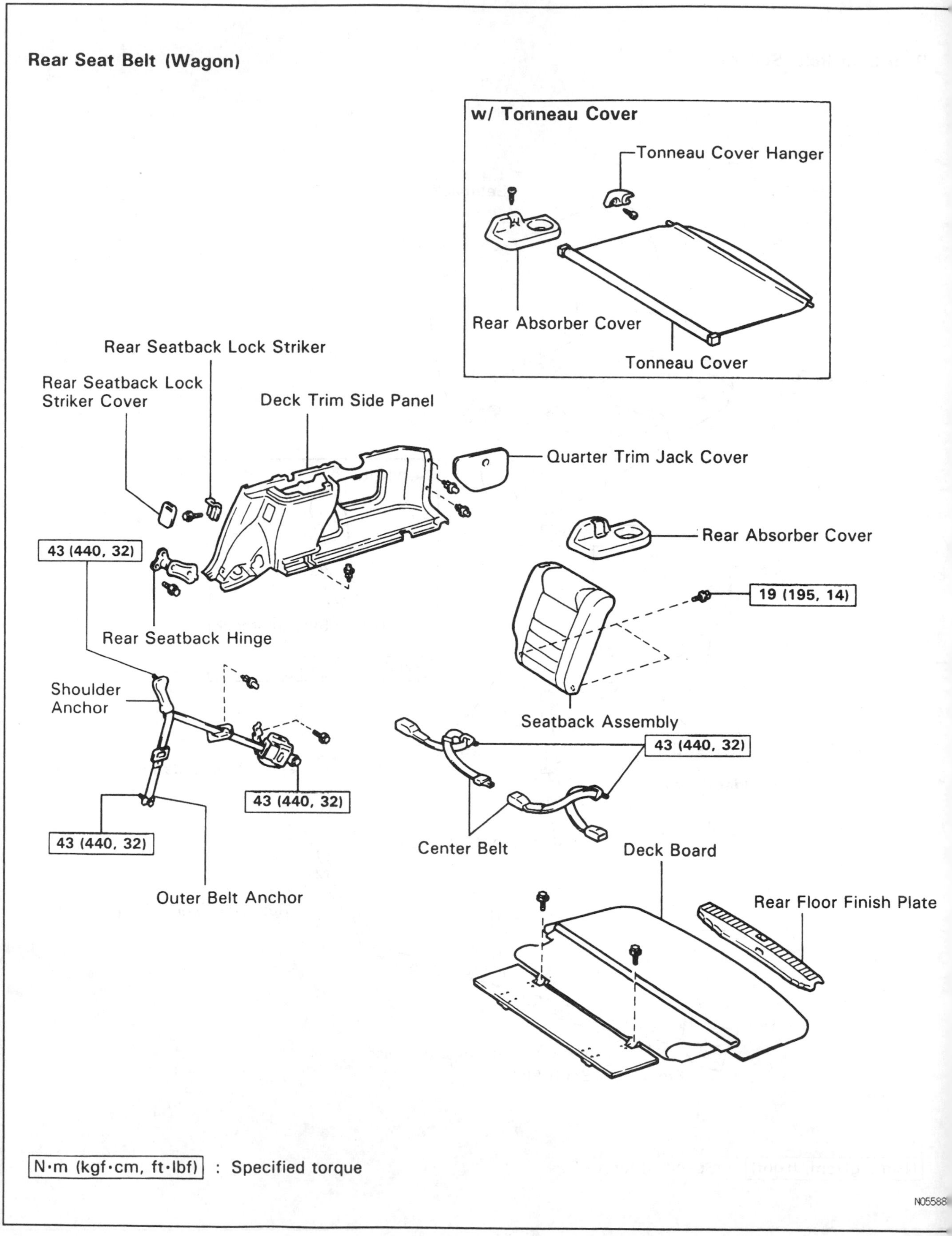

Rear Seat Belt (Wagon)

w/ Tonneau Cover

Tonneau Cover Hanger

Rear Absorber Cover

Tonneau Cover

Rear Seatback Lock Striker

Rear Seatback Lock Striker Cover

Deck Trim Side Panel

Quarter Trim Jack Cover

Rear Absorber Cover

43 (440, 32)

19 (195, 14)

Rear Seatback Hinge

Shoulder Anchor

Seatback Assembly

43 (440, 32)

43 (440, 32)

Center Belt

Deck Board

43 (440, 32)

Outer Belt Anchor

Rear Floor Finish Plate

BO

N·m (kgf·cm, ft·lbf) : Specified torque

N05588

BO03F—04

SEAT BELT INSPECTION
[Emergency Locking Retractor (ELR) Type]

BO0632

1. RUNNING TEST (IN SAFE AREA)
(a) Fasten the front seat belts.

(b) Drive the car at 10 mph (16 km/h) and make a very hard stop.

(c) Check that the belt is locked and cannot be extended at this time.

HINT: Conduct this test in a safe area. If the belt does not lock, remove the belt mechanism assembly and conduct the following static check. Also, whenever installing a new belt assembly, verify the proper operation before installation.

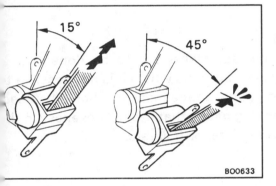

BO0633

2. STATIC TEST
(a) Remove the locking retractor assembly.

(b) Tilt the retractor slowly.

(c) Verify that the belt can be pulled out at a tilt of 15 degrees or less, and cannot be pulled out at over 45 degrees of tilt.

If a problem is found, replace the assembly.

(Manual Type)

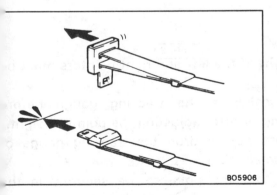

BO5906

TESTING
(a) Adjust the belt to the proper length.

(b) Apply a firm load to the belt.

(c) Verify that the belt does not extend.

BO

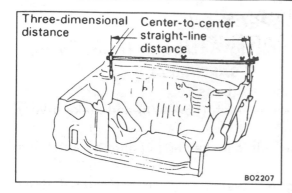

Three-dimensional distance   Center-to-center straight-line distance

BO2207

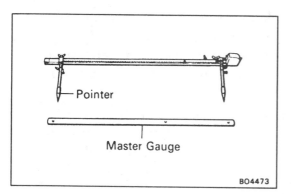

Two-dimensional distance   Center-to-center Horizontal distance in forward/rearward

Vertical distance in center   Vertical distance in lower surface

Imaginary Standard Line

BO2208

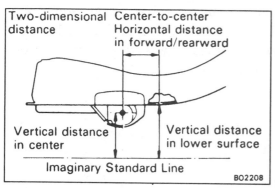

Pointer

Master Gauge

BO4473

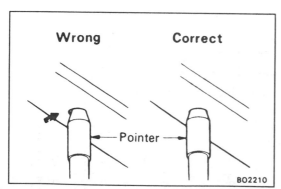

Wrong   Correct

Pointer

BO2210

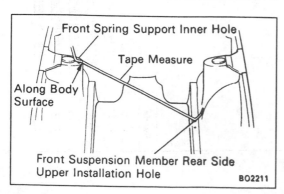

Front Spring Support Inner Hole

Tape Measure

Along Body Surface

Front Suspension Member Rear Side Upper Installation Hole

BO2211

BODY DIMENSIONS
GENERAL INFORMATION

BO03G–0

1. BASIC DIMENSIONS

(a) There are two types of dimensions in the diagram. (Three—dimensional distance)

- Straight—line distance between the centers c two measuring points.

(Two—dimensional distance)

- Horizontal distance in forward / rearward be tween the centers of two measuring points.
- The height format imaginary standard line.

(b) In cases in which only one dimension is given, left an right are symmetrical.

(c) The dimensions in the following drawing indicat actual distance. Therefore, please use the dimension as a reference.

2. MEASURING

(a) Basically, all measurements are to be done with tacking gauge. For portions where it is not possible t use a tracking gauge, a tape measure should be used

(b) Use only a tracking gauge that has no looseness in th body, measuring plate, or pointers.

HINT:

1. The height of the left and right pointers must b equal.
2. Always calibrate the tracking gauge befor measuring or after adjusting the pointer height.
3. Take care not to drop the tracking gauge o otherwise shock it.
4. Confirm that the pointers are securely in th holes.

(c) When using a tape measure, avoid twists and bends i the tape.

(d) When tracking a diagonal measurement from th front spring support inner hole to the suspensio member upper rear installation hole, measure along the front spring support panel surface.

BO

BODY DIMENSIONS
ENGINE COMPARTMENT

BO09E—01

(Three-Dimensional Distance)

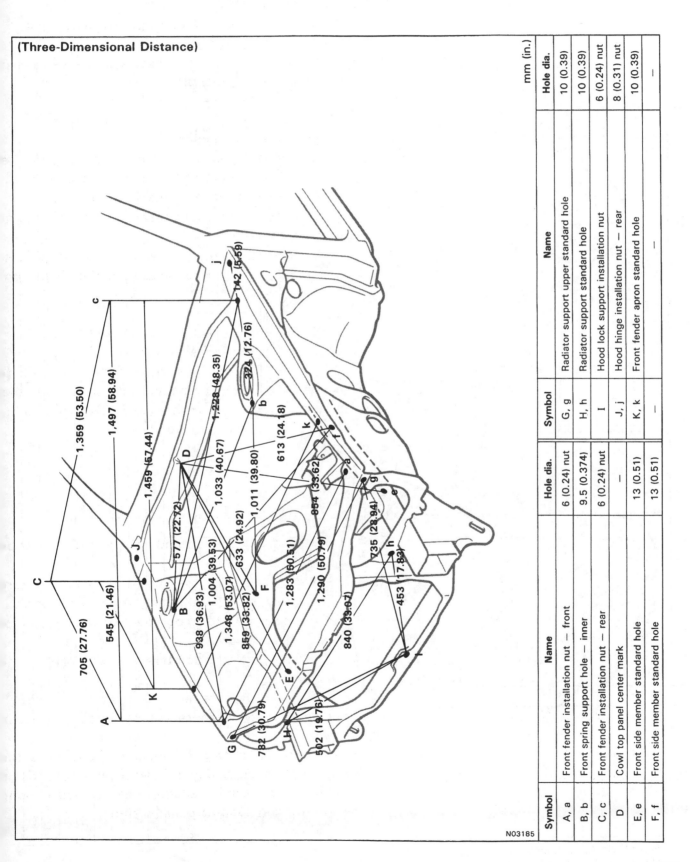

mm (in.)

Symbol	Name	Hole dia.
A, a	Front fender installation nut — front	6 (0.24) nut
B, b	Front spring support hole — inner	9.5 (0.374)
C, c	Front fender installation nut — rear	6 (0.24) nut
D	Cowl top panel center mark	—
E, e	Front side member standard hole	13 (0.51)
F, f	Front side member standard hole	13 (0.51)

Symbol	Name	Hole dia.
G, g	Radiator support upper standard hole	10 (0.39)
H, h	Radiator support standard hole	10 (0.39)
I	Hood lock support installation nut	6 (0.24) nut
J, j	Hood hinge installation nut — rear	8 (0.31) nut
K, k	Front fender apron standard hole	10 (0.39)
—	—	—

N03185

V00592

BO

BODY OPENING AREAS (Side View: Front)

(Three-Dimensional Distance)

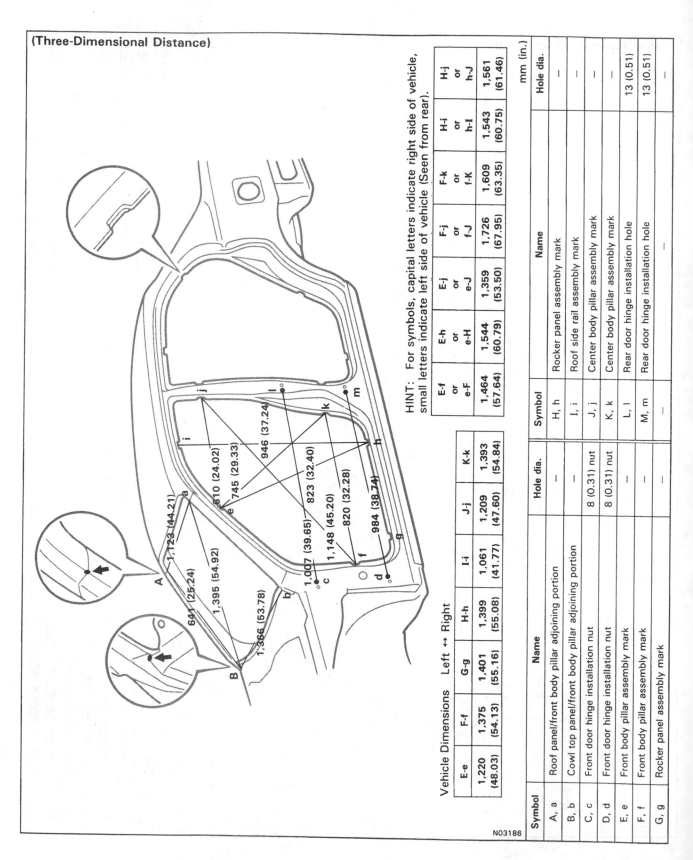

HINT: For symbols, capital letters indicate right side of vehicle, small letters indicate left side of vehicle (Seen from rear).

mm (in.)

Symbol	E-f or e-F	E-h or e-H	E-j or e-J	F-j or f-J	F-k or f-K	H-i or h-I	H-j or h-J	Name	Hole dia.
H, h	1,464 (57.64)	1,544 (60.79)	1,359 (53.50)	1,726 (67.95)	1,609 (63.35)	1,543 (60.75)	1,561 (61.46)	Rocker panel assembly mark	—
I, i								Roof side rail assembly mark	—
J, j								Center body pillar assembly mark	—
K, k								Center body pillar assembly mark	—
L, l								Rear door hinge installation hole	13 (0.51)
M, m								Rear door hinge installation hole	13 (0.51)
—								—	—

Vehicle Dimensions Left ↔ Right

Symbol	E-e	F-f	G-g	H-h	I-i	J-j	K-k	Name	Hole dia.
A, a	1,220 (48.03)	1,375 (54.13)	1,401 (55.16)	1,399 (55.08)	1,061 (41.77)	1,209 (47.60)	1,393 (54.84)	Roof panel/front body pillar adjoining portion	—
B, b								Cowl top panel/front body pillar adjoining portion	—
C, c								Front door hinge installation nut	8 (0.31) nut
D, d								Front door hinge installation nut	8 (0.31) nut
E, e								Front body pillar assembly mark	—
F, f								Front body pillar assembly mark	—
G, g								Rocker panel assembly mark	—

N03186

V00593

BODY OPENING AREAS (Side View: Rear)

(Three-Dimensional Distance)

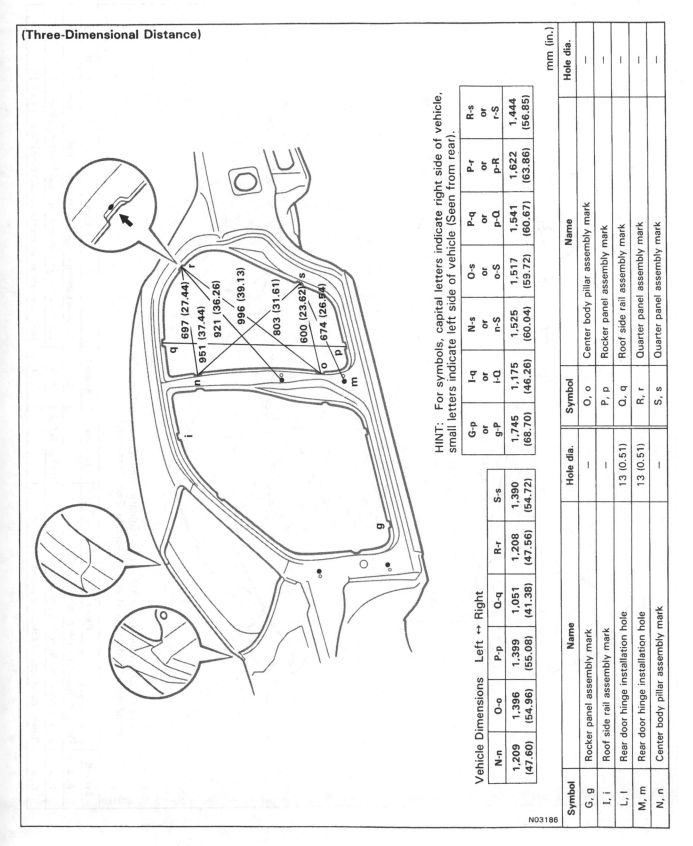

HINT: For symbols, capital letters indicate right side of vehicle, small letters indicate left side of vehicle (Seen from rear).

mm (in.)

Symbol		Name	Hole dia.
G-p or g-P	1,745 (68.70)		—
I-q or i-Q	1,175 (46.26)		—
N-s or n-S	1,525 (60.04)		—
O-s or o-S	1,517 (59.72)		—
P-q or p-Q	1,541 (60.67)		—
P-r or p-R	1,622 (63.86)		—
R-s or r-S	1,444 (56.85)		—

Symbol	Name	Hole dia.
O, o	Center body pillar assembly mark	—
P, p	Rocker panel assembly mark	—
Q, q	Roof side rail assembly mark	13 (0.51)
R, r	Quarter panel assembly mark	13 (0.51)
S, s	Quarter panel assembly mark	—

Vehicle Dimensions Left ↔ Right

	N-n	O-o	P-p	Q-q	R-r	S-s
	1,209 (47.60)	1,396 (54.96)	1,399 (55.08)	1,051 (41.38)	1,208 (47.56)	1,390 (54.72)

Symbol	Name	Hole dia.
G, g	Rocker panel assembly mark	—
I, i	Roof side rail assembly mark	—
L, l	Rear door hinge installation hole	13 (0.51)
M, m	Rear door hinge installation hole	13 (0.51)
N, n	Center body pillar assembly mark	—

N03186

V00594

BODY OPENING AREA (Rear View)

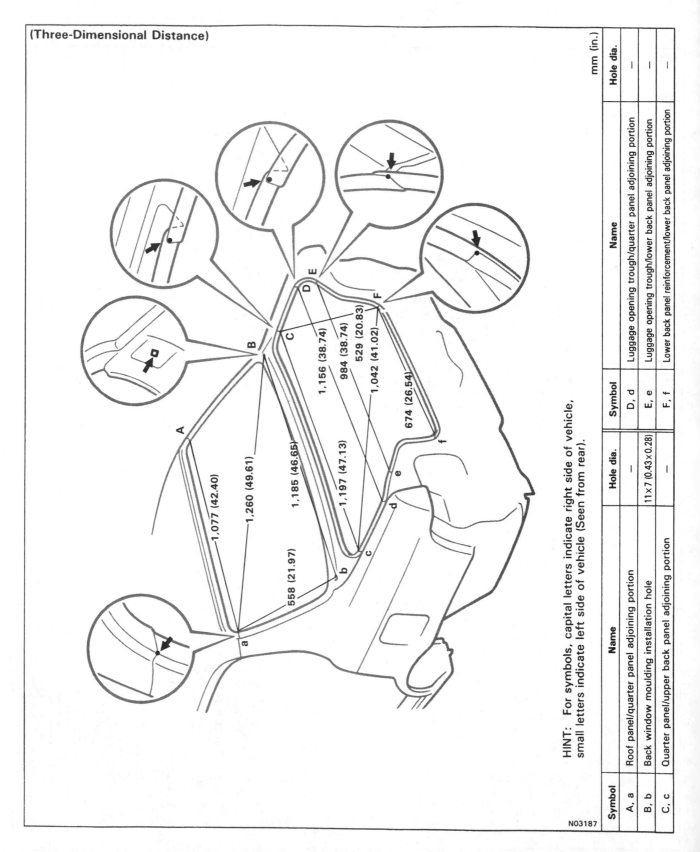

(Three-Dimensional Distance)

mm (in.)

HINT: For symbols, capital letters indicate right side of vehicle, small letters indicate left side of vehicle (Seen from rear).

Symbol	Name	Hole dia.
A, a	Roof panel/quarter panel adjoining portion	—
B, b	Back window moulding installation hole	11×7 (0.43×0.28)
C, c	Quarter panel/upper back panel adjoining portion	—

Symbol	Name	Hole dia.
D, d	Luggage opening trough/quarter panel adjoining portion	—
E, e	Luggage opening trough/lower back panel adjoining portion	—
F, f	Lower back panel reinforcement/lower back panel adjoining portion	—

N03187

V00595

UNDER BODY

(Three-Dimentional Distance)

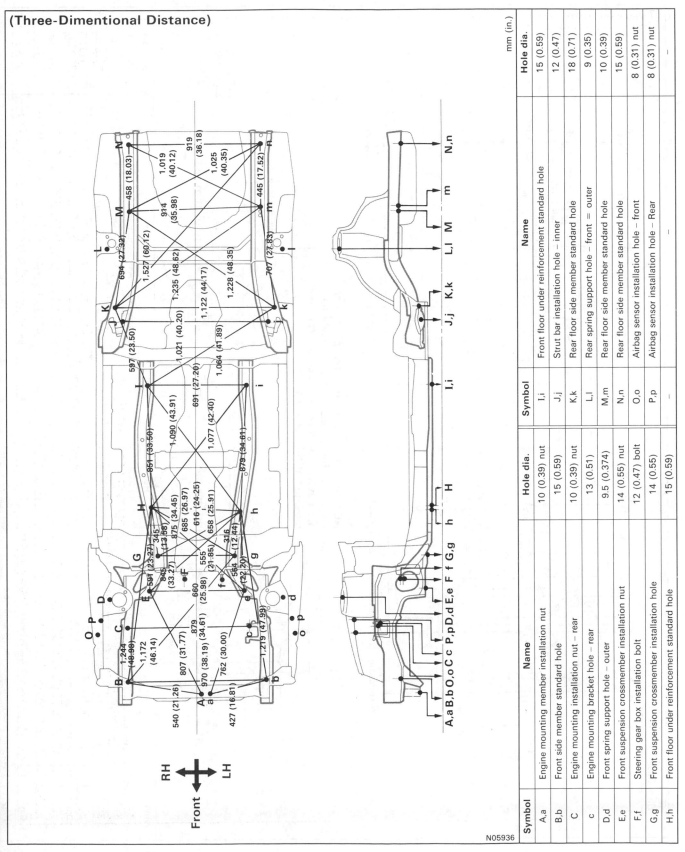

mm (in.)

Symbol	Name	Hole dia.
I,i	Front floor under reinforcement standard hole	15 (0.59)
J,j	Strut bar installation hole – inner	12 (0.47)
K,k	Rear floor side member standard hole	18 (0.71)
L,l	Rear spring support hole – front = outer	9 (0.35)
M,m	Rear floor side member standard hole	10 (0.39)
N,n	Rear floor side member standard hole	15 (0.59)
O,o	Airbag sensor installation hole – front	8 (0.31) nut
P,p	Airbag sensor installation hole – Rear	8 (0.31) nut
	–	–

Symbol	Name	Hole dia.
A,a	Engine mounting member installation nut	10 (0.39) nut
B,b	Front side member standard hole	15 (0.59)
C	Engine mounting installation nut – rear	10 (0.39) nut
c	Engine mounting bracket hole – rear	13 (0.51)
D,d	Front spring support hole – outer	9.5 (0.374)
E,e	Front suspension crossmember installation nut	14 (0.55) nut
F,f	Steering gear box installation bolt	12 (0.47) bolt
G,g	Front suspension crossmember installation hole	14 (0.55)
H,h	Front floor under reinforcement standard hole	15 (0.59)

N05936

V01593

UNDER BODY (Cont'd)

(Two- Dimentional Distance)

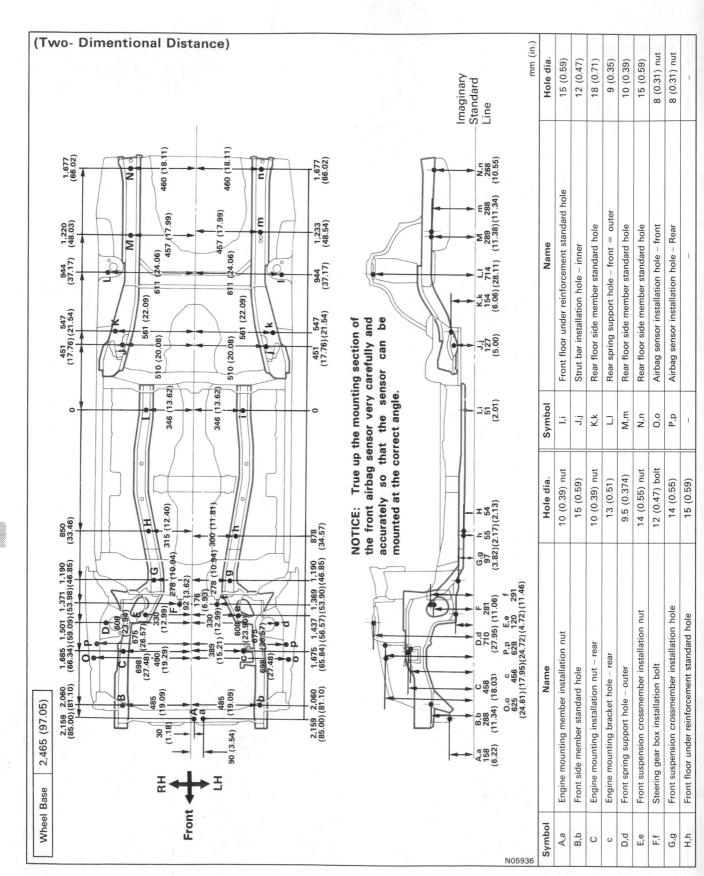

NOTICE: True up the mounting section of the front airbag sensor very carefully and accurately so that the sensor can be mounted at the correct angle.

mm (in.)

Symbol	Name	Hole dia.
A,a	Engine mounting member installation nut	10 (0.39) nut
B,b	Front side member standard hole	15 (0.59)
C	Engine mounting installation nut – rear	10 (0.39) nut
c	Engine mounting bracket hole – rear	13 (0.51)
D,d	Front spring support hole – outer	9.5 (0.374)
E,e	Front suspension crossmember installation nut	14 (0.55) nut
F,f	Steering gear box installation bolt	12 (0.47) bolt
G,g	Front suspension crossmember installation hole	14 (0.55)
H,h	Front floor under reinforcement standard hole	15 (0.59)
I,i	Front floor under reinforcement standard hole	15 (0.59)
J,j	Strut bar installation hole – inner	12 (0.47)
K,k	Rear floor side member standard hole	18 (0.71)
L,l	Rear spring support hole – front = outer	9 (0.35)
M,m	Rear floor side member standard hole	10 (0.39)
N,n	Rear floor side member standard hole	15 (0.59)
O,o	Airbag sensor installation hole – front	8 (0.31) nut
P,p	Airbag sensor installation hole – Rear	8 (0.31) nut
		–

Wheel Base	2,465 (97.05)

N05936

V01594

SERVICE SPECIFICATIONS
TORQUE SPECIFICATIONS

BO09F—04

Part tightend	N·m	kgf·cm	ft·lbf
HOOD	—	—	—
Hood hinge x Hood	14	145	10
Hood lock x Body	8.3	85	74 in.·lbf
FRONT DOOR	—	—	—
Door hinge x Body	28	290	21
Door hinge x Door panel	28	290	21
Door check x Body	33	340	25
Door lock x Door panel	5.4	55	48 in.·lbf
Window regulator x Door inside panel frame	5.4	55	48 in.·lbf
Window regulator x Door panel	5.4	55	48 in.·lbf
REAR DOOR	—	—	—
Door hinge x Body	28	290	21
Door hinge x Door panel	28	290	21
Door check x Body	33	340	25
Door lock x Door panel	5.4	55	48 in.·lbf
Window regulator x Door panel	5.4	55	48 in.·lbf
BACK DOOR	—	—	—
Back door hinge x Body	13	130	9
Back door hinge x Back door	13	130	9
Back door damper stay x Body	8.8	90	78 in.·lbf
Back door damper stay x Back door	8.8	90	78 in.·lbf
LUGGAGE COMPARTMENT	—	—	—
Luggage compartment door hinge x Body	5.4	55	48 in.·lbf
Luggage compartment door hinge x Luggage compartment door	8.3	85	74 in.·lbf
WIPER AND WASHER	—	—	—
Front Wiper	—	—	—
Wiper arm x Wiper link	20	204	15
Rear Wiper	—	—	—
Wiper arm x Wiper motor	5.4	55	48 in.·lbf
FRONT SEAT	—	—	—
Seat adjuster x Body	37	375	27
Seat track x Body	37	375	27
Seat adjuster x Seatback	37	375	27
Seat adjuster x Seat cushion frame	18	185	13
Seat track x Seat cushion frame	18	185	13

TORQUE SPECIFICATIONS (Cont'd)

Part tightend	N·m	kgf·cm	ft·lbf
REAR SEAT	—	—	—
Seatback x Body	7.8	80	69 in.·lbf
Seat side cushion x Body	7.8	80	69 in.·lbf
Seatback hinge x Seatback	19	195	14
Seatback hinge x Body	7.8	80	69 in.·lbf
Seat cushion hinge x Seat cushion	5.4	55	48 in.·lbf
Seat cushion hinge x Body	19	195	14
Seatback lock x Seatback	20	200	14
Seatback x Center armrest hinge	7.8	80	69 in.·lbf
SEAT BELT	—	—	—
Front Seat Belt	—	—	—
Shoulder anchor x Adjustable anchor	43	440	32
Outer belt anchor x Body	43	440	32
ELR x Body (Upper Side)	5.4	55	48 in.·lbf
ELR x Body (Lower Side)	43	440	32
Adjustable anchor x Body	43	440	32
Inner belt x Seat	43	440	32
Rear Seat Belt	—	—	—
Shoulder anchor x Body	43	440	32
Outer belt anchor x Body	43	440	32
ELR x Body	43	440	32
Center belt x Body	43	440	32

BO

BO

AIR CONDITIONING SYSTEM

AC

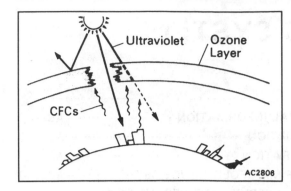

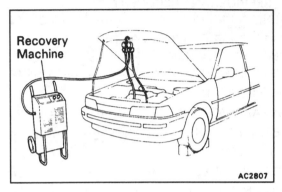

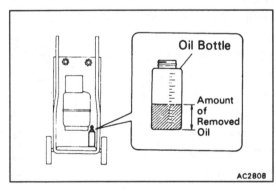

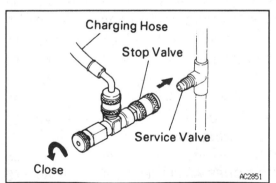

GENERAL INFORMATION
REFRIGERATION SYSTEM

ACOGV–01

Prevention of Refrigerant Release and Excessive Quantities

Refrigerant (CFCs) for automobile air conditioners is believed to cause harm by depleting the ozone layer which helps to protect us from the ultraviolet rays of the sun.

Therefore, it is necessary to prevent release of refrigerant to the atmosphere and to use the minimum amount when servicing the air conditioner.

1. **USE RECOVERY MACHINE TO RECOVER REFRIGERANT**

   When discharging refrigerant from the system as follows, use a recovery machine to recover the refrigerant.
   - Before replacing parts on the refrigerant line.
   - When moisture or air gets in the refrigerant line
   - When excess refrigerant is charged.

   NOTICE:
   - **When handling the recovery machine, always follow the directions given in the instruction manual.**
   - **After recovery, the amount of compressor oil removed must be measured and the same amount added to the system.**

2. **USE CHARGING HOSES WITH STOP VALVE WHEN INSTALLING MANIFOLD GAUGE SET**

   To prevent release of refrigerant, use charging hoses with a stop valve when installing the manifold gauge set to the service valves on the refrigerant line.

3. **TIGHTEN CONNECTION PARTS SECURELY**

   Follow the notices about tightening connecting parts in step 6 on page AC–4.

4. **PROPERLY EVACUATE AIR FROM REFRIGERANT SYSTEM**

   To prevent release and wasteful use of refrigerant, evacuate air with care from refrigeration system as follows:
   - Do not evacuate before recovering refrigerant in system.
   - Do not perform repeat evacuation of system.

AC

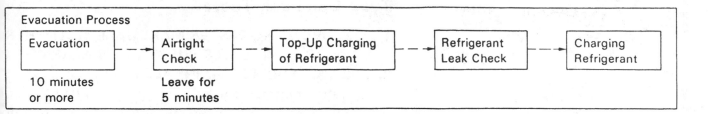

Evacuation Process

Evacuation		Airtight Check		Top-Up Charging of Refrigerant		Refrigerant Leak Check		Charging Refrigerant
10 minutes or more		Leave for 5 minutes						

V00117

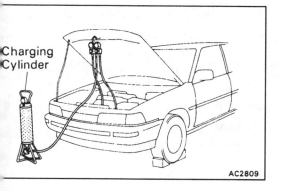

5. USE CHARGING CYLINDER TO CHARGE PROPER AMOUNT OF REFRIGERANT

To prevent excessive use of refrigerant due to overcharging, use a charging cylinder to charge the proper amount of refrigerant.

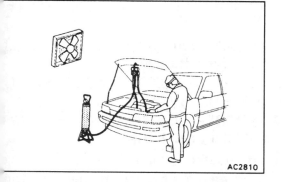

Handling Precautions for Refrigerant

1. DO NOT HANDLE REFRIGERANT IN AN ENCLOSED AREA OR NEAR AN OPEN FLAME

2. ALWAYS WEAR EYE PROTECTION

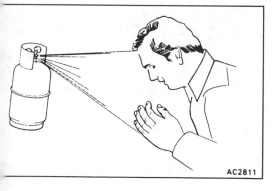

3. BE CAREFUL THAT LIQUID REFRIGERANT DOES NOT GET IN YOUR EYES OR ON YOUR SKIN

If liquid refrigerant gets in your eyes or on your skin:

(a) Wash the area with lots of cool water.

CAUTION: Do not rub your eyes or skin.

(b) Apply clean petroleum jelly to the skin.

(c) Go immediately to a physician or hospital for professional treatment.

CAUTION: Do not attempt to treat yourself.

Handling Precautions for Refrigerant Container

1. NEVER HEAT CONTAINER OR EXPOSE IT TO NAKED FLAME

2. BE CAREFUL NOT TO DROP CONTAINER AND NOT TO APPLY PHYSICAL SHOCKS TO IT

AC

AC

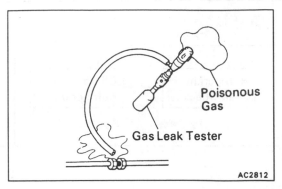

Handling Precautions for Gas—Cylinder Type Gas Leak Tester

1. **BEFORE USING TESTER MAKE SURE THAT THER[E] ARE NO FLAMMABLE SUBSTANCES NEARBY**
2. **BE CAREFUL NOT TO INHALE POISONOUS GAS**
   If refrigerant gas comes in contact with flame, a po[i]sonous gas is produced. During leak tests, do n[ot] inhale any gas.

Precautions When Replacing Parts in Refrigerant Line

1. **RECOVER REFRIGERANT IN SYSTEM BEFOR[E] REMOVING PARTS**
   Using a recovery machine, recover refrigerant i[n] system before removing the parts.
   NOTICE: Do not release refrigerant to atmosphere.

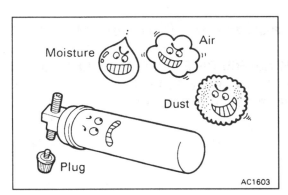

2. **INSERT PLUG IMMEDIATELY IN DISCONNECTE[D] PARTS**
   Insert a plug immediately in the disconnected parts t[o] prevent the entry of moisture and dust.
3. **DO NOT REMOVE PLUG FROM NEW PARTS UNTI[L] IMMEDIATELY BEFORE INSTALLATION**
4. **DO NOT USE BURNER FOR BENDING OR LENG[T] HENING OPERATIONS ON TUBE**
   If the tubes are heated with a burner, a layer [of] oxidation forms inside the tube, causing the same kin[d] of trouble as an accumulation of dust.
5. **DISCHARGE GAS IN NEW COMPRESSOR FRO[M] CHARGING VALVE BEFORE INSTALLING IT**
   If the gas in new compressor is not discharged firs[t], compressor oil will spray out with gas when the plu[g] is removed.

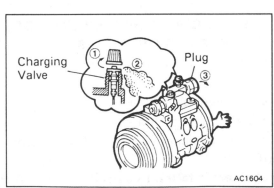

6. **TIGHTEN CONNECTING PARTS SECURELY**
   Securely tighten the connecting parts to prevent le[a]king of refrigerant gas.
   - Apply a few drops of compressor oil to O—rin[g] fittings for easy tightening and to prevent le[a]king of refrigerant gas.
   - Tighten the nuts using two wrenches to avo[id] twisting the tube.

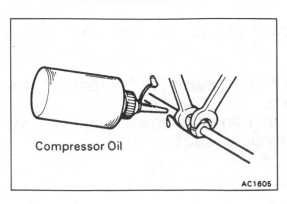

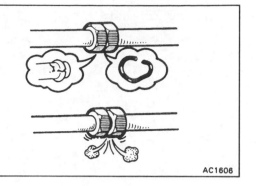

AC1606

- Tighten the O—ring fittings or the bolted type fittings to the specified torque.

Precautions When Charging Refrigerant

1. **DO NOT OPERATE COMPRESSOR WITHOUT ENOUGH REFRIGERANT IN REFRIGERANT CYCLE**
   If there is not enough refrigerant in the refrigerant cycle, oil lubrication will be insufficient and compressor burnout may occur, so take care to avoid this.

AC2813

2. **DO NOT OPEN HIGH PRESSURE VALVE OF MANIFOLD WITH COMPRESSOR OPERATING**
   If the high pressure valve is opened, refrigerant flows in the reverse direction and could cause the charging cylinder to rupture, so open and close the low pressure valve only.

3. **BE CAREFUL NOT TO OVERCHARGE WITH REFRIGERANT IN SYSTEM**
   If refrigerant is overcharged, it causes trouble such as insufficient cooling, poor fuel economy, engine overheating etc.

ACOGW—01

ELECTRICAL PARTS

Before removing and inspecting the electrical parts, set the ignition switch to the LOCK position and disconnect the negative (—) terminal cable from battery.

CAUTION: Work must not be started until after at least 30 seconds or longer from the time the negative (—) terminal cable is disconnected.

—MEMO—

AC

DESCRIPTION
PARTS LOCATION

AC0GX–01

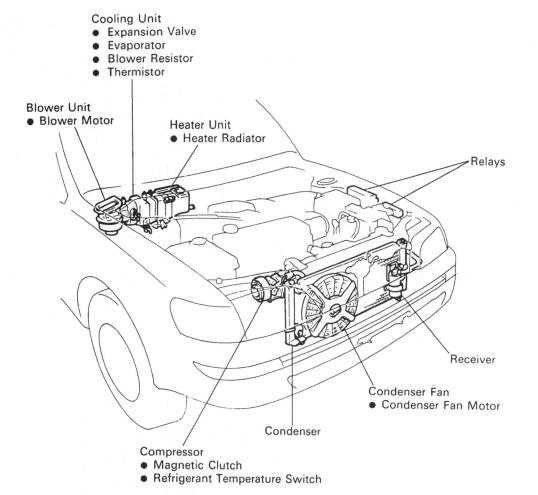

Cooling Unit
- Expansion Valve
- Evaporator
- Blower Resistor
- Thermistor

Blower Unit
- Blower Motor

Heater Unit
- Heater Radiator

Relays

Receiver

Condenser Fan
- Condenser Fan Motor

Condenser

Compressor
- Magnetic Clutch
- Refrigerant Temperature Switch

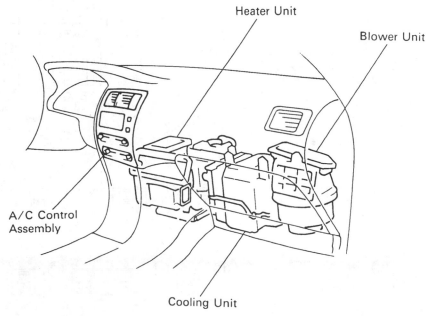

Heater Unit

Blower Unit

A/C Control Assembly

Cooling Unit

AC

N05842

ELECTRICAL WIRING DIAGRAM

ACOGY–01

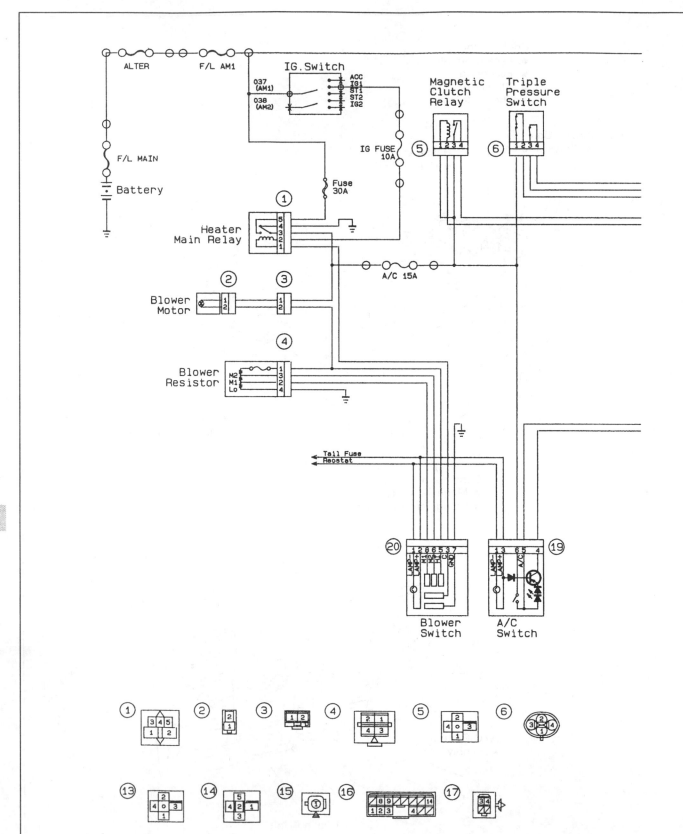

ELECTRICAL WIRING DIAGRAM(CONT'D)

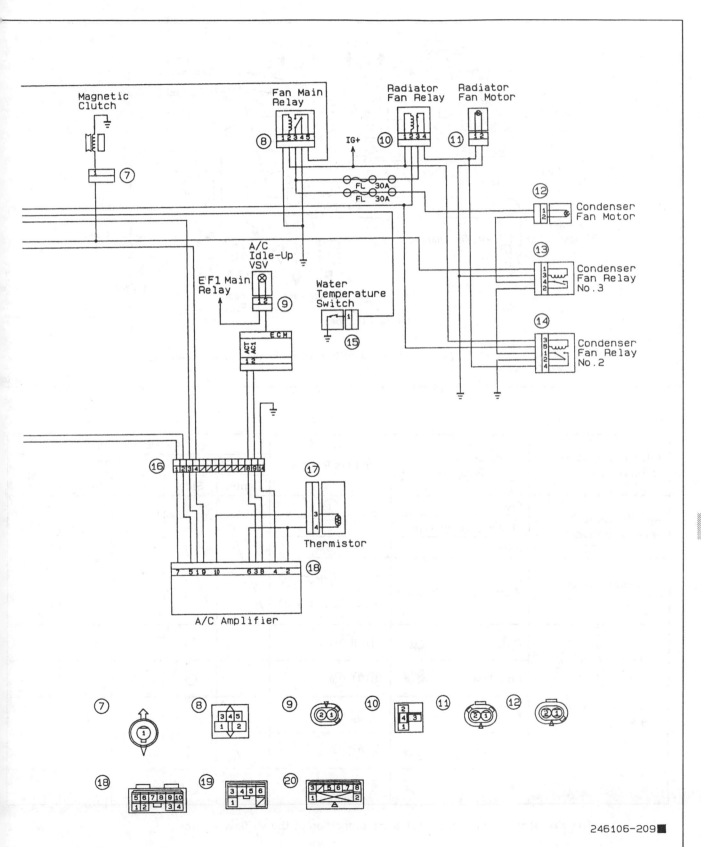

DAMPERS POSITION

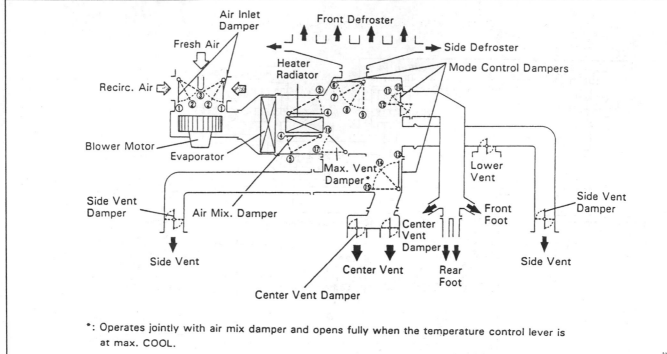

*: Operates jointly with air mix damper and opens fully when the temperature control lever is
at max. COOL.

A/C Control Lever and Switch	A/C Control Lever Position		Dampers Position	Air Flow Vents				
				FACE		FOOT		DEF
				Center	Side	Front	Rear	
Air Inlet Control Lever and Switch	Fresh		①					
	■ (Only Lever Type)		②					
	Recirc		③					
Temperature Control Lever	Warm ⟸⟹ Cool		⑰ ⟺ ⑯					
			⑤ ⟺ ④					
Mode Control Lever and Switch	Def.	〰	⑨ ⑩ ⑮		○			○
	Foot/Def.	〰	⑧ ⑪ ⑮		○	○	○	○
	Foot	〰	⑦ ⑫ ⑮		○	○	○	○
	Bi-Level	〰	⑥ ⑪ ⑭	○	○	○	○	
	Face	〰	⑥ ⑩ ⑬	○	○			

The size of the circle (○) indicates the proportion of the air flow volume.

AC

PREPARATION
SST(SPECIAL SERVICE TOOLS)

ACOHO—01

 07110—58011	Air Conditioner Service Tool Set	
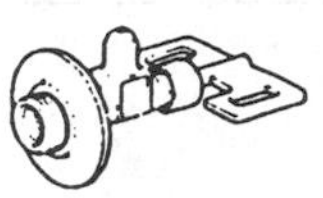 (07117—58010)	Refrigerant Drum Service Valve	
 (07117—78011)	Refrigerant Charging Gauge	
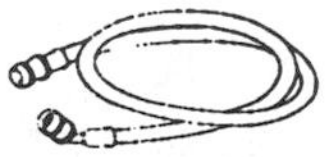 (07117—88013)	Refrigerant Charging Hose	Green color
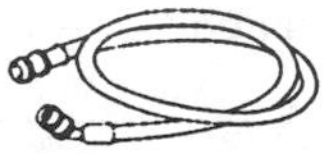 (07117—88022)	Refrigerant Charging Hose	Blue color
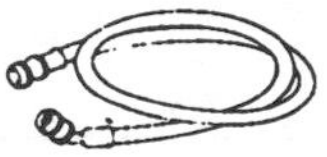 (07117—88040)	Refrigerant Charging Hose	Orange color
 (——————)	Stop Valve	
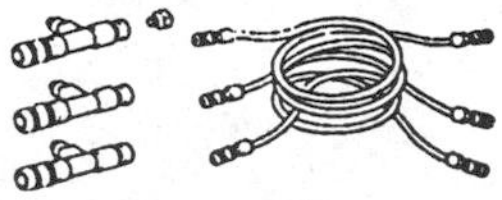 07110—58040	Charging Hose Kit With Stop Valve	The stop valve can be ordered only in this kit form.
 07110—61050	Wrench Set	
 07112—66040	Magnetic Clutch Remover	
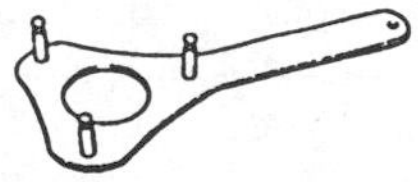 07112—76060	Magnetic Clutch Stopper	
 07114—84020	Snap Ring Pliers	
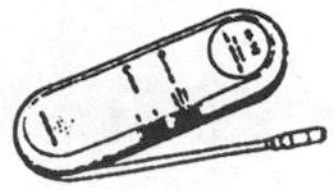 07116—38330	Gas Leak Detector Assembly	

AC

	07117–48050 Vacuum Pump Assembly	Rated voltage AC220V

RECOMMENDED TOOLS

	09082–00015 TOYOTA Electrical Tester	

LUBRICANT

Item	Capacity		Classification
	cm³	fl. oz	
Compressor oil			ND-OIL 6
When replacing receiver	20	0.7	
When replacing condenser	40 – 50	1.4 – 1.7	
When replacing evaporator	40 – 50	1.4 – 1.7	

AC

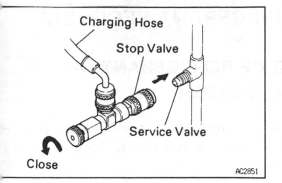

Charging Hose
Stop Valve
Service Valve
Close
AC2851

USE OF MANIFOLD GAUGE SET
MANIFOLD GAUGE SET INSTALLATION

ACOH4-01

HINT: To prevent releasing refrigerant, use charging hoses with a stop valve when installing the manifold gauge set to service valves on the refrigerant line.

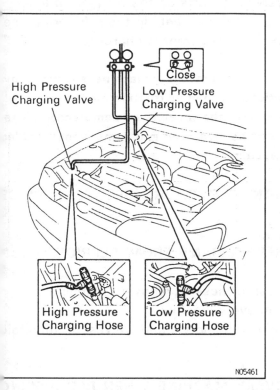

High Pressure
Charging Valve

Low Pressure
Charging Valve

Close

High Pressure
Charging Hose

Low Pressure
Charging Hose

N05461

1. **CONNECT CHARGING HOSES WITH A STOP VALVE TO MANIFOLD GAUGE SET**
   Tighten the nuts by hand.
   CAUTION:
   - Do not connect the wrong hoses to the high pressure and the low pressure sides.
   - To prevent loosening the nuts, do not apply compressor oil to seat of the connection.
2. **CLOSE HAND VALVES OF BOTH STOP VALVES**
3. **CLOSE BOTH HAND VALVES OF MANIFOLD GAUGE SET**
4. **REMOVE CAPS FROM SERVICE VALVES ON REFRIGERANT LINE**
5. **CONNECT STOP VALVES TO SERVICE VALVES**
   Tighten the nuts by hand.
   CAUTION:
   - Do not connect the wrong hoses to the high pressure and the low pressure sides.
   - To prevent loosening the nuts, do not apply compressor oil to seat of the connection.
6. **OPEN HAND VALVES OF BOTH STOP VALVES**

AC

MANIFOLD GAUGE SET REMOVAL

ACOH5-01

1. **CLOSE BOTH HAND VALVES OF MANIFOLD GAUGE SET**

2. **CLOSE HAND VALVES OF BOTH STOP VALVES**

3. **DISCONNECT STOP VALVES FROM SERVICE VALVES ON REFRIGERANT LINE**

4. **INSTALL CAPS TO SERVICE VALVES ON REFRIGERANT LINE**

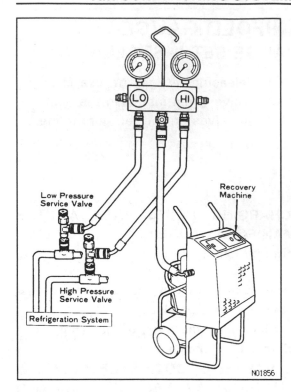

Low Pressure Service Valve

Recovery Machine

High Pressure Service Valve

Refrigeration System

N01856

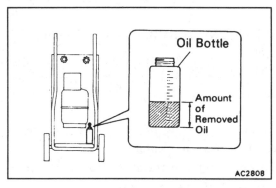

Oil Bottle

Amount of Removed Oil

AC2808

USE OF REFRIGERANT RECOVERY MACHINE

ACOH6-01

RECOVERING OF REFRIGERANT IN REFRIGERANT SYSTEM

When discharging refrigerant from the system as follows, use a recovery machine to recover the refrigerant.

- Before replacing parts on the refrigerant line.
- When moisture or air gets in the refrigerant line
- When excess refrigerant is charged.

NOTICE:

- **When handling the recovery machine, always follow the directions given in instruction manual.**
- **After recovery, the amount of compressor oil removed must be measured and same amount added into the system.**

1. **INSTALL MANIFOLD GAUGE SET TO SERVICE VALVES**

2. **RECOVER REFRIGERANT FROM REFRIGERATION SYSTEM**
(a) Connect the center hose to recovery machine.
(b) Operate the recovery machine.
(c) Open both high and low hand valves of manifold gauge set.

3. **STOP RECOVERY MACHINE WHEN RECOVERING HAS FINISHED**

4. **REMOVE MANIFOLD GAUGE SET FROM SERVICE VALVES**

AC

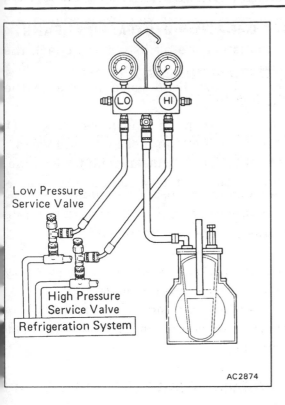

Low Pressure
Service Valve

High Pressure
Service Valve

Refrigeration System

AC2874

EVACUATING AIR IN REFRIGERATION SYSTEM AND CHARGING WITH REFRIGERANT

ACOH7—01

HINT: Before charging the system with refrigerant, be sure carry out a complete evacuation of the system.

1. **INSTALL MANIFOLD GAUGE SET TO SERVICE VALVES**
   (See page AC—13)

2. **EVACUATE AIR IN REFRIGERATION SYSTEM**

(a) Connect the center hose of the manifold gauge set to the vacuum pump.

(b) Open both the high and low hand valves and run the vacuum pump.
   HINT: When opening the low pressure valve in the manifold gauge causes the high pressure gauge to read into the vacuum range, there is no blockage in the system.

(c) After ten minutes or more, check that the low pressure gauge indicates 99.99 kPa (750 mmHg, 29.53 in. Hg) or more of vacuum.
   HINT: If the reading is not 99.99 kPa (750 mmHg, 29.53 in.Hg) or more of vacuum, close both the high and low hand valves of the manifold gauge set and stop vacuum pump. Then, check the system for leaks and repair as necessary.

(d) Close both the high and low hand valves and stop the vacuum pump.

(e) Leave the system in this condition for five minutes or longer and check that there is no change in the gauge indicator.

3. **INSTALL CHARGING CYLINDER**
   NOTICE: When handling the charging cylinder, always follow the directions given in the instruction manual.

(a) Charge the proper amount of refrigerant in charging cylinder.

(b) Connect the center hose to charging cylinder.
   NOTICE: Do not open both high and low hand valves of manifold gauge set.

(c) Press on the schrader valve on the side of manifold gauge and expel the air inside of the center hose.

AC

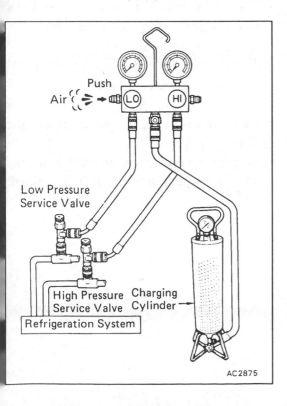

Push

Air

Low Pressure
Service Valve

High Pressure
Service Valve

Charging
Cylinder

Refrigeration System

AC2875

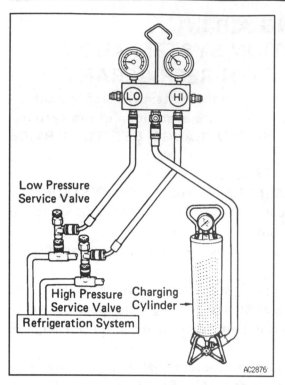

4. INSPECT REFRIGERATION SYSTEM FOR LEAKS

HINT: After evacuating the air in system, check the system for leakage.

(a) Open the high pressure hand valve to charge the system with refrigerant.

(b) When the low pressure gauge indicates 98 kPa (1 kgf/cm², 14psi), close the high pressure hand valve.

(c) Using a gas leak tester, check the system for leakage. If leak is found, repair the faulty component or connection.

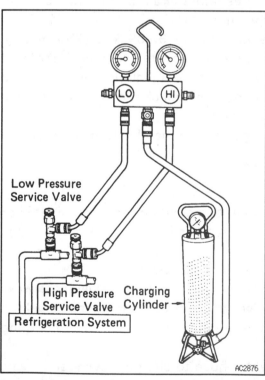

5. CHARGE EMPTY REFRIGERATION SYSTEM WITH REFRIGERANT (LIQUID)

HINT: This step is used to charge an empty system through the high pressure side with refrigerant in a liquid state.

NOTICE:

- **Never run the engine when charging the system through the high pressure side with refrigerant in a liquid state.**

- **Do not open the low pressure hand valve when the system is being charged with liquid refrigerant.**

(a) Open the high pressure hand valve fully.

(b) Charge the system with specified amount of refrigerant, then close the high pressure hand valve.

HINT:

- A fully charged system is indicated by the sight glass being free of any bubbles.

- If the low pressure gauge does not show a reading the system is clogged and must be repaired.

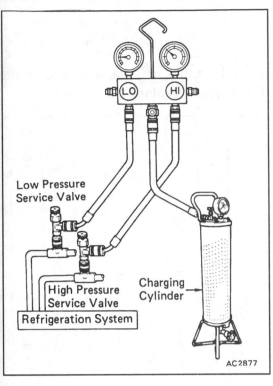

Low Pressure
Service Valve

High Pressure
Service Valve

Charging
Cylinder

Refrigeration System

AC2877

6. CHARGE PARTIALLY REFRIGERATION SYSTEM WITH REFRIGERANT (VAPOR)

HINT: This step is used to charge the system through the low pressure side with refrigerant in a vapor state.

NOTICE: Do not open the high pressure hand valve when running the engine.

(a) Run the engine at idling speed and operate the air conditioner.

(b) Open the low pressure hand valve.

NOTICE: Adjust the hand valve so that the low pressure gauge does not indicate over limited pressure of charging cylinder.

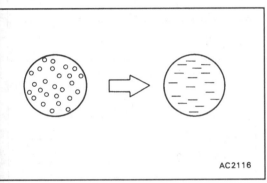

AC2116

(c) Close the low pressure hand valve when the sight glass is free of any bubbles and stop the engine.

NOTICE: Be careful not to overcharge the system with refrigerant.

7. REMOVE MANIFOLD GAUGE SET FROM SERVICE VALVES

(See page AC—13)

AC

TROUBLESHOOTING
TROUBLESHOOTING

ACOH8—01

You will find the troubles easier using the table well shown. In this table, each number shows the priority of causes in troubles. Check each part in order. If necessary, replace these parts.

Trouble \ Part Name	Inspect volume of refrigerant	Inspect drive belt tension	Inspect engine coolant volume	Inspect A/C control lever adjustment	Inspect outlet air control	Heater main relay	Blower speed control switch	Blower resistor	Blower motor	Inspect cooling system for refrigerant	Condenser fan fuse	Radiator fan main relay	Condenser fan relay No. 2	Condenser fan relay No. 3	Condensor fan motor
See Page	AC-23	AC-24	—	AC-58		AC-54	AC-60	AC-52	AC-48		—	—	AC-53	AC-54	AC-47
No blower operation						1	4	3	2						
No air temperature control			1	2											
No compressor operation	1					7	9								
Compressor operates intermittently	1									2					
No condenser fan operation											1	2	3	4	6
No cool air comes out	1	2													
Cool air comes out intermittently	1	2													
Cool air comes out only at high engine rpm	1	2													
Insufficient cooling	1	2								3					
No engine idle up when A/C switch on															
No warm air comes out			1	2											

V00626

Pressure switch	Water temperature switch	Inspect refrigerant lines	Compressor	Magnetic clutch	Condenser	Receiver	Evaporator	Expansion valve	Inspect refrigeration control	A/C fuse	A/C switch	Magnetic clutch relay	Pressure switch	Thermistor	A/C amplifier	Wiring and wiring connections	Vacuum switching valve (VSV)	Heater radiator
AC-56	—	—	AC-34	AC-34	AC-43	AC-42	AC-46	AC-49		—	AC-60	AC-53	AC-56	AC-55	AC-62	—	AC-50	AC-46
			5	4						2	8	3	6	11	10	12		
												3	5	4	6			
7	8											5			9			
			4	3				5										
							5	4					6		3	7		
		3																
		5											6	4				
															2	3	1	
																		3

V00627

AC

REFRIGERANT SYSTEM INSPECTION WITH MANIFOLD GAUGE SET

ACOH9-01

This is a method in which the trouble is located by using a manifold gauge set. (See "MANIFOLD GAUGE SET INSTALLATION" on page AC–13) Read the manifold gauge pressure when the following conditions are established:

(a) Temperature at the air inlet with the switch set at RECIRC is 30 – 35°C (86 – 95°F)
(b) Engine running at 2,000 rpm
(c) Blower fan speed control switch set at high speed
(d) Temperature control switch set at max. cool side

HINT: It should be noted that the gauge indications may vary slightly due to ambient temperature conditions.

NOTICE:

• **Always recover refrigerant before removing the parts in the refrigerant line and evacuating air.**

• **Evacuate air and charge proper amount of purified refrigerant after installing the parts in the refrigerant line.**

No.	Gauge reading kPa (kgf/cm², psi)	Condition	Probable cause	Remedy
1	LO: 147 – 196 (1.5 – 2.0, 21 – 28) HI: 1,422 – 1,471 (14.5 – 15.0, 206 – 213) AC0067	Normal cooling	Normally functioning system	
2	During operation, pressure at low pressure side sometimes becomes a vacuum and sometimes normal AC0068	Periodically cools and then fails to cool	Moisture present in refrigeration system	(1) Replace receiver (2) Remove moisture in system through repeatedly evacuating air

V00110

NOTICE:
- Always recover refrigerant before removing the parts in the refrigerant line and evacuating air.
- Evacuate air and charge proper amount of purified refrigerant after installing the parts in the refrigerant line.

No	Gauge reading kPa (kgf/cm², psi)	Condition	Probable cause	Remedy
3	Pressure low at both low and high pressure sides AC0069	• Insufficient cooling • Bubbles seen in sight glass	Insufficient refrigerant	(1) Check for gas leakage with gas leak tester and repair if necessary (2) Add refrigerant until bubbles disappear
		• Insufficient cooling • Frost on tubes from receiver to unit	Refrigerant flow obstructed by dirt in receiver	Replace receiver
4	Pressure too high at both low and high pressure sides	Insufficient cooling	Insufficient cooling of condenser	(1) Clean condenser (2) Check fan motor operation
5			Refrigerant overcharged	(1) Check amount of refrigerant If refrigerant is overcharged (2) Recover refrigerant (3) Evacuate air and charge proper amount of purified refrigerant
6			Air present in system	(1) Replace receiver (2) Check compressor oil to see if dirty (3) Remove air in system through repeatedly evacuating air
7	AC0070	• Insufficient cooling • Frost or Large amount of dew on piping at low pressure side	Expansion valve improperly mounted, heat sensing tube defective (Opens too wide)	(1) Check heat sensing tube installation condition If (1) is normal (2) Check expansion valve and replace if defective

V00109

AC

HINT at 6:
These gauge indications are for when the refrigeration system has been opened and the refrigerant charged without evacuating air.

NOTICE:
- Always recover refrigerant before removing the parts in the refrigerant line and evacuating air.
- Evacuate air and charge amount of purified refrigerant after installing the parts in the refrigerant line.

No	Gauge reading kPa (kgf/cm², psi)	Condition	Probable cause	Remedy
8	Vacuum indicated at low pressure side, very low pressure indicated at high pressure AC0156	• Does not cool (Cools from time to time in some cases) • Front or dew seen on piping before and after receiver or expansion valve	Refrigerant does not circulate	(1) Check heat sensing tube for gas leakage and replace expansion valve if defective If (1) is normal (2) Clean out dirt in expansion valve by blowing with air If not able to remove dirt, replace expansion valve (2) Replace receiver
9	Pressure too high at low pressure side, pressure too low at high pressure side AC0157	Does not cool	Insufficient compression	Repair or replace compressor

AC

V00103

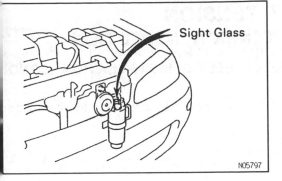

Sight Glass

N05797

REFRIGERANT VOLUME
REFRIGERANT VOLUME INSPECTION

ACOHA–02

1. **SET TEMPERATURE CONTROL AT MAX. COOL**
2. **SET BLOWER SWITCH AT "HI"**
3. **SET AIR INLET CONTROL AT "RECIRC"**
4. **A/C SWITCH ON**
5. **FULLY OPEN DOORS**
6. **RUN ENGINE AT APPROX. 1,500 RPM**
7. **INSPECT AMOUNT OF REFRIGERANT**
   Observe the sight glass on the liquid tube.

Item	Symptom	Amount of refrigerant	Remedy
1	Bubbles present in sight glass	Insufficient*	(1) Check for gas lakage with gas leak tester and repair if necessary (2) Add refrigerant until bubbles disapear
2	No bubbles present in sight glass	None, sufficient or too much	Refer to items 3 and 4
3	No temperature difference between compressor inlet and outlet	Empty or nearly empty	(1) Check for gas leakage with gas leaktester and repair if necessary (2) Add refrigerant until bubbles disappear
4	Temperature between compressor inlet and outlet is noticeably different	Correct or too much	Refer to items 5 and 6
5	Immediately after air conditioner is turned off, refrigerant in sight glass stays clear	Too much	(1) Recover refrigrant (2) Evacuate air and charge proper amounto of purified refrigerant
6	When air conditioner is turned off, refrigerant foams and then stay clear	Correct	–

* Bubbles in the sight glass with ambient temperatures higher can be considered normal if cooling is sufficient.

REFRIGERANT CHARGE VOLUME

ACOHB–01

Specified amount:
   750 ± 50 g (26.45 ± 1.76 oz.)

AC

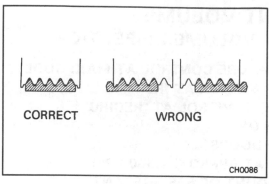

CORRECT   WRONG

CH0086

DRIVE BELT TENSION
DRIVE BELT TENSION INSPECTION

ACOHC—01

1. **INSPECT DRIVE BELT'S INSTALLATION CONDI-TION**

   Check that the drive belt fits properly in the ribbed grooves.

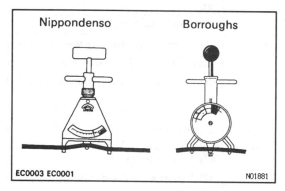

Crank Shaft Pulley   Idle Pulley

7A-FE

Compressor

4A-FE

N05707

2. **INSPECT DRIVE BELT TENSION**

   Using SST, check the drive belt tension.
   SST 09216—00020 and 09216—00030
   New belt   160±20 lbf
   Used belt   100±20 lbf
   HINT:
   - "New belt" refers to a belt which has been used less than 5 minutes on a running engine.
   - "Used belt" refers to a belt which has been on a running engine for 5 minutes or more.
   - After installing the drive belt, check that it fits properly in the ribbed grooves.

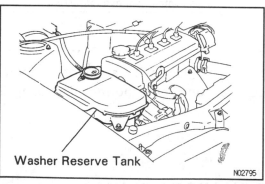

Nippondenso   Borroughs

EC0003 EC0001   N01881

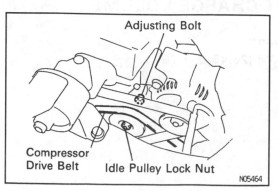

Washer Reserve Tank

N02795

DRIVE BELT REMOVAL

ACOHD—01

1. **REMOVE WASHER RESERVE TANK**
2. **LOOSEN ALTERNATOR AND REMOVE ALTERNATOR DRIVE BELT**

Adjusting Bolt

Compressor Drive Belt   Idle Pulley Lock Nut

N05464

3. **LOOSEN IDLE PULLEY LOCK NUT**
4. **LOOSEN AND REMOVE COMPRESSOR DRIVE BELT**

ACOHE—01

DRIVE BELT INSTALLATION

1. **INSTALL COMPRESSOR DRIVE BELT AND ADJUST ITS TENSION WITH ADJUSTING BOLT**
   Tension: See DRIVE BELT TENSION INSPECTION on page AC—24
2. **TIGHTEN IDLE PULLEY LOCK NUT**
   Torque: 39 N·m (400 kgf·cm, 29 ft·lbf)
3. **INSTALL ALTERNATOR DRIVE BELT AND ADJUST ITS TENSION**
4. **INSTALL WASHER RESERVE TANK**

IDLE—UP SPEED
IDLE UP SPEED INSPECTION

ACOJZ—01

1. **WARM UP ENGINE**
2. **SET VEHICLE IN FOLLOWING CONDITION**
   - Blower switch high position
   - A/C switch on
   - Magnetic clutch on
3. **INSPECT IDLE UP SPEED**
   Standard: 900 rpm

AC

REFRIGERANT LINES
TIGHTENING TORQUE OF REFRIGERATION LINES

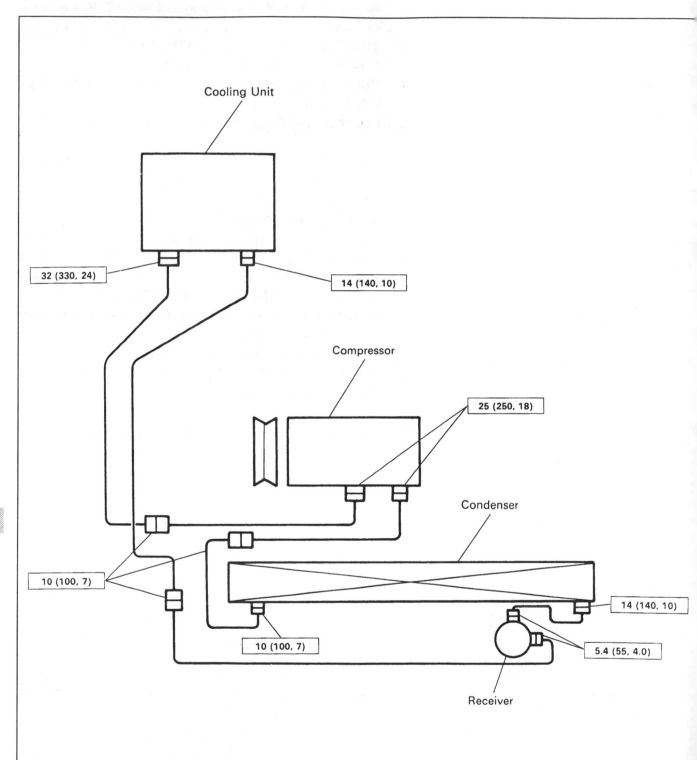

N·m (kgf·cm, ft·lbf) : Specified torque

ON−VEHICLE INSPECTION

ACOHH−01

1. **INSPECTION HOSE AND TUBE CONNECTIONS FOR LOOSENESS**
2. **INSPECT HOSES AND TUBES FOR LEAKAGE**
   Using a gas leak tester, check for leakage of refrigerant.

REFRIGERANT LINES REPLACEMENT

ACOHJ−01

1. **RECOVER REFRIGERANT IN REFRIGERATION SYSTEM**
2. **REPLACE FAULTY TUBE OR HOSE**
   HINT: Cap the open fittings immediately to keep moisture or dirt out of the system.
3. **TORQUE CONNECTIONS TO SPECIFIED TORQUE**
   NOTICE: Connections should not be torqued tighter than the specified torque.
4. **EVACUATE AIR IN REFRIGERATION SYSTEM AND CHARGE WITH REFRIGERANT**
   Specified amount:750 ± 50 g (26.45 ± 1.76 oz.)
5. **INSPECT FOR LEAKAGE OF REFRIGERANT**
   Using a gas leak tester, check for leakage of refrigerant.
6. **INSPECT AIR CONDITIONER OPERATION**

AC

COOLING UNIT
COOLING UNIT REMOVAL

ACOHK-0

1. **DISCONNECT NEGATIVE CABLE FROM BATTERY**
2. **RECOVER REFRIGERANT FROM REFRIGERATION SYSTEM**

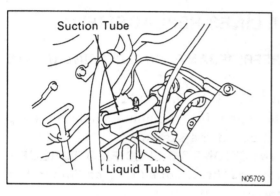

3. **DISCONNECT SUCTION TUBE AND LIQUID TUBE FROM COOLING UNIT FITTING**
   HINT: Cap the open fittings immediately to keep moisture out of the system.
4. **REMOVE FRONT DOOR SCUFF PLATE AND GLOVE BOX ASSEMBLY**
5. **DISCONNECT TWO CONNECTORS**
6. **REMOVE COOLING UNIT AND A/C AMPLIFIER**
   Remove three nuts and four tapping screws.

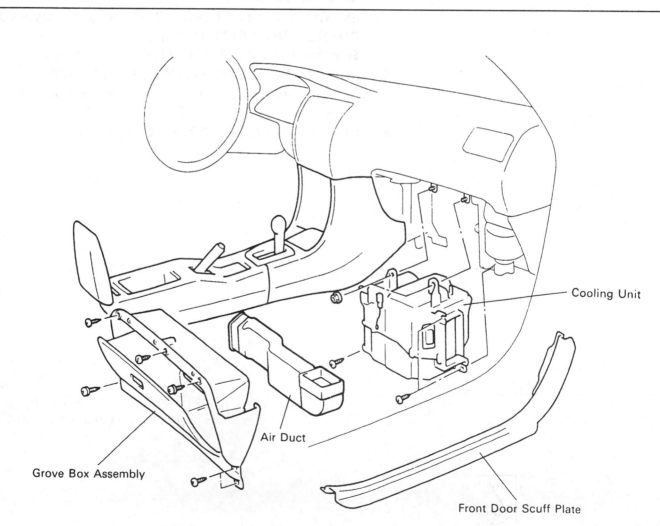

COOLING UNIT DISASSEMBLY

ACOHL—01

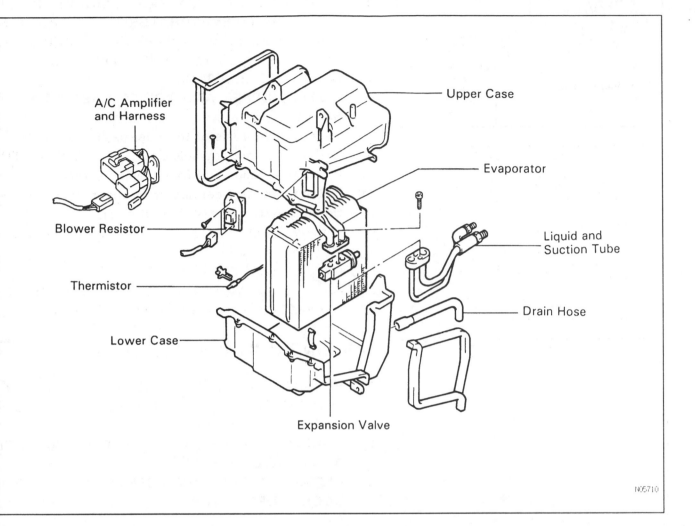

A/C Amplifier
and Harness

Upper Case

Evaporator

Blower Resistor

Liquid and
Suction Tube

Thermistor

Lower Case

Drain Hose

Expansion Valve

N05710

AC

1. REMOVE UPPER AND LOWER CASE
(a) Disconnect A/C harness from thermistor.
(b) Remove thermistor connector from upper case.
(c) Remove three clips and four tapping screws.
(d) Remove upper and lower case.
(e) Remove blower resistor from upper case.

2. REMOVE THERMISTOR FROM EVAPORATOR
3. REMOVE EXPANSION VALVE, LIQUID AND SUCTION TUBE
Remove two bolts from evaporator.

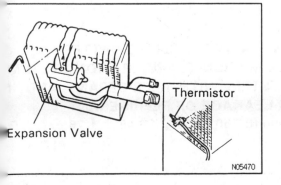

Thermistor

Expansion Valve

N05470

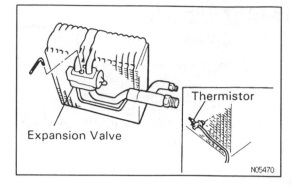

Expansion Valve

Thermistor

N05470

COOLING UNIT ASSEMBLY

1. **CONNECT EXPANSION VALVE, LIQUID AND SUCTION TUBE TO EVAPORATOR**
   Tighten the bolts.
   Torque: 5.4 N·m (55 kgf·cm, 48 in.·lbf)
2. **INSTALL THERMISTOR**
3. **INSTALL UPPER AND LOWER CASE TO EVAPORATOR**
   (a) Install blower resistor to upper case.
   (b) Install upper and lower case.
   (c) Install three clips and four tapping screws.
   (d) Install thermistor connector to upper case.
   (e) Connect A/C harness to thermistor.

COOLING UNIT INSTALLATION

1. **INSTALL COOLING UNIT AND A/C AMPLIFIER**
   Install cooling unit and A/C amplifier with three nut and four tapping screws.
2. **CONNECT TWO CONNECTORS TO A/C AMPLIFIE AND BLOWER RESISTOR**
3. **INSTALL GLOVE BOX ASSEMBLY AND FRON DOOR SCUFF PLATE**

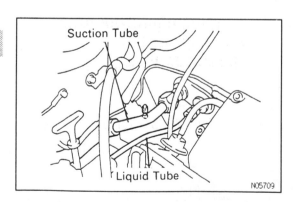

Suction Tube

Liquid Tube

N05709

4. **CONNECT LIQUID TUBE TO COOLING UNIT INLE FITTING**
   Tighten the nut.
   Torque: 14 N·m (140 kgf·cm, 10 ft·lbf)
5. **CONNECT SUCTION TUBE TO COOLING UNI OUTLET FITTING**
   Tighten the nut.
   Torque: 32 N·m (330 kgf·cm, 24 ft·lbf)
6. **IF EVAPORATOR WAS REPLACED, ADD COM PRESSOR OIL TO COMPRESSOR**
   Add 40−50 cc (1.4−1.7 fl.oz.)
   Compressor oil: ND−OIL 6
7. **CONNECT NEGATIVE CABLE TO BATTERY**
8. **EVACUATE AIR FROM REFRIGERATION SYSTEM**
9. **CHARGE SYSTEM WITH REFRIGERANT AND I SPECT FOR LEAKAGE OF REFRIGERANT**
   Specified amount: 750 ± 50 g (26.45 ± 1.76 oz.)

AC

HEATER UNIT
HEATER UNIT REMOVAL

ACOHP-01

1. **REMOVE COOLING UNIT**
   (See page AC—28)
2. **DRAIN ENGINE COOLANT FROM RADIATOR**
   HINT: It is not necessary to drain out all the coolant.

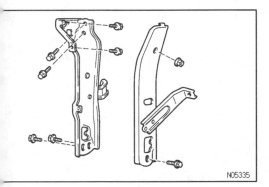

3. **DISCONNECT WATER HOSES FROM HEATER RA-DIATOR PIPES**
(a) Grip the claws of the hose clip with pliers and slide the clip along the hose to a place where it does not clamp the hose to the pipe.
(b) Disconnect the water hoses.
4. **REMOVE PIPE GROMMETS**

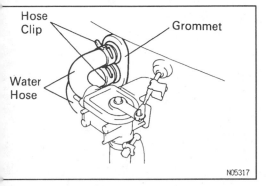

5. **REMOVE INSTRUMENT PANEL**
   (See page BO—62)
6. **REMOVE INSTRUMENT PANEL REINFORCEMENT NO.1 BRACE**
   Remove the six bolts and the No.1 brace.
7. **REMOVE INSTRUMENT PANEL REINFORCEMENT NO.2 BRACE**
   Remove the bolt, the nut and the No.2 brace.

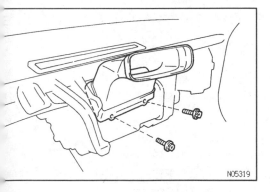

8. **REMOVE DUCT HEATER TO REGISTER NO.3**
   Remove the two screws and the duct.
9. **REMOVE FRONT DEFROSTER NOZZLE**

AC

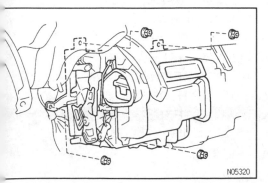

10. **REMOVE HEATER UNIT**
    Remove the four nuts and the heater unit.

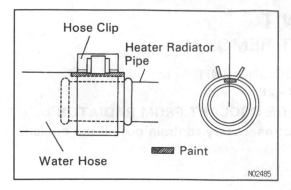

Hose Clip

Heater Radiator Pipe

Water Hose

▨ Paint

N02485

HEATER UNIT INSTALLATION

Install by following the removal procedure in rever‌s‌
order.
HINT:
● Push the water hose onto the heater radiator pi‌p‌
as far as the ridge on the pipe.
● Install the hose clip in a position as shown to t‌h‌
left.

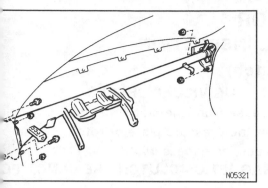

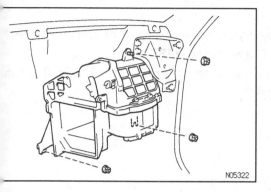

BLOWER UNIT
BLOWER UNIT REMOVAL

ACOHQ-01

1. **REMOVE INSTRUMENT PANEL**
(See page BO−62)

2. **REMOVE INSTRUMENT PANEL REINFORCEMENT**
Remove the four nuts, two screws and the instrument panel reinforcement.

3. **REMOVE COOLING UNIT**
(See page AC−28)

4. **REMOVE BLOWER UNIT**
(a) Disconnect the connector from the blower motor.
(b) Disconnect the air inlet damper control cable from the blower unit.
(c) Remove the three nuts and the blower unit.

BLOWER UNIT INSTALLATION

ACOHR-01

1. **INSTALL BLOWER UNIT**
(a) Install the blower unit with the three nuts.
(b) Connect the air inlet damper control cable to the blower unit.
HINT: For installing the control cable, refer to "A/C CONTROL CABLES ADJUSTMENT" on page AC−58.
(c) Connect the connector to the blower motor.

2. **INSTALL COOLING UNIT**
(See page AC−28)

3. **INSTALL INSTRUMENT PANEL REINFORCEMENT**
Install the four nuts, two screws and the instrument panel reinforcement.

4. **INSTALL INSTRUMENT PANEL**
(See page BO−62)

AC

COMPRESSOR

ON—VEHICLE INSPECTION

(Magnetic Clutch)

1. MAKE FOLLOWING VISUAL CHECKS

(a) Leakage of grease from the clutch bearing.

(b) Signs of oil on the pressure plate or rotor.

Repair or replace, as necessary.

2. INSPECT MAGNETIC CLUTCH BEARING FC NOISE

(a) Start engine.

(b) Check for abnormal noise from near the compress when the A/C switch is OFF.

If abnormal noise is being emitted, replace the ma netic clutch.

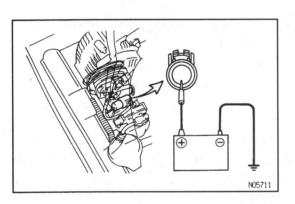

3. INSPECT MAGNETIC CLUTCH

(a) Disconnect the connector from the magnetic clutc

(b) Connect the positive (+) lead from the battery to t terminal on the magnetic clutch connector and t negative (−) lead to the body ground.

(c) Check that the magnetic clutch is energized.

If operation is not as specified, replace the magne clutch.

(Compressor)

1. INSTALL MANIFOLD GAUGE SET

(See page AC—13)

2. START ENGINE

3. INSPECT COMPRESSOR FOR METALLIC SOUND

Check that there is a metallic sound from the co pressor when the A/C switch is turn on.

If metallic sound is heard, replace the compress assembly.

4. INSPECT PRESSURE OF REFRIGERATION SYSTE

See "REFRIGERANT SYSTEM INSPECTION WI MANIFOLD GAUGE SET" on page AC—20.

5. STOP ENGINE

6. INSPECT VISUALLY FOR LEAKAGE OF REFRIGE ANT FROM SAFETY SEAL

If there is any leakage, replace the compressor sembly.

COMPRESSOR REMOVAL

ACOHT–01

1. **RUN ENGINE AT IDLE SPEED WITH A/C ON FOR TEN MINUTES**
2. **STOP ENGINE**
3. **DISCONNECT NEGATIVE CABLE FROM BATTERY**
4. **RECOVER REFRIGERANT FROM REFRIGERATION SYSTEM**

5. **REMOVE WASHER RESERVE TANK**

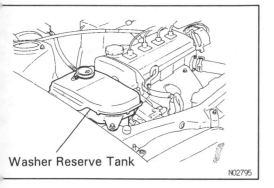

Washer Reserve Tank

N02795

6. **LOOSEN IDLE PULLEY LOCK NUT AND COMPRESSOR DRIVE BELT**

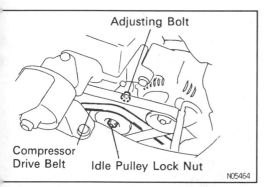

Adjusting Bolt

Compressor Drive Belt   Idle Pulley Lock Nut

N05464

7. **DISCONNECT COMPRESSOR HARNESS FROM COMPRESSOR**
8. **DISCONNECT DISCHARGE TUBE FROM CONDENSER**
   HINT: Cap the open fittings immediately to keep the moisture and dust out of the system.
9. **DISCONNECT SUCTION HOSE FROM SUCTION TUBE**
   HINT: Cap the open fittings immediately to keep the moisture and dust out of the system.

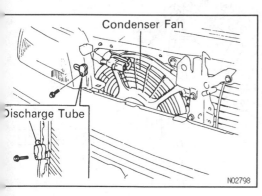

Condenser Fan

Discharge Tube

N02798

AC

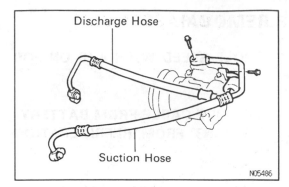

Discharge Hose

Suction Hose

N05486

10. REMOVE TWO HOSES FROM COMPRESSOR

11. REMOVE COMPRESSOR

Remove compressor mounting bolts and compresso

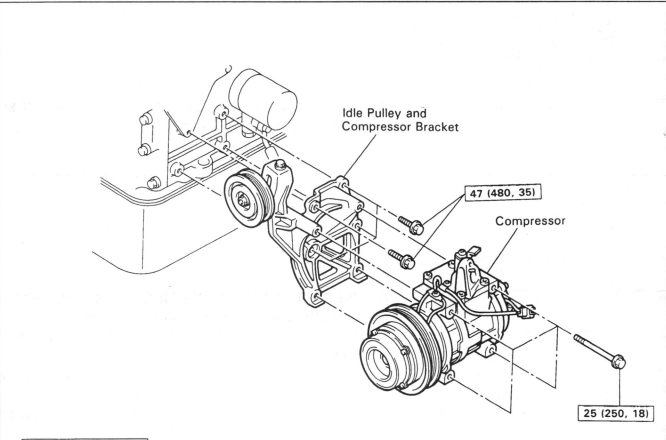

Idle Pulley and
Compressor Bracket

47 (480, 35)

Compressor

25 (250, 18)

N·m (kgf·cm, ft·lbf) : Specified torque

N04446

Z04

MAGNETIC CLUTCH DISASSEMBLY

AC00T-03

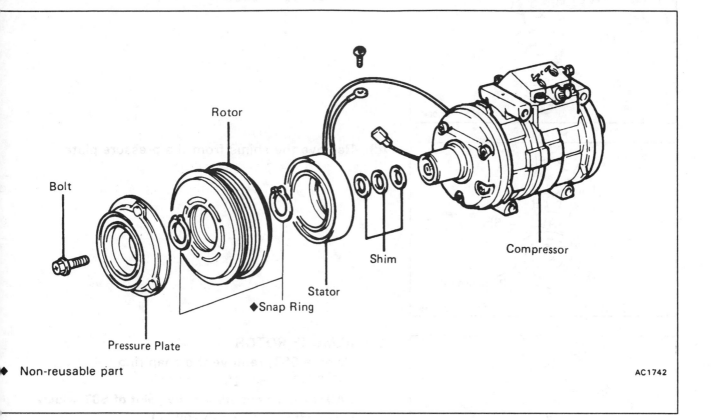

Bolt

Rotor

Shim

Compressor

◆Snap Ring

Stator

Pressure Plate

◆ Non-reusable part

AC1742

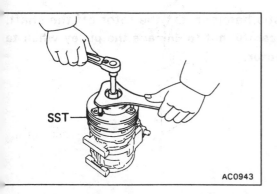

SST

AC0943

1.   REMOVE PRESSURE PLATE

(a)   Using a SST and socket wrench, remove the shaft bolt.
SST 07112—76060

AC

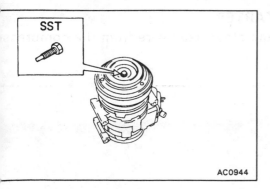

SST

AC0944

(b)   Install a SST on the pressure plate.
SST 07112—66040

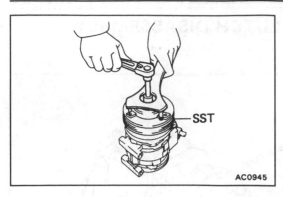

AC0945

(c) Using a SST and socket wrench, remove the pressur
plate.
SST 07112−76060

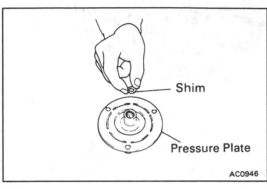

AC0946

(d) Remove the shims from the pressure plate.

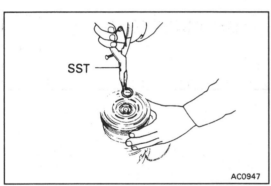

AC0947

2. REMOVE ROTOR
(a) Using a SST, remove the snap ring.
SST 07114−84020
CAUTION: Do not spread the point of SST widely.
Max width: 23.1 mm (0.909 in.)

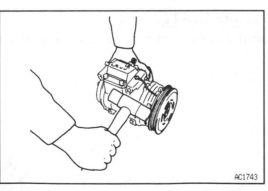

AC1743

(b) Using a plastic hammer, tap the rotor off the shaft.
NOTICE: Be careful not to damage the pulley when ta
ping on the rotor.

AC1744

3. REMOVE STARTER
(a) Disconnect the stator lead wire from the compress
housing.

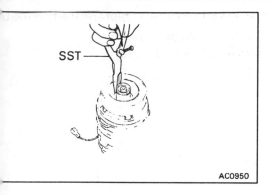

AC0950

(b) Using a SST, remove the snap ring.
SST 07114—84020

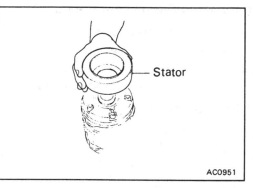

AC0951

(c) Remove the stator.

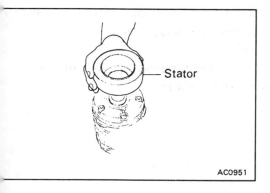

AC0951

MAGNETIC CLUTCH ASSEMBLY

ACOHU—01

1. INSTALL STATOR
(a) Install the stator on the compressor.

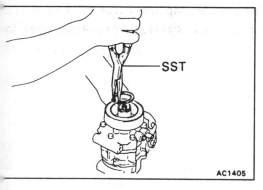

AC1405

(b) Using SST, install the new snap ring.
SST 07114—84020

AC

NOTICE: The snap ring should be installed so that its beveled side faces up.

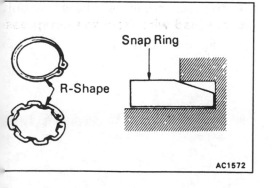

Snap Ring

R-Shape

AC1572

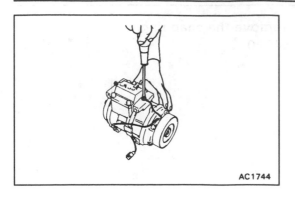

AC1744

(c) Using a SST and torque wrench, fasten the magneti
clutch lead wire to the clynder block.
Torque: 3.4 N·m (35 kgf·cm, 30 in.·lbf)
SST 07110–61050

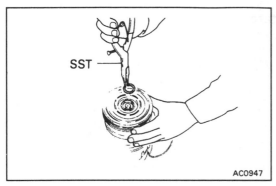

SST

AC0947

2. INSTALL ROTOR
(a) Install the rotor on the compressor shaft.
(b) Using SST, install the new snap ring.
SST 07114–84020
NOTICE: Do not spread the point of SST widely.
Max width: 23.1mm (0.909 in.)

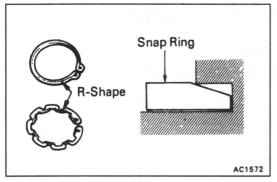

Snap Ring

R-Shape

AC1572

**NOTICE: The snap ring should be installed so that i
beveled side faces up.**

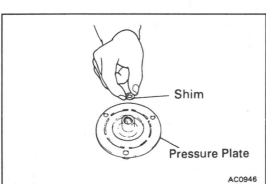

Shim

Pressure Plate

AC0946

3. INSTALL PRESSURE PLATE
(a) Adjust the clearance between the pressure plate ar
rotor by putting shims on the compressor shaft.

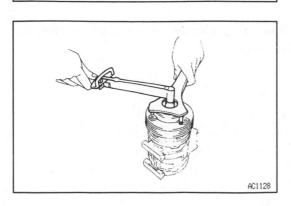

AC1128

(b) Using SST and torque wrench, install the shaft bolt
SST 07112–76060
Torque: 13 N·m (135 kgf·cm, 10 ft·lbf)

AC

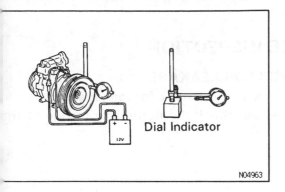

Dial Indicator

N04963

4. CHECK CLEARANCE OF MAGNETIC CLUTCH

(a) Set the dial indicator to the pressure plate of the magnetic clutch.

(b) Connect the magnetic clutch lead wire to the positive (+) terminal of the battery.

(c) Check the clearance between the pressure plate and rotor, when connect the negative (−) terminal of the battery.

Standard clearance:
    0.5 ± 0.15 mm (0.020 ± 0.0059 in.)

If the clearance is not within standard clearance, adjust the clearance using shims to obtain the standard clearance.

Shim Thickness:
    0.1 mm (0.004 in.)
    0.3 mm (0.012 in.)
    0.5 mm (0.020 in.)

ACOHV-01

COMPRESSOR INSTALLATION

1. **CONNECT TWO HOSES TO COMPRESSOR**
   Torque: 25 N·m (250 kgf·cm, 18 ft·lbf)

2. **INSTALL COMPRESSOR WITH MOUNTING BOLTS**
   Torque: 25 N·m (250 kgf·cm, 18 ft·lbf)

3. **CONNECT DISCHARGE TUBE TO CONDENSER**
   Torque: 10 N·m (100 kgf·cm, 7 ft·lbf)

4. **CONNECT SUCTION HOSE TO SUCTION TUBE**
   Torque: 10 N·m (100 kgf·cm, 7 ft·lbf)

5. **CONNECT COMPRESSOR HARNESS TO COMPRESSOR**

6. **INSTALL AND ADJUST COMPRESSOR DRIVE BELT**
   (See page AC−25)

7. **CONNECT BATTERY NEGATIVE CABLE TO BATTERY**

8. **EVACUATE AIR FROM REFRIGERATION SYSTEM**

9. **CHARGE SYSTEM WITH REFRIGERANT AND INSPECT FOR LEAKAGE OF REFRIGERANT**
   Specified amount: 750 ± 50 g (26.45 ± 1.76 oz.)

AC

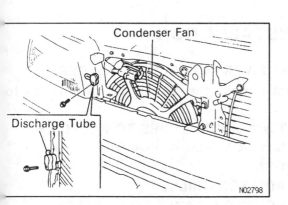

Condenser Fan

Discharge Tube

N02798

RECEIVER
ON-VEHICLE INSPECTION

INSPECT FITTINGS FOR LEAKAGE
Using a gas leak tester, check for leakage.
If there is leakage, check the tightening torque at the joints.

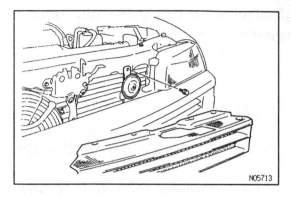

RECEIVER REMOVAL

1. **RECOVER REFRIGERANT FROM REFRIGERATION SYSTEM**
2. **REMOVE NEGATIVE CABLE FROM BATTERY**
3. **REMOVE RADIATOR GRILLE**
4. **REMOVE HORN**
5. **DISCONNECT TWO LIQUID TUBES FROM RECEIVER**
   HINT: Cap the open fittings immediately to keep moisture out of the system.
6. **REMOVE RECEIVER FROM RECEIVER HOLDER**

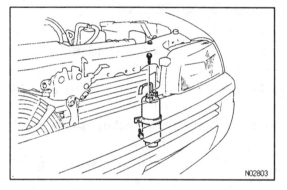

RECEIVER INSTALLATION

1. **INSTALL RECEIVER IN RECEIVER HOLDER**
   HINT: Do not remove the blind plugs until ready for connection.
2. **CONNECT TWO LIQUID TUBES TO RECEIVER**
   Torque: 5.4 N·m (55 kgf·cm, 48 in.·lbf)
3. **INSTALL HORN**
4. **INSTALL RADIATOR GRILLE**
5. **CONNECT NEGATIVE CABLE TO BATTERY**
6. **IF RECEIVER WAS REPLACED, ADD COMPRESSOR OIL TO COMPRESSOR**
   Add 20 cc (0.71 fl.oz.)
   Compressor oil: ND-OIL 6 or equivalent
7. **EVACUATE AIR FROM REFRIGERATION SYSTEM**
8. **CHARGE SYSTEM WITH REFRIGERANT AND INSPECT FOR LEAKAGE OF REFRIGERANT**
   Specified amount: 750 ± 50 g (26.45 ± 1.76 oz.)

CONDENSER
ON-VEHICLE INSPECTION

ACOHZ-01

1. **INSPECT CONDENSER FINS FOR BLOCKAGE OR DAMAGE**
   If the fins are clogged, wash them with water and dry with compressed air.
   NOTICE: Be careful not to damage the fins.
   If the fins are bent, straighten them with a screwdriver or pliers.
2. **INSPECT CONDENSER FITTINGS FOR LEAKAGE**
   Repair as necessary.

CONDENSER REMOVAL

ACOJO-01

1. **RECOVER REFRIGERANT FROM REFRIGERATION SYSTEM**
2. **DISCONNECT NEGATIVE CABLE FROM BATTERY**
3. **REMOVE FOLLOWING PARTS**
   - Radiator Grille
   - Horn
   - Hood Lock
   - Center Brace
   - Battery
   - Radiator Reserve Tank and Bracket

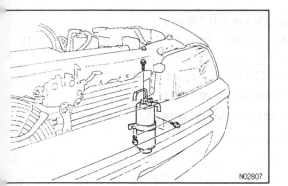

4. **DISCONNECT LIQUID TUBES AND REMOVE RE-CEIVER WITH BRACKET**
   HINT: Cap the open fittings immediately to keep moisture out of the system.

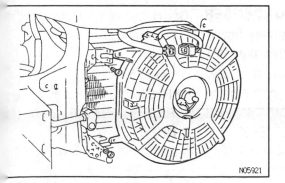

5. **REMOVE CONDENSER FAN**
   (a) Disconnect condenser fan harness.
   (b) Remove two clips.
   (c) Pull condenser fan out.

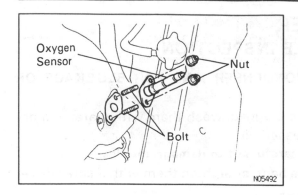

6. **REMOVE OXYGEN SENSOR**
(a) Disconect oxygen sensor harness.
(b) Remove two nuts, two bolts and oxygen sensor.

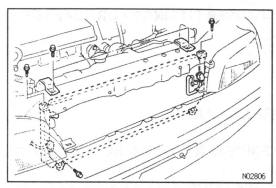

7. **DISCONNECT DISCHARGE HOSE FROM CON-
DENSER FITTING**
HINT: Cap the open fittings immediately to keep
moisture out of the system.
8. **REMOVE RADIATOR SUPPORT BRACKETS**
9. **REMOVE CONDENSER**
(a) Remove two condenser mounting bolts.
(b) Lean the radiator back and pull the condenser out.

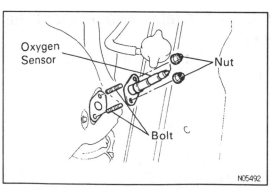

CONDENSER INSTALLATION

1. **INSTALL CONDENSER**
Install the condenser with two condenser mounting
bolts.
2. **CONNECT DISCHARGE HOSE TO CONDENSER
FITTING**
Torque: 10 N·m (100 kgf·cm, 7 ft·lbf)
3. **INSTALL RADIATOR SUPPORT BRACKETS**

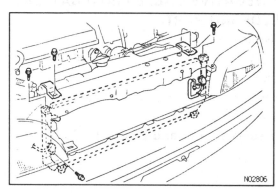

4. **INSTALL OXYGEN SENSOR**
(a) Install oxygen sensor with two bolts and two nuts.
Torque:
Bolts: 19.7N·m (201 kgf·cm, 15 ft·lbf)
Nuts : 20N·m (204 kgf·cm, 15 ft·lbf)
(b) Connect oxygen sensor harness.

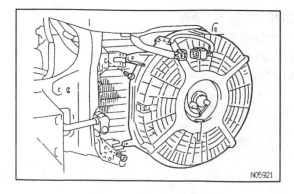

5. **INSTALL CONDENSER FAN**
(a) Install condenser fan with two clips.
(b) Connect condenser fan harness.

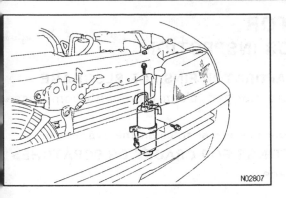

6. **INSTALL RECEIVER WITH BRACKET**
7. **CONNECT LIQUID TUBES TO RECEIVER**
   Torque: 5.4 N·m (55 kgf·cm, 48 in.·lbf)

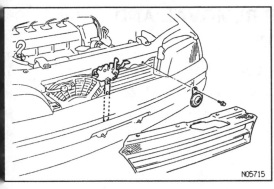

8. **INSTALL FOLLOWING PARTS**
   - Hood Lock
   - Center Brace
   - Horn
   - Radiator Grille
   - Radiator Reserve Tank and Bracket
   - Battery
9. **CONNECT NEGATIVE CABLE TO BATTERY**
10. **IF CONDENSER WAS REPLACED, ADD COMPRESSOR OILR TO COMPRESSO**
    Add 40−50 cc (1.4−1.7 fl.oz.)
    Compressor oil: ND−OIL 6
11. **EVACUATE AIR FROM AIR CONDITIONING SYSTEM**
12. **CHARGE SYSTEM WITH REFRIGERANT AND INSPECT FOR LEAKAGE**
    Specified amount: 750 ± 50 g (26.45 ± 1.76 oz.)

AC

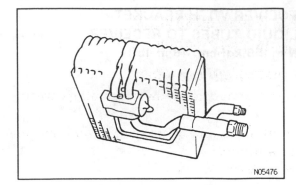

EVAPORATOR
EVAPORATOR INSPECTION

ACOJ2–01

1. **CHECK EVAPORATOR FINS FOR BLOCKAGE**
   If the fins are clogged, clean them with compressed air.
   NOTICE: Never use water to clean the evaporator.
2. **CHECK FITTINGS FOR CRACKS OR SCRATCHES**
   Repair as necessary.

EVAPORATOR REMOVAL AND INSTALLATION

ACOJ3–01

(See page AC–29)

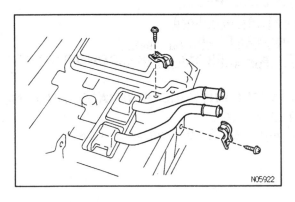

HEATER RADIATOR
HEATER RADIATOR REMOVAL

ACOJ4–0

1. **REMOVE HEATER UNIT**
   (See page AC–31)
2. **REMOVE HEATER RADIATOR**
(a) Remove the screws and plates.
(b) Pull the heater radiator out.

HEATER RADIATOR INSPECTION

INSPECT FINS FOR BLOCKAGE
If the fins are clogged, clean them with compressed air.

HEATER RADIATOR INSTALLATION

1. **INSTALL HEATER RADIATOR**
(a) Insert the heater radiator to the heater unit.
(b) Install the plates with screws.
2. **INSTALL HEATER UNIT**
   (See page AC–32)

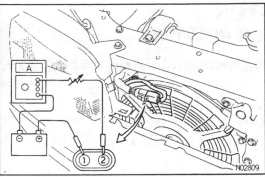

CONDENSER FAN MOTOR
ON−VEHICLE INSPECTION

ACOJ5−01

INSPECT CONDENSER FAN MOTOR
(a) Using the wire harness, apply battery voltage to the connector.
(b) Confirm smooth rotation of the motor within the specified c urrent flow.
Standard current: 6.7 ± 0.7 A

If current is not as specified, replace the motor.

ACOJ6−01

CONDENSER FAN REMOVAL

1. **DISCONNECT NEGATIVE CABLE FROM BATTERY**
2. **REMOVE RADIATOR GRILLE, HOOD LOCK AND CENTER BRACE**

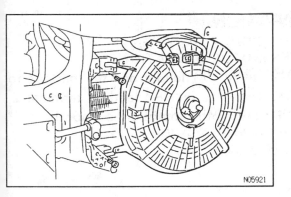

3. **REMOVE CONDENSER FAN**
(a) Disconnect condenser fan harness.
(b) Remove two clips and condensor fan.

CONDENSER FAN INSTALLATION

1. **INSTALL CONDENSER FAN**
(a) Install the condenser fan with two clips.
(b) Connect the condenser fan harness.
2. **INSTALL CENTER BRACE, HOOD LOCK AND RA-DIATOR GRILLINSTALL CENTER BRACE, HOOD LOCK AND FRONT GRILLE**
3. **CONNECT NEGATIVE CABLE TO BATTERY**

AC

BLOWER MOTOR
BLOWER MOTOR REMOVAL

ACOJ7—01

1. **DISCONNECT NEGATIVE (−) CABLE FROM BATTERY**
2. **REMOVE GLOVE BOX ASSEMBLY**
   (See page BO−62)

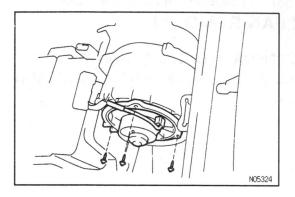

3. **REMOVE BLOWER MOTOR**
   (a) Disconnect the connector from the blower motor.
   (b) Remove the three screws and the blower motor.

MOTOR INSPECTION

ACOJ8—01

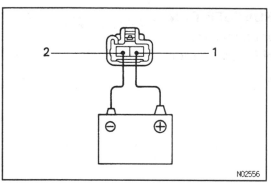

INSPECT BLOWER MOTOR OPERATION
Connect the positive (+) lead from the battery to terminal 1 and the negative (−) lead to terminal 2, then check that the motor operation is smooth.

MOTOR INSTALLATION

ACOJ9—01

1. **INSTALL BLOWER MOTOR**
   (a) Install the blower motor with the three screws.
   (b) Connect the connector to blower motor.
2. **INSTALL GLOVE BOX ASSEMBLY**
3. **CONNECT NEGATIVE (−) CABLE TO BATTERY**

EXPANSION VALVE
ON—VEHICLE INSPECTION

ACOJA-01

1. **CHECK QUANTITY OF GAS DURING REFRIGERA-TION CYCLE**
2. **INSTALL MANIFOLD GAUGE SET**
3. **RUN ENGINE**
   Run the engine at 2,000 rpm for at least 5 minutes. Then check that the high pressure reading is 1,275 — 1,471 kPa (13 — 15 kgf/cm², 185 — 213 psi).
4. **CHECK EXPANSION VALVE**
   If the expansion valve is faulty, the low pressure reading will drop to 0 kPa (0 kgf/cm², 0 psi).
   HINT: When the low pressure drops to 0 kPa (0 kgf/cm², 0 psi), feel the receiver's IN and OUT sides for no temperature difference.

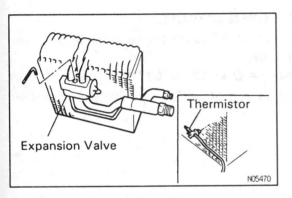

Expansion Valve

Thermistor

N05470

ACOJB-01

EXPANSION VALVE REMOVAL AND INSTALLATION

(See page AC—29)

AC

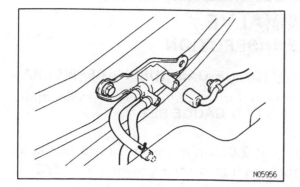

N05956

VACUUM SWITCHING VALVE (VSV)
VSV INSPECTION
ACOJC–01

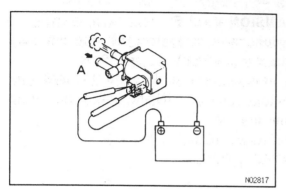

N02817

1. **INSPECT VACUUM CIRCUIT CONTINUITY IN VSV BY BLOWING AIR INTO PIPES**
(a) Connect the VSV terminals to the battery terminals as illustrated.
(b) Blow into pipe "A" and check that air comes out of pipe "C".

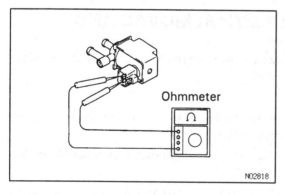

Ohmmeter

N02818

2. **INSPECT FOR OPEN CIRCUIT**
Using an ohmmeter, measure the resistance between the two terminals.
Resistance: 30–34 Ω at 20 °C (68 °F)
If the resistance is not within specification, replace the VSV.

WATER VALVE
WATER VALVE REMOVAL

ACOJD-01

1. **DRAIN ENGINE COOLANT FROM RADIATOR**
    HINT: It is not necessary to drain out all the coolant.

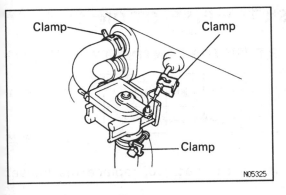

2. **DISCONNECT WATER VALVE CONTROL CABLE**
3. **DISCONNECT WATER HOSES FROM HEATER RADIATOR PIPE AND WATER VALVE**
(a) Grip the claws of the hose clip with pliers and slide the clip along the hose to a place where it does not clamp the hose to the pipe.
(b) Disconnect the water hoses.
4. **REMOVE WATER VALVE**

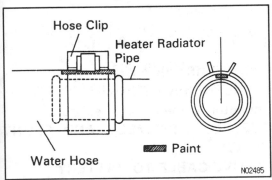

WATER VALVE INSTALLATION

Install by following the removal procedure in reverse order.
HINT:
- Push the water hose onto the heater radiator pipe as far as the ridge on the pipe.
- Install the hose clip in a position as shown to the left.
- For installing the control cable, refer to "A/C CONTROL CABLES ADJUSTMENT".

AC

BLOWER RESISTOR
BLOWER RESISTOR REMOVAL

ACOK0-01

1. **DISCONNECT NEGATIVE CABLE FROM BATTERY**
2. **REMOVE COWL SIDE PANEL AND GLOVE BOX ASSEMBLY**
3. **REMOVE BLOWER RESISTOR**
(a) Disconnect connector from the blower resistor.
(b) Remove two screws and the blower resistor.

BLOWER RESISTOR INSPECTION

INSPECT BLOWER RESISTOR CONTINUITY

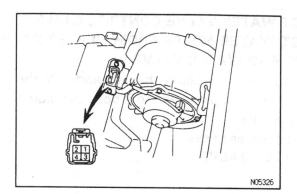

N05326

Terminal / Condition	4	3	2	1
Constant	o——WW——o	——WW——o	——WW——o	——o

V01568

If continuity is not as specified, replace the blower resistor.

BLOWER RESISTOR INSTALLATION

1. **INSTALL BLOWER RESISTOR**
(a) Install blower resistor with two screws.
(b) Connect the connector to the blower resistor.
2. **INSTALL GLOVE BOX ASSEMBLY AND FRONT DOOR SCUFF PLATE**
3. **CONNECT NEGATIVE CABLE TO BATTERY**

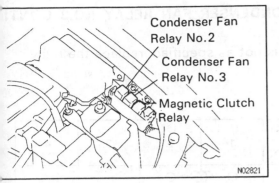

Condenser Fan Relay No.2

Condenser Fan Relay No.3

Magnetic Clutch Relay

N02821

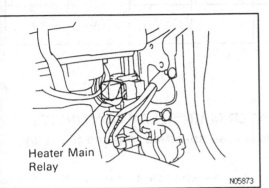

Heater Main Relay

N05873

RELAYS
RELAYS REMOVAL

ACOJF–01

1. **DISCONNECT NEGATIVE (−) CABLE FROM BATTERY**
2. **REMOVE RELAYS**

RELAYS INSPECTION

ACOJG–01

1. **INSPECT MAGNETIC CLUTCH RELAY CONTINUITY**

   If continuity is not as specified, replace the relay.

N02833

Terminal / Condition	1	2	3	4
Constant	o—OOO—o			
Apply battery voltage to terminals 1 and 2			o———o	

V00509

2. **INSPECT CONDENSER FAN RELAY NO.2 CONTINUITY**

   If continuity is not as specified, replace the relay.

N02832

Terminal / Condition	1	2	3	4	5
Constant	o—OOO—o		o———o		
Apply battery voltage to terminals 1 and 2			o———o		

V00510

AC

3. **INSPECT CONDENSER FAN RELAY NO.3 CONTINUITY**

If continuity is not as specified, replace the relay.

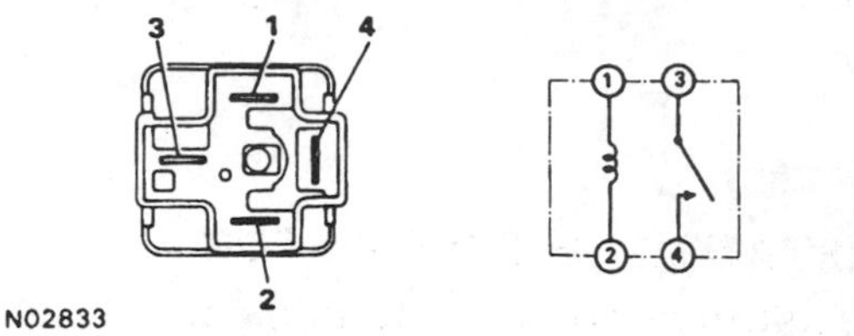

Terminal / Condition	1	2	3	4
Constant	O——OOO——O			
Apply battery voltage to terminals 1 and 2			O———O	

N02833

V00609

4. **INSPECT HEATER MAIN RELAY CONTINUITY**

If continuity is not as specified, replace the relay.

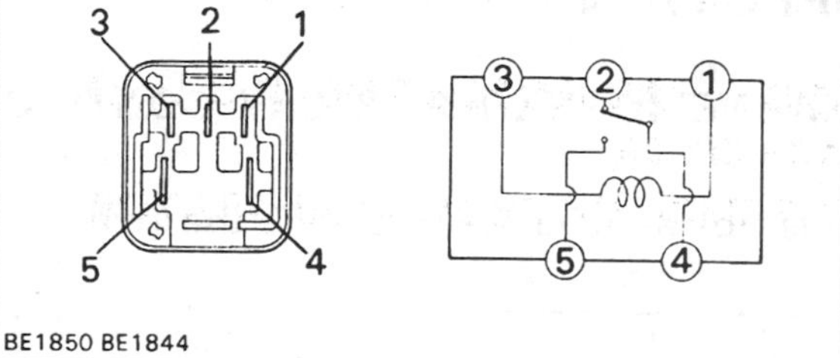

Terminal / Condition	1	2	3	4	5
Constant	O——OOOO——O		O———O		
Apply battery voltage to terminals 1 and 3.				O———O	

BE1850 BE1844

V00612

ACOJH–01

RELAYS INSTALLATION

1. **INSTALL RELAYS**
2. **CONNECT NEGATIVE (–) CABLE TO BATTERY**

AC

THERMISTOR
THERMISTOR
ON-VEHICLE INSPECTION

1. **DISCONNECT NEGATIVE CABLE FROM BATTERY**
2. **REMOVE FRONT DOOR SCUFF PLATE AND GLOVE BOX ASSEMBLY**

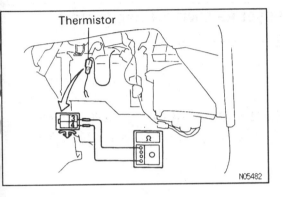

3. **INSPECT RESISTANCE OF THERMISTOR**
   Measure the resistance between terminals.
   Standard resistance: 1,500 Ω at 25 °C (77 °F)
   If resistance is not as specified, replace the thermistor.

THERMISTOR REMOVAL

1. **REMOVE AND DISASSEMBLE COOLING UNIT**
   (See pages AC–28, 29)
2. **REMOVE THERMISTOR FROM EVAPORATOR**

THERMISTOR INSPECTION

INSPECT THERMISTOR RESISTANCE
(a) Place the thermistor in cold water, while varying the temperature of the water, measure the resistance at the connector and at the same time, measure the temperature of the water with a thermometer.
(b) Compare the two readings on the chart.
   If the resistance value is not as specified, replace the thermistor.

THERMISTOR INSTALLATION

1. **INSTALL THERMISTOR TO EVAPORATOR**
2. **ASSEMBLE AND INSTALL COOLING UNIT**
   (See page AC–30)

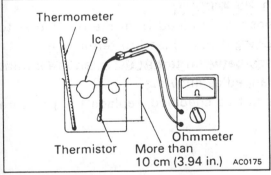

PRESSURE SWITCH
ON—VEHICLE INSPECTION

ACOJK–01

1. **INSTALL MANIFOLD GAUGE SET**
2. **DISCONNECT CONNECTOR FROM PRESSURE SWITCH**
3. **RUN ENGINE AT APPROX. 2,000 RPM**

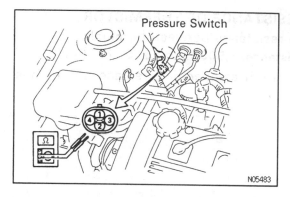

4. **INSPECT PRESSURE SWITCH OPERATION**

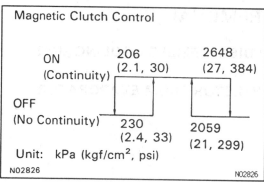

(Magnetic Clutch Control)

(a) Connect the positive (+) lead from the ohmmeter to terminal 2 and negative (−) lead to terminal 1.

(b) Check continuity between terminals when refrigerant pressure is changed as shown.
If operation is not as specified, replace the pressure switch.

(Condenser Fan Control)

(a) Connect the positive (+) lead from the ohmmeter to terminal 3 and negative (−) lead to terminal 4.

(b) Check continuity between terminals when refrigerant pressure is changed as shown.
If operation is not as specified, replace the pressure switch.

5. **STOP ENGINE AND REMOVE MANIFOLD GAUGE SET**
6. **CONNECT CONNECTOR TO PRESSURE SWITCH**

ACOJL-01

PRESSURE SWITCH REMOVAL

1. **RECOVER REFRIGERANT IN REFRIGERATION SYSTEM**
2. **REMOVE PRESSURE SWITCH**
(a) Disconnect the connector.
(b) Remove the pressure switch from the liquid tube.

ACOJM-01

PRESSURE SWITCH INSTALLATION

1. **INSTALL PRESSURE SWITCH**
(a) Install the pressure switch to the liquid tube.
   Torque: 9.8 N·m (100 kgf·cm, 7 ft·lbf)
(b) Connect the connector.
2. **EVACUATE AIR IN REFRIGERATION SYSTEM AND CHARGE WITH REFRIGERANT**
   Specified amount:750 ± 50 g (26.45 ± 1.76 oz.)
3. **INSPECT FOR LEAKAGE OF REFRIGERANT**
   Using a gas leak tester, check for leakage of refrigerant from the pressure switch mount.
4. **INSPECT A/C OPERATION**

AC

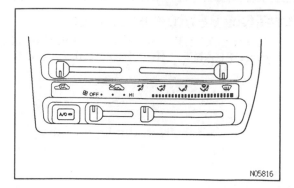

AIR CONDITIONING CONTROL ASSEMBLY
ON-VEHICLE INSPECTION
INSPECT A/C CONTROL LEVERS OPERATION
Move the control levers left and right and check for stiffness and binding through the full range of the levers.

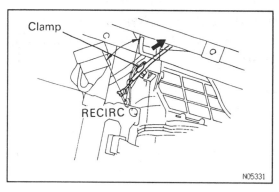

A/C CONTROL CABLES ADJUSTMENT

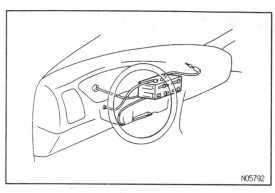

1. ADJUST AIR INLET DAMPER CONTROL CABLE
Set the air inlet damper on "RECIRC" position, install the control cable and lock the clamp.

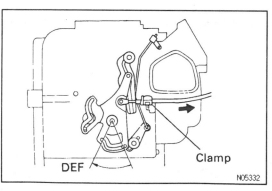

2. ADJUST MODE DAMPER CONTROL CABLE
Set the mode damper on "DEFE" position, install the control cable and lock the clamp.

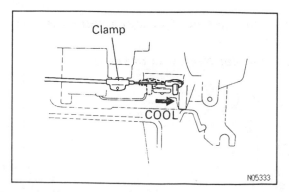

3. ADJUST AIR MIX DAMPER CONTROL CABLE
Set the air mix damper on "COOL" position, install the control cable and lock the clamp.

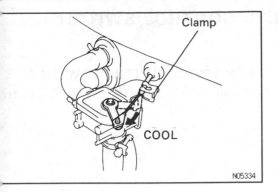

4. **ADJUST WATER VALVE CONTROL CABLE**
Set the water valve on "COOL" position, install the control cable lock the clamp.

A/C CONTROL ASSEMBLY REMOVAL

1. **REMOVE CENTER CLUSTER FINISH LOWER PANEL AND STEREO OPENING COVER**
(See page BO–62)
2. **REMOVE CENTER CLUSTER FINISH PANEL AND RADIO**
(See page BO–62)

3. **REMOVE A/C CONTROL ASSEMBLY**
(a) Disconnect the control cables from the heater unit and the water valve.

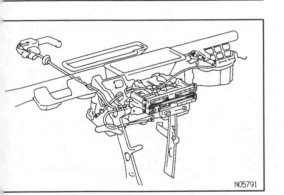

(b) Remove the four screws and the A/C control assembly.

 AC

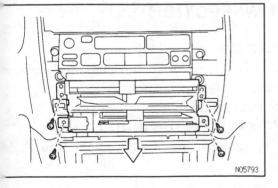

(c) Disconnect the air inlet control cable from the A/C control assembly.
(d) Disconnect the blower switch connector.

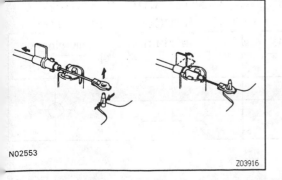

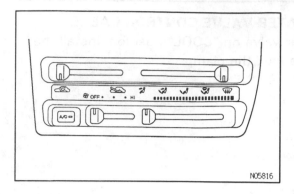

N05816

BLOWER SPEED CONTROL SWITCH INSPECTION

1. REMOVE BLOWER SPEED CONTROL SWITCH

(a) Remove the illumination light from the A/C contro assembly.

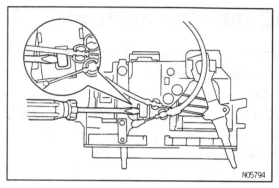

N05794

(b) Using a screwdriver, pry loose the clip and push ou the blow er speed control switch to rear of the A/ control assembly.

2. INSPECT BLOWER SPEED CONTROL SWITC CONTINUITY

If continuity is not as specified, replace the blowe speed control switch.

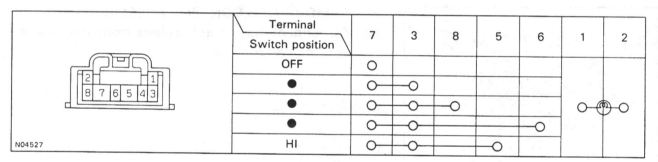

Terminal / Switch position	7	3	8	5	6	1	2
OFF	○						
●	○—	—○					
●	○—	—○—	—○			○—(⊗)—○	
●	○—	—○—		—○			
HI	○—	—○—			—○		

N04527   V0103

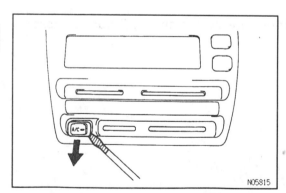

N05815

A/C SWITCH INSPECTION

1. REMOVE A/C SWITCH

Using a screwdriver, pry loose the clips and remov the A/C switch.

HINT: Tape the screwdriver tip before use.

2. INSPECT A/C SWITCH CONTINUITY

If continuity is not as specified, replace the A / switch.

Terminal / Condition	5	6	Illumination 1	Illumination 3
A/C switch off			○—(⊗)—○	
A/C switch on	○—————○			

N02830   V00613

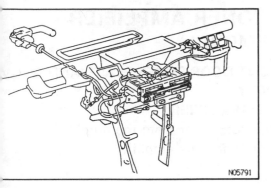

A/C CONTROL ASSEMBLY INSTALLATION

1. INSTALL A/C CONTROL ASSEMBLY

(a) Install the blower switch and illumination light to the A/C control assembly.

(b) Connect the blower switch connector.

(c) Wire the control cables as shown the illustration.

(d) Connect the air inlet cable to the A/C control assembly.

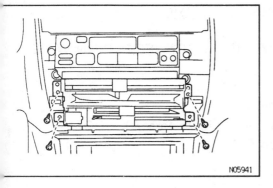

(e) Install the A/C control assembly with the four screws.

(f) Connect the control cables to the heater unit and the water valve.

HINT: For installing the control cables, refer to "A/C CONTROL CABLES ADJUSTMENT".

2. INSTALL RADIO AND CENTER CLUSTER FINISH PANEL

3. INSTALL STEREO OPENING COVER AND CENTER CLUSTER FINISH LOWER PANEL

AC

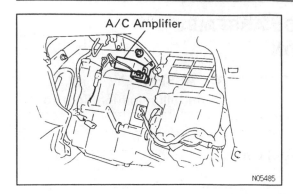

AIR CONDITIONER AMPLIFIER
AMPLIFIER REMOVAL

1. **REMOVE FRONT DOOR SCUFF PLATE AND GLOV**
   BOX ASSEMBLY
2. **REMOVE A/C AMPLIFIER**
(a) Disconnect the connector from the amplifier.
(b) Remove two nuts and the amplifier.

AMPLIFIER INSTALLATION

1. **INSTALL A/C AMPLIFIER**
(a) Connect the connector.
(b) Install the amplifier with two nuts.
2. **INSTALL GLOVE BOX ASSEMBLY AND FRON**
   DOOR SCUFF PLATE

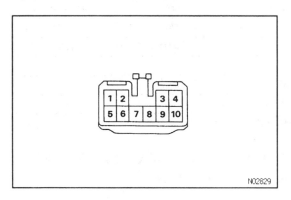

AMPLIFIER INSPECTION

**INSPECT A/C AMPLIFIER CONNECTOR ON WIRE
HARNESS SIDE**
Test conditions:
- Ignition switch ON
- Temperature control lever to MAX COOL
- Blower switch ON

Check for	Tester Connection	Condition	Specified Value
Voltage	1 – Ground	Ignition switch on	Approx. 10 to 14 V
	5 – Ground	A/C switch on	Approx. 10 to 14 V
	7 – Ground	A/C switch on	Below 1 V
	9 – Ground	Magnetic clutch on	0 V
	8 – Ground	Magnetic clutch on	Below 1V
Resistance	4 – 10	Constant	Approx. 1.5 kΩ at 25°C (77°F)
Continuity	4 – Ground	Constant	Continuity

SERVICE SPECIFICATIONS
SERVICE DATA

ACOJW—01

Refrigerant charge volume		750±50 g (26.45±1.76oz.)
Drive belt tension		
7A—FE and 4A—FE	New belt	160±20 lbf
	Used belt	100±20 lbf
Magnetic clutch clearance		0.5±0.15 mm (0.020±0.0059 in.)

TORQUE SPECIFICATIONS

ACOJX—01

Part tightened		N·m	kgf·cm	ft·lbf
Compressor x Suction hose		25	250	18
Compressor x Discharge hose		25	250	18
Compressor x Compressor bracket		25	250	18
Compressor bracket x Engine		47	480	35
Receiver x Liquid tube		5.4	55	48 in.-lbf
Condenser x Discharge hose		10	100	7
Cooling unit x Liquid tube		14	140	10
Cooling unit x Suction tube		32	330	24
Oxygen sensor	Bolts	19.7	201	15
Oxygen sensor	Nuts	20	204	15

AC

AC

ELECTRICAL WIRING DIAGRAMS

ABBREVIATION

The following abbreviations are used in this wiring diagram.

ABS	= Anti-Lock Brake System
A/C	= Air Conditioner
A/T	= Automatic Transaxle
COMB.	= Combination
ECT	= Electronic Controlled Transmission
ECU	= Electronic Control Unit
EFI	= Electronic Fuel Injection
EGR	= Exhaust Gas Recirculation
Ex.	= Except
FL	= Fusible Link
IIA	= Integrated Ignition Assembly
ISC	= Idle Speed Control
LH	= Left-Hand
MFI	= Multiport Fuel Injection
M/T	= Manual Transaxle
O/D	= Overdrive
RH	= Right-Hand
S/D	= Sedan
SW	= Switch
TEMP.	= Temperature
VSV	= Vacuum Switching Valve
W/G	= Wagon
w/	= With
w/o	= Without

EWD

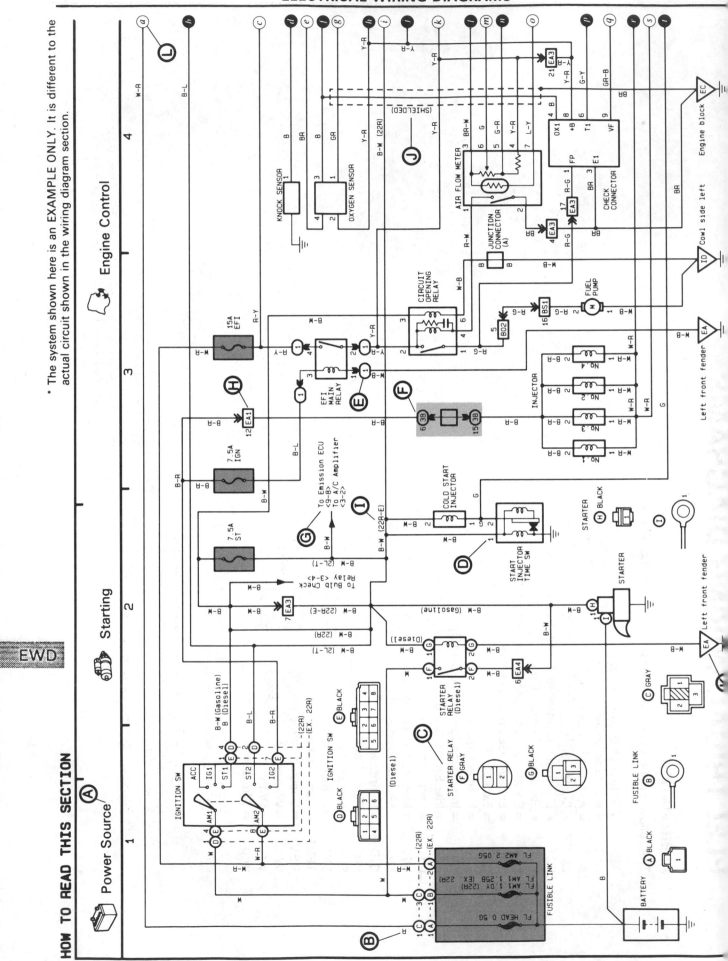

* The system shown here is an EXAMPLE ONLY. It is different to the actual circuit shown in the wiring diagram section.

Ⓐ: System Title

Ⓑ: Indicates the wiring color.

Wire colors are indicated by an alphabetical code.

B = Black   L = Blue   R = Red
BR = Brown   LG = Light Green   V = Violet
G = Green   O = Orange   W = White
GR = Gray   P = Pink   Y = Yellow

The first letter indicates the basic wire color and the second letter indicates the color of the stripe.

Example: L – Y

L – Y
(Blue) (Yellow)

Ⓒ: Indicates the connector to be connected to a part (the numeral indicates the pin No.)

Ⓓ: Indicates the pin number of the connector. The numbering system is different for female and male connectors.

Example: Numbered in order from upper left to lower right   Numbered in order from upper right to lower left

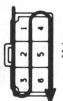

Female   Male

The numbering system for the overall wiring diagram is the same as above.

Ⓔ: Indicates a Relay Block. No shading is used and only the Relay Block No. is shown to distinguish it from the J/B.

Example: ① Indicates Relay Block No. 1.

Ⓕ: Junction Block (The number in the circle is the J/B No. and the connector code is shown beside it). Junction Blocks are shaded to clearly separate them from other parts (different junction blocks are shaded differently for further clarification).

Example:

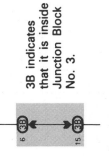

3B indicates that it is inside Junction Block No. 3.

Ⓖ: Indicates related system.

Ⓗ: Indicates the wiring harness and wiring harness connector. The wiring harness with male terminal is shown with arrows (≫). Outside numerals are pin numbers.

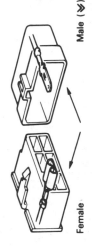

Male (≫)

Female

Ⓘ: ( ) is used to indicate different wiring and connector, etc. when the vehicle model, engine type, or specification is different.

Ⓙ: Indicates a shielded cable.

Ⓚ: Indicates a ground point.

Ⓛ: The same code occuring on the next page indicates that the wire harness is continuous.

EWD

SYSTEM INDEX

1993 Model (Location No. 1 to 27)

SYSTEMS	LOCATION	SYSTEMS	LOCATION	SYSTEMS	LOCATION
ABS (Anti-Lock Brake System)	19-2	Horn	11-4	Stop Light	8-3
Air Conditioner	23-4	Ignition	1-3	Sun Roof	16-3
Back Door Lock (W/G w/o Power Window)	7-4	Interior Light	10-4	Taillight and Illumination	9-2
Back-Up Light	8-2	Light Auto Turn Off	12-2	Theft Deterrent and Door Lock	17-2
Charging	1-4	Power Source	1~23-1	Turn Signal and Hazard Warning Light	11-2
Cigarette Lighter	21-2	Power Window	14-2	Unlock and Seat Belt Warning	12-3
Clock	21-2	Radiator Fan	23-2	Wiper and Washer	15-2
Combination Meter	22-2	Radio and Player	21-3	Junction Block and Wire Harness Connector	24-1
Cruise Control	20-2	Rear Window Defogger	10-2	Connector Joining Wire Harness and Wire Harness	25~27-1
Door Lock	18-2 (w/o Theft Deterrent System)	Remote Control Mirror	16-2		
ECT (Electronic Controlled Transmission)	5-2	Shift Lock	13-2		
Engine Control	2-2 (for 7A-FE A/T) 3-2 (for 7A-FE M/T) 4-2 (for 4A-FE)	SRS Airbag	13-3		
Headlight	6-2 (w/ Daytime Running Light) 7-2 (w/o Daytime Running Light)	Starting	1-2		

EWD

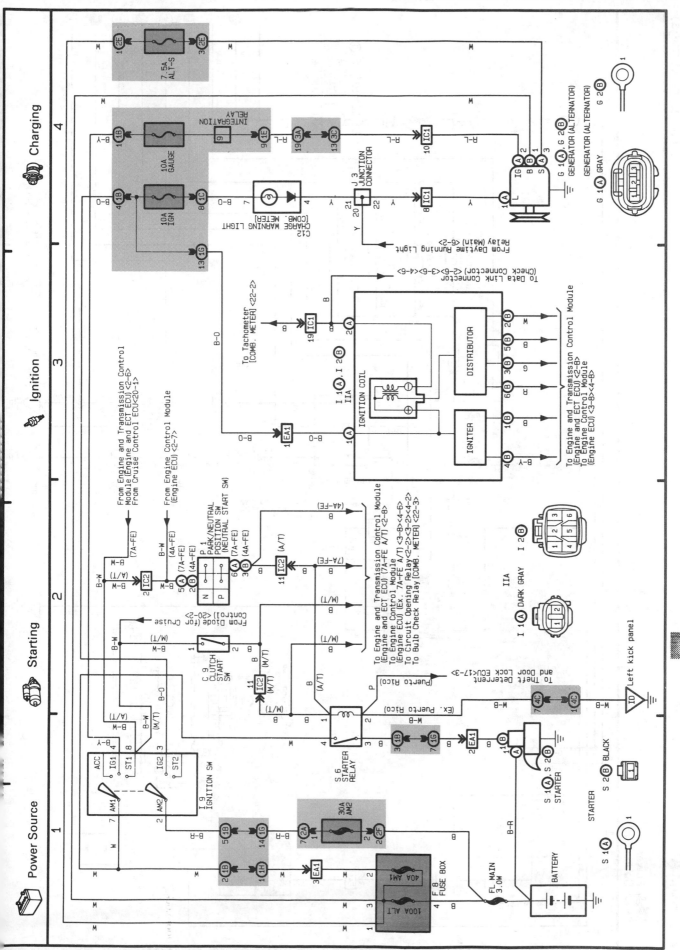

EWD

(Cont. next page)

2 COROLLA

EWD

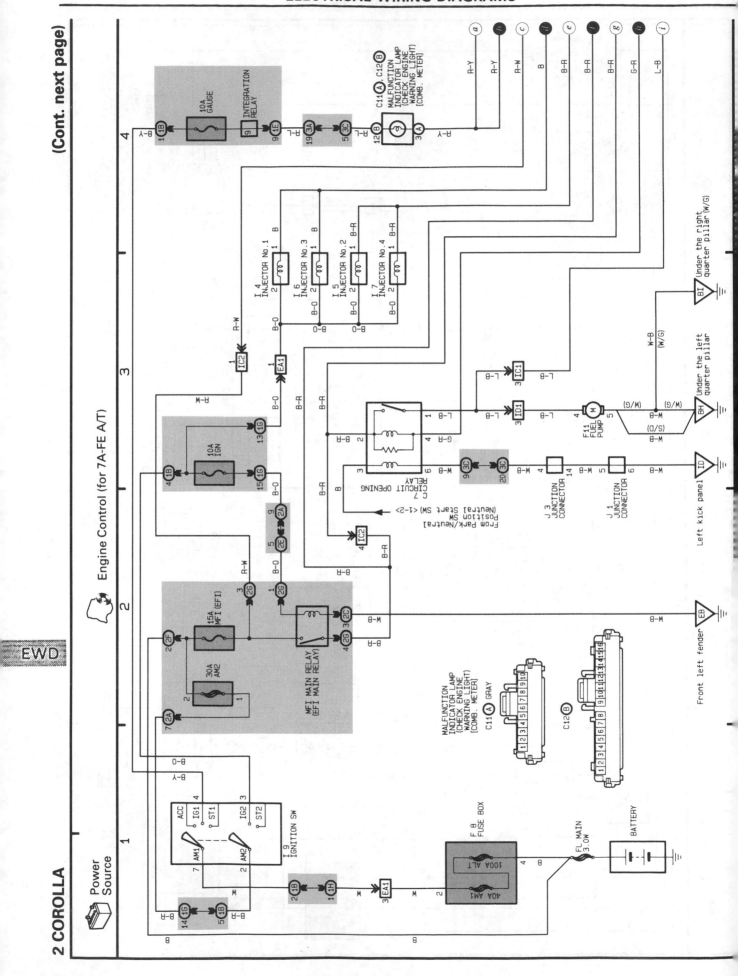

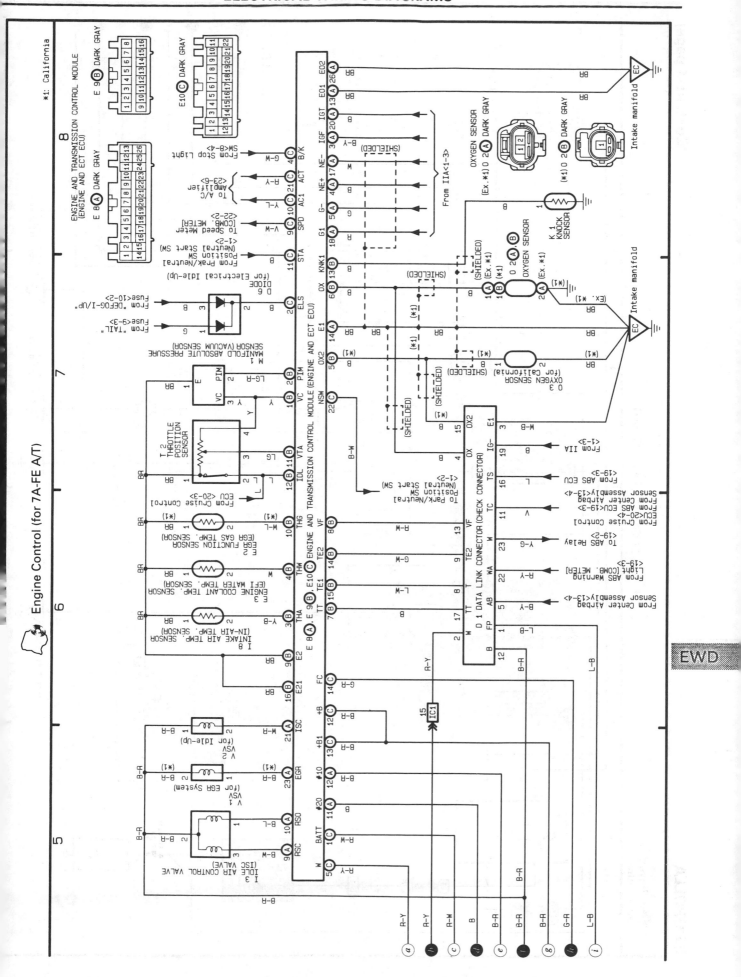

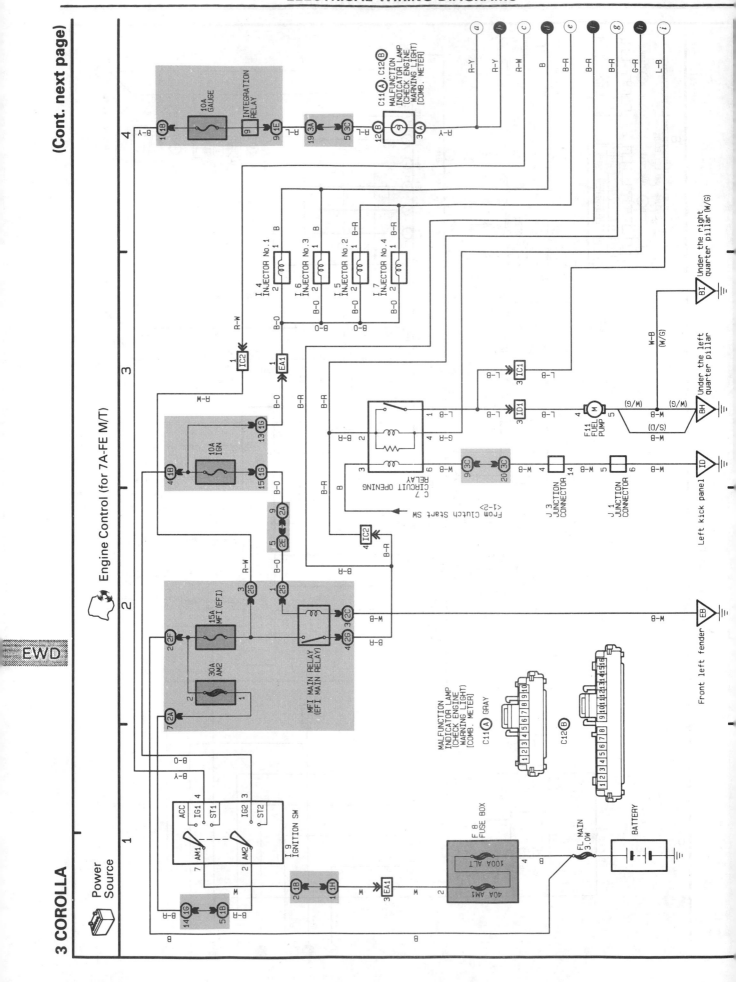

(Cont. next page)

EWD

3 COROLLA

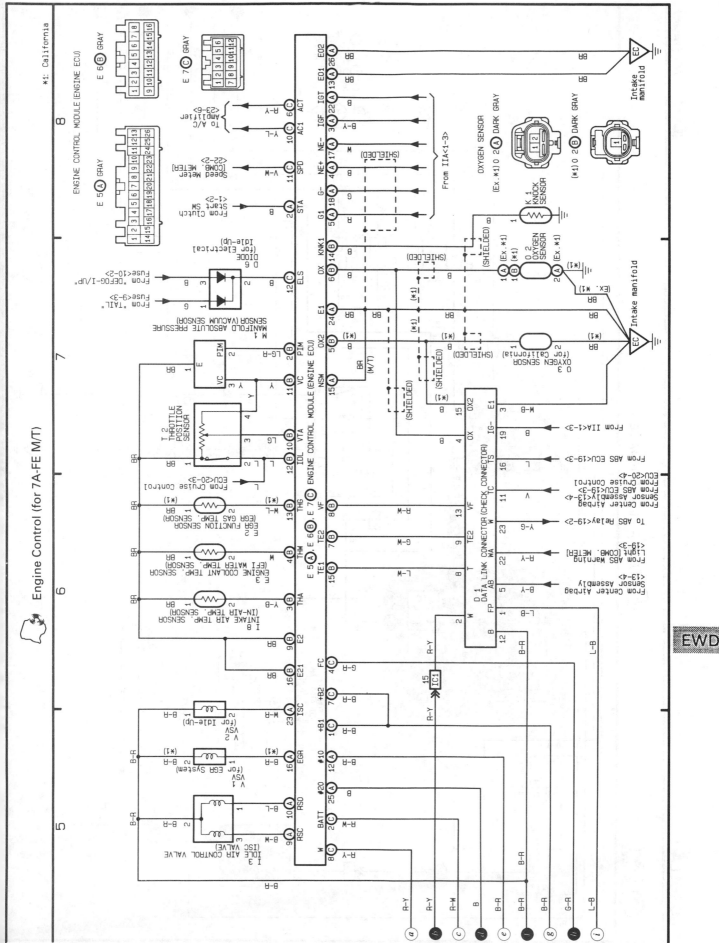

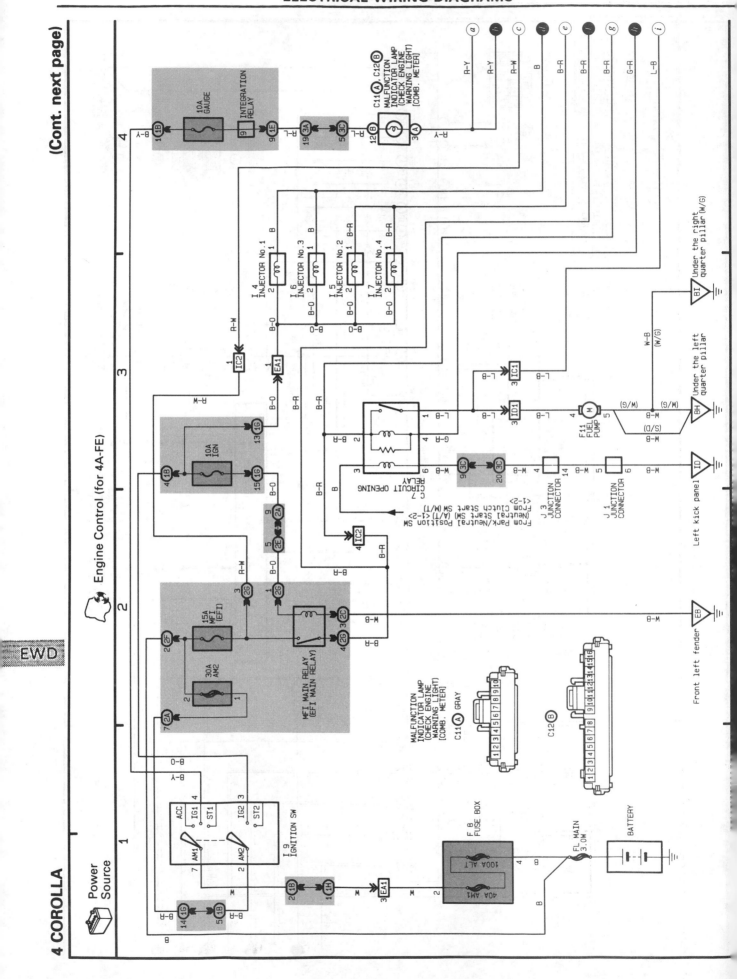

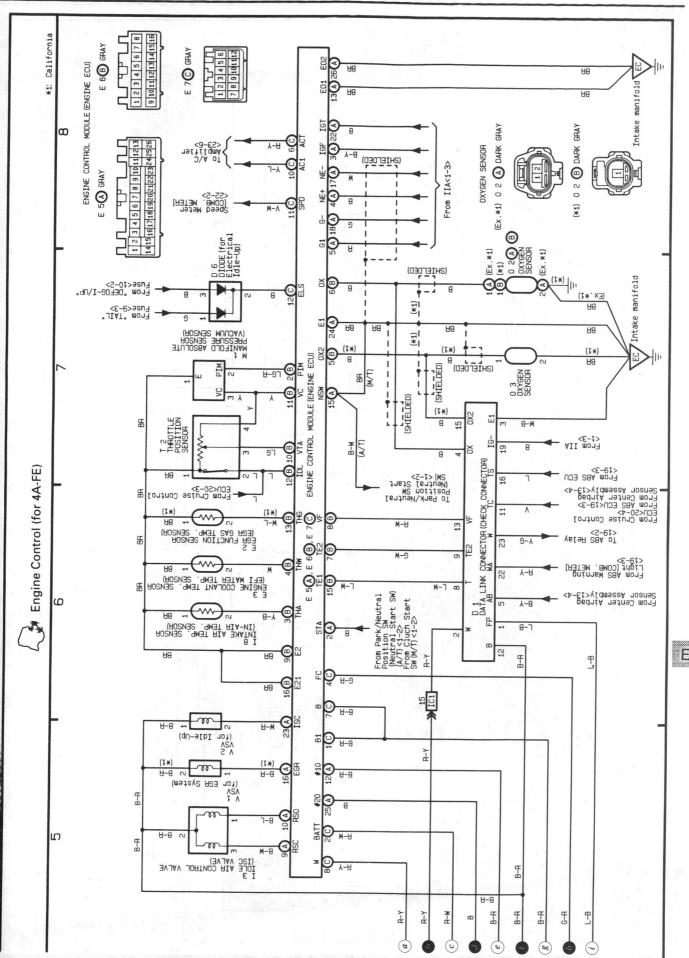

Engine Control (for 4A-FE)

EWD

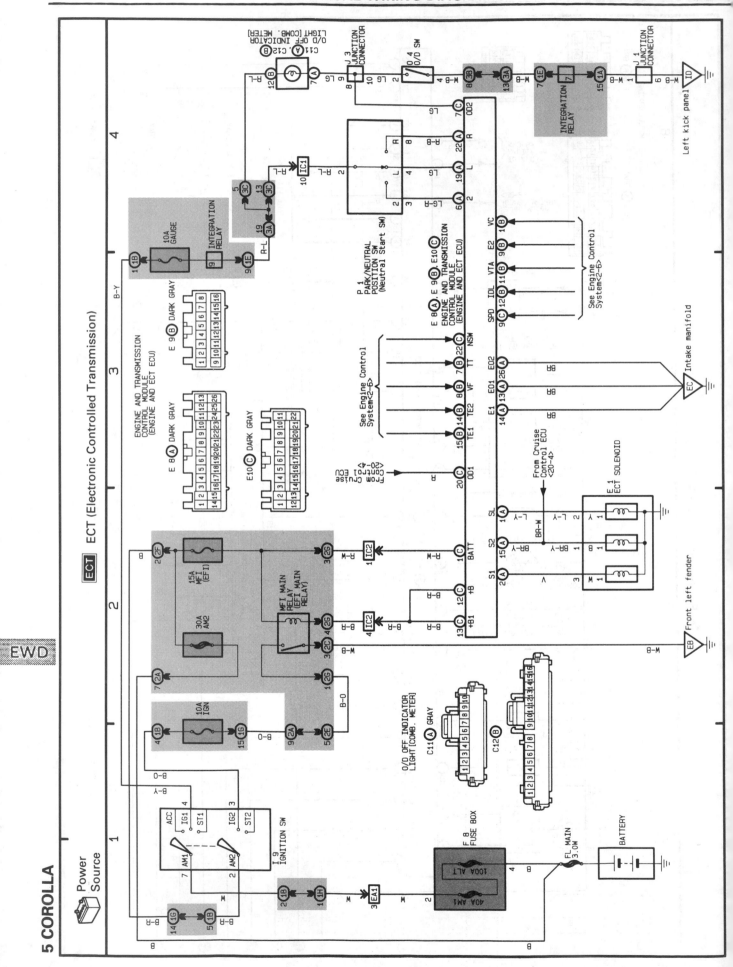

5 COROLLA

ECT (Electronic Controlled Transmission)

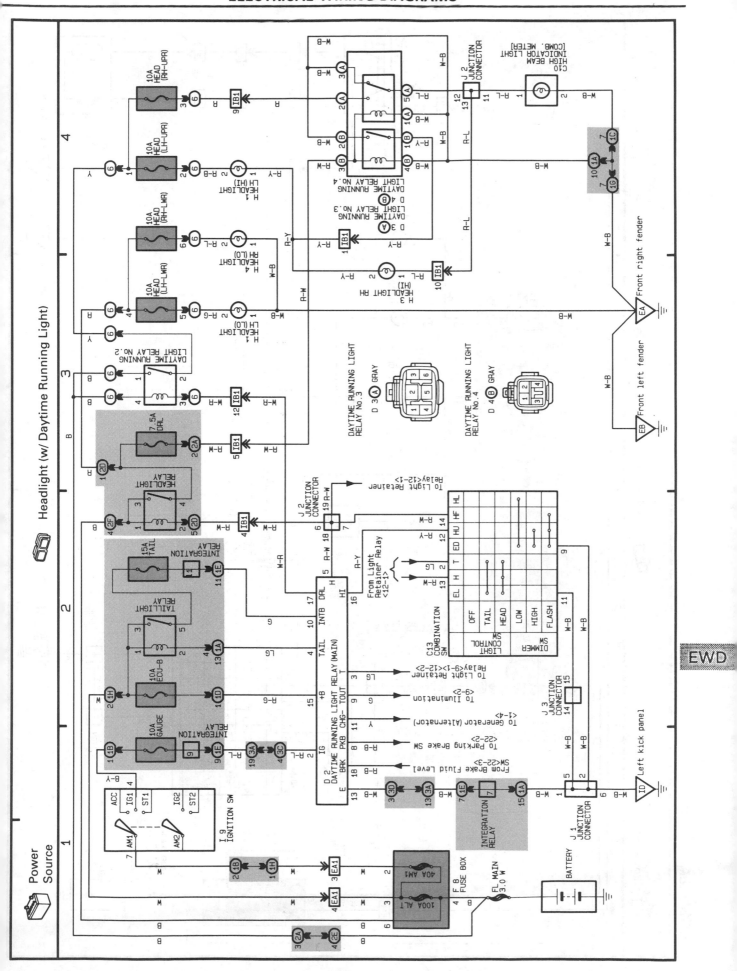

Headlight (w/ Daytime Running Light)

Power Source

EWD

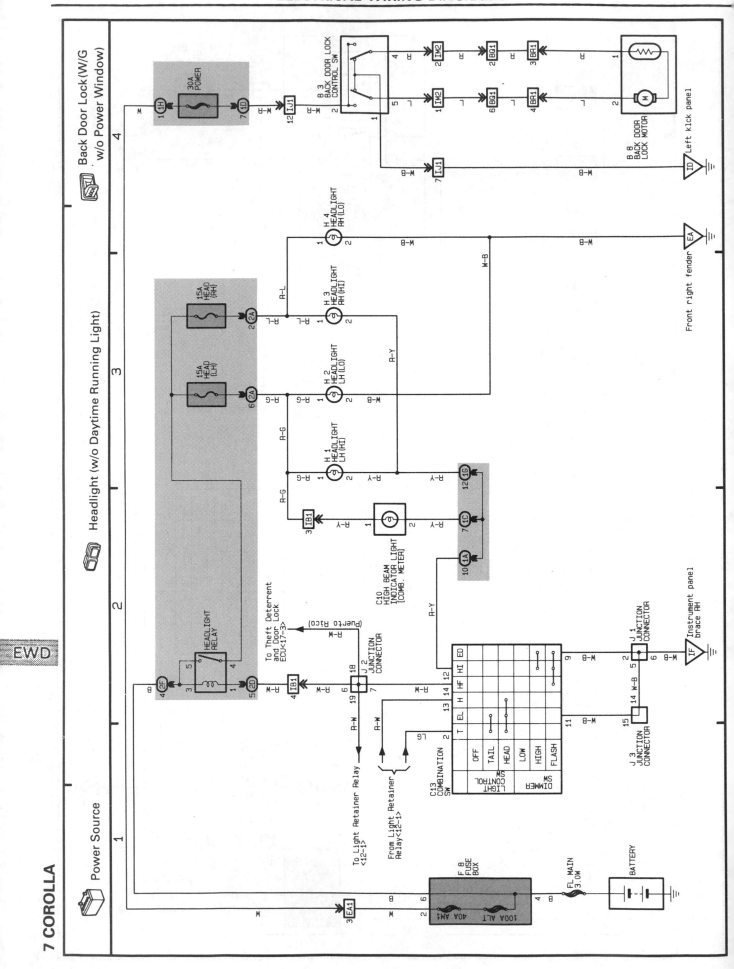

7 COROLLA

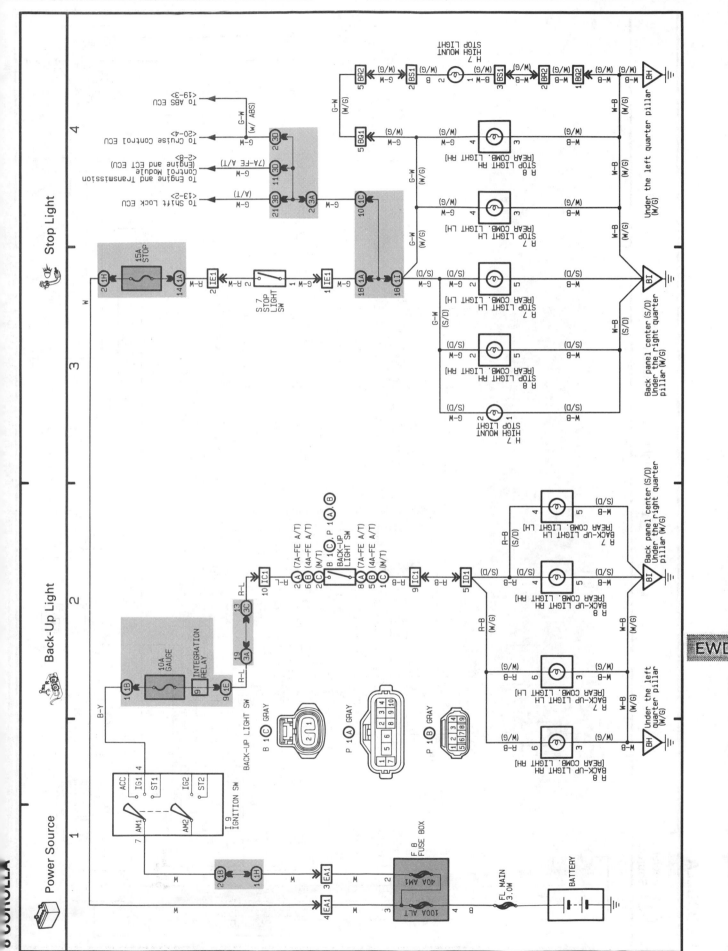

EWD

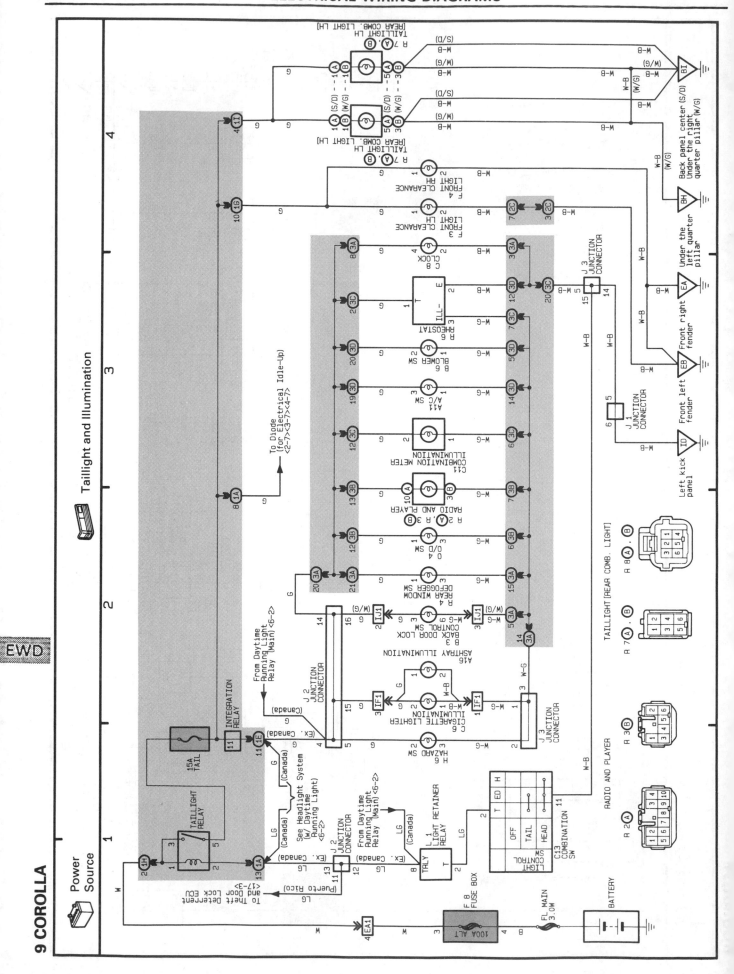

9 COROLLA

Power Source

Taillight and Illumination

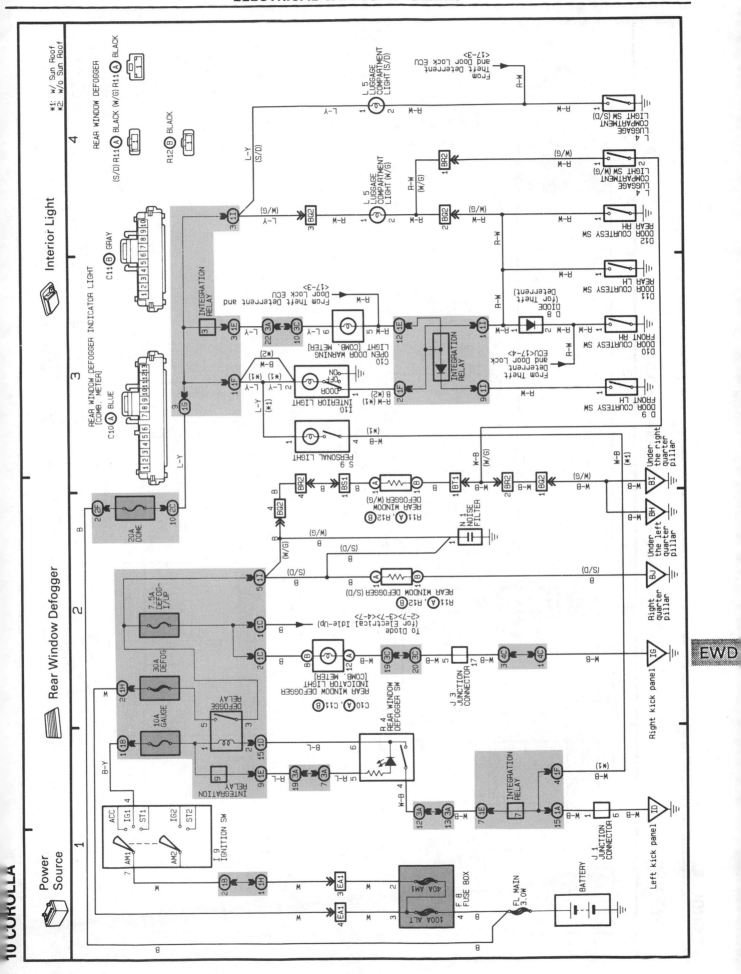

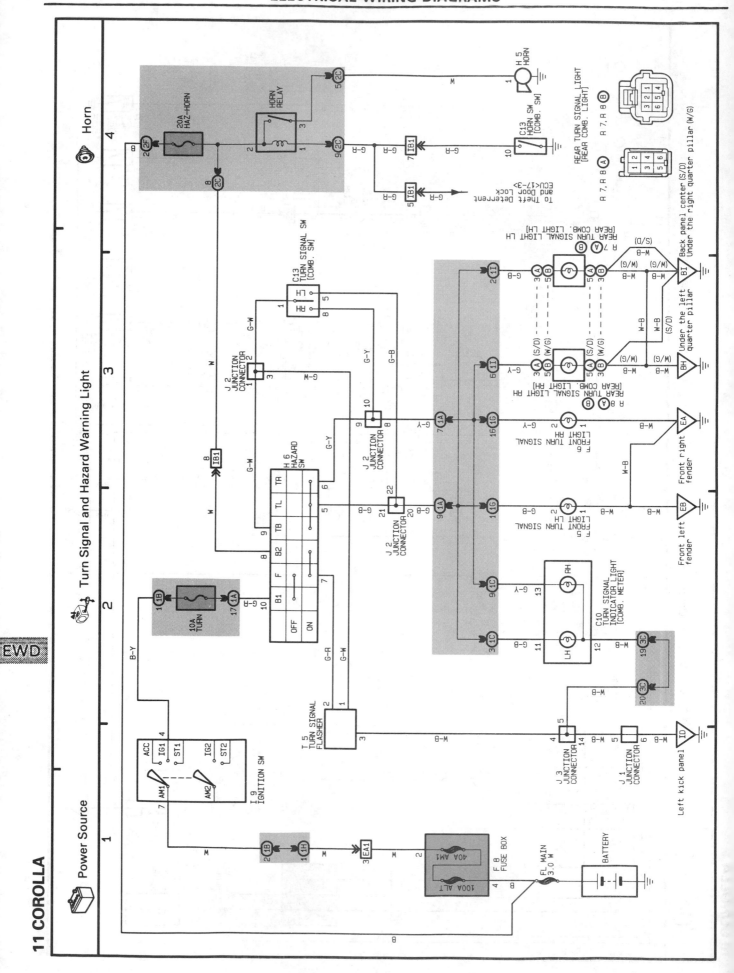

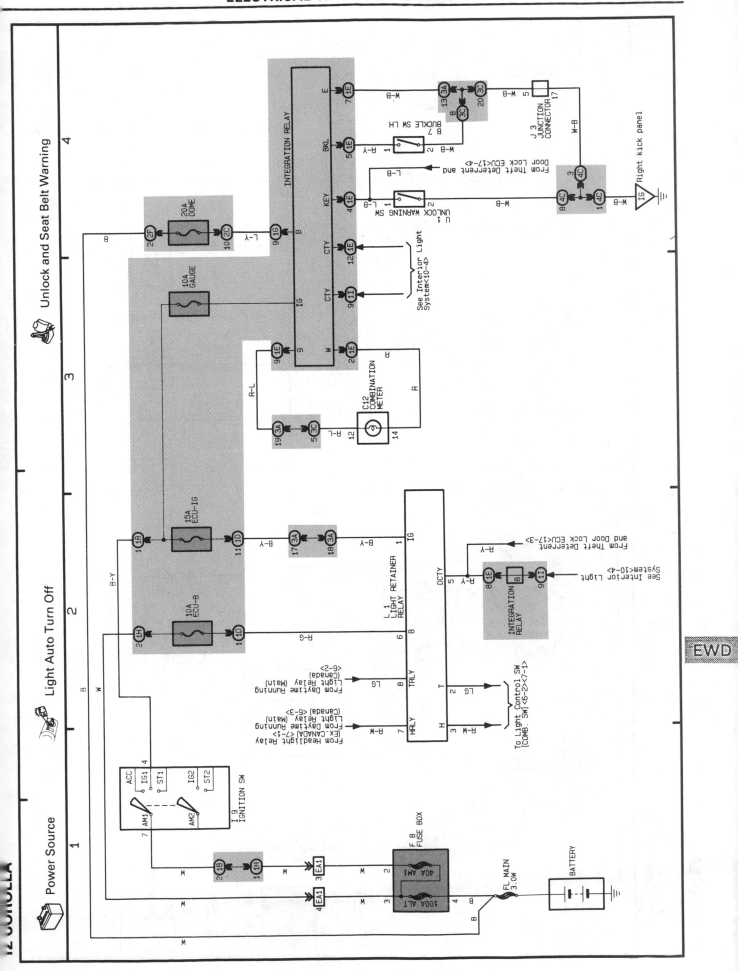

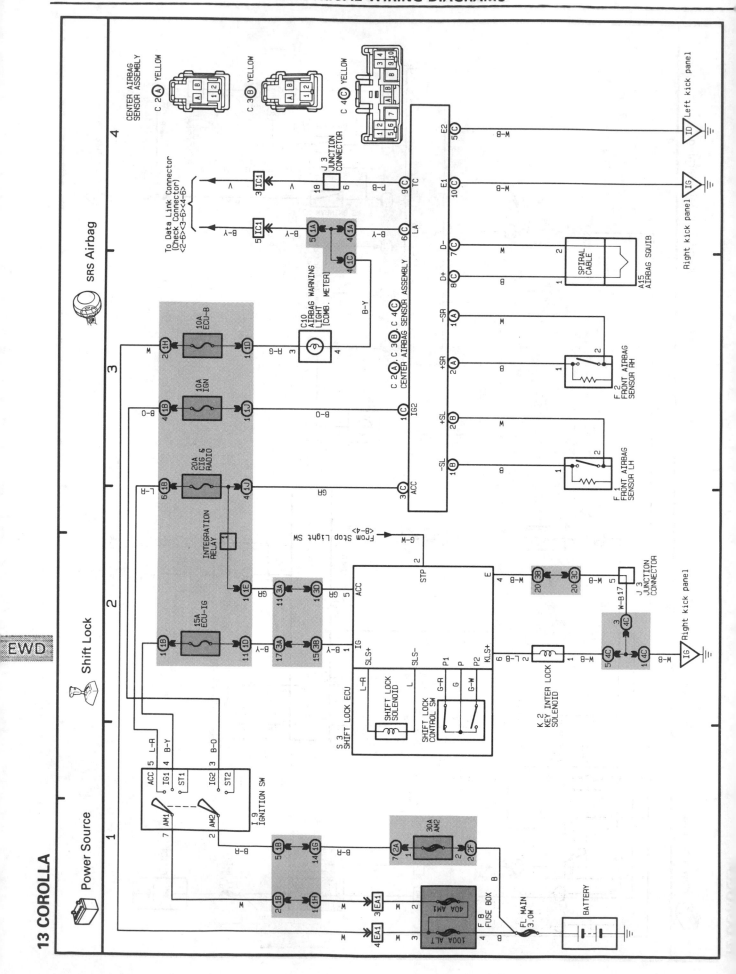

13 COROLLA

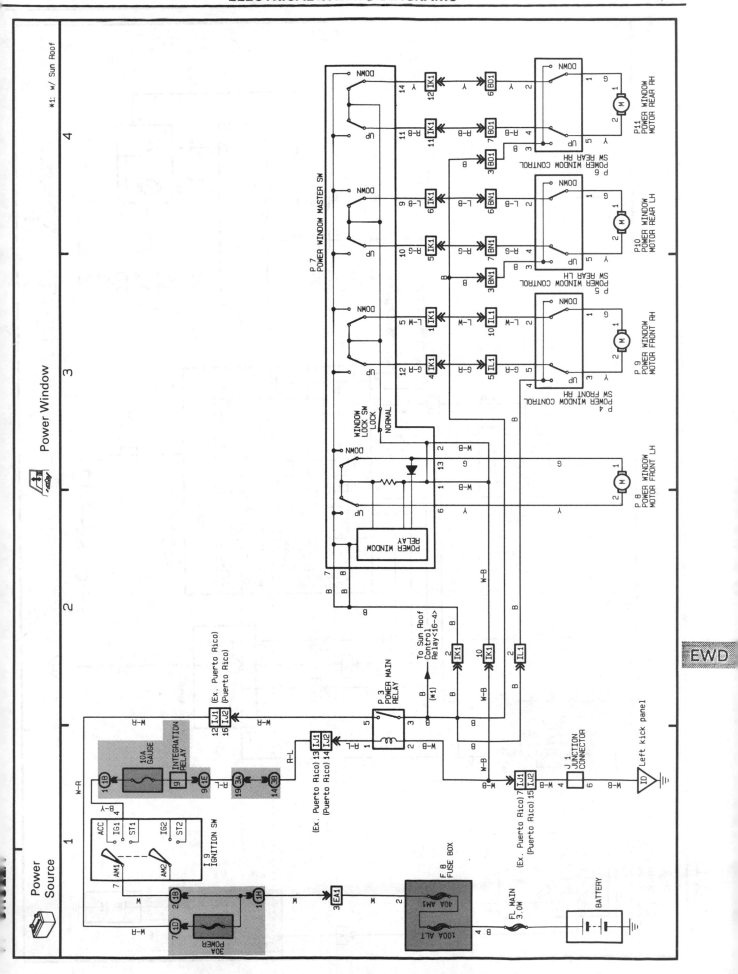

EWD

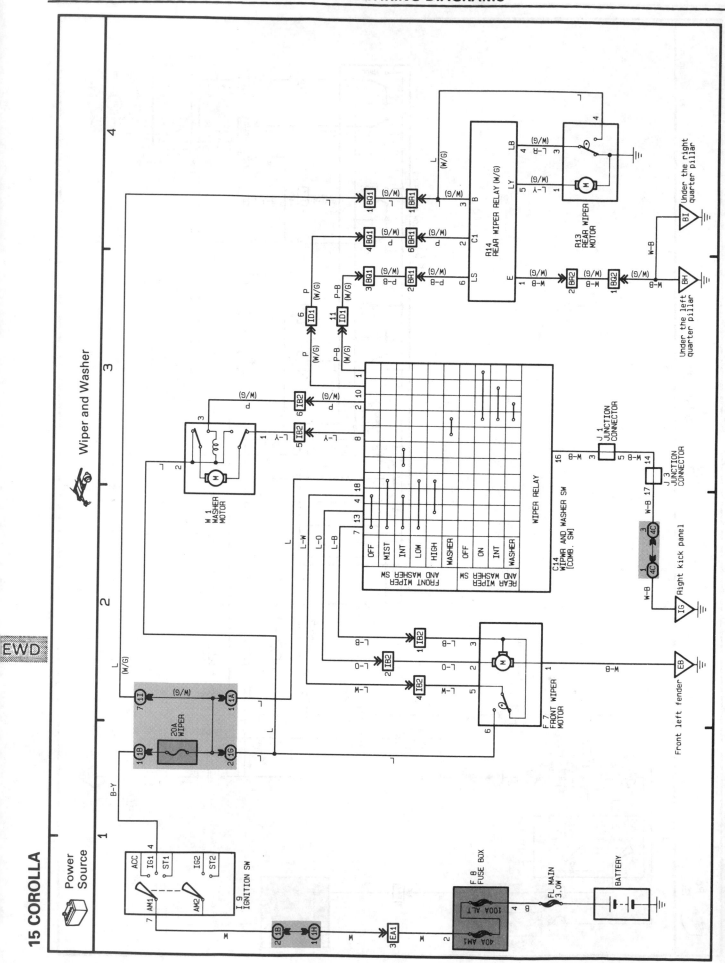

15 COROLLA

Power Source

Wiper and Washer

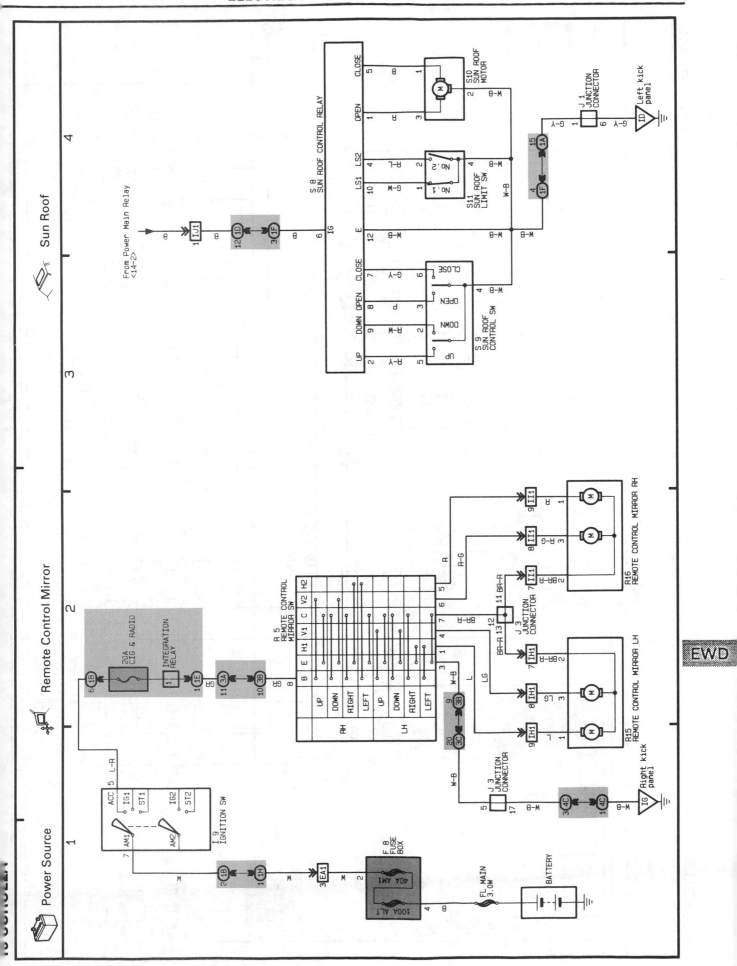

(Cont. next page)

17 COROLLA

Theft Deterrent and Door Lock

Power Source

EWD

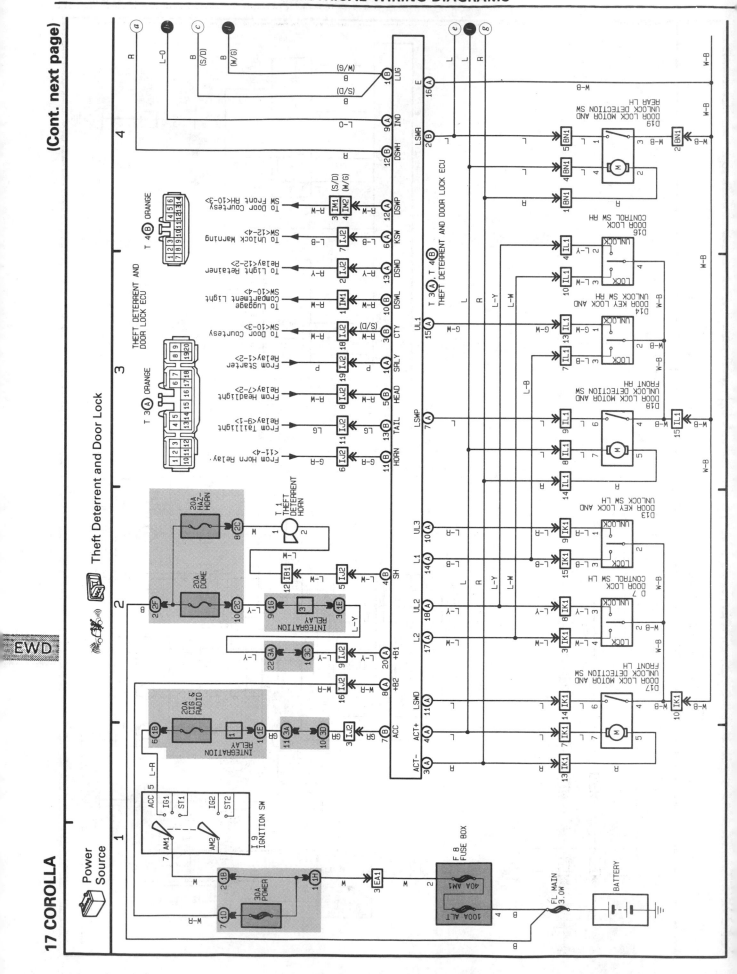

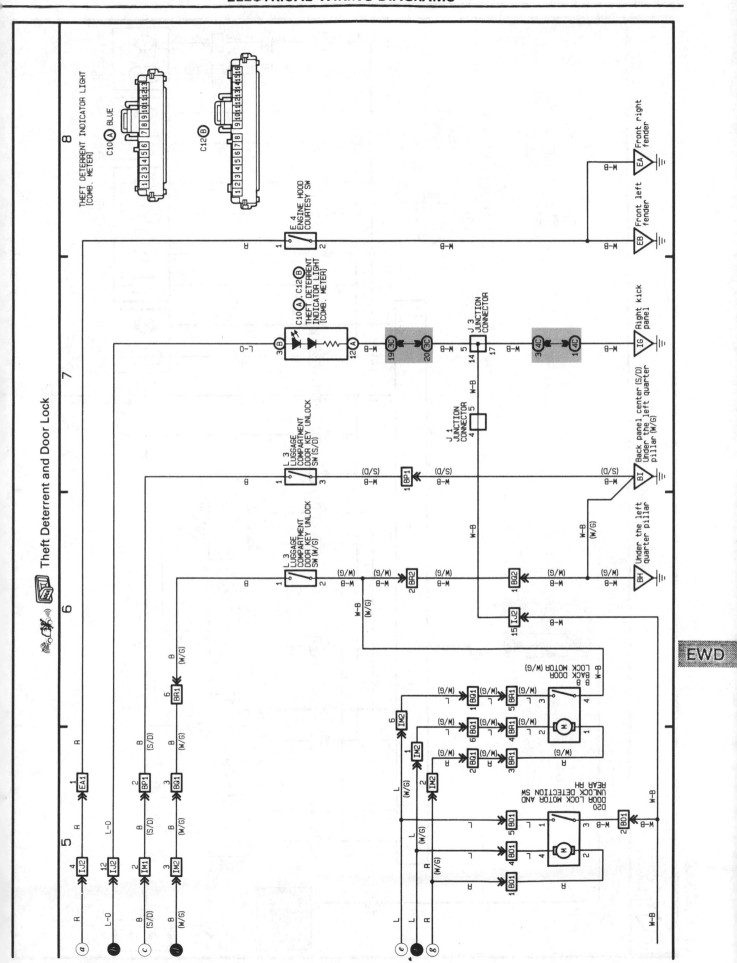

Theft Deterrent and Door Lock

EWD

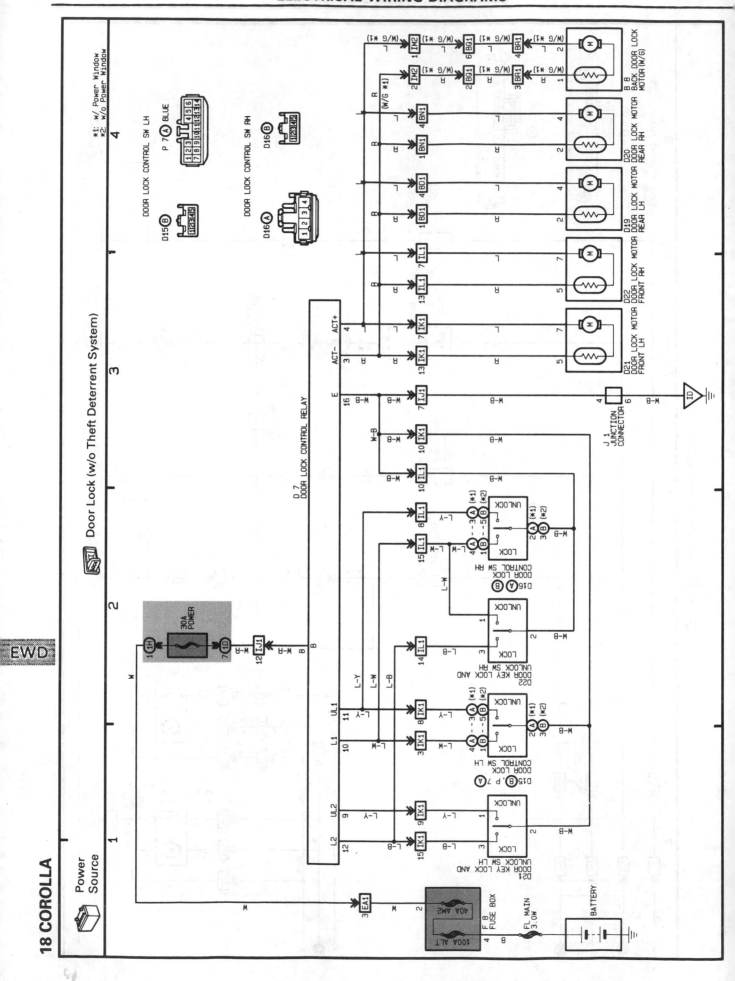

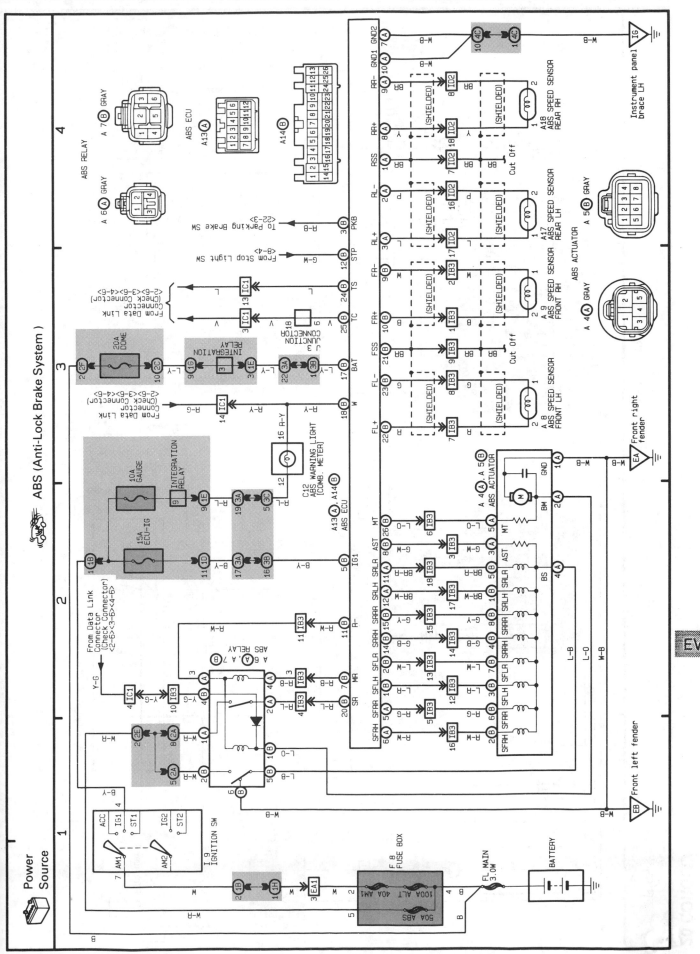

ABS (Anti-Lock Brake System)

EWD

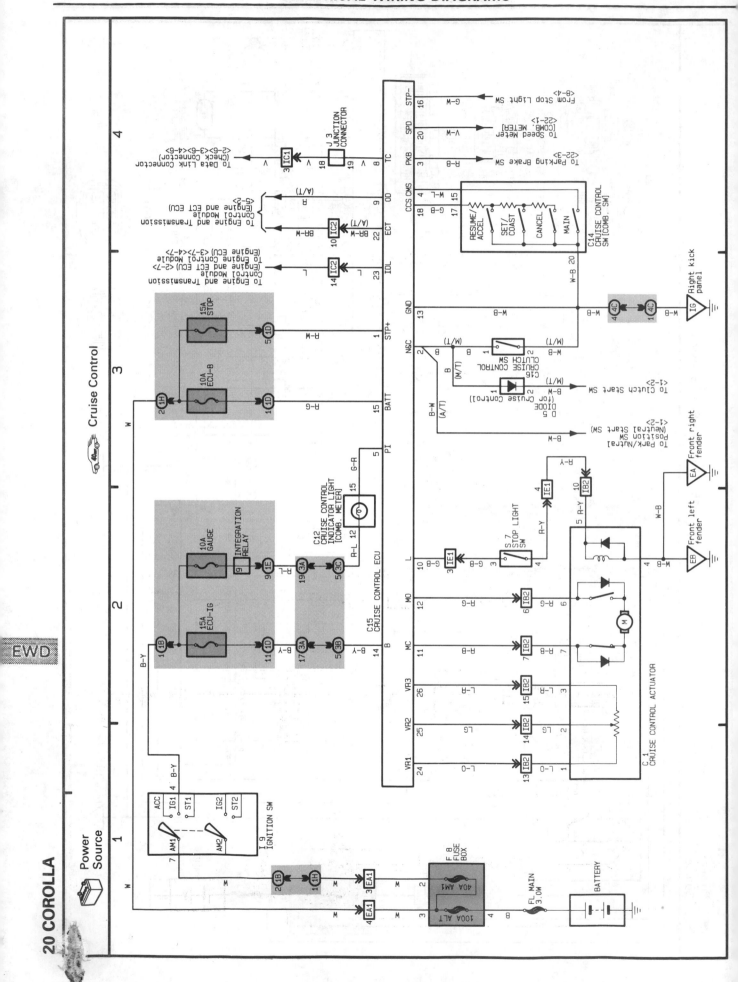

EWD

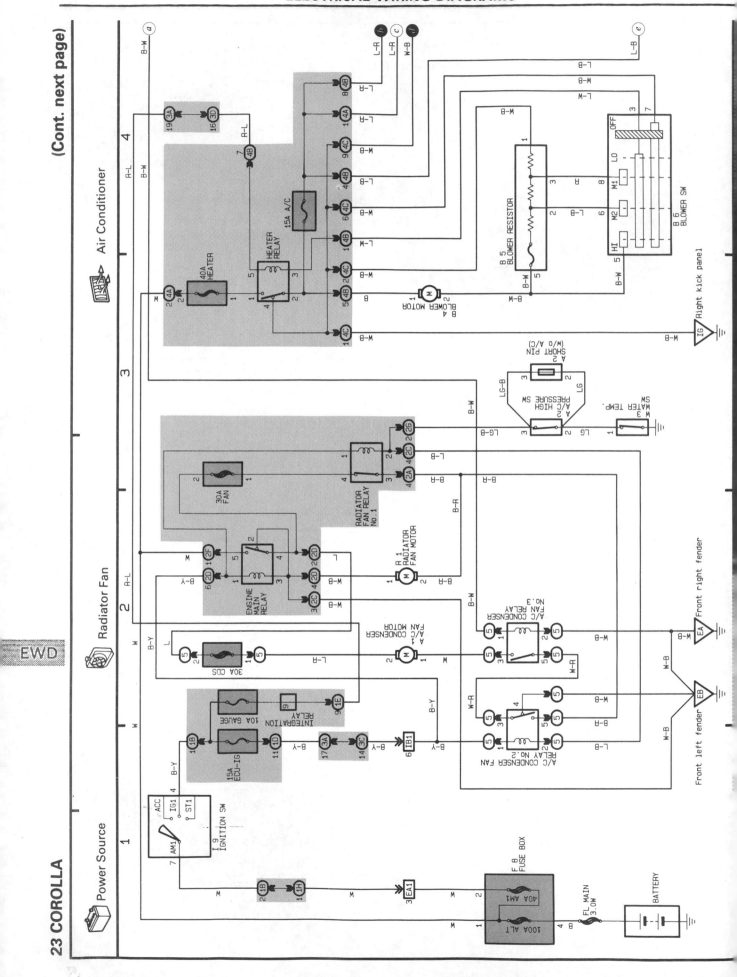

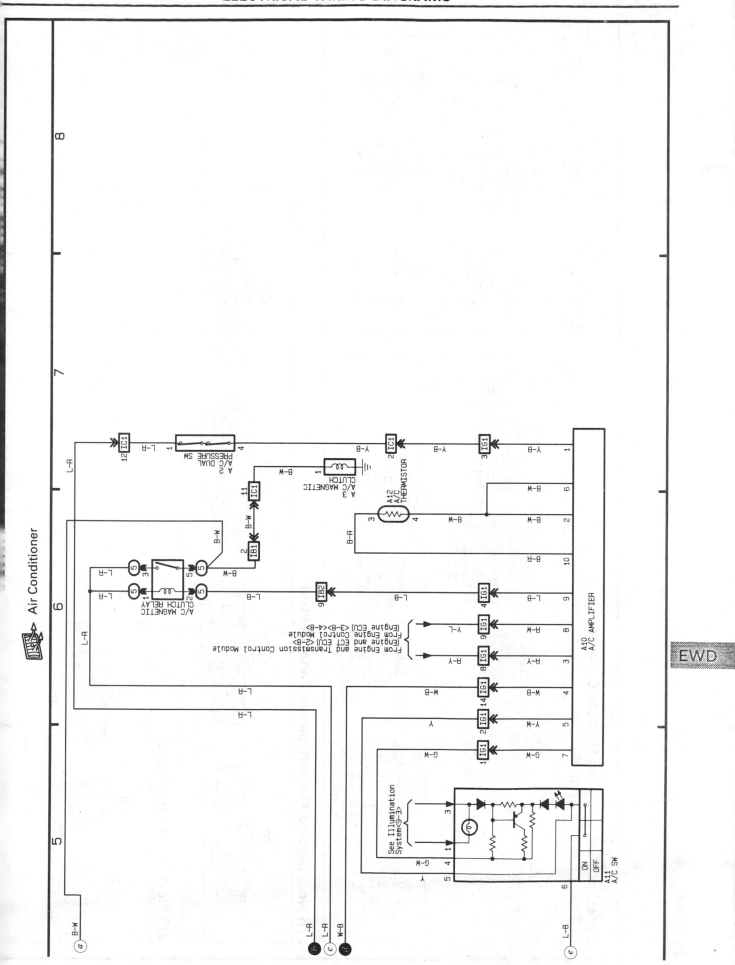

EWD

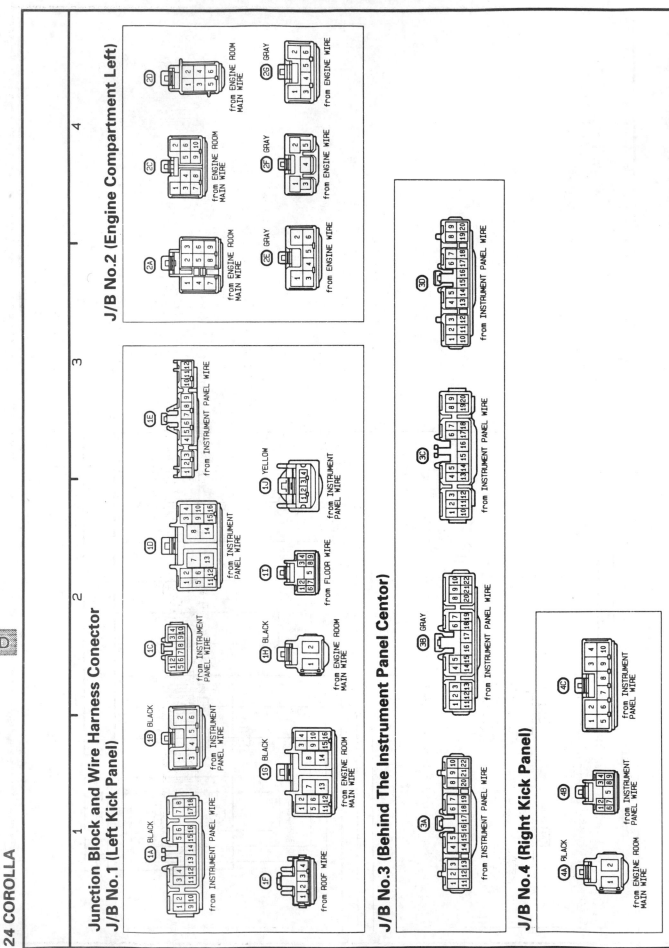

Junction Block and Wire Harness Conector
J/B No.1 (Left Kick Panel)

J/B No.2 (Engine Compartment Left)

J/B No.3 (Behind The Instrument Panel Center)

J/B No.4 (Right Kick Panel)

EWD

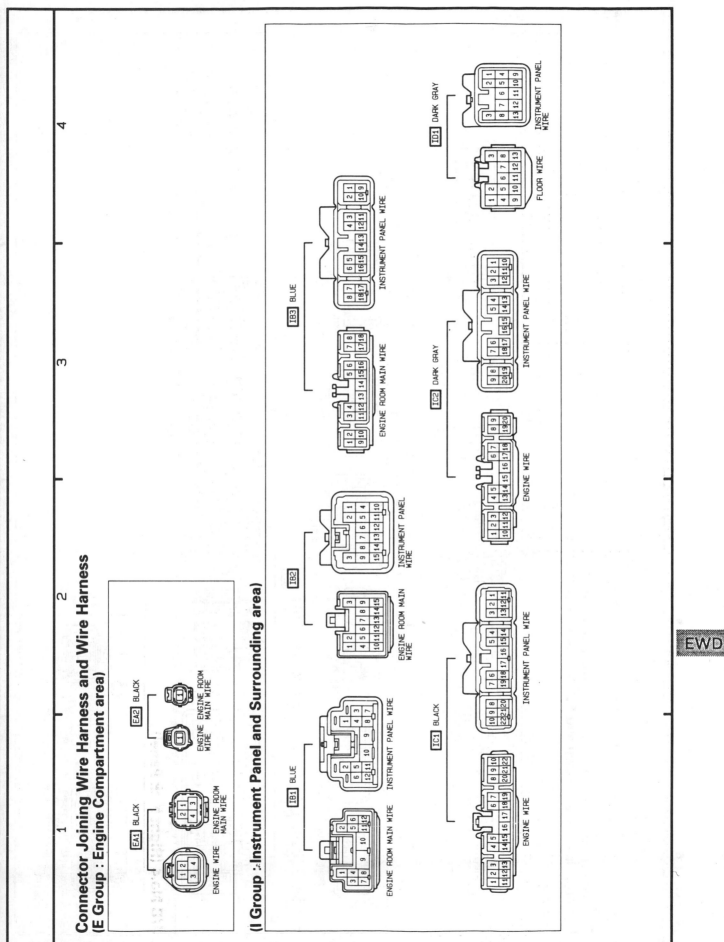

Connector Joining Wire Harness and Wire Harness
(E Group : Engine Compartment area)

(I Group : Instrument Panel and Surrounding area)

EWD

ELECTRICAL WIRING DIAGRAMS

EWD

Connector Joining Wire Harness and Wire Harness
(I Group : Instrument Panel and Surrounding area)(Cont'd)

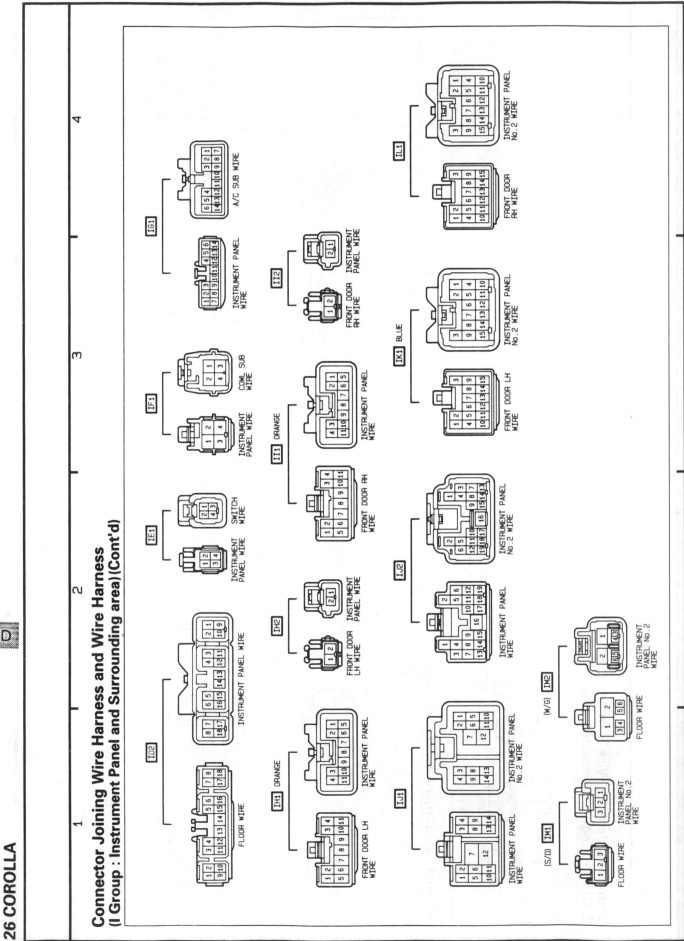

Connector Joining Wire Harness and Wire Harness
(B Group : Body and Surrounding area)

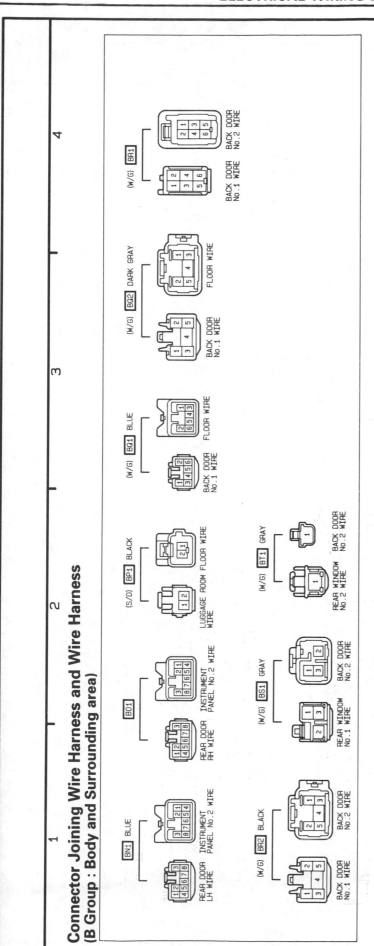

EWD

EWD